T0300573

Adaptive Technologies for Training and Education

This edited volume provides an overview of the latest advancements in adaptive training technology. Intelligent tutoring has been deployed for well-defined and relatively static educational domains such as algebra and geometry. However, this adaptive approach to computer-based training has yet to come into wider usage for domains that are less well defined or where student-system interactions are less structured, such as during scenario-based simulation and immersive serious games. In order to address how to expand the reach of adaptive training technology to these domains, leading experts in the field present their work in areas such as student modeling, pedagogical strategy, knowledge assessment, natural language processing, and virtual human agents. Several approaches to designing adaptive technology are discussed for both traditional educational settings and professional training domains. This book will appeal to anyone concerned with educational and training technology at a professional level, including researchers, training systems developers, and designers.

Paula J. Durlach is a research psychologist at the U.S. Army Research Institute for the Behavioral Social Sciences. After receiving her Ph.D. in experimental psychology from Yale University in 1983, she held fellowship positions at the University of Pennsylvania and the University of Cambridge. From 1987 to 1994, she was an assistant professor of psychology at McMaster University and went on to lead the exploratory consumer science team at Unilever Research Colworth Laboratory in the United Kingdom. Dr. Durlach has received recognition for her work in experimental psychology and cognitive science at the Army Science Conference and from the Department of Army Research and Development. She has recently published her research in the *International Journal of Artificial Intelligence in Education, Military Psychology, and Human-Computer Interaction*.

Alan M. Lesgold is professor and dean of the School of Education at the University of Pittsburgh and professor of psychology and intelligent systems. He received his Ph.D. in psychology from Stanford University in 1971 and holds an honorary doctorate from the Open University of the Netherlands. In 2001, he received the APA award for distinguished contributions in the application of psychology to education and training and was also awarded the Educom Medal. Dr. Lesgold is a Lifetime National Associate of the National Research Council and was appointed by Pennsylvania Governor Edward Rendell as a member of the Governor's Commission on Preparing America's Teachers. He serves on the boards of A+ Schools and Youthworks and is chair of the National Research Council committee on adolescent and adult literacy.

Adaptive Technologies for Training and Education

Edited by

PAULA J. DURLACH

U.S. Army Research Institute

ALAN M. LESGOLD

University of Pittsburgh

CAMBRIDGE UNIVERSITY PRESS
Cambridge, New York, Melbourne, Madrid, Cape Town,
Singapore, São Paulo, Delhi, Mexico City

Cambridge University Press
32 Avenue of the Americas, New York, NY 10013-2473, USA

www.cambridge.org
Information on this title: www.cambridge.org/9780521769037

First published 2012
Reprinted 2013

A catalog record for this publication is available from the British Library.

Library of Congress Cataloging in Publication Data

Adaptive technologies for training and education / [edited by]
Paula J. Durlach, Alan M. Lesgold.
    p. cm.
Includes bibliographical references and index.
ISBN 978-0-521-76903-7
1. Computer-assisted instruction.   2. Assistive computer technology.   3. Internet in education.
I. Durlach, Paula J.   II. Lesgold, Alan M.
LB1028.5.A135   2012
004.67'8071–dc23   2011030487

ISBN 978-0-521-76903-7 Hardback

Contents

Figures

Tables

Contributors

Vincent Aleven
Human-Computer Interaction Institute
Carnegie Mellon University

Kevin D. Ashley
University of Pittsburgh

Marie Bienkowski
SRI International

Ami E. Bolton
Office of Naval Research

Peter Brusilovsky
School of Information Sciences
University of Pittsburgh

Gwendolyn Campbell
Training and Human Performance
   R&D
Naval Air Warfare Center Training
   Systems Division

Min Chi
Machine Learning Department
Carnegie Mellon University

Cristina Conati
Department of Computer Science
University of British Columbia

Sidney D'Mello
University of Memphis

Paula J. Durlach
U.S. Army Research Institute

John Flynn
Raytheon BBN Technologies

Jared Freeman
Aptima, Inc.

LeeEllen Friedland
Alelo Inc.

Cleotilde Gonzalez
Dynamic Decision Making Laboratory
Social and Decision Sciences Department
Carnegie Mellon University

Art Graesser
University of Memphis

W. Lewis Johnson, Ph.D.
Alelo Inc.

Judy Kay
School of Information Technologies J12
University of Sydney

Kenneth R. Koedinger
Human-Computer Interaction
    Institute
Carnegie Mellon University

Bob Kummerfeld
School of Information Technologies J12
University of Sydney

H. Chad Lane
USC Institute for Creative
    Technologies

Alan M. Lesgold
School of Education
University of Pittsburgh

Georgiy Levchuk
Aptima, Inc.

Matthew Lineberry
Training & Human Performance R&D
    Branch
Naval Air Warfare Center, Training
    Systems Division

Diane Litman
Department of Computer Science
    and Learning Research and
    Development Center
University of Pittsburgh

Collin Lynch
University of Pittsburgh

Phillip M. Mangos
Kronos Incorporated

Niels Pinkwart
Department of Informatics
Clausthal University of Technology

Ido Roll
Carl Wieman Science Education
    Initiative
University of British Columbia

Wayne Shebilske
Psychology Department
Wright State University

Valerie J. Shute
Educational Psychology & Learning
    Systems Department
Florida State University

Eric A. Surface
SWA Consulting Inc.

Diana Tierney
Army Research Institute Scientific
    Coordination Office,
    HQs TRADOC

Kurt VanLehn
School of Computing, Informatics and
    Decision Systems Engineering

Aaron M. Watson
SWA Consulting Inc.

Robert E. Wray
Soar Technology

Diego Zapata-Rivera
Educational Testing Service

Preface

Adaptive instruction is instruction that can change to suit the needs of individual learners, with the potential to alter aspects like time on task, content, practice examples, and pedagogical strategy. One-on-one human tutoring is the epitome of adaptive instruction and is the gold standard against which developers of adaptive training technology measure the success of their systems; however, it is unclear which aspects of expert human tutoring are necessary to embed in technology to approximate this benchmark. There are many different ways in which technology could deliver instruction adaptively, but at present, it is not entirely clear (based on empirical evidence) which ways are the most effective in terms of learning outcomes. If we take the example of a television documentary as completely non-adaptive instruction, there are many ways in which adaptation could be added. For example, we could give the student control over the presentation, allowing them to replay or skip parts of the film; or we could allow the student to request subtitles in a different language; or we could follow up the presentation with a question-and-answer period; or we could decide to assign different documentaries to different students, based on an assessment of what they already know. So, an important question is: Which methods of adaptation can be realized in technology, and which are effective at enhancing learning outcomes such that they are worth the extra effort and expense of designing into technology-based training systems?

The purpose of this book is to make a serious examination of what we know and what we do not know with respect to this question. The book is based on a 2009 workshop sponsored by the U.S. Army Research Institute for the Behavioral and Social Sciences. It may be surprising to some that this is a critical question for the U.S. Army; however, many factors have converged to foster an interest by the U.S. Army (as well as other military services) in tailored training enabled by technology. These factors include the nature of the current operational environment and its demand for repeated deployments, which limit time for formal training; the breadth and diversity of the skills and knowledge soldiers and leaders require, fed by the continual introduction of new equipment and rapidly changing tactics and procedures; a shift in the training paradigm to provide on-demand training; and the size and diversity of the soldier trainee population.

Of these factors, the most compelling is the operational environment. The scope and unpredictable nature of the operational demands on the U.S. military underlie many of the other factors that will shape future training. The U.S. Department of Defense (DOD) Capstone Concept for Joint Operations Version 3 (2009) states that "The future operating environment will be characterized by uncertainty, complexity, rapid change, and persistent conflict" (p. 2). Joint forces will face a range of national security challenges (p. 7) that will require a weighted mix of military actions including combat aimed at defeating armed enemies, security activities to protect and manage civil populations, engagement to improve capabilities of or cooperation with other governments, and relief and reconstruction (pp. 14–18).

Making training more adaptive is a current aspiration within the U.S. Army training community; however, it is important to distinguish three different ways in which the term "adaptive training" is used. One way refers to training people to be adaptable; that is, to train people so that they can respond creatively to unexpected or unfamiliar challenges (Fletcher, 2004; see VanLehn & Chi, Chapter 2, this volume). A second sense in which adaptive training is used concerns the nature of the training bureaucracy and its systems. Traditionally, Army institutional training is based on career tracks, in which, over time, the individual participates in a set of predefined courses linked to promotion steps; however, converting this linear model of training to one allowing more spontaneity and responsiveness to immediate needs makes sense given the unpredictability of future Army missions. The future Army training system aims to become a "learner-centric

system of education"(Training and Doctrine Command [TRADOC], 2008). Soldier proficiency and developmental needs, as well as specific operational circumstances and requirements, will be used to shape the content, timing, delivery, and duration of training. This type of instructional adaptability is similar to what Lee and Park (2008) refer to as "macro-adaptive," and what Hannafin and Hill (2008) call "resource-based learning."

The third meaning of adaptive training is the one on which the chapters in this book concentrate primarily. This meaning refers to the ability of training to mold itself to the learner, *within a training episode or event*. It is thus analogous to what Lee and Park (2008) refer to as "micro-adaptive," or what VanLehn (2006) refers to as the "inner loop." From the Army's point of view, less time for training and constraints on resources will necessitate greater reliance on technology-based training. Not only is there less time, but there is a wider skill set to train. The Army is faced with the need to maintain a steady stream of soldiers and leaders trained and ready to perform an ever-increasing set of complex tasks, now including such things as cultural competence, adaptability (both of training environments to individual trainee needs and of trainees to environments they will face in their work), critical and creative thinking, effective team leadership, and effective use of new equipment and information technologies. The vision for micro-adaptive technology-based training is that it will be responsive to time constraints by tailoring training to the learner's current level of knowledge or skill and by applying principles of learning science, thus making training more efficient. The intent is to accelerate learning compared to more traditional modes of training and/or to increase the percentage of trainees achieving standards-based mastery. It is also to enhance the availability of training for the entire training audience, by reducing reliance on face-to-face training and increasing it on technology-based techniques. The aim is to ensure that the best methods are used to give the military learner just what is needed, when it is needed, and where it is needed (Scales, 2006).

With regard to the provision of training on-demand, it is intended that "embedded" training and performance support will provide much of the needed deployed capability for technical and tactical training involving equipment systems. The DOD defines embedded training as "[c]apabilities built into, strapped onto, or plugged into operational materiel systems to train, sustain, and enhance individual and crew skill proficiencies necessary to operate and maintain the equipment" (Pilgrim, 2008, chart 4). However, advances in training technology that adapt coaching, feedback, and content to a soldier's or unit's proficiency level are required to help realize the full potential of embedded training. In addition to embedding training in equipment, distributing learning to a soldier's computer and/or mobile device can greatly increase their access to needed training while at home station or deployed. The Army continues to push in this direction as time for instructor-led classroom training shrinks and the need to optimize the efficiency of training delivered to units grows. The Army envisions that in the future, "[i]n lieu of the subject matter and instructional expertise of trainers, artificially intelligent tutors, coaches and mentors will monitor and track soldier learning needs, assessing and diagnosing problems and providing other assistance, as appropriate" (TRADOC, 2008, p. 118).

Finally, it is important to consider how characteristics of the Army's trainee population drive the need for adaptive training technologies. In fiscal year 2008, the TRADOC's 5 Army Training Centers and 33 schools conducted about 1,500 courses for more than 500,000 trainees. In addition, TRADOC reaches about 90,000 trainees annually via distributed learning. TRADOC faces many challenges to delivery of effective and efficient training across this vast enterprise. In particular, with a trainee population as large and dispersed as the Army's, it is not possible to make on-site, expert human tutors or coaches available to every trainee.

Automated intelligent tutors and coaches, integrated into the delivery of distributed learning courses, could cover at least some of this need. Similarly, the characteristics of soldiers, their training and task proficiency inside and outside of their specialty, their operational and leadership experiences, and the skills needed by any given individual soldier or team for a specific mission vary tremendously across individuals across the force. Thus, a one-size-fits-all approach to training may be ineffective and inefficient in meeting individual or team training needs in a timely manner. For this reason, and for the many reasons mentioned previously, TRADOC has made tailored training enabled by adaptive training technology a high priority for science and technology research.

In summary, many factors intersect to make each trainee and their training requirements unique. Adaptive training technologies could respond to this diversity of experience and learning needs by providing dynamic learning environments that adjust to the requirement of the individual soldier. These technologies can help meet the demands created by the current operational tempo to accelerate learning and help keep training current. In lieu of human tutors, intelligent technology-based tutors can help guide trainees and provide assessment of and feedback on their performance.

The U.S. Army training system is at an important crossroads. Fundamental changes, such as those enabled by adaptive training technologies, will be needed to gain the most out of every training opportunity (U.S. Army Memorandum, 2009). The new U.S. Army Training Concept 2012–2020 (U.S. Army, 2009, p.7), drawing on lessons learned from recent persistent and complex operations, concludes that increasing innovation in training will be essential to *develop the versatile units and agile leaders required for the future*" (emphasis in the original). Advances in adaptive training technologies will make a critical contribution to realization of that concept. Where do those advances need to be to meet these ambitious goals? The purpose of this book is to "plant a flag in the ground," indicating where the cutting edge of adaptive training technology is today, and determining in which directions it will need to be pushed to meet the Army vision for tomorrow.

Drs. Paula J. Durlach
and Diana Tierney

References

Fletcher, J. D. (2004). Cognitive Readiness: Preparing for the Unexpected. Institute for Defense Analysis document D-3061, Log 06–000702. Alexandria, VA. Downloaded on January 13, 2010, from http://www.dtic.mil/cgi-bin/GetTRDoc?AD=ADA458683&Location=U2&doc=GetTRDoc.pdf.

Hannafin, M. J. and Hill, J. R. (2008). Resource-based learning. In J. M. Spector, M. D. Merrill, J. V. Merrienboer, and M. P. Driscoll (Eds.) *Handbook of Research on Educational Communication and Technology, third edition* (pp. 525–536). New York: Lawrence Erlbaum Associates.

Lee, J. and Park, O. (2008). Adaptive instructional systems. In J. M. Spector, M. D. Merrill, J. V. Merrienboer, and M. P. Driscoll (Eds.) *Handbook of Research on Educational Communication and Technology, third edition* (pp. 469–484). New York: Lawrence Erlbaum Associates.

Pilgrim, Kevin H. (2008). Value of Embedded Training – Future Combat Systems Example. Briefing to Military Operations Research Society Symposium, June 10–12, 2008. Retrieved January 15, 2010, from http://www.dtic.mil/cgi-bin/GetTRDoc?AD=ADA490129&Location=U2&doc=GetTRDoc.pdf.

Scales, R. H. (2006). The Second Learning Revolution, *Military Review, 86 (January–February)*, 37–44. http://www.au.af.mil/au/awc/awcgate/milreview/scales2.pdf.

TRADOC (2008). U.S. Army Study of the Human Dimension in the Future 2015–2024. TRADOC PAM 525–3-7–01. Retrieved January 15, 2010, from http://www.TRADOC.Army.mil/tpubs/pams/p525-3-7-01.pdf.

U.S. Army (2009). U.S. Army Training Concept 2012–2020, Coordinating Draft (December 9, 2009). Available from HQs Combined Arms Command, executive offices, Fort Leavenworth, KS.

U.S. Army Memorandum (2009). Army Training and Leader Development Guidance FY10–11. Available from Department of the Army, Office of the Chief of Staff, Pentagon.

U.S. Department of Defense (2009). Capstone Concept for Joint Operations (version 3.0). Retrieved January 15, 2010, from http://www.jfcom.mil/newslink/storyarchive/2009/CCJO_2009.pdf.

VanLehn, K. (2006). The behavior of tutoring systems. *International Journal of Artificial Intelligence in Education, 16* (3), 227–265.

Acknowledgments

The editors wish to thank the U.S. Army Research Institute for supporting both the workshop on which this volume is based and subsequent efforts to bring this book to publication. We wish to thank all the workshop participants. Although not all are represented here by name as contributors, they all made valuable contributions and supported lively, thoughtful discussion. We also wish to thank Pamela Wells of Alion Science and Technology for conducting the myriad administrative tasks required for the workshop. Finally, our thanks to Cambridge University Press editors and staff who provided assistance and patience throughout the publication process.

Introduction

This book addresses the use of technology to provide training adapted to the individual needs of different trainees. The use of technology for training has become commonplace, as a way to increase training effectiveness at reduced cost. Pressures on time and resources have impelled organizations responsible for the education and training of large numbers of people to adopt technology-based training. Initially, technological approaches replicated classroom methods (mass instruction) and generally provided either no tuning of instruction to individual student needs, simple branching schemes, or mastery approaches in which instruction essentially was repeated until a mastery test was passed.

But as the use of computer-based instructional materials has grown, so has disenchantment with one-size-fits-all passive learning solutions and the inadequate mastery-assessment methods that often accompany them. More advanced technology-based learning environments can provide tailored and personal interaction opportunities and allow students to learn by doing, supported by feedback. Still, they might not meet the needs of a varied target audience because they typically fail to integrate prerequisite or remedial instruction, which may be required for a heterogeneous user population, and they are still primarily one-size-fits-all solutions, unable to adapt their behaviors to learner backgrounds.

The need for more adaptive training and instruction arises from today's fast pace of change, both in societal complexity and in the content that needs to be learned. Historically, a great deal of training and education was personalized. The elite had private tutors, and craftsmen learned through apprenticeship. Group approaches to education and training often originated from institutional needs (e.g., religious or military) to maintain their ranks and carry out their agendas.

Less specialized education for wider audiences was aimed mainly at enculturation, to make sure that everyone shared a common body of everyday knowledge and expectations, social values, and religion. In these cases, a relatively uniform approach to training or teaching worked pretty well because there was so much shared everyday experience that the instructor could assume a lot about what the learner already knew.

The environment for instruction and training in the developed world today is quite different from the homogeneous, closed, small-scale society or institution. Society is multicultural, and education and training are undertaken by students with varied experiences and motivations. This makes it much harder to know what prior knowledge or level of motivation any individual student might have. Inaccurate instructor knowledge of each student's current level of knowledge and skill can in turn can lead to large variations in instructional effectiveness and rates of mastery. One way to cope has been to stream students into different class tracks, where the pace of progress through the material (and the ultimate end state) differs across tracks. Although this still leaves the logistic problem of multiple tracks going on at once, it represents an improvement because groups are relatively homogeneous in the characteristics that impact learning. Today, however, when students come from so many different backgrounds, learning must adapt not only to learning pace, but also to differing underlying knowledge and differing prior experience – the ontological base of different students can easily be quite different.

Within institutions such as the military, there is the additional challenge that training needs can emerge on short notice, as the result of changes in world events and affairs, as well the emergence of new technologies. Personnel without recent deployment experience may require different training from those with firsthand knowledge of a particular situation or piece of equipment. Such heterogeneity may be difficult for an instructor to cope with. Moreover, the knowledge may be required by personnel not participating currently in formal education (e.g., already deployed personnel). Technology-based training has the potential to reach a wider audience, but it needs to be appropriately tailored to the learner's prior knowledge.

Developers of learning and training systems today realize that it can be beneficial for a system to encode information about each student and to use that information to adapt the training regimen to better support mastery on an individual-by-individual basis. The information about each student – the student model – typically includes some subset of the student's experiences, knowledge, skills, and abilities in the domain of instruction, measured prior to and/or during instruction. It can also include information about student traits (e.g., spatial ability) and states (e.g., confusion) that are relevant to setting an adaptive pedagogical strategy. Various parts of this information occur and suggest adaptations on different time scales. Parts of the student model may change even within an exercise, whereas other parts may endure for much longer periods, even years.

Training system behaviors adapted on the basis of the student model can include sequencing of content, selection of content, and the type and timing of coaching and feedback provided during the learning experience. For a system to adapt effectively (i.e., better promote mastery than a one-size-fits-all version), it needs both good rules about how and what to adapt (pedagogical model) and accurate data in the student model to guide these rules. The accuracy requirement implies the need for valid and sensitive measures of student knowledge, skills, abilities, traits, and states. In addition, effective adaptation requires a thorough understanding and systematization of the instructional content itself, as well as significant insights about the knowledge structures possessed by domain experts and the cognitive processes they use to solve problems in the domain.

Given all these requirements, the dearth of adaptive instructional technology in practical use is hardly surprising. Typically it has had high development costs and required multiple generations of tryout and refinement over years (for further discussion see Chapter 15 in this volume, by Lesgold). Only a few intelligent adaptive systems have made it past the development stage because of this. Mostly, they have been well-defined and relatively static educational domains (i.e., where the content remains stable), such as algebra and geometry, because this is where all the needed elements most readily coalesce (expert cognitive models, problems sets with known psychometric properties, systematized content, and step-based problems with objectively correct or incorrect solutions). The other real applications have been in areas where no deep training existed before and much was needed, as in the language and cultural training described by Johnson and colleagues in Chapter 14 of this volume.

The success of the extant applications and the findings that one-on-one human tutoring provides an advantage over classroom instruction suggest that adaptive training technology should produce superior learning outcomes compared with nonadaptive technology. The purpose of this volume is to provide an overview of the latest advancements in adaptive training technology and to provide a basis for determining what further advancements would be required to make this approach more amenable to wider practical usage.

Part I, "Adaptive Training Technology," provides the reader with a foundational understanding of adaptive training technology. In Chapter 1, Shute and Zapata-Rivera provide an overview of adaptive training technology: why to adapt, how to adapt, and what to adapt. In Chapter 2, VanLehn and Chi present a case study of how adaptive technology can produce accelerated learning. In Chapter 3, Brusilovsky reviews the application of adaptive techniques to Web-based systems, specifically adaptive educational hypermedia.

Part II, "Student Modeling Beyond Content Mastery," presents work focusing on student modeling. The title of the section was chosen to acknowledge the core role that students' domain knowledge and skill play in a student model, but also to suggest that other elements of student-associated data may contribute to adaptive strategies. Aleven, Roll, and Koedinger in Chapter 4 and Conati in Chapter 5, respectively, discuss their research on using adaptive training technology to foster metacognitive learning skills, such as help seeking and

self-explanation. In Chapter 6, D'Mello and Graesser describe the interaction of learning and affect, the measurement of affect during learning, and the design of affect-sensitive intelligent tutors (see also Litman's Chapter 13). Concluding the section, the potential benefits and challenges involved in creating persistent student models – long-term models that the learner takes along from one training application to the next – are explored by Kay and Kummerfeld in Chapter 7.

As previously mentioned, adaptive intelligent training technology (e.g., intelligent tutors) has been successfully applied in well-defined domains and step-based problem solving. Many domains and fields requiring training are not so well-defined, nor characterized by step-based problems. Part III, "Experiential Learning and Ill-Defined Domains," turns the focus toward how adaptive training technology might handle domains that are less well-defined and/or where the employment of a less structured interface (compared with step-based problem solving) bestows a greater latitude of activities, and thus greater challenges for interpreting student state from overt behavior. In Chapter 8, Gonzalez describes models of dynamic decision making where there is uncertainty about when events will occur and alternative options unfold over time. She describes her research investigating the decision-making process and provides implications for the training of decision making for dynamic environments. Lynch, Ashley, Pinkwart, and Aleven in Chapter 9 explore what exactly it means for a domain or problem to be ill-defined, and the implications for education and training strategies. In Chapter 10, Lane and Wray discuss experiential training designed to promote the acquisition of social and intercultural skills and describe a framework for adapting the behavior of virtual humans to support this type of learning. Similarly, Flynn in Chapter 12 is concerned with the behavior of virtual characters, and describes how semantic-web technology could be harnessed to create virtual humans for training, based on "person ontologies" and "action agents."

Mangos, Campbell, Lineberry, and Bolton in Chapter 11 lay out the challenges of designing pedagogically sound experiential training and focus on methods to orchestrate the interplay of student assessment and content selection, which adaptive experiential training requires.

There are multiple ways in which the ability to use language supports training and education. This is obviously the case when the goal is to teach reading, writing, language skills, and tasks that are inherently language based (e.g., negotiation or legal argumentation). Additionally, language can play a crucial role in a teacher's assessment of student mastery and stimulation of student cognitive processing. Part IV, "Natural Language Processing for Training," includes two chapters providing examples of both of these functions. In Chapter 13, Litman discusses the role of natural language processing during interactive tutorial dialogues, not just for purposes of content understanding, but also for monitoring student affect. Johnson, Friedland, Watson, and Surface bring the issues of experiential learning and language processing together in Chapter 14, describing language and culture training systems aimed at adult learners for whom foreign language and intercultural competency must be learned to conduct their work.

The last group of chapters in Part V address various "Culminations" for adaptive training development. In Chapter 15, Lesgold presents lessons learned during the development of five generations of intelligent coached apprenticeship systems. In Chapter 16, Levchuk, Shebilske, and Freeman present the challenges of designing adaptive technology for team training. In Chapter 17, Bienkowski describes and advocates the Design-Based Research approach to the study of technology-based learning. This approach draws on engineering, software, and industrial design practices, such as agile design rapid prototyping, participatory design, and user-centered design. Finally, in Chapter 18, Durlach describes discussions held by contributors to this book (and others) regarding the current state and the future of adaptive training technology. Four topics were targeted for discussion: student models, pedagogical models for experiential learning, training efficiency, and military training applications.

Part I

ADAPTIVE TRAINING TECHNOLOGY

CHAPTER 1

Adaptive Educational Systems

Valerie J. Shute and Diego Zapata-Rivera

Introduction

Adaptive educational systems monitor important learner characteristics and make appropriate adjustments to the instructional milieu to support and enhance learning. The goal of adaptive educational systems, in the context of this chapter, is to create an instructionally sound and flexible environment that supports learning for students with a range of abilities, disabilities, interests, backgrounds, and other characteristics. The challenge of accomplishing this goal depends largely on accurately identifying characteristics of a particular learner or group of learners – such as type and level of knowledge, skills, personality traits, affective states – and then determining how to leverage the information to improve student learning (Conati, 2002; Park & Lee, 2004; Shute et al., 2000; Snow, 1989, 1994).

We present a general evidence-based framework for analyzing adaptive learning technologies. We then describe experts' thoughts on: (1) the variables to be taken into account when implementing an adaptive learning system (i.e., *what* to adapt)

and (2) the best technologies and methods to accomplish adaptive goals (i.e., *how* to adapt). We conclude with a summary of key challenges and future applications of adaptive learning technologies. These challenges include: (1) obtaining useful and accurate learner information on which to base adaptive decisions, (2) maximizing benefits to the learner while minimizing costs associated with adaptive technologies, (3) addressing issues of learner control and privacy, and (4) figuring out the bandwidth problem, which has to do with the amount of relevant learner data that can be acquired at any time.

Rationale for Adapting Content

The attractiveness of adaptive technologies derives from the wide range of capabilities that these technologies afford. One capability involves the real-time delivery of assessments and instructional content that adapt to learners' needs and preferences. Other technology interventions include simulations of dynamic events, extra practice opportunities on emergent skills, and alternative multimedia options, particularly those that allow greater access to individuals with disabilities. We now provide evidence that supports the importance of adapting content to students to improve learning. These arguments concern individual and group differences among students.

Differences in Incoming Knowledge, Skills, and Abilities

The first reason for adapting content to the learner has to do with general individual differences in relation to incoming knowledge and skills among students. These differences are real, often large, and powerful; however, our educational system's traditional approach to teaching is not working well in relation to the diverse population of students in U.S. schools today (Shute, 2007). Many have argued that incoming knowledge is the *single* most important determinant of subsequent learning (Alexander & Judy, 1988; Glaser, 1984; Tobias, 1994). Thus, it makes sense to assess students' incoming knowledge and skills to provide a sound starting point for teaching. A second reason to adapt content to learners has to do with differences among learners in terms of relevant abilities and disabilities. This addresses issues of equity and accessibility. To illustrate, a student with visual disabilities will have great difficulty acquiring visually presented material, regardless of prior knowledge and skill in the subject area. Student abilities and disabilities can usually be readily identified and content adapted to accommodate the disability or leverage an ability to support learning (Shute et al., 2005).

Differences in Demographic and Sociocultural Variables

Another reason to adapt content to learners relates to demographic and sociocultural differences among students, which can affect learning outcomes and ultimately achievement (Conchas, 2006; Desimone, 1999; Fan & Chen, 2001). For example, training on a foreign language may contain different content depending on whether the learner is a child or an adult.

Differences in Affective Variables

In addition to cognitive, physical, and sociocultural differences, students' affective states fluctuate both within and across individuals. Some of these states – such as frustration, boredom, motivation, and confidence – may influence learning (Conati, 2002; Craig et al., 2004; D'Mello & Graesser, Chapter 6 in this volume; Ekman, 2003; Kapoor & Picard, 2002; Litman & Forbes-Riley, 2004; Picard, 1997; Qu et al., 2005).

In summary, there are a number of compelling reasons to adapt content to learners. We now provide context and coherence for adaptive technologies by way of a general evidence-based, four-process model. This model has been extended from (1) a simpler two-process model that lies at the heart of adaptive technology (diagnosis and prescription) and (2) a process model to support assessment (Mislevy et al., 2003).

Four-Process Adaptive Cycle

The success of any adaptive technology to promote learning requires accurate *diagnosis* of learner characteristics (e.g., knowledge, skill, motivation, persistence). The collection of learner information can then be used as the basis for the *prescription* of optimal content, such as hints, explanations, hypertext links, practice problems, encouragement, and metacognitive support. Our framework involves a *four-process cycle* connecting the learner to appropriate educational materials and resources (e.g., other learners, learning objects, applications, and pedagogical agents) through the use of a learner model (LM) (see Figure 1.1).[1] The components

---

[1] The terms "student model" and "learner model" are used interchangeably in this chapter. They are abbreviated as either SM or LM. Because this chapter focuses on the educational functions of adaptive systems, we limit our modeling discussion to the context of students or learners rather than more broadly defined users.

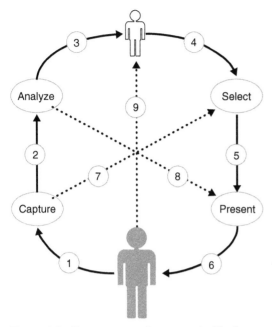

Figure 1.1. Four-process adaptive cycle. The larger human icon represents the student. The smaller human icon represents the student model.

Source: From "Adaptive technologies," by V. J. Shute and D. Zapata-Rivera, 2007, in J. M. Spector, D. Merrill, J. van Merriënboer, & M. Driscoll (Eds.), *Handbook of research on educational communications and technology* (3rd Ed.) (pp. 277–294). New York: Lawrence Erlbaum Associates, Taylor & Francis Group. Copyright © 2007 by the Taylor & Francis Group; reprinted by permission of the publisher.

of this four-process cycle include capture, analyze, select, and present.

CAPTURE

This process entails gathering information about the learner as the learner interacts with the environment (depicted in Figure 1.1 by the larger human figure). Relevant information can include cognitive data (e.g., solution to a given problem) as well as noncognitive aspects of the learner (e.g., engagement). This information is used to update internal models maintained by the system.

ANALYZE

This process requires the creation and maintenance of a model of the learner in relation to the domain, typically representing information in terms of inferences on current

states. That is, the computer can infer what the learner knows or can do directly from aspects of the learner's performance in the learning domain (e.g., if the learner solves a relatively difficult problem correctly, the inference is that his/her knowledge and/or skill related to the topic is likely pretty good, and if he/she solves another difficult problem correctly, the confidence in the inference that he/she knows the content well increases). In Figure 1.1, this is depicted as the smaller human figure and is often referred to as the student model or the LM.

SELECT

Information (i.e., content in the broadest sense) is selected for a particular learner according to: (1) his/her current status as represented in the student model and (2) the purpose(s) of the system (e.g., next learning object or test item). This process is often required to determine how and when to intervene.

PRESENT

Based on results from the select process, specific content is presented to the learner. This entails appropriate use of media, devices, and technologies to efficiently convey information to the learner.

This model accommodates alternative types and levels of adaptation. Table 1.1 describes some of the different possibilities, starting with a completely adaptive cycle and continuing to a nonadaptive presentation.

In general, the architecture of adaptive applications has evolved in a way that reflects the evolution of software systems architecture; for example, it is possible to find *stand-alone* adaptive applications where the complete adaptive system – including its student model – resides in a single machine. Also, adaptive applications have been implemented using a *distributed* architecture model. Some examples of distributed applications include: (1) client-server adaptive applications that make use of student modeling servers and shells (Fink & Kobsa, 2000); (2) distributed agent-based platforms (Azambuja et al., 2002; Vassileva et al., 2003); (3) hybrid approaches

Table 1.1. Scenarios Represented in the Four-Process Adaptive Cycle

Scenario	Description
A complete outer cycle, automated adaptation (1, 2, 3, 4, 5, and 6)	All processes of the cycle are exercised: capturing relevant information, analyzing it, updating the variables that are modeled in the learner model, selecting appropriate learning resources and strategies that meet the current needs of the learner, and making them available to the student in an appropriate manner. This cycle will continue until the goals of the instructional activity have been met.
Automated adaptation with user input (1, 2, 3, 4, 5, 6, and 9)	The learner is allowed to interact with the learner model. The nature of this interaction and the effects on the learner model can vary (e.g., overwriting the value of a particular variable). Allowing student input to the model may help reduce the complexity of the diagnostic and selection processes by decreasing the level of uncertainty inherent in the processes. It can also benefit the learner by increasing learner awareness and supporting self-reflection.
Diagnosis only (1, 2, and 3)	The learner is continuously monitored; information gathered is analyzed and used to update learner profiles, but not to adapt content. This may be seen as analogous to student assessment.
Short (or temporary) memory cycle (1, 7, 5, and 6)	The selection of content and educational resources is done by using the most recent information gathered from the learner (e.g., current test results and navigation commands). Adaptation is performed using information gathered from the latest interaction between learner and the system.
Short (or temporary) memory, no selection cycle (1, 2, 8, and 6)	A predefined path on the curriculum structure is followed. No learner model is maintained. This predefined path dictates which educational resources and testing materials are presented to the learner.

involving distributed agents and a student modeling server (Brusilovsky et al., 2005; Zapata-Rivera & Greer, 2004); (4) peer-to-peer architectures (Bretzke & Vassileva, 2003); and (5) service-oriented architectures (Fröschl, 2005; González et al., 2005; Kabassi & Virvou, 2003; Trella et al., 2005; Winter et al., 2005).

To illustrate how our four-process adaptive model can accommodate more distributed scenarios, Figure 1.2 depicts an extended version of our model. Agents (e.g., application, personal, and pedagogical agents) maintain a personal view of the learner using their own representation of the "four-process adaptive cycle" (see Figure 1.1). Agents share (or negotiate) personal information with other agents to accomplish goals on behalf of the learner. A common LM is maintained in a learner modeling server. The term "common learner model" refers to a subset of the LM that is common

to all the agents (e.g., identification information) and other information the agents share (e.g., long-term goals and interests).

Summary of Current Adaptive Technologies

This section describes adaptive technologies currently in use and relevant to the context of this chapter. The technologies have been divided into two main sections: soft and hard technologies; this distinction may be likened to *program* versus *device* and may be used across the array of processes described in the previous section (i.e., capturing student information, analyzing it, selecting content, and presenting it). The technologies selected for inclusion in this section are those that make use of, to some extent, an LM in its formulation. Also, this listing is intended to be illustrative and not

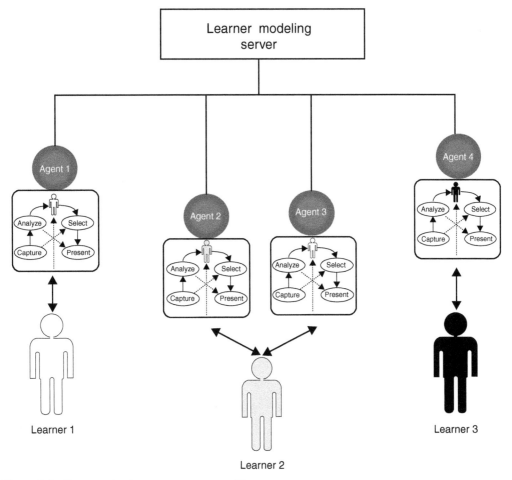

Figure 1.2. Communication among agents and learners.

Source: From "Adaptive technologies," by V. J. Shute and D. Zapata-Rivera, 2007, in J. M. Spector, D. Merrill, J. van Merriënboer, & M. Driscoll (Eds.), *Handbook of research on educational communications and technology* (3rd Ed.) (pp. 277–294). New York: Lawrence Erlbaum Associates, Taylor & Francis Group. Copyright © 2007 by the Taylor & Francis Group; reprinted by permission of the publisher.

exhaustive. For a more thorough description of adaptive technologies in the context of e-learning systems, see Buxton (2006), Fröschl (2005), Jameson (2008), and Kobsa (2006), the first of these for a directory of sources for input technologies.

Figure 1.3 provides examples of both soft and hard technologies (in shaded boxes) operating within an adaptive learning environment in relation to our four-process adaptive cycle; for example, technologies for *analyzing* and *selecting* LM information include Bayesian networks and machine-learning techniques. These technologies are examined in relation to both learner variables (cognitive and noncognitive) and modeling approaches (quantitative and qualitative). Similarly, examples of soft and hard technologies are provided for the processes of *capturing* and *presenting* information.

Soft Technologies

Soft technologies represent programs or approaches that capture, analyze, select, or present information. Their primary goals are to create LMs (diagnostic function) and to utilize information from LMs (prescriptive function).

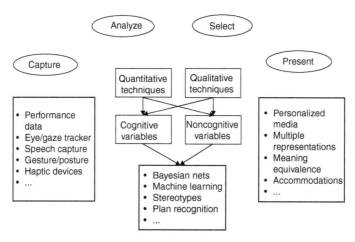

Adaptive Learning Environments

Figure 1.3. Overview of technologies to support learner modeling

Source: From "Adaptive technologies," by V. J. Shute and D. Zapata-Rivera, 2007, in J. M. Spector, D. Merrill, J. van Merriënboer, & M. Driscoll (Eds.), *Handbook of research on educational communications and technology* (3rd Edition) (pp. 277–294). New York: Lawrence Erlbaum Associates, Taylor & Francis Group. Copyright © 2007 by the Taylor & Francis Group; adapted by permission of the publisher.

QUANTITATIVE MODELING

In general, quantitative modeling of learners obtains estimates about the current state of some attribute. This involves models and datasets, as well as typically complex relationships and calculations. To begin modeling, relationships are established and tested, in line with a hypothesis that forms the basis of the model and its test. To quantify the relationships, one can use graphical models to create graphs of the relationships and statistical models that will define quantitative equations of expected relationships to model uncertainty (for more, see Jameson, 1995).

QUALITATIVE MODELING

Qualitative modeling supports learners by constructing conceptual models of systems and their behavior using qualitative formalisms. According to Bredeweg and Forbus (2003), qualitative modeling is a valuable technology because much of education is concerned with conceptual knowledge (e.g., causal theories of physical phenomena). Environments using qualitative models may use diagrammatic representations to facilitate understanding of important concepts and relationships. Evaluations in educational settings provide support for the hypothesis that qualitative modeling tools can be valuable aids for learning (Frederiksen & White, 2002; Leelawong et al., 2001).

COGNITIVE MODELING

Cognitive models may be quantitative or qualitative. They help predict complex human behaviors, including skill learning, problem solving, and other types of cognitive activities. Generally, cognitive models may apply across various domains, serve different functions, and model well- or ill-defined knowledge (e.g., design problems). The range of cognitive modeling approaches includes, for example, symbolic, connectionist, hybrid, neural, probabilistic, and deterministic mathematical models. Probably the best-known examples of cognitive models come from the cognitive tutoring research by John Anderson and colleagues (Anderson, 1993; Anderson & Lebiere, 1998; Anderson et al., 1990, 1995; Koedinger & Anderson, 1998; Koedinger et al., 1997; Matsuda et al., 2005).

MACHINE LEARNING

Machine-learning methods applicable for learner modeling include rule/tree (analogy) learning methods, probabilistic learning methods, and instance- or case-based learning approaches. An LM can take advantage of machine-learning methods and thus increase accuracy, efficiency, and extensibility in areas not modeled before (Sison & Shimura, 1998). According to Webb et al. (2001), machine-learning methods can be used to model: (1) cognitive processes underlying the learner's actions, (2) differences between the learner's skills and expert skills, (3) the learner's behavioral patterns or preferences, and (4) other characteristics of the learner.

BAYESIAN NETWORKS

Bayesian networks are graphs composed of nodes and directional arrows (Pearl, 1988). Nodes represent variables, and directed edges (arrows) between pairs of nodes indicate probabilistic relationships between variables (Pearl, 1988). Bayesian networks are related to the machine-learning methods (see preceding subsection) and are used within LMs to handle uncertainty by using probabilistic inference to update and improve belief values (e.g., regarding learner proficiencies). The inductive and deductive reasoning capabilities of Bayesian nets support "what if" scenarios by activating and observing evidence that describes a particular case or situation and then propagating that information through the network using the internal probability distributions that govern the behavior of the Bayesian net. Resulting probabilities inform decision making, as needed in, for example, our select process. Examples of Bayesian net implementations for LMs may be found in Conati et al. (2002), Shute, Hansen, and Almond (2008), and VanLehn et al. (2005).

STEREOTYPE METHODS

A stereotype is a collection of frequently occurring characteristics of users (e.g., physical characteristics, social background, computer experience). Adaptive methods are used to initially assign users to specific classes (stereotypes), so previously unknown characteristics can be inferred on the basis of the assumption that they will share characteristics with others in the same class (Kobsa, 2006). Creating stereotypes is a common approach to user modeling, whereby a small amount of initial information is used to assume a large number of default assumptions. When more information about individuals becomes available, the default assumptions may be altered (Rich, 1979). The two types of stereotyping are *fixed* and *default*. In fixed stereotyping, learners are classified according to their performance into a predefined stereotype that is determined by, for example, an academic level. Default stereotyping is a more flexible approach. At the beginning of a session, learners are stereotyped to default values, but as the learning process proceeds and learner performance data is obtained, the settings of the initial stereotype are gradually replaced by more individualized settings (Kay, 2000).

OVERLAY METHODS

An overlay model is a novice-expert difference model representing missing conceptions, often implemented as either an expert model annotated for missing items or an expert model with weights assigned to each element in the expert knowledge. The weights represent the probability of a student knowing a particular concept or having a misconception. One of the first uses of an overlay model was done with the WUSOR program (Stansfield et al., 1976). More recent applications of this overlay approach can be found in a variety of research projects (e.g., Kay, 1999; Vassileva, 1998; Zapata-Rivera & Greer, 2000).

PLAN RECOGNITION

A plan is a sequence of actions (which may include choice points) to achieve a certain goal, thus reflecting the learner's intentions and desires. Plan recognition is based on observing the learner's input actions and the system, and then inferring all possible learner plans based on the observed actions. According to Kobsa (1993), two main techniques are used to recognize the learner's plan: (1) establishing a *plan library* containing all possible plans where the selection of the actual plan is based on the match between observed actions and a set of actions in the library; and (2) *plan construction* where the system controls a library of all possible learner actions combined with the effects and the preconditions of these actions. Possible next actions may be calculated by comparing the effects of preceding actions with the preconditions of actions stored in the actions library. To read more about applying plan-recognition techniques in relation to instructional planning efforts, see Kobsa (1993) and Vassileva and Wasson (1996).

CUMULATIVE/PERSISTENT STUDENT MODEL

The cumulative student model represents the more traditional approach where the LM is analyzed and updated in response to the learner's activities. This involves building a student model that captures and represents emerging knowledge, skills, and other attributes of the learner, with the computer responding to updated observations with modified content that can be minutely adjusted. The selection and presentation of subsequent content are dependent on individual response histories (Shute & Psotka, 1996; VanLehn et al., 2005; Wenger, 1987). Student models can last for a long time and provide valuable information for various applications that keep track of long-term goals and interests. Some researchers have explored these ideas in the context of lifelong user models (e.g., Kay & Kummerfeld, Chapter 7 in this volume).

TEMPORARY STUDENT MODEL

Temporary student models usually do not persist in the system after the learner has logged out. In artificial intelligence, formalisms used to describe the world often face something called the *frame problem*, which is the problem of inferring whether something that was true is still true; for example, the accuracy of cumulative (or persistent) student models can degrade as students forget

things. Brooks (1999) and others have circumvented the frame problem by using the world as its own model (i.e., if you want to know if a window is closed, check the actual window rather than consult an internal model). The same idea applies to student modeling; that is, if you want to know if a student can still multiply two fractions, ask the student to multiply two fractions. This kind of student model is always up to date and corresponds to the short memory cycle scenario shown in Table 1.1.

PEDAGOGICAL AGENTS

Pedagogical means that these programs are designed to teach, and *agent* suggests that the programs are semiautonomous, possessing their own goals and making decisions on what actions to take to achieve their goals (i.e., a programmer has not predefined every action for them). The current generation of pedagogical agents is interactive and sometimes animated; for example, students can speak to agents that can speak back, often have faces and bodies, use gestures, and can move around a computer screen. Some well-known agents include Steve (Johnson et al., 2000), AutoTutor (Graesser et al., 2001), AdeLE (Shaw et al., 1999), and the Tactical Language Training System (Johnson et al., 2004). An interesting application of agent technologies is *teachable agents*, which have been successfully used to promote student learning of mathematics and science (Biswas et al., 2001). This computer-based environment involves a multi-agent system (Betty's Brain) that implements a learning-by-teaching paradigm. Students teach Betty by using concept map representations with a visual interface. Betty is intelligent, not because she learns on her own but because she can apply qualitative-reasoning techniques to answer questions that are directly related to what she has been taught. Another class of agents is *emotional agents* (affective computing), which have been employed to support student learning (Picard, 1997; Wright, 1997). Getting students motivated and sustaining their motivation have historically been major obstacles in education. Emotional (or affective) agents create a learning environment involving learners and interactive characters (or believable agents). Two important aspects of such characters are that they appear emotional and can engage in social interactions. This requires a broad agent architecture and some degree of modeling of other agents in the environment. Finally, pedagogical or virtual agents can collaborate with students, enabling new types of interactions and support for learning (Johnson et al., 2000).

Hard Technologies

In this section, we review several hardware-based technologies. These are mainly used for input (i.e., data capture) and output (presentation).

BIOLOGICALLY BASED DEVICES

So-called biologically based devices obtain physical measures of the student's body or physical activity. They were originally developed to support learners with disabilities (i.e., assistive technologies); however, many are being created or repurposed to support LMs for both cognitive and noncognitive student data. As an example, obtaining information about where on the computer the learner is looking during learning provides evidence about the learner's current state and attentiveness (for good reviews of eye-tracking research, see Conati et al., 2005; Merten & Conati, 2006). This information can inform the system about what is the next optimal path to take for this particular learner. In terms of eye-tracking technology, eye movements, scanning patterns, and pupil diameter are indicators of thought and mental processing that occur during learning from visual sources (Rayner, 1998); consequently, eye-tracking data can be used as the basis for supporting and guiding learners during the learning process. To illustrate the approach, consider a novel application of this technology known as AdeLE (García-Barrios et al., 2004). This introduces a real-time eye-tracking procedure for intelligent user profile deduction, as well as the use of a dynamic background library to support learning.

SPEECH-CAPTURE DEVICES

These devices allow users to interact with the computer via speech instead of relying on typing their input; consequently, this approach is valuable for individuals with physical disabilities that preclude typing, for young children who cannot yet type, and so on. The devices can also analyze speech profiles and obtain information on other aspects of the person, such as stress. One example project using speech-capture technology is Project LISTEN (Literacy Innovation that Speech Technology ENables) by Jack Mostow and colleagues. This is an automated reading tutor that displays stories on a computer screen and listens to children read aloud. It intervenes when the reader makes mistakes, gets stuck, clicks for help, or is likely to encounter difficulty (Project LISTEN, 2006). See also D'Mello and Graesser, Chapter 6 in this volume, and Litman, Chapter 13 in this volume.

HEAD-GESTURE CAPTURE DEVICES

Many computers are currently equipped with video cameras. Processing the image provides a means to track head position and movement. Software by Visionics Corp., for example, provides this capability. Zelinsky and Heinzmann (1996) developed a system that can recognize thirteen different head and face gestures. In addition, researchers in areas such as animated pedagogical and conversational agents have used sensors and a video camera for recognizing facial gestures (e.g., Kanade, Cohn, & Tian, 2000). This information is used to facilitate human-agent interaction (Cassell et al., 2001).

ASSISTIVE TECHNOLOGIES

Disabilities and nonnative language status can be major obstacles to learning from a computer. Examining adaptations in light of a validity framework can be valuable, if not essential, for ensuring effectiveness (for more on this topic, see Hansen & Mislevy, 2005; Hansen et al., 2005). Currently, a growing number of sites on the Web provide information for persons with special needs. See the Special Needs Opportunity Window (SNOW, 2006) Web site for information about the different kinds of adaptive technologies for people with disabilities.

Adaptive Environments

When technologies (soft and hard) are integrated into a single environment or platform to accomplish the goal of enhancing student learning via adaptation, this is called an *adaptive environment*. We now examine several well-known types of adaptive environments.

ADAPTIVE HYPERMEDIA ENVIRONMENT

Adaptive hypermedia environments or systems (AHSs) are extended from an intelligent tutoring system foundation and combine adaptive instructional systems and hypermedia-based systems (Brusilovsky, 1996; Chapter 3 in this volume). An AHS combines hypertext and hypermedia, utilizes features of the learner in the model, and applies the LM during adaptation of visible aspects of the system to the learner. Brusilovsky (2001) distinguished between two different types of AHS: (1) adapting the presentation of content (i.e., different media formats or orderings), and (2) adapting the navigation or learning path, via direct guidance; hiding, reordering, or annotating links; or even disabling or removing links (Kinshuk & Lin, 2004).

ADAPTIVE EDUCATIONAL HYPERMEDIA ENVIRONMENT

A particular type of AHS is an adaptive educational hypermedia system (AEHS). The hyperspace of AEHS is kept relatively small given its focus on a specific topic; consequently, the focus of the LM is entirely on the domain knowledge of the learner (Brusilovsky, 1996). Henze and Nejdl (2003) have described AEHS as consisting of a document space, an LM, observations, and an adaptation component that recommends content and changes the appearance of links and icons. The document space belongs to the hypermedia system and is enriched with associated information (e.g., annotations, domain or knowledge graphs). The LM stores, describes, and infers information, knowledge, and preferences about a learner. Observations represent the information about the interaction between the learner and the AEHS and are used for updating the LM.

COLLABORATIVE LEARNING ENVIRONMENT

An alternative approach to individualized learning is collaborative learning – that is, the notion that students, working together, can learn more than by themselves, especially when they bring complementary, rather than identical, contributions to the joint enterprise (Cumming & Self, 1989). Collaboration is a process by which "individuals negotiate and share meanings relevant to the problem-solving task at hand" (Teasley & Roschelle, 1993, p. 229). Research in this area examines methods to accurately capture and analyze student interactions in collaborative or distance learning environments; for example, Soller (2004) described various techniques (e.g., probabilistic machine learning) for modeling knowledge-sharing interactions among different learners.

SIMULATION AND IMMERSIVE ENVIRONMENT

Although simulations and immersive environments (e.g., virtual reality) change in response to specific user actions, typically the change is not due to an underlying LM but rather is a function of a predefined set of rules. Some simulations and immersive environments, however, do maintain an LM (Rickel & Johnson, 1997). Smithtown (Shute & Glaser, 1990; Shute et al., 1989) is a simulated environment where students change parameters in the hypothetical town – such as per-capita income, population, the price of gasoline – and see immediate changes in various markets, thus learning the laws of supply and demand. Smithtown actually maintains two LMs: one to model students' microeconomic knowledge and skills and the other to model their scientific inquiry skills.

As we have just shown, many different programs and devices are available to capture, analyze, select, or present information to a learner based on current or perceived needs or wants. We now turn our attention to what some experts in the field have to say about adaptive technologies. Our goal is to provide additional perspectives on relevant topics.

Experts' Thoughts on Adaptive Technologies

To supplement our literature review on adaptive technologies, we asked leading adaptive-technology experts to address two questions: (1) *what to adapt* (i.e., what variables should be taken into account when implementing an adaptive system?) and (2) *how to adapt* (i.e., what are the best technologies and methods that you use or recommend?). The experts who responded to our e-mail queries include Cristina Conati, Jim Greer, Tanja Mitrovic, Julita Vassileva, and Beverly Woolf.

What To Adapt?

Our experts responded to the what-to-adapt question in two ways: (1) input data or *learner variables* to be measured and used as the basis for adaptation, and (2) output or *instructional variables* that adapt to learners' needs and occasionally to preferences. Table 1.2 summarizes their collective responses and illustrates a wide range of student variables and adaptive pedagogical responses.

How To Adapt?

Responses to this question tended to focus on domain-independent approaches and technologies based on analysis of student and pedagogical models. Table 1.3 lists the methods suggested by our experts, which represent innovative implementations of the adaptive technologies discussed earlier.

In this section, we have presented a variety of learner traits and states that are judged relevant to modeling in educational contexts. In addition to these variables to be captured and analyzed in the LM, new data-mining technologies permit the discovery of even more learning variables for

Table 1.2. What to Adapt

Variables	Examples
Learner Variables	
Cognitive abilities	Math skills, reading skills, cognitive development stage, problem solving, analogical reasoning.
Metacognitive skills	Self-explanation, self-assessment, reflection, planning.
Affective states	Motivated, attentive, engaged, frustrated.
Additional variables	Personality traits, learner styles, social skills, perceptual skills.
Instructional Variables	
Feedback	Types: hints, explanations. Timing: immediate, delayed.
Content sequencing	Concepts, learning objects, tasks, items, cases or problems to solve.
Scaffolding	Support and fading as warranted; rewards.
View of material	Overview, preview, review, as well as visualization of goal and/or solution structure.

a more refined just-in-time collection of student information (for more, see Baker & Yacef, 2009; Beck & Woolf, 2000). This will allow systems to discover new things about a learner based on multiple sources of information from a single learner as well as from different learners. This sets the stage for accomplishing more accurate individual as well as distributed and collaborative learner modeling in the future. Challenges and envisioned futures are discussed next.

Challenges and Future of Adaptive Technologies

Several major obstacles must be overcome for the area of adaptive technologies to move forward. As in the previous section, we

Table 1.3. How to Adapt

Adaptive Approach	Rationale
Probability and decision theory	Rule-based approaches are typically used in adaptive systems, but using probabilistic learner models provides formal theories of decision making for adaptation. Decision theory takes into account the uncertainty in both model assessment and adaptation actions' outcome, and combines it with a formal representation of system objectives to identify optimal actions (Conati, 2006).
Constraint-based tutoring	The domain model is represented as a set of constraints on correct solutions, the long-term student model contains constraint histories, and these can be used to generate the system's estimate of students' knowledge. Constraint histories can also be used to generate a population student model (e.g., probabilistic model), which can later be adapted with the student's data to provide adaptive actions (e.g., problem or feedback selection) (Mitrovic, 2006).
Concept mapping	In order to adapt content (e.g., sequences of concepts, learning objects, hints) to the student, employ a concept map with prerequisite relationships, an overlay model of the students' knowledge, and a reactive planning algorithm (Vassileva, 2006).
Unsupervised machine learning	Most existing student models are built by relying on expert knowledge, either for direct model definition or for labeling data to be used by supervised machine-learning techniques. But relying on expert knowledge can be very costly and for some innovative applications it may be even impossible because the necessary knowledge does not exist. An alternative is to use unsupervised machine learning to build student models from unlabeled data using clustering techniques for defining classes of user behaviors during learning environment interactions (Conati, 2006).
Exploiting learning standards	Adapting around standardized content packages can make use (and reuse) of large quantities of high-quality content. This can be done by extending the Shareable Content Object Reference Model (SCORM) Runtime Environment specification to include user-modeling functionality. This permits content authors to take advantage of (and update) LMs in a content-management system. Content recommendations to students are based on the LM and recommendation is done in a lightweight manner with minimal demands on content developers (Greer & Brooks, 2006).
Analyzing expert teachers	Studying expert teachers/tutors is an invaluable source of information on how to adapt instructional content, but it is not always possible. Moreover, for some innovative systems (e.g., educational games), human tutors may not know how to provide effective pedagogical support. An alternative is to run so-called Wizard of Oz studies to test adaptation strategies defined via pedagogical and/or cognitive theories and/or through intuition (Conati, 2006).
Matching instructional support to cognitive ability	Adapting instructional support to match students' cognitive needs (i.e., developmental stage and different abilities) has been shown to promote better learning in a couple of experimental studies (e.g., Arroyo, Beal, Murray, Walles, & Woolf, 2004; Arroyo, Woolf, & Beal, 2006). The rationale is that if students receive instructional support that they are not cognitively ready to use, it will be less effective in promoting learning (Woolf, 2006).

have augmented this section by directly asking leading researchers in the field of adaptive technologies to summarize their views on challenges and the future of adaptive technologies. Our experts include Anthony Jameson, Judy Kay, and Gord McCalla.

Practical and Technical Challenges

The main barriers to moving ahead in the area of adaptive educational technologies are obtaining useful and accurate learner information on which to base adaptive decisions, maximizing benefits to learners while minimizing costs associated with adaptive technologies, addressing issues relating to learner control and privacy, and figuring out the bandwidth problem, relating to the scope of learner data. Each of these is now described.

DEVELOPING USEFUL LEARNER
MODELS
A core challenge of developing effective adaptive technologies is building useful LMs. According to Judy Kay (2006), collecting meaningful learning traces (i.e., data obtained from records and student log files) should help overcome this challenge; that is, the large and increasing volume of learning trace data associated with individuals is generally trapped within logs of individual tools. As a consequence, these data represent a wasted, untapped resource that might be used to build rich LMs. To transform learning trace data into an LM, a process must interpret the data to infer relevant learner attributes, such as knowledge and preferences. This would require the addition of a knowledge layer that maps learner trace data (evidence) to a set of inferences about the learner's knowledge.

ACQUIRING VALID LEARNER DATA
A related barrier to overcome involves the acquisition of valid learner data, particularly when accomplished via self reports (Kay, 2006). Self-report information has at least two problems. First, learners may enter inaccurate data either purposefully

(e.g., based on concerns about privacy or a desire to present themselves in a flattering light) or by accident (e.g., lack of knowledge about the characteristics they are providing). This problem may be solved by maintaining separate views of the LM (e.g., the learner's view) and providing mechanisms for reconciling different views into one LM. Second, when additional interactions are required during the learning process (e.g., completing online questionnaires), this increases the time imposition and can lead to frustration (Kay, 2006) as well as potentially invalid data from students simply trying to get to the content quickly (Greer & Brooks, 2006). Gathering such information, however, can not only reduce the complexity of diagnosis, but also encourage students to become more active participants in learning and assume greater responsibility for their own LMs.

MAXIMIZING BENEFITS
Currently, the cost of developing and employing adaptive technologies is often quite high, while the return on investment is equivocal. This challenge is a practical one – how to maximize the benefit-to-cost ratio of adaptive technologies. Despite a growing number of adaptive technologies available today, there are too few controlled evaluations of the technologies and systems.

According to Jameson (2006), addressing this problem should begin with the identification of specific conditions that warrant adaptation. There are at least two standards of comparison for adaptivity: (1) fixed sequencing and (2) learner control of content. The question is whether these comparison conditions accomplish the same goals that could be achieved via adaptation. Jameson (2006) offers a strategy for finding appropriate adaptivity applications – look for cases where the learner is in a poor position to select content herself, such as: (1) the learner wants to choose an item from a very large set of items whose properties the learner is not familiar with, and (2) the learner is in a situation lacking in the resources that would be required for effective performance.

MINIMIZING COSTS

One straightforward way to minimize the technical costs associated with adaptivity involves the use of more or less off-the-shelf technology for user adaptivity (Fink & Kobsa, 2000; Jameson, 2006). Another cost-minimizing option has been suggested by Greer and Brooks (2006), which involves leveraging existing content. They note that adaptive algorithms are often domain-specific, requiring the hand-coding of content to fit the specific form of adaptation. But, with the growing use of standardized content management systems and content available with descriptive metadata, the adaptive learning community has the opportunity to get in on the ground floor in creating standards for content adaptation (see Flynn, Chapter 12 in this volume). Their approach involves creating formal ontologies to capture content, context, and learning outcomes. Instances of these ontologies can be reasoned over by a learning environment to provide content (and peer help) recommendations. Formal ontologies may then be shared (e.g., via Semantic Web specifications) and provide a clear set of deduction rules as well as extensive tool support.

DEALING WITH LEARNER CONTROL ISSUES

Learners often want to control their learning environment. One strategy that addresses this desire is to allow them partial control of the process. According to Jameson (2006), there are several ways to divide the job of making a learning-path decision by the system versus the learner (see Wickens & Hollands, 2000, chapter 13). The system can (1) recommend several possibilities and allow the learner to choose from that list; (2) ask the learner for approval of a suggested action; or (3) proceed with a particular action but allow the learner to interrupt its execution of the action.

ADDRESSING PRIVACY AND OBTRUSIVENESS CONCERNS

When a system has control of the learning environment and automatically adapts, its behavior may be viewed by learners as relatively unpredictable, incomprehensible, or uncontrollable (Jameson, 2008). Moreover, the actions that the system performs to acquire information about the learner or to obtain confirmation for proposed actions may make the system seem obtrusive or threaten the learner's privacy (Kobsa, 2002). According to Kay (2006), one way to address this concern is to build all parts of the learner modeling system in a transparent manner to ensure that the learner can scrutinize the system's management of their data and the way in which those data are interpreted (Cook & Kay, 1994).

CONSIDERING THE SCOPE OF THE LEARNER MODEL

According to McCalla (2006), adapting to individual differences is essential to making adaptive systems more effective. Despite some support for this claim (Arroyo et al., 2004, 2006), significantly more experimental studies are needed. The traditional approach to achieving adaptivity has required the system to maintain an LM that captures certain characteristics of each learner and then use those data as the basis for adapting content (Greer & McCalla, 1994). One major problem concerns obtaining sufficient bandwidth of learner interactions to allow the capture of a sufficient range of characteristics to paint an accurate picture of the learner for appropriate adaptation. Bandwidth in this case refers to the amount of relevant learner data that can be passed along a communications channel in a given period of time. The bad news is that it is difficult to maintain a consistent model as learners' knowledge and motivations change over time; but the good news is that the bandwidth problem is diminishing as learners are currently spending more time interacting with technology (McCalla, 2006), and it is possible to gather a broad range of information about them. Moreover, learners' interactions can now be recorded at a fine enough grain size to produce more depth in the LM. The maintenance problem may be addressed by the simple expedient of not trying to maintain a persistent LM but instead making sense of a learner's interactions with an adaptive system just in time to achieve particular pedagogical goals.

Having summarized the main challenges surrounding adaptive technologies and possible ways to overcome them, we now present some visions of where the field may be heading in the future. These views have been crafted from the answers provided by three experts to our questions.

The Future of Adaptive Technology

JUDY KAY'S VIEWS

A long-term vision for adaptive technologies involves the design and development of life-long LMs under the control of each learner. This idea draws on the range of learning traces available from various tools and contexts. Learners could release relevant parts of their lifelong LMs to new learning environments. Realizing such a vision requires that all aspects of the LM and its use are amenable to learner control. Part of the future for LMs of this type must include the aggregation of information across models. This relates back to two major challenges: privacy and user control of personal data, as well as its use and reuse. An important part of addressing these issues will be to build LMs and associated applications so learners can always access and control their LMs and their use. This approach must go beyond just making the LM more open and inspectable, to ensuring that learners actually take control of its use.

GORD MCCALLA'S VIEWS

The next envisioned future of adaptive technologies relates to the ecological approach. The learning environment is assumed to be a repository of known learning objects, but both learning object and repository are defined broadly to include a variety of learning environments. To further enhance flexibility, the repository may also include: (1) artificial agents representing learning objects, and (2) personal agents representing users (e.g., learners, tutors, and teachers). In this vision, each agent maintains models of other agents and users that help the agent achieve its goals. The models contain raw data tracked during interactions between the agents and users (and other agents), as well as inferences drawn from the raw data. Such inferences are only made as needed (and as resources allow) while an agent is trying to achieve a pedagogical goal. This is called *active modeling* (McCalla et al., 2000). After a learner has interacted with a learning object, a copy of the model that his or her personal agent has been keeping can be attached to the learning object. This copy is called a *learner model instance* and represents the agent's view of the learner during this particular interaction, both what the personal agent inferred about the learner's characteristics and how the learner interacted with the system. Over time, each learning object slowly accumulates LM instances that collectively form a record of the experiences of many different learners as they have interacted with the learning object. To achieve various pedagogical goals, agents can *mine* LM instances – attached to one or more learning objects – for patterns about how learners interacted with the learning objects. The approach is called *ecological* because the agents and objects in the environment must continuously accumulate information, and there can be natural selection as to which objects are useful or not. Useless objects and agents can thus be pruned. Moreover, ecological niches may exist that are based on goals (e.g., certain agents and learning objects are useful for a given goal whereas others are not). Finally, the whole environment evolves and changes naturally through interaction among the agents and ongoing attachment of LM instances to learning objects. The ecological approach will require research into many issues (e.g., experimentation to discover algorithms that work for particular kinds of pedagogical goals).

ANTHONY JAMESON'S VIEWS

Although there are many improvements that can and should be made in terms of tools and techniques for adaptation, it is even more important to focus on the central problem of getting the benefits to exceed the costs. Adaptivity, like many other novel technologies, is a technology that is worthwhile, albeit within a restricted range of settings. It is thus critically important to clearly identify these settings and to solve the adaptation problems therein. The ultimate goal is to enhance (in the short or middle term) the usability and effectiveness of real systems in the real world.

Summary and Discussion

Adaptive systems have been and will continue to evolve as new technologies appear in the field and old ones transform and become more established. The future of the field is wide open in that it can evolve in different ways depending on factors such as the emergence of new technologies, new media, advances in learning, measurement, and artificial intelligence, and general policies and standards that take hold (or not) in relation to adaptive instruction and learning. One shift that we see as critically important to the field, particularly in the near term, is toward conducting controlled evaluations of adaptive technologies and systems. This will enable the community to gauge the value-added of these often expensive technologies in relation to improving student learning or other valued proficiencies (e.g., self-esteem, motivation). Our review has shed light on a range of technologies, but the bottom line has not yet been addressed: What works, for whom, and under which conditions and contexts? Conati (2006) asserts and we agree that *learners' traits targeted for adaptation should clearly improve the pedagogical effectiveness of the system.* This depends on whether or not: (1) a given trait is relevant to achieve the system's pedagogical goals; (2) there is enough learner variability on the trait to justify the need for individualized interaction; and (3) there is sufficient knowledge on how to adapt to learner differences along this trait. Along the same lines, Jameson (2006) argues that the benefits of adaptation should be weighed against the cost of modeling each candidate trait, to focus on traits that provide the highest benefit given the available resources.

A similar appeal for conducting controlled evaluations was made more than a decade ago, during the heyday of intelligent tutoring system development. Now, as then, the call for evaluations of adaptive technologies and systems is crucial for future development efforts to succeed in terms of promoting learning. Building adaptive systems and not evaluating them is like "building a boat and not taking it in the water" (Shute & Regian, 1993, p. 268). Evaluation is not only important to the future of the field, but can also be as exciting as the process of developing the tools and systems. And although the results may be surprising or humbling, they will always be informative.

Acknowledgments

We gratefully acknowledge the experts cited herein who provided us with thoughtful and insightful responses to our adaptive-technology queries: Chris Brooks, Cristina Conati, Jim Greer, Anthony Jameson, Judy Kay, Gord McCalla, Tanja Mitrovic, Julita Vassileva, and Beverly Woolf. We also thank Paula J. Durlach and Alan M. Lesgold for their very sage comments on an earlier draft of this chapter.

References

Alexander, P. A., & Judy, J. E. (1988). The interaction of domain-specific and strategic knowledge in academic performance. *Review of Educational Research, 58(4)*, 375–404.

Anderson, J. R. (1993). *The adaptive character of thought.* Hillsdale, NJ: Lawrence Erlbaum.

Anderson, J. R., Boyle, C. F., Corbett, A. T., & Lewis, M. (1990). Cognitive modeling and intelligent tutoring. *Artificial Intelligence, 42,* 7–49.

Anderson, J. R, Corbett, A. T., Koedinger, K. R., & Pelletier, R. (1995). Cognitive tutors: Lessons learned. *Journal of the Learning Sciences, 4,* 167–207.

Anderson, J. R., & Lebiere, C. (1998). *The atomic components of thought.* Mahwah, NJ: Lawrence Erlbaum.

Arroyo, I., Beal, C. R., Murray, T., Walles, R. & Woolf, B. P. (2004). Web-based intelligent multimedia tutoring for high stakes achievement tests. *Intelligent Tutoring Systems, 7th International Conference, ITS 2004*, Maceió, Alagoas, Brazil, Proceedings. Lecture Notes in Computer Science *3220* (pp. 468–477). Berlin: Springer Verlag.

Arroyo, I., Woolf, B. P., & Beal, C. R. (2006). Addressing cognitive differences and gender during problem solving. *Technology, Instruction, Cognition & Learning, 3(1)*, 31–63.

Azambuja Silveira, R., & Vicari, R. M. (2002). Developing distributed intelligent learning environment with JADE – Java Agents for Distance Education Framework. *Intelligent Tutoring Systems, 2363*, 105–118.

Baker, R. S., & Yacef, K. (2009). The state of educational data mining in 2009: A review and future visions. *Journal of Educational Data Mining, 1*, 3–17.

Beck, J., & Woolf, B. (2000). High-level student modeling with machine learning. *Proceedings of the 5th International Conference on Intelligent Tutoring Systems*, 584–593.

Biswas, G., Schwartz, D., Bransford, J., & the Teachable Agent Group at Vanderbilt (TAG-V) (2001). Technology support for complex problem solving: From SAD environments to AI. In K. D. Forbus & P. J. Feltovich (Eds.), *Smart machines in education: The coming revolution in educational technology* (pp. 71–97). Menlo Park, CA: AAAI/MIT Press.

Bredeweg, B., & Forbus, K. (2003). Qualitative modeling in education. *AI Magazine, 24(4)*, 35–46.

Bretzke H., & Vassileva J. (2003) Motivating cooperation in peer-to-peer networks. *Proceedings from the User Modeling UM03 Conference* (pp. 218–227). Berlin: Springer Verlag.

Brooks, R. A. (1999). *Cambrian intelligence: The early history of the new AI*. Cambridge, MA: MIT Press.

Brusilovsky, P. (1996). Methods and techniques of adaptive hypermedia. *User Modeling and User-Adapted Interaction, 6(2–3)*, 87–129.

Brusilovsky, P. (2001). Adaptive hypermedia. *User Modeling and User-Adapted Interaction, 11(1/2)*, 87–110.

Brusilovsky, P., Sosnovsky, S., & Shcherbinina, O. (2005). User modeling in a distributed e-learning architecture. In L. Ardissono, P. Brna, & A. Mitrovic (Eds.), *Proceedings of 10th International User Modeling Conference* (pp. 387–391). Berlin: Springer Verlag.

Buxton, W. (2006). A directory of sources for input technologies. Retrieved October 3, 2006 from http://www.billbuxton.com/InputSources.html

Cassell, J., Nakano, Y., Bickmore, T., Sidner, C., & Rich, C. (2001). Non-verbal cues for discourse structure. *Proceedings of the 41 Annual Meeting of the Association of Computational Linguistics* (pp. 106–115), July 17–19, Toulouse, France.

Chu, C., & Cohen, I. (2005). Posture and gesture recognition using 3D body shapes decomposition. *IEEE Workshop on Vision for Human-Computer Interaction (V4HCI)*. Retrieved October 2, 2006 from, http://iris.usc.edu/~icohen/pdf/Wayne-v4hci05.pdf

Conati, C. (2002). Probabilistic assessment of user's emotions in educational games. *Journal of Applied Artificial Intelligence, 16(7–8)*, 555–575.

Conati, C. (2006). *What to Adapt, and How?* Personal communication, May 18, 2006, 1–2.

Conati, C., Gertner, A., & VanLehn, K. (2002). Using Bayesian networks to manage uncertainty in student modeling. *Journal of User Modeling and User-Adapted Interaction, 12(4)*, 371–417.

Conati, C., Merten, C., Muldner, K., & Ternes, D. (2005). Exploring eye-tracking to increase bandwidth in user modeling. In *Proceedings of UM2005 User Modeling: Proceedings of the Tenth International Conference*, Edinburgh, UK. Retrieved October 29, 2006 from http://www.cs.ubc.ca/~conati/my-papers/um05-eyetracking-camera.pdf

Conchas, G. (2006). *The color of success: Race and high achieving urban youth*. New York: Teachers College Press.

Cook, R., & Kay, J. (1994). The justified user model: A viewable, explained user model. In A. Kobsa, & D. Litman (Eds.), *Proceedings of the Fourth International Conference on User Modeling UM94* (pp. 145–150). Hyannis, MA: MITRE, UM Inc.

Craig, S. D., Graesser, A. C., Sullins, J., & Gholson, B. (2004). Affect and learning: An exploratory look into the role of affect in learning with AutoTutor. *Journal of Educational Media, 29(3)*, 241–250.

Cumming, G., & Self, J. (1989). Collaborative intelligent educational systems. In D. Bierman, J. Breuker, & J. Sandberg (Eds.), *Proceedings of Artificial Intelligence and Education* (pp. 73–80). Amsterdam: IOS.

Desimone, L. (1999). Linking parent involvement with student achievement: Do race and income matter? *The Journal of Educational Research, 93(1)*, 11–30.

Ekman, P. (2003). *Emotions revealed: Recognizing faces and feelings to improve communication and emotional life*. New York: Henry Holt.

Fan, X., & Chen, M. (2001). Parental involvement and students' academic achievement: A meta-analysis. *Educational Psychology Review, 13*(1), 1–22.

Fink, J., & Kobsa, A. (2000). A review and analysis of commercial user modeling servers for personalization on the world wide web. *User Modeling and User-Adapted Interaction, 10*, 209–249.

Frederiksen, J., & White, B. (2002). Conceptualizing and constructing linked models: Creating coherence in complex knowledge systems. In P. Brna, M. Baker, K. Stenning, & A. Tiberghien (Eds.), *The role of communication in learning to model* (pp. 69–96). Mahwah, NJ: Lawrence Erlbaum.

Fröschl, C. (2005). *User modeling and user profiling in adaptive e-learning systems: An approach for a service-based personalization solution for the research project AdeLE* (Adaptive e-Learning with Eye-Tracking). Unpublished master's thesis, Graz University of Technology, Graz, Austria.

García-Barrios, V. M., Gütl, C., Preis, A., Andrews, K., Pivec, M., Mödritscher, F., Trummer, C. (2004). AdELE: A Framework for Adaptive E-Learning through Eye Tracking. In *Proceedings of I-KNOW '04* (pp. 609–616). Graz, Austria.

Glaser, R. (1984). Education and thinking: The role of knowledge. *American Psychologist, 39*(2), 93–104.

González, G., Angulo, C., López, B., & de la Rosa, J. L. (2005). Smart user models: Modelling the humans in ambient recommender systems. In *Proceedings of the Workshop on Decentralized, Agent Based and Social Approaches to User Modelling* (DASUM 2005), pp. 11–20.

Graesser, A. C., Person, N., Harter, D., & TRG (2001). Teaching tactics and dialog in AutoTutor. *International Journal of Artificial Intelligence in Education, 12*, 257–279.

Greer, J., & Brooks, C. (2006). *What to Adapt, and How?* Personal communication, May 16, 2006, 1–2.

Greer, J. E., & McCalla, G. I. (Eds.) (1994). *Student Modelling: The Key to Individualized Knowledge-Based Instruction*. Berlin: Springer Verlag.

Hansen, E. G., & Mislevy, R. J. (2005). Accessibility of computer-based testing for individuals with disabilities and English language learners within a validity framework. In M. Hricko & S. Howell (Eds.), *Online assessment and measurement: Foundation, challenges, and issues*. Hershey, PA: Idea Group Publishing.

Hansen, E. G., Mislevy, R. J., Steinberg, L. S., Lee, M. J., & Forer, D. C. (2005). Accessibility of tests for individuals with disabilities within a validity framework. *System: An International Journal of Educational Technology and Applied Linguistics, 33*(1), 107–133.

Henze, N., & Nejdl, W. (2003). Logically characterizing adaptive educational hypermedia systems. In *Proceedings of the AH 2003 – Workshop on Adaptive Hypermedia and Adaptive Web-Based Systems*, Budapest, Hungary.

Jameson, A. (1995). Numerical uncertainty management in user and student modeling: An overview of systems and issues. *User Modeling and User-Adapted Interaction, 5*(3–4), 193–251.

Jameson, A. (2006). *Challenges and future of learner modeling*. Personal communication, May 24, 2006, 1–4.

Jameson, A. (2008). Adaptive interfaces and agents. In A. Sears & J. A. Jacko (Eds.), *The human-computer interaction handbook: Fundamentals, evolving technologies and emerging applications* (2nd ed.) (pp. 433–458). Mahwah, NJ: Lawrence Erlbaum.

Johnson, W. L., & Rickel, J. (1997). Steve: An animated pedagogical agent for procedural training in virtual environments. *ACM SIGART Bulletin, 8*(1–4), 16–21.

Johnson, W. L., Rickel, J. W., & Lester, J. C. (2000). Animated Pedagogical Agents: Face-to-Face Interaction in Interactive Learning Environments. *International Journal of Artificial Intelligence in Education, 11*(1), 47–78.

Johnson. W. L., Beal, C., Fowles-Winkler, A., Narayanan, S., Papachristou, D., Marsella, S., & Vilhjálmsson, H. (2004). Tactical Language Training System: An interim report. *Proceedings of Intelligent Tutoring Systems 2004 (ITS 2004)*. Berlin: Springer Verlag.

Kabassi, K., & Virvou, M. (2003). Using web services for personalised web-based learning. *Educational Technology & Society, 6*(3), 61–71. Retrieved October 10, 2006 from http://ifets. ieee.org/periodical/6_3/8.html

Kanade, T., Cohn, J. F., & Tian, Y. (2000). Comprehensive database for facial expression analysis. *Proceedings of the Fourth IEEE International Conference on Automatic Face and Gesture Recognition (FG'00)*. Grenoble, France, pp. 46–53.

Kapoor, A., & Picard, R. W. (2002). Real-time, fully automatic upper facial feature tracking. Paper presented at the *5th International Conference on Automatic Face and Gesture Recognition*, Washington, DC.

Kay, J. (1999). A scrutable user modelling shell for user-adapted interaction. Ph.D. Thesis, Basser Department of Computer Science, University of Sydney, Sydney, Australia.

Kay, J. (2000). Stereotypes, student models and scrutability. In G. Gauthier, G., Frasson, C., & K. VanLehn (Eds.), *Lecture Notes in Computer Science* (pp. 19–30). Berlin: Springer Verlag.

Kay, J. (2006). *Challenges and future of learner modeling*. Personal communication, June 6, 2006, 1–4.

Kettebekov, S., Yeasin, M, & Sharma, R. (2003). Improving continuous gesture recognition with spoken prosody. In IEEE *Computer Society Conference on Computer Vision and Pattern Recognition (CVPR)*, pp. 565–570.

Kinshuk, & Lin, T. (2004). Cognitive profiling towards formal adaptive technologies in Web-based learning communities. *International Journal of WWW-based Communities, 1*(1), 103–108.

Kobsa, A. 1993. User modeling: Recent work, prospects and hazards. In T. K. M. Schneider-Hufschmidt, & U. Malinowski (Eds.), *Adaptive User Interfaces: Principles and Practice* (pp. 111–128). Amsterdam: North-Holland.

Kobsa, A. (2002). Personalization and international privacy. *Communications of the ACM 45*(5), 64–67.

Kobsa, A. (2006). Generic user modeling systems and servers. In P. Brusilovsky, A. Kobsa, & W. Neijdl (Eds.), *The adaptive web: Methods and strategies of web personalization*. Berlin: Springer Verlag.

Koedinger, K. R., & Anderson, J. R. (1998). Illustrating principled design: The early evolution of a cognitive tutor for algebra symbolization. *Interactive Learning Environments, 5*, 161–180.

Koedinger, K. R., Anderson, J. R., Hadley, W. H., & Mark, M. A. (1997). Intelligent tutoring goes to school in the big city. *International Journal of Artificial Intelligence in Education, 8*, 30–43.

Leelawong, K., Wang, Y., Biswas, G., Vye, N., & Bransford, J. (2001). Qualitative reasoning techniques to support learning by teaching: The teachable agents project. In G. Biswas (Ed.), *Proceedings of the Fifteenth International Workshop on Qualitative Reasoning*, St. Mary's University, San Antonio, TX.

Litman, D. J., & Forbes-Riley, K. (2004). Predicting student emotions in computer-human tutoring dialogues. *Proceedings of the 42nd Annual Meeting of the Association for Computational Linguistics (ACL)* (pp. 351–358). Barcelona, Spain.

Matsuda, N., Cohen, W. W., & Koedinger, K. R. (2005). Applying programming by demonstration in an intelligent authoring tool for cognitive tutors. In *AAAI Workshop on Human Comprehensible Machine Learning* (Technical Report WS-05-04) (pp. 1–8), Menlo Park, CA: AAAI Association.

McCalla, G. I. (2004). The ecological approach to the design of e-learning environments: Purpose-based capture and use of information about learners. In T. Anderson & D. Whitelock (Guest Eds.), *Journal of Interactive Media in Education*, Special Issue on the Educational Semantic Web (pp. 1–23). Retrieved September 22, 2006 from http://www-jime.open.ac.uk/2004/7/mccalla-2004-7.pdf

McCalla, G. I. (2006). *Challenges and future of learner modeling*. Personal communication, May 26, 2006, 1–4.

McCalla, G. I., Vassileva, J., Greer, J. E., & Bull, S. (2000). Active learner modeling. In G. Gauthier, C. Frasson, & K. VanLehn (Eds.), *Proceedings of the International Conference on Intelligent Tutoring Systems* (pp. 53–62). Berlin: Springer Verlag.

Merten, C., & Conati, C. (2006). Eye-tracking to model and adapt to user meta-cognition in Intelligent Learning Environments. *Proceedings of International Conference on Intelligent User Interfaces* (IUI 06), Sydney, Australia. Retrieved October 31, 2006 from http://www.cs.ubc.ca/~conati/my-papers/IUI06eyetrackingCamera.pdf

Mislevy, R. J., Steinberg, L. S., & Almond, R. G. (2003). On the structure of educational assessments. *Measurement: Interdisciplinary Research and Perspectives, 1*(1), 3–62.

Mitrovic, A. (2006). *What to adapt, and how?* Personal communication, May 17, 2006, 1–2.

Park, O., & Lee, J. (2004). Adaptive instructional systems. In D. H. Jonassen (Ed.), *Handbook of research for educational communications and technology* (pp. 651–685). Mahwah, NJ: Lawrence Erlbaum.

Pearl, J. (1988). *Probabilistic reasoning in intelligent systems: Networks of plausible inference*. San Mateo, CA: Kaufmann.

Picard, R. W. (1997). *Affective computing*. Cambridge, MA: MIT Press.

Potamianos, A., Narayanan, S., & Riccardi, G. (2005). Adaptive categorical understanding for spoken dialogue systems. In *IEEE Transactions on Speech and Audio Processing, 13,* 321–329.

Project LISTEN (2006). Retrieved October 28, 2006 from http://www.cs.cmu.edu/~listen/

Qu, L., Wang N., & Johnson, W. L. (2005). Detecting the learner's motivational states in an interactive learning environment. In C.-K. Looi et al. (Eds.), *Artificial intelligence in education* (pp. 547–554). Amsterdam: IOS Press.

Rayner, K. (1998). Eye movements in reading and information processing: 20 years of research. *Psychological Bulletin, 124,* 372–422.

Rich, E. (1979). User modeling via stereotypes. *Cognitive Science, 3*(4), 329–354.

Rickel, J., & Johnson, W. L. (1997). Intelligent tutoring in virtual reality. In *Proceedings of Eighth World Conference on AI in Education* (pp. 294–301), Kobe, Japan.

Seo, K., Cohen, I., You, S., & Neumann, U. (2004). Face pose estimation system by combining hybrid ICA-SVM learning and re-registration. *Asian Conference on Computer Vision (ACCV),* Jeju, Korea.

Shaw, E., Johnson, W. L., & Ganeshan, R. (1999). Pedagogical agents on the Web. In *Proceedings of the Third International Conference on Autonomous Agents* (pp. 283–290).

Shute, V. J. (2007). Tensions, trends, tools, and technologies: Time for an educational sea change. In C. A. Dwyer (Ed.), *The future of assessment: Shaping teaching and learning* (pp. 139–187). New York: Lawrence Erlbaum Associates, Taylor & Francis Group.

Shute, V. J., & Glaser, R. (1990). Large-scale evaluation of an intelligent tutoring system: Smithtown. *Interactive Learning Environments, 1,* 51–76.

Shute, V. J., Glaser, R., & Raghavan, K. (1989). Inference and discovery in an exploratory laboratory. In P. L. Ackerman, R. J. Sternberg, & R. Glaser (Eds.), *Learning and individual differences* (pp. 279–326). New York: W.H. Freeman.

Shute, V. J., Graf, E. A., & Hansen, E. (2005). Designing adaptive, diagnostic math assessments for individuals with and without visual disabilities. In L. PytlikZillig, R. Bruning, & M. Bodvarsson (Eds.), *Technology-based education: Bringing researchers and practitioners together* (pp. 169–202). Greenwich, CT: Information Age Publishing.

Shute, V. J., Hansen, E. G., & Almond, R. G. (2008). You can't fatten a hog by weighing it – or can you? Evaluating an assessment for learning system called ACED. *International Journal of Artificial Intelligence and Education, 18*(4), 289–316.

Shute, V. J., Lajoie, S. P., & Gluck, K. A. (2000). Individualized and group approaches to training. In S. Tobias & J. D. Fletcher (Eds.), *Training and retraining: A handbook for business, industry, government, and the military* (pp. 171–207). New York: Macmillan.

Shute, V. J., & Psotka, J. (1996). Intelligent tutoring systems: Past, present, and future. In D. Jonassen (Ed.), *Handbook of research for educational communications and technology* (pp. 570–600). New York: Macmillan.

Shute, V. J., & Regian, J. W. (1993) Principles for evaluating intelligent tutoring systems. *Journal of Artificial Intelligence in Education, 4*(3), 245–271.

Sison, R., & Shimura, M. (1998). Student modeling and machine learning. *International Journal of Artificial Intelligence in Education, 9,* 128–158.

Snow, C. E., & Biancarosa, G. (2003). *Adolescent literacy and the achievement gap: What do we know and where do we go from here?* New York: Carnegie Corporation of New York.

Snow, R. E. (1989). Toward assessment of cognitive and conative structures in learning. *Educational Researcher, 18*(9), 8–14.

Snow, R. E. (1994). Abilities in academic tasks. In R. J. Sternberg & R. K. Wagner (Eds.), *Mind in context: Interactionist perspectives on human intelligence* (pp. 3–37). New York: Cambridge University Press.

SNOW (2006). Retrieved October 28, 2006 from http://snow.utoronto.ca/technology/

Soller, A. (2004). Computational modeling and analysis of knowledge sharing in collaborative distance learning, *User Modeling and User-Adapted Interaction, 14(4),* 351–381.

Stansfield, J., Carr, B., & Goldstein, I. (1976). *Wumpus advisor: A first implementation of a program that tutors logical and probabilistic reasoning skills.* (Technical Report 381). MIT, Artificial Intelligence Laboratory, Cambridge, MA.

Teasley, S. D., & Rochelle, J. (1993). Constructing a joint problem space: The computer as a tool for sharing knowledge. In S. P. Lajoie & S. J. Derry (Eds.), *Computers as cognitive tools* (pp. 229–258). Hillsdale, NJ: Lawrence Erlbaum.

Tobias, S. (1994). Interest, prior knowledge, and learning. *Review of Educational Research, 64(1),* 37–54.

Trella, M., Carmona, C., & Conejo, R. (2005). MEDEA: An open service-based learning platform for developing intelligent educational systems for the Web. In *Proceedings of Workshop on Adaptive Systems for Web based Education at 12th International Conference on Artificial Intelligence in Education* (pp. 27–34). Amsterdam: IOS Press.

VanLehn, K., Lynch, C., Schulze, K., Shapiro, J. A., Shelby, R., Taylor, L., Treacy, D., Weinstein, A., & Wintersgill, M. (2005). The Andes physics tutoring system: Lessons learned. *International Journal of Artificial Intelligence and Education, 15(3)*, 147–204.

Vassileva, J. (1998). DCG +GTE: Dynamic courseware generation with teaching expertise. *Instructional Science, 26(3/4)*, 317–332.

Vassileva, J. (2006). *What to adapt, and how?* Personal communication, May 15, 2006, 1–2.

Vassileva, J., McCalla, G. I., & Greer, J. E., (2003). Multi-agent multi-user modeling in I-help. *User Modeling and User-Adapted Interaction, 13(1–2)*, 179–210.

Vassileva, J., & Wasson, B. (1996). Instructional planning approaches: From tutoring towards free learning. *Proceedings of EuroAIED* (pp. 1–8). Lisbon, Portugal.

Webb, G., Pazzani, M. J., & Billsus, D. (2001). Machine learning for user modeling. *User Modeling and User-Adapted Interaction, 11*, 19–29.

Wenger, E. (1987). *Artificial intelligence and tutoring systems*. Los Altos, CA: Morgan Kaufmann Publishers.

Wickens, C. D., & Hollands, J. G. (2000). *Engineering psychology and human performance* (3rd Ed). Upper Saddle River, NJ: Prentice Hall.

Winter, M., Brooks, C., & Greer, J. (2005). Towards best practices for semantic web student modelling. In the *12th International Conference on Artificial Intelligence in Education (AIED 2005)*, July 18–22, Amsterdam, The Netherlands.

Woolf, B. (2006). *What to adapt, and how?* Personal communication, May 22, 2006, 1–2.

Wright, I. (1997). *Emotional agents*. PhD thesis, University of Birmingham. Retrieved May 25, 2006 from http://citeseer.ist.psu.edu/wright97emotional.html

Yang, M., Zapata-Rivera, D., & Bauer, M. (2006). E-Grammar: An assessment-based learning environment for English grammar. In E. Pearson & P. Bohman (Eds.), *Proceedings of World Conference on Educational Multimedia, Hypermedia and Telecommunications* (pp. 2474–2479). Chesapeake, VA: AACE.

Yeasin, M., & Bullot, B. (2005). Comparison of linear and non-linear data projection techniques in recognizing universal facial expressions. In *Proceedings of International Joint Conference on Neural Networks, 5*, 3087–3092.

Zapata-Rivera, D., & Greer, J. (2000). Inspecting and visualizing distributed Bayesian student models. *Proceedings of the 5th International Conference on Intelligent Tutoring Systems* (pp. 544–553). Berlin: Springer Verlag.

Zapata-Rivera, D., & Greer, J. (2004). Inspectable Bayesian student modelling servers in multi-agent tutoring systems. *International Journal of Human-Computer Studies, 61(4)*, 535–563.

Zelinsky, A., & Heinzmann, J. (1996). Real-time visual recognition of facial gestures for human-computer interaction. *Proceedings of the Second International Conference on Automatic Face and Gesture Recognition* (pp. 351–356), Killington, VT.

CHAPTER 2

Adaptive Expertise as Acceleration of Future Learning

A Case Study

Kurt VanLehn and Min Chi

This chapter begins with an extensive examination of the various ways that adaptive expertise can be measured. Most of them have fairly well-known theoretical explanations, which are reviewed briefly. On the other hand, theoretical explanations are not easily found for one particularly valuable manifestation of adaptive expertise: acceleration of future learning. Acceleration of future learning is valuable because the growth of knowledge anticipated for the twenty-first-century demands that experts be able to learn new task domains quickly. That is, their training *now* should raise their learning rates *later*. It accelerates their future learning.

We present a case study where accelerated future learning was achieved. The trick was to use an intelligent tutoring system that focused students on learning domain principles. Students in this condition of the experiment apparently realized that principles were more easily learned and more effective than problem schemas, analogies, and so forth. Thus, when given the freedom to choose their own learning strategy while learning a second task domain, they seem to

have focused on the principles of the new task domain. This caused them to learn faster than the control group, who were not focused on principles during their instruction on the initial task domain. In short, the metacognitive learning strategy/policy of focusing on principles seems to have transferred from one domain (probability) to another (physics), thus causing accelerated future learning of the second task domain (physics).

A Framework for Understanding Adaptive Expertise

Adaptive expertise has been discussed for at least twenty-five years (Hatano & Inagaki, 1986), and there seems to be consensus on what differentiates it from routine expertise. A widely quoted definition is: "Whereas routine experts are able to solve familiar types of problems quickly and accurately, they have only modest capabilities in dealing with novel types of problems. Adaptive experts, on the other hand, may be able to invent new procedures derived from their expert knowledge" (Holyoak, 1991, p. 312). According to Hatano and Inagaki (1986), a routine expert has mere procedural skill whereas an adaptive expert has some type of conceptual understanding of the procedures as well. Whatever this conceptual understanding may be, it allows the adaptive expert to be more effective in nonroutine situations than the routine expert.

This introduction will present a framework for understanding adaptive expertise by first presenting a fairly mundane classification system for studies. It classifies studies first along their design (cross-sectional vs. training) and second along their method of assessment. Although these are textbook classifications that can be applied to almost any experiment, they set the stage for speculating on the underlying knowledge structures that differentiate adaptive expertise from routine expertise. It will turn out that almost every type of study is easily interpreted using familiar theoretical concepts such as schemas and domain principles. However, one type of study (a training study that uses acceleration of future learning as its assessment) is not so easily explained. Thus, we conducted a study of that type, and describing it occupies the rest of the chapter.

Dimension 1: Cross-Sectional versus Training Studies

Two study designs are commonly used for understanding adaptive expertise: cross-sectional and training. The cross-sectional design is like an expert-novice study, except that the groups being compared are both experts: routine versus adaptive experts. For instance, when Barnett and Koslowski (2002) compared the behaviors of two groups of experts – experienced restaurant managers and business consultants – they found that the business consultants were more adaptive than the restaurant managers. Other studies compare experts with varying degrees of experience (e.g., Lesgold et al., 1988).

The other common design is a training study, where experimental and control groups are both trained to mastery on a small task domain, then tested for adaptive expertise. For instance, Pandy, Petrosino, Ausin, and Barr (2004) studied adaptive expertise in biomechanics that developed after a training period of about three hours.

The advantage of cross-sectional studies is that they focus on knowledge and skills that unarguably qualify as expertise, whereas training studies must use small task domains and short training periods in order to be feasible. On the other hand, training studies focus on instructions and conditions that can cause trainees to acquire adaptive expertise as opposed to routine expertise. This is an important question that cross-sectional studies address only indirectly at best. The chapter focuses exclusively on training studies of adaptive expertise.

Dimension 2: Methods for Assessing Adaptive Expertise

The difference between adaptive and routine expertise can be subtle, so methods of assessment are an important dimension for classifying studies of adaptive expertise. This section presents a simple taxonomy, which is summarized later in Figure 2.2.

The Hatano/Holyoak definition of adaptive expertise refers to a single type of assessment, wherein participants are asked to solve problems that are novel and cannot be solved with routine problem-solving procedures. In the context of training studies, such problems are often called far-transfer problems. As participants are solving the far-transfer problems, they are not allowed to access instructional resources. That is, they are *sequestered*, as are American juries, which led Bransford and Schwartz (1999) to call this "sequestered problem solving."

Bransford and Schwartz point out that transfer can also be measured by replacing sequestered problem solving with a situation where students can learn, a technique called *dynamic assessment* (Haywood & Tzuriel, 2002). That is, participants learn twice. First, they acquire some prior knowledge, then they are instructed in a second task domain as their progress is monitored.

Progress monitoring typically measures the rate of learning, the amount of help required during learning, or both. If the two task domains have the right relationship, then adaptive experts should master the second task domain faster and with less help than routine experts.

In addition to measures of transfer, some studies of adaptive expertise have used measures of the conceptual quality of solutions (e.g., Martin, Petrosino, Rivale, & Diller, 2006). This assessment assumes the theoretical position mentioned earlier, namely that routine experts have mere procedural skills whereas adaptive experts have a conceptual understanding of their procedures. The assessment procedure is merely to ask participates to solve problems that both routine and adaptive experts find challenging but solvable. Students either speak aloud or provide rich explanations of their reasoning in some other way. The participants' utterances are coded for conceptual depth and quality.

So far, three classes of assessment have been defined: (1) sequestered assessment: solving far-transfer problems without instructional resources or other help; (2) dynamic assessment: measuring how fast students learn or how much help they need while learning; (3) direct conceptual assessment. Although there is little more to say about the third type of assessment, there is much to discuss about the first two, so the discussion is broken into two subsections.

Sequestered Assessment of Adaptive Expertise

One way to measure adaptive expertise involves training students on one kind of task then giving students transfer tasks to solve in a sequestered situation. Bransford and Schwartz (1999) call this type of transfer Direct Application.

Direct Application also can be subclassified according the relationship between the transfer tasks and the training tasks. A standard theoretical framework is to assume that students acquire problem-solving schemas that have retrieval cues, slots, and

solution procedures, and these correspond to difficulties with *access*, *application*, and *adaptation* of the schemas. Let us examine each briefly.

Access-impeding transfer problems have features that are not typical of the training tasks, and some students have trouble even noticing that their schemas are relevant. For instance, Gick and Holyoak (1983) showed that students who knew how to apply Dunker's convergence schema in one context (marching armies across weak bridges over a circular moat) failed to notice its application to an X-ray convergence problems. However, if reminded of the schema, they were easily able to solve the X-ray problem.

Application-impeding transfer occurs when a known schema has several slots, and students have difficulty figuring out which slots go with which objects in the problem. It can also occur when students have accessed two or more similar schemas and are not sure which one to apply. For instance, several studies first taught students schemas for permutation and combination (Catrambone, 1994; Ross, 1987; VanderStoep & Seifert, 1993). These two schemas have similar applicability conditions and each schema has two numerical slots. The training problems are designed so that irrelevant features (e.g., students choosing lockers; balls placed in urns) are strongly correlated with the choice of schema and the filling of slots. Students are trained to mastery on such problems, so in a sense, they have become routine experts on these schemas. The transfer problems use new features or reverse the correlations, and this causes such students difficulty.

Lastly, adaptation-impeding transfer problems require that students modify the solution procedure. This is the only assessment method mentioned by the Hatano/Holyoak definition. To do such modifications, the expert must access some other kind of knowledge than the schema itself. As an illustration of such "extra knowledge" and how it can be used to modify a procedure, let us consider an especially obvious case. Kieras and Bovair (1984) taught two groups of subjects some complex procedures for operating an unfamiliar device (the phasor cannons on the Starship *Enterprise*). One group of subjects could access a schematic of the device as they learned. They were able to invent shortcuts for the procedures. The group that knew nothing of the schematic performed like routine experts; they could follow the procedures accurately and quickly, but could not modify them. Clearly, the additional knowledge possessed by the adaptive experts was the schematic of the device.

When experts are required to operate or troubleshoot a physical device or system, it is widely believed that they must understand its anatomy (structure) and physiology (function) in addition to mastering the standard operating procedures. Such "mental models" are a standard explanation for adaptive expertise in medicine, troubleshooting, and other domains where participants work with physical systems or devices.

Some mathematical and scientific task domains include explicit domain principles that are composed to form schemas. For instance, in kinematics, there are three common schemas for identifying acceleration. They apply when objects are (1) moving in a straight line and speeding up, (2) moving in a straight line and slowing down, and (3) moving in a circle. When experts are asked to identify the acceleration of a pendulum during the ascending part of its swing, routine experts apply the third schema, circular motion, which produces an incorrect answer (Reif & Allen, 1992). Adaptive experts produce a correct answer by retreating to first principles, namely the definition of acceleration as the first derivative of velocity. This behavior suggests that the "extra knowledge" that adaptive experts use is merely knowledge of the first principles of the task domain. This obviously is not quite right, as all experts "know" the first principles of their task domain; apparently, that knowledge is more inert for routine experts than adaptive experts. Perhaps the adaptive expert's retrieval cues for accessing first principles are more general, stronger, or somehow better than those of the routine expert. Anyway, we have at least the outline of an explanation for adaptive expertise

in principle-rich task domains when such expertise is assessed by adaptation-impeding far-transfer problems.

As illustrated by these two types of task domain, adaptive experts modify their schemas' procedures by using extra knowledge. For procedures that operate or troubleshoot systems, that extra knowledge was a mental model: the structure and function of the system. For principle-rich math and science task domains, it was noninert knowledge of the domain's first principles. Unless a task domain's procedures are completely arbitrary, they have some rational derivation, so adaptive experts may simply possess noninert knowledge of the original derivations of the procedures that they follow, whereas routine experts have somehow lost access to such knowledge or never have learned it.

Dynamic Assessment of Adaptive Expertise

Dynamic assessment features two learning periods, and the second learning period is monitored to provide an assessment of the knowledge produced during the first learning period. Logically, transfer measured via dynamic assessment can be divided into two types based on the students' performance during the second learning period. *Savings* occurs when some students have a head start in learning. *Acceleration of Future Learning* (AFL) occurs when prior knowledge increases the rate at which some students learn, relative to others. These are independent measures, so students could exhibit both Savings and AFL. For instance, suppose we are comparing two methods to train a skill, A and B. Figure 2.1 maps our terminology onto the relative performance of A (dashed line) and B (solid line) during the second learning period. The next few paragraphs present more concrete illustrations of Savings and AFL, albeit not in the context of measuring adaptive expertise.

Singley and Anderson (1989) monitored students as they learned the Microsoft Word text editing. Half of the students were familiar with WordPerfect, which is similar to Word, and the other half were familiar with

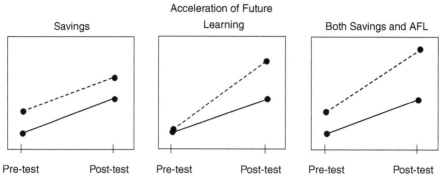

Figure 2.1. Performance during the second learning period for three types of transfer.

a line-oriented editor. Singley and Anderson observed Savings but not AFL That is, the students who knew WordPerfect did much better than the other students on a pre-test of Word skills, and they maintained exactly that advantage and no more throughout their training on Word. As Thorndike, Anderson, and many others have pointed out, this kind of transfer is easily explained by assuming that the two bodies of knowledge (Word and WordPerfect usage, in this case) share some elements. When students have mastered one, they have a head start on learning the other.

An example of AFL is Slotta and Chi's (2006) study. They taught half their students the emergence schema, which is an explanatory schema for certain types of scientific phenomena. Students were then taught about the flow of electricity in wires, an emergent phenomena. The electricity pre-test scores of the two groups were not significantly different, but the post-test scores of the emergence group were much higher than the post-test scores of the control group. Thus, this is evidence of AFL without Savings.

AFL can also be caused by teaching metacognitive skills and learning-to-learn skills (Hattie, Biggs, & Purdie, 1996). These are domain-independent skills (e.g., self-monitoring, note taking, self-explanation), in that they can in principle accelerate the learning of almost any content. If domain-independent skills were the whole explanation for the competence of adaptive experts, then such people would be universal experts:

Adaptive experts could learn *any* content much more rapidly than routine experts. Thus, the secret of adaptive expertise probably lies more toward domain-specific knowledge, such as the emergence schema taught by Slotta and Chi.

A type of AFL, called Preparation for Future Learning (Bransford & Schwartz, 1999; Schwartz & Bransford, 1998; Schwartz, Bransford, & Sears, 2005), focuses on just one task domain but still uses two learning periods. During the first learning period, students engage is some kind of preparatory activity that does not involve explicit domain instruction. During the second learning period, their knowledge is dynamically assessed. For instance, during the first learning period, Schwartz and Martin (2004) had the experimental group try to answer the question, "Was Bill a better high-jumper than Joe was a long-jumper?" Students had not yet been taught about z-scores, but they were given the appropriate distributions of high jumpers and long jumpers' performance, so they could have invented the z-score concept, although none did. Thus, this preparatory exercise did not contain explicit instruction on z-scores, nor did students successfully discover the z-score concept. On the other hand, the control group engaged in a filler activity during the first learning period. During the second learning period, both groups were taught explicitly about z-scores. The experimental group's learning was faster during the second learning period than the control group's learning. This experiment demonstrated Preparation

- Direct measures of conceptual understanding
- Sequestered assessment
    - Access-impeding problems
    - Application-impeding problems
    - Adaptation-impeding problems
- Dynamic assessment
    - Savings
    - Acceleration of future learning (AFL)
        - Transfer of meta-cognitive or learning-to-learn skills
        - Transfer of explicitly taught knowledge
        - Preparation for future learning (PFL)
        - Other

Figure 2.2. A taxonomy of assessments of adaptive expertise.

for Future Learning. Unlike the first earlier types of AFL where the to-be-transferred knowledge was explicitly taught (e.g., a metacognitive skill, a learning-to-learn skill, or Chi's emergence schema), Preparation for Future Learning does not teach anything explicitly, so it is less clear what knowledge is being transferred. What transfers may not be knowledge per se, but instead be interest, commitment, or some other persistent affective state.

In summary, we have defined a taxonomy of commonly used adaptive expertise assessments, shown in Figure 2.2. As mentioned earlier, AFL is an especially important manifestation of adaptive expertise, because as the amount of knowledge increases in the twenty-first century, experts will repeatedly be called on to master new knowledge. Moreover, as the work on Preparation for Future Learning shows, there are aspects of AFL that are not well understood. Thus, we chose to focus on AFL for the study described next.

The Study's Design and Findings

The study is complex, but it can be easily described now that the taxonomy of studies of adaptive expertise has been presented. This study is a training study rather than a contrast of two types of experts. It used both sequestered and dynamic assessment. The sequestered assessment used application-impeding and adaptation-impeding transfer problems, but it did not use access-impeding transfer problems. The dynamic assessment showed both Savings and AFL.

On all these measures, the experimental group performed significantly better than the control group. In the context of this experiment, adaptive expertise turned out to be a unified phenomenon: Whatever it was that the experimental group learned and the control group did not learn, that knowledge, meta-knowledge, motivation, and so on probably caused them to do better on *every* assessment.

Although the success of the experimental group is surprising, even more surprising is that the knowledge that we taught them, and not the control group, does not seem to be the source of their success. This raises the very interesting question: What did they transfer? Why did they become such adaptive experts?

Rather than extend this introduction, which is quite long already, we will describe the experiment itself. Afterward, we will discuss what it implies for adaptive expertise.

Methods

Many scientific task domains have equation-based principles. For instance, mechanics has a principle called Conservation of Mechanical Energy, which states that under certain conditions, the total mechanical energy of a system does not change over time. This can be more formally expressed by the equation TME1 = TME2, where TME1 and TME2 are the total mechanical energy of the system at times 1 and 2, respectively. Similarly, in the task domain of elementary probability, the addition law says that $P(A \cup B) = P(A) + P(B) - P(A \cap B)$.

In such task domains, a common way to get students to learn the principles is to give them problems where they are expected to apply some principles, then solve the resulting set of equations algebraically. That is, each application of a principle generates an equation expressed in terms of problem-specific variables. Some of those variables have already been given values in the statement of the problem. The student's job is to write enough equations so that a certain variable, often called the sought variable, can have its value determined algebraically. Such problems are common in textbooks for introductory physics, probability, circuits, thermodynamics, statics, and many other task domains.

Although it is not widely known, there is an effective, complete strategy for solving such problems. It is a specialization of a well-known weak method for deductive problem solving, called backwards chaining (Russell & Norvig, 2003). As far as we know, Bhaskar and Simon (1977) were the first to study its properties, but it is undoubtedly older than that. The basic idea is relatively straightforward:

1. If there are no goal variables left, then go to step 4. Otherwise, pick a goal variable as the target variable.
2. Considering all the principle applications that are possible for this problem and have not yet been done, pick one whose equation contains the target variable. Write that equation down.
3. Some of the variables in the equation may have known values and some may be goal variables now or in the past. If there are any others that are neither

known nor goal variables, then add them to the set of goal variables. Go to step 1.
4. Solve the set of equations that have been written down. This is most easily done via substitution, working backward through the list of equations.

We call this strategy the Target Variable Strategy, and we implemented an intelligent tutoring system called Pyrenees (VanLehn et al., 2004), which teaches students how to apply it. Pyrenees also teaches students the task domain's principles. From the students' point of view, learning the principles is probably much more difficult than learning the Target Variable Procedure. There are often dozens of principles, and some of the principles have subtle conditions on when they may and may not be applied. We view Pyrenees mostly as scaffolding for teaching principles. The Target Variable Strategy is part of that scaffolding.

The hypothesis tested by this experiment is that the Target Variable Strategy can be transferred. That is, when students learn one task domain using the Target Variable Strategy and Pyrenees, then they will more rapidly learn a second task domain without the aid of Pyrenees because they will apply the Target Variable Strategy by themselves. The hypothesis really hinges on motivation. That is, after several hours of following the Target Variable Strategy while using Pyrenees, they have probably mastered the procedure. However, they may or may not be motivated to use it in a new task domain. To paraphrase Pintrich and de Groot (1990), they have the *skill* but do they have the *will*?

Design

Two task domains, probability and physics, were taught. As students learned the first task domain, probability, half the students learned the Target Variable Strategy. The rest of the students were free to solve problems any way they liked. We call these two groups the strategy and no-strategy groups. The second task domain, physics, was taught the same way to all students and was used to

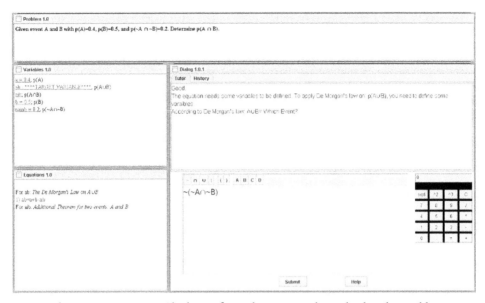

Figure 2.3. The Pyrenees screen. Clockwise from the top: windows display the problem statement, dialogue with the tutor, a workspace for composing and submitting an entry, equations and variables.

measure AFL. Each domain contained ten major principles.

Participants

Data were collected over four months during the fall of 2005 and the early spring of 2006. We recruited ninety-one college students. They were required to have basic knowledge of high-school algebra, but not to have taken college-level statistics or physics courses. Students were randomly assigned to the strategy and no-strategy groups. Each student took from two to three weeks to complete the study over multiple sessions. All the materials were online, and when students came back each time, they would continue from the point where they left off previously. Because of the winter break and length of the experiment, only forty-four participants completed the experiment. Two students were eliminated because of a perfect performance on the probability pre-test and a lack of time consistency, respectively. Of the remaining forty-two participants (59.5% female), twenty were assigned to the strategy group and twenty-two to the no-strategy group.

Three Intelligent Tutoring Systems

To control and measure the students' learning, three Intelligent Tutoring Systems were used: two for probability instruction, Pyrenees and Andes-probability, and one for physics, Andes-physics. Apart from the declarative knowledge, Andes-probability and Andes-physics were identical, and we will use Andes to refer to both of them. All the tutoring systems provided a screen that consisted of a problem statement window, a variable window for listing defined variables, an equation window, and a dialog window (see Figure 2.3).

Both Andes and Pyrenees are step-based tutoring systems (VanLehn, 2006). That is, the student can get feedback and hints on every step leading up to the final answer. Pyrenees explicitly taught the Target Variable Strategy and required the student to follow it during problem solving, so at any given time, only a few steps were acceptable to it, namely the steps consistent with the Target Variable Strategy. On the other hand, Andes provided no explicit strategic instruction, nor did it require students to follow any particular strategy. Students using Andes could input any entry, and Andes colored it green if it was correct and red if it was incorrect. Students could enter an equation that was the algebraic combination of several principle applications on Andes but not on Pyrenees.

Beside providing immediate feedback, both Pyrenees and Andes provided help when students asked. When an entry was incorrect, students could either fix it on their own or ask for *what's-wrong help*. When they did not know what to do next, they could ask for *next-step help*. Both Pyrenees and Andes gave the same *what's-wrong help*, but their *next-step help* differed. Because Pyrenees required students to follow the Target Variable Strategy, it knew exactly what step the student should be doing next so it gave specific hints. In Andes, on the other hand, students could enter correct equations in any order, and an equation was considered correct if it was true, regardless of whether it was useful for solving the problem. So Andes did not attempt to figure out the student's problem-solving plans or intentions. Instead, it picked a step that it would most like to do next and hinted at that step. Both *next-step help* and *what's-wrong help* were provided via a sequence of hints that gradually increased in specificity. The last hint in the sequence, called the *bottom-out hint*, told the student exactly what to do.

In summary, the strategy students were required to study and use the Target Variable Strategy to learn probability on Pyrenees and then learned physics on Andes-physics. The no-strategy students were not required to use any specific strategy and they learned both probability and physics on Andes.

Procedure

The study had four main parts: a background survey, probability instruction, Andes interface training, and physics instruction (see Table 2.1, left column). The background survey included high-school GPA, Math SAT, Verbal SAT score, and experience with algebra, probability, and physics, as well as other information.

The probability instruction had the five main phases: (1) pre-training, (2) pre-test, (3) watching a video introduction to the tutoring system, (4) training, and (5) post-test. The pre-training phase taught students individual probability principles, whereas the training phase taught students how to solve moderately complex problems involving multiple-principle applications. The experimental manipulation occurred only during the training phase. The pre-test and post-test used problems similar to the training problems. The pre-test was given *after* the pre-training and just before the training phase, so that the tests would more reliably measure differences in learning due to the manipulation, which occurred only during the training phase.

During phase 1 (pre-training), students studied the domain principles. For each principle, they read a general description, reviewed some examples, and solved some single- and multiple-principle problems. During this training, students were tutored by an answer-based tutoring system (VanLehn, 2006). For instance, suppose the system asked them to solve a problem: "Given that A and B are mutually exclusive events such that p(A) = 0.3 and p(B) = 0.4, what is the value of p(A∩B)?" If the students enter the correct answer, 0, the system would show it in green; if it was incorrect, the system would show it in red and then ask the student to solve an isomorphic problem. They will not go onto the next domain principle or solve the next problem until they have solved such a problem correctly. If they failed three times, then the correct answer (which is similar in all three problems) was explained to them and they were allowed to move on. The purpose of pre-training was to familiarize students with the principles, not necessarily to master them. They were expected to continue learning about the principles during the training phase as it taught them how to apply several principles in combination order to solve moderately complex problems.

During phase 2, students took the pre-test. Students were not given feedback on

Table 2.1. Procedure for the Experiment

	Strategy Group	No-Strategy Group
Background Survey	Background survey	
Probability instruction	Probability pre-training	
	Probability pre-test	
	Pyrenees video	Andes-Probability video
	Probability Training on Pyrenees	Probability Training on Andes-Probability
	Probability post-test	
Andes interface training	Andes-Probability video	
	Solve a problem with Andes-Probability.	
Physics instruction	Physics pre-training	
	Physics pre-test	
	Andes-Physics video	
	Physics Training on Andes-Physics	
	Physics Post-test	

their answers or allowed to go back to earlier questions. (This was also true for the post-tests.)

During phase 3, students watched a video about how to use their tutoring system. In particular, the strategy group read a text description of the Target Variable Strategy, then watched a video on how use the Pyrenees. The no-strategy group watched a video on how to use the Andes.

During phase 4, students in both conditions solved the same twelve probability problems in the same order on either Pyrenees (strategy condition) or Andes (no-strategy condition). Each main domain principle was applied at least twice. All students could access the corresponding textbook and the strategy students could also access the description of the Target Variable Strategy. Finally, students took the post-test.

After completing the probability instruction, the strategy students were taught how to use Andes without introducing any new domain knowledge. The user interface training, which was the same as the one given earlier to the no-strategy students, comprised a video and a probability problem to be solved. The problem was one of the twelve problems that the strategy students had solved earlier on Pyrenees. The pilot studies showed that solving one probability problem on Andes was enough for most students to become familiar with the Andes' user interface.

Finally, all students learned physics using exactly the same instruction. The instruction consisted of the same five phases as the probability instruction. That is, it consisted of (1) pre-training on individual principles, (2) pre-testing, (3) user interface training for Andes-Physics, (4) training on solving moderately complex problems using Andes, and (4) post-testing. To measure AFL, the strategy group and the no-strategy group received exactly the same physics instruction.

Table 2.2 shows the number of single- and multiple-principle problems in the experiment. In each post-test, five of the multiple-principle problems were isomorphic to training problems in phase 4. These functioned as near-transfer problems for assessing routine expertise. The other post-test problems (five for probability; eight for physics) were novel, nonisomorphic multiple-principle problems. Most of the multiple-principle problems had dead-end search paths so that the Target Variable Strategy could show an advantage in search efficiency. These functioned as far-transfer problems for sequestered assessment of adaptive expertise.

Table 2.2. Numbers of Problems for Each Phase of the Experiment

		Single-Principle Problems	Multiple-Principle Problems	Total Problems
Probability	Pre-Training	14	5	19
	Pre-test	10	4	14
	Training	0	12	12
	Post-test	10	10	20
Physics	Pre-Training	11	3	14
	Pre-test	9	5	14
	Training	0	8	8
	Post-test	5	13	18

To summarize, the main procedural difference between the two conditions was that during the probability instruction, the strategy students used Pyrenees while the no-strategy students used Andes. However, because familiarity with Andes might give the no-strategy students an unfair advantage during the physics instruction, where both groups used Andes, the strategy students were given a brief introduction to the Andes' user interface before the physics instruction.

Scoring Criteria

Three scoring rubrics were used: binary, partial credit, and one point per principle. Under the binary rubric, a solution was worth 1 point if it was completely correct and 0 otherwise. Under the partial-credit scoring rubric, the score was the proportion of correct principle applications evident in the student's solution – a student who correctly applied four of five possible principles would get a score of 0.8. One-point-per-principle scoring rubric gave a student a point for each correct principle application. Solutions were scored by a single grader who did not know which student or condition the solution came from. For comparison purposes, all of the scores were normalized to fall in the range of [0,1].

Results

Several measures showed that the incoming student competence was balanced across conditions: (1) there was no significant difference on the background survey between two conditions; (2) the two groups did not differ on the probability pre-test with respect to their scores on single-principle, multiple-principle, and overall problems across all three scoring rubrics; (3) during the probability pre-training, wherein students solved problems embedded in the textbook, the conditions did not differ on single-principle, multiple-principle, and overall scores. Thus, despite the high attrition, the conditions remained balanced in terms of incoming competence.

The two conditions did not differ on any of the training times: (1) the probability pre-training; (2) probability training on either Pyrenees or Andes-probability; (3) physics pre-training; and (4) physics training on Andes-physics. This is fortuitous as it implies that any difference in post-training test scores was due to the effectiveness of the instruction rather than differences in time-on-task.

The main outcome (dependent) variables are the students' scores on the probability post-test, the physics pre-training, the physics pre-test, and the physics post-test. We discuss each in turn.

First, on the probability post-test using the binary scoring rubric, the strategy students scored significantly higher than the no-strategy students: $t(40) = 3.765; p = 0.001$ (see Figure 2.4). Cohen's effect size (difference in mean post-test scores divided by pooled standard deviation) was 1.17, and is denoted "d" subsequently. Moreover, the

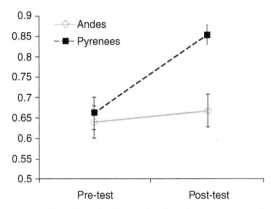

Figure 2.4. Results from the first learning period (probability task domain).

strategy students scored higher than the no-strategy students on both single-principle problems, $t(40)=3.960$; $p<0.001$; $d=1.24$, and multiple-principle ones, $t(40)=2.829$; $p=0.007$; $d=0.87$. The same pattern was found with using the partial-credit and one-point-per-principle scoring rubrics. Thus, the strategy students learned more probability than the no-strategy students.

Next we consider performance during the physics pre-training, reporting the binary scoring rubric only. The strategy students solved significantly more single-principle problems correctly in the first try than the no-strategy students: $t(40)=2.072$, $p=0.045$; $d=0.64$. No significant difference was found between the two groups on the number of multiple-principle problems solved correctly. This result could be due to an unlucky assignment of students to conditions, so that the strategy students happened to know more physics before the experiment began. Although we cannot rule this interpretation out, it does seem unlikely due to the use of random assignment and to the lack of difference in background questionnaire items that asked about the students' physics experience and grades. It is more likely that the strategy students were, even at this early stage, learning physics faster than the no-strategy students. This is consistent with the results presented next.

On the physics pre-test, the strategy students scored higher than the no-strategy students under the binary scoring rubric, $t(40)=2.217$, $p=0.032$, $d=0.69$. The same

pattern was found with the other two scoring rubrics. On the single-principle problems, the two conditions did not differ significantly regardless of the scoring rubric, probably due to a ceiling effect. For example, under the binary scoring rubric, we have $M = .93$, $SD = .097$ (maximum is 1) for the strategy students and $M = .86$, $SD = .11$ for the no-strategy students. On the multiple-principle problems, the strategy students scored higher than the no-strategy students on the partial-credit rubric, $t(40)=2.913$, $p=0.0058$, $d=0.90$ and one-point-per-principle rubric $t(40)=.800$, $p=0.008$, $d=0.86$, but not on the binary rubric $t(40)=1.148$, $p=0.147$. This could be due to the inherently less sensitive nature of the binary rubric. Anyway, the overall physics pre-test scores indicate that the strategy students learned more effectively during the physics pre-training than the no-strategy students. It appears that the strategy training during probability accelerated the strategy group's future learning, that is, their physics learning.

On the last assessment, the physics post-test, the strategy students' score was much larger than the no-strategy student's scores under the binary scoring rubric, $t(40)=4.130$, $p<0.0002$, $d=1.28$ and the two other rubrics (see Figure 2.5). More specifically, the strategy students outperformed the no-strategy students on single-principle problems under the binary rubric, $t(40)=3.211$, $p=0.003$, $d=1.00$ and on the multiple-principle problems as well, $t(40)=3.395$, $p<0.001$, $d=1.23$. Similar pattern was also found under the other two rubrics. Thus, the strategy students scored much higher than the no-strategy students on the physics post-test scores as well as on the single- and multiple-principle problems under all scoring rubrics.

The results presented so far are consistent with two kinds of transfer: *Savings*: the strategy students had a head start over the no-strategy students when learning physics; and *AFL*: the strategy students learned physics faster than the no-strategy students. To determine whether it was a head start or a learning rate, we ran an ANCOVA on the physics post-test scores using the physics pre-test scores as a covariant. This yielded a post-test

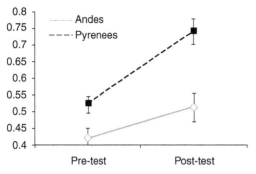

Figure 2.5. Results from the second learning period (physics task domain).

score for each student, adjusted for the difference in his/her physics pre-test score. With the binary scoring rubric, the strategy students had higher adjusted post-test score (M = 0.705, SD = 0.21) than the no-strategy students (M = 0.478, SD = 0.22). This difference was large and reliable $F(39) = 11.079$, $p = 0.002$, $d = 1.05$. A similar pattern held for the other rubrics: $F(39) = 6.155$, $p = 0.0175$, $d = 0.81$ for the partial-credit rubric and $F(39) = 5.290$, $p = 0.0269$, $d = 0.75$ for the one-point-per-principle rubric. This suggests that learning the Target Variable Strategy in one task domain caused AFL of the second task domain. This is intuitively satisfying, as we chose task domains that had very little overlap, making a Savings-style transfer unlikely.

What Was Transferred?

The overarching goal of our study was to determine whether teaching students the Target Variable Strategy explicitly in one deductive task would improve their learning performance not only in that task domain, but also in a new one. We found evidence for learning in both task domains. First of all, consistent with our previous study of physics (VanLehn et al., 2004), the Target Variable Strategy improved students' learning significantly in the initial domain, probability. Because the Target Variable Strategy increased learning in two initial domains, it may be an effective strategy in other deductive domains as well. Second, teaching students the Target

Variable Strategy in probability also significantly accelerated their learning during a second learning period, when they were not constrained to follow it.

Let us consider three hypotheses about *why* teaching the Target Variable Strategy improved learning in both domains. In particular, what did students learn during probability instruction that they transferred and used to improve their learning of physics? It will turn out that only the third hypothesis is supported by the data.

The first hypothesis, unsurprisingly, is that the strategy students learned the Target Variable Strategy and that they applied it during physics problems solving, which improved their search efficiency. The multiple-principle problems were constructed so that using the strategy would reduce the average number of steps required to solve the problems, and hence reduce both time and the likelihood of error. If the search-efficiency hypothesis is true, the strategy students should have performed better than the no-strategy students on the multiple-principle problems but not on the single-principle problems, where search is not required. However, the latter prediction was false (see Table 2.2). The strategy students outscored no-strategy students on single-principle post-test problems in both probability and physics.

The second hypothesis is that strategy students learned probability problem schemas better than no-strategy students, and that (somehow) they also learned physics problem schemas better than no-strategy students. A problem schema is a generalization formed as a by-product of problem solving by analogy that matches a whole problem and proposes a whole solution (VanLehn, 1989). Although students can construct problem schemas from only a few examples and are quite facile at using them to solve near-transfer problems, problem schemas often will not solve far-transfer problems (Gerjets, Scheiter, & Catrambone, 2004). Suppose the strategy students were better at learning problem schemas than the no-strategy students. This hypothesis would explain the strategy students' superior performance on near-transfer problems (i.e., test problems isomorphic to the training problems). However, this hypothesis predicts that on far-transfer problems, the two groups should perform equally poorly. The latter prediction is false. On the nonisomorphic multiple-principle problems (five in probability post-test and eight in physics post-test), the strategy students performed significantly better than the no-strategy students: $t(40) = 2.27$, $p = 0.029$ in probability post-test and $t(40) = 3.803$, $p < 0.0005$ in physics post-test.

The third hypothesis is that the strategy group learned both probability and physics principles better than the no-strategy group. The knowledge that was transferred could not be the principles themselves, because probability and physics share no principles. What may have transferred was the meta-knowledge that principles were the best thing to focus attention on when learning a new domain. That is, instead of trying to recall problem schemas, solved problems, equations, definitions of terms, and so forth, one should just focus on learning the principles.

Although this may seem implausible, examining the details of the strategy versus no-strategy training suggests otherwise. In Pyrenees, the Target Variable Strategy requires students to apply one principle at a time by selecting the desired principle from a menu, whereas Andes did not force them to apply one principle at a time, and seldom had students select principles from a menu. In Pyrenees, when students made a mistake, they got principle-specific feedback, but such feedback was rarely given by Andes because the no-strategy policy made it difficult for Andes to determine what principle the student was trying (and failing) to apply. Essentially, Pyrenees taught students over and over that if they could recall and apply the principles accurately, the Target Variable Strategy would take care of the rest of the problem solving. In particular, there was no use doing the usual schema building: recalling a solved problem, forming an analogy to this problem, mapping over the old problem's solution, using it to solve this

problem, and forming a general schema that paired a general problem description with a generalization of the solution. This focus on principles during probability instruction may have convinced the strategy students to approach physics differently than they otherwise would – that is, to forgo schema building and to concentrate instead to memorizing, understanding, and becoming fluent in applying physics principles.

Anyway, the principle-learning hypothesis predicts that on all problems, the strategy students should have performed better than the no-strategy students. This is exactly what occurred, which suggests that the main effect of teaching the strategy was to get students to focus on learning the domain principles in both probability and physics.

Unfortunately, because the strategy students outperformed the no-strategy students on every measure, the findings are consistent with any hypothesis that predicts a general increase in ability. For instance, using Pyrenees could have increased the strategy students' self-efficacy, interest in science, or even intelligence.

As a further test, we coded the Andes-physics log files for the solution strategies being used by students. Although the details are presented elsewhere (M. Chi & VanLehn, 2007), we found that no-strategy students tended to use the same mixture of problem-solving strategies on both easy and difficulty problems, and about 55 percent of the mixture was consistent with the Target Variable Strategy. On the other hand, the strategy students tended to use the Target Variable Strategy on hard problems and a step-skipping strategy on easy problems. This suggests that the strategy students had begun to learn the physics principles well enough that they can combine two principle applications in working memory, as physics experts often do (Priest & Lindsay, 1992). However, on difficult problems, they fell back on the scaffolding afforded by the (well-known to them) Target Variable Strategy. This is consistent with the hypothesis that strategy students transferred a predilection to study the principles, which caused them to master the details of each principle more rapidly, which in turn allowed them to start apply- ing principles in working memory instead of on paper, at least on easy problems.

To summarize, we have shown that teach- ing students an explicit problem-solving strategy improved their performance in the initial domain; more importantly, it seems to have caused AFL of a new domain. Because the improvement occurred with all types of problems, it may be due to the strategy instruction convincing students to focus on learning domain principles, as opposed to problem schemas.

Discussion

These results are unusually good. It is rare to observe interdomain transfer at all, and espe- cially one with such a large effect size. AFL is also uncommon. Lastly, getting students to stop focusing on problems and start focus- ing on principles is probably rare. Despite all the good news, there are limitations to this study that need to be considered.

First, the initial step in both physics and probability problems is to idealize the given situation and view it in terms of point masses, connectors and contacts between them (physics), or events conditioned on other events (probabilities). In this study, the idealizations were obvious for most problems. When a problem's idealization was not obvious, the problem told students the key idealizations (e.g., what the events are). Problems that "give away" the idealiza- tions are typical of introductory courses on physics and probability, so the idealization phase was tutored by neither Andes nor Pyrenees.

Second, experts in physics can plan solu- tions mentally without writing principle applications down on paper. This allows them to sort problems by their solution principles (M. T. H. Chi, Feltovich, & Glaser, 1981), articulate a principled basic approach (M. T. H. Chi, Glaser, & Rees, 1982), and determine when two problems' solutions use the same principles (Hardiman, Dufresne, & Mestre, 1989). Even though the strategy group in this experiment exhibited AFL, and that is

a manifestation of adaptive expertise, they were not physics experts. Indeed, they were selected to have had no university physics and were given only a few hours' training, so they are not even close to being physics experts. Nonetheless, according to one the- ory of the development of physics expertise (VanLehn & van de Sande, 2009), they were on their way to becoming experts. It would be interesting to see how adaptive they eventually become.

Third, it may seem that these results are limited to task domains that have both equation-based principles and problem schemas, and that students tend to ignore the principles and focus on acquiring the problem schemas. These properties are key to explaining the AFL results. When the strategy group used Pyrenees to master the probability principles, they also learned that mastering principles was better than learn- ing schemas. Thus, whereas the no-strategy group skimmed the pre-training discussions of physics principles so that they could get to the examples and problems, the strategy group probably paid a great deal of atten- tion to the initial presentation of the physics principles. When no-strategy students got stuck during physics problem solving, they probably hunted for an example that was similar to their problem so that they could map its solution over, whereas the strategy students started using the Target Variable Strategy and their list of principles (available in the help system and the textbook). This manipulation worked, one might say, only because the task domains happened to have both principles and problem schemas.

Hatano and Inagaki (1986) were well aware that adaptive expertise only makes sense when a task domain has both problem schemas (which they called procedures) and conceptual knowledge. Although they sometimes referred to conceptual knowl- edge as principles, their major examples of conceptual knowledge were mental models, such as the schematic of the phasor bank mentioned earlier. Regardless of the epis- temology type of conceptual knowledge, there must exist at least *something extra* beyond procedural skills (schemas) so that the adaptive experts can have it and the routine experts can lack it. Moreover, this extra knowledge must be able to derive or justify the procedures because that allows the adaptive expert to modify and adapt the procedures. In short, our requirement that a task domain have both schemas and principles that derive them is rather close to Hatano and Inagaki's requirement that the task domain have both procedures and a certain kind of conceptual knowledge.

This suggests that the instructional method of Pyrenees could be generalized. The basic idea is to explicate the conceptual knowledge in the declarative (pre-training) materials; then, during problem-solving practice, both compel students to use conceptual knowledge to solve problems and block their use schemas.

Mathematics educators may roll their eyes and exclaim that they have already tried that, and it seldom works. For instance, the principles of the base-10 numeration system plus the principles of set theory can be used to derive the multicolumn subtraction procedure (VanLehn & Brown, 1980). Many instructors and mathematics researchers have tried with little success to get students to understand this conceptual knowledge, often by using Dienes blocks and other concrete base-10 notations. However, the derivation of the written procedure from the principles is extremely long and complex (VanLehn & Brown, 1980). It is well beyond the capabilities of elementary school children. Thus, instructors often end up simply teaching an intermediate procedure (e.g., subtraction using Dienes blocks) that is almost as opaque as the written procedure, even though it is "halfway" between the first principles and the written procedure.

Although the third limitation (that a task domain have both schemas and principles) is not very constraining because many task domains probably have both schemas and principles, we now have a fourth limitation that probably *is* quite constraining. For novices, solving problems with first principles must be feasible and not too much more difficult than solving problems with schemas (procedures). For instance, if novice students must spend twice as much time using principles as schemas to solve problems, then they will probably stop using principles as soon as the tutoring system stops nagging them, and they are not likely to pay much attention to principles when they are taught another task domain. In our task domains, the strategy students, who we assume were using principles, took the same amount of time to solve problems as the no-strategy students, who we assume were using schemas and analogies to past problems. Thus, our task domains meet the criterion that principle-based problem solving is efficient. Multicolumn subtraction does not meet this criterion, so explicitly teaching its principles and blocking its schemas has not worked well.

To summarize, our instructional method is to teach principles explicitly and to require students to solve problems with principles instead of problem schemas. We speculate that it should lead to adaptive expertise when the following conditions are met:

1. The idealization phase of problem solving does not play a major role in this task domain.
2. The students are novices. It is not clear what happens after thousands of hours of training.
3. The task domain has principles or some other conceptual knowledge in addition to procedural knowledge, and the conceptual knowledge can be used to solve problems and modify procedures.
4. For novices, solving problems with conceptual knowledge is only a little more work than solving the problems with schemas.

In collaboration with Jared Freeman and Zachary Horn, these hypotheses are being tested in the task domain of naval force protection tactics.

Acknowledgments

This research was supported by several grants from NSF (EIA-0325054, PSLC-0354420, and DRL-0910221) and an STTR contract from ONR (N00014–09-M-0327).

References

Barnett, S. M., & Koslowski, B. (2002). Adaptive expertise: Effects of type of experience and the level of theoretical understanding it generates. *Thinking and Reasoning, 8(4)*, 237–267.

Bhaskar, R., & Simon, H. A. (1977). Problem solving in semantically rich domains: An example from engineering thermodynamics. *Cognitive Science, 1*, 193–215.

Bransford, J. D., & Schwartz, D. L. (1999). Rethinking transfer: A simple proposal with multiple implications. In A. Iran-Nejad & P. D. Pearson (Eds.), *Review of research in education, Vol. 24* (pp. 61–100). Washington, DC: American Educational Research Association.

Catrambone, R. (1994). Improving examples to improve transfer to novel problems. *Memory and Cognition, 22(5)*, 606–615.

Chi, M., & VanLehn, K. (2007). The impact of explicit strategy instruction on problem-solving behaviors across intelligent tutoring systems. In D. S. McNamara & G. Trafton (Eds.), *Proceedings of the 29th Conference of the Cognitive Science Society* (pp. 167–172). Mahway, NJ: Erlbaum.

Chi, M. T. H., Feltovich, P., & Glaser, R. (1981). Categorization and representation of physics problems by experts and novices. *Cognitive Science, 5(2)*, 121–152.

Chi, M. T. H., Glaser, R., & Rees, E. (1982). Expertise in problem solving. In R. J. Sternberg (Ed.), *Advances in the Psychology of Human Intelligence, Vol. 1* (pp. 7–75). Hillsdale, NJ: Lawrence Erlbaum Associates.

Gerjets, P., Scheiter, K., & Catrambone, R. (2004). Designing instructional examples to reduce intrinsic cognitive load: Molar versus modular presentation of solution procedures. *Instructional Science, 32*, 33–58.

Gick, M. L., & Holyoak, K. J. (1983). Schema induction and analogical transfer. *Cognitive Psychology, 15*, 1–38.

Hardiman, P. T., Dufresne, R. J., & Mestre, J. P. (1989). The relation between problem categorization and problem solving among experts and novices. *Memory & Cognition, 17(5)*, 627–638.

Hatano, G., & Inagaki, K. (1986). Two courses of expertise. In H. Stevenson, H. Azuma, & K. Hakuta (Eds.), *Child development and education in Japan* (pp. 262–272). New York: Freeman.

Hattie, J., Biggs, J., & Purdie, N. (1996). Effects of learning skills interventions on student learning: A meta-analysis of findings. *Review of Educational Research, 66*, 99–136.

Haywood, H. C., & Tzuriel, D. (2002). Applications and challenges in dynamic assessment. *Peabody Journal of Education, 77(2)*, 40–63.

Holyoak, K. J. (1991). Symbolic connectionism: Toward third-generation theories of expertise. In K. A. Ericsson & J. Smith (Eds.), *Toward a general theory of expertise: Prospects and limits* (pp. 301–336). New York: Cambridge University Press.

Kieras, D. E., & Bovair, S. (1984). The role of a mental model in learning to operate a device. *Cognitive Science, 8*, 255–273.

Lesgold, A., Rubinson, H., Feltovich, P., Glaser, R., Klopher, D., & Wang, Y. (1988). Expertise in a complex skill: Diagnosing X-Ray Pictures. In M. T. H. Chi, R. Glaser, & M. J. Farr (Eds.), *The nature of expertise*. Mahway, NJ: Erlbaum.

Martin, T., Petrosino, A., Rivale, S., & Diller, K. R. (2006). The development of adaptive expertise in biotransport. *New Directions for Teaching and Learning, 108*, 35–47.

Pandy, M. G., Petrosino, A., Austin, B. A., & Barr, R. E. (2004). Assessing adaptive expertise in undergraduate biomechanics. *Journal of Engineering Education* (July), 1–12.

Pintrich, P. R., & De Groot, E. V. (1990). Motivational and self-regulated learning components of classroom academic performance. *Journal of Educational Psychology, 82(1)*, 33–40.

Priest, A. G., & Lindsay, R. O. (1992). New light on novice-expert differences in physics problem solving. *British Journal of Psychology, 83*, 389–405.

Reif, F., & Allen, S. (1992). Cognition for interpreting scientific concepts: A study of acceleration. *Cognition and Instruction, 9(1)*, 1–44.

Ross, B. (1987). This is like that: The use of earlier problems and the separation of similarity effects. *Journal of Experimental Psychology: Learning, Memory and Cognition, 13*, 629–639.

Russell, S., & Norvig, P. (2003). *Artificial intelligence: A modern approach* (2nd ed.). Upper Saddle River, NJ: Prentice Hall.

Schwartz, D. L., & Bransford, J. D. (1998). A time for telling. *Cognition and Instruction, 16(4)*, 475–522.

Schwartz, D. L., Bransford, J. D., & Sears, D. (2005). Efficiency and innovation in transfer. In J. P. Mestre (Ed.), *Transfer of learning from a modern multidisciplinary perspective* (pp. 1–51). Charlotte, NC: Information Age Publishing.

Schwartz, D. L., & Martin, T. (2004). Inventing to prepare for future learning: The hidden efficiency of encouraging original student production in statistics instruction. *Cognition and Instruction, 22(2)*, 129–184.

Singley, M. K., & Anderson, J. R. (1989). *The transfer of cognitive skill.* Cambridge, MA: Harvard University Press.

Slotta, J. D., & Chi, M. T. H. (2006). Helping students understand challenging topics in science through ontology training. *Cognition and Instruction, 24(2)*, 261–289.

VanderStoep, S. W., & Seifert, C. M. (1993). Learning "how" versus learning "when": Improving transfer of problem-solving principles. *The Journal of the Learning Sciences, 3(1)*, 93–111.

VanLehn, K. (1989). Problem solving and cognitive skill acquisition. In M. I. Posner (Ed.), *Foundations of Cognitive Science* (pp. 526–579). Cambridge, MA: MIT Press.

VanLehn, K. (2006). The behavior of tutoring systems. International Journal of Artificial Intelligence and Education, 16, 227–265.

VanLehn, K., Bhembe, D., Chi, M., Lynch, C., Schulze, K., Shelby, R., et al. (2004). Implicit vs. explicit learning of strategies in a non-procedural skill. In J. C. Lester, R. M. Vicari, & F. Paraguaca (Eds.), *Intelligent tutoring systems: 7th International Conference* (pp. 521–530). Berlin: Spring-Verlag.

VanLehn, K., & Brown, J. S. (1980). Planning nets: A representation for formalizing analogies and semantic models of procedural skills. In R. E. Snow, P. A. Frederico, & W. E. Montague (Eds.), *Aptitude learning and instruction: Cognitive process analyses* (pp. 95–138). Hillsdale, NJ: Lawrence Erlbaum Associates.

VanLehn, K., & van de Sande, B. (2009). Acquiring conceptual expertise from modeling: The case of elementary physics. In K. A. Ericsson (Ed.), *Development of professional expertise: Toward measurement of expert performance and design of optimal learning environments* (pp. 356–378). Cambridge: Cambridge University Press.

CHAPTER 3

Adaptive Hypermedia for Education and Training

Peter Brusilovsky

Adaptive hypermedia (AH) is an alternative to the traditional, one-size-fits-all approach in the development of hypermedia systems. AH systems build a model of the goals, preferences, and knowledge of each individual user; this model is used throughout the interaction with the user to adapt to the needs of that particular user (Brusilovsky, 1996b). For example, a student in an adaptive educational hypermedia system will be given a presentation that is adapted specifically to his or her knowledge of the subject (De Bra & Calvi, 1998; Hothi, Hall, & Sly, 2000) as well as a suggested set of the most relevant links to proceed further (Brusilovsky, Eklund, & Schwarz, 1998; Kavcic, 2004). An adaptive electronic encyclopedia will personalize the content of an article to augment the user's existing knowledge and interests (Bontcheva & Wilks, 2005; Milosavljevic, 1997). A museum guide will adapt the presentation about every visited object to the user's individual path through the museum (Oberlander et al., 1998; Stock et al., 2007).

Adaptive hypermedia belongs to the class of *user-adaptive* systems (Schneider-Hufschmidt, Kühme, & Malinowski, 1993).

A distinctive feature of an adaptive system is an explicit user model that represents user knowledge, goals, and interests, as well as other features that enable the system to adapt to different users with their own specific set of goals. An adaptive system collects data for the user model from various sources that can include implicitly observing user interaction and explicitly requesting direct input from the user. The user model is applied to provide an adaptation effect, that is, tailor interaction to different users in the same context. In different kinds of adaptive systems, adaptation effects could vary greatly. In AH systems, it is limited to three major adaptation technologies: adaptive content selection, adaptive navigation support, and adaptive presentation. The first of these three technologies comes from the fields of adaptive information retrieval (IR) and intelligent tutoring systems (ITS). When the user searches for information, the system adaptively selects and prioritizes the most relevant items (Brajnik, Guida, & Tasso, 1987; Brusilovsky, 1992b). *Adaptive navigation support* was introduced in early AH systems (de La Passardiere & Dufresne,

1992; Kaplan, Fenwick, & Chen, 1993) and is specifically associated with browsing-based access to information. When the user navigates from one item to another, the system can manipulate the links (e.g., hide, sort, annotate) to guide the user adaptively to the most relevant information items. *Adaptive presentation* stems from research on adaptive explanation and adaptive presentation in intelligent systems (Boyle & Encarnacion, 1994; Paris, 1988). When the user gets to a particular page, the system can present its content adaptively.

The goal of this chapter is to provide an overview of adaptive educational hypermedia (AEH). The chapter, however, doesn't offer a detailed classification of AH technologies, because these reviews can be found elsewhere (Brusilovsky, 2001, 2004, 2007; Bunt, Carenini, & Conati, 2007; Knutov, De Bra, & Pechenizkiy, 2009). Instead, this work attempts to give a developer-oriented insight into the internal structure of AEH systems. The remaining part of the chapter focuses on three educational hypermedia design approaches of increasing complexity, illustrating the presentation with examples from the past research projects of the author. We conclude with a brief discussion of challenges in the field of adaptive educational hypermedia.

Adaptive Educational Hypermedia: From Classic Hypertext to the Adaptive Web

From the very early days of AH, educational hypermedia was one of its major application areas. In an educational context, users with alternative learning goals and knowledge of the subjects require essentially different treatment. In educational hypermedia, the problem of "being lost in hyperspace" is especially critical. A number of pioneer adaptive educational hypermedia systems were developed between 1990 and 1996. These systems can be roughly divided into two research streams. The systems of one of these streams were created by researchers in the area of ITS,

who were trying to extend traditional student modeling and adaptation approaches developed in this field to ITS with hypermedia components (Beaumont, 1994; Brusilovsky, 1993; Gonschorek & Herzog, 1995; Pérez, Gutiérrez, & Lopistéguy, 1995). The systems of another stream were developed by researchers working on educational hypermedia in an attempt to make their systems adapt to individual students (De Bra, 1996; de La Passardiere & Dufresne, 1992; Hohl, Böcker, & Gunzenhäuser, 1996).

Adaptive Educational Hypermedia: The Second Generation

Despite the number of creative ideas explored and evaluated in the early educational AH systems, it was not until 1996 that this research area attracted attention from a larger community of researchers. This process was stimulated by the accumulation and consolidation of research experience in the field. The research in AH performed and reported on up to 1996 provided a good foundation for the new generation of research. Many papers published since 1996 were clearly based on earlier research. These papers cite earlier work and usually propose an elaboration or an extension of techniques suggested earlier. In addition, the Web, with its clear demand for personalization served to boost AH research, providing both a challenge and an attractive platform. Almost all the papers published before 1996 describe classic pre-Web hypertext and hypermedia. In contrast, the majority of papers published since 1996 are devoted to Web-based AH systems.

In the field of educational AH, the major driving factor behind second-generation adaptive educational hypermedia was Web-based education. The imperative to address the needs of the heterogeneous audience for Web-based courses individually was clear to many researchers and practitioners. A few early AH systems developed for Web-based education context by 1996, such as ELM-ART (Brusilovsky, Schwarz,

& Weber, 1996b), InterBook (Brusilovsky, Schwarz, & Weber, 1996a), and 2L670 (De Bra, 1996), provided "proof of existence" and influenced a number of more recent systems. The majority of adaptive educational hypermedia systems developed since 1996 are Web-based systems that were developed for Web-based education context. Some earlier examples are: ADI (Schöch, Specht, & Weber, 1998), RATH (Hockemeyer, Held, & Albert, 1998), ACE (Specht & Oppermann, 1998), TANGOW (Carro, Pulido, & Rodríguez, 1999), Arthur (Gilbert & Han, 1999), CAMELEON (Laroussi & Benahmed, 1998), KBS-Hyperbook (Henze et al., 1999), AHA! (De Bra & Calvi, 1998), and Multibook (Steinacker et al., 1999).

The choice of the Web as a development platform turned out to be a wise one for educational hypermedia systems. It extended the life of a number of pioneer systems. In particular, the first Web-based adaptive educational hypermedia systems developed before 1996, such as ELM-ART, InterBook, and 2L670, are still in use and have been significantly updated and extended to incorporate a number of new techniques, and were used for several experimental studies (Brusilovsky & Eklund, 1998; De Bra & Calvi, 1998; Weber & Brusilovsky, 2001) that further guided development of the field.

The work on second-generation adaptive educational hypermedia was performed mainly between 1996 and 2002. It can be roughly split into three different streams that lack clear-cut borders. The largest group of work (produced mainly by researchers coming from the Web-based education side) focused on creating adaptive Web-based educational systems with elements of AH. The main motivation was to produce systems to be used in teaching, not in developing new technologies. As a result, the works of this stream broadly reused already existing technologies and explored various subject areas and approaches. A smaller stream of work (produced mainly by researchers who were very familiar with ITS or the AH area) focused on producing new techniques for AH. For example, the early AHA! project (De Bra & Calvi, 1998) explored several approaches to link removal. MetaLinks (Murray et al., 2000) explored advanced approaches to hyperspace structuring. INSPIRE explored the use of learning styles (Papanikolaou et al., 2003) and MANIC (Stern & Woolf, 2000) explored innovative approaches for user modeling and adaptive presentation. Finally, another stream of work (which was small, but rapidly expanded) focused on developing frameworks and authoring tools for producing AH systems. The majority of this work produce what we can call *frameworks* for adaptive Web-based education: KBS-Hyperbook (Henze et al., 1999), Multibook (Steinacker et al., 1999), ACE (Specht & Oppermann, 1998), CAMELEON (Laroussi & Benahmed, 1998), MediBook (Steinacker et al., 2001), and ECSAIWeb (Sanrach & Grandbastien, 2000). Although not resulting in end-user authoring tools, a framework typically introduces a generic reusable architecture and approach that could be used to produce a range of adaptive systems with low overhead. A few of the most experienced teams, those working on AH projects for several years, introduced practical authoring systems that could be utilized by end-users to develop AH systems and courses. Examples are InterBook (Brusilovsky et al., 1998), ART-Web/NetCoach (Weber, Kuhl, & Weibelzahl, 2001), AHA! (De Bra & Calvi, 1998) and MetaLinks (Murray et al., 2000).

Adaptive Educational Hypermedia: The Third Generation

Altogether, the systems of the second-generation adaptive educational hypermedia demonstrated a variety of ways to integrate adaptation technologies into Web-based education systems, as well as the value of these technologies. Yet, they failed to influence practical Web-based education. Almost ten years after the appearance of the first adaptive Web-based educational systems, just a handful are used for teaching real courses, typically for a class led by one of the authors of the adaptive system. Instead, the absolute majority of Web-enhanced courses rely on so-called learning management systems (LMS). LMS are powerful integrated systems that support a number of needs of both teachers and students. Teachers can use an LMS to develop Web-based course notes and quizzes, to communicate with students, and to monitor their progress. Students can use it for communication and collaboration. The complete dominance of LMS over adaptive systems may look surprising. Actually, for every function that a typical LMS performs, we can find an adaptive Web-based Educational System (AWBES) that can significantly outperform the LMS. Adaptive textbooks created with systems like the previously mentioned AHA!, InterBook, or NetCoach can help students learn faster and better. Adaptive quizzes delivered by such systems as SIETTE (Conejo, Guzman, & Millán, 2004) and QuizGuide (Hsiao, Sosnovsky, & Brusilovsky, 2010) evaluate student knowledge more precisely with fewer questions. Adaptive class monitoring systems (Oda, Satoh, & Watanabe, 1998) give the teachers more opportunities to notice students that are lagging behind. Adaptive collaboration support systems (Soller, 2007) can reinforce the power of collaborative learning. It seems obvious that the drawback to modern adaptive systems is not the quality of their performance, but their inability to meet the needs of practical Web-enhanced education. The challenge of integrating AH technologies into the regular educational process has defined the current third generation of adaptive educational hypermedia research.

Various research groups stress different reasons for the domination of LMS, and thus pursue different research directions. One research stream focused on the versatility of LMS, attempting to provide in one system as many teacher and learner support features (from content authoring to quizzes to discussion forums) as provided by a modern LMS, plus the ability to adapt to the user (Morimoto et al., 2007; Specht

et al., 2002; Ueno, 2005). A different stream addressed another superior feature of an LMS – the ability to integrate open-corpus Web content. The systems in this stream explored several approaches to integrating open-corpus content in an AH system while providing adaptive guidance for this content (Brusilovsky, Chavan, & Farzan, 2004; Brusilovsky & Henze, 2007; Henze & Nejdl, 2001). Most recent projects, however, choose not to compete with present-day LMS, but instead to focus on adaptive features of the coming generation of Web-based educational systems. This new generation, which will replace modern LMS, is based on system interoperability and reusability of content and supported by a number of emerging e-learning interoperability. A number of research teams are trying now to integrate existing AH technologies with the ideas of standard-based reusability (Conlan, Dagger, & Wade, 2002; Dolog et al., 2003; Morimoto et al., 2007). However, other teams argue that the current generation of standards is not able to support the needs of adaptive learning (Mödritscher, García Barrios, & Gütl, 2004; Rey-López et al., 2008). Yet another direction of work attempts to explore the ideas of the Semantic Web for content representation and resource discovery, capitalizing on standards such as Resource Description Framework (RDF) and Topic Maps (Denaux, Dimitrova, & Aroyo, 2005; Dichev, Dicheva, & Aroyo, 2004; Dolog & Nejdl, 2007; Dolog et al., 2003; Henze, 2005; Jacquiot, Bourda, & Popineau, 2004).

Adaptive Educational Hypermedia: A Designer's View

Knowledge behind Pages

Despite an amazing diversity of existing AEH systems, almost all of them are based on the same set of design principles. It is important for those who are interested in applying or developing AEH systems to understand these principles. The key to intelligence and adaptivity in these systems is the presence of a *knowledge space* (formed

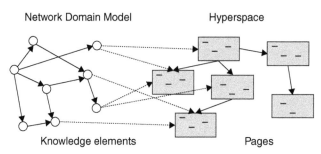

Figure 3.1. The key to adaptivity in AEH systems is the knowledge layer behind the traditional hyperspace.

by topics, concepts, rules, or other kinds of *knowledge elements*) beyond the traditional hyperspace formed by interconnected pages (Figure 3.1).

The knowledge space (also known as the *domain model*) serves as the backbone for AEH systems. It is used to structure the information about individual user's knowledge and goals (known as the *user model* or *student model* in AEH systems). It is also used to describe the content of information pages in these systems. In this capacity, the knowledge space empowers a range of specific AH technologies (such as adaptive sequencing or adaptive link annotation) to bridge the gap between user knowledge and goals on one side and the information content on the other side. Such technologies help the user receive the most appropriate educational or training content. Although the general principles of knowledge structuring and user modeling are shared by the majority of AES systems, practical system may differ a great deal in their complexity and the range of supported adaptation techniques. More specifically, larger and more diverse information spaces typically require more sophisticated approaches to information indexing (i.e., connecting information pages with knowledge elements) and user modeling. For example, systems with a small information space (such as those developed in the early days of AH) frequently use just one concept to describe an information fragment. Larger information spaces – with many pages related to the same concept – demand more precise multi-concept indexing to make pages more distinct from the system's point of view. In turn, these more sophisticated

approaches enable a wider range of adaptation techniques. Following earlier reviews (Brusilovsky, 1996a, 2003), three groups of information indexing approaches of increasing complexity are identified. The analysis of these three groups is the focus of the second part of this chapter. After a brief introduction to the principles of domain modeling and student modeling in AEH systems, the remaining part of the paper analyzes these major information indexing approaches one by one, illustrating each with a detailed practical example.

The Domain Model

The heart of the knowledge-based approach to developing AH systems is a structured *domain model* composed of a set of small domain knowledge elements (KE). Each KE represents an elementary fragment of knowledge for the given domain. KE can be named differently in different systems – concepts, knowledge items, topics, knowledge elements, learning objectives, learning outcomes; however, in all cases, they denote elementary fragments of domain knowledge. Depending on the domain, the application area, and the choice of the designer, KE can represent bigger or smaller pieces of domain knowledge. A set of KE forms *a domain model*. More exactly, a set of independent KE is the simplest form of domain model. It is typically called a *set model* or a *vector model* (Brusilovsky, 2003), because the set of KE has no internal structure. In a more advanced form of domain model, KE are related to each other, thus forming a semantic network. This network represents the structure of the domain covered by a hypermedia system. This kind of model is known as a *network model* (shown on the left part of Figure 3.1).

The structured domain model was inherited by adaptive educational hypermedia systems from the field of ITS, where it was used mainly by systems with task sequencing, curriculum sequencing, and instructional planning functionality (Brecht, McCalla, & Greer, 1989; Brusilovsky, 1992a). This model proved to be relatively simple and powerful and was later accepted as the de facto standard by almost all educational and many noneducational AH systems.

Domain models in AEH systems seriously differ in complexity. Some systems developed for teaching practical university courses employed only the simplest vector domain model (Brusilovsky & Anderson, 1998; De Bra, 1996). At the same time, a number of modern AEH systems use sophisticated ontology-based networked models with several kinds of links that represent different kinds of relationships between the KE. The most popular kind of links in AEH are *prerequisite links* between the KE. A prerequisite link represents the fact that one of the related KE has to be learned before another. Prerequisite links are relatively easy to understand by authors of educational systems and can support several adaptation and user-modeling techniques. In many AEH systems, prerequisite links are the only kind of links between KE (Davidovic, Warren, & Trichina, 2003; Farrell et al., 2003; Henze & Nejdl, 2001; Papanikolaou et al., 2003). Other types of links popular in many systems are the classic semantic links, "is-a" and "part-of" (De Bra, Aerts, & Rousseau, 2002a; Hoog et al., 2002; Steinacker et al., 2001; Trella, Conejo, & Bueno, 2002; Vassileva, 1998). The popularity of these links is currently increasing following the expanded use of more formal ontologies in place of domain models (Dagger, Wade, & Conlan, 2004; Mitrovic & Devedzic, 2004; Trausan-Matu, Maraschi, & Cerri, 2002).

Another difference in complexity is related to the internal structure of concepts. For the majority of AEH systems, the domain concepts are nothing more than names that denote fragments of domain knowledge. At the same time, some AH systems use a more advanced frame-like knowledge representation – that is, represent the internal structure of each concept as a set of attributes or aspects (Beaumont, 1994; Brusilovsky & Cooper, 2002; Hohl et al., 1996; Weber & Brusilovsky, 2001).

The Student Model

One of the most important functions of the domain model is to provide a framework for representation of the user's domain knowledge. The majority of AEH systems use an *overlay model* of user knowledge (also known as an overlay student model). The overlay model was also inherited from the field of ITS. The key principle of the overlay model is that for each domain KE, the individual user knowledge model stores some data that is an estimation of the user's knowledge level for this KE. In the simplest (and oldest) form, it is a binary value (known – not known) that enables the model to represent the user's knowledge as an overlay of domain knowledge. Although some successful AEH systems (De Bra, 1996) use this classic form of an overlay model, the majority of systems use a weighted overlay model that can distinguish several levels of the user's knowledge of a KE through a qualitative value (Brusilovsky & Anderson, 1998; Papanikolaou et al., 2003) (for example, good-average-poor), an integer numeric value (for example, from 0 to 100) (Brusilovsky et al., 1998; De Bra & Ruiter, 2001), or a probability that the user knows the concept (Henze & Nejdl, 1999; Specht & Klemke, 2001). A few AEH systems use an even more sophisticated *layered overlay model* (Brusilovsky & Millán, 2007) to store multiple evidences about the user's level of knowledge separately (Brusilovsky & Cooper, 2002; Brusilovsky, Sosnovsky, & Yudelson, 2005; Weber & Brusilovsky, 2001). The level of sophistication in student modeling has been constantly increasing to support increasingly sophisticated personalization needs, and we expect this process will continue in the context of lifelong modeling (Kay & Kummerfeld, 2010).

All kinds of weighted overlay models are known to be powerful personalization tools due to their ability to independently assess and store the evidences of the user's knowledge about different KE. This power can be further extended by taking into account connections between KE represented in the domain model and using them for weight propagation between KE. Weight propagation increases the impact of a single observation (such as answering a single question) on the student model and decreases student modeling *sparsity*. Good examples of student models incorporating weight propagation are Bayesian student models (Brusilovsky & Millán, 2007; Conati, 2010; Conati, Gertner, & VanLehn, 2002; Zapata-Rivera & Greer, 2003).

Connecting Knowledge with Educational Material

The complexity of an AEH system depends to a large extent on the complexity of the *knowledge-indexing* approach it uses. In the AEH literature, *indexing* denotes the process of connecting domain knowledge with educational content – in other words, specifying a set of underlying KE for every page or fragment of educational content. This process is very similar to traditional indexing of a page using a set of keywords. The literature distinguishes four aspects of indexing approaches: cardinality, granularity, navigation, and expressive power (Brusilovsky, 2003). The first two are most important in the context of this paper.

From the *cardinality* aspect, there are essentially two different cases: single-KE indexing where each fragment of educational material is related to one and only one domain model concept; and multi-concept indexing where each fragment can be related to many concepts. Single-KE indexing is simpler and more intuitive for the authors. Multi-concept indexing is more powerful, but it makes the system more complex and requires more skilled authoring teams.

Expressive power concerns the amount of information that the authors can associate with every link between a concept and a page. Of course, the most important information is the very presence of the link. This case is called *flat indexing* and is used in the majority of existing systems. Still, some systems with a large hyperspace and advanced adaptation techniques want to associate more information with every link by using roles and/or weights. Assigning a role to a link helps distinguish several kinds of connections between concepts and pages. For example, some systems want to distinguish between a case where a page provides an introduction, a core explanation or a summary of a KE, and a case where it provides only a core explanation of the KE (Brusilovsky, 2000) or even some domain-specific aspects of a KE (Brusilovsky & Cooper, 2002). Other systems use the *prerequisite* role to mark the case where the KE is not presented on a page but is required to understand it (Brusilovsky et al., 1998; Holden, 2003).

Existing AH systems suggest various ways of indexing that differ in all aspects listed previously. However, all this variety can be described in terms of three basic approaches that are explored in the remaining part of this chapter. Systems using the same indexing approach have similar hyperspace structure and share specific adaptation techniques that are based on this structure. Thus, the indexing approach selected by developers to a large extent defines the functionality of an AEH system.

Concept-Based Hyperspace: The Case of QuizGuide

The simplest approach to organizing connections between knowledge space and hyperspace is known as *concept-based hyperspace*. This is the organization approach used in an AEH system that uses single-KE indexing. In systems with *simple concept-based hyperspace*, the hyperspace is built as an exact replica of the domain model. Each KE (concept) of the domain model is represented by exactly one node of the hyperspace, whereas the links between the KE constitute main paths between hyperspace nodes. This approach was quite popular among early AEH systems (Brusilovsky, Pesin, & Zyryanov, 1993; Hohl et al., 1996). Its current use is limited to developing encyclopedically structured learning material such as encyclopedias (Bontcheva & Wilks, 2005; Milosavljevic, 1997) and glossaries (Brusilovsky et al., 1998; Weibelzahl & Weber, 2003). For other kinds of practical AEH systems, multiple pages of educational material can be created to teach the same domain model concept.

A typical AEH system with rich content and single-concept indexing uses an *enhanced concept-based hyperspace* design approach. With this design approach, multiple pages describing the same concept are connected to this concept in both the information space and hyperspace. Each concept has a corresponding "hub" page in the hyperspace. The concept hub page is connected by links to all educational hypertext pages related to this concept. The links can be typed and weighted (Papanikolaou et al., 2003), although it is not necessary for using the approach. The student can navigate between hub concept pages along conceptual links and from hub pages to the pages with educational material. An even faster approach to navigate to specific KE and associated educational content can be provided by a visual representation of the domain model (also known as a domain map), which is used in AEH systems such as AES-CS (Triantafillou, Pomportis, & Demetriadis, 2003). The enhanced concept-based hyperspace approach was used to create relatively large AEH systems with quite straightforward structure, and allows for a number of adaptation techniques (Kavcic, 2004; Papanikolaou et al., 2003; Steinacker et al., 2001).

Either form of concept-based hyperspace design approach provides excellent opportunities for adaptive navigation support technologies such as link annotation. For example, ISIS-Tutor (Brusilovsky & Pesin, 1998), InterBook (Brusilovsky et al., 1998), and INSPIRE (Papanikolaou et al., 2003) used annotated links to the concept

hub page featuring special font colors and icons to express the current educational state of the concept (not known, known, well known). ISIS-Tutor (Brusilovsky & Pesin, 1998), AES-CS (Triantafillou et al., 2003), ELM-ART (Weber & Brusilovsky, 2001), and a number of other systems use annotation to show that a concept page is not ready to be learned (i.e., its prerequisite concepts are not yet learned). Hiding technology can be used to hide links to pages representing KEs, which have prerequisites not yet learned (Brusilovsky & Pesin, 1998; Kavcic, 2004) or which do not belong to the current educational goal (Brusilovsky et al., 1998; Papanikolaou et al., 2003).

A good example of a practical system with enhanced concept-based hyperspace is QuizGuide (Brusilovsky, Yudelson, & Sosnovsky, 2004), an adaptive front end to a collection of interactive self-assessment questions in the domain of C programming. The domain model in QuizGuide was formed by twenty-two *topics* such as *variables, constants,* or *character processing.* In contrast to more traditionally used *concepts,* topics are coarse-grain knowledge elements: Each topic covers a relatively large fraction of domain knowledge. QuizGuide topics were connected by prerequisite relationships forming a network domain model. The educational content in the system was formed by a set of more than forty programming quizzes (each comprised of several questions). Each quiz was classified under one of the domain topics. Most of the topics have several quizzes associated with them, thus forming a clean example of enhanced concept-based hyperspace.

The topic-level domain model was made visible in the QuizGuide interface (Figure 3.2) in the form of a linear topic map. Each topic name works as a link. When a student clicks on the link, the topic opens and expands the links to quizzes available for this topic. A click on a quiz link loads the first question in the quiz presentation area. A click on an opened topic collapses the list of topic questions.

Adaptive navigation support is provided in the quiz navigation area through

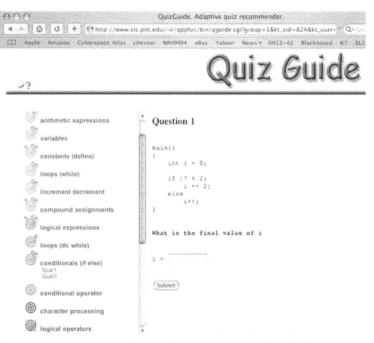

Figure 3.2. Links to topics in QuizGuide interface were annotated with adaptive target-arrow icons displaying educational states of the topics.

adaptive icons shown to the left of each topic. QuizGuide adapts to the most critical characteristics of the user: the knowledge level and the learning goal. To reflect both the goal and knowledge relevance of each topic in one icon, QuizGuide uses the "target-arrow" abstraction (Figure 3.2). The number of arrows in the target reflects the level of knowledge the student has acquired on the topic: The more arrows the target has, the higher the level of knowledge. The intensity of the target's color shows the relevance of the topic to the current learning goal: The more intense the color is, the more relevant the topic. Current topics are indicated by the bright blue targets, their direct prerequisites are indicated by dimmer blue targets, and so on. Topics that are not ready to be studied are annotated with the crossed target. In total, there are four levels of knowledge (from zero to three arrows) and four levels of goal relevance (not ready, important, less important and non-important). Because the student goals and knowledge are constantly changing, different icons will be shown practically each time the student accesses QuizGuide. To reflect changes in

the user model that happened during the same session, the student can click on the refresh icon.

Despite a relatively simple hyperspace structure and adaptation approach, the navigation support provided by QuizGuide resulted in a remarkable impact on student performance and motivation to work with the system. In comparison with QuizPACK (Brusilovsky & Sosnovsky, 2005b), an earlier version of the system that provided access to the same quizzes with no navigation support, the average knowledge gain (a difference between post-test and pre-test results on a 10-point test) for the students using QuizGuide increased from 5.1 to 6.5. By guiding students to the right topics at the right time, the system caused a significant increase in the percentage of correctly answered questions, from 35.6 percent to 44.3 percent (Brusilovsky & Sosnovsky, 2005a). Most remarkable, however, was an increase in the students' interest in working with the system. The number of attempts, the percentage of students using the system actively, and the percentage of attempted topics increased significantly (Brusilovsky & Sosnovsky, 2005a).

The remarkable effects of QuizGuide on student performance and motivation were discovered first in 1994 and confirmed in several other studies (Brusilovsky, Sosnovsky, & Yudelson, 2009). Moreover, a re-implementation of QuizGuide's adaptive navigation support approach for SQL (Sosnovsky et al., 2008) and Java programming (Hsiao, Sosnovsky, & Brusilovsky, 2009) confirmed this impact in two other domains.

Page Indexing: The Case of InterBook

The *page indexing* approach is typically used in cases when the volume of educational content is relatively large and when it is desirable to increase the precision of user modeling using finer-grained KE (which are most frequently referred to as *concepts*). In these cases, page indexing (the most straightforward implementation of multi-concept indexing) becomes very attractive. With this approach, the whole hypermedia page (node) is indexed with domain model concepts. In other words, links are created between a page and each concept related to the content of the page (as shown in Figure 3.1). The simplest indexing approach is flat content-based indexing, where a concept is included in a page index if some part of this page presents the piece of knowledge corresponding to the concept (Brusilovsky & Pesin, 1998; Henze & Nejdl, 2001). A more general – but less often used – way to index the pages is to add the role for each concept in the page index (role-based indexing). The most popular role is "prerequisite": A concept is included in a page index if a student has to know this concept to understand the content of the page (Brusilovsky et al., 1998; De Bra, 1996; Holden, 2003). Other roles can be used to specify the kind of contribution that the page is providing to learning this concept (introduction, main presentation, example, etc.). Weights also can be used in multi-concept page indexing to show how much the page contributes to learning the concept (De Bra et al., 2002b).

A good example of the page-indexing approach is provided by InterBook (Brusilovsky et al., 1998), one of the first authoring systems for developing AEH. InterBook allowed the authors to create a domain-based *bookshelf* containing a set of *electronic textbooks* on the same subject. All books on the same bookshelf were indexed by concepts from the domain model associated with this bookshelf using the page indexing approach. For example, each section (page) of each textbook was connected to all concepts related to that section. The original version of InterBook supported role-based indexing with two roles: a concept can be either a prerequisite or an outcome of a page. The domain model also defined the structure for an overlay *student model*. As an authoring system, InterBook allowed flexibility in defining thresholds for the different states of domain knowledge; however, almost all AEH systems produced with InterBook distinguished four states of student knowledge of a concept: unknown, known (learning started), learned, and well-learned.

The hyperspace of each bookshelf was formed by a set of *electronic textbooks* and a bookshelf *glossary*. Textbooks were hierarchically structured into units of different levels: chapters, sections, and subsections. As explained earlier, each of these units was indexed with prerequisite and outcome concepts. Unless hidden by settings, this indexing was clearly visible on the border of the textbook page of InterBook (Figure 3.3).

The glossary was simply the visualized domain network. Each node of the domain network was represented by a glossary page with links between domain model concepts serving as navigation paths between corresponding glossary pages. Thus, the structure of the glossary resembled the pedagogic structure of the domain knowledge. In addition to providing a description of a concept, each glossary page provided links to all of the book sections that introduced or required the concept (Figure 3.4). This means that the glossary integrated traditional features of an index and a glossary. Vice versa, concept names mentioned in the text or on the border of textbook pages served as links to glossary pages.

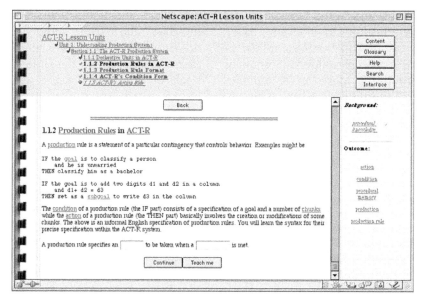

Figure 3.3. A textbook page in InterBook. Links to textbook sections are annotated with colored bullets indicating educational states of the pages. Links to glossary pages are annotated with checkmarks of different sizes indicating the current knowledge level of the explained concept.

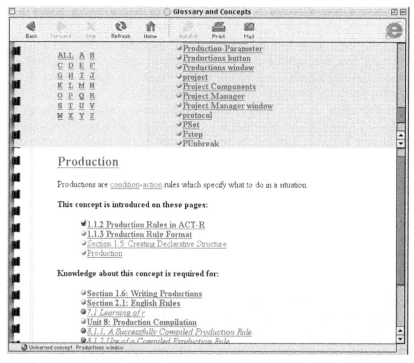

Figure 3.4. A glossary page in InterBook represents a domain concept. It provides links to all of the textbook sections that introduce or require the concept. The links are annotated with colored bullets indicating educational states of the pages.

The hypertext-structuring approach supported by InterBook produced a rich interlinking space with many links both within the textbook and glossary components and between these components. To help guide users to the most appropriate information in this multitude of links, InterBook used two types of link annotation. Links to glossary pages were annotated with checkmark icons of several sizes: The more knowledge of this concept registered in the student model, the larger the size of the annotating checkmark. Links to book sections were annotated with bullet icons of three different colors. The bullet color (and the link font) indicated the current educational state of the section, which was determined through tracking of user reading. White bullets indicated pages with already learned outcome concepts. Green bullets indicated "ready to be learned" pages (some new outcome concepts, but all prerequisite concepts learned already). Red bullets marked those pages that the system considered "not ready to be learned" (some prerequisite concepts were not yet learned). The icon and the font of each link presented to the student were computed dynamically from the individual student model. The goal of the latter approach was to guide the users to interesting "ready to be learned" pages, while discouraging them from spending too much time on "already learned" or "not ready to be learned" pages. To provide additional guidance, the educational state of the current page was shown by a bar of the corresponding color at the top of the page. Needless to say, these link and text annotations were generated dynamically taking into account the current state of individual student knowledge.

Even though the adaptive navigation support provided in InterBook was relatively simple, it had a significant impact on student navigation and learning (Brusilovsky & Eklund, 1998). It increased student nonsequential navigation (i.e., use of links beyond "back" and "continue") and helped students who followed the system's guidance gain better knowledge of the subject. The prerequisite-based "traffic light" annotation approach introduced originally in

ELM-ART (Weber & Brusilovsky, 2001) and, popularized by InterBook, was later successfully applied in a number of other systems (Carmona et al., 2002; Henze & Nejdl, 2001; Kavcic, 2004).

Fragment Indexing: The Case of ADAPTS

Fragment indexing is still a relatively rare indexing approach, but it is the most precise one. The idea is to divide the content of each hypermedia page into a set of fragments and to index some (or even all) of these fragments with domain model concepts related to the content of these fragments. Similar to the page-indexing approach, it can be used even with unstructured vector domain models. The difference is that indexing is done on a more fine-grained level. Generally, multi-concept indexing is used. With smaller fragments, it is often possible to use exactly one concept to index a fragment. In both cases, the fragment indexing approach gives the system more precise knowledge about the content of the page: The system knows what is presented in each indexed fragment. This knowledge can be effectively used for advanced adaptive presentations. Depending on the level of user knowledge about the concepts presented in a particular fragment, the system can hide the fragment from the user (De Bra & Calvi, 1998; Stern & Woolf, 2000), shade it (Hothi et al., 2000), or choose one of several alternative ways to present it (Beaumont, 1994).

One of the problems in fragment-based content adaptation, especially in its versions that hide some part of the page from users, is the lack of control from the user side. In case of user modeling or adaptation errors, a user may miss some valuable information without knowing of its existence. Several approaches were suggested to return ultimate control over the process to the user. For example, Kay (2006) argues for *scrutable* content adaptation where a user can opt to see all content along with an explanation of which parts were hidden and why. Tsandilas and Schraefel (2004) suggest sliders as a way for the user to control fragment adaptation. Höök (1996) explored *adaptive*

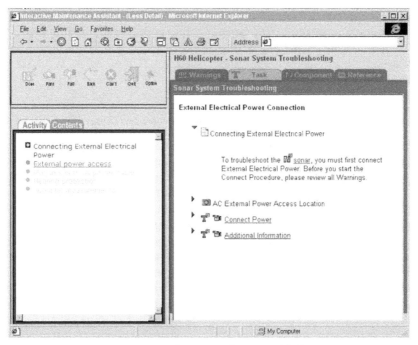

Figure 3.5. When presenting supporting information for a troubleshooting step, ADAPTS uses the stretchtext approach (right): depending on user goal and knowledge, fragments can be shown or hidden; however, the user can override system's selection.

stretchtext – a specific kind of hypertext where both the user and the system can decide which fragments are hidden or visible.

A good example of a system with fragment indexing and adaptive stretchtest is ADAPTS (Brusilovsky & Cooper, 2002), a system for workplace training and performance support developed for avionics technicians. ADAPTS is able to guide the user through the troubleshooting process building a plan of action adapted to the users' knowledge. At each step of the plan, the system uses adaptive content selection and adaptive stretchtext to bring up the most relevant information (i.e., the information that matches user goals and knowledge) from gigabytes of information stored in an interactive electronic technical manual (IETM). The goal of this information is to help the user in performing this step and to expand his knowledge (Figure 3.5).

As in other AEH systems, the key to the intelligent performance of ADAPTS is the domain model. ADAPTS uses a standard concept network approach to domain

modeling; however, because of the complexity of the domain, its domain network is very large. The network is formed by two main types of domain concepts: a component and a task, which form two separate hierarchies. One hierarchy is a tree of components: from the whole aircraft at the top, to subsystems, to sub-subsystems, down to elementary components called addressable units. Another hierarchy is a tree of tasks: from big diagnostic tasks that are handled by the diagnostic engine, to subtasks, and then to elementary steps. The two hierarchies are tightly interconnected because each task is connected with all components involved in performing the task.

To support the user in performing a diagnostic task, ADAPTS uses *rich content* stored in the IETM database. In addition to textual documents and diagrams, the rich content includes various pieces of multimedia: color photos, training videos, animations, and simulations. Moreover, the rich content includes variations of the same information fragments oriented to users with different levels of experience. One of the functions of ADAPTS is to find pieces of the rich content relevant to the selected subtask and to adaptively present them to the user. To deal with large volumes of rich content, ADAPTS uses a very elaborate indexing approach, explained in detail in Brusilovsky and Cooper (2002). In addition to other types of indexing, ADAPTS uses role-based indexing with components. Conceptually, this means that each fragment of the rich content is linked by *typed* (categorized) links with all components *involved in* this fragment. The type of link indicates the kind of involvement (i.e., its role). For example, a piece of video that shows how to remove a component is indexed with a component-role pair *(component ID, role=removal)*. Similarly, a figure that shows the location of a component is indexed with a component-role pair *(component ID, role=location)*.

To match the complexity of the domain model and content indexing, ADAPTS uses a layered multi-aspect overlay user model. A technician's experience with a concept can be judged on many aspects, each weighted to indicate its relative influence on the decision. The user model independently accumulates several aspects (roles) of the experience as well as the knowledge of each technician about each concept as defined in the domain model. From this record, ADAPTS uses a weighted polynomial to estimate the proficiency of a user in locating, operating, and repairing equipment or performing each step of a recommended procedure. The weighting of aspects can be adjusted for different individuals. Factors measured in the ADAPTS prototype include whether and how often a technician has reviewed, observed, simulated, expressed understanding (self- evaluation), previously worked on, or received certification on specific equipment or procedures.

Adaptive Educational Hypermedia in a Broader Context

This chapter provided a brief overview of adaptive educational hypermedia. As shown by multiple examples cited here, AEH technology is rich and flexible. It supports a range of personalization scenarios and offers multiple ways to guide a student to the most relevant learning context – presentation, examples, problems, and so forth. Although it works well in multiple contexts, AEH is not a silver bullet and has to be applied with an understanding of its limitations. To start with, AEH needs to work with a hyperspace. Hyperspace provides the best fit for educational applications that already use hypertext to present various education-oriented information (i.e., educational encyclopedia) or to provide access to rich learning content (i.e., a typical Web-based education system). It is also a good choice for any educational system that needs to operate with a large number of information items, examples, or tasks. Even if this information is not yet hyperlinked, it is typically not hard to structure it as a hyperspace and AEH technologies can provide additional help by offering semantic links. At the same time, AEH is just one of many kinds of adaptive educational systems (Shute & Zapata-Rivera, 2010). AEH provides neither a step-by-step problem-solving support, as many ITS do, nor tools for groupwork or collaboration as collaborative learning systems. It means that a really versatile educational and training system should not be limited to AEH technology alone, but should wisely use a combination of technologies to support multiple needs of students and trainees. We hope that this book as a whole provides a well-balanced overview of many technologies and will enable the designers of educational and training systems to create rich and balanced systems in which AEH serves as one of the primary components.

References

Beaumont, I. (1994) User modeling in the interactive anatomy tutoring system ANATOM-TUTOR. *User Modeling and User-Adapted Interaction 4* (1), 21–45.

Bontcheva, K. and Wilks, Y. (2005) Tailoring automatically generated hypertext. *User*

Modeling and User Modeling and User-Adapted Interaction 15 (1–2), 135–168.

Boyle, C. and Encarnacion, A. O. (1994) MetaDoc: an adaptive hypertext reading system. *User Modeling and User-Adapted Interaction 4* (1), 1–19.

Brajnik, G., Guida, G., & Tasso, C. (1987) User modeling in intelligent information retrieval. *Information Processing and Management 23* (4), 305–320.

Brecht, B. J., McCalla, G., & Greer, J. (1989) Planning the content of instruction. In D. Bierman, J. Breuker & J. Sandberg (eds.) *Proceedings of 4th International Conference on AI and Education*, Amsterdam, May 24–26. Amsterdam: IOS, pp. 32–41.

Brusilovsky, P. (1992a) A framework for intelligent knowledge sequencing and task sequencing. In C. Frasson, G. Gauthier & G. McCalla (eds.) *Proceedings of Second International Conference on Intelligent Tutoring Systems*, ITS'92, Montreal, Canada, June 10–12. Berlin: Springer-Verlag, pp. 499–506.

Brusilovsky, P. (1993) Student as user: Towards an adaptive interface for an intelligent learning environment. In P. Brna, S. Ohlsson & H. Pain (eds.) *Proceedings of AI-ED'93, World Conference on Artificial Intelligence in Education*, Edinburgh, August 23–27. Charlottesville, NC: AACE, pp. 386–393.

Brusilovsky, P. (1996a) Adaptive hypermedia, an attempt to analyze and generalize. In P. Brusilovsky, P. Kommers & N. Streitz (eds.) *Multimedia, Hypermedia, and Virtual Reality*. Lecture Notes in Computer Science, Vol. *1077*, Berlin: Springer-Verlag, pp. 288–304.

Brusilovsky, P. (1996b) Methods and techniques of adaptive hypermedia. *User Modeling and User-Adapted Interaction 6* (2–3), 87–129.

Brusilovsky, P. (2000) Concept-based courseware engineering for large scale Web-based education. In G. Davies and C. Owen (eds.) *Proceedings of WebNet'2000, World Conference of the WWW and Internet*, San Antonio, TX, October 30–November 4. Charlottesville, NC: AACE, pp. 69–74.

Brusilovsky, P. (2001) Adaptive hypermedia. *User Modeling and User-Adapted Interaction 11* (1/2), 87–110.

Brusilovsky, P. (2003) Developing adaptive educational hypermedia systems: From design models to authoring tools. In T. Murray, S. Blessing & S. Ainsworth (eds.) *Authoring Tools for Advanced Technology Learning Environments: Toward cost-effective adaptive,*

interactive, and intelligent educational software. Kluwer: Dordrecht, pp. 377–409.

Brusilovsky, P. (2004) Adaptive educational hypermedia: From generation to generation. In *Proceedings of 4th Hellenic Conference on Information and Communication Technologies in Education*, Athens, Greece, September 29–October 3, pp. 19–33.

Brusilovsky, P. (2007) Adaptive navigation support. In P. Brusilovsky, A. Kobsa & W. Neidl (eds.) *The Adaptive Web: Methods and Strategies of Web Personalization*. Lecture Notes in Computer Science, Vol. 4321, Berlin Heidelberg New York: Springer-Verlag, pp. 263–290.

Brusilovsky, P. & Anderson, J. (1998) ACT-R electronic bookshelf: An adaptive system for learning cognitive psychology on the Web. In H. Maurer and R. G. Olson (eds.) *Proceedings of WebNet'98, World Conference of the WWW, Internet, and Intranet*, Orlando, FL, November 7–12. AACE, pp. 92–97.

Brusilovsky, P., Chavan, G., & Farzan, R. (2004) Social adaptive navigation support for open corpus electronic textbooks. In P. De Bra & W. Nejdl (eds.) *Proceedings of Third International Conference on Adaptive Hypermedia and Adaptive Web-Based Systems* (AH'2004), Eindhoven, the Netherlands, August 23–26. Berlin: Springer-Verlag, pp. 24–33, also available at http://www2.sis.pitt.edu/~peterb/papers/AH2004Final.pdf

Brusilovsky, P. & Cooper, D. W. (2002) Domain, task, and user models for an adaptive hypermedia performance support system. In Y. Gil & D. B. Leake (eds.) *Proceedings of 2002 International Conference on Intelligent User Interfaces*, San Francisco, CA, January 13–16. New York: ACM Press, pp. 23–30.

Brusilovsky, P. & Eklund, J. (1998) A study of user-model based link annotation in educational hypermedia. *Journal of Universal Computer Science 4* (4), 429–448.

Brusilovsky, P., Eklund, J., & Schwarz, E. (1998) Web-based education for all: A tool for developing adaptive courseware. In H. Ashman and P. Thistewaite (eds.) *Proceedings of Seventh International World Wide Web Conference*, Brisbane, Australia, April 14–18. Amsterdam: Elsevier Science B. V., pp. 291–300.

Brusilovsky, P. & Henze, N. (2007) Open corpus adaptive educational hypermedia. In P. Brusilovsky, A. Kobsa, & W. Neidl (eds.) *The Adaptive Web: Methods and Strategies of Web Personalization*. Lecture Notes in Computer

Science, Vol. 4321, Berlin Heidelberg. New York: Springer-Verlag, pp. 671–696.

Brusilovsky, P. & Millán, E. (2007) User models for adaptive hypermedia and adaptive educational systems. In P. Brusilovsky, A. Kobsa & W. Neidl (eds.) *The Adaptive Web: Methods and Strategies of Web Personalization*. Lecture Notes in Computer Science, Vol. 4321, Berlin Heidelberg. New York: Springer-Verlag, pp. 3–53.

Brusilovsky, P. & Pesin, L. (1998) Adaptive navigation support in educational hypermedia: An evaluation of the ISIS-Tutor. *Journal of Computing and Information Technology* 6 (1), 27–38.

Brusilovsky, P., Pesin, L., & Zyryanov, M. (1993) Towards an adaptive hypermedia component for an intelligent learning environment. In L. J. Bass, J. Gornostaev & C. Unger (eds.) *Proceedings of 3rd International Conference on Human-Computer Interaction*, EWHCI'93, Berlin, August 3–7. Berlin: Springer-Verlag, pp. 348–358.

Brusilovsky, P., Schwarz, E., & Weber, G. (1996a) A tool for developing adaptive electronic textbooks on WWW. In H. Maurer (ed.) *Proceedings of WebNet'96, World Conference of the Web Society*, San Francisco, CA, October 15–19. Charlottesville, NC: AACE, pp. 64–69.

Brusilovsky, P., Schwarz, E., & Weber, G. (1996b) ELM-ART: An intelligent tutoring system on World Wide Web. In: C. Frasson, G. Gauthier & A. Lesgold (eds.) *Proceedings of Third International Conference on Intelligent Tutoring Systems*, ITS-96, Montreal, Canada, June 12–14. Berlin: Springer Verlag, pp. 261–269, also available at http://www.contrib.andrew.cmu.edu/~plb/ITS96.html

Brusilovsky, P. & Sosnovsky, S. (2005a) Engaging students to work with self-assessment questions: A study of two approaches. In *Proceedings of the 10th Annual Conference on Innovation and Technology in Computer Science Education*, ITiCSE'2005, Monte de Caparica, Portugal, June 27–29. New York: ACM Press, pp. 251–255, also available at http://www2.sis.pitt.edu/~peterb/papers/ITICSE05.pdf

Brusilovsky, P. & Sosnovsky, S. (2005b) Individualized exercises for self-assessment of programming knowledge: An Evaluation of QuizPACK. *ACM Journal on Educational Resources in Computing* 5 (3), Article No. 6.

Brusilovsky, P., Sosnovsky, S., & Yudelson, M. (2005) Ontology-based framework for user model interoperability in distributed learning environments. In G. Richards (ed.) *Proceedings of World Conference on E-Learning*, E-Learn 2005, Vancouver, Canada, October 24–28. Charlottesville, NC: AACE, pp. 2851–2855.

Brusilovsky, P., Sosnovsky, S., & Yudelson, M. (2009) Addictive links: The motivational value of adaptive link annotation. *New Review of Hypermedia and Multimedia* 15 (1), 97–118.

Brusilovsky, P., Yudelson, M., & Sosnovsky, S. (2004) An adaptive E-learning service for accessing Interactive examples. In J. Nall and R. Robson (eds.) *Proceedings of World Conference on E-Learning*, E-Learn 2004, Washington, DC, November 1–5. AACE, pp. 2556–2561.

Brusilovsky, P. L. (1992b) Student models and flexible programming course sequencing. In *Proceedings of ICCAL'92, 4th International Conference on Computers and Learning*, Wolfville, Canada, June 17–20, pp. 8–10.

Bunt, A., Carenini, G., & Conati, C. (2007) Adaptive content presentation for the Web. In P. Brusilovsky, A. Kobsa & W. Neidl (eds.) *The Adaptive Web: Methods and Strategies of Web Personalization*. Lecture Notes in Computer Science, Vol. 4321, Berlin Heidelberg. New York: Springer-Verlag, pp. 409–432.

Carmona, C., Bueno, D., Guzmán, E., & Conejo, R. (2002) SIGUE: Making web courses adaptive. In P. De Bra, P. Brusilovsky & R. Conejo (eds.) *Proceedings of Second International Conference on Adaptive Hypermedia and Adaptive Web-Based Systems* (AH'2002), Málaga, Spain, May 29–31. Berlin: Springer-Verlag, pp. 376–379.

Carro, R. M., Pulido, E., & Rodríguez, P. (1999) An adaptive driving course based on HTML dynamic generation. In P. D. Bra & J. Leggett (eds.) *Proceedings of WebNet'99, World Conference of the WWW and Internet*, Honolulu, HI, October 24–30. AACE, pp. 171–176.

Conati, C. (2011) Student modeling and intelligent tutoring beyond coached problem solving. In this volume, Chapter 5.

Conati, C., Gertner, A., & VanLehn, K. (2002) Using Bayesian networks to manage uncertainty in student modeling. *User Modeling and User-Adapted Interaction* 12 (4), 371–417.

Conejo, R., Guzman, E., & Millán, E. (2004) SIETTE: A Web-based tool for adaptive teaching. *International Journal of Artificial Intelligence in Education* 14 (1), 29–61.

Conlan, O., Dagger, D., & Wade, V. (2002) Towards a standards-based approach to e-Learning personalization using reusable learning objects. In M. Driscoll & T. C. Reeves (eds.) *Proceedings of World Conference on E-Learning*, E-Learn 2002, Montreal, Canada, October 15–19. AACE, pp. 210–217.

Dagger, D., Wade, V., & Conlan, O. (2004) A framework for developing adaptive personalized elearning. In J. Nall & R. Robson (eds.) *Proceedings of World Conference on E-Learning*, E-Learn 2004, Washington, DC, November 1–5. AACE, pp. 2579–2587.

Davidovic, A., Warren, J., & Trichina, E. (2003) Learning benefits of structural example-based adaptive tutoring systems. *IEEE Transactions on Education 46* (2), 241–251.

De Bra, P., Aerts, A., & Rousseau, B. (2002a) Concept relationship types for AHA! 2.0. In M. Driscoll & T. C. Reeves (eds.) *Proceedings of World Conference on E-Learning*, E-Learn 2002, Montreal, Canada, October 15–19. AACE, pp. 1386–1389.

De Bra, P., Aerts, A., Smits, D., & Stash, N. (2002b) AHA! version 2.0: More adaptation flexibility for authors. In M. Driscoll & T. C. Reeves (eds.) *Proceedings of World Conference on E-Learning*, E-Learn 2002, Montreal, Canada, October 15–19. AACE, pp. 240–246.

De Bra, P. & Calvi, L. (1998) AHA! An open Adaptive Hypermedia Architecture. *The New Review of Hypermedia and Multimedia 4*, 115–139.

De Bra, P. & Ruiter, J.-P. (2001) AHA! Adaptive hypermedia for all. In W. Fowler and J. Hasebrook (eds.) *Proceedings of WebNet'2001, World Conference of the WWW and Internet*, Orlando, FL, October 23–27. AACE, pp. 262–268.

De Bra, P. M. E. (1996) Teaching hypertext and hypermedia through the web. *Journal of Universal Computer Science 2* (12), 797–804.

de La Passardiere, B. & Dufresne, A. (1992) Adaptive navigational tools for educational hypermedia. In I. Tomek (ed.) *Proceedings of ICCAL'92, 4th International Conference on Computers and Learning*, Berlin, June 17–20. Berlin: Springer-Verlag, pp. 555–567.

Denaux, R., Dimitrova, V., & Aroyo, L. (2005) Integrating open user modeling and learning content management for the semantic web. In L. Ardissono, P. Brna & A. Mitrovic (eds.) *Proceedings of 10th International User Modeling Conference*, Edinburgh, Scotland, July 24–29. Berlin: Springer Verlag, pp. 9–18.

Dichev, C., Dicheva, D., & Aroyo, L. (2004) Using topic maps for Web-based education. *Advanced Technology for Learning 1* (1), 1–7.

Dolog, P., Gavriloaie, R., Nejdl, W., & Brase, J. (2003) Integrating adaptive hypermedia techniques and open RDF-based environments. In *Proceedings of The Twelfth International World Wide Web Conference*, WWW 2003, Budapest, Hungary, May 20–24, 2003, pp. 88–98.

Dolog, P. & Nejdl, W. (2007) Semantic Web technologies for the adaptive Web. In P. Brusilovsky, A. Kobsa & W. Neidl (eds.) *The Adaptive Web: Methods and Strategies of Web Personalization*. Lecture Notes in Computer Science, Vol. 4321, Berlin Heidelberg. New York: Springer-Verlag, pp. 697–719.

Farrell, R., Thomas, J. C., Dooley, S., Rubin, W., Levy, S., O'Donnell, R., & Fuller, E. (2003) Learner-driven assembly of Web-based courseware. In A. Rossett (ed.) *Proceedings of World Conference on E-Learning*, E-Learn 2003, Phoenix, AZ, November 7–11. AACE, pp. 1052–1059.

Gilbert, J. E. & Han, C. Y. (1999) Arthur: Adapting instruction to accommodate learning style. In P. D. Bra & J. Leggett (eds.) *Proceedings of WebNet'99, World Conference of the WWW and Internet*, Honolulu, HI, October 24–30. AACE, pp. 433–438.

Gonschorek, M. & Herzog, C. (1995) Using hypertext for an adaptive helpsystem in an intelligent tutoring system. In J. Greer (ed.) *Proceedings of AI-ED'95, 7th World Conference on Artificial Intelligence in Education*, Washington, DC, August 16–19. AACE, pp. 274–281.

Henze, N. (2005) Personal readers: Personalized learning object readers for the semantic Web. In C.-K. Looi, G. McCalla, B. Bredeweg & J. Breuker (eds.) *Proceedings of 12th International Conference on Artificial Intelligence in Education*, AIED'2005, Amsterdam, July 18–22. Amsterdam: IOS Press, pp. 274–281, also available at http://www.kbs.uni-hannover.de/Arbeiten/Publikationen/2005/aied05.pdf

Henze, N., Naceur, K., Nejdl, W., & Wolpers, M. (1999) Adaptive hyperbooks for constructivist teaching. *Künstliche Intelligenz* (4), 26–31.

Henze, N. & Nejdl, W. (1999) Student modeling for KBS hyperbook system using Bayesian networks. Technical report, Report, University of Hannover.

Henze, N. & Nejdl, W. (2001) Adaptation in open corpus hypermedia. *International Journal of Artificial Intelligence in Education 12* (4), 325–350.

Hockemeyer, C., Held, T., & Albert, D. (1998) RATH – A relational adaptive tutoring hypertext WWW-environment based on knowledge space theory. In C. Alvegård (ed.) *Proceedings of CALISCE'98, 4th International Conference on Computer Aided Learning and Instruction in Science and Engineering*, Göteborg, Sweden, June 15–17, pp. 417–423.

Hohl, H., Böcker, H.-D., & Gunzenhäuser, R. (1996) Hypadapter: An adaptive hypertext system for exploratory learning and programming. *User Modeling and User-Adapted Interaction 6* (2–3), 131–156.

Holden, S. (2003) *Architecture for scrutable adaptive hypermedia teaching from diverse document collection.* PhD thesis, the University of Sydney.

Hoog, R. d., Wielinga, B., Kabel, S., Anjewierden, A., Verster, F., Barnard, Y., PaoloDeLuca, Desmoulins, C., & Riemersma, J. (2002) Re-using technical manuals for instruction: Document analysis in the IMAT project. In Y. Barnard (ed.) *Proceedings of Workshop on integrating technical and training documentation held in conjucntion with ITS'02 conference*, San Sebastian, Spain, June 3, pp. 15–25.

Höök, K., Karlgren, J., Wærn, A., Dahlbäck, N., Jansson, C. G., Karlgren, K., & Lemaire, B. (1996) A glass box approach to adaptive hypermedia. *User Modeling and User-Adapted Interaction 6* (2–3), 157–184.

Hothi, J., Hall, W., & Sly, T. (2000) A study comparing the use of shaded text and adaptive navigation support in adaptive hypermedia. In P. Brusilovsky, O. Stock & C. Strapparava (eds.) *Proceedings of Adaptive Hypermedia and Adaptive Web-based systems*, Berlin, August 28–30. Berlin: Springer-Verlag, pp. 335–342.

Hsiao, I.-H., Sosnovsky, S., & Brusilovsky, P. (2009) Adaptive navigation support for parameterized questions in object-oriented programming. In U. Cress, V. Dimitrova & M. Specht (eds.) *Proceedings of 4th European Conference on Technology Enhanced Learning* (ECTEL 2009), Nice, France, September 29–October 2. Berlin: Springer-Verlag, pp. 88–98.

Hsiao, I.-H., Sosnovsky, S., & Brusilovsky, P. (2010) Guiding students to the right questions: Adaptive navigation support in an e-learning system for Java programming. *Journal of Computer Assisted Learning, 26*(4), 270–283.

Jacquiot, C., Bourda, Y., & Popineau, F. (2004) GEAHS: A generic educational adaptive hypermedia system. In L. Cantoni & C. McLoughlin (eds.) *Proceedings of ED-MEDIA'2004 – World Conference on Educational Multimedia, Hypermedia and Telecommunications*, Lugano, Switzerland, June 21–26. AACE, pp. 571–578.

Kaplan, C., Fenwick, J., & Chen, J. (1993) Adaptive hypertext navigation based on user goals and context. *User Modeling and User-Adapted Interaction 3* (3), 193–220.

Kavcic, A. (2004) Fuzzy user modeling for adaptation in educational hypermedia. *IEEE Transactions on Systems, Man, and Cybernetics 34* (4), 439–449.

Kay, J. (2006) Scrutable adaptation: Because we can and must. In V. Wade, H. Ashman & B. Smyth (eds.) *Proceedings of 4th International Conference on Adaptive Hypermedia and Adaptive Web-Based Systems* (AH'2006), Dublin, Ireland, June 21–23. Berlin: Springer Verlag, pp. 11–19.

Kay, J. & Kummerfeld, B. (2011) Lifelong learner modeling. In this volume, Chapter 7.

Knutov, E., De Bra, P., & Pechenizkiy, M. (2009) AH 12 years later: A comprehensive survey of adaptive hypermedia methods and techniques. *New Review of Hypermedia and Multimedia 15* (1), 5–38.

Laroussi, M. & Benahmed, M. (1998) Providing an adaptive learning through the Web case of CAMELEON: Computer Aided MEdium for LEarning on Networks. In C. Alvegård (ed.) *Proceedings of CALISCE'98, 4th International Conference on Computer Aided Learning and Instruction in Science and Engineering*, Göteborg, Sweden, June 15–17, pp. 411–416.

Milosavljevic, M. (1997) Augmenting the user's knowledge via comparison. In A. Jameson, C. Paris & C. Tasso (eds.) *Proceedings of 6th International Conference on User Modeling*, UM97, Chia Laguna, Sardinia, Italy, June 2–5. New York: SpringerWien, pp. 119–130.

Mitrovic, A. & Devedzic, V. (2004) A model of multitutor ontology-based learning environments. *Continuing Engineering Education and Life-Long Learning 14* (3), 229–245.

Mödritscher, F., García Barrios, V. M., & Gütl, C. (2004) Enhancement of SCORM to support adaptive e-learning within the scope of the research project AdeLE. In J. Nall & R. Robson (eds.) *Proceedings of World Conference on E-Learning*, E-Learn 2004, Washington, DC, November 1–5. AACE, pp. 2499–2505.

Morimoto, Y., Ueno, M., Kikukawa, I., Yokoyama, S., & Miyadera, Y. (2007) SALMS: SCORM-compliant adaptive LMS. In T. Bastiaens & S. Carliner (eds.) *Proceedings of World Conference on E-Learning*, E-Learn 2007, Quebec City, Canada, October 15–19. AACE, pp. 7287–7296.

Murray, T., Piemonte, J., Khan, S., Shen, T., & Condit, C. (2000) Evaluating the need for intelligence in an adaptive hypermedia system. In G. Gauthier, C. Frasson & K. VanLehn (eds.) *Proceedings of 5th International Conference on Intelligent Tutoring Systems* (ITS'2000), Berlin, June 21–23. Berlin: Springer-Verlag, pp. 373–382.

Oberlander, J., O'Donell, M., Mellish, C., & Knott, A. (1998) Conversation in the museum: Experiments in dynamic hypermedia with the intelligent labeling explorer. *The New Review of Multimedia and Hypermedia 4*, 11–32.

Oda, T., Satoh, H., & Watanabe, S. (1998) Searching deadlocked Web learners by measuring similarity of learning activities. In *Proceedings of Workshop "WWW-Based Tutoring" at 4th International Conference on Intelligent Tutoring Systems* (ITS'98), San Antonio, TX, August 16–19, also available at http://www.sw.cas.uec.ac.jp/~watanabe/conference/its98workshop1.ps.

Papanikolaou, K. A., Grigoriadou, M., Kornilakis, H., & Magoulas, G. D. (2003) Personalising the interaction in a Web-based educational hypermedia system: The case of INSPIRE. *User Modeling and User-Adapted Interaction 13* (3), 213–267.

Paris, C. L. (1988) Tailoring object description to a user's level of expertise. *Computational Linguistics 14* (3), 64–78.

Pérez, T., Gutiérrez, J., & Lopistéguy, P. (1995) An adaptive hypermedia system. In J. Greer (ed.) *Proceedings of AI-ED'95, 7th World Conference on Artificial Intelligence in Education*, Washington, DC, August 16–19, 1995. AACE, pp. 351–358.

Rey-López, M., Brusilovsky, P., Meccawy, M., Díaz-Redondo, R. P., Fernández-Vilas, A., & Ashman, H. (2008) Resolving the problem of intelligent learning content in learning management systems. *International Journal on E-Learning 7* (3), 363–381.

Sanrach, C. & Grandbastien, M. (2000) ECSAIWeb: A Web-based authoring system to create adaptive learning systems. In P. Brusilovsky, O. Stock & C. Strapparava

(eds.) *Proceedings of Adaptive Hypermedia and Adaptive Web-based Systems*, AH2000, Trento, Italy, August 28–30. Berlin: Springer-Verlag, pp. 214–226.

Schneider-Hufschmidt, M., Kühme, T., & Malinowski, U. (eds.) (1993) Adaptive user interfaces: Principles and practice. In *Human Factors in Information Technology*. Amsterdam: North-Holland.

Schöch, V., Specht, M., & Weber, G. (1998) "ADI" – an empirical evaluation of a tutorial agent. In T. Ottmann and I. Tomek (eds.) *Proceedings of ED-MEDIA/ED-TELECOM'98–10th World Conference on Educational Multimedia and Hypermedia and World Conference on Educational Telecommunications*, Freiburg, Germany, June 20–25. AACE, pp. 1242–1247.

Shute, V. J. & Zapata-Rivera, D. (2011) Adaptive educational systems. In this volume, Chapter 1.

Soller, A. (2007) Adaptive support for distributed collaboration. In P. Brusilovsky, A. Kobsa & W. Neidl (eds.) *The Adaptive Web: Methods and Strategies of Web Personalization*. Lecture Notes in Computer Science, Vol. 4321, Berlin Heidelberg. New York: Springer-Verlag, pp. 573–595.

Sosnovsky, S., Brusilovsky, P., Lee, D. H., Zadorozhny, V., & Zhou, X. (2008) Re-assessing the value of adaptive navigation support in e-learning. In W. Nejdl, J. Kay, P. Pu & E. Herder (eds.) *Proceedings of 5th International Conference on Adaptive Hypermedia and Adaptive Web-Based Systems* (AH'2008), Hannover, Germany, July 29–August 1. Berlin: Springer Verlag, pp. 193–203, also available at http://dx.doi.org/10.1007/978-3-540-70987-9_22

Specht, M. & Klemke, R. (2001) ALE – adaptive learning environment. In W. Fowler & J. Hasebrook (eds.) *Proceedings of WebNet'2001, World Conference of the WWW and Internet*, Orlando, FL, October 23–27. AACE, pp. 1155–1160.

Specht, M., Kravcik, M., Klemke, R., Pesin, L., & Hüttenhain, R. (2002) Adaptive learning environment (ALE) for teaching and learning in WINDS. In *Proceedings of Second International Conference on Adaptive Hypermedia and Adaptive Web-Based Systems* (AH'2002), Berlin, May 29–31. Berlin: Springer-Verlag, pp. 572–581.

Specht, M. & Oppermann, R. (1998) ACE – adaptive courseware environment. *The New*

Review of Hypermedia and Multimedia 4, 141–161.

Steinacker, A., Faatz, A., Seeberg, C., Rimac, I., Hörmann, S., Saddik, A. E., & Steinmetz, R. (2001) MediBook: Combining semantic networks with metadata for learning resources to build a Web based learning system. In *Proceedings of ED-MEDIA'2001 – World Conference on Educational Multimedia, Hypermedia and Telecommunications,* Tampere, Finland, June 25–30. AACE, pp. 1790–1795.

Steinacker, A., Seeberg, C., Rechenberger, K., Fischer, S., & Steinmetz, R. (1999) Dynamically generated tables of contents as guided tours in adaptive hypermedia systems. In P. Kommers and G. Richards (eds.) *Proceedings of ED-MEDIA/ED-TELECOM'99–11th World Conference on Educational Multimedia and Hypermedia and World Conference on Educational Telecommunications,* Seattle, WA. AACE, pp. 640–645.

Stern, M. K. & Woolf, B. P. (2000) Adaptive content in an online lecture system. In P. Brusilovsky, O. Stock & C. Strapparava (eds.) *Proceedings of Adaptive Hypermedia and Adaptive Web-based Systems,* Berlin, August 28–30. Berlin: Springer-Verlag, pp. 225–238.

Stock, O., Zancanaro, M., Busetta, P., Callaway, C., Krüger, A., Kruppa, M., Kuflik, T., Not, E., & Rocchi, C. (2007) Adaptive, intelligent presentation of information for the museum visitor in PEACH. *User Modeling and User-Adapted Interaction 17* (3), 257–304.

Trausan-Matu, S., Maraschi, D., & Cerri, S. A. (2002) Ontology-centered personalized presentation for knowledge extracted from the Web. In S. A. Cerri, G. Gouardères & F. Paraguaçu (eds.) *Proceedings of 6th International Conference on Intelligent Tutoring Systems* (ITS'2002), Berlin, June 2–7. Berlin: Springer-Verlag, pp. 259–269.

Trella, M., Conejo, R., & Bueno, D. (2002) An autonomous component architecture to develop WWW-ITS. In P. Brusilovsky, N. Henze & E. Millán (eds.) *Proceedings of Workshop on Adaptive Systems for Web-Based Education at the 2nd International Conference on Adaptive Hypermedia and Adaptive Web-Based Systems* (AH'2002), Málaga, Spain, May 28, pp. 69–80.

Triantafillou, E., Pomportis, A., & Demetriadis, S. (2003) The design and the formative evaluation of an adaptive educational system based on cognitive styles. *Computers and Education,* 87–103.

Tsandilas, T. & Schraefel, M. C. (2004) Usable adaptive hypermedia systems. *New Review in Hypermedia and Multimedia 10* (1), 5.

Ueno, M. (2005) Intelligent LMS with an agent that learns from log data. In G. Richards (ed.) *Proceedings of World Conference on E-Learning,* E-Learn 2005, Vancouver, Canada, October 24–28. AACE, pp. 2068–2074.

Vassileva, J. (1998) DCG + GTE: Dynamic courseware generation with teaching expertise. *Instructional Science 26* (3/4), 317–332.

Weber, G. & Brusilovsky, P. (2001) ELM-ART: An adaptive versatile system for Web-based instruction. *International Journal of Artificial Intelligence in Education 12* (4), 351–384.

Weber, G., Kuhl, H.-C., & Weibelzahl, S. (2001) Developing adaptive internet based courses with the authoring system NetCoach. In P. D. Bra, P. Brusilovsky & A. Kobsa (eds.) *Proceedings of Third Workshop on Adaptive Hypertext and Hypermedia,* Sonthofen, Germany, July 14, pp. 35–48, also available at http://wwwis.win.tue.nl/ah2001/papers/GWeber-UM01.pdf

Weibelzahl, S. & Weber, G. (2003) Evaluating the inference mechanism of adaptive learning systems. In P. Brusilovsky, A. Corbett & F. D. Rosis (eds.) *Proceedings of 9th International User Modeling Conference,* Johnstown, PA, June 22–26. Berlin: Springer Verlag, pp. 154–162.

Zapata-Rivera, J.-D. & Greer, J. E. (2003) Student model accuracy using inspectable Bayesian student models. In U. Hoppe, F. Verdejo & J. Kay (eds.) *Proceedings of AI-Ed'2003,* Amsterdam, July 22–24. Amsterdam: IOS Press, pp. 65–72.

Part II

STUDENT MODELING BEYOND CONTENT MASTERY

CHAPTER 4

Progress in Assessment and Tutoring of Lifelong Learning Skills

An Intelligent Tutor Agent that Helps Students Become Better Help Seekers

Vincent Aleven, Ido Roll, and Kenneth R. Koedinger

Introduction

Intelligent Tutoring Systems (ITSs) have been shown to enhance learning in a range of domains, including mathematics, physics, computer programming, electronics troubleshooting, database design, medical diagnosis, and others (Beal, Walles, Arroyo, & Woolf, 2007; Crowley et al., 2007; Gott & Lesgold, 2000; Graesser, Chipman, Haynes, & Olney, 2005; Koedinger & Aleven, 2007; Koedinger, Anderson, Hadley, & Mark, 1997; Martin & Mitrovic, 2002; Mitrovic et al., 2008; Mostow & Beck, 2007; Rickel & Johnson, 1999; VanLehn et al., 2005). In this chapter we take up the question whether ITSs can help learners foster *lifelong learning skills*. By this term we refer to skills and strategies that enable people to be effective learners in a range of domains. Domain-general learning skills are important "tools" for learners, because the formal schooling system cannot prepare students for all knowledge or skills they will ever need. Prior to the study reported in the current chapter, there was limited evidence that ITSs can support learners in acquiring lifelong learning

skills. We feel we have interesting progress to report: We found evidence that an ITS can support students in becoming better at seeking help as they work with an ITS.

Researchers have long studied the self-regulatory processes that effective learners exhibit in a range of learning environments, with and (primarily) without computers. This line of work has produced a number of comprehensive theoretical frameworks for self-regulated learning (Pintrich, 2004; Winne & Hadwin, 1998; Zimmerman, 2008). Other work has focused on creating instructional interventions that emphasize self-regulatory or metacognitive aspects of learning, including successful classroom programs for: learning to read with understanding through reciprocal teaching (Palincsar & Brown, 1984); self-assessment and classroom discussion thereof related to a science inquiry cycle (White & Frederiksen, 1998); using self-addressed metacognitive questions in the domain of mathematics learning (Mevarech & Fridkin, 2006); and reflecting on quiz feedback in college-level remedial mathematics (Zimmerman & Moylan, 2009).

Researchers in the field of ITSs have begun to develop and evaluate ways of supporting lifelong learning skills. Probably the most-researched lifelong learning skill in the ITS arena is self-explanation. Following a large body of work on self-explanation without computers (Bielaczyc, Pirolli, & Brown, 1995; Chi, Bassok, Lewis, Reimann, & Glaser, 1989; Chi, de Leeuw, Chiu, & LaVancher, 1994; Renkl, Stark, Gruber, & Mandl, 1998), ITS researchers have developed and evaluated a variety of ways of supporting self-explanation within ITS (Aleven & Koedinger, 2002; Aleven, Ogan, Popescu, Torrey, & Koedinger, 2004; Conati, Muldner, & Carenini, 2006; Conati & VanLehn, 2000; Corbett, Wagner, & Raspat, 2003; McNamara, O'Reilly, Rowe, Boonthum, & Levinstein, 2007; Rau, Aleven, & Rummel, 2009; Weerasinghe & Mitrovic, 2006; Wylie, Koedinger, & Mitamura, 2009). A number of these studies found that support for self-explanation in ITS can lead to better learning, as perhaps a first demonstration that ITSs can be effective in supporting lifelong learning skills. In addition to self-explanation, ITSs researchers have focused on supporting other aspects of lifelong learning, such as error detection and correction (Mathan & Koedinger, 2005) and self-assessment (El Saadawi et al., 2009; Gama, 2004). Finally, a substantial amount of work has focused on reducing ineffective learning behaviors (gaming the system) and disengagement (Arroyo et al., 2007; Baker et al., 2006, 2008; Beck, 2005; Cocea, Hershkovitz, & Baker, 2009; Walonoski & Heffernan, 2006a, 2006b).

These studies underline a view of the users of ITSs as self-regulated learners, and identified relations between specific learning behaviors and resulting learning outcomes. A number of studies demonstrated improved learning outcomes due to support for lifelong learning skills. However, none of these studies investigated whether the support offered by the system had a *lasting effect* on students' lifelong learning skills. The distinction between supporting effective *application* of learning skills versus supporting the *acquisition* of such skills is very important

from an educational perspective. An instructional intervention may support effective learning behaviors, with a positive effect on domain-level learning, while not necessarily causing students to internalize these behaviors so they can produce them in subsequent learning situations or in other learning environments, when there is no support for these learning behaviors. For example, in most of the studies on self-explanation mentioned earlier, the system channeled students into effective learning behaviors by prompting them to self-explain. In most cases, the system also provided feedback on students' self-explanations. It is possible that due to this support for self-explanation, the students became more inclined to spontaneously self-explain even when not prompted, resulting in more robust *future* domain-level learning even without support for self-explanation. However, we should not assume that most students internalized the self-explanation support in this manner. It is possible, perhaps even likely, that the majority of students treated the self-explanation prompts simply as more steps that the tutoring system wanted them to fill in, rather than as practice with a helpful lifelong learning strategy. The previously cited research is silent on this issue because it did not evaluate students' propensity to self-explain after the self-explanation support had been removed. A similar point can be made about the other ITS research on lifelong learning skills. We know of two notable exceptions. A study involving the Betty's Brain system showed that combined support for metacognition and learning by teaching can have a lasting influence on students' propensity for information seeking and monitoring solution quality (Leelawong & Biswas, 2008; Wagster, Tan, Biswas, & Schwartz, 2007). Second, the research presented in the current chapter addresses this issue head on.

Our research focuses on help seeking, a lifelong learning skill that has been identified in the theories of self-regulated learning mentioned earlier (e.g., Pintrich, 2004) and has been studied extensively in social learning situations (e.g., Karabenick & Newman,

2006; Newman, 2008; Zusho, Karabenick, Bonney, & Sims, 2007). Help seeking is viewed as an important developmental skill that self-regulated learners use to good effect in challenging learning situations (Nelson-Le Gall, 1981). Good help seekers have a sense for when they need help with a given learning task and for when they may be better off trying to succeed on their own. When they seek help, they do so in ways aimed at enhancing learning rather than simply getting through the present difficulty. However, there is evidence that many learners do not seek help when needed or do so in ways not conducive to learning (e.g., Puustinen, 1998). Also, learners frequently avoid seeking help altogether (Ryan, Gheen, & Midgeley, 1998; Ryan, Pintrich, & Midgley, 2001). A small number of studies found positive relations between adaptive help seeking and academic achievement, such as grades or standardized test scores in actual classrooms (Karabenick, 2003). One study found that teachers' assessment of student help seeking in grade 5 predicted academic achievement in grade 7 (Ryan, Patrick, & Shim, 2005). A number of lab studies also yielded evidence that more adaptive help seeking on early training tasks is associated with better performance on later training tasks (Butler, 1998; Butler & Neuman, 1995).

There is a relatively small body of research on help seeking and learning in various kinds of computer-based learning environments, including ITSs. On-demand help is a standard feature of ITSs (Anderson, 1993; Koedinger & Aleven, 2007; VanLehn, 2006) and is widely thought to influence learning with ITSs. There is some, although limited, evidence that on-demand help in computer-based learning environments can enhance student learning (Aleven, Stahl, Schworm, Fischer, & Wallace, 2003). An experimental study by Renkl (2002) established a causal connection between help seeking and learning. This study, which involved a computer-based learning environment for studying examples, showed a positive effect of principle-based instructional explanations, given by the system at the student's request. A later study by Schworm and

Renkl (2006) largely confirmed this finding, but also uncovered a limitation of this type of help facility, discussed later in this chapter. We note that these studies were lab studies and therefore had limited ecological validity. Other work uncovered correlational evidence for a link between help seeking and learning with an ITS: Wood and Wood (1999) found a positive correlation between help seeking and learning in a small-scale ITS (Wood & Wood, 1999). Beck, Chang, Mostow, and Corbett (2008), using educational data-mining techniques, found a positive relation between help use and learning in a large data set from a tutor that helps elementary students learn to read. In a study with an ITS based on Vygotskian principles, Luckin and Hammerton (2002) found that students with above-average learning gains tended to seek more and deeper help than students with below-average learning gains. Other studies found relations between help seeking and performance (although not necessarily learning) in a large hypertext system for biology (Bartolomé, Stahl, Pieschl, & Bromme, 2006) and a computer-based learning environment for problem-based learning of statistics (Mercier & Frederiksen, 2007). In addition to this evidence of a positive relation between help seeking and learning, however, there is evidence that students often do not make effective use of the help facilities offered by computer-based learning environments (e.g., Aleven et al., 2003). Also, there is evidence that apparently poor help use, such as clicking through hints to quickly get to a hint that gives away the answer, is associated with poorer learning outcomes (Baker et al., 2006). In our own prior work, we found evidence of substantial suboptimal use of the help facilities of the Geometry Cognitive Tutor (Aleven & Koedinger, 2000). In sum, both the educational psychology literature and the literature on ITS provide evidence that adaptive help seeking can be a positive influence on student learning, but show also that ineffective help seeking is quite widespread.

Given this evidence, help seeking seems a promising area to investigate for ITSs researchers. In the work reported in this chapter, we investigate whether an ITS can help students acquire effective help-seeking skills. We focus on the hypothesis that giving students feedback on the way they use the system's help facilities will help them become more effective help seekers and better learners, not just while the support for help seeking is in effect, but also in the long run, on future learning opportunities. To test this hypothesis, we created and evaluated a tutor agent (called the "Help Tutor") to foster help-seeking skill. As part of this effort, we created a computer-executable model of help-seeking skill. This model captures a simple recurrent metacognitive cycle in tutored problem solving, of which help seeking is an integral part. The Help Tutor uses this model to assess students' help-seeking behavior. We integrated the Help Tutor with an existing commercial ITS, the Geometry Cognitive Tutor (Koedinger, Corbett, Ritter, & Shapiro, 2000), and ran two classroom studies to evaluate its effect on students' help seeking and learning.

Our project differs in a number of important ways from other efforts that have focused on helping students become better help seekers, and from related work focused on reducing ineffective help use and guessing behaviors in ITS (Arroyo et al., 2007; Baker et al. 2006; Luckin & Hammerton, 2002; Walonoski & Heffernan, 2006b). As mentioned, none of this work tested whether an ITS can help bring about a *lasting* improvement in students' help-seeking behavior. The nature of the metacognitive support differs as well between projects. First, in the current work, the Help Tutor gives feedback to students based on a *highly specific* assessment of their metacognitive behaviors. Other systems recognize only very broad categories of gaming behaviors (Baker et al., 2006; Walonoski & Heffernan, 2006b) or do not assess students' lifelong learning behaviors at all (Arroyo et al., 2007), or assess them in a fine-grained manner closely tied to a domain model (Luckin & Hammerton, 2002). Second, in the current work, the Help Tutor provides feedback at the *metacognitive* level, pointing out specific ways in which student's help-seeking behavior is not ideal. Prior efforts more often focus on providing feedback that is related to the *domain level* – for example, by providing supplemental exercises at the domain level (Baker et al., 2006) or presenting information about the individual student's performance at the *domain* level (Arroyo et al., 2007). Finally, in the current work, the Help Tutor provides metacognitive feedback messages in the context of problem solving as soon as it detects ineffective help-seeking behaviors. Other efforts delegate the metacognitive messages to a separate phase in between tutor problems (Arroyo et al., 2007; Baker et al., 2006), or present feedback in a graphical display without interrupting the student (Baker et al., 2006; Walonoski & Heffernan, 2006b). At this point it is not fully known which of these design features matter the most in terms of helping students' acquire lifelong learning skills.

In this chapter, we give a retrospective overview of our project. We describe the computer-executable model of help-seeking skill that we created to assess student help-seeking behavior and give feedback. We provide a rationale for the main design decisions we made as we created the Help Tutor. We illustrate the behavior of the Help Tutor agent, integrated with the Geometry Cognitive Tutor. We present results from a classroom study aimed at evaluating the long-term effect of automated feedback on students' help-seeking behavior. Finally, we reflect on the design of the Help Tutor, reconceptualize the role of help seeking in learning with ITS, and outline some promising directions for future work.

Background: The Geometry Cognitive Tutor

We used the Geometry Cognitive Tutor, shown in Figure 4.1, as platform to investigate the effect of tutoring students with respect to their help-seeking behavior. The Geometry Cognitive Tutor is a commercially available ITS, an integrated part of a full-year high-school geometry course. It has

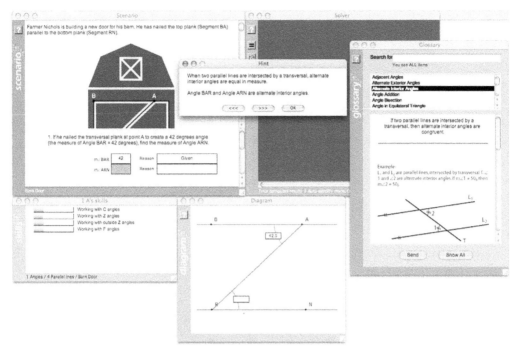

Figure 4.1. The Geometry Cognitive Tutor as it looked in 2005.

a track record of improving student learning (Koedinger et al., 2000). Like all Cognitive Tutors (Koedinger & Corbett, 2006), it is grounded in cognitive theory (Anderson, 1993). This type of ITS has successfully made the transition out of the research lab and into the real world (Corbett, Koedinger, & Hadley, 2001; Koedinger, Anderson, Hadley, & Mark, 1997), with currently about half a million users annually (see http://www. carnegielearning.com). Like other ITSs (VanLehn, 2006), the Geometry Cognitive Tutor provides step-by-step guidance with complex multistep problem-solving activities; a simple tutor problem is shown in Figure 4.1. More specifically, it provides the following types of step-by-step guidance, most of them typical of ITSs (cf. VanLehn, 2006):

1. a series of problem-type-specific interfaces with multiple representational tools, carefully designed to make thinking steps visible (e.g., Anderson, Corbett, Koedinger, & Pelletier, 1995); specifically, the Geometry Cognitive Tutor provides a worksheet tool (labeled

"Scenario"), a diagram tool, and a tool for symbolic equation solving;
2. correctness feedback on problem-solving steps, not just final solutions;
3. feedback messages for commonly occurring errors;
4. on-demand hints about what to do next, available at any point during problem solving;
5. a freely accessible online Glossary of geometry knowledge with descriptions and examples of all relevant definitions and theorems;
6. an open-learner model (dubbed "skill meter") that displays the system's estimates of an individual student's skill mastery, as an indication of his/her progress toward his/her learning goals; and
7. individualized problem selection (by the system) based on each student's performance with the tutor as summarized in the student model.

As part of its step-by-step guidance, the Geometry Cognitive Tutor offers two main help facilities (items 4 and 5 on the preceding list). First, on-demand next-step hints

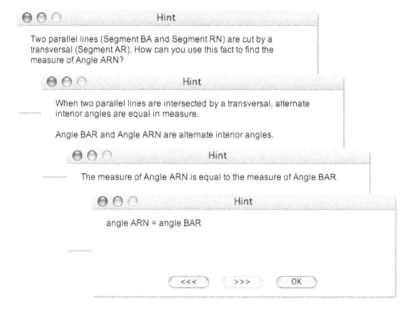

Figure 4.2. An example of a hint sequence, with hint levels sequenced from the general (top) to the specific (bottom).

provide context-specific advice on what to do next. For any step in a tutor problem, multiple levels of principle-based advice are available. The hint levels are sequenced from the general to the specific (see Figure 4.2). The hint levels identify features of the problem that determine which problem-solving principle applies, state the principle, discuss how the principle maps onto the problem, and what inferences and calculations follow. The last hint level, often referred to as the "bottom-out hint," states the answer for the given step or an expression that evaluates to the answer. Most steps have between three and five levels of hints.

The students have control over when they request help and over how many hint levels they read before attempting a given step. The motivation for this policy is that the student may be in a better position than the system to judge when help is needed and how much of it is needed, especially after errors (Anderson, 1993, summarized in Aleven et al., 2003). It was thought also that sequencing hints from general to specific helps learning because this policy enables students to generate answers themselves with a minimal amount of help

(e.g., the expectation is that they read only as many help levels as is needed). Generating answers is thought to enhance learning more than being given answers (e.g., Roediger & Karpicke, 2006).

In addition to context-sensitive hints, the Geometry Cognitive Tutor offers a Glossary of geometry knowledge (item 5 on the earlier list, shown on the right in Figure 4.1). The Glossary is an online browse-able resource that can be accessed at any time during the problem-solving process. The information in the Glossary is not context-sensitive, nor does the tutor offer any help to students as they search the Glossary for information relevant to the problem step at hand. The Glossary is representative of many real-life sources of help, such as Wikipedia or the many Web sites devoted to math learning. It was added to the tutor because being able to use a resource like the Glossary is a valuable lifelong learning skill in and of itself.

"Under the hood," each Cognitive Tutor uses a rule-based cognitive model that captures the ways in which competent students solve problems within the given subject area and the typical errors novices make (Anderson et al., 1995;

Koedinger & Aleven, 2007; Koedinger & Corbett, 2006). The model enables the tutor to guide students within a given problem and to track progress over a sequence of problems, in a process called *model tracing* (Anderson et al., 1995). In addition, the tutor keeps track, over time and across multiple problems, of how well the student masters the modeled skills, using a Bayesian student-modeling technique called *knowledge tracing* (Corbett, McLaughlin, & Scarpinatto, 2000). The estimates of skill mastery are the basis for the individualized problem selection. As described later in the chapter, the tutor agent for help seeking uses these estimates to help determine what the appropriate help-seeking behavior is on any given step in a tutor problem.

Novel Approach: A Tutor Agent for Help Seeking

Studying log data of student sessions with the Geometry Cognitive Tutor, we came to the conclusion that a large majority of students tend to use the tutor's help facilities in ways that do not seem conducive to learning (Aleven & Koedinger, 2000). For example, making multiple errors does not always increase the likelihood of seeking help on the given problem step, even though objectively it should. Further, in the majority of cases when students do ask for help, they request to see all hint levels, spending little time with all but the last one, which, as mentioned, gives away the answer. In other words, they tend to use hints in ways that get them through problems but are unlikely to help them learn with understanding. Because the tutor's student model reflects whether students complete steps without hints or errors, students cannot get through entire problem sets by relying on the hints to get answers, without much learning. Nonetheless, this kind of hint abuse may hamper learning.

We also had some anecdotal evidence that students may not be aware of good strategies for help seeking (as opposed to being aware of these strategies but not

bothering to implement them). For example, one day, one of us took an out-of-town visitor to a Cognitive Tutor lab session in a school where the Geometry Cognitive Tutor was being used as part of the regular geometry instruction. The visitor was invited to try out a tutor problem or two but had some trouble making progress on the tutor. The student sitting next to the visitor pointed out a useful tutor feature: If you do not know the answer, you can just click through the tutor's hints. We interpreted this student's advice as a genuine effort to be helpful rather than as communicating a strategy to game the system. She must have not been aware of better ways of using the tutor's help facilities.

The kinds of hint (ab)use that we observed are likely to lead to a somewhat implicit and/or shallow learning process, not guided by solid conceptual knowledge of the underlying problem-solving principles, or a good grasp of exactly what features need to be present for a problem-solving principle to apply. Better use of the tutor's help facilities might lead to deeper learning. Thus the idea was born to enhance the tutor so it could give feedback on students' help-seeking behavior. As mentioned, we hypothesized that a tutor agent that provides feedback on help seeking would help students become more aware of effective help-seeking strategies, become more effective help seekers, and become better learners.

Assessing Help Seeking: A Computer-Executable Model

We decided early on that in creating this tutor agent we would take an ITS approach. Specifically, we decided to apply the same tutoring technology at the metacognitive level that we use at the domain level, namely, the Cognitive Tutor technology (Koedinger & Aleven, 2007; Koedinger & Corbett, 2006). Thus, the Help Tutor would be a Cognitive Tutor, meaning that it would use a model of desired help-seeking behavior to interpret and assess student's behavior at the metacognitive level. A key step in creating the tutor was to create an executable model of help seeking that could be used for tutoring. Developing this model turned out to be an interesting challenge. There were some theoretical models of help seeking in the literature (Gross & McMullen, 1983; Nelson-Le Gall, 1981; Newman, 1994), but these models were not nearly detailed enough for implementation on a computer. Nor did typical instructional practice provide sufficiently detailed models. As described elsewhere (Aleven et al., 2006), we combined theoretical and empirical cognitive task analysis techniques (Lovett, 1998). Specifically, we created an initial model based on theoretical task analysis and informal observations of students using tutors and then refined this model using tutor log data and pre/post-test data. In this latter phase we made sure that the metacognitive errors captured in the model were defined in such a way that they correlated negatively with learning.

The help-seeking model that we created captures a recurrent metacognitive cycle in a tutored problem-solving environment. It focuses on completing a single step in a problem with the typical kinds of guidance that an ITS offers: hints, feedback, and online information resources such as a Glossary.

The *preferred* metacognitive behavior, according to this model, is summarized in the flow chart of Figure 4.3. When faced with a step in a tutor problem, the preferred behavior is to work deliberately at all times. That is, the student is expected to take sufficient time to understand the problem statement and carefully read and process any hint levels that he or she may request. She is to avoid quick attempts at solving the step at hand and quick hint requests. The decision whether to seek help or not depends in the first place on the student's self-assessed familiarity with the step (or more precisely, the skill involved in the step). Initially, when starting a new tutor unit, students will have only a fleeting familiarity with the skills that are targeted in that unit. Typically, they have encountered each skill at least briefly as part of their classroom activities but may not have seen many examples and

are not likely to have exercised the skill in problem-solving activities. The skills gradually become more familiar as they have multiple opportunities to practice them with the tutor. When a student recognizes that a step is not familiar, she is expected to use the tutor's hints even before attempting the step. By contrast, when the student, after thinking deliberately about the step, has a sense of what to do, she is expected to try the step. When a step is familiar but the student does not have a sense of what to do, she is expected to access the tutor's Glossary, and to use hints only when Glossary use turns out not to be helpful. Regardless of whether a step is familiar or not, a student is expected to request a hint after making an error that he/she is not clear how to fix. When taking hints, a student is expected to ask only for as many hint levels as is needed to get a clear sense of what to do (i.e., until she judges a hint to be "helpful"). If after the last hint has been seen, it is still not clear what to do, the student is expect to consult with their teacher.

The model has precise and detailed criteria for the key decision points, represented by diamonds in the flowchart (Figure 4.3). For the self-monitoring steps such as determining whether a step is familiar or whether the student has a sense of what to do, the model relies on the Cognitive Tutor's assessment of the student's skill mastery. As mentioned, for each of the (domain-level) skills targeted in the instruction, the (domain-level) Cognitive Tutor maintains an estimate of the probability that the student masters the skill. We defined a familiar step as one for which the estimated probability of skill mastery is above .6, and an unfamiliar step as one for which the skill estimate is below .4. The determination whether an error is easy to fix also depends on the familiarity of the step, as follows: Errors on familiar steps are assumed to be easy to fix until the student exceeds a certain threshold number of errors. Errors on unfamiliar steps, by contrast, are never assumed to be easy to fix. For example, it is likely that an error on a familiar step is a slip, a miscalculation, or a typo, whereas an error on an unfamiliar step

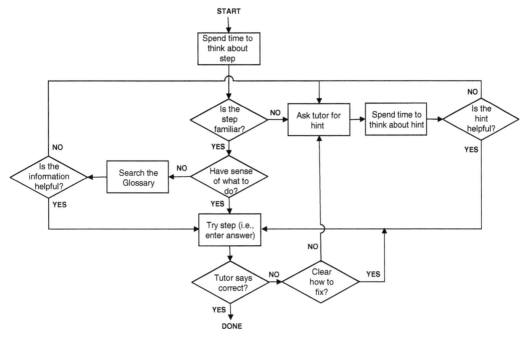

Figure 4.3. The preferred metacognitive behavior captured in the model.

is likely to represent a genuine conceptual difficulty. Finally, the number of hint levels a student needs to see before she is expected to have a good sense for how to solve the step also depends on the familiarity of the step. On familiar steps, only the first one-third of the hint sequence for the step is assumed to be needed. On unfamiliar steps, by contrast, the student is expected to read all hint levels before attempting the step.

The model's criterion for deliberate reading of problem statements and hints is based on basic results in the literature on reading rates. We assumed that deliberate reading can only be done at a rate below 600 words/minute, a level that is significantly above average reading rates reported in the literature (e.g., Card, Moran, & Newell, 1983). This criterion is lenient; it is meant to only catch egregious instances of skimming problem statements and hints, or of skipping them altogether.

A large part of the model is devoted to capturing specific incorrect metacognitive behaviors that do not fall within the preferred and acceptable behaviors outlined earlier (Aleven et al., 2006). The model has an extensive taxonomy of incorrect

help-seeking behaviors, which enables the metacognitive tutor agent to respond with specific feedback messages, as illustrated later in the chapter. As we developed the model, we ran it offline against tutor log data and tried to design it in such a way that the major error categories in the taxonomy correlate negatively with learning (Aleven et al., 2006). Based on our analysis of offline log data, the taxonomy captures three broad classes of metacognitive errors: Help Abuse, Help Avoidance, and Try-Step Abuse. For each of these categories, the model defines many specific manifestations. For example, one (frequent) type of Help Abuse is clicking through hints quickly to get to the last hint level that gives away the answer.[1] A specific form of Help Avoidance is trying an unfamiliar step without asking for a hint first.

The model consists of seventy-six production rules, of which forty-six rules (60%)

---

[1] Although clicking through hints is strongly negatively correlated with learning (Aleven et al., 2006), later research revealed that a focus on bottom-out hints is not always maladaptive (Shih, Koedinger, & Scheines, 2008). This point is taken up in the discussion section.

represent incorrect help-seeking behavior. The model was validated using a separate measure of help seeking in a transfer environment. Specifically, in a classroom experiment with the Help Tutor (not described in the current chapter), we assessed students' ability to take advantage of help by embedding help messages in geometry problem-solving items on a paper-and-pencil post-test (Roll et al., 2011). In addition, this test included hypothetical help-seeking dilemmas that asked about appropriate help-seeking behavior in situations commonly encountered during tutor use. We found that students who demonstrated better help-seeking behavior while they worked with the tutor (i.e., whose help-seeking behavior with the tutor conformed more closely to the model) also tended to demonstrate better help-seeking behavior on the paper-and-pencil test and better understanding of appropriate help-seeking behavior in the hypothetical scenarios.

Tutoring Help Seeking: A Novel Tutor Agent Based on the Model

The next step was to create a tutor agent that provides guidance with respect to students' help-seeking behavior and to integrate it into an existing ITS. In deciding how to integrate cognitive and metacognitive tutoring, one faces a number of interesting design decisions. Should multiple tutor agents be identified and shown in the interface? If multiple tutor agents are to be reified in the interface, what should they look like? What kind of guidance should the metacognitive tutor agent give? And *when* should it provide guidance?

As mentioned, we decided early on that in creating the Help Tutor, we would apply the Cognitive Tutor methodology at the metacognitive level (Roll, Aleven, McLaren, & Koedinger, 2007b). This decision meant that the Help Tutor would be a model-tracing tutor, using the model of help seeking to assess and interpret students' help-seeking behavior. It also meant that, as

we tackled the design questions listed earlier, we let ourselves be guided primarily by the Cognitive Tutor principles (Anderson et al., 1995; Koedinger & Corbett, 2006), which distill some of the key features of Cognitive Tutors.

A key decision was to provide immediate feedback on help seeking in the context of learning (geometry) by doing. This decision follows Cognitive Tutor principle #6: "Provide immediate feedback on errors relative to the model of desired performance" (Koedinger & Corbett, 2006). Thus, the Help Tutor provides feedback potentially after each student action (attempt at solving, hint request, access of Glossary items). With respect to the content of the Help Tutor feedback, we decided that the Help Tutor would give specific feedback messages in response to help-seeking errors, but would not provide positive feedback when the student exhibited desirable help-seeking behavior. We had no obvious place to present low-key positive feedback and were concerned that repeated congratulatory messages would be distracting and annoying – we expected they would be given about 80 percent of the time. Further, we decided that there would not be on-demand hints at the metacognitive level. We figured that if poor help use is a problem, then a tutor agent designed to help students improve their help use should not depend on students' ability or propensity to use on-demand help effectively. A second reason was that we did not want to increase cognitive load (Cognitive Tutor principle #5, Koedinger & Corbett, 2006). Finally, as for the tutor agent's looks, we opted for the unspectacular: the metacognitive feedback messages appear in the same messages window as the tutor's hint and feedback messages. They are somewhat visually distinct from regular tutor messages, so as to help students interpret tutor advice more easily (e.g., Alpert, Singley, & Carroll, 1999). Specifically, they are shown in blue, italic font.

Given our decision to provide immediate feedback on help seeking, integrated with immediate feedback and hints at the domain level, we needed a policy for coordinating the tutoring moves of the two tutor agents. A student action can be correct at the domain level but erroneous at the metacognitive level, and vice versa. Or it could be wrong at both levels, but for different reasons. Some key features of the coordination policy we designed are (Aleven, Roll, McLaren, Ryu, & Koedinger, 2005):

- Feedback from at most one tutor agent is shown at any given time (i.e., when the two tutor agents both have a message to present to the student, a choice is made). This decision was made to reduce cognitive load (Cognitive Tutor principle #5).
- Positive feedback from the domain-level tutor (i.e., feedback indicating that a student attempt at solving a step is correct) preempts error feedback from the Help Tutor, because feedback pointing out metacognitive shortcomings of a successful domain-level action is likely to be ineffective.
- Error feedback from the domain-level tutor preempts Help Tutor feedback, because this domain-level information helps students get through problems.
- Metacognitive feedback on hint requests (saying e.g., that the hint request was too fast or that a hint may not have been necessary) preempts the display of the requested hint message, given our commitment to not displaying cognitive and metacognitive messages at the same time. Further, we thought it would be ineffective to provide feedback saying that the student should not need a (domain-level) hint message when that feedback is accompanied by the very hint message that the student purportedly does not need.
- Even if a (domain-level) hint was preempted by Help Tutor feedback, it would be shown if the student repeated the hint request. In other words, a hint request following a hint request is always metacognitively acceptable. (Strictly speaking, this decision was not part of the coordination policy, but is built into the model of help seeking.)

Having decided on the behavior of the metacognitive tutor agent, the next step was the technical integration of the tutor agent into the existing Cognitive Tutor architecture (Aleven et al., 2005). Our goal was to make the Help Tutor an independent plug-in agent that could be combined with any Cognitive Tutor. We created a two-agent architecture akin to the multi-agent architecture proposed by Ritter (1997). In this architecture, multiple tutor agents are combined in such a way that they maintain their independence. All coordination and conflict resolution among tutor agents is done by a mediator module. This integration did not require any changes to the specific Cognitive Tutor with which it was being integrated, nor did it require that the Help Tutor was in any way specific to this Cognitive Tutor. It did require the creation of a specific mediator module. The mediator module collects information for the Help Tutor (from the domain-level Cognitive Tutor) and implements the coordination policy described previously. A key factor in achieving ease of integration was that the Help Tutor has been designed from the start so that it requires only information that the Cognitive Tutor generates in its normal course of operations, suitably abstracted so that no domain-specific information is needed.

Examples of Feedback of Lifelong Learning Skill: Help Seeking

We illustrate the Help Tutor's metacognitive feedback in response to the main categories of help-seeking errors discussed earlier. The examples illustrate how the preferred behavior (and, consequently, what counts as a help-seeking error) depends on how familiar the student is with the type of problem-solving step under consideration. We consider a hypothetical student during his or her learning trajectory, and we focus on the skill of applying one of the geometry theorems targeted in the tutor, the alternate interior angles theorem. We contrast a situation in which this skill is not familiar and one in which it is.

Figure 4.4. Help Tutor message in response to Try Step Abuse and Help Avoidance on an unfamiliar step.

Figure 4.5. Help Tutor message in response to Help Abuse (clicking through hints).

First, consider the first tutor problem that involves the skill (i.e., a scenario in which the skill is likely to be unfamiliar). In the situation depicted in Figure 4.1, the student has already entered the measure of the first angle in the problem (see the answer table in the tutor's scenario window shown at the top left in Figure 4.1). The next step is to figure out the measure of a second angle, which together with the first angle forms a pair of alternate interior angles. The Help Tutor considers the step to be unfamiliar to the student. As mentioned, the Help Tutor's assessment of whether a step is familiar to the student depends on the (domain-level) Cognitive Tutor's assessment of the student's mastery of the skill involved. As can be seen in the tutor's skill window at the bottom left, the relevant skill bar, labeled "Working with Z angles" is below the Help Tutor's .4 threshold.

The preferred metacognitive behavior on unfamiliar steps is for the student to spend time thinking about the step and, upon realizing that the step is unfamiliar, ask for hints, read all of them carefully, and then try the step. If the student approaches the problem in this manner, the Help Tutor will remain silent.

Let us consider what happens when our hypothetical student does not follow the preferred metacognitive behavior but instead commits various help-seeking errors. For example, suppose that the student quickly types a wrong answer, "90–42" (the correct answer is "42"). This metacognitive error is an instance of Try-Step Abuse because the attempt at solving is hasty. It is also an instance of Help Avoidance because on unfamiliar steps, the preferred behavior is to seek help rather than attempt the step. The Help Tutor recognizes both metacognitive errors and provides appropriate feedback (see Figure 4.4).

Second, let us consider an instance of Help Abuse. If the student were to ask for a hint but then quickly clicks through the hint levels, the Help Tutor will let the student know that he/she might learn more if he/she processes the hints more deliberately (see Figure 4.5).

Now let us follow the same hypothetical student at a later point in time, at which the student has had more practice with the given skill (see Figure 4.6; the fourth step in this more complex tutor problem involves the alternate interior angles theorem). Note that the tutor's assessment of the student's

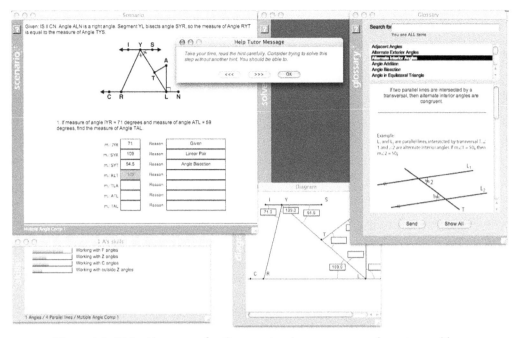

Figure 4.6. Help Abuse on a familiar step in a later, more complex tutor problem.

mastery of the skill is above the .6 threshold. Therefore, at this stage in the given student's learning progression, the Help Tutor considers steps involving this theorem to be familiar steps.

The preferred behavior on familiar steps contrasts in a number of ways with that on unfamiliar steps. Quick initial attempts at familiar steps are acceptable, unless they are so quick as to be near-instantaneous. On familiar steps, the student should ask for hints only if he/she makes a (domain-level) error and cannot readily figure out how to fix it, whereas on unfamiliar steps, the student is expected to ask for hints right off the bat. Further, on a familiar step, when the student requests hints, he/she is expected to get a sense for what to do with only a small number of the hint levels, although requesting all hint levels is acceptable. On unfamiliar steps, it is assumed that all hint levels will be needed.

Let us consider an example of Help Abuse on familiar steps. If our hypothetical student requests a hint before attempting the step, or after making an error without trying to repair the error, the Help Tutor will protest

(see Figure 4.7). This action is a form of Help Abuse, because on familiar steps, the student is supposed to try the step without help, at least until making an error for which it is not clear how to fix it. It is assumed that initial errors on familiar steps are likely due to slips rather than deep conceptual misunderstanding. On the other hand, a hint request (even if it is not preceded by multiple errors) is an indication that the student does not have a strong sense of what to do. Therefore, the Help Tutor recommends Glossary use, consistent with its preferred strategy shown in the flowchart.

Finally, let us consider Help Avoidance, which in general is rare on familiar steps, because the student is expected to use help sparingly. However, if the student makes more than a threshold number of errors without asking for a hint, the Help Tutor will assume that it is not clear to this student how to fix the error, and will deem this behavior to be a form of Help Avoidance (Figure 4.8). On unfamiliar steps, the student would have received a similar message even after making a single error without requesting a hint.

Figure 4.7. Help Tutor responses to Help Abuse (using on-demand hints prior to trying the step or using the Glossary) when a step is familiar.

Figure 4.8. Help Avoidance on a familiar step.

Classroom Evaluation Study

We conducted two classroom studies to examine the effect of giving feedback in response to students' help-seeking errors as they work with an ITS. We hypothesized that such feedback will have a positive effect on (1) students' help-seeking behavior while the feedback is in effect, (2) students' domain-level learning while the feedback is in effect, and (3) students' help-seeking behavior during subsequent tutor units, when the feedback is no longer given. Following the first classroom study involving the Help Tutor (Roll et al., 2006; Roll et al., 2011), we conducted a second, more extensive, quasi-experimental study (Roll, Aleven, McLaren, & Koedinger, 2007a; 2011). In this chapter we focus on the second study.

The study evaluated the effect of a package of three support elements for help seeking. First, it included the Help Tutor. Second, we added a brief in-class video presentation aimed at helping students understand the principles underlying the Help Tutor messages. We conjectured that students would be more accepting of these messages if they understood the principles. Third, we added within-tutor self-assessment activities, in which students self-assessed their knowledge of the geometry principles targeted in the tutor units and reflected on the accuracy of their self-assessment. These new tutor activities, which also included feedback on the student's reflections, were created with the Cognitive Tutor Authoring Tools (CTAT) (Aleven, McLaren, Sewall, & Koedinger, 2009). We thought the self-assessment exercises might make students more aware of their need for help, with a positive influence on their help-seeking behavior, as has been found by other researchers (Nelson

Le Gall, Kratzer, Jones, & DeCooke, 1990; Tobias & Everson, 2002).

The study took place over a period of four months in a vocational school in a rural area in Western Pennsylvania, where the Geometry Cognitive Tutor is used as part of the regular geometry instruction. The participants were 67 students in grades 10 and 11, in four classes taught by two teachers. We assigned the students to an experimental condition and a control condition. The assignment of students to conditions was done on a class-by-class basis, because the experimental group but not the control group had in-class instructional sessions dealing with help seeking. We made sure that each teacher had one class in the experimental condition and one class in the control condition.

During the four months of the study, the students used the tutor two days a week, as is customary in Cognitive Tutor courses. The intervention took place during months 1 and 3. During these two one-month periods, all students worked on the two units of the tutor curriculum targeted in the experiment, dealing with the geometric properties of angles and with quadrilaterals, respectively. During these two months, the students in the control condition worked with the standard tutor and the students in the experimental condition worked with a tutor version that was enhanced with the help-seeking support package described earlier. During months 2 and 4, the students resumed their normal work on the standard tutor. Different students worked on different tutor units, but not on angles or quadrilaterals. During these two months, all students used the standard version of the tutor, without extra support for help seeking.

We administered paper-and-pencil tests at three different points in time: before month 1 (test-0), at the end of month 1 (test-1), and at the end of month 3 (test-2). All tests included four types of items to assess students' domain-level learning: problem-solving and explanation items, similar to the types of steps the students had encountered within the tutor; procedural transfer items, in which the students were asked to make

solvability judgments; and finally conceptual transfer items, in which students were asked to match particular geometric shapes (e.g., a parallelogram) with their properties. Test-0 served as the pre-test for the material targeted in month 1 (angles). Test-1 served both as a post-test related to the material covered in month 1 (angles) and as a pre-test related to the material covered in month 3 (quadrilaterals). Specifically, it included conceptual items related to quadrilaterals, although not problem-solving items. Test-2, finally, served as the post-test related to material taught in month 3.

To test our second hypothesis, that help-seeking support leads to greater domain-level learning, we analyzed student performance on the domain-level test items. The data and analysis are presented in more detail in Roll et al. (2007a). Here we state only the main conclusions. First, significant learning gains were observed, both with respect to the material targeted in month 1 and that targeted in month 3, with respect to the problem-solving items, explanation items, and conceptual transfer items. However, we found no significant differences between the conditions in any of the domain-level measures, nor did we find any interactions with condition. Therefore, the hypothesis that support for help seeking in the context of tutored problem solving leads to better domain-level learning could not be confirmed.

To test our first and third hypotheses – that students' help-seeking behavior would improve due to the feedback on help seeking – we assessed students' help-seeking behavior while they worked on the tutor both during the intervention (months 1 and 3) and after (month 4). We looked at five key variables related to how adaptively the students used the tutor's hints and how deliberately they worked with the tutor (see Tables 4.1 and 4.2). Three of these variables measure the time taken for various categories of metacognitive actions: the time taken before requesting a first hint on a step, the time taken to read a hint level and then to request a subsequent hint level, and the time taken before an attempt at solving.

Table 4.1. Students' Help-Seeking Behavior During the Intervention

	Month 1 (Unit: Angles)			Month 3 (Unit: Quadrilaterals)		
	Exp. Group	Ctrl. Group	Effect Size	Exp. Group	Ctrl. Group	Effect Size
Time before first hint (seconds)	18	16	.2	24	22	.2
Time before subsequent hint (seconds)	6	5	.7*	8	6	.6*
Time before trying a step (seconds)	16	14	.6*	22	19	.7**
Depth of hint sequences (hint levels)	3.1	3.7	−1.1**	3.3	3.9	−1.3**
Hint sequences ending in bottom-out hint (percentage of hint sequences)	45	60	−.6*	47	59	−.6*

Note: The effect sizes (Cohen's *d*) measure the difference between the experimental group and control group. It is assumed that the more adaptive behavior is to spend more time with hints and to request fewer hint levels.
$* - p < .05; ** - p < .01$

The other two variables relate to students' hint requests: the average hint depth (i.e., the highest hint level reached on any given problem step) and the percentage of hint sequences in which the student reached the bottom-out hint. For this last variable, the percentage of bottom-out hints, we were able to ascertain values during the intervention (months 1 and 3) but not after (month 4). Given the students' natural propensity to work quickly, we made the simplifying assumption that working slower is always better. Also, we made the assumption that requesting fewer hint levels on a step is better, representing a sign that the student is processing the hint levels more carefully and is generating inferences/answers, rather than relying on being given them by the tutor, as foreseen in the original design of the hint facility, described by Anderson (1993) and summarized by Aleven et al. (2003).

During the intervention, the students in the experimental condition took more time than their counterparts in the control condition before attempting a step and also took more time to read a hint before moving on to the next hint level (see Table 4.1). Further, students in the experimental condition went less deeply into the tutor's hint sequences and reached the bottom-out

hint on a significantly lower percentage of the hint sequences than the students in the control condition. In sum, there was a statistically significant difference in favor of the experimental group on four of the five measures, often with substantial effect sizes. The differences are consistent across the two tutor units. The one variable for which we found no difference while the intervention was in effect is average time before a first hint. The values for this variable shown in Table 4.1 suggest that the students in both conditions spent an adequate amount of time before requesting a first hint, and that therefore there was no room (or need) for the Help Tutor to help students improve with respect to this measure. These results provide support for our first hypothesis, that feedback on help seeking influences students' help-seeking behavior over the period during which the feedback is given. More detail about the study can be found in Roll et al. (2006; 2011).

After the intervention, we saw that students who had previously received feedback on their help-seeking behavior spent more time with the tutor's hints and went less deeply into the tutor's hint sequences, compared to students who had received no such feedback (see Table 4.2). The first

Table 4.2. Students' Help-Seeking Behavior Subsequent to the Intervention (i.e., During Month 4, While Working with the Unmodified Cognitive Tutor)

	Experimental Group	Control Group	Effect Size (Cohen's d)
Time before first hint (seconds)	24	22	.2
Time before subsequent hint (seconds)	12	8	.9**
Time before trying a step (seconds)	24	22	.3
Depth of hint sequences (hint levels)	2.2	2.6	$-.5^{\dagger}$

$^{\dagger} - p < .1; ** - p < .01$

effect was statistically significant and the second was marginally statistically significant. The effect sizes (Cohen's d) were .9 standard deviations and .5 standard deviations, respectively, which should be considered as large and medium effect sizes. There was no difference between the conditions with respect to time before the first hint, but there is little reason to expect that there would be a difference *after* the intervention, given that there was no difference in this variable *during* the intervention (as described above). There was also no difference with respect to the time before trying a step. Again, judging by the average value of this variable in the control group, it looks like there is little room for improvement. These findings provide support for our third hypothesis, that feedback on help seeking leads to more adaptive help-seeking behavior even after the feedback is no longer in effect. The lasting improvement can be attributed to students' having internalized the Help Tutor feedback, so that in subsequent learning opportunities, they were capable of independently generating the help-seeking behaviors that the Help Tutor was advocating.

The improvement in students' help-seeking behavior *while the Help Tutor was in effect* may to some degree be attributable to the fact that the Help Tutor was impeding certain help-seeking behaviors thought to be ineffective. For example, the Help Tutor made it more difficult (although not impossible) to quickly click through a sequence of hints; after a quick click, the Cognitive Tutor's next hint level was intercepted and a Help Tutor message was displayed instead.

However, for the other variables shown in Tables 4.1 and 4.2, there is no similar impeding effect of the Help Tutor. More importantly, the *lasting* improvement on students' help-seeking behavior cannot be attributed to the Help Tutor's impeding ineffective help-seeking behaviors.

Given our experimental design, we can conclude that the combination of three support elements – classroom instruction, a self-assessment tutor, and feedback on help seeking – is *sufficient* to cause a lasting improvement in student help seeking (although not in students' domain learning, as discussed further below). Our experimental design does not allow us to conclude that any individual element is *necessary* or to single out any element as being more influential than the others. We think it is unlikely, however, that the effect could have been achieved without the Help Tutor's feedback on help seeking, because the Help Tutor was by far the most "intense" of the three support elements. The other two elements may have amplified the effect of the Help Tutor. In fact, we suspect that the in-class introduction of help-seeking principles was largely ineffective. The TV monitors were small, the video quality low, the teachers did not engage students in a discussion, and many students seemed to be surfing the Web or playing games while the video was running.

Discussion

Our classroom study yielded an interesting and novel result: Students who were given feedback on their help-seeking behavior learned to use the tutor's hints more carefully; they asked for fewer hint levels and spent more time with the levels that they saw. The fact that the effect lasted even after the feedback was turned off means that the students must have internalized some of the help-seeking behaviors that this feedback was advocating. A key contribution of the current project, therefore, is that it demonstrates that an intelligent tutor agent can bring about a *lasting* improvement in key aspects of students' metacognitive behavior, specifically help seeking. A number of ITS projects have attempted to improve students' help-seeking behaviors or reduce students' "gaming the system." These projects, however, did not measure whether the effect lasted beyond the intervention. More broadly, we are aware of only one other ITS project that measured whether there were improvements in student metacognition not just during the intervention, but also afterward. A study involving the Betty's Brain found a lasting improvement on students' propensity for information seeking and monitoring solution quality (Leelawong & Biswas, 2008).

Our studies have not confirmed the hypothesis that student learning at the domain level would improve as a result of students' improved (more deliberate) help-seeking skill. Under the view of help seeking with an ITS, embodied in the model of help seeking presented in this chapter, more deliberate hint use should relate to improved domain learning. Students' more deliberate processing of the tutor's principle-based hints should lead to an improved understanding of the problem-solving principles that are the target of the instruction. This understanding should guide students' learning-by-doing process away from shallow strategies or guessing toward more deliberate application of problem-solving principles. Furthermore, the fact that the students request fewer hint levels suggests that they are more successful at generating steps for themselves, using the more abstract hints from the tutoring system. *Generating* answers, as opposed to being given answers, is often thought to enhance learning (e.g., Roediger & Karpicke, 2006).

As we considered possible reasons why we did not see an improvement in students' domain-level learning, we were led to reflect on three broad issues: (1) the design of principle-based hints, (2) the design of metacognitive tutoring agents, and (3) the role of help seeking in learning with ITSs. Our experiment does not enable us to single out any particular factor why students' domain learning did not improve, but we hope this discussion identifies opportunities for follow-up research.

Design of Hints and Hinting Facilities

First, could it be that the Geometry Cognitive Tutor's principle-based hints may not have been good enough to support learning? If so, then students' help-seeking attempts could be made more effective simply by rewriting the hints. At one level, we find little reason to accept that substantially more effective hints could be written while staying within the genre of text-based, principle-based hints. The complexity of the hints stems largely from the complexity of the geometry principles themselves. As one tries to write principle-based hints that are accurate, one has a lot of ground to cover: The hints should probably include a general statement of the problem-solving principle, should describe how the principle applies, what inferences follow, and what calculations are needed. The principles themselves are complex: They often have multiple conditions and often refer to geometry concepts that are themselves complex. It may be that principle-based hints are especially complex in the domain of geometry, as compared to other domains. The principles tend to contain jargon. Further, many concepts in this domain have a strong visual component and are thus hard to describe in words.

To craft more effective hints, one may have to look beyond text-based, principle-based hints that are sequenced from the general to the specific. If the main issue is that novices have great difficulty understanding general statements of abstract concepts or principles, then one place to start might be by relaxing or abandoning the general-to-specific sequencing. The *contingent tutoring* approach pioneered by Wood and Wood (1999), based on their empirical studies of human tutors, may be a good place to start. In this approach, hints are sequenced from the general to the specific, but the level at which the hint sequences start varies depending on the individual student's recent performance. In this approach, more knowledgeable students start at a more abstract hint level than less knowledgeable students. It is possible that the contingent hinting scheme is a key reason why Wood and Wood observed a positive correlation between help use and learning, whereas with the Geometry Cognitive Tutor, a negative correlation was observed (Aleven, McLaren, & Koedinger, 2006),[2] although other explanations cannot be ruled out.

An alternative approach would be to start with the hint that gives the answer, based on the idea that it is easier to interpret specific examples than it is to interpret abstract statements of general rules and principles (Charney & Reder, 1986; van der Meij & Carroll, 1995). Under this assumption, the bottom-out hint should come first, because it essentially turns the problem step into a worked example. Subsequent hint levels would then explain the answer. It is an interesting question whether the subsequent hint levels should be sequenced from the general to the specific or the other way around. Both ideas seem viable. A possible risk of a hinting scheme in which the answer is given first may be that it leads to increased instances of "gaming the system," although, if it really serves students better, perhaps the opposite will turn out to be true. Beyond these ideas, one might design interactive hints (e.g., Arroyo et al., 2000) that take advantage of multiple media and multimedia principles (e.g., Clark & Mayer, 2007).

Design Choices in Creating an Agent for Metacognitive Tutoring

In addition to considering the design of the help itself, it is useful to reflect on the design of the Help Tutor and that of metacognitive

tutor agents more generally. Although the Help Tutor was based on proven tutoring principles (Roll et al., 2007b), could it be that a better-designed Help Tutor would have been more successful? Although the Help Tutor actually led to an improvement in students' help-seeking behavior with medium to large effect sizes, one might argue that the Help Tutor needs to be even more effective to yield domain-learning improvement. We therefore look at some of the key design choices that were made.

One way the Help Tutor differs from related systems is that it gives specific feedback based on a detailed diagnosis of student metacognition. Even if other projects were able to achieve an improvement in domain-level learning and student engagement or metacognition without such detailed feedback (Arroyo et al., 2007; Baker et al., 2006), we still view the ability to do detailed metacognitive diagnosis as a strength. It is unknown whether these simpler approaches can have a *lasting* effect on lifelong learning skills and domain learning. An advantage of specific feedback based on detailed diagnosis is that it gives students a clear notion of the desired learning behaviors, which more coarse-grained approaches cannot do.

A second difference is that the Help Tutor focuses almost entirely on feedback with *metacognitive* content, whereas other work suggests that emphasizing domain-level learning can be a helpful aspect of metacognitive support or feedback. As mentioned, Baker et al. (2006) give remedial domain-level exercises in response to students' gaming the system. These exercises are selected so that they involve the same skill(s) as the step on which the gaming occurred, thus making up for learning opportunities lost due to gaming. Arroyo et al.'s (2007) system also made connections with domain-level learning: it periodically presented information to the student about his/her own domain-level performance, accompanied by brief metacognitive tips. It may be telling that the tips alone, without the domain-level performance feedback, did not have an effect on student engagement. Connecting the metacognitive message to

---

[2] This possibility was pointed out by Shaaron Ainsworth.

(domain-level) learning goals students care about seems key.

Finally, in the current work, the metacognitive feedback is given "on the spot," that is, in the context of (domain-level) problem solving, at the moment that the nondesirable metacognitive behavior happens. Immediate, in-context feedback is supported by one of the Cognitive Tutor principles, distilled from the success of this line of ITS in enhancing domain-level learning (Koedinger & Corbett, 2006). When feedback is given in the specific context in which it is relevant, it may be easier for students to encode the specific conditions under which a recommended action is appropriate, leading to better-contextualized knowledge. A contrasting approach is to provide feedback during an "after-action review." This approach has been successful in enhancing learning at the domain level (Katz, Allbritton, & Connelly, 2003; Katz et al., 1998). In VanLehn's (2006) catalog of ITS behaviors, after-action review is therefore considered a key form of (domain-level) within-problem support. The record of after-action review of metacognitive aspects of problem solving within ITSs is mixed, however. Some approaches focused on improving help seeking gave feedback, tips, or remedial problems at the problem boundaries (e.g., Arroyo et al., 2007; Baker et al., 2006). These approaches improved student domain learning (but provided no evidence about *future* domain learning). On the other hand, Gama (2004) found that metacognitive feedback at the end of a problem is meaningless because students ignored it. The question of how in-context and after-action feedback and review can best be employed and combined to help foster lifelong learning skills clearly has not been settled yet.

Somewhat relatedly, permanently visible but low-key graphical displays of aspects of an individual student's metacognition (e.g., Baker et al., 2006; Walonoski & Heffernan, 2006b) seem to enable students to reflect on their metacognitive behavior at moments convenient to them. At the same time, as Walonoski and Heffernan (2006b) point out, because these displays are available for bystanders (including the teacher) to see, they may provide effective social pressure for students to engage in learning behaviors that are evaluated more positively. However, the effect of these displays has not been separated from that of other features.

Role of Help Seeking in Learning with an ITS

The third and final factor we considered as we thought about why an improvement in help seeking was not accompanied by improved domain-level learning was the following: Could it be, at least in the domain of geometry, that help seeking may not be as strong an influence on domain learning as previously thought? As mentioned, principle-based explanations (which typically form the content of hints presented by ITSs) are challenging forms of instructional text. It may be that deeply processing and understanding principle-based hints is so challenging that it is beyond all but the most advanced learners in the target population. This notion may seem to be at odds with prior work in the area of help seeking in ITSs, cited in the introduction of the chapter, namely, the finding by Beck et al. (2008) that help in an ITS for reading (LISTEN) was helpful, the positive correlation between help use and learning found by Wood and Wood (1999), and the work by Schworm and Renkl (2006) indicating that principle-based instructional explanations are helpful in the context of example studying. Perhaps these seeming inconsistencies can be resolved by saying that Beck and colleagues did not focus on *principle-based* explanations. The hints provided by the LISTEN reading tutor may not be as challenging as the principle-based hints in geometry, even taking into account that the target population of that system was much younger. Further, neither the Beck et al. study nor the Wood and Wood study presented causal data; therefore, these studies have not ruled out the possibility of a common cause of both better help seeking and better learning results. Only Schworm and Renkl provided causal data related to on-demand principle-based explanations (Renkl, 2002; Schworm & Renkl, 2006), but theirs were principle-based explanations in the context of example studying (rather than problem solving) and their study was a lab study. It is conceivable that these factors make a real difference. Perhaps more importantly, their second study showed that instructional explanations are not as effective as prompting students to give self-explanations. These findings are in line with those from studies that suggest that learning from instructional explanations is difficult (Gerjets, Scheiter, & Catrambone, 2006; Wittwer & Renkl, 2008). Similarly, a number of studies have shown that students tend to learn more by giving explanations, compared to receiving them (Brown & Kane, 1988; Webb, 1989), depending on the quality of their explanations (Lovett, 1992).

If learning from instructional explanations is inherently difficult, then perhaps instead of providing principle-based hints, an ITS should, when a student requests a hint, provide the bottom-out hint (thereby turning the problem step into an example step) and prompt the student to explain the step. It should then provide some help and feedback with answering these prompts. This approach is designed to capitalize on the fact that studying examples seems easier than studying rules or principle-based explanations. This notion finds support in the large literature on worked examples. It also is reflected in, for example, medical education practice and in recent findings by ITS researchers in a medical domain. For example, Yudelson et al. (2006) found that medical students in a leading medical school successfully learned by quickly getting to the bottom-out hints. This kind of behavior would be considered help abuse by the Help Tutor. However, if we make the reasonable assumption that this population of students has strong metacognitive skills, it is likely that they preferred seeing the answer first, so that they could self-explain it. Similarly, in recent educational data-mining work using log data from the Geometry Cognitive Tutor, Shih, Koedinger, and Scheines (2008)

found that the time students spend with the bottom-out hint is positively correlated with learning. They interpret this finding as evidence that students learn by self-explaining bottom-out hints, which essentially turn the problem step into an example step. An issue that needs to be resolved when pursuing this idea is that for some students, especially those with low prior knowledge, prompts for self-explanations may not be very effective. Thus, there may still be a role for principle-based explanations; the challenge is to find out how best to combine them with prompts for self-explanations (cf. Renkl, 2002).

Conclusion

Help seeking has long been regarded as an important influence on student learning (Nelson-Le Gall, 1981). Because ITSs typically offer on-demand hints (e.g., VanLehn, 2006), help seeking plays an important role in learning with an ITS. These types of learning environments therefore may provide a good platform to study the influence of this lifelong learning skill on student learning. Of particular interest is the question of whether ITSs are capable of improving this particular lifelong learning skill. As a platform for our investigations we used the Geometry Cognitive Tutor, a commercially available ITS. We feel we made three main contributions along the way.

First, we created a detailed, computer-executable model of help seeking (Aleven et al., 2006), based on extensive theoretical and empirical cognitive task analysis. This model is, to the best of our knowledge, the first computer model of help seeking in the literature on educational psychology or ITS. The model captures a recurrent metacognitive cycle during tutored problem solving. It describes how to approach a step in tutor problem while using the help and feedback from the tutoring environment in a manner consistent with the (self-assessed) familiarity with the step. The model clarifies what it means for students to seek help adaptively with an ITS and provides an extensive taxonomy of help-seeking errors. We are not aware of other work that provides this level of detail about desirable or undesirable learning behaviors. We validated the model using other independent and direct measures of help seeking (Roll et al., 2011). As we put the model to the test in our research, we have identified ways in which it can be refined. For example, the model does not account for use of bottom-out hints to support spontaneous self-explanation on the part of students (Shih et al., 2008). We would not be surprised to see further refinements in the future, but they do not subtract from the fact that articulating a model was a significant first contribution.

Second, we used this model, combined with a standard ITS technique – model tracing – to automatically assess how adaptively students seek help as they work with an ITS. The fact that the system can, automatically and unobtrusively, assess a lifelong learning skill is a significant technical contribution. The use of the model for the purpose of assessment has yielded much insight into learners' help-seeking behavior and the relation between help seeking and learning. For example, we know much more about the relative frequency of specific help-seeking behaviors and errors as well as about their correlations with learning.

The third contribution is a demonstration that feedback on students' help-seeking behavior within the context of tutored problem solving leads to a lasting improvement in this lifelong learning skill. Thus, the work provides evidence that an ITS can foster lifelong learning skills in the context of learning by doing. Improvements in learners' self-regulation are notoriously difficult to sustain (e.g., Zimmerman & Schunk, 2008), so to demonstrate any improvement at all is a significant contribution.

Along the way, we have come to understand that much of the difficulty in help seeking may stem from the fact that interpreting and understanding principle-based explanations is harder than we thought originally. Although this point seems to be in line with findings from other researchers studying learning from instructional explanations

(e.g., Wittwer & Renkl, 2008), it is contrary to the assumptions made by many developers of ITSs (Koedinger & Aleven, 2007; VanLehn, 2006). We caution against over-interpreting this finding, however. It is possible that geometry is a particularly difficult domain for learning from principle-based explanations, compared to other domains. Further, although learning from principle-based explanations is difficult, being able to do so is an important lifelong learning skill. ITS researchers wanting to take our findings seriously could look for ways in which the system could support students in interpreting these types of explanations, or follow some of the other suggestions for future research made earlier. It would be interesting as well to probe how far help-seeking skills acquired by using an ITS transfer, for example, to more active help seeking in the classroom.

The current work and related work are yielding interesting insight into what lifelong learning skills are especially relevant to learning with an ITS and what the exact nature is of these learning skills. This line of work shows that paying close attention to these skills helps improve the effectiveness of learning with an ITS. It raises the possibility that soon ITS will support the acquisition of lifelong learning skills that have an influence not just on future learning with ITS but that transfer to other types of learning environments as well.

References

Aleven, V., & Koedinger, K. R. (2000). Limitations of student control: Do students know when they need help? In G. Gauthier, C. Frasson, & K. VanLehn (Eds.), *Proceedings of the 5th international conference on intelligent tutoring systems, ITS 2000* (pp. 292–303). Berlin: Springer.

Aleven, V., & Koedinger, K. R. (2002) . An effective meta-cognitive strategy: learning by doing and explaining with a computer-based Cognitive Tutor . *Cognitive Science, 26* (2), 147–179.

Aleven, V., McLaren, B. M., & Koedinger, K. R. (2006). Towards computer-based tutoring of help-seeking skills. In S. Karabenick & R. Newman (Eds.), *Help seeking in academic settings: Goals, groups, and contexts* (pp. 259–296). Mahwah, NJ: Erlbaum.

Aleven, V., McLaren, B. M., Roll, I., & Koedinger, K. R. (2006). Toward meta-cognitive tutoring: A model of help seeking with a cognitive tutor. *International Journal of Artificial Intelligence in Education, 16*, 101–128.

Aleven, V., McLaren, B. M., Sewall, J., & Koedinger, K. R. (2009). A new paradigm for intelligent tutoring systems: Example-tracing tutors. *International Journal of Artificial Intelligence in Education, 19*(2), 105–154.

Aleven, V., Ogan, A., Popescu, O., Torrey, C., & Koedinger, K. (2004). Evaluating the effectiveness of a tutorial dialogue system for self-explanation. In J. C. Lester, R. M. Vicario, & F. Paraguaçu (Eds.), *Proceedings of seventh international conference on intelligent tutoring systems, ITS 2004* (pp. 443–454). Berlin: Springer Verlag.

Aleven, V., Roll, I., McLaren, B., Ryu, E. J., & Koedinger, K. R. (2005). An architecture to combine meta-cognitive and cognitive tutoring: Pilot testing the Help Tutor. In C. K. Looi, G. McCalla, B. Bredeweg, & J. Breuker (Eds.), *Proceedings of the 12th international conference on artificial intelligence in education, AIED 2005* (pp. 17–24). Amsterdam: IOS Press.

Aleven, V., Stahl, E., Schworm, S., Fischer, F., & Wallace, R. M. (2003). Help seeking and help design in interactive learning environments. *Review of Educational Research, 73*(2), 277–320.

Alpert, S. R., Singley, M. K., & Carroll, J. M. (1999). Multiple instructional agents in an intelligent tutoring system. In *Proceedings of the workshop on animated and personified pedagogical agents*. Workshop held during AI-ED '99: 9th International Conference on Artificial Intelligence in Education, July. Le Mans: France.

Anderson, J. R. (1993). *Rules of the mind*. Hillsdale, NJ: Lawrence Erlbaum Associates.

Anderson, J. R., Corbett, A. T., Koedinger, K. R., & Pelletier, R. (1995). Cognitive tutors: Lessons learned. *The Journal of the Learning Sciences, 4*(2), 167–207.

Arroyo, I., Beck, J. E., Woolf, B. P., Beal, C. R., & Schultz, K. (2000). Macroadapting animalwatch to gender and cognitive differences with respect to hint interactivity and symbolism. In G. Gauthier, C. Frasson, & K. VanLehn (Eds.), *Proceedings of the 5th international conference on intelligent tutoring systems, ITS 2000* (pp. 574–83). Berlin: Springer.

Arroyo, I., Ferguson, K., Johns, J., Dragon, T., Meheranian, H., Fisher, D., et al. (2007). Repairing disengagement with non-invasive interventions. In R. Luckin, K. R. Koedinger, & J. Greer (Eds.), *Proceedings of the 13th international conference on artificial intelligence in education, AIED 2007* (pp. 195–202). Amsterdam: IOS Press.

Baker, R. S. J. d., Corbett, A. T., Koedinger, K. R., Evenson, S., Wagner, A. Z., Naim, M., et al. (2006). Adapting to when students game an intelligent tutoring system. In M. Ikeda, K. D. Ashley, & T. W. Chan (Eds.), *Proceedings of the 8th international conference on intelligent tutoring systems, ITS 2006* (pp. 392–401). Berlin: Springer.

Baker, R., Walonoski, J., Heffernan, N., Roll, I., Corbett, A., & Koedinger, K. (2008). Why students engage in "gaming the system" behavior in interactive learning environments. *Journal of Interactive Learning Research, 19*(2), 185–224.

Bartholomé, T., Stahl, E., Pieschl, S., & Bromme, R. (2006). What matters in help-seeking? A study of help effectiveness and learner-related factors. *Computers in Human Behavior, 22*(1), 113–129.

Beal, C. R., Walles, R., Arroyo, I., & Woolf, B. P. (2007). Online tutoring for math achievement: A controlled evaluation. *Journal of Interactive Online Learning, 6*, 43–55.

Beck, J. (2005). Engagement tracing: Using response times to model student disengagement. In C. K. Looi, G. McCalla, B. Bredeweg, & J. Breuker (Eds.), *Proceedings of the 12th international conference on artificial intelligence in education, AIED 2005*, (pp. 88–95). Amsterdam: IOS Press.

Beck, J. E., Chang, K., Mostow, J., & Corbett, A. T. (2008). Does help help? Introducing the Bayesian evaluation and assessment methodology. In B. P. Woolf, E. Aimeur, R. Nkambou, & S. Lajoie (Eds.), *Proceedings of the 9th international conference on intelligent tutoring systems, ITS 2008* (pp. 383–394). Berlin: Springer.

Bielaczyc, K., Pirolli, P. L., & Brown, A. L. (1995). Training in self-explanation and self-regulation strategies: Investigating the effects of knowledge acquisition activities on problem solving. *Cognition and Instruction, 13*(2), 221–252.

Brown, A. L., & Kane, M. J. (1988). Preschool children can learn to transfer: Learning to learn and learning from example. *Cognitive Psychology, 20*, 493–523.

Butler, R. (1998). Determinants of help seeking: Relations between perceived reasons for classroom help-avoidance and help-seeking behaviors in an experimental context. *Journal of Educational Psychology, 90*(4), 630–643.

Butler, R., & Neuman, O. (1995). Effects of task and ego achievement goals on help-seeking behaviors and attitudes. *Journal of Educational Psychology, 87*(2), 261–271.

Card, S., Moran, T., & Newell, A. (1983). *The psychology of human-computer interaction.* Mahwah, NJ: Erlbaum.

Charney, D. H., & Reder, L. M. (1986). Designing interactive tutorials for computer users. *Human-Computer Interaction, 2*(4), 297–317.

Chi, M. T. H., Bassok, M., Lewis, M. W., Reimann, P., & Glaser, R. (1989). Self-Explanations: How students study and use examples in learning to solve problems. *Cognitive Science, 13,* 145–182.

Chi, M. T. H., de Leeuw, N., Chiu, M., & LaVancher, C. (1994). Eliciting self-explanations improves understanding. *Cognitive Science, 18,* 439–477.

Clark, R. C., & Mayer, R. E. (2007). *E-Learning and the science of instruction* (2nd ed.). San Francisco: Pfeiffer.

Cocea, M., Hershkovitz, A., & Baker, R. S. J. d. (2009). The impact of off-task and gaming behaviors on learning: Immediate or aggregate? In V. Dimitrova, R. Mizoguchi, B. du Boulay, & A. Graesser (Eds.), *Proceedings of the 14th international conference on artificial intelligence in education, AIED 2009* (pp. 507–514). Amsterdam: IOS Press.

Conati, C., Muldner, K., & Carenini, G. (2006). From example studying to problem solving via tailored computer-based meta-cognitive scaffolding: Hypotheses and design. *Technology, Instruction, Cognition, and Learning, 4*(2), 139–190.

Conati, C., & VanLehn, K. (2000). Toward computer-based support of meta-cognitive skills: A computational framework to coach self-explanation. *International Journal of Artificial Intelligence in Education, 11*(4), 389–415.

Corbett, A. T., Koedinger, K. R., & Hadley, W. H. (2001). Cognitive tutors: From the research classroom to all classrooms. *Technology Enhanced Learning: Opportunities for Change,* 235–263.

Corbett, A., McLaughlin, M., & Scarpinatto, K. C. (2000). Modeling student knowledge: Cognitive tutors in high school and college. *User Modeling and User-Adapted Interaction, 10,* 81–108.

Corbett, A., Wagner, A., & Raspat, J. (2003). The impact of analysing example solutions on problem solving in a pre-algebra tutor. In U. Hoppe, F. Verdejo, & J. Kay (Eds.), *Proceedings of the 11th international conference on artificial intelligence in education, AIED 2003* (pp. 133–140). Amsterdam: IOS Press.

Crowley, R. S., Legowski, E., Medvedeva, O., Tseytlin, E., Roh, E., & Jukic, D. (2007). Evaluation of an intelligent tutoring system in pathology: Effects of external representation on performance gains, metacognition, and acceptance. *Journal of the American Medical Informatics Association, 14*(2), 182–190.

El Saadawi, G. M., Azevedo, R., Castine, M., Payne, V., Medvedeva, O., Tseytlin, E., et al. (2009). Factors affecting feeling-of-knowing in a medical intelligent tutoring system: The role of immediate feedback as a metacognitive scaffold. *Advances in Health Sciences Education: Theory and Practice, 15,* 9–30.

Gama, C. (2004). Metacognition in interactive learning environments: The Reflection Assistant model. In J. C. Lester, R. M. Vicario, & F. Paraguaçu (Eds.), *Proceedings of seventh international conference on intelligent tutoring systems, ITS 2004* (pp. 668–677). Berlin: Springer.

Gerjets, P., Scheiter, K., & Catrambone, R. (2006). Can learning from molar and modular worked examples be enhanced by providing instructional explanations and prompting self-explanations? *Learning and Instruction, 16*(2), 104–121.

Gott, S. P., & Lesgold, A. M. (2000). Competence in the workplace: How cognitive performance models and situated instruction can accelerate skill acquisition. In R. Glaser (Ed.), *Advances in instructional psychology* (pp. 239–327). Hillsdale, NJ: Erlbaum.

Graesser, A. C., Chipman, P., Haynes, B. C., & Olney, A. (2005). AutoTutor: An intelligent tutoring system with mixed-initiative dialogue. *IEEE Transactions in Education, 48,* 612–618.

Gross, A. E., & McMullen, P. A. (1983). Models of the help-seeking process. In J. D. Fisher, N. Nadler, & B. M. DePaulo (Eds.), *New directions in helping, Vol. 2* (pp. 45–61). New York: Academic Press.

Karabenick, S. A. (2003). Seeking help in large college classes: A person-centered approach. *Contemporary Educational Psychology, 28*(1), 37–58.

Karabenick, S., & Newman, R. (Eds.) (2006). *Help seeking in academic settings: Goals, groups, and contexts.* Mahwah, NJ: Erlbaum.

Katz, S., Allbritton, D., & Connelly, J. (2003). Going beyond the problem given: How human tutors use post-solution discussions to support transfer. *International Journal of Artificial Intelligence and Education, 13*(1), 79–116.

Katz, S., Lesgold, A., Hughes, E., Peters, D., Eggan, G., Gordin, M., & Greenberg, L. (1998). Sherlock II: An intelligent tutoring system built upon the LRDC tutor framework. In C. P. Bloom & R. B. Loftin (Eds.), *Facilitating the development and use of interactive learning environments* (pp. 227–258). Mahwah, NJ: Erlbaum.

Koedinger, K. R., & Aleven V. (2007). Exploring the assistance dilemma in experiments with Cognitive Tutors. *Educational Psychology Review, 19*(3), 239–264.

Koedinger, K. R., Anderson, J. R., Hadley, W. H., & Mark, M. A. (1997). Intelligent tutoring goes to school in the big city. *International Journal of Artificial Intelligence in Education, 8*(1), 30–43.

Koedinger, K. R., & Corbett, A. T. (2006). Cognitive tutors: Technology bringing learning sciences to the classroom. In R. K. Sawyer (Ed.), *The Cambridge handbook of the learning sciences* (pp. 61–78). Cambridge: Cambridge University Press.

Koedinger, K. R., Corbett, A. T., Ritter, S., & Shapiro, L. (2000). Carnegie learning's Cognitive Tutor: Summary research results. White paper. Pittsburgh, PA. Available at http://www.carnegielearning.com

Leelawong, K., & Biswas, G. (2008). Designing learning by teaching agents: The Betty's Brain system. *International Journal of Artificial Intelligence in Education, 18*(3), 181–208.

Lovett, M. C. (1992). Learning by problem solving versus by examples: The benefits of generating and receiving information. In *Proceedings of the fourteenth annual meeting of the cognitive science society* (pp. 956–961). Hillsdale, NJ: Erlbaum.

Lovett, M. C. (1998). Cognitive task analysis in the service of intelligent tutoring system design: A case study in statistics. In B. P. Goettle, H. M. Halff, C. L. Redfield, & V. J. Shute (Eds.), *Intelligent tutoring systems, proceedings of the fourth international conference* (pp. 234–243). Berlin: Springer Verlag.

Luckin, R., & Hammerton, L. (2002). Getting to know me: Helping learners understand their own learning needs through metacognitive scaffolding. In S. A. Cerri, G. Gouardères, & F. Paraguaçu (Eds.), *Proceedings of the sixth international conference on intelligent tutoring systems, ITS 2002* (pp. 759–71). Berlin: Springer.

Martin, B., & Mitrovic, A. (2002). Automatic problem generation in constraint-based tutors. In S.A. Cerri, G. Gouardères & F. Paraguaçu (Eds.) *Intelligent tutoring systems: 6th international conference (ITS-2002)* (p. 388–398). Berlin: Springer.

Mathan, S. A., & Koedinger, K. R. (2005). Fostering the intelligent novice: Learning from errors with metacognitive tutoring. *Educational Psychologist, 40*(4), 257–265.

McNamara, D., O'Reilly, T., Rowe, M., Boonthum, C., & Levinstein, I. (2007). Istart: A Web-based tutor that teaches self-explanation and metacognitive reading strategies. In D. McNamara (Ed.), *Reading comprehension strategies: Theories, interventions, and technologies* (pp. 397–420). New York: Lawrence Erlbaum.

Mercier, J., & Frederiksen, C. H. (2007). Individual differences in graduate students' help-seeking process in using a computer coach in problem-based learning. *Learning and Instruction, 17*(2), 184–203.

Mevarech, Z., & Fridkin, S. (2006). The effects of IMPROVE on mathematical knowledge, mathematical reasoning and meta-cognition. *Metacognition and Learning, 1*(1), 85–97.

Mitrovic, A., McGuigan, N., Martin, B. Suraweera, P., Milik, N., & Holland, J. (2008). Authoring constraint-based tutors in ASPIRE: A case study of a capital investment tutor. *In world conference on educational multimedia, hypermedia & telecommunications (ED-MEDIA 2008).*

Mostow, J., & Beck, J. (2007). When the rubber meets the road: Lessons from the in-school adventures of an automated Reading Tutor that listens. In B. Schneider & S.-K. McDonald (Eds.), *Conceptualizing scale-up: Multidisciplinary perspectives, Vol. 2* (pp. 183–200). Lanham, MD: Rowman & Littlefield.

Nelson-Le Gall, S. (1981). Help-seeking: An understudied problem-solving skill in children. *Developmental Review, 1,* 224–246.

Nelson-Le Gall, S., Kratzer, L., Jones, E., & DeCooke, P. (1990). Children's self-assessment of performance and task-related help-seeking. *Journal of Experimental Child Psychology, 49,* 245–263.

Newman, R. S. (1994). Adaptive help seeking: A strategy of self-regulated learning. In D. H. Schunk & B. J. Zimmerman (Eds.), *Self-regulation of learning and performance: Issues* and educational applications (pp. 283–301). Hillsdale: Erlbaum.

Newman, R. S. (2008). The motivational role of adaptive help seeking in self-regulated learning. In D. H. Schunk & B. J. Zimmerman (Eds.), Motivation and self-regulated learning: Theory, research, and applications (pp. 315–337). New York: Erlbaum.

Palincsar, A. S., & Brown, A. L. (1984). Reciprocal teaching of comprehension-fostering and comprehension-monitoring activities. Cognition and Instruction, 1(2), 117–175.

Pintrich, P. R. (2004). A conceptual framework for assessing motivation and self-regulated learning in college students. Educational Psychology Review, 16(4), 385–407.

Puustinen, M. (1998). Help-seeking behavior in a problem-solving situation: Development of self-regulation. European Journal of Psychology of Education, 13(2), 271–282.

Rau, M., Aleven, V., & Rummel, N. (2009). Intelligent tutoring systems with multiple representations and self-explanation prompts support learning of fractions. In V. Dimitrova, R. Mizoguchi, B. du Boulay, & A. Graesser (Eds.), Proceedings of the 14th international conference on artificial intelligence in education, AIED 2009 (pp. 441–448). Amsterdam: IOS Press.

Renkl, A. (2002). Worked-out examples: Instructional explanations support learning by self-explanations. Learning and Instruction, 12(5), 529–556.

Renkl, A., Stark, R., Gruber, H., & Mandl, H. (1998). Learning from worked-out examples: The effects of example variability and elicited self-explanations. Contemporary Educational Psychology, 23(1), 90–108.

Rickel, J., & Johnson, W. L. (1999). Animated agents for procedural training in virtual reality: Perception, cognition, and motor control. Applied Artificial Intelligence, 13, 343–382.

Ritter, S. (1997). Communication, cooperation and competition among multiple tutor agents. In B. du Boulay & R. Mizoguchi (Eds.), Artificial intelligence in education, proceedings of AI-ED 97 world conference (pp. 31–38). Amsterdam: IOS Press.

Roediger, H. L., & Karpicke, J. D. (2006). Test-enhanced learning: Taking memory tests improves long-term retention. Psychological Science, 17(3), 249–255.

Roll, I., Aleven, V., McLaren, B. M., & Koedinger, K. R. (2011). Improving students' help-seeking skills using metacognitive feedback in an intelligent tutoring system. Learning and Instruction, 21 (2), 267–280.

Roll, I., Aleven, V., McLaren, B., & Koedinger, K. (2007a). Can help seeking be tutored? Searching for the secret sauce of metacognitive tutoring. In R. Luckin, K. Koedinger, & J. Greer (Eds.), Proceedings of the 13th international conference on artificial intelligence in education (pp. 203–210). Amsterdam: IOS Press.

Roll, I., Aleven, V., McLaren, B., & Koedinger, K. (2007b). Designing for metacognition – applying Cognitive Tutor principles to metacognitive tutoring. Metacognition and Learning, 2(2–3), 125–140.

Roll, I., Aleven, V., McLaren, B. M., Ryu, E., Baker, R. S., & Koedinger, K. R. (2006). The Help Tutor: Does metacognitive feedback improve students' help-seeking actions, skills and learning? In M. Ikeda, K. D. Ashley, & T. W. Chan (Eds.), Proceedings of 8th international conference on intelligent tutoring systems (ITS 2006) (pp. 360–369). Berlin: Springer.

Ryan, A. M., Gheen, M. H., & Midgley, C. (1998). Why do some students avoid asking for help? An examination of the interplay among students' academic efficacy, teachers' social-emotional role, and the classroom goal structure. Journal of Educational Psychology, 90(3), 528–535.

Ryan, A. M., Patrick, H., & Shim, S. O. (2005). Differential profiles of students identified by their teacher as having avoidant, appropriate, or dependent help-seeking tendencies in the classroom. Journal of Educational Psychology, 97(2), 275–285.

Ryan, A. M., Pintrich, P. R., & Midgley, C. (2001). Avoiding seeking help in the classroom: Who and why? Educational Psychology Review, 13(2), 93–114.

Schworm, S., & Renkl, A. (2006). Computer-supported example-based learning: When instructional explanations reduce self-explanations. Computers & Education, 46(4), 426–445.

Shih, B., Koedinger, K. R., & Scheines, R. (2008). A response time model for bottom-out hints as worked examples. In R. S. J. d. Baker, T. Barnes, & J. Beck (Eds.), Educational Data Mining 2008: 1st International Conference on Educational Data Mining, Proceedings (pp. 117–126). Montreal, Canada.

Tobias, S., & Everson, H. T. (2002). Knowing what you know and what you don't: Further research on metacognitive knowledge monitoring. College Board Research Report 2002–2003.

van der Meij, H., & Carroll, J. M. (1995). Principles and heuristics for designing minimalist instruction. *Journal of the Society for Technical Communication, 42*(2), 243–261.

VanLehn, K. (2006). The behavior of tutoring systems. *International Journal of Artificial Intelligence in Education, 16*(3), 227–265.

VanLehn, K., Lynch, C., Schultz, K., Shapiro, J. A., Shelby, R. H., Taylor, L., et al. (2005). The Andes physics tutoring system: Lessons learned. *International Journal of Artificial Intelligence in Education, 15*(3), 147–204.

Wagster, J., Tan, J., Biswas, G., & Schwartz, D. (2007). How metacognitive feedback affects behavior in learning and transfer. In R. Luckin, K. Koedinger, & J. Greer (Eds.), *Proceedings of the 13th international conference on artificial intelligence in education, AIED 2007.* Amsterdam: IOS Press.

Walonoski, J. A., & Heffernan, N. T. (2006a). Detection and analysis of off-task gaming behavior in intelligent tutoring systems. In M. Ikeda, K. Ashley, & T. W. Chan (Eds.), *Proceedings of the eighth international conference on intelligent tutoring systems* (pp. 382–91). Berlin: Springer.

Walonoski, J. A., & Heffernan, N. T. (2006b). Prevention of off-task gaming behavior in intelligent tutoring systems. In M. Ikeda, K. Ashley, & T. W. Chan (Eds.), *Proceedings of the 8th international conference on intelligent tutoring systems, ITS 2006* (pp. 722–724). Berlin: Springer.

Webb, N. M. (1989). Peer interaction and learning in small groups. *International Journal of Education Research, 13*, 21–39.

Weerasinghe, A., & Mitrovic, A. (2006). Facilitating deep learning through self-explanation in an open-ended domain. *International Journal of Knowledge-Based and Intelligent Engineering Systems, 10*(1), 3–19.

White, B. Y., & Frederiksen, J. R. (1998). Inquiry, modeling, and metacognition: Making science accessible to all students. *Cognition and Instruction, 16*(1), 3–118.

Winne, P. H., & Hadwin, A. F. (1998). Studying as self-regulated learning. In D. J. Hacker, J. Dunlosky, & A. C. Graesser (Eds.), *Metacognition in educational theory and practice* (pp. 279–306). Hillsdale, NJ: Erlbaum.

Wittwer, J., & Renkl, A. (2008). Why instructional explanations often do not work: A framework for understanding the effectiveness of instructional explanations. *Educational Psychologist, 43*(1), 49–64.

Wood, H., & Wood, D. (1999). Help seeking, learning and contingent tutoring. *Computers and Education, 33*(2–3), 153–169.

Wylie, R., Koedinger, K. R., & Mitamura, T. (2009). Is self-explanation always better? The effects of adding self-explanation prompts to an English grammar tutor. In N. A. Taatgen & H. van Rijn (Eds.), *Proceedings of the 31st annual conference of the cognitive science society* (pp. 1300–1305). Austin, TX: Cognitive Science Society.

Yudelson, M. V., Medvedeva, O., Legowski, E., Castine, M., Jukic, D., & Crowley, R. S. (2006). Mining student learning data to develop high level pedagogic strategy in a medical ITS. In *Proceedings of a workshop on educational data mining at AAAI 2006.* Menlo Park, CA: AAAI Press.

Zimmerman, B. J. (2008). Investigating self-regulation and motivation: Historical background, methodological developments, and future prospects. *American Educational Research Journal, 45*(1), 166–183.

Zimmerman, B. J., & Moylan, A. R. (2009). Self-regulation: Where metacognition and motivation intersect. In D. J. Hacker, J. Dunlosky, & A. C. Graesser (Eds.), *Handbook of metacognition in education* (pp. 299–315). New York: Routledge.

Zimmerman, B. J., & Schunk, D. H. (2008). Motivation: An essential dimension of self-regulated learning. In D. H. Schunk & B. J. Zimmerman (Eds.), *Motivation and self-regulated learning: Theory, research, and applications.* Mahwah, NJ: Lawrence Erlbaum.

Zusho, A., Karabenick, S. A., Bonney, C. R., & Sims, B. C. (2007). Contextual determinants of motivation and help seeking in the college classroom. In R. P. Perry, & J. C. Smart (Eds.), *The scholarship of teaching and learning in higher education: An evidence-based perspective* (pp. 611–659). Dordrecht: Springer.

CHAPTER 5

Student Modeling and Intelligent Tutoring Beyond Coached Problem Solving

Cristina Conati

Introduction

Given our society's increasing need for high-quality teaching and training, computer-supported education is becoming critical to complementing human tutoring in a large variety of fields and settings. Research in Intelligent Tutoring Systems (ITS) leverages advances in Artificial Intelligence (AI), Cognitive Science and Education to increase the ability of computer-supported education to autonomously provide learners with effective educational experiences tailored to their specific needs, as good human tutors may do.

ITS research has successfully delivered techniques and systems that provide adaptive support for student problem-solving or question-answering activities in a variety of domains (e.g., programming, physics, algebra, geometry, Structural Query Language [SQL] and introductory computer science). The support is usually in the form of *coached problem solving*. The tutor has a representation of one or more acceptable solutions to a problem. This representation is used to monitor the student's solution and provide feedback and guidance in case the student's solution deviates from the tutor's known solutions. Several of these systems are actively used in real-world settings (e.g., Mitrovic et al., 2007, http://www.carnegie-learning.com/products.cfm) and have even contributed to changing traditional school curricula (Koedinger et al., 1995).

Although coached problem solving is an important form of instruction, other educational activities can foster understanding at different stages of the learning process or for learners with different preferences/abilities, such as learning from examples, exploring interactive simulations, playing educational games, and learning with a group of peers. Like for problem solving, providing individualized support for these activities can be highly beneficial. However, providing this support via an ITS poses unique challenges because it requires modeling domains as well as student behaviors and mental states that may not be as structured and well-defined as those involved in coached problem solving. For instance, an ITS that provides support for exploration-based learning must be able to "understand" exploratory activities so that it can propose them to students. It also needs to know what it means to explore a given concept or domain effectively, so that it can monitor the student's exploration process and provide adequate feedback when needed. In recent years, the ITS community has actively taken on these new challenges, aided by advances in AI research. The remainder of this chapter will focus on one specific endeavor to push ITS research beyond support for coached problem solving: devising intelligent tutors that can scaffold and enhance the learner's metacognitive skills. In particular, we describe work we have done on providing student-adaptive scaffolding for metacognitive skills relevant to successfully learning from studying examples and exploring interactive simulations.

Intelligent Tutors That Scaffold Metacognition

Metacognition refers to *"one's knowledge concerning one's own cognitive processes and products or anything related to them"* (Flavell 1976); more informally, metacognition has been referred to as *"thinking about thinking"* (emphasis added). Examples include, among others, the ability to monitor one's learning progress (*self-monitoring*), the tendency to explain instructional material to oneself in terms of the underlying domain knowledge (*self-explanation*), the ability to learn from examples (*analogical reasoning*), and the ability to appropriately seek tutoring help. Individuals vary significantly in these abilities (e.g., Bielaczyc et al., 1995; Chi, 2000; Shute & Glaser, 1990; Veermans et al., 2000), and thus several researchers have been investigating how to devise tutors that can help students acquire the relevant metacognitive skills.

Whereas some researchers have focused on creating tools that can scaffold metacognition by design (e.g., Aleven & Koedinger, 2002; Azevedo et al., 2009; Chi & VanLehn,

2007; Leelawong & Biswas, 2008; Luckin & Hammerton, 2002; van Joolingen, 2000) others have started investigating how to capture a user's need for metacognitive support in real time during interaction, to enable the ITS to respond accordingly. For instance, Normit-SE (Mitrovic, 2003) is an ITS designed to stimulate students to self-explain while they solve problems on data normalization in the database domain. Scaffolding for self-explanation is provided by asking students to explain every new or incorrect problem-solving step they generate, using a set of menu-based tools. The Geometry tutor is an ITS designed to support self-explanation during geometry problem solving by allowing students to type free-form self-explanations and providing feedback on their correctness (Aleven et al., 2004). Roll and colleagues have devised a model that enables an ITS to track and scaffold a student's tendency to effectively use the available help facilities (Aleven et al., Chapter 4 in this volume; Roll et al., 2007). In our work, we have focused on modeling and scaffolding students' metacognitive skills related to learning from examples, as well as skills related to learning effectively from exploration. The two subsequent sections in this chapter describe these two endeavors, respectively.

Arguably, the higher the level of the user's states to be captured, the more difficult they are to assess unobtrusively from basic interaction events. Our approach to dealing with the difficulty of these user-modeling tasks has been twofold. First, we use formal methods for probabilistic reasoning to deal with the uncertainty inherent in going from users' interaction behaviors to users' mental states. Second, we try to increase the bandwidth of the information available to the user model by including input beyond interaction events. In particular, in the fourth section we illustrate how we have successfully used information on user attention captured via an eye-tracking device to increase the accuracy of a user model for adaptive support to learning from exploration.

An Intelligent Tutor for Example-Based Learning

Research in cognitive science has provided extensive evidence of the utility of worked-out example solutions as learning aids (e.g., Anderson et al., 1984; VanLehn, 1996). However, this research also indicates that there is great variation in how effectively different students learn from examples because of individual differences in the metacognitive skills relevant to succeeding in this activity. Two of these metacognitive skills are *self-explanation* and *min-analogy*. Self-explanation involves elaborating and clarifying available instructional material to oneself (e.g., Chi, 2000). Min-analogy involves transferring from an example only the minimum amount of information necessary to enable successful problem solving, as opposed to copying indiscriminately (VanLehn, 1998). We have devised ExBL, an ITS that takes into account individual differences in these metacognitive skills to provide user-adaptive support to example-based learning (Conati et al., 2006). ExBL complements Andes, an ITS that supports physics problem solving at the college level (Conati et al., 2002), and includes two components. The first component, known as the SE (Self-Explanation)-Coach, supports example studying *prior* to problem solving. The second component, known as the EA (Example-Analogy)-Coach, supports the effective use of examples *during* problem solving (i.e., analogical problem solving, or APS from now on). Each component provides interactive tools for students to use examples in the corresponding modality, as well as proactive scaffolding adapted to each student's assessed needs.

To adapt its scaffolding to a student's needs, ExBL must be capable of monitoring and assessing each student's performance with respect to the target pedagogical tasks. Thus, the framework needs an internal representation of these tasks, against which to compare the student's problem-solving and example-studying behaviors. It also needs to encode in a student model its assessment of the student's domain knowledge and

relevant metacognitive skills. In ExBL, the representation of each problem-solving task (known as the *solution graph*) is automatically built by the system before run-time from a knowledge base of physics principles and a formal description of the problem situation (Conati & VanLehn, 2000). Each solution graph is a dependency network that represents how each solution step derives from previous steps and physics knowledge.

Both SE-Coach and EA-Coach use the solution graph as guidance to provide feedback on students' performance during example studying and analogical problem solving, by matching students' interface actions to elements in the solution graph. In addition to serving as the basis for the ExBL's ability to provide feedback, the solution graph is used to build its student models. Each time a student opens a new exercise, the corresponding solution graph provides the structure for a Bayesian network that forms the student model for the currently active Coach. The Bayesian network uses information on the student's interface actions to generate a probabilistic assessment of the student's knowledge and relevant metacognitive tendencies at any given point during the interaction. This procedure allows the system to generate tailored interventions to foster effective metacognitive skills when the model assesses the student as having knowledge gaps or requiring improvement in her metacognitive behaviors (Conati et al., 2006; Muldner & Conati 2007).

In the next subsections, we will describe for each Coach the interface used to support the target learning skills and the type of adaptive support enabled by that Coach's student model. We will also report the results of empirical evaluations of each Coach, providing encouraging evidence that adaptive support to metacognition is both feasible and desirable.

Studying Examples with the SE-Coach

The SE-Coach provides individualized support to help a student better understand a given example, based on its current assessment of the student's *knowledge, reading*

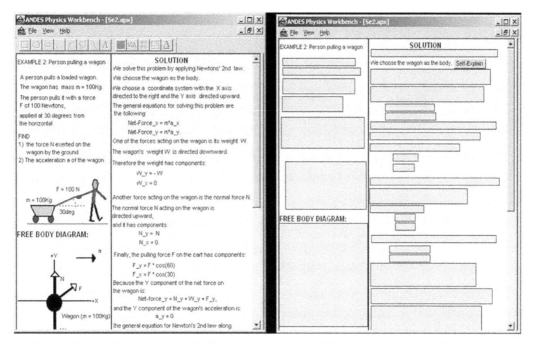

Figure 5.1. A physics example (left) presented with the SE-Coach masking interface (right).

patterns, and *explanations* that the student can generate via dedicated interface tools.

Based on this assessment, the SE-Coach guides the student to more carefully explain parts of the example that may not be fully understood. The general philosophy underlying the design of the ExBL framework is to provide guidance incrementally, to encourage students to rely on their own initiative rather than on the tutor and to interfere as little as possible with a student's spontaneous behaviors. In the SE-Coach, incremental guidance is embedded in three different levels of scaffolding for effective self-explanation, as we describe in the next section

THE SE-COACH INTERFACE TO
SCAFFOLD SELF-EXPLANATION
The different levels of scaffolding embedded in the SE-Coach's interface are designed to help students with different degrees of self-explanation capabilities self-explain more, while maintaining as much as possible the spontaneous, constructive nature of this learning activity.

The first level of scaffolding is given by a masking interface that presents different

parts of the example covered by grey boxes (see Figure 5.1). To read the hidden text or graphics, the student must move the mouse over the corresponding box. The fact that not all the example parts are visible at once helps students focus their attention and reflect on individual example parts. In addition, requiring a student to mouse over an example line to view it allows the SE-Coach to track students' attention (Conati & VanLehn 2000). The second level of scaffolding is provided by explicit prompts to self-explain. These prompts go from a generic reminder to self-explain, which appears next to each example part when it is uncovered (see *self-explain* button in Figure 5.2, next to the uncovered line in the screenshot on the right), to more specific prompts that encourage the student to elaborate a given solution step in terms of

1. how that step derived from domain theory (*step correctness* self-explanation);
2. the role that it plays in the overall solution (*step utility* self-explanation);
3. missing steps (*gaps*) in the example solution that led to the current step (*gap-filling* self-explanation).

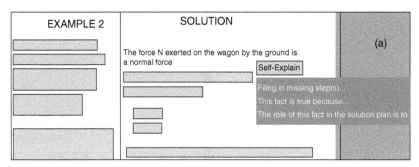

Figure 5.2. SE-Coach prompts for specific types of self-explanation.

These prompts appear when a student clicks on the *self-explain* button for a given line (see Figure 5.2).

The third level of scaffolding consists of menu-based tools designed to provide constructive but controllable ways to generate the above self-explanations, to help those students that would be unable to properly self-explain if left to their own devices (Conati & Carenini 2001; Conati & VanLehn 2000). For instance, as Figure 5.2 shows, one of the prompts that appears in the self-explain menu for a given example part reads: "This fact is true because...." This prompt aims to trigger self-explanations that justify why a step is correct in terms of domain principles (physics principles in the case of the SE-Coach). If a student selects it, a Rule Browser is displayed in the right half of the window (see Figure 5.3, left). The rule browser contains a hierarchy of physics rules, reflecting the content of ExBL's knowledge base. The student can browse the rule hierarchy to find a rule that justifies the currently uncovered part. The SE-Coach will use a green check or a red cross to provide feedback on the correctness of the student's selection (see Figure 5.3, left). To determine the correctness of a selection, the selection is matched to the rule that derives the uncovered example step in the solution graph for this example.

To explain more about a rule, the student can click on the "Template" button at the bottom of the Rule Browser (see Figure 5.3, left). A dialog box comes up, containing a template with a partial definition of the rule that has blanks for the student to fill in (see Figure 5.3, right). Clicking on a blank brings up a menu of possible fillers (see menu below the "EXERTED BY" blank in Figure 5.3, right). The rule definition consists of the preconditions that allow for the application of the rule, as well as the effects of applying the rule. This format derives from findings showing that defining a principle in terms of preconditions and effects is the spontaneous way in which students tend to express self-explanations for correctness (Chi & VanLehn 1991).

After completing a template, the student can select "submit" to get immediate feedback. The SE-Coach retrieves the definition of the corresponding rule from the ExBL's knowledge base and uses it to verify the correctness of the student's selections. Student performance in filling a given template is treated by the system as evidence of the student's knowledge on the corresponding rule (or lack thereof), and is therefore used to update the SE-Coach's assessment of this knowledge in the SE-Coach's student model. Similar sequences of incremental, tailored scaffolding help students (1) explain the function of each example solution step in a high-level plan underlying the example solution (this sequence is initiated by clicking on the prompt *"the role of this fact in the solution plan is ..."* in Figure 5.3); and (2) derive solution steps that can lead to the current step but that have been "hidden" by the SE-Coach (this sequence is initiated by clicking on the prompt *"filling in missing steps"* in Figure 5.3).

The interface tools described in this section are designed to provide incremental

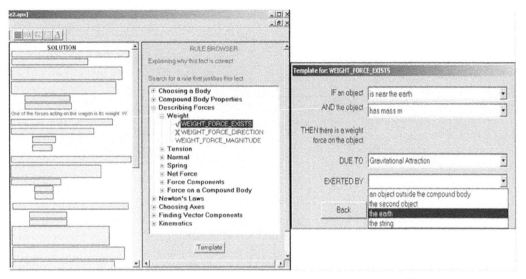

Figure 5.3. (a) Selections in the Rule Browser; (b) Template filling.

scaffolding for self-explanation that students can access at their own discretion, to adhere to our goal of providing an environment that stimulates as much as possible the student's initiative in the learning process. However, to help those students who are not receptive to interface scaffolding because of their low tendency for self-explanation, the SE-Coach can also provide more direct tutorial interventions, targeting specific limitations in a student's self-explanation behavior, as described in the next section.

THE SE-COACH'S ADAPTIVE
INTERVENTIONS
Initially, self-explanation is voluntary. However, the SE-Coach keeps track of each student's progress through an example, including how much time the student looked at each solution line (through the masking interface), what the student chose to self-explain via the interface tools, and whether or not the self-explanations were correct. This information is collected in the SE-Coach's student model as evidence to assess which example lines may benefit from further self-explanation (Conati & VanLehn 2001). Then, when the student tries to close the example, the SE-Coach generates interventions to make the student

self-explain those parts. These interventions include:

1. A generic warning: "*You may learn more by self-explaining further items. These items are indicated by pink covers.*" The warning is accompanied by changing the color of the relevant boxes to pink (shown in darker grey in Figure 5.4).
2. A specific prompt attached to each pink box, such as "*Self-explain with the Rule Browser,*" "*Self-explain with both the Rule and the Plan Browser,*" or "*Read more carefully,*" depending on what self-explanation the student model predicts to be missing for that item.

When a solution item is uncovered, the corresponding specific prompts appear in place of the simple *self-explain* button (see Figure 5.4). The color of the boxes and the related prompts change dynamically as the student performs more reading and self-explanation actions that change the probabilities in the student model. The student is not forced to follow the SE-Coach suggestions and can close the example whenever desired.

One of the challenges of designing the SE-Coach tutorial interventions is that they must motivate to self-explain those students with low propensity to do so. The current

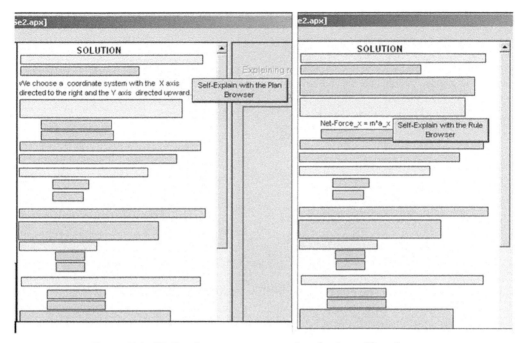

Figure 5.4. SE-Coach interventions to elicit further self-explanation.

design was selected through pilot-testing of various alternatives (Conati & VanLehn 2000) because it allows the students to see at once all the parts that they should further self-explain, as well as which interface tools they should use for that purpose. It also gives students suitable feedback on the progress they are making, because the color of the example lines and the attached hints change dynamically as students generate more self-explanations.

EVALUATION OF THE SE-COACH

The SE-Coach component of ExBL was evaluated in a controlled study with fifty-six college students. The study involved an earlier version of the SE-Coach that covered two of the three types of self-explanations currently included in the system: step correctness (justify why a solution step is correct in terms of domain principles) and step utility (explain what role a solution step plays in the high-level plan underlying an example solution). The participants were college students taking introductory physics, who had just recently covered Newton's Laws (the topic of the examples used in the

study). The rational for this selection criterion was to have participants who could understand the topic of the examples but would still need to work on it, so that they would find studying examples useful. The students came from four different colleges.

During the one-session study, students first took a pre-test on Newton's Laws, then studied related examples with the SE-Coach and finally took a post-test equivalent to the pre-test. The study had two conditions. In the *experimental (SE)* condition, twenty-nine students studied examples with the complete SE-Coach. In the *control* condition, twenty-seven students studied examples with the masking interface including the *self-explain* prompts that appear when a line is uncovered. However, these students had no access to the subsequent levels of scaffolding, nor to the adaptive coaching.

As we reported in Conati and VanLehn (2000), the analysis of the log data file from the study shows that the SE-Coach's interface is easy to use and explicit tutorial interventions are quite successful at stimulating self-explanation. The analysis of the students' learning gains from pre-test to post-test show that the SE-Coach's multiple levels of scaffolding for self-explanation improve students' problem solving when students are in the early stage of cognitive-skill acquisition. In particular, students who had just started covering Newton's laws (late-start students from now on) learned significantly better with the adaptive version of the tutor. On the other hand, the adaptive version was not as effective for students who had started covering Newton's laws earlier in the term (early-start students). Although these students did not have significantly better performance in the pre-test, the different exposure they had had to the example topics did seem to impact how they interacted with examples. We have indications that the milder form of scaffolding provided by the SE-Coach in the control condition (i.e., the masking interface and untailored reminders) might have been sufficient to trigger effective self-explanation for these students. On the other hand, it appears that the more complex form of scaffolding available to students in the experimental condition was not suitable for early-start students. Although these students accessed the SE tools as often as the late-start ones, they on average engaged in significantly fewer attempts to correctly fill Rule templates (Conati et al., 2006). This difference suggests that the early-start students were less motivated and put less effort in learning from the SE-Coach tools, perhaps because they overestimated their understanding of the subject matter. In other words, it appears that these tools are overkilled for students who have already had substantial exposure to the examples' topics, whereas they are beneficial for students who have just started learning a topic. In summary, our results provide encouraging evidence that it is possible and useful, if done at the right time, to provide students with individualized guidance to studying examples before moving to problem solving. In the next section, we describe the ExBL component that aims to provide analogous support to help students use examples effectively *during* problem solving.

Using Examples to Aid Problem Solving with the EA-Coach

The EA-Coach uses the ExBL's reasoning mechanisms to support effective analogical problem solving by providing students with adaptively selected examples that encourage two metacognitive skills known to trigger learning:

1. *min-analogy*: solving the problem on one's own as much as possible instead of copying from examples (e.g., VanLehn, 1998);
2. self-explanation that relies on common-sense or overly general knowledge to infer a domain principle that allows the student to justify how a given example solution step is derived.

Min-analogy and self-explanation are beneficial for learning because they allow students to discover and fill their knowledge gaps, as well as strengthen their knowledge through practice. Unfortunately, some students prefer more shallow processes that hinder learning, such as copying as much as possible from examples without any proactive reasoning on the underlying domain principles (e.g., VanLehn, 1998). The EA-Coach uses both interface mechanisms and adaptive example selection to discourage these shallow behaviors and foster effective APS.

THE EA-COACH INTERFACE

The EA-Coach's interface allows students to solve problems and refer to worked-out examples for help. The student selects a problem to work on from the EA-Coach's pool, which opens the problem window. The problem-solving interface (see Figure 5.5, left) is directly based on the design used in the Andes ITS for coached problem solving (Conati et al., 2002) and consists of a diagram and an equation pane, which students can use to draw free-body diagrams and type equations. To help the system assess the correctness of students' equations, any variables that students include in their equations must first be added to the variable

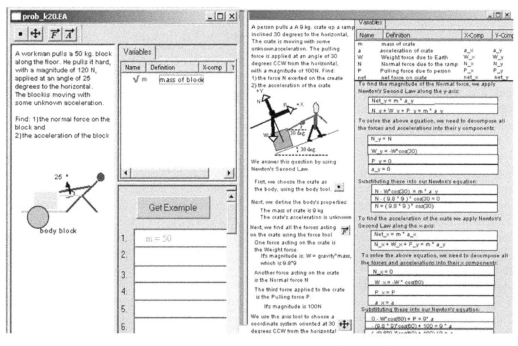

Figure 5.5. EA-Coach problem (left) and example (right) interface.

definition pane (see top of problem window in Figure 5.5, left).

During problem solving, students can ask the system to provide an example, which the EA-Coach presents in the example window (see Figure 5.5, right). Note that the EA-Coach example format differs slightly from the SE-Coach design. We initially intended to use the SE-Coach format in the EA-Coach, which is loosely based on the presentation of worked-out examples in physics text books. However, a pilot study with the EA-Coach revealed that students felt this format was not sufficiently similar to the problem-solving window. One common complaint was related to the lack of a variable definition pane in the example window. Although this lack of similarity could be a form of scaffolding to discourage copying, we found that for several participants it hindered problem solving. To address this issue, we decided to change the example format to more closely mirror the problem-solving format.

As is the case with the SE-Coach, ExBL's general principle of providing support at incremental levels of detail is realized in the EA-Coach by offering several levels of scaffolding to trigger min-analogy and self-explanation in the presence of an example. One form of interface scaffolding corresponds to providing immediate feedback for students' problem-solving entries, realized by coloring these entries as either red or green. Evidence in cognitive science shows that some students lack self-monitoring skills and so are unable to diagnose their own misconceptions or errors (e.g., Chi 2000). Immediate problem-solving feedback can help trigger the right APS behaviors in these students, who would otherwise continue on incorrect solution paths. For instance, if a problem-solving error is due to a student indiscriminately copying from an example, immediate feedback can discourage this behavior by making the student aware of its limitations. If the error is the result of a knowledge gap, then the immediate feedback can help the student detect the gap and encourage him/her to use an available example to overcome it.

A second form of interface scaffolding is provided by the same masking interface used by the SE-Coach. As for the SE-Coach, this interface can help focus a student's attention on individual solution lines. In the context of the EA-Coach, this interface also serves a second function: It is intended to discourage copying because of the effort needed to explicitly uncover example solution steps. To further discourage copying, the interface does not include "Cut" and "Paste" functionalities. This design is based on findings from an earlier pilot study, showing that students abused cutting and pasting to copy entire example solutions.

The last form of scaffolding provided by the EA-Coach is the adaptive selection of examples that discourage indiscriminate copying and facilitate min-analogy and self-explanation. The selection is based on a process that allows the EA-Coach to assess which of their available examples is more likely to help the student both solve the problem and learn from the process (Muldner & Conati 2007). In the next section, we first summarize the example-selection mechanism and then describe a study to evaluate its effectiveness

THE EA-COACH'S ADAPTIVE INTERVENTIONS

To find examples that best trigger effective APS behaviors for each student, the EA-Coach takes into account both student characteristics (domain knowledge and pre-existing tendencies for min-analogy and self-explanation), as well as the similarity between a problem and a candidate example. In particular, the Coach relies on the assumption that certain types of differences between a problem and an example may actually be beneficial in helping students learn from APS because they promote the necessary APS metacognitive skills (Muldner & Conati 2005).

A challenge of this assumption is how to balance learning with problem-solving success. Examples that are not too similar to the target problem naturally discourage copying because they make it difficult to transfer example lines to the problem

solution. However, for the same reason they may fail to help generate a problem solution because they do not provide enough scaffolding for students who cannot solve the problem on their own. Our solution is to use the EA-Coach's probabilistic student model to *simulate* how a student will solve a target problem and learn in the presence of a candidate example, given the problem/example similarities. The result of this simulation is then used by a decision-theoretic process to select the example that has the highest overall utility in terms of both learning and problem-solving success. As for the SE-Coach, the EA-Coach's assessment of the relevant student's characteristics (knowledge and tendency for min-analogy and self-explanation) is based on tracing the student's actions in the The EA-Coach interface (Muldner & Conati 2005). The example-selection process is summarized in Figure 5.6.

EVALUATION OF THE EA-COACH

As we pointed out earlier, one of the challenges for the EA-Coach is to choose examples that trigger learning by encouraging effective APS behaviors (*learning goal*), and at the same time help the student generate the problem solution (*problem-solving success goal*). To verify how well the EA-Coach's example-selection mechanism meets these goals, we ran a study that compared it with selecting the most similar example (the standard approach used by other ITS that support APS, such as ELM-ART [Weber 1996]). The study involved sixteen university students. We used a within-subject design, where each participant : (1) completed a pencil-and-paper physics pretest; (2) was introduced to the EA-Coach interface (*training* phase); (3) solved two Newton's Second Law problems using the EA-Coach interface (*experimental* phase); and (4) completed a pencil-and-paper physics post-test. For each problem, participants had access to one example. For one of the problems, the example was selected by the EA-Coach (*adaptive-selection condition*), whereas for the other (*static-selection condition*), an example most similar to the target

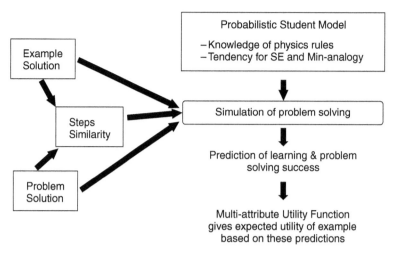

Probabilistic Student Model

– Knowledge of physics rules
– Tendency for SE and Min-analogy

Example
Solution

Steps
Similarity

Problem
Solution

Simulation of problem solving

Prediction of learning & problem
solving success

Multi-attribute Utility Function
gives expected utility of example
based on these predictions

◆ Done for every example known by the EA-Coach

• Select example with maximum expected utility

Figure 5.6. Example-selection process.

problem was provided. To account for car-ryover effects, the orders of the problems/ selection conditions were counterbalanced. Participants were given sixty minutes to solve the two problems. All actions in the interface were logged. They were asked to verbalize their thoughts while working with the EA-Coach and we videotaped all sessions. The results from the study are based on the data from the fourteen participants who used an example in *both* conditions (two participants used an example in only one condition: one subject used the example only in the static condition, another subject used the example only in the adaptive condition).

Learning goal results. To assess how well the EA-Coach's adaptively selected examples satisfied the *learning goal* as compared to the statically selected ones, we assessed how each study condition influenced students' copying and self-explanation. To obtain these measures, we mined both the action logs for each session and the corresponding verbal protocols, obtaining *copy* and *self-explanation (SE)* rates for each subject in the adaptive and the static condition. The data was analyzed using univariate ANOVAs with *condition* (*adaptive* vs. *static*) as within-subject factor and two between-

subject factors resulting from the counterbalancing of selection and problem types. The results show that students copied significantly less from the adaptively selected examples than from the statically selected examples ($F(1,14) = 7.2$, $p = 0.023$; on average, 5.9 vs. 8.1, respectively). In addition, students expressed significantly more self-explanations in the adaptive-selection condition ($F(1, 10) = 6.4$, $p = 0.03$; on average, 4.07 vs. 2.57, respectively).

Assessing the impact of the adaptive-selection mechanism on topic learning measured as pre/post-test differences is not straightforward. Because there was overlap between the two problems in terms of domain principles, the within-subject design makes it difficult to attribute learning to a particular selection condition. The only approach we could use to make the attribution with our data involves, for each student: (1) isolating rules that were unknown prior to the study (as assessed from the pre-test) and that appeared in one condition only; and (2) determining from post-test results how many of these rules the student learned after working with the EA-Coach. Unfortunately, this procedure left us with very sparse data, making formal statistical analysis infeasible. However, we found encouraging trends: There was a higher percentage of rules learned, given each student's learning opportunities in the adaptive condition, as compared to the static one (on average, 77% vs. 52%, respectively).

Results on problem solving success. The *problem-solving success goal* is fulfilled if students generate a required problem solution. In the static condition, all sixteen students generated a correct problem solution, whereas in the adaptive condition, fourteen students did so (the other two students generated a partial solution; both used the example in both conditions). This difference between conditions, however, is not statistically significant (sign test, p = 0.5), indicating that overall, both statically and adaptively selected examples helped students generate the problem solution. We also performed univariate ANOVAs on the dependent variables *error rate* and *task time* to analyze how the adaptively selected examples affected the problem-solving *process*, in addition to the problem-solving *result*. Students took significantly longer to generate the problem solution in the adaptive than in the static-selection condition (F(1, 10) = 31.6, $p < 0.001$; on average, 42 min., 23 sec. vs. 25 min., 35 sec., respectively). Similarly, students made significantly more errors *while* generating the problem solution in the adaptive than in the static-selection condition (F(1, 10) = 11.5, $p = 0.007$; on average, 22.35 vs. 7.57 respectively). The fact that students took longer/made more errors in the adaptive condition is not a negative finding from a pedagogical standpoint, because these are *by-products* of learning. Specifically, learning takes time and may require multiple attempts before the relevant pieces of knowledge are inferred/correctly applied, as we saw in our study and as is backed up by cognitive science findings (e.g., Chi 2000).

Still, a point of future research is how to mediate this process so that the benefit of taking extra time to learn from one's errors does not turn into hopeless *floundering* down incorrect solution paths. This research relates to a long-standing debate in educational technology on if, when, and how to provide feedback for correctness during problem solving. Some systems have taken the extreme approach of not allowing students to go down an incorrect solution path. To ensure that students can correct erroneous steps as soon as they are taken, these systems provide hints at incremental levels of detail, ending with the correct answer (e.g., Koedinger et al., 1995). Although this strategy can speed up learning because it avoids student floundering altogether, it may interfere with the development of important self-regulatory skills crucial for becoming independent learners. Other systems, like the EA-Coach, flag errors but do not force students to correct them. Although many of these systems still make hints available for students who feel they need help (e.g., Conati et al., 2002), the current version of the EA-Coach does not include any form of proactive scaffolding in addition to that provided by tailored examples. So when a student is unable to solve a problem on one's own or with the aid of the proposed example, problem solving fails, as it happened with the two students who did not complete the problem in the adapting condition of our study. This finding suggests that the EA-Coach's effectiveness could be improved by the addition of more explicit scaffolding on self-explanation that can help students reconcile example/problem differences when they cannot do it on their own.

Discussion

In this section, we discussed research on devising ExBL, an ITS that provides tailored support to learning from examples. Example-based learning is a perfect example of an educational activity that complements problem solving because it can be useful in the early stages of learning, when students still do not have enough knowledge to engage in unaided problem solving. The need for adaptive support is grounded in the abundance of cognitive science findings indicating that effective learning from examples is mediated by both student expertise and preexisting metacognitive skills.

A formal evaluation of the ExBL's component that provides adaptive support for example studying (the SE-Coach) showed that it can help students learn more effectively than a version with no adaptive support, when students are in the early stages of learning a new topic (Conati et al., 2006). A formal evaluation of the ExBL's component that provides adaptive support for analogical problem solving (EA-Coach) showed that it can increase the number of appropriate student metacognitive behaviors, more than presenting the example most similar to the current problem. These results, although obtained in controlled laboratory studies as opposed to classroom settings, represent encouraging evidence that it is feasible to devise intelligent tutors that can model, adapt, and support student activities less well-defined and structured than problem solving.

The example-based activities discussed in the previous section were directly related to problem solving in the sense that they engage students in using worked-out solutions of problems in a given domain (physics in our case). One important implication of this factor is that the technology underlying the provision of adaptive support could reuse some of the solutions we had previously devised to provide coached problem solving in that domain (e.g., the solution graph representation, the backbone of the probabilistic student models, some interface elements).

In the next section, we present work we have done to provide adaptive support for an activity farther removed from problem solving: learning from exploration of interactive simulations. In the context of this work, we will discuss how we are using eye-tracking technology to increase the amount and quality of the information available to the ITS to monitor the relevant student behaviors. In ExBL, relevant attention patterns (e.g., how a student reads the different components of an example solution) were captured via an interface artifact, the masking interface, for lack of better means. In the next section, we show how eye tracking can be a valid alternative, especially in light of the fact that eye-tracking technology is becoming unobtrusive and increasingly affordable.

ACE: Supporting Learning via Exploration of Interactive Simulations

This research seeks to provide intelligent support for exploratory learning. The capability to explore effectively is relevant to many tasks involving interactive systems, but not all users possess this capability in equal measure (e.g., Shute & Glaser 1990). We developed a model of exploratory behavior that an ITS can use to improve user exploration via interventions tailored to the user's needs. This task is challenging because it requires assessing the effectiveness of behaviors for which there is no formal definition of correctness. We tackled the challenge with a probabilistic model that assesses exploration effectiveness by integrating information on user actions, knowledge, and whether a user actually reasons about (self-explains) his/her exploratory actions. Self-explanation is a well-known metacognitive skill in cognitive science, but this work is the first to model self-explanation in the context of exploration-based learning. We developed the model in the context of Adaptive Coach for Exploration (ACE), an ITS that supports student exploration of mathematical functions via a set of interactive simulations and via adaptive hints that provide individualized scaffolding for the exploration process.

The ACE's Interface

Ace's interactive simulations are designed to illustrate function-related concepts such as the relationship between the input and the output of a function, or between a function's equation and its graph. ACE presents the learner with various activities, divided into units and exercises. Units are collections of exercises with a common theme, whereas exercises within the units differ in function type and equation.

Figure 5.7 is a screenshot of the complete interface for one of ACE's units. The top-left window is the main interaction window, where the learner works on the exercises that ACE provides to explore various function

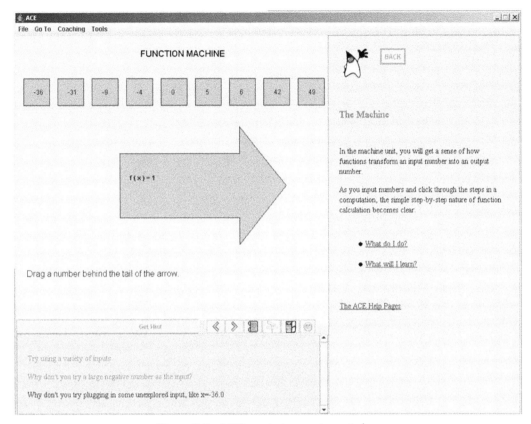

Figure 5.7. ACE's main interaction window.

concepts. The right panel is a set of hypertext help pages that contain instructions on how to use ACE and function-related definitions. The bottom panel displays messages containing the tailored feedback that can be obtained from the ACE's coaching component. A toolbar separates the main interaction panel from the feedback panel, containing access points to several help features and navigation tools.

Currently, ACE has three units: the Machine Unit, the Arrow Unit, and the Plot Unit. The Machine Unit (see Figure 5.7) provides the learner with the opportunity to explore the relationship between the input and output of a given function. The learner can explore this relationship by dragging any number of inputs displayed at the top of the screen to the tail of the function "machine" (the large arrow shown in Figure 5.7). The machine computes the output and spits it out at the other end of the arrow by encasing the output in an animated pink ball.

If there are multiple steps involved in the computation (e.g., substitution and algebraic operations), the learner must repeatedly click the "step" button that will appear below the machine to view the equation being resolved.

The Arrow Unit (Figure 5.8) is also designed to help the learner explore the input-output relationship, but requires more active thought on the part of the learner, who must both select which input to experiment with and connect it to the correct output. ACE gives feedback on the learner's actions by turning correctly connected arrows green and incorrectly connected arrows red. This is the only activity within ACE that has a clear definition of correct and incorrect knowledge application and for which ACE's Coach provides feedback on the correctness of the learner's actions

The Plot Unit (Figure 5.9) aims to help the learner gain an understanding of the relationship between the graph of a function

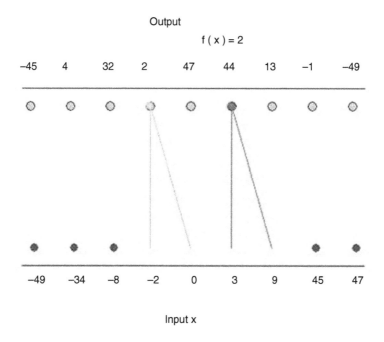

Function Switchboard

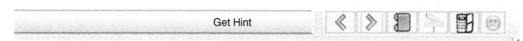

Figure 5.8. ACE's arrow unit.

and its equation, as well as to become famil-iar with different properties of graphs, including slopes and intercepts. The learner can manipulate a function's graph by either dragging it around the screen (using the mouse) or by editing the equation box (shown in the area just below the graph panel in Figure 5.9, to the right of the mag-nifying glass symbol). Changes in the posi-tion of the graph are immediately visible in the function's equation, and changes in the equation immediately update the graph. As an example, the learner could change the first coefficient in the equation from −2 to 2. This action would change the shape of the graph from concave upward to concave

downward, illustrating the effect of posi-tive and negative leading coefficients on the shape of the graph.

Whereas the Plot Unit is ACE's most interesting unit in terms of the range of exploration that it permits, the Machine and Arrow units are still exploratory in the sense that there are a number of inputs to choose from. This element of choice can cause a variety of learner behaviors, ranging from being too rushed or timid, to exploring thor-oughly, to methodically selecting all of the inputs. The learner has two ways to navigate through the curriculum. The first is by click-ing on the forward and backward arrows on the toolbar (see Figure 5.7). The second way

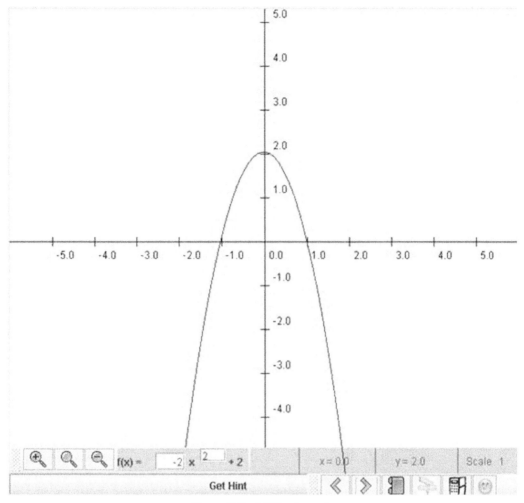

Figure 5.9. ACE's plot unit.

is by using the curriculum browser, a tool that lets the learner move to any exercise in the curriculum.

ACE continuously monitors the student's interaction with its simulations and generates interventions to improve those behaviors that its probabilistic student model deems to be suboptimal. The next section illustrates this process and the model that supports it.

ACE's Adaptive Interventions

ACE provides learners with tailored feedback on their exploration process through hints, which the student can request by clicking on the "Get Hint" button (see tool bar in Figure 5.7). ACE also generates unsolicited hints when the learner tries to move to a new exercise before he/she has explored the current exercise sufficiently (as assessed by the ACE's student model). Hints are supplied to the learner at increasing levels of detail, ranging from a generic suggestion to explore the current exercise more thoroughly to exactly what things to explore. Because the system is designed to give the learner as much control as possible, the learner can either choose to follow ACE's advice or to move on.

To judge the effectiveness of a student's exploratory behaviors and to provide hints on how to improve this behavior, ACE relies on a probabilistic student model. The

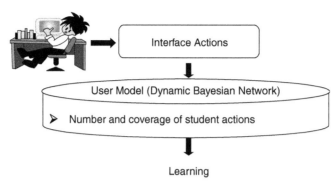

Figure 5.10. First version of the SE-Coach's student model.

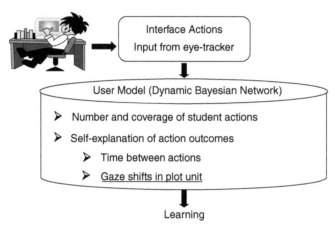

Figure 5.11. Version of the ACE's model including eye-tracking information.

first version of the model was a Dynamic Bayesian Network (DBN) that included (1) nodes representing student exploration cases; (2) nodes representing student understanding of related mathematical concepts; and (3) links representing how exploration of relevant cases relates to concept understanding. To assess whether an exercise has been explored effectively, this version of the ACE model just used evidence from the student's interface action (see Figure 5.10).

Initial studies of this version of the system generated encouraging evidence that it could help students learn better from exploration (Bunt & Conati 2003). However, these studies also showed that ACE sometimes overestimated students' exploratory behavior because it considered interface actions to be sufficient evidence of good exploration, without taking into account whether a student was reasoning, or *self-explaining* the outcome

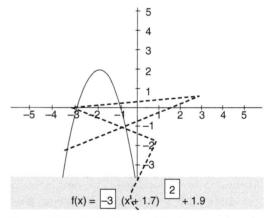

Figure 5.12. Tracked gaze shift from equation to plot panel.

of these actions. For instance, a student who quickly moves a function plot around the screen but never reflects on how these movements change the function equation

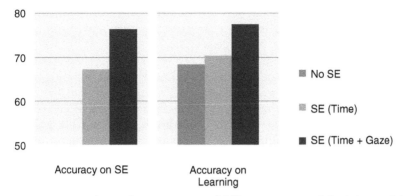

Figure 5.13. Results on the comparison of different versions of the ACE model.

is performing many exploratory actions but can hardly learn from them. Still, the first ACE student model would likely judge this type of behavior as good exploration.

To circumvent this problem, we devised a new version of the student model that includes an assessment of the student's self-explanation behavior during exploration-based learning (Conati & Merten 2007). To assess self-explanation, this model uses evidence derived from both the time a student spent on each exploratory action and the student's attention patterns monitored via an eye-tracking system (see Figure 5.11). In particular, we tracked the occurrence of *gaze shifts* between the equation and the graph panel in the Plot Unit after the student had made a change in either panel (see Figure 5.12).

We formally evaluated the model using both time and eye-tracking information (SE time + gaze in Figure 5.13) against (1) a model using only time as a predictor of self-explanation (SE time in Figure 5.13) and (2) the earlier ACE model that ignores self-explanation and uses only the number of user-interface actions as a predictor of effective exploration (No SE in Figure 5.13). Model performance in assessing occurrence of self-explanation was compared to assessment of self-explanation behavior provided by human judges (see Conati et al., 2005 for details on this process). Model performance in assessing the learning effectiveness of student exploratory behavior was compared to student performance in the study post-test. We found that:

- The model including both gaze and time data provides better assessment of student self-explanation than the model using only time (Figure 5.13, left). The difference is statistically significant.
- Assessing self-explanation significantly improves the assessment of student exploratory behavior, and the accuracy of the latter increases with increased accuracy of self-explanation assessment. All improvements are statistically significant (Figure 5.13, right).

This work shows that it is possible to increase the bandwidth of an ITS that needs to capture high-level user mental states by using information on user attention. Because eye-tracking technology is becoming increasingly more precise and unobtrusive, this result opens many opportunities for devising intelligent tutors that can understand and adapt to complex user reasoning processes. In the context of the ACE's research, we are working on devising adaptive interventions that rely on the above model to scaffold students' self-explanation while they interact with ACE, as an additional means to improve the students' exploration behaviors.

Conclusions

In this chapter, we have provided examples of one current direction of ITS research aimed at extending the reach of this technology toward new forms of computer-based instruction beyond coached problem solving: providing intelligent tutoring for metacognitive skills. This endeavor is only one of several new directions in ITS research. Other new forms of intelligent computer-based tutoring that have been actively investigated include, among others: support for collaborative learning (e.g., Isotami & Mizoguchi 2008); emotionally intelligent tutors that take into account both student learning and affect when deciding how to act (e.g., Conati & Maclaren 2009; D'Mello & Graesser, Chapter 6 in this volume); teachable agents that can help students learn by acting as peers that students can tutor (e.g., Leelawong & Biswas 2008); intelligent support for learning from educational games (e.g., Johnson 2007; Manske & Conati 2005); and intelligent tutoring for ill-defined domains (e.g., Lynch et al., Chapter 9 in this volume). Providing these forms of intelligent tutoring, like providing intelligent support for metacognition, poses unique challenges because it requires an ITS that can model domains as well as student behaviors and mental states often not as structured and well-defined as those involved in coached problem solving. In this chapter, we have provided initial evidence that students' metacognitive skills can be scaffolded via tailored interventions during interaction, and that the scaffolding can improve learning. Some researchers have also provided initial results along these lines, showing partial or full transfer of meta-strategies acquired while working with a metacognitive ITS in one domain to a different domain without tutoring (e.g., Chi & VanLehn 2007; Leelawong & Biswas 2008). In this work, however, the metacognitive scaffolding provided by the tutor was not tailored to a student's specific needs; all students were required to engage in the target metacognitive behaviors. We are interested in exploring if and how tailoring the metacognitive scaffolding will impact long-term student abilities, compared to less-individualized approaches. We are also planning to include in our metacognitive student models information on the student's affective states (Conati & Maclaren 2009) to study the relationships between affect, metacognition, and learning outcomes.

Acknowledgments

We thank Andrea Bunt, Cristina Mertner, Kasia Mudlner, and David Ternes for their invaluable contributions to this research. The research was funded by the National Sciences and Engineering Research Council of Canada.

References

Aleven, V., & Koedinger, K. (2002). An effective meta-cognitive strategy: Learning by doing & explaining with a computer-based cognitive tutor. *Cognitive Science, 26*(2), 147–179.

Aleven, V., Ogan, A., Popescu, O., Torrey, C., & Koedinger, K. (2004). Evaluating the effectiveness of a tutorial dialogue system for self-explanation. *Intelligent Tutoring Systems: 7th International Conference*, Maceió, Alagoas, Brazil, 443–454.

Anderson, J. R., Farrell, R., & Saurers, R. (1984). Learning to program in Lisp. *Cognitive Science, 8*, 87–129.

Azevedo, R., Witherspoon, A. M., Graesser, A., McNamara, D. S., Chauncey, A., Siler, E., Cai, Z., Rus, V., & Lintean, M. C. (2009). MetaTutor: Analyzing Self-Regulated Learning in a Tutoring System for Biology. *AIED 2009:* 635–637.

Bielaczyc, K., Pirolli, P., & Brown, A. L. (1995). Training in self-explanation and self-regulation strategies: Investigating the effects of knowledge acquisition activities on problem-solving. *Cognition and Instruction, 13(2)*, 221–252.

Bunt, A., & Conati C. (2003). Probabilistic student modeling to improve exploratory behaviour. *Journal of User Modeling and User-Adapted Interaction, 13*(3), 269–309

Chi, M., & VanLehn, K. (2007). The impact of explicit strategy instruction on problem solving behaviors across intelligent tutoring systems. In D. McNamara & G. Trafton (Eds.), *Proceedings of the 29th Annual Conference of the Cognitive Science Society.* (pp. 167–172). Mahwah, NJ: Lawrence Erlbaum.

Chi, M. T. H. (2000). Self-explaining expository texts: The dual processes of generating inferences and repairing mental models.

In R. Glaser (Ed.), *Advances in instructional psychology* (pp. 161–238). Mahwah, NJ: Lawrence Erlbaum.

Chi, M. T. H., & VanLehn, K. (1991). The content of physics self-explanations. *The Journal of the Learning Sciences, 1,* 69–105.

Conati, C., & Carenini, G. (2001) Generating tailored examples to support learning via self-explanation. In *Proceedings of IJCAI '01, the Seventeenth International Joint Conference on Artificial Intelligence,* Seattle, WA, 1301–1306.

Conati, C., Gertner A., & VanLehn, K. (2002). Using Bayesian networks to manage uncertainty in student modeling. *User Modeling and User-Adapted Interaction, 12*(4), 371–417.

Conati, C., & Maclaren, H. (2009). Empirically building and evaluating a probabilistic model of user affect. *User Modeling and User-Adapted Interaction, 19*(3): 267–303.

Conati, C., & Merten, C. (2007). Eye-tracking for user modeling in exploratory learning environments: An empirical evaluation. *Knowledge Based Systems, 20*(6), 557–574. Amsterdam: Elsevier.

Conati, C., Merten, C., Muldner, K., & Ternes, D. (2005). Exploring eye tracking to increase bandwidth in user modeling. *Proceedings of UM2005 User Modeling: Proceedings of the Tenth International Conference.* Lecture Notes in Computer Science, Vol. 3538/2005 (pp. 357–366). Berlin/Heidelberg: Springer.

Conati, C., Muldner, K., & Carenini, G. (2006). From example studying to problem solving via tailored computer-based meta-cognitive scaffolding: Hypotheses and design. *Technology, Instruction, Cognition and Learning (TICL): Special Issue on Problem Solving Support in Intelligent Tutoring Systems, 4*(2), 139–190.

Conati, C., & VanLehn, K. (2000). Toward computer-based support of meta-cognitive skills: a computational framework to coach self-explanation. *International Journal of AI in Education, 11,* 389–415.

Flavell, J. H. (1976). Metacognitive aspects of problem solving. In L. Resnick (Ed.), *The Nature of Intelligence* (pp. 231–235). Hillsdale, NJ: Lawrence Erlbaum.

Isotani, S., & Mizoguchi, R. (2008). Theory-driven group formation through ontologies. *Intelligent Tutoring Systems 2008*: 646–655.

Johnson, W. L. (2007). Serious use for a serious game on language learning. In *Proceedings of the 13th International Conference on Artificial Intelligence in Education,* Los Angeles, CA, 67–74.

Koedinger, K. R., Anderson, J. R., Hadley, W. H., & Mark, M. A. (1995). Intelligent tutoring goes to school in the big city. *International Journal of Artificial Intelligence in Education, 8,* 30–43.

Leelawong, K., & Biswas, G. (2008). Designing learning by teaching agents: The Betty's Brain System. *International Journal of Artificial Intelligence in Education, 18*(3), 181–208.

Luckin, R., & Hammerton, L. (2002). Getting to know me: Helping learners understand their own learning needs through metacognitive scaffolding. In *Intelligent Tutoring Systems: Proceedings of the 6th International Conference, ITS 2002* (pp. 759–771). Springer Berlin/Heidelberg: Springer.

Manske, M., & Conati, C. (2005). Modeling learning in educational games in AIED 05. *Proceedings of the 12th International Conference on AI in Education.* Amsterdam, 411–418.

Mitrovic, T. (2003). Supporting self-explanation in a data normalization tutor. *Supplementary Proceedings of AIED 2003,* 565–577.

Mitrovic, A., Martin, B., & Suraweera, S. (2007). Constraint-based tutors: Past, present and future. *IEEE Intelligent Systems, Special Issue on Intelligent Educational Systems, 22*(4), 38–45.

Muldner, K., & Conati, C. (2005). Using similarity to infer meta-cognitive behaviors during analogical problem solving. *Proceedings of UM2005 User Modeling: Proceedings of the Tenth International Conference,* Lecture Notes in Computer Science, Vol. 3538/2005. Berlin/Heidelberg: Springer.

Muldner, K., & Conati, C. (2007). Evaluating a decision-theoretic approach to tailored example selection. In *Proceedings of the 20th International Joint Conference on Artificial Intelligence (IJCAI'07),* 483–489.

Roll I., Aleven, V., McLaren, B., & Koedinger, K. (2007). Can help seeking be tutored? Searching for the secret sauce of metacognitive tutoring. In R. Luckin, K. Koedinger, & J. Greer (Eds.), *Proceedings of the 13th International Conference on Artificial Intelligence in Education,* 203–210.

Shute, V. J., & Glaser, R. (1990). A large-scale evaluation of an intelligent discovery world: Smithtown. *Interactive Learning Environments, 1,* 51–77.

van Joolingen, W. (2000). Designing for collaborative discovery learning. *Proceedings of the Fifth International Conference on Intelligent Tutoring Systems (ITS 2000).* Montreal, Canada, 202–211.

VanLehn, K. (1996). Cognitive skill acquisition. *Annual Review of Psychology, 47*, 513–539.

VanLehn, K. (1998). Analogy events: How examples are used during problem solving. *Cognitive Science, 22*(3), 347–388.

Veermans, K., de Jong, T., & van Joolingen, W. (2000). Promoting self-directed learning in simulation-based discovery learning environments through intelligent support. *Interactive Learning Environments 8*(3), 229–255.

Weber, G. (1996). Individual selection of examples in an intelligent learning environment. *Journal of Artificial Intelligence in Education 7*(1), 3–33.

CHAPTER 6

Emotions during Learning with AutoTutor

Sidney D'Mello and Art Graesser

Deep learning and problem solving are emotionally rich experiences. Students experience boredom when the material does not appeal to them, confusion when they have difficulty comprehending the material and are unsure about how to proceed, frustration when they make mistakes and get stuck, and perhaps even despair and anxiety when their efforts seem to be futile and the big exam is creeping around the corner. This negative picture of the emotional experiences that accompany learning has a complementary positive side. Students experience curiosity when they encounter topics that interest them, eureka moments when insights are unveiled and major discoveries made, delight when challenges are conquered, and perhaps even flow-like states (Csikszentmihalyi, 1990) when they are so engaged in learning that time and fatigue disappear.

In general, emotion and cognition are complementary processes in learning environments that require students to generate inferences, demonstrate causal reasoning, diagnose and solve problems, make conceptual comparisons, produce coherent explanations, and show application and transfer of acquired knowledge. Contemporary theories of emotion and cognition assume that cognitive processes such as memory encoding and retrieval, causal reasoning, deliberation, goal appraisal, and planning operate continually throughout the experience of emotion (Barrett, Mesquita, Ochsner, & Gross, 2007; Bower, 1981; Mandler, 1984, 1999; Ortony, Clore, & Collins, 1988; Scherer, Schorr, & Johnstone, 2001; Stein, Hernandez, & Trabasso, 2008; Stein & Levine, 1991). The inextricable link between emotion and cognition is sufficiently compelling that some claim the scientific distinction between emotion and cognition to be artificial, arbitrary, and of limited value (Lazarus, 1991, 2000).

The last decade has witnessed a burst of research investigating the links between emotions and learning from the fields of psychology (Beilock & DeCaro, 2007; Deci & Ryan, 2002; Dweck, 2002; Stein et al., 2008), education (Lepper & Woolverton, 2002; Meyer & Turner, 2006; Pekrun, Elliot, & Maier, 2006), computer science (Arroyo et al., 2009; Conati & Maclaren,

(a)

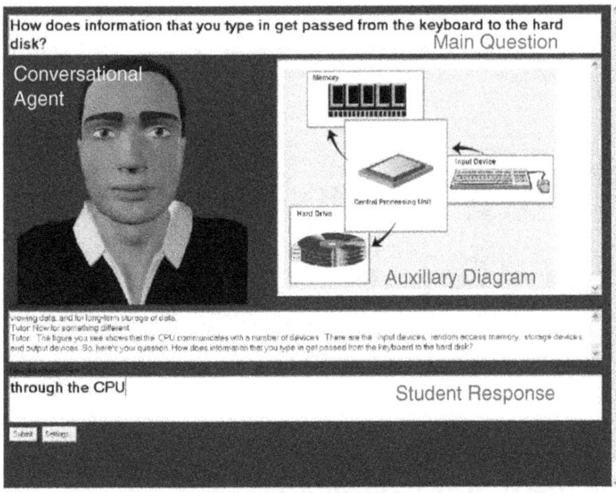

(b)

T: When you turn on the computer, how is the operating system first activated and loaded into RAM? *[main question]*
S: When the computer is turned on a file is automatically booted up.

T: Anything else? *[pump for info]*
S: This file contains the operating system.

T: What about storage? [hint]
S: The operating system is then read into RAM and activated.

T: Right. The CPU executes instructions in ROM, which helps the operating system to start.
[after positive feedback, there is an assertion]

Figure 6.1. (a) AutoTutor interface. The main question stays on the computer screen throughout the conversation. The animated conversational agent speaks the content of AutoTutor's turns via synthesized speech. The image window is either blank or has auxiliary diagrams pertaining to the main question. The dialogue history contains the conversational exchange between the student and the tutor. The student response window displays the student's answers as they are typed in. (b) Sample dialogue from an actual tutorial session, with annotated tutor dialogue moves displayed in brackets.

2009), and neuroscience (Damasio, 2003; Immordino-Yang & Damasio, 2007). Some of the research has focused on student emotions in classrooms, where a broad array of affective responses are elicited in a number of contexts. These affect-inducing contexts include classroom activities such as lectures and discussions that may evoke curiosity and boredom, examinations and quizzes that may induce anxiety and joy, and peer interactions where some of the social emotions such as pride and shame play a major role (Meyer & Turner, 2006; Schultz & Pekrun, 2007). Other research has focused on a more in-depth analysis of a smaller set of emotions that arise during deep learning in more restricted contexts and over shorter time spans (Baker, D'Mello, Rodrigo, & Graesser, 2010; Conati & Maclaren, 2009). Our own research, which we describe in this chapter, aligns with the latter group, and has explored emotion-learning connections in the context of advanced learning environments such as AutoTutor.

AutoTutor is a validated intelligent tutoring system (ITS) that helps students learn topics in Newtonian physics, computer literacy, and critical thinking via a mixed-initiative conversational dialogue between the student and the tutor (Graesser, Chipman, Haynes, & Olney, 2005; Graesser et al., 2004; VanLehn et al., 2007). AutoTutor's dialogues are organized around difficult questions and problems (called main questions) that require reasoning and explanations in the answers. AutoTutor actively monitors learners' knowledge states and engages them in a turn-based dialogue as they attempt to answer these questions. It adaptively manages the tutorial dialogue by providing feedback (e.g., "good job," "not quite"), pumping the learner for more information (e.g., "What else"), giving hints (e.g., "What about X"), prompts (e.g., "X is a type of what"), identifying and correcting misconceptions, answering questions, and summarizing answers. Using these strategies, AutoTutor adheres to constructivist theories of pedagogy (Biggs, 1995; Chi, Roy, & Hausmann, 2008; Jonassen, Peck, & Wilson, 1999; Moshman, 1982) by allowing students to chart their own course through the tutorial dialogue and to build their own answers to difficult questions. The AutoTutor interface along with a sample dialogue between a college student and AutoTutor is presented in Figure 6.1.

Intelligent tutoring systems (ITSs) such as AutoTutor (Graesser et al., 2004), Andes physics tutor (VanLehn et al., 2005), and Cognitive Tutor (Koedinger & Corbett, 2006) have come a long way toward modeling and responding to learners' cognitive states. This allows ITSs to implement some of the ideal tutoring strategies such as error identification and correction, building on prerequisites, frontier learning (expanding on what the learner already knows), student modeling (inferring what the student knows and having that information guide tutoring), and building coherent explanations (Aleven & Koedinger, 2002; Anderson, Douglass, & Qin, 2005; Gertner & VanLehn, 2000; Koedinger, Anderson, Hadley, & Mark, 1997; Lesgold, Lajoie, Bunzo, & Eggan, 1992; Sleeman & Brown, 1982).

However, ITSs can be more than mere cognitive machines, and the link between emotions and learning suggests that they should be affective processors as well (Issroff & del Soldato, 1996; Picard, 1997). Affect sensitivity is important for ITSs that aspire to model human tutors because it has been claimed that expert teachers are able to recognize a student's emotional state and respond in an appropriate manner that has a positive impact on the learning process (Goleman, 1995; Lepper & Woolverton, 2002). An affect-sensitive ITS would incorporate assessments of the students' cognitive and affective states into its pedagogical and motivational strategies to keep students engaged, boost self-confidence, heighten interest, and presumably maximize learning.

Therefore, in addition to investigating links between emotions and learning with AutoTutor, our research also focused on developing a version of AutoTutor that is dynamically responsive to learners' affective states in addition to their cognitive states. Our research program involving emotions and learning with AutoTutor has encompassed:

1. identifying the emotions that occur during learning with AutoTutor and other learning environments (Baker et al., in review; Craig, Graesser, Sullins, & Gholson, 2004; D'Mello, Craig, Sullins, & Graesser, 2006; Graesser, Chipman, King, McDaniel, & D'Mello, 2007; Graesser et al., 2006; Lehman, D'Mello, & Person, 2008; Lehman, Matthews, D'Mello, & Person, 2008);

2. investigating relationships between emotions and learning (Craig et al., 2004; D'Mello, Taylor, & Graesser, 2007; D'Mello & Graesser, in press; Graesser, Chipman et al., 2007);

3. modeling the temporal dynamics of emotions (D'Mello & Graesser, in review; D'Mello, Taylor et al., 2007);

4. assessing how reliably humans detect emotions (D'Mello, Taylor, Davidson, & Graesser, 2008; Graesser et al., 2006);

5. identifying cognitive, bodily, and linguistic correlates of emotional expressions and developing systems to automatically detect emotions (D'Mello, Craig, Witherspoon, McDaniel, & Graesser, 2008; D'Mello, Dale, & Graesser, in review; D'Mello, Dowell, & Graesser, 2009; D'Mello & Graesser, 2009; McDaniel et al., 2007); and

6. developing computer systems that detect, respond to, and synthesize emotions (D'Mello, Craig, Fike, & Graesser, 2009; D'Mello, Jackson et al., 2008; D'Mello, Picard, & Graesser, 2007; D'Mello et al., 2005).

This chapter provides a synopsis of our research on emotions and learning by focusing on students' emotions during learning sessions with AutoTutor. We discuss: (1) theories on emotions and learning; (2) the emotions that learners experience during interactions with AutoTutor and correlational links between emotions and learning gains; (3) the temporal dynamics of the emotional states; (4) how contextual events influence learners' emotions; and (5) new versions of AutoTutor that detect and respond to learners' emotions.

Theories of Emotions and Learning

The major theories of emotion and cognition have primarily focused on affective taxonomies (Izard & Ackerman, 2000; Ortony et al., 1988), valence-arousal frameworks (Barrett et al., 2007; Russell, 2003), cognitive-affective associative networks (Bower, 1981, 1992; Forgas, 1991), attributions (Gotlib & Abramson, 1999; Heider, 1958; Weiner, 1986), appraisals (Lazarus, 1991; Scherer et al., 2001; Smith & Ellsworth, 1985), and physiological and behavioral correlates of emotional experience (Ekman, 1984, 2003; Scherer, 2003). These theories convey general links between cognition and emotions, but they do not directly explain and predict the sort of emotions that occur during complex learning, such as attempts to master physics, biology, or critical thinking skills.

Fortunately, theoretical frameworks that predict systematic relationships between affective and cognitive processes during complex learning are beginning to emerge in fields of psychology (Barrett, 2006; Deci & Ryan, 2002; Dweck, 2002; Russell, 2003), education (Lepper & Chabay, 1988; Lepper & Woolverton, 2002; Linnenbrink & Pintrich, 2002; Meyer & Turner, 2006; Stein et al., 2008), and even artificial intelligence (Conati, 2002; Dragon et al., 2008; Forbes-Riley, Rotaru, & Litman, 2008; Kort, Reilly, & Picard, 2001). The theories that have emerged highlight the contributions of academic risk-taking, motivation, mood states, flow, goals, and cognitive disequilibrium, as we elaborate later in the chapter.

The academic risk theory and intrinsic motivation literature address how individual differences in risk-taking behavior and motivation influence learners' emotional states and behavior choices. The academic risk theory contrasts (1) adventuresome learners who want to be challenged with difficult tasks, take risks of failure, and manage negative emotions when they occur with (2) cautious learners who tackle easier tasks, take fewer risks, and minimize failure and its resulting negative emotions (Clifford, 1988). Risk takers choose challenging tasks to maximize learning; they perceive failure and the resulting negative emotions as necessary steps toward content mastery (Meyer & Turner, 2006). In contrast, risk

avoiders settle for emotional well-being at the expense of learning; they select tasks that are easier than their capabilities and that result in positive feedback on their performance (Boekaerts, 1993; Meyer & Turner, 2006).

The intrinsic motivation literature has identified affective states such as curiosity as indicators of motivation level and learning (Harter, 1992; Stipek, 1988). Intrinsically motivated learners derive pleasure from the task itself (e.g., enjoyment from problem solving), whereas learners with extrinsic motivation rely on external rewards (e.g., receiving a good grade). Learners with more intrinsic motivation display greater levels of pleasure, more active involvement in tasks (Harter, 1992; Tobias, 1994), more task persistence (Miserandino, 1996), lower levels of boredom (Miserandino, 1996), less anxiety, and less anger (Patrick, Skinner, & Connell, 1993). Because a person's affective state is linked to their motivation level, intrinsically motivated learners who are affectively engaged should demonstrate more active involvement in tasks and greater task persistence. One consequence of this engaged persistence is a deeper understanding of the material (Jonassen et al., 1999).

Whereas theories of academic risk-taking and intrinsic motivation address individual differences, mood theories and flow theory are concerned with how mood states impact emotions and performance. Mood theories highlight the important role of baseline mood states (positive, negative, or neutral) on learning, particularly for creative problem solving. In particular, flexibility, creative thinking, and efficient decision making in problem solving have been linked to experiences of positive affect (Bless & Fielder, 1995; Fielder, 2001; Isen, 2001; Isen, Daubman, & Nowicki, 1987), whereas negative affect has been associated with a more methodical approach to assessing the problem and finding the solution (Hertel, Neuhof, Theuer, & Kerr, 2000; Schwarz, 2000; Schwarz & Skurnik, 2003). Mood states also influence emotional reactions by performing a threshold reduction function on emotional elicitation (Rosenberg, 1998).

For example, repetitive failure is more likely to trigger frustration when the learner is in a negative rather than positive mood.

According to flow theory, learners are in a state of flow (Csikszentmihalyi, 1990) when they are so deeply engaged in learning the material that time and fatigue disappear. The zone of flow occurs when the structure of the learning environment matches a learner's zone of proximal development (Brown, Ellery, & Campione, 1998; Vygotsky, 1978), so that the learner is presented with just the right sort of materials, challenges, and problems to the point of being totally absorbed. The state of flow is characterized by a focus on goals, unbridled attention, a virtual disappearance of time and fatigue, and a critical balance between skills and challenge (Csikszentmihalyi, 1990; Meyer & Turner, 2006); all factors that make flow the optimal state for learning.

Goal theory and cognitive disequilibrium theory specify how particular events predict emotional reactions and are pitched at a finer temporal resolution than theories that highlight individual differences and mood states. Goal theory emphasizes the role of goals in predicting emotions. Consistent with contemporary appraisal theories, the arousal level (intense/weak) of an emotional episode is dependent on how great the interruption is to the person's goal, whereas the valence (positive/negative) depends on the person's evaluation of the interruption (Lazarus, 1991; Mandler, 1984). Hence, outcomes that achieve challenging goals result in positive emotions, whereas outcomes that jeopardize goal accomplishment result in negative emotions (Dweck, 2002; Stein & Levine, 1991; Stein et al., 2008). For example, getting stuck and not being able to move past an obstacle would be interpreted as intensely negative, because goal attainment is obstructed (Dweck, 2002). Obstacles to goals are particularly diagnostic of both learning and emotions.

The cognitive disequilibrium theory postulates an important role for impasses (VanLehn, Siler, Murray, Yamauchi, & Baggett, 2003) in comprehension and learning processes. Cognitive disequilibrium

is a state that occurs when learners face obstacles to goals, contradictions, incongruities, anomalies, uncertainty, and salient contrasts (Graesser, Lu, Olde, Cooper-Pye, & Whitten, 2005; Graesser & Olde, 2003; Otero & Graesser, 2001; Piaget, 1952; Schwartz & Bransford, 1998). Cognitive equilibrium is restored after thought, reflection, problem solving, and other effortful deliberations. This theory states that the complex interplay between external events that trigger impasses and the resultant cognitive disequilibrium are the key to understanding the cognitive-affective processes that underlie deep learning. In particular, the affective states of confusion and perhaps frustration are likely to occur during cognitive disequilibrium because confusion indicates an uncertainty about what to do next or how to act (Keltner & Shiota, 2003; Rozin & Cohen, 2003).

These theoretical perspectives make a number of predictions about the affective experiences during learning. We have tested some of these predictions in our analysis of emotion-learning connections in the context of advanced learning environments. We begin with a description of studies that attempted to identify the emotions that are prominent in learning sessions with ITSs, problem-solving environments, and human tutors.

Identifying the Learning-Centered Emotions and Assessing Their Relationship with Learning

Researchers in different fields are familiar with Ekman's pioneering work on the detection of emotions from facial expressions (Ekman, 1984; Keltner & Ekman, 2000). However, the emotions that Ekman intensely investigated (e.g., sadness, happiness, anger, fear, disgust, surprise), although ubiquitous to everyday experience, are not expected to be relevant to learning sessions that span thirty minutes to two hours. The theoretical perspectives described earlier recommend a somewhat different set of emotions during learning. These include

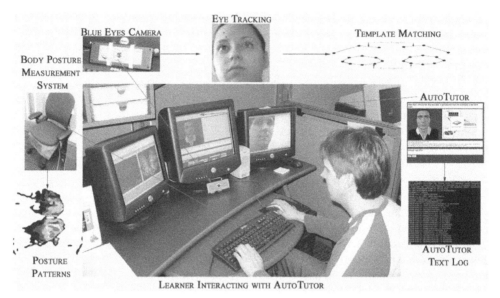

Figure 6.2. Sensors used in the multiple-judge study. The leftmost and rightmost monitors were turned off during the tutoring session.

boredom, flow/engagement, confusion, frustration, delight, and surprise. We refer to these states as *learning-centered emotions*. We conducted four studies in an attempt to identify the major emotions that accompany deep learning with AutoTutor, and presumably similar learning environments. These are briefly described in the following subsection.

Brief Description of Studies

In Study 1 (Observational study), affective states of thirty-four participants were coded by observers every five minutes during interactions with AutoTutor (Craig et al., 2004). The affective states were boredom, flow, confusion, frustration, eureka, and neutral. All coders were given a training session lasting at least thirty minutes to ensure they understood and were comfortable with coding the affective states of interest.

Study 2 (Emote-aloud study) adopted an emote-aloud procedure, a variant of the think-aloud procedure (Ericsson & Simon, 1993), as an online measure of the learners' emotions. Seven college students were asked to state the affective states they were feeling while working on a task, in this case

being tutored in computer literacy with AutoTutor. This method allowed for online identification of emotions while working on a task with minimal task interference. The affective states in this study were anger, boredom, confusion, contempt, curiosity, disgust, eureka, and frustration. Flow was not included in this study because of the concern that asking people to report on their flow experiences would disrupt those experiences.

Whereas the observational and emote-aloud studies used online methods to monitor learners' emotions, Studies 3 and 4 used an offline retrospective affect-judgment protocol for emotion measurement. Study 3 (Multiple-judge study) had twenty-eight college students who interacted with the AutoTutor system for thirty-five minutes (Graesser et al., 2006). Videos of the learners' faces, their computer screens, and posture patterns were recorded for offline analyses, as shown in Figure 6.2.

Participant's affective states (boredom, flow/engagement, confusion, frustration, delight, surprise, and neutral) were measured in a retrospective affect-judgment procedure that commenced after their AutoTutor session. The judging process was initiated by synchronizing the video streams from the screen and the face (center and right monitors in Figure 6.2) and displaying them to the judges. The screen capture included the tutor's synthesized speech, printed text, students' responses, dialogue history, and images, thereby providing the context of the tutorial interaction.

Judges were instructed to make judgments on what affective states were present in twenty-second intervals (*fixed* judgments), at which time the video automatically paused. They were also instructed to indicate any affective states that were present in between the twenty-second stops (*spontaneous* judgments). Judgments were provided by the learners themselves (self-reports), untrained peers, and two researchers (trained judges) with considerable experience interacting with AutoTutor and with the Facial Action Coding System (Ekman & Friesen, 1978). The judges were provided with a list of emotions with definitions. Boredom was defined as being weary or restless through lack of interest. Confusion was defined as a noticeable lack of understanding, whereas flow was a state of interest that results from involvement in an activity. Frustration was defined as dissatisfaction or annoyance. Delight was a high degree of satisfaction. Surprise was wonder or amazement, especially from the unexpected. Neutral was defined as no apparent emotion or feeling.

Study 4 (Speech recognition study) was a replication of the multiple-judge study with the exception that thirty learners spoke their responses to a new speech-enabled version of AutoTutor (D'Mello, King, Entezari, Chipman, & Graesser, 2008). This study also utilized a retrospective affect-judgment procedure with judgments provided by the self and peers.

The Emotions That Occur during Learning with AutoTutor

Figure 6.3 shows descriptive statistics on the proportional occurrence of the various affective states in the four studies. There are important differences in the reliability by which different judges (self, peer, trained judges) can classify learners' emotions; these are discussed in previous publications (D'Mello, Taylor et al., 2008; Graesser et al., 2006). In Figure 6.3, proportional scores for the multiple-judge study and the speech recognition study were computed by averaging across the different judges. The results indicate that boredom, flow/engagement, confusion, and frustration were the major affective states observed during learning sessions with AutoTutor.

These learner-centered emotions have also been found in learning environments other than AutoTutor and with populations other than college students. For example, the learning-centered emotions comprised 86 percent of the observations in a study where thirty-six adolescents from the Philippines solved logic problems with a simulation environment (Baker et al., in review). They comprised 86 percent of the observations in a study where 140 Philippine students were tutored in algebra with an ITS (Baker et al., in review). Confusion, boredom, and frustration were also the dominant states in a study where forty-one aspiring law-school students solved difficult problems from the analytical reasoning section of the Law School Admissions Test (LSAT) (flow was not included in that study) (D'Mello, Lehman, & Person, in review; Lehman, D'Mello et al., 2008).

In contrast, eureka, curiosity, anger, contempt, disgust, delight, and surprise were comparatively infrequent. Eureka was well reported in the emote-aloud study, but there was only one eureka experience identified in the twenty hours of tutoring in the observational study. Hence, we suspect that eureka responses in the emote-aloud study might functionally signify happiness or delight from giving a correct answer rather than a true eureka experience where there is a flash of deep insight. An examination of the videos captured during the tutorial sessions confirmed this suspicion.

Curiosity was also quite rare in the emote-aloud study, presumably because students had no choice of tutoring topics in our experimental environment. If participants

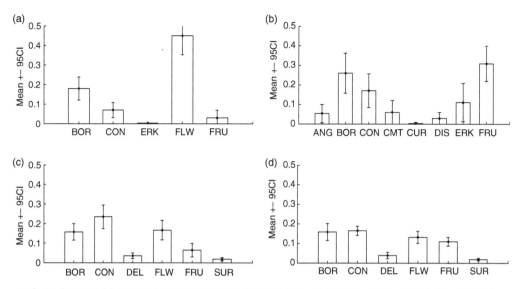

ANGer, BORedom,CONfusion,ConteMpT,CURious,DELight, DISgust, EURka, FLOw, FRUstration, SURprise
(Neutral not depicted)

Figure 6.3. Proportional occurrence of affective states across four studies.

had been given a choice of topics, they might have picked one more relevant to their interests and displayed more curiosity (Lepper & Woolverton, 2002). There is some evidence to support this assertion. In particular, curiosity was the dominant emotion when aspiring law-school students solved problems from the LSAT (D'Mello, Lehman, & Person, in review).

It is interesting to note that four of the six low-frequency emotions were basic emotions, namely anger, disgust, surprise (Ekman, 1992; Izard, 1971), and contempt (Izard, 1971). Although the studies with AutoTutor did not incorporate the full set of basic emotions (i.e., happiness and sadness were excluded), two studies that compared the full set of basic emotions to the learning-centered emotions indicated that the basic emotions were infrequent in learning sessions (D'Mello, Lehman, & Person, in review; Lehman, Matthews et al., 2008). For example, 67 percent of students' emotions in forty tutoring session with human tutors were the learning-centered emotions. The six basic emotions comprised 32 percent of the observations (Lehman, Matthews et al., 2008), with happiness accounting for 29 percent of the emotional expressions.

Similarly, the basic and learning-centered emotions accounted for 26 percent and 74 percent of the observations, respectively, when students solved analytical reasoning problems for the LSAT (D'Mello, Lehman, & Person, in review; Lehman, D'Mello et al., 2008).

Taken together, the results substantiate the claim that the basic emotions, although ubiquitous in everyday experience, may not be particularly relevant to learning, at least for the short learning sessions of these studies. It is possible that they might be more relevant during learning in more extended time spans (such as completing a dissertation) or high-stakes tests (e.g., final exams in courses). However, this hypothesis needs to be substantiated with some empirical evidence.

Relationship between Emotions and Learning

The previously discussed theoretical perspectives make a number of predictions regarding relationships between emotions and learning gains. According to the zone-of-flow theory, the state of flow should also show a positive correlation with learning

(Csikszentmihalyi, 1990), whereas boredom should be negatively correlated with learning (Csikszentmihalyi, 1990; Miserandino, 1996). If constructivist theory and the claims about cognitive disequilibrium are correct, we should observe a positive relationship between confusion and learning gains if the learning environment productively helps the learners regulate their confusion (Graesser & Olde, 2003; Kort et al., 2001). Similarly, a negative correlation is predicted between frustration and learning (Kort et al., 2001; Patrick et al., 1993).

We tested these predictions by correlating the proportional occurrence of boredom, confusion, flow, and frustration with learning measures collected in each study. Correlations were not performed for the emote-aloud study due to the small number of participants ($N = 7$). Learning gains were obtained from knowledge tests administered both before and after the tutorial session (pre-test and post-test, respectively). The testing materials were adapted from computer literacy tests used in previous experiments involving AutoTutor (Graesser et al., 2004). These tests had a four-alternative multiple-choice format and consisted of questions that required inferences and deep reasoning, such as *why, how, what-if, what if not, how is X similar to Y.*

With the exception of frustration, the predictions were supported in the observational study. As predicted, learning gains were positively correlated with confusion and flow and negatively correlated with boredom. There was no correlation between learning gains and frustration (Craig et al., 2004). The positive correlation between confusion and learning was replicated in the multiple-judge study (D'Mello & Graesser, in review) and in the speech recognition study (Graesser, Chipman et al., 2007). Learning was not correlated with boredom, flow, and frustration in these studies.

It was somewhat of a surprise to discover that boredom and flow were not correlated with learning gains in the multiple-judge and speech recognition studies. It might be the case that these states operate on longer timescales, so their effects on learning could not be observed in short thirty- to thirty-five-minute learning sessions. Longer learning sessions would be required before the effects of these states can be observed.

These emotions were correlated with learning in the predicted directions in the observational study, with approximately similar training times, so a comparison of methodologies is warranted. The major differences between studies included (1) the version of AutoTutor (improved version in multiple-judge and speech recognition studies), (2) the population of learners (low-domain-knowledge students in the observational study), (3) the emotion judgment frequency (five minutes in observational study versus less than twenty seconds in the multiple-judge and speech recognition studies), and (4) the emotion judges (observers in observational study versus self, peers, and trained judges in the multiple-judge study, and self and peer in speech recognition study). Additional data and analyses would be needed to isolate which of these factors contributed to the discrepant findings between studies.

Another surprising finding was that frustration was not correlated with learning gains in any of the studies. Frustration is a state that occurs when learners fail to resolve an impasse, they get stuck, and important goals are blocked. The apparent lack of a relationship between frustration and learning might be attributed to the fact that AutoTutor does not let a learner perseverate in an impasse. When AutoTutor tries to get a learner to articulate an idea, it first provides a hint (e.g., "What about X"). The hint is followed by a prompt (e.g., "X is a type of what?") if the learner's response to the hint was unsatisfactory. AutoTutor simply asserts the information when the learner cannot answer the prompt. Hence, impasses presumably caused by hints and prompts are eliminated with assertions. Withholding assertions and repeating hint-prompt cycles would presumably increase frustration and possibly impact learning.

There is some evidence to support this claim. For example, negative affect (amalgamation of frustration, anxiety, and annoyance) was negatively correlated with post-tests scores when the task was to read a passage in physics without any interference from a tutor (Linnenbrink & Pintrich, 2002). Frustration was also negatively linked to performance outcomes when students solved analytical reasoning problems in the absence of a tutor (D'Mello, Lehman, & Person, in review).

Perhaps the most important finding is that the positive correlation between confusion and learning was discovered in all three studies. This relationship is consistent with the model discussed earlier, which claims that cognitive disequilibrium is one precursor to deep learning (Graesser, Lu et al., 2005; Graesser & Olde, 2003), with theories that highlight the merits of impasses during learning (Brown & VanLehn, 1980; VanLehn et al., 2003), and with models that help students learn how to overcome failure from getting stuck (Burleson & Picard, 2004). According to these models, confusion naturally occurs in the learning session when learners are confronted with information that is inconsistent with existing knowledge. Learners are in the state of cognitive disequilibrium, heightened physiological arousal, and more intense thought when they attempt to resolve impasses, discard misconceptions, and actively solve problems. Confusion itself does not cause learning gains, but the cognitive activities that accompany confusion, cognitive disequilibrium, and impasse resolution are presumably linked to learning.

Modeling the Temporal Dynamics of Learners' Emotions

Identification of the affective states that occur during learning is undoubtedly very important, but it could be argued that there is limited utility in merely knowing *what* states occur and their overall impact on learning. What is missing is a specification of *how* these states evolve, morph, interact, and influence learning and engagement. An analysis of mood states during a learning session will not suffice, because states such as confusion, frustration, surprise, and delight arise and decay at much faster timescales (a few seconds) compared to moods (several minutes or a few hours) (Ekman, 1984; Rosenberg, 1998). Simply put, the affective experiences that accompany learning are seldom static and persistent; instead, they are dynamic and highly transient.

This point is exemplified in the affective trajectory of a sample learner presented in Figure 6.4. The learner settles into flow after initially oscillating between flow and delight. An impasse or perturbation jerks the learner out of the flow state into a state of confusion. Repetitive oscillations between confusion and flow are observed, presumably as problem solving proceeds. Sometimes the learner gets stuck and experiences frustration. Success in problem solving yields delight and extreme novelty triggers surprise. This is the dominant pattern of emotional transitions until boredom kicks in toward the end of the session.

This example illustrates two interesting phenomena pertaining to the temporal dynamics of learners' emotions. First, learners tend to perseverate in some states, whereas others are more transitory. For example, one would expect boredom to be more persistent than surprise, which is undoubtedly a transitory state. It would be difficult to imagine a learner sustaining a state of surprise for more than a few seconds. The second interesting phenomenon is that some emotional transitions are more likely than others. For example, we would not expect flow to transition into boredom, whereas a flow-to-confusion transition is expected when an impasse is detected.

We investigated these questions by analyzing the persistence of individual states and transitions between states (D'Mello & Graesser, in review; D'Mello & Graesser, in review). The data from the multiple-judge and speech recognition studies were used for this analysis because the sampling methodology in the observational and emote-aloud studies did not have the requisite sampling rate to warrant a temporal analysis.

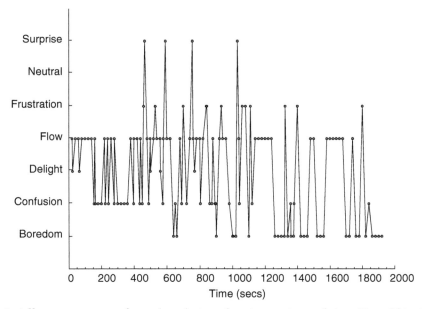

Figure 6.4. Affective trajectory of a student during a learning session with AutoTutor. This time series is from a student in the multiple-judge study. The student self-reported their affective states at twenty-second intervals as well as in between the twenty-second blocks.

Persistence of Emotions

Although the scientific literature on the persistence of the learning-centered emotions is sparse, it is possible to theoretically align them on the following temporal scale in increasing order of persistence: (Delight = Surprise) < (Confusion = Frustration) < (Boredom = Engagement/Flow). These predictions can be understood from the perspective of goal-appraisal theories of emotion (Mandler, 1976, 1999; Stein & Levine, 1991; Stein et al., 2008). In general, learners are typically in a *prolonged* state of either (1) engagement/flow as they pursue the superordinate learning goal of mastering the material or (2) disengagement (boredom) when they abandon pursuit of the superordinate learning goal. When they are deeply engaged, they attempt to assimilate new information into existing knowledge schemas. However, when new or discrepant information is detected, attention shifts to the discrepant information, the autonomic nervous systems increases in arousal, and the learner experiences a variety of possible states depending on the context, the amount of change, and whether important goals are blocked. In the case of extreme novelty, the event evokes surprise. When the novelty triggers the achievement of a goal, the emotion is positive, such as delight or even one of those rare *eureka* experiences (Knoblich, Ohlsson, & Raney, 2001). Previous research on delight and surprise has indicated that these emotions are typically quite brief (Ekman, 1984, 1992). In contrast, confusion and frustration occur when the discrepancy or novelty trigger an impasse that blocks the superordinate learning goal and possibly results in the student getting stuck. The learner initiates a subgoal of resolving the impasse through effortful reasoning and problem solving. Confusion and frustration address a subgoal, so they should be shorter than the states of flow and boredom that address the major goal. However, confusion and frustration are expected to persist longer than the short-lived reactions of delight and surprise.

We developed a set of exponential decay models to capture graded differences in the decay rates of the various emotions (D'Mello & Graesser, in review). The

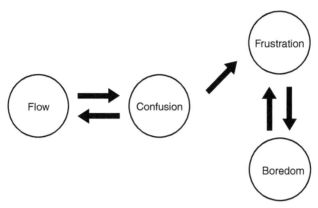

Figure 6.5. Observed pattern of transitions between emotions.

models supported a tripartite classification of learning-centered emotions along a temporal dimension: persistent emotions (boredom, flow, and confusion), transitory emotions (delight and surprise), and an intermediate emotion (frustration). This pattern somewhat confirms the aforementioned predictions stemming from goal-appraisal theories of emotion, with the exception that confusion was categorized as a persistent rather than an intermediate emotion.

Transitions between Emotions

Cognitive disequilibrium theory makes a number of predictions about the transitions between the learning-centered emotions. Learners who are in a flow/engaged state will experience confusion when an impasse is detected. They engage in effortful problem-solving activities to resolve the impasse and restore equilibrium. Equilibrium is restored when the impasse is resolved and learners revert back into the flow/engaged state. However, confusion transitions into frustration when the impasse cannot be resolved, the student gets stuck, and important goals are blocked (Burleson & Picard, 2004). Furthermore, persistent frustration may transition into boredom, a crucial point at which the learner disengages from the learning process.

The major hypotheses of the model were tested by performing time-series analyses on the data from the multiple-judge study and the speech recognition study (D'Mello

& Graesser, in review; D'Mello, Taylor et al., 2007). The results confirmed the presence of confusion–flow/engagement and boredom–frustration oscillations as well as confusion-to-frustration transitions (see Figure 6.5). Hence, students in the state of engagement/ flow are continuously being challenged within their zones of optimal learning (Brown et al., 1998; Vygotsky, 1978) and are experiencing two-step episodes alternating between confusion and insight. In contrast to these *beneficial* flow-confusion-flow cycles, there are the *harmful* oscillations between boredom and frustration. As cognitive disequilibrium theory asserts, confusion plays a central role in the learning process because it is the gateway to positive (flow) or negative (frustration) emotions.

Assessing Contextual Influences on Learners' Emotions

An investigation into the emotions that occur during learning will not be complete without a discussion of the context surrounding the emotional experiences (Aviezer et al., 2008; Barrett, 2006; Russell, 2003; Stemmler, Heldmann, Pauls, & Scherer, 2001). In many cases, examining the context of an emotional expression can lead to a deeper (and sometimes even causal) explanation of the emotional experience. For example, confusion *while* solving a problem can be contrasted with confusion *after* receiving feedback for the solution. The first

(a)

(b)

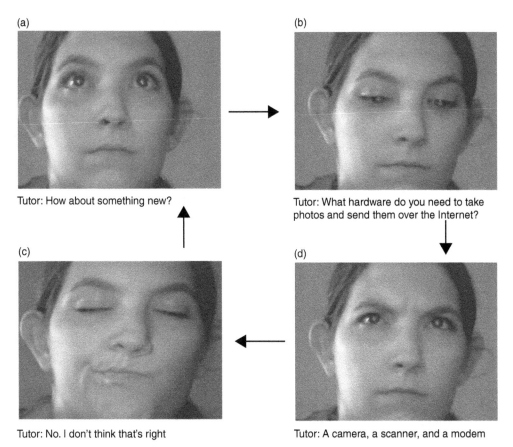

Tutor: How about something new?

Tutor: What hardware do you need to take photos and send them over the Internet?

(c)

(d)

Tutor: No. I don't think that's right

Tutor: A camera, a scanner, and a modem

Figure 6.6. Sequence of affective states annotated with the text of student or tutor dialogue move when the emotions were experienced (a) neutral, (b) flow/engagement, (c) confusion, and (d) frustration.

form of confusion can be causally attributed to being perplexed with the problem itself, whereas confusion after feedback is more related to the problem-solving outcome. Although similar, these two forms of confusion might have distinct manifestations (i.e., intensity, valence) and different pedagogical virtues.

In general, the context is critical because it helps disambiguate between various exemplars of an emotion category (Russell, 2003). For example, the two forms of confusion discussed earlier are different exemplars of the "confusion" category. Examining confusion (i.e., the category) out of context (i.e., without the exemplar) runs the risk of being meaningless.

One advantage of investigating emotions with a dialogue-based ITS like AutoTutor is that the dialogue history provides a rich

trace into the contextual underpinnings of learners' emotional experiences. For example, consider a four-turn segment of the dialogue history, the accompanying facial expressions, and self-reported emotions of a learner from an actual tutorial session (Figure 6.6). The learner is in the neutral state when the tutor discusses a change of topic (Figure 6.6a). She is then engaged while she tries to answer the question (Figure 6.6b). She experiences an impasse when she is uncertain about her answer (Figure 6.6c). The answer is incorrect and the tutor responds with negative feedback, which frustrates the student (Figure 6.6d).

We examined the tutorial dialogue (i.e., the context) over fifteen-second intervals that culminated in episodes of boredom, flow/engagement, confusion, and frustration that were reported by the self, peers, and trained judges (D'Mello et al., 2006; D'Mello, Craig et al., 2008). An event triggering an emotional reaction could either be tutor-generated (i.e., boredom because the tutor is providing a long-winded explanation), student-generated (i.e., boredom because the student has no interest in computer literacy), or a session-related event (i.e., boredom because the tutorial session is dragging on).

We discovered a number of interesting patterns that provide some insights into the emotional experiences during learning with AutoTutor (D'Mello & Graesser, in review; D'Mello, Taylor et al., 2007). In particular, boredom occurs later in the session, after multiple attempts to answer a question. Boredom also occurs when AutoTutor gives more direct dialogue moves (i.e., assertions or summaries are more direct than pumps or hints). In contrast, confusion occurs earlier in the session, within the first few attempts to answer a question, with slower and less verbose responses, with poor answers, with frozen expressions (instead of domain-related contributions), when the tutor is less direct, and when the tutor provides negative feedback. Flow occurs within the first few attempts to answer a question, with quicker, longer, proficient responses, and is accompanied by positive feedback from the tutor. Frustration was prevalent later in the temporal span of a session, with longer response times, with good answers to the immediate question but poor answers to the broader topic, and after negative tutor feedback. In summary, the relationships between the various dialogue features and the affective states described earlier are generally intuitive and in the expected directions.

Programming AutoTutor to be Responsive to Learners' Emotions

Now that we have a better understanding of what emotions are relevant to learning and how they arise and decay within the context of a learning session, we turn our attention to the practical problem of developing an ITS that is responsive to learners' affective

and cognitive states. We have recently developed two new versions of AutoTutor that detect and respond to learners' affective and cognitive states (D'Mello, Craig et al., 2009; D'Mello, Jackson et al., 2008). These affect-sensitive variants of AutoTutor detect and respond to boredom, confusion, and frustration. Appropriate responses to these states could potentially have a positive impact on engagement and learning outcomes. These affect-sensitive versions of AutoTutor have a set of production rules that were designed to map dynamic assessments of the student's cognitive and affective states with tutor actions to address the presence of the negative emotions (see Figure 6.7). Hence, the learner and the tutor are embedded into an affective loop that involves *detecting* the learner's affective states, *responding* to the detected states, and *synthesizing* emotional expressions via animated pedagogical agents. These processes are briefly described in the following subsections.

Detecting Affective and Cognitive States

The affect-detection system monitors conversational cues, gross body language, and facial features to detect boredom, confusion, frustration, and neutral (no affect). Automated affect-detection systems that detect these emotions have been integrated into AutoTutor (see D'Mello, Craig et al., 2008; D'Mello & Graesser, 2009; D'Mello, Picard & Graesser, 2007). Each channel independently provides its own diagnosis of the student's affective state. These individual diagnoses are combined with a decision-level fusion algorithm that selects a single affective state (see Current State and Next State in Figure 6.7) and a confidence value (see Detection Probability in Figure 6.7).

The tutor's model of learners' cognitive states include a global measure of student ability (dynamically updated throughout the session) and the conceptual quality of the student's immediate response (Global Ability and Local Ability, respectively, in Figure 6.7). These parameters are computed by performing a syntactic and semantic analysis of the student's past and immediate

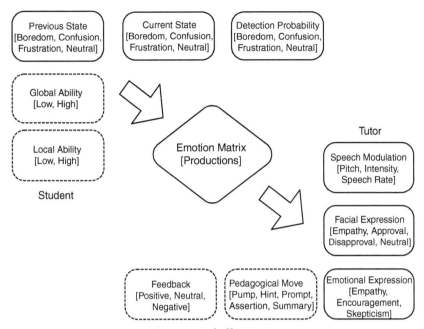

Figure 6.7. Architecture of affect-sensitive AutoTutor.

utterances (Graesser, Penumatsa, Ventura, Cai, & Hu, 2007; Graesser et al., 2000).

Responding to Affective and Cognitive States

AutoTutor provides short feedback to each student response. In addition to articulating the verbal content of the feedback, the affective AutoTutor also modulates its facial expressions and speech prosody. Positive feedback is delivered with an *approval* expression (big smile and big nod). Neutral positive feedback receives a *mild approval* expression (small smile and slight nod). Negative feedback is delivered with a *disapproval* expression (slight frown and head shake); the tutor makes a *skeptical* face when delivering neutral-negative feedback (see Figure 6.8). No facial expression accompanies the delivery of neutral feedback.

After delivering the feedback, the affective AutoTutor delivers an emotional statement if it senses that the student is bored, confused, or frustrated. A nonemotional discourse marker (e.g., "Moving on," "Try this one") is selected if the student is neutral. AutoTutor's strategies to respond to boredom, confusion, and frustration are motivated by attribution theory (Batson, Turk, Shaw, & Klein, 1995; Heider, 1958; Weiner, 1986), cognitive disequilibrium during learning (Craig et al., 2004; Festinger, 1957; Graesser & Olde, 2003; Piaget, 1952), and recommendations by pedagogical experts. These perspectives are integrated in two pedagogically distinct variants of the affect-sensitive AutoTutor. These include a Supportive and a Shakeup AutoTutor.

Supportive AutoTutor. The supportive AutoTutor responds to the learners' affective states via empathetic and motivational responses. These responses always attribute the source of the learners' emotion to the material instead of the learners themselves. So the supportive AutoTutor might respond to mild boredom with "This stuff can be kind of dull sometimes, so I'm gonna try and help you get through it. Let's go." A response to confusion would include attributing the source of confusion to the material ("Some of this *material* can be confusing. Just keep going and I am sure you will get it.") or the tutor itself ("I know I do not always convey things clearly. I am always happy to repeat myself if you need it. Try this one.").

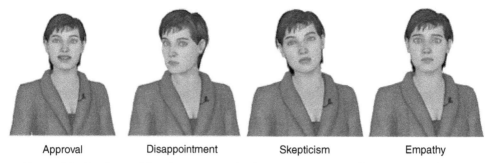

| Approval | Disappointment | Skepticism | Empathy |

Figure 6.8. Synthesized facial expressions by AutoTutor's animated conversational agent.

Shakeup AutoTutor. The major difference between the shakeup AutoTutor and the supportive AutoTutor lies in the source of emotion attribution. Whereas the supportive AutoTutor attributes the learners' negative emotions to the material or itself, the shakeup AutoTutor directly attributes the emotions to the learners. For example, possible shakeup responses to confusion are "This material has got *you* confused, but I think you have the right idea. Try this ..." and "You are not as confused as you might think. I'm actually kind of impressed. Keep it up."

Another difference between the two versions lies in the conservational style. Whereas the supportive AutoTutor is subdued and formal, the shakeup tutor is edgier, flaunts social norms, and is witty. For example, a supportive response to boredom would be "Hang in there a bit longer. Things are about to get interesting." The shakeup counterpart of this response is "Geez this stuff sucks. I'd be bored too, but I gotta teach what they tell me."

Synthesizing Affective Expressions

The affect-sensitive versions of AutoTutor synthesize affect with facial expressions and emotionally modulated speech. These affective expressions include: approval, mild approval, disapproval, empathy, skepticism, mild enthusiasm, and high enthusiasm (Figure 6.8). The supportive and shakeup responses are always paired with the appropriate expression, which can be neutral in some cases. The facial expressions in each

display were informed by Ekman's work on the facial correlates of emotion expression (Ekman & Friesen, 1978).

The facial expressions of emotion displayed by AutoTutor are augmented with emotionally expressive speech synthesized by the agent. The emotional expressivity is obtained by variations in pitch, speech rate, and other prosodic features. Previous research has led us to conceptualize AutoTutor's affective speech on the indices of pitch range, pitch level, and speech rate (Johnstone & Scherer, 2000).

Evaluating the Affect-Sensitive AutoTutor

We have recently conducted an experiment that evaluated the pedagogical effectiveness of the supportive AutoTutor when compared to the original tutor (D'Mello, Lehman, Sullins et al., in review). This original AutoTutor has a conventional set of fuzzy production rules that are sensitive to cognitive states of the learner, but not to the emotional states of the learner. The supportive AutoTutor is sensitive to learners' affective and cognitive states. The obvious prediction is that learning gains should be superior for the supportive AutoTutor.

The experiment utilized a between-subjects design where learners (1) completed a pretest on topics in computer literacy, (2) were tutored on two computer literacy topics with either the affective or the regular AutoTutor, and (3) completed a post-test. The tests and tutorial sessions were pitched at deeper levels of comprehension with questions that required reasoning and inference instead of the recall of shallow facts and definitions. The tutorial session consisted of two thirty-minute sessions on different computer literacy topics but with the same version of AutoTutor (i.e., either supportive or original).

The results of this experiment indicated that the supportive AutoTutor was more effective than the regular tutor for low-domain-knowledge students in the second session ($d = .713$), but not the first session. This suggests that it is inappropriate for the tutor to be supportive to these students before there has been enough context to show there are problems. Simply put, do not be supportive until the students need support. Second, the students with more knowledge never benefited from the supportive AutoTutor. These students do not need the emotional support; rather they need to go directly to the content. Third, there are conditions when emotional support is detrimental, if not irritating, to the learner. There appears to be a liability to quick support and empathy compared to no affect-sensitivity.

The central message is that there is an appropriate time for affect-sensitivity in the form of supportive dialogues. Just as there is a "time for telling," there is a "time for emoting." We could imagine a strategy where low-knowledge students start out with a nonemotional regular tutor until they see there are problems. After that they need support, as manifested in the second tutorial session. Regarding high-knowledge students, they are perfectly fine working on content for an hour or more and may get irritated with an AutoTutor showing compassion, empathy, and care. But later on there may be a time when they want a shakeup AutoTutor for stimulation, challenge, and a playful exchange. Or maybe even a supportive AutoTutor. These are all questions to explore in future research.

Conclusions

The idea of having a tutoring system detect, respond to, and synthesize emotions was once a seductive vision (Picard, 1997). This vision is now a reality as affect-sensitive learning environments are coming online. Our research on emotions during learning with AutoTutor represents one out of a handful of related efforts made by researchers who have a vision of enhancing engagement and motivation, boosting self-efficacy, and promoting learning gains by designing intelligent learning environments that optimally coordinate cognition and emotion (Arroyo et al., 2009; Burleson & Picard, 2007; Chaffar, Derbali, & Frasson, 2009; Conati & Maclaren, 2009; D'Mello, Craig et al., 2009; Forbes-Riley & Litman, 2009; Robison, McQuiggan, & Lester, 2009; Woolf, 2009).

Despite the impressive progress on affect-sensitive ITSs, it should be noted that affect detectors and reactors (i.e., they detect and respond to learners' emotions) are not the panacea for the problem of promoting learning gains. Our research suggests that they need to be affect *anticipators, forestallers*, and *inducers* as well. Affect anticipators and forestallers would be required to predict and prevent the occurrence of persistent negative affective states like boredom and presumably frustration. Prediction and prevention is necessary to address boredom because boredom begets frustration and even more boredom (D'Mello & Graesser, in review; D'Mello, Taylor et al., 2007). More importantly, tutorial interventions are not very effective in alleviating boredom when learners tend to experience harmful oscillations between boredom and frustration (D'Mello & Graesser, in review), indicating that advanced prediction is very important to regulate boredom.

Proactively responding to boredom would involve engaging the learner in a task that increases interest and cognitive arousal, such as a challenge, an interactive simulation, or a seductive embedded serious game. These difficult tasks have a high likelihood of getting students to reengage with the material. Another strategy is to provide participants with a choice of tasks and topics so they might pick one that is more relevant to their interests. Curiosity and engagement are enhanced by the learner's freedom of choices (Lepper & Woolverton, 2002).

On the other hand, the positive link between confusion and learning suggests that learning environments need to substantially challenge students to illicit critical thought and deep inquiry. Therefore, a promising strategy to promote opportunities for deep learning is to develop affect-induction interventions that jolt students out of their perennial state of blasé comprehension by presenting challenges with contradictions, incongruities, anomalies, system breakdowns, and difficult decisions (Bjork & Linn, 2006; Festinger, 1957; Graesser & Olde, 2003; Schwartz & Bransford, 1998). Learners experience impasses, cognitive disequilibrium, and confusion in these conditions. Cognitive equilibrium is restored after thought, reflection, problem solving, self-explanations, and other effortful cognitive activities that force learners to pause and think.

In summary, the scientific research on affect and learning is an exciting research direction that we believe will be a priority for the next decade or longer. Progress will depend on breakthroughs in the development of affective computing technologies, such as affect detectors, reactors, synthesizers, anticipators, forestallers, and inducers. Future research will hopefully unveil novel insights into the intricate dance among emotions, cognition, motivation, individual differences, pedagogical interventions, and learning gains.

Acknowledgments

This research was supported by the National Science Foundation (REC 0106965, ITR 0325428, HCC 0834847). Any opinions, findings, conclusions, or recommendations expressed in this paper are those of the authors and do not necessarily reflect the views of NSF.

We thank our research colleagues in the Emotive Computing Group and the Tutoring Research Group (TRG) at the University of Memphis (http://emotion.autotutor.org). We gratefully acknowledge our partners in the Affective Computing group at the MIT Media Lab.

The Tutoring Research Group (TRG) is an interdisciplinary research team comprised of researchers from psychology, computer science, physics, linguistics, engineering, and education (visit http://www.autotutor.org, http://emotion.autotutor.org, http://fedex.memphis.edu/iis/).

References

Aleven, V., & Koedinger, K. (2002). An effective metacognitive strategy: Learning by doing and explaining with a computer-based Cognitive Tutor. *Cognitive Science, 26*(2), 147–179.

Anderson, J., Douglass, S., & Qin, Y. (2005). How should a theory of learning and cognition inform instruction? In A. Healy (Ed.), *Experimental cognitive psychology and its applications* (pp. 47–58). Washington, DC: American Psychological Association.

Arroyo, I., Woolf, B., Cooper, D., Burleson, W., Muldner, K., & Christopherson, R. (2009). Emotion sensors go to school. In V. Dimitrova, R. Mizoguchi, B. Du Boulay, & A. Graesser (Eds.), *Proceedings of 14th International Conference on Artificial Intelligence in Education.* Amsterdam: IOS Press.

Aviezer, H., Hassin, R., Ryan, J., Grady, C., Susskind, J., Anderson, A., et al. (2008). Angry, disgusted, or afraid? Studies on the malleability of emotion perception. *Psychological Science, 19*(7), 724–732.

Baker, R., D'Mello, S., Rodrigo, M., & Graesser, A. (2010). Better to be frustrated than bored: The incidence and persistence of affect during interactions with three different computer-based learning environments. *International Journal of Human-Computer Studies, 68*(4), 223–241.

Barrett, L. (2006). Are emotions natural kinds? *Perspectives on Psychological Science, 1,* 28–58.

Barrett, L., Mesquita, B., Ochsner, K., & Gross, J. (2007). The experience of emotion. *Annual Review of Psychology, 58,* 373–403.

Batson, C., Turk, C., Shaw, L., & Klein, T. (1995). Information function of empathic emotion – learning that we value the others' welfare. *Journal of Personality and Social Psychology, 68*(2), 300–313.

Beilock, S. L., & DeCaro, M. S. (2007). From poor performance to success under stress: Working memory, strategy selection, and mathematical problem solving under pressure. *Journal of Experimental Psychology-Learning Memory and Cognition, 33*(6), 983–998.

Biggs, J. (1995). *Enhancing teaching through constructive alignment*. Paper presented at the 20th International Conference on Improving University Teaching, Hong Kong, Hong Kong, July.

Bjork, E. L., & Bjork, R. A. (2011). Making things hard on yourself, but in a good way: Creating desirable difficulties to enhance learning. In M. A. Gernsbacher, R. W. Pew, L. M. Hough, & J. R. Pomeranz (Eds.), *Psychology and the real world: Essays illustrating fundamental contributions to society* (pp. 56–64). New York: Worth Publishers.

Bless, H., & Fielder, K. (1995). Affective states and the influence of activated general knowledge. *Personality and Social Psychology Bulletin, 21*, 766–778.

Boekaerts, M. (1993). Being concerned with well-being and with learning. *Educational Psychologist, 28*(2), 149–167.

Bower, G. (1981). Mood and memory. *American Psychologist, 36*, 129–148.

Bower, G. (1992). How might emotions affect learning. In S. A. Christianson (Ed.), *The handbook of emotion and memory: Research and theory* (pp. 3–31). Hillsdale, NJ: Erlbaum.

Brown, A., Ellery, S., & Campione, J. (1998). Creating zones of proximal development electronically in thinking practices in mathematics and science learning. In J. Greeno & S. Goldman (Eds.), *Thinking practices in mathematics and science learning* (pp. 341–368). Mahwah, NJ: Lawrence Erlbaum.

Brown, J., & VanLehn, K. (1980). Repair theory: A generative theory of bugs in procedural skills. *Cognitive Science, 4*, 379–426.

Burleson, W., & Picard, R. (2004). *Affective agents: Sustaining motivation to learn through failure and a state of "stuck."* Paper presented at the ITS 2004 Workshop Proceedings on Social and Emotional, Maceio, Brazil.

Burleson, W., & Picard, R. (2007). Evidence for gender specific approaches to the development of emotionally intelligent learning companions. *IEEE Intelligent Systems, 22*(4), 62–69.

Chaffar, S., Derbali, L., & Frasson, C. (2009). *Inducing positive emotional state in intelligent tutoring systems*. Paper presented at the 14th International Conference on Artificial Intelligence in Education. Brighton, U.K.

Chi, M., Roy, M., & Hausmann, R. (2008). Observing tutorial dialogues collaboratively: Insights about human tutoring effectiveness from vicarious learning. *Cognitive Science, 32*(2), 301–341.

Clifford, M. (1988). Failure tolerance and academic risk-taking in ten- to twelve-year-old students. *British Journal of Educational Psychology, 58*, 15–27.

Conati, C. (2002). Probabilistic assessment of user's emotions in educational games. *Applied Artificial Intelligence, 16*(7–8), 555–575.

Conati, C., & Maclaren, H. (2009). Empirically building and evaluating a probabilistic model of user affect. *User Modeling and User-Adapted Interaction, 19*(3), 267–303.

Craig, S., Graesser, A., Sullins, J., & Gholson, B. (2004). Affect and learning: An exploratory look into the role of affect in learning. *Journal of Educational Media, 29*, 241–250.

Csikszentmihalyi, M. (1990). *Flow: The psychology of optimal experience*. New York: Harper and Row.

D'Mello, S., Craig, S., Fike, K., & Graesser, A. (2009). Responding to learners' cognitive-affective states with supportive and shakeup dialogues. In J. Jacko (Ed.), *Human-computer interaction. Ambient, ubiquitous and intelligent interaction* (pp. 595–604). Berlin/Heidelberg: Springer.

D'Mello, S., Craig, S., Gholson, B., Franklin, S., Picard, R., & Graesser, A. (2005). Integrating affect sensors in an intelligent tutoring system. In *The Computer In The Affective Loop Workshop At 2005 International Conference On Intelligent User Interfaces* (pp. 7–13), San Diego, CA.

D'Mello, S., Craig, S., Sullins, J., & Graesser, A. (2006). Predicting affective states expressed through an emote-aloud procedure from AutoTutor's mixed-initiative dialogue. *International Journal of Artificial Intelligence in Education, 16*(1), 3–28.

D'Mello, S., Craig, S., Witherspoon, A., McDaniel, B., & Graesser, A. (2008). Automatic detection of learner's affect from conversational cues. *User Modeling and User-Adapted Interaction, 18*(1–2), 45–80.

D'Mello, S., Dale, R., & Graesser, A. (in press). Disequilibrium in the mind, disharmony in the body. *Cognition and Emotion*. Online version available at: http://www.tandfonline.com/doi/abs/10.1080/02699931.2011.575767.

D'Mello, S., Dowell, N., & Graesser, A. (2009). Cohesion relationships in tutorial dialogue as predictors of affective states. In V. Dimitrova, R. Mizoguchi, B. du Boulay, & A. Graesser (Eds.), *Proceedings of 14th International Conference on*

Artificial Intelligence In Education (pp. 9–16). Amsterdam: IOS Press.

D'Mello, S., & Graesser, A. (2009). Automatic detection of learners' affect from gross body language. *Applied Artificial Intelligence, 23*(2), 123–150.

D'Mello, S., & Graesser, A. (2010). Modeling cognitive-affective dynamics with hidden Markov models. In R. Catrambone & S. Ohlsson (Eds.), *Proceedings of the 32nd Annual Cognitive Science Society* (pp. 2721–2726). Austin, TX: Cognitive Science Society.

D'Mello, S., & Graesser, A. (in review). The half-life of emotions.

D'Mello, S., Jackson, G., Craig, S., Morgan, B., Chipman, P., White, H., et al. (2008). *AutoTutor detects and responds to learners affective and cognitive states.* Paper presented at the Workshop on Emotional and Cognitive issues in ITS held in conjunction with the Ninth International Conference on Intelligent Tutoring Systems, Montreal, Canada.

D'Mello, S., King, B., Entezari, O., Chipman, P., & Graesser, A. (2008). *The impact of automatic speech recognition errors on learning gains with AutoTutor.* Paper presented at the Annual meeting of the American Educational Research Association, New York, New York, March.

D'Mello, S., Lehman, B., & Person, N. (in review). Monitoring affect states during effortful problem solving activities. *International Journal of Artificial Intelligence in Education.*

D'Mello, S., Lehman, B., Sullins, J., Daigle, R., Combs, R., Vogt, K., et al. (2010). A time for emoting: When affect-sensitivity is and isn't effective at promoting deep learning. In J. Kay & V. Aleven (Eds.), *Proceedings of the 10th International Conference on Intelligent Tutoring Systems* (pp. 245–254). Berlin/Heidelberg: Springer.

D'Mello, S., Picard, R., & Graesser, A. (2007). Towards an affect-sensitive AutoTutor. *Intelligent Systems, IEEE, 22*(4), 53–61.

D'Mello, S., Taylor, R., Davidson, K., & Graesser, A. (2008). Self versus teacher judgments of learner emotions during a tutoring session with AutoTutor. In B. Woolf, E. Aimeur, R. Nkambou, & S. Lajoie (Eds.), *Proceedings of the 9th International Conference on Intelligent Tutoring Systems.* Berlin, Heidelberg: Springer-Verlag.

D'Mello, S., Taylor, R., & Graesser, A. (2007). Monitoring affective trajectories during complex learning. In D. McNamara & G. Trafton (Eds.), *Proceedings of the 29th Annual Cognitive Science Society* (pp. 203–208). Austin, TX: Cognitive Science Society.

Damasio, A. (2003). *Looking for Spinoza: Joy, sorrow, and the feeling brain.* New York: Harcourt.

Deci, E., & Ryan, R. (2002). The paradox of achievement: The harder you push, the worse it gets. In J. Aronson (Ed.), *Improving academic achievement: Impact of psychological factors on education* (pp. 61–87). Orlando, FL: Academic Press.

Dragon, T., Arroyo, I., Woolf, B. P., Burleson, W., el Kaliouby, R., & Eydgahi, H. (2008). Viewing student affect and learning through classroom observation and physical sensors. In B. Woolf, A. E. N. R., & L. S. (Eds.), *Proceedings of the 9th International Conference on Intelligent Tutorin Systems* (pp. 29–39). Berlin/Heidelberg: Springer-Verlag.

Dweck, C. (2002). Messages that motivate: How praise molds students' beliefs, motivation, and performance (in surprising ways). In J. Aronson (Ed.), *Improving academic achievement: Impact of psychological factors on education* (pp. 61–87). Orlando, FL: Academic Press.

Ekman, P. (1984). Expression and the nature of emotion. In K. Scherer & P. Ekman (Eds.), *Approaches to emotion* (pp. 319–344). Hillsdale, NJ: Erlbaum.

Ekman, P. (1992). An argument for basic emotions. *Cognition & Emotion, 6*(3–4), 169–200.

Ekman, P. (2003). *Emotions revealed: Recognizing faces and feelings to improve communication and emotional life.* New York: Henry Holt.

Ekman, P., & Friesen, W. (1978). *The facial action coding system: A technique for the measurement of facial movement.* Palo Alto, CA: Consulting Psychologists Press.

Ericsson, K., & Simon, H. (1993). *Protocol analysis: Verbal reports as data* (Rev. ed.). Cambridge, MA: The MIT Press.

Festinger, L. (1957). *A theory of cognitive dissonance.* Stanford, CA: Stanford University Press.

Fielder, K. (2001). Affective states trigger processes of assimilation and accommodation. In K. Martin & G. Clore (Eds.), *Theories of mood and cognition: A user's guidebook* (pp. 85–98). Mahwah, NJ: Erlbaum.

Forbes-Riley, K., & Litman, D. (2009). Adapting to student uncertainty improves tutoring dialogues. In V. Dimitrova, R. Mizoguchi, & B. Du Boulay (Eds.), *Proceedings of the 14th*

International Conference on Artificial Intelligence in Education (pp. 33–40). Amsterdam: IOS Press.

Forbes-Riley, K., Rotaru, M., & Litman, D. (2008). The relative impact of student affect on performance models in a spoken dialogue tutoring system. User Modeling and User-Adapted Interaction, 18(1–2), 11–43.

Forgas, J. (1991). Affect and cognition in close relationships. In J. Fletcher & J. Fincham (Eds.), Cognition in close relationships (pp. 151–174). Hillsdale, NJ: Erlbaum.

Gertner, A., & VanLehn, K. (2000). Andes: A coached problem solving environment for physics. In G. Gauthier, C. Frasson & K. VanLehn (Eds.), Proceedings of the International Conference on Intelligent Tutoring Systems (pp. 133–142). Berlin/Heidelberg: Springer.

Goleman, D. (1995). Emotional intelligence. New York: Bantam Books.

Gotlib, I., & Abramson, L. (1999). Attributional theories of emotion. In T. Dalgleish & M. Power (Eds.), Handbook of cognition and emotion. Sussex: John Wiley & Sons.

Graesser, A., Chipman, P., Haynes, B., & Olney, A. (2005). AutoTutor: An intelligent tutoring system with mixed-initiative dialogue. IEEE Transactions on Education, 48(4), 612–618.

Graesser, A., Chipman, P., King, B., McDaniel, B., & D'Mello, S. (2007). Emotions and learning with AutoTutor. In R. Luckin, K. Koedinger, & J. Greer (Eds.), 13th International Conference on Artificial Intelligence in Education (pp. 569–571). Amsterdam: IOS Press.

Graesser, A., Lu, S., Olde, B., Cooper-Pye, E., & Whitten, S. (2005). Question asking and eye tracking during cognitive disequilibrium: Comprehending illustrated texts on devices when the devices break down. Memory and Cognition, 33, 1235–1247.

Graesser, A., Lu, S. L., Jackson, G., Mitchell, H., Ventura, M., Olney, A., et al. (2004). AutoTutor: A tutor with dialogue in natural language. Behavioral Research Methods, Instruments, and Computers, 36, 180–193.

Graesser, A., McDaniel, B., Chipman, P., Witherspoon, A., D'Mello, S., & Gholson, B. (2006). Detection of emotions during learning with AutoTutor. Paper presented at the 28th Annual Conference of the Cognitive Science Society, Vancouver, Canada.

Graesser, A., & Olde, B. (2003). How does one know whether a person understands a device? The quality of the questions the person asks when the device breaks down. Journal of Educational Psychology, 95(3), 524–536.

Graesser, A., Penumatsa, P., Ventura, M., Cai, Z., & Hu, X. (2007). Using LSA in AutoTutor: Learning through mixed-initiative dialogue in natural language. In T. Landauer, D. McNamara, S. Dennis, & W. Kintsch (Eds.), Handbook of latent semantic analysis (pp. 243–262). Mahwah, NJ: Erlbaum.

Graesser, A., Wiemer-Hastings, P., Wiemer-Hastings, K., Harter, D., Person, N., & TRG. (2000). Using latent semantic analysis to evaluate the contributions of students in AutoTutor. Interactive Learning Environments, 8(2), 129–147.

Harter, S. (1992). The relationship between perceived competence, affect, and motivational orientation within the classroom: process and patterns of change. In A. Boggiano & T. Pittman (Eds.), Achievement and motivation: A social-developmental perspective (pp. 77–114). New York: Cambridge University Press.

Heider, F. (1958). The psychology of interpersonal relations. New York: John Wiley & Sons.

Hertel, G., Neuhof, J., Theuer, T., & Kerr, N. (2000). Mood effect on cooperation in small groups: Does positive mood simply lead to more cooperation? Cognition and Emotion, 14, 441–472.

Immordino-Yang, M. H., & Damasio, A. R. (2007). We feel, therefore we learn: The relevance of affective and social neuroscience to education. Mind, Brain and Education, 1(1), 3–10.

Isen, A. (2001). An influence of positive affect on decision making in complex situations: Theoretical issues with practical implications. Journal of Consumer Psychology, 11, 75–85.

Isen, A., Daubman, K., & Nowicki, G. (1987). Positive affect facilitates creative problem solving. Journal of Personality and Social Psychology, 52, 1122–1131.

Issroff, K., & del Soldato, T. (1996). Incorporating motivation into computer-supported collaborative learning. In Proceedings of European conference on Artificial Intelligence in Education. Ficha Tecnica, Lisbon.

Izard, C. (1971). The face of emotion. New York: Appleton-Century-Crofts.

Izard, C., & Ackerman, B. (2000). Motivational, organizational, and regulatory functions of discrete emotions. In M. Lewis & J. Haviland-Jones (Eds.), Handbook of emotions (2nd ed.). New York: Guilford Press.

Johnstone, T., & Scherer, K. (2000). Vocal communication of emotion. In M. Lewis & J. Haviland-Jones (Eds.), Handbook of *emotions* (2nd ed., pp. 220–235). New York: Guilford Press.

Jonassen, D., Peck, K., & Wilson, B. (1999). *Learning with technology: A constructivist perspective.* Upper Saddle River, NJ: Prentice Hall.

Keltner, D., & Ekman, P. (2000). Facial expression of emotion. In R. Lewis & J. M. Haviland-Jones (Eds.), *Handbook of emotions* (2nd ed., pp. 236–264). New York: Guilford.

Keltner, D., & Shiota, M. (2003). New displays and new emotions: A commentary on Rozin and Cohen (2003). *Emotion, 3,* 86–91.

Knoblich, G., Ohlsson, S., & Raney, G. (2001). An eye movement study of insight problem solving. *Memory & Cognition, 29*(7), 1000–1009.

Koedinger, K., Anderson, J., Hadley, W., & Mark, M. (1997). Intelligent tutoring goes to school in the big city. *International Journal of Artificial Intelligence in Education, 8,* 30–43.

Koedinger, K., & Corbett, A. (2006). Cognitive tutors: Technology bringing learning sciences to the classroom. In R. K. Sawyer (Ed.), *The Cambridge handbook of the learning sciences* (pp. 61–78). New York: Cambridge University Press.

Kort, B., Reilly, R., & Picard, R. (2001). *An affective model of interplay between emotions and learning: Reengineering educational pedagogy-building a learning companion.* Paper presented at the IEEE International Conference on Advanced Learning Technologies. Madison, WI, (U.S).

Lazarus, R. (1991). *Emotion and adaptation.* New York: Oxford University Press.

Lazarus, R. (2000). The cognition-emotion debate: A bit of history. In M. Lewis & J. Haviland-Jones (Eds.), *Handbook of emotions* (2nd ed., pp. 1–20). New York: Guilford Press.

Lehman, B., D'Mello, S., & Person, N. (2008). *All alone with your emotions: An analysis of student emotions during effortful problem solving activities.* Paper presented at the Workshop on Emotional and Cognitive issues in ITS at the Ninth International Conference on Intelligent Tutoring Systems. Montreal, Canada.

Lehman, B., Matthews, M., D'Mello, S., & Person, N. (2008). What are you feeling? Investigating student affective states during expert human tutoring sessions. In B. Woolf, E. Aimeur, R. Nkambou, & S. Lajoie (Eds.), *Proceedings of the 9th International Conference on Intelligent Tutoring Systems* (pp. 50–59). Berlin/Heidelberg: Springer.

Lepper, M., & Chabay, R. (1988). Socializing the intelligent tutor: Bringing empathy to computer tutors. In H. Mandl & A. Lesgold (Eds.), *Learning issues for intelligent tutoring systems* (pp. 242–257). Hillsdale, NJ: Erlbaum.

Lepper, M., & Woolverton, M. (2002). The wisdom of practice: Lessons learned from the study of highly effective tutors. In J. Aronson (Ed.), *Improving academic achievement: Impact of psychological factors on education* (pp. 135–158). Orlando, FL: Academic Press.

Lesgold, A., Lajoie, S., Bunzo, M., & Eggan, G. (1992). SHERLOCK: A coached practice environment for an electronics troubleshooting job. In J. H. Larkin & R. W. Chabay (Eds.), *Computer-assisted instruction and intelligent tutoring systems* (pp. 201–238). Hillsdale, NJ: Erlbaum.

Linnenbrink, E., & Pintrich, P. (2002). The role of motivational beliefs in conceptual change. In M. Limon & L. Mason (Eds.), *Reconsidering conceptual change: Issues in theory and practice* (pp. 115–135). Dordretch: Kluwer Academic Publishers.

Mandler, G. (1976). *Mind and emotion.* New York: Wiley.

Mandler, G. (1984). *Mind and body: Psychology of emotion and stress.* New York: W.W. Norton & Company.

Mandler, G. (1999). Emotion. In B. M. Bly & D. E. Rumelhart (Eds.), *Cognitive science. Handbook of perception and cognition* (2nd ed.). San Diego, CA: Academic Press.

McDaniel, B., D'Mello, S., King, B., Chipman, P., Tapp, K., & Graesser, A. (2007). Facial features for affective state detection in learning environments. In D. McNamara & G. Trafton (Eds.), *Proceedings of the 29th Annual Meeting of the Cognitive Science Society* (pp. 467–472). Austin, TX: Cognitive Science Society.

Meyer, D., & Turner, J. (2006). Re-conceptualizing emotion and motivation to learn in classroom contexts. *Educational Psychology Review, 18*(4), 377–390.

Miserandino, M. (1996). Children who do well in school: Individual differences in perceived competence and autonomy in above-average children. *Journal of Educational Psychology, 88*(2), 203–214.

Moshman, D. (1982). Exogenous, endogenous, and dialectical constructivism. *Developmental Review, 2*(4), 371–384.

Ortony, A., Clore, G., & Collins, A. (1988). *The cognitive structure of emotions.* New York: Cambridge University Press.

Otero, J., & Graesser, A. (2001). PREG: Elements of a model of question asking. *Cognition and Instruction, 19*(2), 143–175.

Patrick, B., Skinner, E., & Connell, J. (1993). What motivates children's behavior and emotion – joint effects of perceived control and autonomy in the academic domain. *Journal of Personality and Social Psychology*, 65(4), 781–791.

Pekrun, R., Elliot, A., & Maier, M. (2006). Achievement goals and discrete achievement emotions: A theoretical model and prospective test. *Journal of Educational Psychology*, 98(3), 583–597.

Piaget, J. (1952). *The origins of intelligence*. New York: International University Press.

Picard, R. (1997). *Affective computing*. Cambridge, MA: MIT Press.

Robison, J., McQuiggan, S., & Lester, J. (2009). *Evaluating the consequences of affective feedback in intelligent tutoring systems*. Paper presented at the International Conference on Affective Computing & Intelligent Interaction, Amsterdam.

Rosenberg, E. (1998). Levels of analysis and the organization of affect. *Review of General Psychology*, 2(3), 247–270.

Rozin, P., & Cohen, A. (2003). High frequency of facial expressions corresponding to confusion, concentration, and worry in an analysis of naturally occurring facial expressions of Americans. *Emotion*, 3, 68–75.

Russell, J. (2003). Core affect and the psychological construction of emotion. *Psychological Review*, 110, 145–172.

Scherer, K. (2003). Vocal communication of emotion: A review of research paradigms. *Speech Communication*, 40(1–2), 227–256.

Scherer, K., Schorr, A., & Johnstone, T. (Eds.). (2001). *Appraisal processes in emotion: Theory, methods, research*. London: London University Press.

Schultz, P., & Pekrun, R. (Eds.). (2007). *Emotion in education*. San Diego, CA: Academic Press.

Schwartz, D., & Bransford, D. (1998). A time for telling. *Cognition and Instruction*, 16(4), 475–522.

Schwarz, N. (2000). Emotion, cognition, and decision making. *Cognition and Emotion*, 14, 433–440.

Schwarz, N., & Skurnik, I. (2003). Feeling and thinking: Implications for problem solving. In J. Davidson & R. Sternberg (Eds.), *The psychology of problem solving* (pp. 263–290). New York: Cambridge University Press.

Sleeman, D., & Brown, J. (Eds.). (1982). *Intelligent tutoring systems*. New York: Academic Press.

Smith, C., & Ellsworth, P. (1985). Patterns of cognitive appraisal in emotion. *Journal of Personality and Social Psychology*, 48(4), 813–838.

Stein, N., Hernandez, M., & Trabasso, T. (2008). Advances in modeling emotions and thought: The importance of developmental, online, and multilevel analysis. In M. Lewis, J. M. Haviland-Jones, & L. F. Barrett (Eds.), *Handbook of emotions* (3rd ed., pp. 574–586). New York: Guilford Press.

Stein, N., & Levine, L. (1991). Making sense out of emotion. In A. O. W. Kessen, & F. Kraik (Eds.), *Memories, thoughts, and emotions: Essays in honor of George Mandler* (pp. 295–322). Hillsdale, NJ: Erlbaum.

Stemmler, G., Heldmann, M., Pauls, C., & Scherer, T. (2001). Constraints for emotion specificity in fear and anger: The context counts. *Psychophysiology*, 38(2), 275–291.

Stipek, D. (1988). *Motivation to learn: From theory to practice*. Boston: Allyn and Bacon.

Tobias, S. (1994). Interest, prior knowledge, and learning. *Review of Educational Research*, 64, 37–54.

VanLehn, K., Graesser, A., Jackson, G., Jordan, P., Olney, A., & Rose, C. P. (2007). When are tutorial dialogues more effective than reading? *Cognitive Science*, 31(1), 3–62.

VanLehn, K., Lynch, C., Schulze, K., Shapiro, J., Shelby, R., Taylor, L., et al. (2005). The Andes physics tutoring system: Five years of evaluations. *International Journal of Artificial Intelligence in Education*, 15, 147–204.

VanLehn, K., Siler, S., Murray, C., Yamauchi, T., & Baggett, W. (2003). Why do only some events cause learning during human tutoring? *Cognition and Instruction*, 21(3), 209–249.

Vygotsky, L. (1978). *Mind in society: The development of higher psychological processes*. Cambridge, MA: Harvard University Press.

Weiner, B. (1986). *An attributional theory of motivation and emotion*. New York: Springer-Verlag.

Woolf, B. (2009). *Building intelligent interactive tutors*. Burlington, MA: Morgan Kaufmann Publishers.

CHAPTER 7

Lifelong Learner Modeling

Judy Kay and Bob Kummerfeld

This chapter explores the potential for improving long-term learning by exploiting the large amounts of data that we can readily collect about learners. We present examples of interfaces to long-term learner models that illustrate both the challenges and potential for them. The challenges include the creation of a suitable technical framework as well as associated interfaces to support a learner in transforming arbitrary collections of learning data into a lifelong learner model. We explain how this can provide new ways to support both the learner and applications in personalizing learning over the long term, taking account of the individual's long-term development.

Lifelong learning deals with the full breadth of learning, be it in a formal classroom or outside (Longworth, 2003), over long periods of time. This contrasts with the current norm for educational technologies, where the learner interacts with many computer-based tools, each operating independently of the others. Each collects its own data about the learner; this means that there are many independent silos of information about the learner and their

learning progress. Commonly, one learning tool holds the data associated with learning a very specific skill, or a single subject, perhaps running over weeks or months. Such silos reduce the possibility for making use of this aggregated data over the long term.

A particularly important aspect of lifelong learning relates to the need to support self-directed learning (Candy, 1991) and learner autonomy (Goodyear, 2000), especially in the case of adult learners. There appears to be a potentially important role for wayfinding systems that can help the learner plan their learning path at each key stage (Tattersall et al., 2005). Personalized learning also has the potential to be important for lifelong learning (Knapper & Cropley, 2000) as does support for collaborative adaptive learning (Klamma et al., 2007), with learner control and choice (Janssen et al., 2007).

This chapter explores the ways that a lifelong learner model can play this role, where we define it as a store for the collection of learning data about an individual learner. To be useful, it must be able to hold many forms of learning data, from diverse sources. It must be able to make that information available in a suitable form to support learning.

Consider the following scenario:

Alice, a forty-year-old pediatrician, has many interests, including playing social netball, primarily to help her keep fit. At one netball training session, the coach recommends NetCoach, a new online training system for netball players. It also provides a smartphone application to help monitor daily exercise and performance.

This scenario illustrates several forms of long-term learner modeling. First, consider Alice's long-term goal for fitness. This is indeed a lifelong goal, with a complex of elements, and it is typical of some of the most important of people's goals, remaining relevant for much of their lives. Alice's long-term model might capture considerable information that is useful for helping her achieve that goal. For example, it could model her knowledge about fitness, about exercises, how to do them correctly, effective training regimes, ways to overcome injuries, and about healthy eating. Success in achieving these is reflected in various measures of health such as weight, blood pressure, strength, cardiac fitness, and performance on physical activities. A system like the hypothetical NetCoach might reuse an existing part of Alice's lifelong learner model. For example, there may be long-term models of her knowledge about fitness and exercise as well as performance data reflecting her changing fitness. This could drive personalization of the coaching. It might also reuse part of her model for past sporting activity and interests.

Whereas a program like NetCoach might reuse parts of her lifelong model, another important role for the model is to support Alice in reflection on her long-term progress and as an aid for her planning new goals. She may also want to be able to share parts of these models with other people, such as her netball coach. In a sense, this would enable the human coach to reuse part of her long-term model. For example, if the coach can see the impact of new learning materials and new training programs on her long-term fitness, this could help the human coach help

Alice devise her plans for improved training and learning. If coaches can aggregate learner models for all the members of all the teams they coach, they can analyze this to improve their understanding of their coaching methods.

A second class of long-term learner model is associated with her knowledge and skills in medicine and pediatrics, from her university days, through the range of her postgraduate specialist education and ongoing training activities and work experience. Alice needs to maintain and develop her expertise as a pediatrician, at the highest level she can. This is representative of an important class of long-term learning, the one required to achieve expertise. It demands long-term, deliberate practice, "a highly structured activity, the explicit goal of which is to improve performance. Specific tasks are invented to overcome weaknesses, and performance is carefully monitored to provide cues for ways to improve it further" (Ericsson et al., 1993, p. 368). A key characteristic of deliberate practice is its long-term nature. This is because it requires "effortful activity that can be sustained only for a limited time each day." So, it takes many days of concerted effort to reach high levels of achievement. Ericsson observed that it requires activity that it is "not inherently motivating." Rather, the learner does it to achieve "improvements in performance." High levels of achievement also appear to require excellent teaching or coaching (Ericsson et al., 2007). This means that Alice should be able to use a diverse set of learning tools. Her lifelong learner model should aggregate model information from these. Then the lifelong learner model can allow many different learning tools to reuse parts of the model. At the same time, if there are suitable interfaces to the right parts of the learner model, they can help Alice reflect on her long-term learning and plan.

The next section establishes a foundation for the new challenges for lifelong learner modeling. It identifies new roles that the lifelong learner model can fulfill and, for each of these, it explores the technical challenges still be be addressed. The following

Table 7.1. Roles for the Lifelong Learner Model and Technical Challenges

Role of Learner Model	Technical Challenges
1. *Open learning modeling (OLM)*	user interfaces for reection and planning, attention, forgetting
2. *Aggregation* of information about the learner from diverse sources	middleware infrastructure for aggregation, user interfaces to control aggregation, ontologies
3. *Sharing* the learner model with people	user interfaces, particularly for privacy management, middleware infrastructure for control of privacy and security, ontologies
4. *Interpretation* of learner information	user interfaces, new tools for different interpretations
5. *Reuse* by different applications for the learner's personal use	user interfaces, middleware infrastructure for controlling release of parts of the model and active delivery of parts; ontologies, standards
6. *Institutional use* of long term learning data from many learners	user interfaces, middleware infrastructure associated with both sharing and reuse of the model, ontologies, standards

two sections present selected examples of our explorations of two of the most important of these. We conclude with a discussion of the particular challenges for lifelong learner modeling.

Roles for Lifelong Learner Models and Technical Challenges

The motivation for lifelong learner modeling is to address important learning needs that are currently unmet. We now identify and discuss these new key roles for the lifelong model. They are summarized in the left column of Table 7.1. In the scenario of the last section, we introduced examples of these. The right column lists the key new technical challenges associated with each goal. Some technical issues are important for multiple roles: User interfaces appear against each role, although the associated demands on them differ; middleware infrastructure also appears for most roles, but with different aspects required for different roles; ontologies and standards are important for all sharing and reuse as well as some forms of aggregation.

Before we discuss each of the roles, we present an architectural overview of the middleware infrastructure and its relationship to many applications that might play a role in supporting a user's long-term learning. This presents a high level overview of

an infrastructure we have created (Kay and Kummerfeld, 2010) based upon a user model server (Assad et al., 2007) but providing additional facilities which we now describe.

Table 7.1 shows the lifelong learner model, with its associated middleware at the bottom. Although the figure shows the model as a single large block, the infrastructure should support distributed models; for example, a user may prefer that particularly sensitive information be kept only on their home computer. This might require the infrastructure to support disconnected operation, gracefully dealing with the situation where a computer is temporarily unavailable, for example when the user's home machine has been turned off. Our Personis (Assad et al., 2007) provides this support for modeling.

However, the lifelong learner model requires much more than this. Consider first the case where the user interacts with an application that provides personalized teaching, such as the Anatomy Tutor, which Alice from our scenario may have used for several semesters of her university studies. This is shown in the center of the figure, with two-way interaction between the user and the Anatomy Tutor. There is also two-way interaction with model, as the

Anatomy Tutor stores its information about the learner in the model, based on recent interactions, and retrieves information

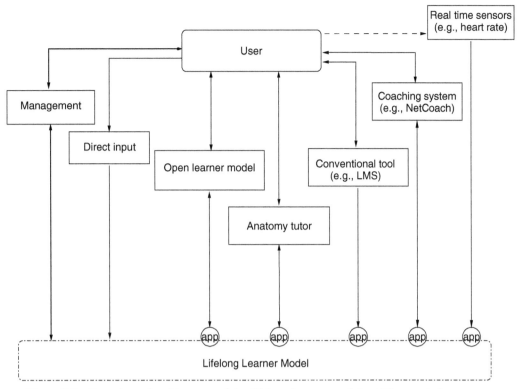

Figure 7.1. Overview of architecture of the lifelong learner model middleware infrastructure.

about the learner, where some of this information might have been contributed by other applications. Note that the figure shows an app – a small glue code application – that manages the actual interaction between the lifelong learner model and the Anatomy Tutor.

Next along to the right, the figure shows a more conventional tool, such as a learner management system (LMS). In this case, we show that the information from the LMS might be harvested into the lifelong learner model. This would be managed by an app that makes use of a standard interface (API) to the LMS. Because current conventional tools cannot yet make use of the lifelong learner model, we show only one-way transfer of information into the model. Next to the right, the figure shows a class of tool that the user interacts with over long periods of time, like the NetCoach of our scenario. This has two-way interaction with the lifelong learner model. It also exploits an emerging class of learner modeling information; this comes from real-time sensors that

automatically capture information about the user. For example, there are already many inexpensive devices that can unobtrusively capture data about exercise, including GPS-based tracking of running and heart rate measures (for example, Garmin watches, http://www.garmin.com/) and weight (for example, http://www.withings.com/). These can send their data wirelessly to a Web-based service. In this case, the app must interact with that service to harvest the learner's data and aggregate it into the lifelong learner model. In the figure, we show a dotted line from the learner to the sensors, because the user does not explicitly interact with it.

In all the cases discussed to this point, the learner has no direct interaction with the learner model. These are important, representing existing as well as emerging learning technology. We now consider three important classes of applications that require the learner to interact directly with the lifelong learner model. These are shown in the upper left quadrant of the figure. We begin with the one with a direct learning role because it provides an interface that enables the learner to view their model. This is coming to be called an open learner model (OLM). We discuss this important class below.

To this point, we have glossed over an important issue: the control over the apps that can interact with the lifelong learner model. Given the personal nature of the information within the lifelong learner model, we consider it essential to give the learner effective ways to control this and other aspects of the model. The management interface is a critical part of the lifelong learner model because it enables the learner to control which apps may interact with the model, thus controlling which classes of information can be aggregated into the learner model and which applications may use and reuse the model.

The final class of tool shown is direct user input, which enables the learner to add information directly to the model. For example, in our scenario, Alice might use this to inform the model of her fitness goals, such as her goal weight, running speed, rate of training, and so forth.

Support Reflection on Progress and Planning to Achieve Long-Term Goals

As learners strive to achieve long-term learning goals, the lifelong learner model could play an important role in helping them monitor their progress and actively plan their future learning. This has been the focus of open learner modeling (OLM) research (Bull & Kay, 2007). Table 7.1 shows three associated technical challenges.

First is the need for effective interfaces such as those from research in Learner Modeling for Reflection (LeMoRe [http://www.eee.bham.ac.uk/bull/lemore]). This has explored many approaches to presenting learner models and supporting interaction with them. For example, Bull et al. (2007b) conducted eye-tracking studies with six different views of learner models. Students were reported to make extensive use of their OLMs, particularly exploring their misconceptions (Bull & Mabbott, 2006; Bull et al., 2008). Careful evaluations of OLMs

have demonstrated important benefits. For example, in the SQL-Tutor, the OLM led to learning gains for weaker students and was generally appreciated by the class as a whole (Mitrovic & Martin, 2007).

There has been little exploration of how to help learners see what deserves their attention in the long term. In many cases, the most recent modeling information may be the most useful. However, other parts may be valuable. For example, suppose that a learner studied a single example repeatedly. An episodic learner model (Weber & Brusilovsky, 2001), which represents the importance of this example for the learner, could ensure it is used as appropriate, even years later, by different teaching systems. Perhaps heavy use of a learning element, in a particular context, might make it stickier, a focus point in the long-term learner model for that context. Another approach, inspired by human episodic memory (Craik & Tulving, 2004), suggests the value of a learner model representation for semantic connections to a particular concept in the model: Rich connections may indicate importance within a particular context. The user's own explicit input seems important, especially if this can be elegantly integrated into the learning environment. For example, a suitable interface might make it easy for learners to mark examples they find most useful, perhaps tagging them with concepts that it helps illustrate or recall.

Now consider the third issue: forgetting, both by the learner and the model. For the learner, we must account for cases where the modeling information is old, for example where there is an accurate model of the user's mathematics knowledge at high school and they are now fifty years old. One way to address this is to create mechanisms for the OLM to interpret old parts of the model appropriately. We will return to this later in the chapter.

From the system's perspective, should it forget very old modeling information, dating back many years? With low-cost storage, it is easy to simply keep all the information in case it one day turns out to be useful. But bloated models with information that is never used may cause problems, particularly for privacy. It may also pose serious problems for scalability. This applies at the system level, as reasoning based on the model may become slow as the learner model grows. It may also become harder to create effective interfaces because these may need to make the model understandable even as it grows larger. So the issue of forgetting may be important for creating effective OLM interfaces. Others have made similar arguments for the value of forgetting for humans (Bannon, 2006; Dodge & Kitchin, 2007).

One intriguing but promising approach is to use a model of cognitive development, perhaps from theories of developmental psychology. More mundanely, but perhaps pragmatically, it might base a useful model on formal syllabus materials (which we might expect to have foundations in best practice, based on educational psychological theory). We have been exploring the latter, creating a pragmatics ontology for generic skills and their different levels, then using this to describe university subjects, so that we can then create curriculum maps for complex university degree programs (Gluga et al., 2010). Our ontology design particularly aimed to support those responsible for the overall curricula to track how well each degree meets institutional goals as well as accreditation requirements. This required an ontology that represents development levels for generic skills. The subsequent models serve as a foundation for an individual learner model (Gluga, 2010) because they define a structure for the model, within the context of the university degree. To populate the individual model, we propose to draw on the learner's results in class assessments as well as other direct input from the learner and formative feedback from teachers. One can envisage similar ontologies and models associated with school curricula. One important benefit of this approach, which links the learner model ontology to developmental models, is the foundation it gives for interpreting older parts of the model. For example, it may be feasible to make interpretations such as "she was an excellent reader for a first grader."

Aggregation Point for the Information for the Learner

This is one of the key new roles that the lifelong learner model takes, as a long-term repository of information about the learner, drawn from a range of sources. To achieve this, one of the key technical challenges is to provide a middleware infrastructure such as the one we have created, as described in Figure 7.1. As discussed earlier, this provides a management interface that enables a learner to control which sources of information should be incorporated into the model. Essentially, this has two parts: selecting and activating the right aggregator app; and linking it to the right part of the model. For example, suppose that Alice (from our scenario) took a course in anatomy, using both a learner management system and the Anatomy Tutor. If these are open, in the sense that there is an API that enables programmers to access their data, our approach requires an aggregation application for each of these sources. Each accesses Alice's data, adding it to her lifelong learner model.

To link a new source of data to the model, it will often be necessary to deal with two different ontologies, or schemas: one from the data sources and the other from the learner model. There has been considerable research on automated approaches for such harmonization. These are particularly important where there is no user in the loop. In the case of the lifelong learner model, the learner may be able to play a role also, if needed. They may also want to have control over this aspect of their model.

Consider an example of learning a complex skill, such as programming. One aspect is knowledge of loops. The term "loops" has an agreed meaning, and it is easy to map this to other synonyms, such as repetition and iteration. This can be automated. By contrast, for the case of Alice's long-term fitness goals, Alice may choose what she considers important as fitness goals and how the various data available should be associated with them. So the system should allow her to establish her model to match her conceptualization of this part of the model.

Sharing the Learner Model with People

With the lifelong learner modeling holding an aggregation of useful information about the learner, it becomes critical that the learner be able to manage its use. This is the complex matter of privacy, and the associated matter of release of information so that it can be useful (Palen & Dourish, 2003). As indicated in the table, the challenge is to create interfaces that can make it easy for the learner to achieve this. A suitable underlying representation and a focus on simplifying the learner model are likely to facilitate the creation of such interfaces.

There has been some exploration of the interfaces for OLMs that enable a learner to control sharing of their model (Bull et al., 2007a). A lab-based evaluation study indicated that there were students who wanted to view the models of their peers and, reciprocally, there were enough students willing to share their models to make this facility useful. To support flexible sharing of arbitrary parts of the lifelong learner model, a key challenge will be the creation of effective user interfaces for the learner to do this safely and easily.

There are other cases where it would be valuable to provide OLM interfaces that share the learner's model with others. For example, for a child, it may be valuable to create one application to present the model to the child and another to the child's parents. Lee and Bull (2008) explored just this, so that parents could help their child with math homework. Similarly, Zapata-Rivera et al. (2007) explored a specialized interface for parents for standardized test results, with personalized explanations of the information.

Interpretation of Learner Information

The lifelong learner model should support a flexible range of interpretations of parts of the model. For example, continuing the example of modeling the learner's knowledge of loops, consider the definition of when a learner knows loops. In a teaching system within a first programming course, it may be reasonable to judge a user as knowing loops if they can read and write simple code in one language (Lister et al., 2004). For a higher-level student, one would expect far more, such as the ability to read and write more complex loop code, in more languages, more quickly, and with fewer errors. For example, Joel Spolsky, a well-known commentator on software and programmers, notes the value of testing potential employees on very straightforward tasks and observing if the person can solve them very quickly and easily, reflecting significant overlearning for that level of knowledge and skill (Spolsky, 2006).

There is no simple and sound basis for defining when something is well enough known. For the case of the individual learner, competency assessments or mastery standards may be useful. The more usual approach in classroom contexts is to provide the learner with comparisons of their own performance against a suitable peer group. For well-calibrated tests, the peer group may be based on age or educational level. More commonly, it is simply the comparison against the students enrolled in the same subject. For long-term models, this may be of decaying usefulness. This is especially true if the student has barely grasped the ideas but was able to demonstrate them adequately on the particular day of an assessment, or with assistance in a classroom or homework setting.

Consider another example of the need for flexible interpretations of the lifelong learner model. If the user returns to the teaching system after several months, or years, how should the old learner model be interpreted? Perhaps older evidence for learning should be treated as less reliable? This, too, depends on whether the learner really mastered the knowledge in the first place, whether there have been practice possibilities, whether it linked to later learning in some way, and the nature of the knowledge.

A somewhat different class of flexibility in interpretation is linked to privacy. Learners may be happy for a very complete model to be available to some people, but for others, they may want to restrict some classes of evidence about their learning. This could be achieved via filters on the evidence, perhaps in combination with specialized interpretations of it.

Reuse by Different Applications

Reuse is one of the major potential benefits of the lifelong learner model. Because multiple programs need to be able to use and reuse parts of the model, each must be able to interpret the model appropriately. Table 7.1 shows three technical challenges.

The user interface challenge relates to providing user control of the reuse of the model. In the discussion of Figure 7.1, we showed that the middleware infrastructure should support this, via the control interfaces so that the user can decide which apps to link to which parts of the model. As illustrated in Figure 7.1, some of these will enable applications to interact with the lifelong learner model to support learning. In the figure, this was the case for the Anatomy Tutor's use of the learner model.

The second challenge shown in Table 7.1 relates to the tasks for the middleware. It must ensure security and manage access to the model, so that the user's privacy requirements are met. The table also shows that active delivery of parts of the model may be needed. For example, an active learner model in conjunction with a fitness application could alert the learner automatically, for example prompting them to do exercise to meet the goals that they had set themselves.

We now consider the third technical challenge of interoperability between application and the lifelong learner model. If an application is to reuse parts of the model that were created by other applications, there needs to be a common ontology or schema for that part of the model or a mechanism for mapping between different schemas. There is also the need to take account of potentially different standards and ways to interpret the value of parts of the model. For example, a teaching system for senior programming students could reuse the model from the earlier stages.

But it would need to "understand" several aspects beyond the semantics of loops: It should take account of the time since the student learned about them, the source of the evidence about their knowledge, and then it would need to interpret these. For some aspects, there may be established competency standards.

Of course, it may turn out that it is simpler not to keep most learning data. Currently, if there is a need to determine what the learner knows, they could be asked to do a test. It will be important to determine what classes of learner-modeling information are better addressed in this way. It seems likely that the long-term learner model will be of real value for the very long-term goals, such as Alice's fitness. It may also be most useful where there are services that act automatically to help the learner achieve these goals.

Institutional Use of Aggregated Long-Term Learning Data

This important possibility for long-term learner models could provide new insights about education, within an institution, or more broadly, based on data mining the long-term learner model. This is a goal for the rather new field of educational data mining, EDM (for an overview, see Romero & Ventura, 2007). There is potential value in mining individual learner models – for example, sequence mining to identify interesting and important patterns of behavior. From the learner's perspective, these might require the learner to authorize applications to use their model. The results of the data mining could be made available to the learner, either by adding them to their model or via applications for viewing the learner model.

In terms of the way that a large organization operates, there is potential for better recognition and exploitation of the knowledge and skills of each person within the organization. Notably, it might help reduce inefficiencies due to the failure to take account of a person's knowledge when they need to undertake new training.

As shown in Table 7.1, there are several technical challenges that need to be addressed if organizations are to make better use of long-term learner models. First is the need for effective interfaces to the models, enabling effective views of the right information while ensuring appropriate respect for individual privacy. There is a need for middleware infrastructure that makes it easy to aggregate the learner model information and to access it as needed, in the form needed. As in many other roles, ontologies and standards have the potential to play an important role in effective management of the user models and reasoning about them. Importantly, these technical elements need to fit seamlessly into the organizational structures – a significant challenge in the large organizations that might potentially gain so much from improved understanding of staff learner models.

In summary, across the range of roles, two the recurring technical challenges relate to user interfaces and the challenges of ontologies. These are the focus of the examples we present in the next sections.

Interfaces to Learner Models

In the scenario presented earlier in the chapter, there were several cases where Alice needed to reflect on her learning progress, by viewing her learner model. In general, there are many hidden learner models within computer systems. In the case of conventional e-learning systems, there is often considerable data about the learner's activity when interacting with the system. Much of this is unused, although it has the potential to contribute to a learner model. Within typical LMSs (e.g., Moodle, Sakai, Blackboard), some information is made available to the learner. (For example, results of assessments are usually available, often with an indication of performance of the rest of the class.) The teacher typically has access to far more detailed information about student activity on the system. In this case, there is some limited use of learner data via the system interfaces and there is

support to export data, such as marks. In addition, more recent versions of LMSs such as Moodle, enable the teacher to associate parts of the site with their subject's learning goals. This is a first step in making current Web-log data, as well as assessment results, ready to be built into a learner model. There has been some work to create useful visualizations of such data, particularly for teachers to track the class and individual activity and progress (e.g., Mazza & Dimitrova, 2007). At the other end of the spectrum, intelligent tutoring systems, with rich learner models, typically keep them completely hidden from the learner, deep within the system.

An OLM aims to exploit the learner model to serve several potential goals, including supporting reflection, planning, and maintaining a sense of control and responsibility (Bull & Kay, 2007).

The remainder of this section discusses two examples of OLM, each representing one important class of research. The first tackles the challenge of large user models, for use over long periods of time for a large learning corpus. The second explores the role of an OLM within a group context. In this case, learning goals include group work skills. These are representative of important generic skills, being particularly highly valued in the workplace. Importantly, such skills can only be developed over several years.

Viewing Large Learner Models

We now describe our work toward interfaces onto large learner models. The initial motivation for this work came from the medical program at Sydney University. This was a four-year graduate program, using problem-based learning (PBL), where students worked in groups on one new problem each week. For each problem, students were presented information about a patient, often spread through the week. They needed to learn enough to conclude what to do in terms of diagnosis, additional tests, and treatment. Importantly, over the course of the program, students needed to learn the essential foundations that were tested in a critical exam at the end of the second year.

The nature of PBL means that students learned many things as they tackled each problem. However, as each problem was designed with particular goals, students needed to check they had learned these. In addition, because many areas of learning interact, students needed to revisit topics, reviewing the links with things learned more recently. It was quite challenging for students to be confident they were making adequate progress. This was partly because there was just so much to learn. As an aid, the students had access to a large database of multiple-choice questions that covered the syllabus and were in a similar format to their actual exams. It had more than 600 learning topics, each with 10 questions. Even with this, it was hard for students to see their progress over the two years of its use.

This situation motivated our exploration of OLM interfaces that could help with this class of problem, involving a large learning corpus, over long periods of time. We created learner models based on evidence from the student's performance on the multiple-choice questions. Then we needed an interface that could open these learner models, enabling students to see how well they were doing and to plan their study to fill gaps. The resulting visualization interface was VLUM (Uther & Kay, 2003) for viewing very large user models. In the first work on VLUM, the model was structured in a graph, created to have suitable levels of fan-out for effective visualization, and based on similarity of the concepts. In later work, we used online dictionary sources to automatically generate the graph based on an ontology for the domain (Apted et al., 2003), with relationships such as synonym, is-a, and is-related. In the case of is-a and synonym relationships, these support inference about the model, most importantly across granularity levels.

We now explain the particular demands for a visualization of this type of large user model and the ways that VLUM addressed them. First, like any visualization of large amounts of information, interfaces to large user models should support the key facilities:

overview first, zoom and filter, then details on demand (Schneiderman, 1996). VLUM achieves an overview with an animated visualization designed to give a quick overview of progress. It enables the student to focus on particular parts of the model (zoom). The user can control the standard required for success (filter). VLUM enables the learner to see the reason for the learner model conclusion, by providing a link to the actual questions and the student's answers (details on demand). In addition, because the learner model is based on reasoning that must take account of correct and incorrect answers, VLUM indicated the certainty of this inference about the level of learning the student has achieved.

An example screen is shown in Figure 7.2. It displays all learning topics at once. Note that on the actual screen, it exploits every pixel, and so it is harder to appreciate in print. The overall appearance, even on the screen, has much of the text very cluttered and not readable. However, the user can see the overall dominant color, and our studies demonstrate that users can also readily see extreme outliers in their model. The reduced-size printed versions of the dynamic VLUM interface are difficult to appreciate. We conducted detailed evaluations of VLUM (Uther, 2002). To be able to run these with a very wide range of participants, we did not use the medical domain learner model. Instead, we created a model of movie preferences, a subject readily understood by most adults. We randomly allocated participants into four groups. The first group saw VLUM displays for 100 concepts; the other groups worked with 300, 500, and 700 concepts each. Participants worked through a short online tutorial introduction and then answered questions requiring them to find concepts strongly liked, strongly disliked, with high or low certainty, and the use of different standards. We measured the correctness of answers as well as the speed (although participants were not told to work quickly). Results indicated that VLUM provides an effective way to scrutinize a large user model, with up to 700 modeled concepts. We now return to the description of

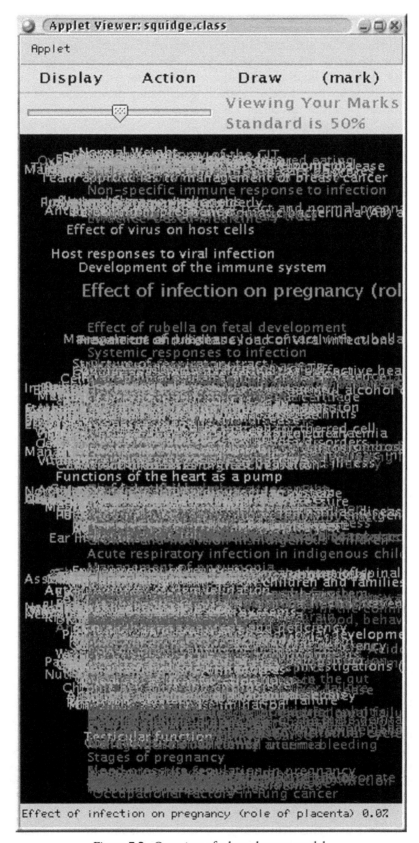

Figure 7.2. Overview of a large learner model.

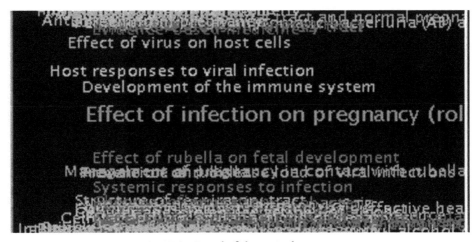

Figure 7.3. Detail of the preceding screen.

its interface, making use of the full screen shown in Figure 7.2 and an enlarged part of it, close to the actual size on the screen, and easier to see in print (Figure 7.3).

If the learner is modeled as knowing a topic, it appears in green, with brighter green for better-known topics. Similarly, if a topic is modeled as not known, it appears in red. At a glance, the user can see an overview of their learning progress. If the display is largely green, as in Figure 7.2, it is easy to see that this learner is modeled as knowing most of the topics. It is also easy to see when there are just a few topics in red, as in the case of the topic "Effect of infection on pregnancy (role of the placenta)," which appears about a fifth of the way down from the top of the screen. Figure 7.3 shows this part of the screen closer to the size in the actual interface.

In VLUM, the display always has one focus topic. This is presented in a larger font and with more space around it than any other topic. VLUM maintains a structure over the learner model, representing which concepts are most closely related to each other. The topics closest to the focus topic are presented in smaller font (and with less space around them) than the focus, but larger than others. This approach has the effect of making the focus topic and those most closely related to it the most visible. At any stage, the learner can click on any concept to make it the focus. The Action

label at the top of the display offers a search, enabling the learner to explore parts of the model they cannot immediately see on the display.

In Figure 7.2, the focus topic is "Effect of infection on pregnancy (role of the placenta)" and it is bright red, indicating lack of knowledge. At the bottom of the display, VLUM shows more details for the topic under the user's mouse, in this case the focus concept. This shows the actual assessed knowledge level (0.07). This makes it easy for a learner to slide the mouse down the display, watching this to see the values of interest. On seeing one, the user can click it to make it the focus.

The learner model makes conclusions about the learner's knowledge of a topic, on a gradient. This can be quantized for presentation in VLUM, for example on a five-, seven-, or more-step scale, from very well known (bright green) down to unknown (bright red). Any such conclusion is uncertain for several reasons: learners may have done very few questions on a topic; they may have made a slip; they may have made a correct guess; they may have done many questions on a topic, some correctly and others not. An important design goal for VLUM was to enable the learner to easily see how certain the learning assessment was.

VLUM shows the certainty using horizontal position. So, for example, a score based on multiple consistently correct answers would appear in bright green at the left. In Figure 7.3, we see that "Effect of infection on pregnancy (role of the placenta)" is further right than "Host responses to viral infection," because the learner model has higher certainty for the latter. If the student has mixed results on questions done for a topic, with some questions for a topic correct and some wrong, VLUM displays this as yellow. So, for example, in Figure 7.3, the topic "Effect of rubella on detail development" is to the right because there is no evidence about it, and it is yellow, indicating that the model treats this as neither a known or unknown topic. Evaluations indicated that users were able to learn and use this information readily (Uther, 2002).

In Figure 7.4, we illustrate the effect of two learner actions. First, they clicked on "Effect of virus on host cells" in Figure 7.2. This is related to "Effect of infection on pregnancy (role of the placenta)," the focus in Figure 7.2. So now, "Effect of virus on host cells" is the focus topic and in the largest font with most space, whereas the former focus is smaller but still visible. In terms of font and space, the two topics have swapped.

The second change is to the standard that the learner wants to set for themselves. In Figure 7.2 and the enlarged part of it in Figure 7.3, VLUM has the standard set at 50 percent. In Figure 7.4, the learner has adjusted this to 10 percent, using the slider just above the actual display of the model. This makes the model greener, with many more topics becoming green and light-green ones becoming brighter green. Also, the formerly bright-red "Effect of infection on pregnancy (role of the placenta)" has become a less-saturated-red (pink). This adjustment to the standard is particularly useful for quickly seeing the least-known topics as very few remain red. Similarly, the user could alter the standard to 90 percent. This makes more topics become red, or brighter red and fewer green. If the learner knew only a few topics, they would be the only green ones and would be easier to see. Of course, another reason the learner may raise the standard is that they may have a high personal standard, especially in the later period of their studies when they aim to do well on most topics. In that case, this display gives an overview of how much of the model is below their standard. In addition, the brightest-red topics are the ones they should consider first in planning their study.

Figure 7.5 shows another example, where the focus is "Structure of heart and great vessels." In this case, various topics related to heart disease are the most visible. Note that VLUM can be configured to use the vertical dimension in a manner that meets particular learning contexts. For example, if the topics have time stamps, provided by the teacher, reflecting when the topic was first encountered in the two years, this vertical dimension may be useful for the students as they may recall the approximate time that they first studied it. Such time-based landmarks have been useful in other contexts (Ringel et al., 2003). This seems a particularly useful approach for visualizing long-term learner models.

VLUM was designed to be at the left of a browser, so that the right of the screen could be used for additional information. For example, we have set it up so that when a learner selects the focus topic, they can see a list of the questions associated with it at the right. In this mode, the VLUM visualisation of the learner model can be used to choose the questions to do. In another mode, the right screen presented a list of links to the learning resources for this topic. In this case, the visualisation can be used as a navigation tool around the large collection of learning resources available for the course.

Long-Term Group Interaction Models

We now turn to a very different example of an open learner model. This was designed to support groups of learners who work over a semester in a team project. We used variants of this form of open learner model in two contexts: a capstone software development project course where students write a substantial piece of software for an authentic client (Upton and Kay, 2009);

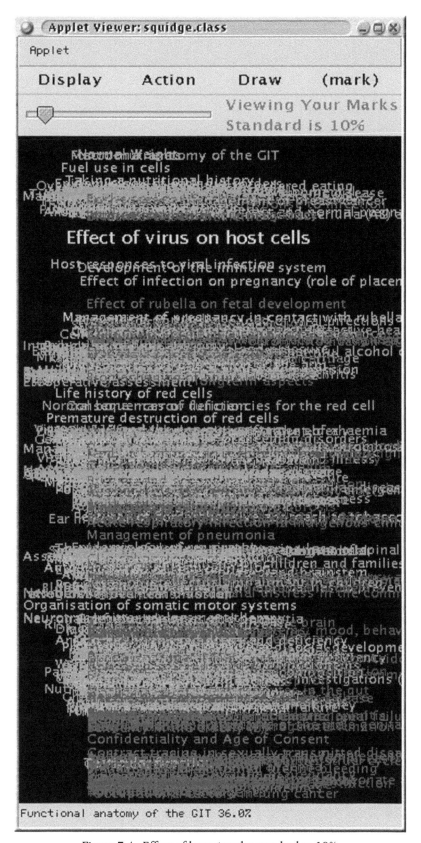

Figure 7.4. Effect of lowering the standard to 10%.

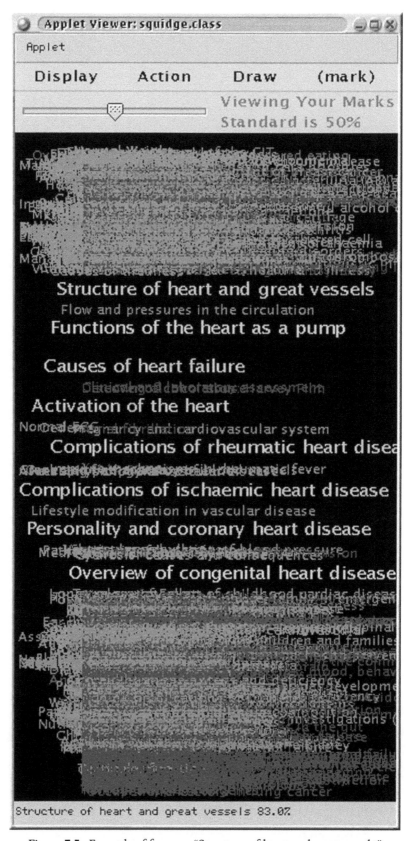

Figure 7.5. Example of focus on "Structure of heart and great vessels."

154

and a postgraduate education subject where students collaboratively write reports (Kay et al., 2006, 2007).

The goal of this work was to exploit the electronic traces of the learner's activity in a conventional tool to build a simple model that would support learning. In our case, our students used trac (http://trac.edgewall.org/), an open-source tool that provides a set of tightly integrated media to support a group project. It was originally designed for teams of programmers. Its basic form provides three media. One helps the team define the tasks that members need to do; each task description (called a ticket) is associated with a higher-level milestone. So, for example, suppose a team needs to find literature related to their project and submit a report summarizing it by a set date. They would define a milestone for this report, due at that date, and then the team members would identify the many tasks to be split among them, creating a ticket for each, allocating these across the team. The second medium is a wiki, useful for collaborative editing of documents, such as reports, meeting minutes, and resources. The third medium, supported by a helpful interface, is a version-controlled repository. (This was not used in the education subject.) Importantly, it is easy to create links between any of these media. So, for example, a ticket description can include a link to the relevant part of the wiki and repository.

As team members use such a tool over many months, their activity can be used to create a learner model. In this sense, it is representative of a large class of widely used online tools. If we can transform such logs of activity into a meaningful learner model, this has the potential to support long-term learning. The most obvious role for such as model is to provide better help and coaching about that tool for the learner – for example, in basic tools such as a word processor (Kay & Thomas, 1995; Linton & Schaefer, 2000).

We created models from trac activity for each group and created a trac plug-in visualization. An example is shown in Figure 7.6. This is for a real group of five students, but has been anonymized. The vertical axis is time, the bottom being the beginning of the time displayed, with one cell for each day. Each of the five blocks represents one student's model. As the legend indicates, the leftmost part of this, in purple, represents wiki activity, the next, in blue, is activity on the svn repository, and the third, in green, shows ticket activity. The intensity of the color indicates the level of activity. (Students can customize the thresholds for the levels.) So, for example, the leftmost student, member1, had quite high levels of activity on all three media on the first day. However, on the last day shown, they had no activity at all, indicated by the grey cells for all three media. Clicking on one of the cells displays the details of the activity on that medium on that day. In the figure, one can see a hand where the user clicked on the svn model for member2. The details appear as the five lines on the right, each to one changeset; clicking on the blue number within any of these presents the precise details of the corresponding changes in the repository.

Below each student's daily details is a summary histogram. This has a grey bar for the group average and a colored one for the individual's activity level. So, a student who does less than the average has a grey bar poking out from their own level. A student who is doing more than average has a pleasing, purer-colored bar visible beyond the grey-backed part. So, for example, member1 had wiki activity similar to the average, but was above average on the other two media.

This visualization has proved particularly useful for meetings between the group facilitator and the students in the group. The students are asked to explain why some members are more active on different media at different times. They are asked to link this to the allocated roles of each student. Narcissus, and its predecessor, enabled teachers to see group problems early enough to help the students improve the function of the group. It also supported the mentor in working with students as they tried to remedy problems in the group management and operation.

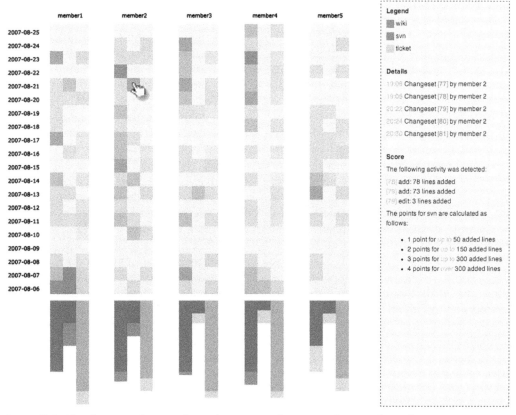

Figure 7.6. Visualization of activity by each team member across three media: wiki, version repository, and tickets defining tasks to be done.

An important goal for this work was to exploit the electronic traces from the activity of team members to create a form of learner model that would enable each member of the team to see their own activity, as a whole, and in relation to other team members. An unintended but valuable side-effect is that the visualization of the learner activity model also serves as a new way to navigate around a very complex information space composed of many-versioned wiki pages, many version-controlled files and tickets.

Our experience indicates that it is quite important that a facilitator helps groups in reviewing the Narcissus models. We briefly considered the possibility of creating a mechanism for sending automated advice; but we rejected this as infeasible. This is partly due

to the complexity of the tasks undertaken by the groups, in building a substantial piece of software over a full semester. It also follows from the fact that each project is different, as each group has their own, real client. This situation would be even worse for general use of a tool like Narcissus, in conjunction with any of the range of group projects that trac is typically used for.

Perhaps even more important is that the actual nature of the ideal contribution is very difficult to formulate. For example, the team leader has very different roles from the person whose main role is as a programmer or a tester. Importantly, groups were asked to write a team contract and as this was under their own control, the ideal behavior should be defined by that. These aspects mitigate against the possibility of a specialized advisory tool. So we opted for the mirroring end of the spectrum that runs from mirroring, to metacognitive tools, to guiding (Soller, 2005). We have explored use of data mining to identify patterns associated with effective performance of a particular role and did find quite promising ones for distinguishing whether the leader is performing that role effectively (Perera et al., 2008). Certainly, our experience is consistent with that of Jermann and Dillenbourg (2008) in the need for supporting learners in judging the appropriateness of the contribution levels of each member of the group.

Ontologies for Lifelong Learner Modeling

This is the second recurring technical challenge of long-term modeling. It is key for aggregation of information from diverse sources and for reuse of the learner model by different applications. A learner model must be defined in terms of an ontology, and the particular challenge for the lifelong learner model is that it must be able to make use of information about the learner where that is framed in terms of the ontologies of the sources. So, for example, if the learner makes use of five different math-teaching systems, the lifelong learner model must be able operate in terms of the ontologies or schemas of each of these. There is a huge body of research on ontologies and the harmonization of different ontologies. In this section, we illustrate a lightweight, highly flexible approach to these problems.

Ontologies Built from Specialized Glossaries and Dictionaries

The work we now describe was motivated by several potential benefits that an ontology could provide, even for short-term learner modeling within a single application. Although we had not considered long-term learner modeling at that time, our motivations and approach turn out to be useful for it, as we now discuss.

One valuable role for an ontology is to provide a structure over a learner model so that it can be presented more effectively in an OLM. For the case of VLUM, we wanted this to structure the graph so that it would present the concepts most closely related to the focus concept. In this case, we need an ontology with the right fan-out from each concept, so that there are neither too few nor too many concepts that were modeled as closely related to any focus.

The enhanced version of VLUM was called Scrutable Inference Viewer (SIV) (Kay & Lum, 2005), its name reflecting another important role for an ontology in supporting inference about the learner model. In particular, we found that it was natural to tag each small learning task with very-fine-grained concepts. For example, consider the case of an exercise designed to help students learn about pointers for string manipulation in C. It is natural to tag this task with this fine-grained concept from the ontology. However, this is part of the coarser-grained, broader topic, pointers in C. Suppose a student wants to know how they are doing on this broader topic, but all the data sources for the learner model are for the finer-grained parts of the model. Then, an ontology could support reasoning that would enable a system to model at both fine and coarse grain. Similarly, when students undertake a large assignment that involves many elements of the course, this must be coded at a coarse grain. An ontology can support (uncertain) reasoning about the learner's finer-grained knowledge. Such inference can be valuable for the task of building comprehensive learner models and for presenting them as OLMs.

We created a flexible mechanism for building ontologies for learner modeling. Importantly, we automated the process of building a basic ontology and also enabled teachers to readily augment the ontology with their own concepts. For example, in a subject on the C programming language and unix, we introduced the notion of Core Material, which included all the concepts required to earn a bare pass. In the context of this subject, which many students

Subject Glossary

SOFT2130

Category/Concept Name	Category/Concept Description
Core	The essential concepts that students must learn to pass SOFT2130. These are *Similar concepts in both C and Java*, *Pointers*, *Pointers with Strings*, *Pointers with Arrays* and *Dynamic Data Structures*
Core/Similar concepts in both C and Java	Similar ideas shared between C and Java
Control Flow	All the elements of the programming language that affect the order of execution of the statement in a program. For both Java and C, these are the selections structures, if, if-else and switch, the looping or iteration structures, for, while and do-while as well as the basic default flow means that statements are executed in the order they appear on the page.
Function Arguments	A value or reference passed to a function or procedure or subroutine or command or program by the caller.
Arrays	A collection or identically typed data items distinguished by their indices. The number of dimensions and array depends on the language but is usually unlimited.
Scope	The scope of an identifier is the region of a program source within which it represents a certain thing. For both C and Java, the basic scope rules are much the same. One of the important things that you will learn in this course is about the runtime storage of data: once you understand this, you will appreciate why scope operates as it does. So, for example, you will realize why the code in one function cannot access data that is declared within another.

Figure 7.7. Subject glossary used to create lightweight ontology.

found difficult but were required to pass, the teacher wanted struggling students to be easily able to determine where to focus.

The learner model was populated with evidence from an online learning system that provided many small learning activities for C programming. All were tagged with fine-grained concepts from the course ontology. Yet, the SIV OLM could use the ontology to infer the learner's progress at the high level. The coarse-grained concept Core Material has child concepts (specialization and part-of) that include about two-thirds of all modeled concepts. The visualization of the Core Material gives the learner an indication of their knowledge at that level, even though there is no direct evidence about learning at this coarse-grain level. SIV infers the value for this part of the model, based on the learner's performance on the full hierarchy of concepts for that part of the subject. In principle, SIV could make use of any ontology and we used it

with several, for teaching different aspects of programming and user interface design (Lum, 2007).

Whereas there are established approaches to building ontologies and many existing ontologies (Noy & McGuinness, 2001), these are based on widely accepted formal approaches. They lack key properties that we wanted. First, we wanted the ontology to be easily extensible by the teacher of a subject. As we have noted, this was important for concepts that were important to the teacher, but not the general area of knowledge. This was the case for the term "Core Material," as discussed earlier. This concept served an important purpose for this subject and it was just this type of concept that we wanted teachers to be able to add to the learner model ontology. This is a problem if one uses formal ontologies because they are not readily understood or managed by a classroom teacher. A second reason for rejecting widespread formal approaches was

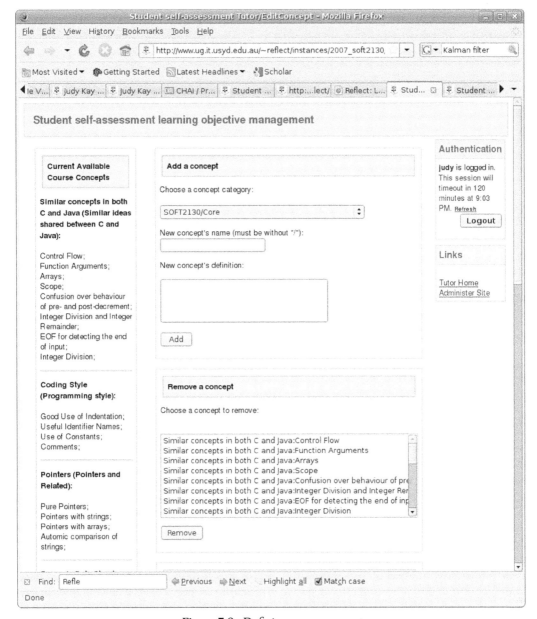

Figure 7.8. Defining a new concept.

that we wanted to create scrutable learner models, meaning that the learner should be able to scrutinize it to determine what it means and how it reasons about their learning. One important aspect of this is to explain the ontological reasoning. This should be feasible with formal ontologies but would involve considerable research to ensure that explanations were at the right level for the learners.

Our approach to building the ontology was to create a tool, called MECUREO, that analyzes a dictionary or glossary to create the ontology (Apted & Kay, 2004). In some of our work, we used substantial online dictionaries (FOLDOC http://foldoc.org/ and Usability Glossary: HCI http://www.usabilityfirst.com/). For the C programming subject, we created a glossary that served both for building the ontology and as a resource

Figure 7.9. Authoring interface for linking concepts from the ontology to learning tasks.

for the students. Part of it is shown in Figure 7.7.

Within the learning system used for this subject, the teacher can add new concepts to the ontology at any time. The interface for this is shown in Figure 7.8. At the left, the system shows the existing ontology. At the top are the Similar concepts in both C and Java, followed by several concepts. The reason the teacher chose this structure is that the students in this subject should have completed two programming courses that used Java. So, both the teacher and the students would find this conceptualization of the domain meaningful and useful. The middle of the screen provides facilities to Add a concept to the ontology. To to do this, the teacher needs to select the concept category from the popup menu (currently on SOFT2130/Core, the course name being SOFT2130). The next box is for the new concept name followed by the definition as it will appear in the glossary. This interface contributes to the definition of the ontology in two ways. First, there is the structure that comes from the hierarchy explicitly defined by the teacher, such as SOFT2130/Core. The second comes from analysis of the dictionary definitions, defining links between all concepts defined by the teacher.

When teachers creates new learning tasks, they select from the available concepts in the ontology, linking them to the task. The interface for this is shown in Figure 7.9. In this case, the teacher has linked four concepts to the task. In this system, these will each be linked to elements of the task in later stages, so that as the students do the task, their actions provide evidence for the learner modeling.

This approach enables a teacher to easily create an ontology based on concepts that are natural for them. When we applied this approach to a user interface subject, we used the SIV visualization of the ontology as part of the interface aiding in the tagging of each learning object with the relevant parts of the ontology (Apted et al., 2004). In that case, we aggregated data for the learner model from different sources (Kay & Lum, 2005): very-fine-grained evidence from each of slides of the online audio lectures for the subject and very-coarse-grained evidence from the larger assessments, such as are commonly stored in LMSs.

The approach can very gracefully handle problems of unstable or changing vocabulary. The teacher simply creates new, local dictionary definitions, where these introduce the new terms and, in normal English, explain that it is the same as, or similar to, other terms from the ontology. These are then available to the students in a class. We used this in the case of our HCI course where some terms are not stable and those used the dictionary were not the ones in our textbook. Simply adding a definition means that the ontology could readily reason in terms of both the terms from the online dictionary and those used in the subject. An additional benefit is that the class glossary could explain this.

Discussion and Conclusions

At some level, all online learning tools can collect data about the learning, at varying levels of accessibility for the learner, or others supporting their learning. At one end of spectrum, there are some emerging teaching systems that maintain a valuable learner model, perhaps with sophisticated interfaces onto it for use by the learner and possibly others who support them. At the other end, there are merely digital footprints in various logs of the user activity. At present, we make little use of most learning data even in the short term and it is rarely pressed into service supporting long-term learning. Typically, it resides in collections of silos, one for each particular system or part of it. The lifelong learner model has the potential to change this situation, making more of this information available in a form that can support learning.

This chapter has explored the new roles that a lifelong learner model might play for open learning modeling, for aggregating information from diverse sources, enabling the sharing of it with other people under the learner's control, supporting flexible interpretation of the model, reuse of it by applications that the learner uses, and institutional use of the models of many learners to improve understanding of their learning. We have also identified key technical challenges that need to be overcome if the lifelong learner model is to fulfill these goals. These take the form of several challenging issues for creating effective interfaces for control over the lifelong learner model and effective views of it, ontological challenges to support effective aggregation, interpretation, and interoperability. We also have identified the need for an effective infrastructure and given an overview of one that we have created.

We began this chapter with a scenario that provided examples of some important classes of very long-term learning goals; those associated with learning related to long-term goals such as fitness; and those associated with development of expertise. Such learning goals, being so long-term, call for the sort of lifelong learner modeling framework we have described, with diverse sources of evidence about the learner and the potential for learning benefits derived from using many teaching and learning systems. Of course, shorter-term learning goals could

also make use of the lifelong learner model, reusing relevant parts of it. This chapter has also focused on the potential role of open learner models, in association with long-term learner models. We have described our exploration of interfaces for large-scale, long-term learner models and lightweight ontological approaches that explore a flexible approach to the challenges of representation of the model. Based on our analysis of the technical challenges of lifelong learner modeling, our work on these two aspects, user interfaces and ontologies, is part of a foundation for supporting lifelong learner modeling.

Acknowledgments

This research was supported by Australian Research Council Projects DP0774532, DP0877665. We are grateful for the insightful comments from the reviewers. Some of these are reflected in important new material that contributes significantly to the paper.

References

Apted, T., and Kay, J. 2004. MECUREO Ontology and Modelling Tools. *International Journal of Continuing Engineering Education and Lifelong Learning* (Special Issue on Concepts and Ontologies in WBES), *14*(3), 191–211.

Apted, T., Kay, J., and Lum, A. 2004. Supporting metadata creation with an ontology built from an extensible dictionary. Pages 4–13 of: de Bra, P., and Nejdl, W. (eds.), *Proceedings of AH 2004, 3rd International Conference on Adaptive Hypermedia and Adaptive Web-Based Systems.* Lecture Notes in Computer Science, vol. 3137. Berlin, Heidelberg: Springer-Verlag.

Apted, T., Kay, J., Lum, A., and Uther, J. 2003. Visualisation of ontological inferences for user control of personal web agents. Pages 306–311 of: Banissi, E., Borner, K., Chen, C., Clapworthy, G., Maple, C., Lobben, A., Moore, C., Roberts, J., Ursyn, A., and Zhang, J. (eds), Proceedings of IV '03, 7th International Conference on Information Visualization. IEEE Computer Society (Washington, DC).

Assad, Mark, Carmichael, David J., Kay, Judy, and Kummerfeld, Bob. 2007. PersonisAD:

Distributed, Active, Scrutable Model Framework for Context-Aware Services. Pages 55–72 of: Proceedings of PERVASIVE 07, 5th International Conference on Pervasive Computing. Lecture Notes in Computer Science, vol. 4480. Springer.

Bannon, L. 2006. Forgetting as a feature, not a bug: The duality of memory and implications for ubiquitous computing. *CoDesign*, 2(1), 3–15.

Bull, S., Cooke, N., and Mabbott, A. 2007b. Visual attention in open learner model presentations: An eye-tracking investigation. *User Modeling*, 4511, 177.

Bull, S., and Kay, J. 2007. Student models that invite the learner in: The SMILI:() open learner modelling framework. *International Journal of Artificial Intelligence in Education*, 17(2), 89–120.

Bull, S., and Mabbott, A. 2006. 20000 inspections of a domain-independent open learner model with individual and comparison views. *Intelligent Tutoring Systems*, 4053, 422–432.

Bull, S., Mabbott, A., and Abu Issa, A.S. 2007a. UMPTEEN: Named and anonymous learner model access for instructors and peers. *International Journal of Artificial Intelligence in Education*, 17(3), 227–253.

Bull, S., Mabbott, A., Gardner, P., Jackson, T., Lancaster, M.J., Quigley, S., and Childs, P.A. 2008. Supporting interaction preferences and recognition of misconceptions with independent open learner models. *Adaptive Hypermedia and Adaptive Web-Based Systems*, 5149, 62–72.

Candy, P.C. 1991. *Self-direction for lifelong learning. A comprehensive guide to theory and practice.* San Francisco: Jossey-Bass.

Craik, F.I.M., and Tulving, E. 2004. Depth of processing and the retention of words in episodic memory. *Journal of Experimental Psychology: General*, 104, 268–294.

Dodge, M., and Kitchin, R. 2007. Outlines of a world coming into existence: Pervasive computing and the ethics of forgetting. *Environment and Planning B: Planning and Design*, 34(3), 431–445.

Ericsson, K.A., Krampe, R.T., and Tesch-Römer, C. 1993. The role of deliberate practice in the acquisition of expert performance. *Psychological Review*, 100, 363.

Ericsson, K.A., Prietula, M.J., and Cokely, E.T. 2007. The making of an expert. *Harvard Business Review*, 85(7/8), 114.

Gluga, Richard. 2010. Long term student learner modeling and curriculum mapping. ITS 2010, Intelligent Tutoring Systems.

Gluga, Richard, Kay, Judy, and Lever, Tim. 2010. Modeling long term learning of generic skills. ITS 2010, Intelligent Tutoring Systems.

Goodyear, P. 2000. Environments for lifelong learning: Ergonomics, architecture and educational design. Integrated and Holistic Perspectives on Learning, Instruction & Technology: Understanding Complexity, 1–18.

Janssen, J., Tattersall, C., Waterink, W., Van den Berg, B., Van Es, R., Bolman, C., and Koper, R. 2007. Self-organising navigational support in lifelong learning: how predecessors can lead the way. *Computers & Education*, 49(3), 781–793.

Jermann, Patrick, and Dillenbourg, Pierre. 2008. Group mirrors to support interaction regulation in collaborative problem solving. *Computer & Education*, 51(1), 279–296.

Kay, J., Maisonneuve, N., Yacef, K., and Reimann, P. 2006. The big five and visualisation of team work activity. Pages 197–206 of: Intelligent Tutoring Systems: *Proceedings of the 8th International Conference*, ITS 2006. Berlin: Springer.

Kay, Judy, and Lum, Andrew. 2005. Exploiting readily available Web data for reflective student models. Pages 338–345 of: *Proceedings of AIED 2005, Artificial Intelligence in Education*. Amsterdam: IOS Press.

Kay, Judy, and Thomas, Richard C. 1995. Studying long-term system use. *Communication & ACM*, 38(7), 61–69.

Kay, Judy, Reimann, Peter, and Yacef, Kalina. 2007. Visualisations for team learning: Small teams working on long-term projects. Pages 351–353 of: Chinn, C, Erkens, G, and Puntambekar, S (eds), Minds, mind, and society. *Proceedings of the 6th International Conference on Computer-supported Collaborative Learning (CSCL 2007)*. International Society of the Learning Sciences.

Klamma, R., Chatti, M.A., Duval, E., Hummel, H., Hvannberg, E.T., Kravcik, M., Law, E., Naeve, A., and Scott, P. 2007. Social software for life-long learning. *Educational Technology & Society*, 10(3), 72–83.

Knapper, C.K., and Cropley, A. 2000. *Lifelong learning in higher education.* Kogan Page.

Lee, S.J.H., and Bull, S. 2008. An open learner model to help parents help their children. *Technology Instruction Cognition and Learning*, 6(1), 29.

Linton, F., and Schaefer, H.P. 2000. Recommender systems for learning: Building user and expert models through long-term observation of application use. *User Modeling and User-Adapted Interaction*, *10*(2), 181–208.

Lister, R, Adams, E S, Fitzgerald, S, Fone, W, Hamer, J, Lindholm, M, McCartney, R, Moström, J E, Sanders, K, Seppälä, O, Simon, B, and Thomas, L. 2004. A multi-national study of reading and tracing skills in novice programmers. *SIGCSE Bulletin*, *36*(4), 119–150.

Longworth, N. 2003. *Lifelong learning in action: transforming education in the 21st century*. New York: Routledge.

Lum, Andrew W. K. 2007. Light-weight ontologies for scrutable user modelling. PhD thesis.

Mazza, R., and Dimitrova, V. 2007. CourseVis: A graphical student monitoring tool for supporting instructors in web-based distance courses. *International Journal of Human-Computer Studies*, *65*(2), 125–139.

Mitrovic, A., and Martin, B. 2007. Evaluating the effect of open student models on self-assessment. *International Journal of Artificial Intelligence in Education*, *17*(2), 121–144.

Noy, N.F., and McGuinness, D.L. 2001. Ontology development 101: A guide to creating your first ontology.

Palen, L., and Dourish, P. 2003. Unpacking "privacy" for a networked world. *Proceedings of the Conference on Human Factors in Computing Systems*, 129–136.

Perera, Dilhan, Kay, Judy, Yacef, Kalina, Koprinska, Irena, and Zaiane, Osmar. 2008. Clustering and sequential pattern mining of online collaborative learning data. IEEE Transactions on Knowledge and Data Engineering.

Ringel, M., Cutrell, E., Dumais, S., and Horvitz, E. 2003. Milestones in time: The value of landmarks in retrieving information from personal stores. Page 184 of: Human-computer Interaction: INTERACT'03; IFIP TC13 International Conference on Human-Computer Interaction, September 1–5, 2003, Zurich, Switzerland. Amsterdam: IOS Press.

Romero, C., and Ventura, S. 2007. Educational data mining: A survey from 1995 to 2005. *Expert Systems with Applications*, *33*(1), 135–146.

Schneiderman, B. 1996. The eyes have it: A task by data type taxonomy for information visualizations. Pages 336–343 of: *Proceedings of the 1996 IEEE Symposium on Visual Languages*, IEEE Computer Society, Washington, DC.

Soller, A. 2005. From mirroring to guiding: A review of state of the art technology for supporting collaborative learning. *International Journal of Artificial Intelligence in Education*, *15*(4), 261–290.

Spolsky, Joel. 2006. The guerrilla guide to interviewing (version 3.0). Retrieved March 2010 from http://www.joelonsoftware.com/articles/GuerrillaInterviewing3.html

Tattersall, C., Manderveld, J., Van den Berg, B., Van Es, R., Janssen, J., and Koper, R. 2005. Self organising wayfinding support for lifelong learners. *Education and Information Technologies*, *10*(1), 111–123.

Upton, Kim, and Kay, Judy. 2009. Narcissus: Interactive activity mirror for small groups. Pages 54–65 of: UMAP09, User Modeling, Adaptation and Personalisation.

Uther, J., and Kay, J. 2003. VlUM, a Web-based visualisation of large user models. Pages 198–202 of: Brusilovsky, P., Corbett, A., and de Rosis, F. (eds), *Proceedings of UM 2003, User Modelling*. Berlin: Springer.

Uther, James. 2002. On the visualisation of large user models in web based systems. PhD thesis, University of Sydney.

Weber, G., and Brusilovsky, P. 2001. ELM-ART: An adaptive versatile system for Web-based instruction. *International Journal of Artificial Intelligence in Education*, *12*(4), 351–384.

Zapata-Rivera, D., Hansen, E., Shute, V.J., Underwood, J.S., and Bauer, M. 2007. Evidence-based approach to interacting with open student models. *International Journal of Artificial Intelligence in Education*, *17*(3), 273–303.

Part III

EXPERIENTIAL LEARNING AND ILL-DEFINED DOMAINS

CHAPTER 8

Training Decisions from Experience with Decision-Making Games

Cleotilde Gonzalez

The research reported here is relevant to human decision making in disaster, emergency, and generally dynamic and changing conditions. In emergency conditions, both external resources and cognitive capabilities are limited. A decision maker must manage his/her cognitive load, that of others in the situation, and allocate the often limited resources in a short period of time. The main job of a decision maker in an emergency situation is to allocate resources wisely where the situation changes constantly, outcomes are delayed, decisions are interdependent, priorities change over time, and there is high uncertainty of outcomes.

These types of decision-making conditions are part of a field of research called Dynamic Decision Making (DDM) (Brehmer, 1990; Edwards, 1962; Rapoport, 1990). Some classical examples of DDM include, among others: firefighting resource allocation and management in real time; triage decisions in a medical emergency room; 911 operators determining relative urgency and deploying resources; and supply-chain management. In general, DDM often involves a dynamic allocation of limited resources in

real time. Disaster and emergency responses are examples of decision making in dynamic conditions. For instance in an emergency room, doctors must allocate limited hospital resources (i.e., nurses, doctors, beds) in the presence of a large number of patients in need of help. The rate and timing of the inflow of patients is unknown, and physicians must make assignments in real time. These allocations are interdependent, perhaps producing suboptimal decisions like when a mildly injured patient is given priority over future unknown severely injured patients.

A common paradigm in the behavioral decision sciences has been that of *decisions from description* (DFD, Hertwig, Barron, Weber, & Erev, 2004). A human is given access to descriptive information, often including probabilities and outcomes, and asked to make a choice based on the conditions described. This is also a common paradigm in the real world. For example, to make an investment decision, people often read brochures with the different pros and cons of the alternatives while considering the risk of the different alternatives. These

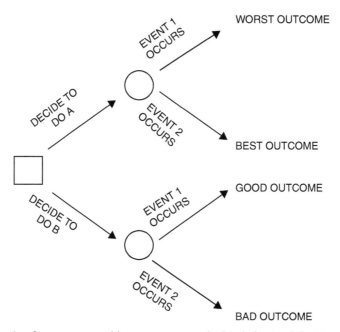

Figure 8.1. Example of a common problem structure studied in behavioral decision-making research.

type of decisions are one-shot (open-loop, no-feedback) decisions, illustrated in Figure 8.1, where people are expected to act "rationally" and select the alternative that results in the best outcome.

In emergency and DDM conditions, DFD are quite uncommon. One rarely finds well-defined alternatives; one rarely understands or is able to correctly predict all possible outcomes; and often high uncertainty prevents one from calculating or estimating any probabilities involved in the occurrence of those alternatives (Gonzalez, Lerch, & Lebiere, 2003; Klein, 1989). Traditional behavioral decision research often makes predictions based on "rational theory," the simple and intuitive idea that people search for the optimal outcome (often monetary outcome) in decision situations. Drawing conclusions from controlled experiments in very simplified decision-making situations has multiple advantages. It allows us to identify clear strategies and measures of human decision making, and thus make theoretical progress by drawing generic inferences about how people make decisions. However, this approach has some limitations, notably their applicability in disaster, emergency, and

dynamic environments in general. Thus, the many years invested in studying DFD in the behavioral decision sciences have resulted in practically no concrete guideline for application to train people that deal with emergency, disaster, and DDM in general.

In contrast, Naturalistic Decision Making is a field that has been concerned with studying decision making in the "wild," in contexts in which proficient decision makers draw conclusions from realistic cases and scenarios that are relevant to their experience and knowledge (Lipshitz, Klein, Orasanu, & Salas, 2001). Those who study naturalistic decision making are confronted with serious challenges. They often study large groups and real decision makers in complex decision situations. Real-world decision makers typically confront many uncertainties about the available options; they have inadequate information about their options; they rarely know the likely costs and benefits, and the value trade-offs they entail. Although one could expect decision makers in the real world to have clear goals and to promote those goals with their decisions, the reality is that decision making in real-world situations is seldom rational, and in fact it

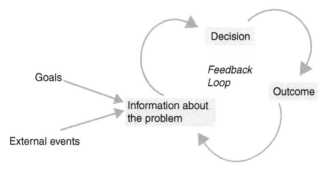

Figure 8.2. A closed-loop view of decision making.

is often hard to understand what constitutes rational choice under such conditions. Thus, these studies have multiple limitations. Realistic studies demonstrate only particular examples of decision-making situations from which general predictions and inferences are hard to derive.

Recently in the behavioral decision sciences, there has been some progress to study decision making in "less ideal" conditions, in situations where there are repeated decisions and uncertainty about the outcomes and probabilities of events. This paradigm, named Decisions from Experience (DFE), has revealed that many assumptions of the perceptions of risk and human preferences in one-shot static decisions do not hold for DFE (Hertwig et al., 2004). Although this work brings a very optimistic view of the application of behavioral decision sciences to DDM situations, there are many years of research ahead to clearly understand all the aspects involved in these tasks in a systematic way (Lejarraga, Dutt, & Gonzalez, in press).

I conceptualize DDM as a control process; a closed-loop learning process where decisions are influenced by goals, external events, and previous decisions. Thus in my view, decision making is a learning process where decisions are made from experience and are feedback-dependent (feedback here is the association that a human makes between actions and their outcomes) (see Figure 8.2). In this paradigm, alternatives are not presented at the same time, but rather unfold over time, and decision making is a learning loop: Decisions depend on previous choices as well as on external events and conditions.

DFE is, very likely, the only method by which decisions can be made in dynamic conditions. In fact, a recent study demonstrates that as the complexity of a problem increases, people prefer to make decisions from experience rather than interpreting the given probabilities and outcomes of a one-shot decision (Lejarraga, 2010). My research has focused on the study of DFE in DDM situations. I have used quite diverse research approaches, different from those used in the behavioral decision sciences and those used in naturalistic decision making, including laboratory experiments with complex interactive decision-making games, and computational cognitive modeling. I believe that these approaches improve the degree of convergence between the traditional behavioral decision sciences experiments and the naturalistic decision-making studies. In what follows I summarize what I have learned in the past years from using these two approaches and present the practical and concrete lessons for application to training decision makers that deal with emergency, disaster, and dynamic environments in general.

Learning in DDM

Research on learning in and about dynamic systems indicate that humans remain suboptimal decision makers even after extended practice and after being given unlimited time and performance incentives (Diehl & Sterman, 1995; Sterman, 1994); that is, humans do not always and frequently do not improve their decisions from experience (Brehmer, 1980). One main impediment to learning in dynamic tasks is the difficulty in processing feedback, particularly delayed feedback (Brehmer, 1992; Sterman, 1989). However, many other difficulties have also been documented, including our abilities to deal with time constraints, high workload, and limitations in our inherent cognitive abilities (Gonzalez, 2004, 2005a; Gonzalez, Thomas, & Vanyukov, 2005).

Various accounts have been proposed regarding how a human learns in dynamic systems (for summaries of these, see Busemeyer, 2002; Gonzalez, 2005b). One theory is that specific instances are used to control dynamic systems (Dienes & Fahey, 1995). This learning model was based on two cognitive mechanisms that compete every time someone encounters a decision-making situation: an algorithm and a set of context-action exemplars. The algorithm is a general heuristic or rule that one uses in a novel situation; the context-action exemplars are discrete representations of knowledge that are called "instances," a name derived from Logan's (1988) instance theory of automatization. In this model, an implicit assumption is that a decision maker stores actions and their outcomes together in memory and retrieves them on the basis of their similarity to subsequently encountered situations.

Another theory of learning is proposed by the connectionist approach, in which decision making is built from interconnected units (Gibson, Fichman, & Plaut, 1997). This model of learning in DDM is based on the control theory approach proposed by Brehmer (1990) and was implemented computationally via neural networks. This theory assumes that decision makers use outcome feedback to form two submodels: the *judgment submodel* that represents how the decision maker's actions affect outcomes, and the *choice submodel* that represents which actions are taken to achieve desired outcomes. The judgment submodel learns by minimizing the differences between the outcomes it predicts

and the outcomes received from feedback, whereas the *choice submodel* learns by minimizing the differences between the alternatives predicted by the judgment model and the alternatives actually selected. This model provides a good account of individuals' learning in dynamic situations and their transfer of knowledge to novel situations (Gibson, 2000).

A third theory is the Instance-Based Learning Theory (IBLT) (Gonzalez & Lebiere, 2005; Gonzalez et al., 2003). IBLT was developed to reproduce decision-making behavior in dynamic tasks. IBLT characterizes learning by storing in memory a sequence of action-outcome links produced by experienced events through a feedback-loop process of human and environment interactions. This process increases knowledge and allows decisions to improve as experience accumulates in memory. IBLT assumes the following components. *Instances* are examples of choices that are stored in memory. Each instance contains cues about the situation in which a decision was made, the decision itself, and the subsequent outcome. Situational cues are relevant in dynamic environments because situations are continuous and variable, and not all experiences are informative for future choice situations. Learning resides in the *Activation* (e.g., frequency and recency) of experienced choices and outcomes. IBLT assumes that the instances experienced by the decision maker are activated in memory as a function of their occurrence. More recent and frequent instances are more active in memory than less recent and less frequent ones. Choice situations are never equivalent in dynamic tasks as environments change over time. Thus, past experiences are not necessarily directly applicable in new conditions. A *similarity* rule, defined on situational cues, is specified to evaluate the resemblance of previous situations with respect to the current situation being evaluated. Finally, IBLT uses *blending* as a mechanism to average the value of different observed outcomes in previous similar situations (Lebiere, 1999). The value of an option is the addition of the subjective value of each possible outcome weighted by its subjective likelihood.

The three learning models summarized earlier incorporate at least two common characteristics; all three models take into account the need for two forms of learning: *explicit* (i.e., decision making based on rules of action) and *implicit* (i.e., decision making based on context-based knowledge and recognition). There is some evidence that individuals who have completed a dynamic task are not always aware of the task structure (i.e., their knowledge is implicit), which suggests that the knowledge they acquired was not in the form of rules about how the system works (Dienes & Fahey, 1995). Often, individuals performing DDM tasks are unable to describe the key elements of the task or verbalize the ways in which they make decisions (Berry & Broadbent, 1987, 1988). Second, these models rely on a similarity process that determines the applicability of accumulated experiences to familiar situations. Research in analogical reasoning has demonstrated the high relevance of analogy to learning and decision-making processes (Kurtz, Miao, & Gentner, 2001; Medin, Goldstone, & Markman, 1995).

In summary, there are well-documented difficulties when humans make decisions in dynamic systems. Humans remain suboptimal or learn very slowly, often due to feedback delays, time constraints, and the cognitive workload required by these environments. To be able to understand and improve training protocols and guidelines, one needs to first understand how humans make decisions in these tasks. Fortunately, the similarities across the most prominent theories of learning in DDM help converge in some issues. All models agree in that humans learn facts, cause-and-effect knowledge related to the context, and none of the models present the main form of learning as being structural knowledge or rules. Also, all of the models agree on the relevance of some form of recognition of familiar patterns from past experience; that decisions are made from experience by retrieving a solution from similar situations in past experience.

Because IBLT is the basis for my proposed guidelines to training decisions from experience with decision-making games, we explain IBLT's principles and its formulations in more detail next.

Instance-Based Learning Theory

An instance in IBLT consists of environmental cues (the situation), the set of actions that are applicable to the situation (the decision), and the evaluation of the goodness of a decision in a particular situation (the utility) (see Figure 8.3). Thus, the accumulation of instances involves storing situation-decision-utility (SDU) triplets in memory. Figure 8.4 presents the generic IBLT process by which decisions are made in an interactive environment, consisting of the Recognition, Judgment, Choice, Execution, and Feedback steps. When faced with a particular decision situation, people are likely to retrieve similar SDUs (SDUs with similar situations) from memory (Recognition step). In a typical situation (situation similar to past SDUs), the expected utility of an action is calculated by combining the utility of similar instances retrieved from memory (a procedure called Blending). In atypical situations, however, people fall back on heuristics in their evaluation of expected utility of the action. The evaluation of the expected utility of a decision in a situation is done in the Judgment step. Alternative actions are evaluated sequentially, and after each evaluation, the decision of whether or not more alternative should be evaluated is determined by a *necessity mechanism*. Necessity may be subjectively determined by the decision maker's own preferences or by exogenous factors such as lack of time or changes in the environmental conditions. The alternative with the highest utility among the evaluated alternatives is then selected (the Choice step) and executed (the Execution step), changing the environment and noting which SDU was executed in memory. Once a decision has been made, the outcome of the decision is

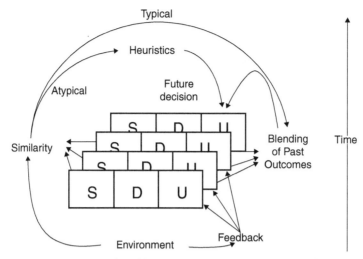

Figure 8.3. Instance-based learning. Instances (SDUs) accumulate over time. At a decision point, a situation is compared to past instances, and based on its similarity to past instances, these are reused and blended to determine the expected utility of the current decision situation. Good instances are reinforced through feedback from the environment.

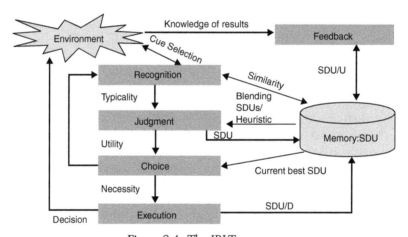

Figure 8.4. The IBLT process.

used as feedback to modify the utility value of the original SDUs (Feedback step).

The computational implementation of the IBLT relies on several mechanisms proposed by the ACT-R cognitive architecture (Anderson & Lebiere, 1998), notably the Activation mechanism. Activation in ACT-R is a value assigned to each "chunk" (i.e., instance) that reflects the estimate of how likely the chunk would be retrieved and the speed of retrieval for the chunk. The activation of a chunk reflects the frequency and recency of use of the chunk and the

degree to which the chunk matches a context (i.e., the extent to which a given chunk is similar to previously presented chunks in each chunk position). ACT-R architectural mechanisms underlie and constrain the various steps of the IBLT process. Learned instances and their accessibility provide for the accumulation of instances in memory; similarity-based retrieval from memory drives the recognition process, and so on. We have used the computational implementation of IBLT to confirm and predict human performance in many tasks. IBLT's computational models' data often agree with human data (e.g., Gonzalez & Lebiere, 2005; Gonzalez et al., 2003; Martin, Gonzalez, & Lebiere, 2004).

Training and Decision-Making Games

Given the similarity of the different theories of learning in DDM and the known difficulties of human learning in these environments, the question we address here is: What are the recommendations that can be drawn from these theories to address the learning difficulties in DDM tasks? Because each DDM situation is unique and the reusability of good past instances from memory depends on the similarity between the current situation and those stored in memory, disaster and emergency situations present a challenge to the improvement of decision performance over time: There are not many similar instances stored in our memories. In addition, the unpredictability of events in dynamic situations makes it difficult to determine the timing of major events, with possibly severe consequences. Thus, our main concern in this section is to present guidelines and suggestions from the IBLT to help individuals become alert and able to perform as best as possible in disaster and emergency situations.

In my view, an essential way to achieve successful training for dynamic tasks is the use of Decision-Making Games (DMGames). DMGames are graphical models (abstractions of reality) used for experimentation with human decision makers. My concept of DMGames has evolved from that of Microworlds, a term commonly used in the DDM field (Brehmer & Dörner, 1993; Gonzalez et al., 2005; Turkle, 1984), and the more recent developments of serious games and serious games initiatives (Cannon-Bowers & Bowers, 2010). Many disciplines are now adopting simulations and games in research, including engineering (Foss & Eikass, 2006), business and management (Zantow, Knowlton, & Sharp, 2005), medicine (Bradley, 2006), and political science (Kelle, 2008; Mintz, Geva, Redd,

& Carnes, 1997). Microworlds were developed to study DDM, and through the years, technological advancements have allowed for the development of more graphical and interactive tools for research, which are also more fun. DMGames may incorporate temporal dependencies among system states (i.e., dynamics), feedback delays, nonlinear relationships among system variables, and uncertainty (in the form of exogenous disturbances). They are interactive and allow repeated, interrelated decisions. They also may incorporate external events and time pressure. Thus, DMGames are essential to compress time and space in the laboratory setting. They reproduce difficult learning in conditions with rare, novel events and unpredictable timing, such as in disaster and emergency situations. DMGames may speed up learning and help people acquire the instances they cannot acquire from the real world. DMGames may help a human acquire the skills needed to be alert and become adaptable in the real world.

The training recommendations that follow are based on the use of DMGames in laboratory experiments where we have manipulated experience (type of instances stored) and the dynamic conditions on which decisions are made, such as timing, workload, and feedback delays. All recommendations come from IBLT and the empirical work done through the years to test IBLT's predictions on ways to speed up learning and facilitate prompt adaptation to novel and rare situations.

Slow Is Fast

IBLT recommends that *slow is fast* when it comes to adapting to time-constrained environments (Gonzalez, 2004). In a dynamic resource allocation task like disaster and emergency situations, it has been demonstrated that individuals trained on a task at a slower pace were able to adapt more successfully to greater time constraints, compared to those who only trained under high time constraints, regardless of exceedingly large number of practice sessions given to those trained under time constraints. Thus, a

few slow practice sessions were more beneficial than a larger number of fast practice sessions because they enable people to acquire
more complex and useful knowledge.

Thirty-three graduate and undergraduate
college students recruited from local uni-
versities were randomly assigned to either
the fast or slow condition group. The Water
Purification Plant simulation™ was used for
this study. The goal in this task is to distrib-
ute all the water in the system on time and
under time constraints by activating and
deactivating pumps. The environment is
opaque, so the user is uncertain about some
key variable values. For example, water
appears in the system according to a scenario
defined by the experimenter and unknown
to the user. The environment changes both
autonomously and in response to the user's
decisions. Because a maximum of five
pumps can be activated at any one time, the
decision maker's actions are interrelated.
This task translates directly to disaster and
emergency situations because it involves
time pressure, limited resources, incomplete
knowledge about the situation, unexpected
events, and the need to coordinate efforts to
meet the demands. Participants did the task
over three consecutive days. Under the fast
condition, each simulation trial lasted eight
minutes. Participants under this condition
completed eighteen trials over the three-
day period (six trials/day). Under the slow
condition, each simulation trial on the first
two days lasted twenty-four minutes (two
trials/day), whereas each trial on the last
day lasted eight minutes (six trials). For all
participants, the first two days were training
days and the last day was the test day. The
results show that slow training led to better
performance than fast training on day three
with fast performance for both groups.

IBLT explains this finding in several ways.
First, learning at a slower pace results in more
alternatives being considered within each
recognition-choice cycle. More instances are
considered and stored in memory during
each evaluation of possible courses of action,
given more time within each cycle. Further,
a greater chance of finding an optimal action
exist, given that more alternatives are being

evaluated. Second, when an individual is
trained at a slower pace and then asked to
perform at a faster pace, she can retrieve and
rely on the larger and possibly more diverse
set of instances in memory, which may be
applied during a time-constrained condition.
In contrast, when someone is trained under
high time constraints, there is no chance of
getting more instances representing different alternatives in memory during training.
Performance under time constraints is thus
limited to the possible retrieval of a few,
selected sets of instances in memory, leading
to poorer performance.

Less Workload Helps Adaptation

Similar to the results on time constraints, it
has been found that individuals who trained
on a task under low workload were able to
perform more accurately during transfer
with a high workload than those trained
under high-workload conditions all along
(Gonzalez, 2005a).

Fifty-one students were recruited and
assigned to conditions that differed in the
amount of workload (number of simultaneous tasks performed at the same time)
during training. In the high-workload condition, participants had to complete the same
Water Purification Plant simulation™ as in
Gonzalez (2004), but also had to simultaneously perform two additional, independent tasks. This group was contrasted to a
low-workload condition in which participants performed the task at the same pace
but with no additional independent tasks.
Participants ran the DMGame on three
consecutive days. The first two days were
the training days, during which participants
worked under one of the workload conditions, and a third day, during which all participants performed the same DMGame
under workload.

Similar to the results in Gonzalez (2004),
the findings indicate that high task workload
during training hindered performance and
transfer compared to low-workload training. Thus, these two studies demonstrated
that it is not a good idea to train individuals
in conditions "close to the real conditions"

when it comes to workload and time constraints. Slower pacing and low workload are best during training for people to perform well in fast and high-workload tasks at test. Once again, from the IBLT perspective, this study demonstrates the effects of workload on the recognition-choice cycle, which under workload inhibits the generation of instances that can then be reused at test.

Heterogeneity Helps Adaptation

In several studies together with my colleagues (Brunstein & Gonzalez, in press; Gonzalez & Madhavan, 2011; Gonzalez & Quesada, 2003; Madhavan & Gonzalez, 2010), I have found that the variation in the situations that people confront during training influences how fast and how well they learn to adapt to novel and unexpected situations, with higher variation leading to better transfer. For example, Gonzalez and Quesada (2003) demonstrated the influence of the similarity of past decisions on future decisions. In this study, decisions became increasingly similar with task practice, but the similarity depended on the interaction of many task features rather than by any single task features. This study demonstrated the relevance of similarity of situations in the IBLT process.

In another study, Madhavan and Gonzalez (2010) used a luggage-screening task to investigate the effects of similarity of experiences during the learning process. In such a task, each piece of luggage could have distractors and targets. Targets could be one of several types: knives, guns, glass objects, liquids, and so on. This task resembles disaster and emergency situations in its key features. For example, disaster responders have to discriminate between patients who would profit most from treatment based on their symptoms and available resources (targets) and patients who would not (distractors). As a dynamic decision-making task, the condition of a patient might change over time, resulting in a different category membership. My work with Brunstein and Madhavan has demonstrated that diverse and heterogeneous conditions of training

lead to better adaptation to novel and unexpected situations. For example, training conditions in which the targets change (targets can be targets in some trials and distractors in others) or training conditions in which targets are drawn from diverse categories result in better adaptation to novel and rare situations, compared to training in consistent conditions (in which the targets set is constant and are items from a narrow set of categories).

Heterogeneity in IBLT increases the chance that a similar instance will be retrieved in future choices. The heterogeneity is defined by the multidimensional space of the cues that form the situation of the instances. The more diverse those instances are, the better the chances will be of finding similarity to past decisions when a novel instance is confronted. Thus, the greater the possibility of reusing well-matching stored instances instead of merely general heuristics.

Feedforward Helps Adaptation

I have found that knowledge of results is not enough for improving learning and adaptation (Gonzalez, 2005b). The provision of outcome feedback was an inferior way of trying to aid learning and performance compared to the viewing of a highly skilled decision maker (e.g., a form of feedforward). Participants were trained in one of four groups during the first day and transfer to the same DDM conditions in the second day. During training, participants were assigned to one of the following four conditions. Control participants only received feedback about the outcome in the task. Process feedback participants received outcome feedback broken down in multiple steps and pieces. Participants in the self-exemplar group ran one trial under the control condition and then viewed a replay of their own performance. Finally, participants in the expert-exemplar condition ran one trial under the control condition and then replayed the trial of a highly skilled participant. On the second day, all participants were asked to perform the DDM task without any feedback (the detailed feed-back, self-exemplar, and expert-exemplar aids were removed).

Results showed that the performance of all groups improved across trials. However, in the early stages of learning, people with the detailed-outcome feedback condition actually showed poorer learning than the control participants. The self-exemplar and the expert-exemplar conditions showed superior performance compared to the detailed-outcome feedback condition; however, when the aid was removed in the testing period, the only treatment that outperformed the control condition was the expert-exemplar group. The expert-exemplar group began to outperform the other groups midway through the training trials, and this superior performance continued throughout the testing period, even after the intervention of seeing the expert performance had been removed.

The results of the detailed feedback are similar to those found in Gonzalez (2005b). Additional detailed feedback increased the workload during training. Because this task was a real-time task, the time left to evaluate more alternatives was used instead in evaluating the detailed feedback. Thus, although presumably the utility of the instances would increase, the number of instances decreased compared to a condition with no detailed feedback. This is clear in the first sessions of the task, in which performance decreased for the self-exemplar group. The effects of self-exemplar and expert-exemplar are also clear from IBLT. In both conditions, people are acquiring more instances without the need of executing the task. The self-exemplar instances, however, are less effective than the expert-exemplar instances. Reflecting on one's own performance only reinforces poor instances, whereas reflecting on expert's performance reinforces instances with higher utility.

Summary and Conclusions

Behavioral scientists, particularly those with interest in human decision making, should pay more attention to the process and skills needed to make decisions in dynamic situations. The majority of research in decision sciences has focused on one-shot (open-loop) decisions that present people with description of hypothetical problems of choice. Very little has been done in the decision sciences to understand the formation of alternatives in the first place and the effects of "closing the loop"; that is, making decisions from experience by reusing past decisions and outcomes.

My research has focused on the study of decisions from experience in dynamic situations. My belief is that experience is the most likely method by which people make decisions in dynamic conditions. I see decision making in dynamic tasks as a learning loop, where decisions are made from experience and are feedback-dependent. In this chapter, I explained current research of learning theories that are directly relevant to DDM. I concentrated particularly on the explanation of IBLT, a theory that has been implemented computationally and from which several training guidelines have been derived. I have illustrated how research on DDM using DMGames and the IBLT can be used to generate practical and concrete training principles. The factors of DDM that are of special relevance for emergency training are time constraints, workload, similarity or diversity of experiences, and types of feedback. For these factors, we found what best prepares people for uncertain and novel situations is to train under conditions that foster skill acquisition and a deeper understanding of the situations confronted.

Some examples of the principles for emergency training derived from DDM research are the diversity of practice and the *slow is fast* principles. Greater diversity of instances during training helped individuals detect unknown and novel targets more accurately at transfer than those trained with a consistent set of targets. In addition, slower training led to better performance than fast training. Thus, training for high-time-pressure tasks is more effective if performed in a slower path before releasing learners to realistic conditions. In laboratory studies, we have demonstrated how these guidelines of training result in better performance and adaptation to unexpected and uncertain conditions. Thus, I suggest that these guidelines could be used to design training protocols for decision makers that have to be prepared to deal with unexpected conditions and possible emergencies in their daily activities.

Acknowledgments

This is a summary of research performed through many years, and thus I owe recognition to a large number of organizations that have trusted and supported my work, including the Army Research Laboratory, the Office of Naval Research, the National Science Foundation, and the Army Research Office, among others. I also owe recognition to doctoral students, postdoctoral fellows, and other research staff of my dynamic decision making laboratory. To all of them, thank you.

References

Anderson, J. R., & Lebiere, C. (1998). *The atomic components of thought*. Hillsdale, NJ: Lawrence Erlbaum Associates.

Berry, D. C., & Broadbent, D. E. (1987). The combination of explicit and implicit learning processes in task control. *Psychological Research*, 49(1), 7–15.

Berry, D. C., & Broadbent, D. E. (1988). Interactive tasks and the implicit-explicit distinction. *British Journal of Psychology*, 79, 251–272.

Bradley, P. (2006). The history of simulation in medical education and possible future directions. *Medical Education*, 40, 254–262.

Brehmer, B. (1980). In one word: Not from experience. *Acta Psychologica*, 45, 223–241.

Brehmer, B. (1990). Strategies in real-time, dynamic decision making. In R. M. Hogarth (Ed.), *Insights in decision making* (pp. 262–279). Chicago: University of Chicago Press.

Brehmer, B. (1992). Dynamic decision making: Human control of complex systems. *Acta Psychologica*, 81(3), 211–241.

Brehmer, B., & Dörner, D. (1993). Experiments with computer-simulated microworlds:

Escaping both the narrow straits of the laboratory and the deep blue sea of the field study. *Computers in Human Behavior*, 9(2–3), 171–184.

Brunstein, A., & Gonzalez, C. (in press). Preparing for novelty with diverse training. *Applied Cognitive Psychology*.

Busemeyer, J. R. (2002). Dynamic decision making. In N. J. Smelser & P. B. Baltes (Eds.), *International encyclopedia of the social and behavioral sciences*, Vol. 6 (pp. 3903–3908). Oxford: Elsevier Press.

Cannon-Bowers, J., & Bowers, C. (2010). *Serious game design and development technologies for training and learning*. Hershey, PA: IGI Global.

Diehl, E., & Sterman, J. D. (1995). Effects of feedback complexity on dynamic decision making. *Organizational Behavior and Human Decision Processes*, 62(2), 198–215.

Dienes, Z., & Fahey, R. (1995). Role of specific instances in controlling a dynamic system. *Journal of Experimental Psychology: Learning, Memory and Cognition*, 21(4), 848–862.

Edwards, W. (1962). Dynamic decision theory and probabilistic information processing. *Human Factors*, 4, 59–73.

Foss, B. A., & Eikaas, T. I. (2006). Game play in engineering education: Concept and experimental results. *International Journal of Engineering Education*, 22(5), 1043–1052.

Gibson, F. P. (2000). Feedback delays: How can decision makers learn not to buy a new car every time the garage is empty? *Organizational Behavior & Human Decision Processes*, 83(1), 141–166.

Gibson, F. P., Fichman, M., & Plaut, D. C. (1997). Learning in dynamic decision tasks: Computational model and empirical evidence. *Organizational Behavior and Human Decision Processes*, 71(1), 1–35.

Gonzalez, C. (2004). Learning to make decisions in dynamic environments: Effects of time constraints and cognitive abilities. *Human Factors*, 46(3), 449–460.

Gonzalez, C. (2005a). The relationship between task workload and cognitive abilities in dynamic decision making. *Human Factors*, 47(1), 92–101.

Gonzalez, C. (2005b). Decision support for real-time dynamic decision making tasks. *Organizational Behavior & Human Decision Processes*, 96, 142–154.

Gonzalez, C., & Lebiere, C. (2005). Instance-based cognitive models of decision making. In D. Zizzo & A. Courakis (Eds.), *Transfer of knowledge in economic decision-making.* New York: Macmillan (Palgrave Macmillan).

Gonzalez, C., Lerch, J. F., & Lebiere, C. (2003). Instance-based learning in dynamic decision making. *Cognitive Science, 27*(4), 591–635.

Gonzalez, C. & Madhavan, P. (2011). Diversity during training enhances detection of novel stimuli. *Journal of Cognitive Psychology, 23*(3), 342–350.

Gonzalez, C., & Quesada, J. (2003). Learning in dynamic decision making: The recognition process. *Computational and Mathematical Organization Theory, 9*(4), 287–304.

Gonzalez, C., Thomas, R. P., & Vanyukov, P. (2005). The relationships between cognitive ability and dynamic decision making. *Intelligence, 33*(2), 169–186.

Hertwig, R., Barron, G., Weber, E. U., & Erev, I. (2004). Decisions from experience and the effect of rare events in risky choice. *Psychological Science, 15*(8), 534–539.

Kelle, A. (2008). Experiential learning in an arms control simulation. *PSOnline, April,* 379–385.

Klein, G. A. (1989). Recognition-primed decisions. In W. B. Rouse (Ed.), *Advances in Man-Machine Systems Research, Vol. 5* (pp. 47–92). Greenwich, CT: JAI Press.

Kurtz, K. J., Miao, C., & Gentner, D. (2001). Learning by analogical bootstrapping. *The Journal of Learning Sciences, 10*(4), 417–446.

Lebiere, C. (1999). *Blending: An ACT-R mechanism for aggregate retrievals.* Paper presented at the Sixth Annual ACT-R Workshop at George Mason University.

Lejarraga, T. (2010). When experience is better than description: Time delays and complexity. *Journal of Behavioral Decision Making, 23*(1), 100–116.

Lejarraga, T., Dutt, V., & Gonzalez, C. (in press). Instance-based learning in repeated binary choice. *Journal of Behavioral Decision Making.*

Lipshitz, R., Klein, G., Orasanu, J., & Salas, E. (2001). Taking stock of naturalistic decision making. *Journal of Behavioral Decision Making, 14*(5), 331–352.

Logan, G. D. (1988). Toward an instance theory of automatization. *Psychological Review, 95*(4), 492–527.

Madhavan, P. & Gonzalez, C. (2010). The relationship between stimulus-response mappings and the detection of novel stimuli in a simulated luggage screening task. *Theoretical Issues in Ergonomics Science, 11*(5), 461–473.

Martin, M. K., Gonzalez, C., & Lebiere, C. (2004). Learning to make decisions in dynamic environments: ACT-R plays the beer game. In M. C. Lovett, C. D. Schunn, C. Lebiere, & P. Munro (Eds.), *Proceedings of the Sixth International Conference on Cognitive Modeling, Vol. 420* (pp. 178–183). Pittsburgh, PA: Carnegie Mellon University/University of Pittsburgh; Lawrence Erlbaum Associates Publishers.

Medin, D. L., Goldstone, R. L., & Markman, A. B. (1995). Comparison and choice: Relations between similarity processing and decision processing. *Psychonomic Bulletin and Review, 2*(1), 1–19.

Mintz, A., Geva, N., Redd, S. B., & Carnes, A. (1997). The effect of dynamic and static choice sets on political decision making: An analysis using the decision board platform. *The American Political Science Review, 91*(3), 553–566.

Rapoport, A. (1990). *The meaning of the built environment: A nonverbal communication approach.* Tucson: University of Arizona Press.

Sterman, J. D. (1989). Modeling managerial behavior: Misperceptions of feedback in a dynamic decision making experiment. *Management Science, 35*(3), 321–339.

Sterman, J. D. (1994). Learning in and about complex systems. *System Dynamics Review, 10,* 291–330.

Turkle, S. (1984). *The second self: Computers and the human spirit.* London: Granada.

Zantow, K., Knowlton, D. S., & Sharp, D. C. (2005). More than fun and games: Reconsidering the virtues of strategic management simulations. *Academy of Management Learning & Education, 4*(4), 451–458.

CHAPTER 9

Adaptive Tutoring Technologies and Ill-Defined Domains

Collin Lynch, Kevin D. Ashley, Niels Pinkwart, and Vincent Aleven

Introduction

Consider the following problems:

Pw: Given a fleet of trucks $F = \{f1, f2, ..., fn\}$ and a shipment of supplies S packed in N crates each weighing $\leq T$ tons, how long would it take to ship the boxes from Bagram AFB to a forward operating base using one of N predefined routes?

Pi: Arrange a logistical distribution system that will provide a sufficient supply of medical and military stores for firebases and patrol units in Helmand province.

Both are standard logistical problems that any hapless staff officer might face on a given day. The former, however, is quite *well-defined* in that the problem is fairly constrained, the relevant knowledge is clear and available to the solver, and the answer is unambiguous. It could easily be approached using standard production rules as employed in GPS (Newell & Simon, 1995) or with a pattern-matching or schema-driven approach (Greeno, 1976).

The latter problem, by contrast, is *ill-defined*. Much of the necessary information is unavailable or underspecified: What supplies are required? How often must they be replenished? Who is available to make the shipments? And so on. To solve the problem, our hapless staffer will be forced to articulate, and answer, a number of related questions, frame and define missing criteria (e.g., what is "sufficient"), and be ready to defend their decisions after the fact. In short, he or she must *recharacterize* the problem to solve it, and that process will define the solution. In doing so, our officer will need to draw on a wide range of information, from the shelf-life of medical supplies, to the status of roads in Helmand, to the local governor's taste in cigars.

Our focus in this chapter is on ill-defined problems and domains. What does it mean for a problem or domain to be ill-defined and what are the implications for adaptive training technologies? We begin by clarifying what we mean by "problem,"

179

"domain," and "adaptation." We will then survey the relevant definitional and educational literature on ill-defined problems and ill-defined domains before presenting our own definition of the term. In so doing we will identify the challenges that ill-defined problems and domains pose for instructors and system developers. We will then survey a number of tutoring strategies and technologies that have been successfully employed in ill-defined domains before concluding with a set of recommendations for future work.

Logistical Problems versus Logistics

Problems are relatively specific task situations in which a student or professional seeks to achieve one or more goals given some initial criteria. Simple puzzle problems such as the "Missionaries and Cannibals" (Jonassen, 1997) are explicit, formal, and self-contained whereas problems such as *Pw* and *Pi* are more open, require external sources of information, and are thus more realistic. In educational settings, problems are tailored to exercise crucial skills or to test pedagogically important domain knowledge that the student is expected to transfer from practice to profession.

Domains are conceptual areas or fields of study such as Newtonian Mechanics, logistics, or law. These are characterized by pedagogical or procedural knowledge, prior examples or cases with which students and professionals should be familiar, and problems that they should be able to address. In educational settings, problems are drawn from a pedagogical domain and often grouped accordingly. In addressing specific problems, students come to understand the domain as a whole and develop skills that can be transferred to novel problems.

Adaptivity

The term "adaptation" is used in a number of contexts relevant to our current topic. As the other chapters in this volume illustrate,

"adaptive training systems" serve a number of functions from guiding students in help seeking (Aleven, Roll, & Koedinger, Chapter 4) to facilitating computer tutoring through natural dialogue-based interaction (D'Mello & Graesser, Chapter 6; Litman, Chapter 13). For a more complete survey, see Shute & Zapata-Rivera (Chapter 1). In case-based reasoning, relevant to many ill-defined domains, prior cases are adapted to meet current needs. Similarly, in recharacterizing ill-defined problems and domains, solvers adapt them so as to make them solvable. For the present chapter we will also be concerned with the educational adaptation by institutions, tutors, and students that adaptive training technologies are meant to support:

Institutional Adaptation: Occurs when training organizations, such as a school district or university, modify their procedures or pedagogy to meet new requirements.

Tutor Adaptation: Occurs when individual instructors or instructional systems respond to new pedagogy, problems, or problem solvers. This includes adapting to the scaffolding or support needs of particular students.

Student Adaptation: Occurs when students adapt to new problems, new domains, or new instructional contexts (e.g., field training versus classroom instruction).

On the other hand, adaptation occurs in response to:

Doctrinal Changes: Where new study domains (e.g., diplomacy, or unmanned aerial reconnaissance) are incorporated, or new research and new experiences render older educational techniques moot.

Task Changes: Where new tasks or study topics – such as new equipment, research, or cases – are incorporated into a field of study.

Novel Solutions: Where student-produced solutions or real-world experiences change the tutor's understanding of a domain or test his own knowledge.

Student Needs: Where a given student brings unique support needs, personal motivations, or background knowledge to the tutoring session.

The adaptive systems we highlighted earlier are chiefly concerned with tutor adaptation in response to students' needs or novel student solutions. However, the role that technology plays in facilitating adaptation is more complex. Educational institutions typically deploy new training technology to respond to new pedagogical needs, new tutoring contexts, or to improve student performance. These systems are in turn used in conjunction with or in lieu of human tutors with the goal of facilitating student adaptation. Thus a single system may in fact support several levels of adaptation.

In the next section we will define the terms *ill-defined problem* and *ill-defined domain* and discuss the unique challenges that they pose for students, tutors, and institutions. In subsequent discussion we will highlight a number of tutoring techniques that have been applied to address these challenges and identify the differing levels of adaptation that they have been designed to support.

Ill-Defined Domains and Ill-Defined Problems

In 1956, John McCarthy outlined a series of procedures for handling *well-defined problems* (McCarthy, 1956). For problems of this type there exists a known recognition function for candidate solutions. If a candidate solution is valid, then the function will terminate in a finite number of steps. If not, then it may loop indefinitely, making them *Turing recognizable languages* (Sipser, 1997). McCarthy noted ill-defined problems in his remarks, stating: "Not every worthwhile problem is well-defined in the sense of this paper. In particular, if there exist more or less satisfactory answers with no way of deciding whether an answer already obtained can be improved on [in] a reasonable time, the problem is not well-defined" (McCarthy, 1956, p. 6). Marvin Minsky then picked up this idea, noting that most

of the problems considered by Artificial Intelligence researchers are well defined, setting up a "frontier" view of definedness (Minsky, 1995). Any problem that has not yet been formalized, not yet been mapped, fenced, and mowed, is *ill-defined*.

This frontier view has been extended by a number of authors including Reitman (1964, 1965), Newell (1969), and Taylor (1974) in decision theory and management science; Voss (2006) in psychology; Simon (1973) in artificial intelligence (AI); Spiro et al. (1987), Jonassen (1997), and Shin et al. (2003) in education; and Goldin et al. (2006), Lynch et al. (2006, 2009), and Mitrovic and Weerasinghe (2009) in Intelligent Tutoring. Related work has also been done on Design problems (Goel & Pirolli, 1992), medical diagnosis (Barrows & Feltovich, 1987; Charlin et al., 2007; Pople, 1982) and unsolvable "Wicked Problems" (Conklin, 2006).

As Reitman, Voss, Jonassen, and the others noted, many, if not most, of the problems addressed by human problem solvers from law to tactics, design, or diagnosis are ill-defined or ill-structured.[1] This lack of structure is an essential feature of real-world problems and domains.

Each author approached the topic of ill-defined problems and domains with a distinct goal. Reitman sought to determine how human problem solvers address ill-defined problems. Newell focused on the relationship between a problem solver's *power* and their perception of a problem's solvability. Simon, by contrast sought to address the potential for automatic problem solving in ill-defined domains. Others such as Shin and colleagues, focused on students' problem-solving abilities and educational goals, whereas Mitrovic and Weerasinghe focused on the role of ill-defined problems and the design of intelligent tutoring systems. Each author has provided their own goal-driven definition that highlighted their areas of interest.

---

[1] The terms "ill-defined" and "ill-structured" are often used interchangeably in the literature. In this work we use the former term and have made substitutions where appropriate.

Ill-Defined Problems and Constraint Propagation

Reitman (1964, 1965) viewed problem solving as state space search. Problems are specified by a *problem requirement* consisting of: the initial or start state; the final state or goal criteria; and a set of acceptable transitions. In his view, problems are ill-defined when one or more of these criteria are un- or underspecified requiring the solver to specify or "close" them during the solution process.

Some components are left unspecified due to missing or implicit solution constraints (e.g., what supplies are needed first, and how quickly will they be used?). Others are unclear because they are defined in terms of *open-textured concepts* such as "sufficient," which cannot be specified in advance but require some measure of judgment (Berman & Hafner, 1985). Open-textured concepts such as "foreseeable" are common in domains such as law where their meaning in a given problem is subject to debate. Indeed, the definitions chosen are motivated by the interlocutor's ultimate goals and determine the final outcome.

Reitman takes a constraint-propagation view of problem solving. As solvers address ill-defined problems, they close the open or underspecified components by seeking out new information, selecting a definition from among a set of alternatives, or imposing them a priori. In some cases, these decisions are made implicitly, even unconsciously, based on the solver's preexisting assumptions or prior experience. Each decision imposes further constraints on the problem and its solutions that are propagated forward, thus limiting future alternatives. As problem solvers proceed, they gradually *recharacterize* the problem, transforming it into a better-defined, and more solvable, one.

In Reitman's view, this constraint propagation is non-monotonic. In observing a composer tasked with producing a fugue, he noted that the composer made multiple thematic decisions and explored the consequences of each before abandoning them in favor of other routes. In some cases the composer later returned to his earlier decisions after evaluating and then rejecting his subsequent choices. Simon (1973) described a similar process of selection and abandonment. He noted that design problems, particularly large-scale ones such as ship design, involve a number of seemingly disparate technical decisions, often made by separate groups (e.g., How deep is the draught? What size crew is required?), which can cause unanticipated conflicts down the road. In some cases this separation is a deliberate consequence of handing design questions to separate experts, whereas in others, such as home design, the conflicts only become apparent to a single designer at a later point in time.

According to Reitman, the presence of unspecified and open-textured components guarantees that there are a number of possible solutions to each ill-defined problem and that no one solution will be universally accepted. The fitness of a candidate solution will be judged based on the problem-solving context, the decisions made by each individual solver, and the judge's personal criteria, both explicit and implicit. This is a solver-centric echo of McCarthy's original comment about the impracticality of distinguishing between alternate answers.

Solutions and Argumentation

In the absence of unambiguously correct solutions, problem solvers must justify their choices and even anticipate potential problems. This is especially true in domains such as public policy or design, where the criteria are often vague and planning for a solution is separate from its implementation. Any solution offered must be backed up by a justification of the choices made and, in absence of an ability to *prove* its validity, an argument in its defense. Indeed for many such problems, no single solution will satisfy all possible stakeholders, a feature that makes them literally unsolvable. These are known as "Wicked Problems" (Conklin, 2006).

Jim Voss and his colleagues have conducted a series of studies on expertise and problem solving in ill-defined domains

(Voss, 2006; Voss et al., 1983). Problem solvers were tasked with articulating a solution to the then-Soviet Union's low agricultural production. The study participants included policy experts, some of whom focused on the Soviet Union, students enrolled in a course on Soviet policy, and faculty in the department of chemistry. In their analyses, Voss and his colleagues articulated a set of criteria that we paraphrase here:

- Ill-defined *problems*:
  1. have vaguely stated goals that require analysis and refinement to define the issue clearly;
  2. usually have no unambiguously right or wrong answers;
  3. have unstated or assumed problem constraints that must be retrieved and examined by the solver through "posting"; and
  4. require a large database of relevant information that is often difficult to access.
- *Solutions* to ill-defined problems:
  5. are typically not "right" or "wrong" but fall on a range of acceptability and plausibility;
  6. often cannot be judged on their own, but require some implementation and evaluation to test; and
  7. may take a substantial amount of time to implement and be affected by changing conditions, particularly for social problems (Voss et al., 1983).
- *Solvers* of ill-defined problems:
  8. typically divide their work into "problem representation" and "problem solving" phases; and
  9. usually justify their solutions by means of verbal argument defending the solution's plausibility, attacking particular constraints, or attempting to refute an anticipated counterargument.

In their view, ill-defined problems are "rhetorical in nature." In Voss et al. (2006), for example, Voss presents an expert's solution structured as an argument. In it the expert sought to identify the key features of the problem and to couple them with an argument for how each feature should be addressed. Problem solvers typically begin by formulating or recharacterizing the problem to make it solvable. They then present their solution along with an argument for its validity, justifying some of the structuring decisions made. The arguments are often formulated to attack particular aspects of the problem that were disputed, and to anticipate potential counterarguments and implementation problems. This process of anticipating counterclaims can also be found in mathematics (Lakatos, 1976).

In Voss's case studies (Voss et al., 1983), the expert problem solvers considered the social and technical sources of the agricultural problems as well as the political climate in which the solutions would be evaluated. One expert specifically noted that implementation would be governed by the kinds of political favors that the agricultural ministers could call in. The novices, by contrast, focused primarily on lower-level problems, presented few arguments to support their proposals, failed to anticipate potential problems in implementation, and, crucially, failed to consider the ideological or political constraints on their solutions. Taking the political and ideological constraints into account allowed domain experts to craft solutions that would be amenable to Soviet planners. The importance of considering the underlying objectives and value systems when solving these problems was noted by Fields (2006) and Checkland (1985).

The structure of justifications varies from domain to domain. Doctors and other diagnostic specialists pose hypothetical causes for observed symptoms and argue about the potential consequences of each course of treatment. Attorneys propose mappings of facts to legal factors and argue that some mappings are more or less consistent and normatively correct. A logistical officer, on the other hand, addressing Pi might focus on describing likely operating conditions, citing tactical and weather reports, estimating the storage capacity of remote firebases, and then arguing that a solution based on helicopter deliveries would be far more secure and adapt better to changing destinations.

Expertise and Ill-Definedness

Alan Newell examined ill-defined problems in management science such as hiring decisions (Newell, 1969). He hypothesized that solvers, both human and machine, will find a problem to be ill-defined if the power of their problem solving methods is low. In his view, the power of a problem-solving method is determined by the number of problems it can solve and the quality of solutions it guarantees relative to the amount of resources required. Blindly generating and testing all possible solutions (*generate and test*), although applicable to all problems, makes no guarantee that it can solve them or that it will produce good solutions in a reasonable amount of time.

Newell presented research on the performance of human problem solvers on ill-defined problems and argued, but did not prove, that human experts perform no better than heuristic search. He conjectured that expert problem solvers outperform novices because they are better at structuring vague problems and recognizing what weak methods apply based on prior experience. Reitman made a similar point about the role of background knowledge and shared assumptions. In his view, problems may appear ill-defined to one community but have a well-defined structure and well-accepted solutions in another (Reitman, 1965). Voss likewise asserted that extensive and well-structured background knowledge is particularly important when addressing ill-defined problems (Voss et al., 1983).

Expert problem solvers may also be better able to identify (implicit or explicit) solution criteria often ignored by novices, and to defend their choices via argument. As we discussed earlier, Voss's experts explicitly identified ideological and political constraints on the problem solutions and incorporated them into their problem-solving and argumentation processes. Thus,

in the musical world, catering to a listener's tastes may be a matter of both patronage and self-preservation. Musical legend holds that Frederick the Great, King of Prussia, once commanded Bach to improvise a fugue on the spot with six obbligato voices and a theme of his choosing. Bach wisely chose Frederick's own "Royal Theme," and the resulting fugue made its way into Bach's "Musical Offering," a set of pieces dedicated to the Emperor (Hofstadter, 1979). In this case, the expert composer drew on both his skills as a composer and his understanding of imperial expectations.

Absence of background information alone, however, does not explain the difference between expert and novice problem solvers. In ill-defined problems, problem solvers have to seek out alternatives (Reitman, 1964). Voss's experts spent more time considering alternative problem formulations and integrating their subsolutions than the novices who quickly focused on lower-level features and routinely failed to consider the consequences of their decisions or the cohesiveness of their overall solutions. This process of considering alternatives includes important metacognitive skills such as plan monitoring and self-assessment. In Fields's work as well as the work of Ge and Land (2004), discussed later in the chapter, the focus is on conscious metacognition such as self-explanation. However, expert problem solvers do not routinely make their reasoning explicit, and make these decisions at an unconscious level.

Pople (1982) presented a similar analysis of expert diagnosticians. Diagnostic reasoning is characterized by hypothesis-driven inquiry (Barrows & Feltovich, 1987; Pople, 1982). When presented with an incomplete or ill-structured case, diagnosticians will generate a number of hypotheses ranging from the general (e.g., "heart problem") to the specific (e.g., "aortic arrhythmia") based on the prevalent symptoms and general diagnostic information. They then contrast these hypotheses to identify useful follow-up questions, diagnostic tests, or productive treatments.

Expert physicians typically generate more early diagnostic hypotheses than novices (Pople, 1982). As a consequence they are less likely to overcommit to an early hypotheses. This early search is crucial for accurate diagnosis. According to Charlin et al. (2007), if a correct diagnostic hypothesis is considered within the first five minutes of treatment, then the diagnostician has a 95 percent chance of making the correct diagnosis. If, however, no correct hypothesis is generated within five minutes, then they have a 95 percent chance of misdiagnosis.

Expert diagnosticians use their prior knowledge to guide hypothesis generation. According to Charlin et al. (2007), prior experiences are encoded mentally as *illness scripts* – cognitive templates that represent disease progressions, likely symptoms, and courses of treatment. When examining a patient, expert diagnosticians will consider illnesses whose scripts are compatible with their diagnostic observations. They will then use these scripts to identify further diagnostic questions or to make treatment decisions. Experienced diagnosticians have better-developed scripts than novices, rely less on "textbook" definitions of disease, and are better able to deal with atypical cases (Barrows & Feltovich, 1987). This is consistent with Pople (1982), who argues that experts are better able to handle important omissions in the diagnostic data.

Voss and Post further noted that the process of ill-defined problem solving varies from one domain to another. In Voss and Post (1988), they contrasted policy decisions with judicial decisions and hiring problems. In law and human resources, the experts also focused on problem representation but relied more on external data to guide their decision making. Fernandes and Simon (1999) presented a detailed comparison of architects, engineers, physicians, and lawyers all tackling a famine relief problem. They concluded that the experts adopted unique reasoning processes typical of their fields. The lawyers, for example, focused on clarifying the facts of the famine and then balancing competing interests in their solution, whereas physicians favored techniques (e.g., diagnosis) and

solutions (e.g., nutritional programs) that were specific to their domain.

Cases and Flexibility

In discussing the role of background knowledge in problem solving, Greeno (1976) noted that ill-defined problem solving is often guided by a process of pattern matching and analogy from prior experience. Spiro and his colleagues have proposed a definition of *ill-defined domains* along these lines, which centers on the role of cases and case-based reasoning (Spiro et al., 1987). In their view, ill-defined domains are characterized by inconsistent cases and an absence of general rules, principles, or concepts general enough to cover them. Key domain features vary in importance from case to case, making prior examples necessary, especially in an educational context.

Their goal in advancing this definition was to focus attention on the limitations of existing educational methodologies in ill-defined domains such as history and medicine. In subsequent work (Spiro et al., 1988), Spiro and his colleagues detailed a number of common student misconceptions, such as a tendency to oversimplify complex domains, to rely on impoverished representations of domain concepts, and to passively receive structural information rather than identify relevant relationships themselves. Although they acknowledge that early or novice students may be better served by more rigid structures, they argue that this emphasis on *prepackaged* knowledge is a key limitation of existing methodologies for advanced instruction in ill-defined domains (Spiro & Jehng, 1990; Spiro et al., 1992).

In response to these limitations they propose a framework for learning called *Cognitive Flexibility Theory*. In their view, education should focus not on information or static schema retrieval but on the dynamic *assembly* of knowledge from prior cases and conceptual sources. They argue that teaching students to recognize complex relationships between cases and to adapt their knowledge as needed will make them better able to transfer that knowledge to new situations. This is consistent with the work of Pople (1982) and Ge and Land (2003, 2004), who noted the importance of active domain structuring in problem solving. To that end, Spiro and his colleagues describe a hypertext methodology of education, centered on presenting multiple interconnected cases to students with active student participation in case linking and retrieval. We will discuss their implementation of this methodology later in the chapter.

Our Definition

Ill-definedness is an open-textured concept. Each of the authors cited previously framed the definition differently to suit their diverse needs. Thus no single definition can really be *definitive*, as each one has its purpose and its merits. Although the definitions vary, they share a common core. With that in mind, we have proposed the following (Lynch et al., 2010):

1. A problem is *ill-defined* when essential concepts, relations, or solution criteria are un- or underspecified, open-textured, or intractable, requiring a solver to frame or *recharacterize* it. This recharacterization and the resulting solution are subject to debate.

2. *Ill-defined domains* lack a single strong domain theory uniquely specifying the essential concepts, relationships, and procedures for the domain and providing a means to validate problem solutions or cases. A solver is thus required to structure or *recharacterize* the domain when working in it. This recharacterization is subject to debate.

This framing or recharacterization is an essential part of the solution process. It may include restating or refining aspects of the problem to align it with specific domain concepts; redefining existing rules according to the present goals; clarifying the solution criteria; or analogizing the problem to and distinguishing it from prior examples. This reasoning process is common in law where advocates frame the case at hand to align it with the precedents (prior cases) and legal rules that will be advantageous for their client. In a notable case, *California v. Carney*,[2] where officers had entered a mobile home without a warrant, the defense argued that the mobile home was a home, thus emphasizing the right to privacy. The state, on the other hand, argued that it was a vehicle, thus emphasizing its potential mobility and the risk of flight. Each characterization aligned the case with a different set of legal principles and precedents carrying with them a different set of implications for the warrant requirement.

Recharacterization may also serve to make the problem more tractable by moving from an intractable or untestable set of standards (e.g., "design the *best possible* home") to ones that can be met and verified. Or it may focus the solver on a more bounded space of relevant concepts, relations, and rules. Both Simon (1973) and Voss (2006) focused on the importance of tractability in problem solving. Policy makers and diplomats, for example, spend a great deal of time seeking to clarify and refine their goals to move from the need to "reduce poverty" to a more specific benchmark. The problems of negotiation are discussed in Chapter 10 in this volume.

Our goal in presenting this definition was to focus on the central role of *recharacterization*, the closing of open constraints, specification of unstated information, or dynamic construction of knowledge in problem solving. This process of recharacterization is essential to the problem-solving process both in making prior cases and high-level information relevant to the present problem and in moving a given problem or domain from vague, intractable, or underspecified (e.g., "achieve a stable security environment," or "what is a modern artist? ") to one that is better specified, more tractable, and therefore more solvable. Due to the presence of unspecified, open-textured, and intractable concepts, and this need for recharacterization, ill-defined domains typically:

1. involve open-textured concepts and competing domain principles that are subject to debate;

[2] Docket #83–859 471 U.S. 386 (1985).

2. lack widely accepted domain theories identifying all of the relevant concepts and functional relations; and
3. have cases that are facially inconsistent.

Similarly, ill-defined problems commonly:

4. cannot be readily partitioned into independent subproblems;
5. involve the need to reason analogically with cases and examples;
6. have a large or complex solution space that prohibits one from enumerating all possible characterizations or solutions;
7. have competing or contradictory solutions that are subject to debate;
8. lack formal or well-accepted methods to verify solutions or clear criteria by which they should be judged;
9. are not considered to be "solved" when one solution is presented but may be readdressed by multiple solvers with distinct outcomes;
10. involve reasonable disagreements among domain experts regarding the adequacy of the solutions; and
11. have apparently successful solutions that are context-dependent (e.g., public policy decisions) and cannot, or should not, be copied uncritically.

On the other hand, solvers of ill-defined problems typically:

12. are required to justify their solutions through argument with reference to prior cases and possible outcomes;
13. often engage in a process of posing conjectures and responding to counterclaims during problem solving; and
14. must recharacterize or closely examine a problem to identify the central conflict or task.

Prior authors have presented these characteristics on par with the absent or underspecified information and the need for recharacterization. In our view, there is a causal relationship between them. The absence of general domain theories, expert disagreement, or facially inconsistent cases arise out of the presence of open-textured, unspecified, and intractable criteria and the consequential need for recharacterization. In recharacterizing the problems, solvers change the concepts that apply as well as the relationships between them, in effect replacing the problem with a closely related, more structured, and therefore more solvable analogue. They will be required to defend these characterization decisions, arguing that, among other things, their better-defined analogue is sufficiently close to the original. As a consequence, prior cases may appear facially inconsistent and preexisting theories will not necessarily hold as the concepts upon which they rest are redefined. This is particularly true of policy debates and other "wicked problems" (Conklin, 2006; Rittel and Webber, 1973) where solvers must recharacterize a problem to transform a mandate to "promote the general welfare" into programs for highway construction and public education. Such problems are, as a consequence, never "solved" in an absolute sense.

Not all ill-defined problems exhibit every one of these characteristics. Doctors or diplomats, for example, are often provided with (reasonably) clear solution criteria, whereas tacticians and architects are not always called on to align their work with prior cases. All of them, however, must recharacterize their problems to identify suitable solutions. Moreover, problem definition is a loose spectrum. On one end lie explicitly formal problems such as the Puzzle Problems (e.g., "Missionaries and Cannibals") described by Jonassen (1997). At the other end lie fully open or debatable arenas like art theory. As one moves across the spectrum, the role of recharacterization changes and the educational goals shift from teaching students mechanical problem-solving tasks to teaching them how to restructure and combine conflicting knowledge.

This is equally true for ill-defined domains. Absent a strong domain theory and rigidly defined domain concepts, ill-defined domains are often defined in terms of a set of mutually conflicting principles (e.g., "The right of people to be secure in their persons" and "The role of the state in preventing crime") or extensionally via representative cases.

When working in these domains, it is necessary to structure the relevant cases and concepts, often delineating what *is not* Dada and what *is* Punk (e.g., Man Ray and NOFX).

This is not to say that ill-defined domains are free of theories. Architects such as Alexander (1977, 1979) and tacticians such as von Clauswitz (1873) have proposed theories for their domains. However, these theories are not always widely accepted, cannot be formally verified, and do not cover all aspects of the domain. No a priori theory can anticipate all possible architectural or tactical problems any more than an attorney can accurately anticipate all future cases. Rather they are conventions used by practitioners and instructors to structure their own discussion or scaffold novices. Even domains with strong formal theories (e.g., Physics) become ill-defined at the fringes where new research is taking place and new theories are formed (Lakatos, 1976). As a result, problems taken from ill-defined domains tend to be ill-defined. Even though it is possible to structure them completely, as in the case of *Pw*, this process makes them less appropriate for advanced study but more tractable for novice problem solvers.

Borderline Cases

Ill-defined and well-defined problems are often facially similar. Both can involve recharacterization and, to novice problem solvers, appear intractable or underspecified. Consider the following problems:

Car: A 1,000 kg car rolls down a 30 degree hill. What is the net force acting on the car?

Checkerboard: Given a checkerboard with the two opposing corners removed, is it possible to tile the board with dominoes each one covering two adjacent tiles?

Fraction: Given a proper fraction, if you add 1 to both the numerator and denominator, will the resulting fraction be larger, smaller, or the same?

The first problem is a mainstay of introductory physics courses. It may be solved using linear kinematics, the Work-Energy Theorem, or a combination of both. Solvers must recharacterize it in terms of some particular set of equations as part of their solution process. However, this characterization is not driven by the presence of open-textured, underspecified, or intractable concepts, nor will it change the outcome of the problem. Both linear kinematics and the Work-Energy Theorem fit into the same theory of classical mechanics, both are equivalent and, if applied correctly, will produce the same result. Neither characterization is, in the context of classical physics, subject to reasonable debate. Thus, although the problem necessitates recharacterization, it is not ill-defined.

The Checkerboard problem has a lengthy history in AI. The common solution recharacterizes the problem in terms of paired tiles and color matching. However, the problem includes no open-textured or unspecified concepts. If one considers all possible board sizes, then the space of possible tilings grows large but is still regular, and thus tractable. No recharacterization of the problem will change the answer, nor will it be subject to reasonable debate. If, however, one seeks the *least-creative* solution as in McCarthy (1999), then it becomes ill-defined, as creativity is an open-textured concept, subject to ongoing debate (Buchanan, 2001).

This is also the case for the fraction problem. The problem itself is well-defined, with a clear logical solution.[3] For students unfamiliar with logic and algebra, the problem may appear ill-defined as they may not know where to begin. This is categorically different, however, from the problems of architecture or ethics where no amount

---

[3] The problem is to determine whether the square should be filled in with >, <, or =.

$$\left(\frac{X}{Y} \square \frac{(X+1)}{(Y+1)}\right) \Rightarrow ((X(Y+1)) \square (Y(X+1)))$$

$$\Rightarrow (XY + X) \square (YX + Y) \Rightarrow X \square Y \quad (1)$$

$$\text{Thus}: (X < Y) \Rightarrow \left(\frac{X}{Y} < \frac{(X+1)}{(Y+1)}\right)$$

$$(X = Y) \Rightarrow \left(\frac{X}{Y} = \frac{(X+1)}{(Y+1)}\right)$$

$$(X > Y) \Rightarrow \left(\frac{X}{Y} > \frac{(X+1)}{(Y+1)}\right) \quad (2)$$

of expertise can provide *the* indisputable answer. Similarly, there exists a number of viable representations for the fraction problem ranging from pieces of pie to glasses of water, each representation taking a different approach but all yielding the same solution. If, as with the checkerboard problem, we seek the most *pedagogically effective* solution or representation, then the problem will be ill-defined. Thus, in making the distinction between ill-defined and well-defined problems, the framing of the problem and assumptions regarding its solution make a crucial difference.

Borderline cases such as these also serve to highlight differences between our characterization of ill-definedness and other researchers. Mitrovic and Weerasinghe (2009), for example, argue that well-defined tasks or problems require clear start states, transitions, and solution criteria. Problems such as the fractions problem would, according to their definition, be ill-defined as they lack a clear algorithm for translating the problem statement into a suitable representation. In our view, however, the problem is well-defined because the essential problem components are well-defined and admit one correct solution irrespective of the representation

Ill-Definedness and Education

Ill-defined problems and domains are pedagogically important on many levels. They are closer to the problems solved by human experts in their professional practice than well-defined ones. Thus they are more motivating to novice students and diagnostic of their abilities. They require deeper and more flexible domain knowledge. They also require unique cognitive, metacognitive, and epistemic skills. In addition to cognitive skills of analogy and justification (Voss & Post, 1988; Voss et al., 1983), a number of other factors have been identified as being important for ill-defined problem solving. These include: well-integrated or "flexible" domain knowledge structured around cases (Ge & Land, 2003, 2004; Shin et al., 2003; Spiro et al., 1987, 1988); the ability to structure

knowledge dynamically for the task at hand (Fields, 2006; Spiro et al., 1987, 1988); and metacognitive skills such as planning and reflective judgment (Fields, 2006; Ge & Land, 2003, 2004).

Some authors have also argued that students' success at ill-defined problems is correlated with their epistemic beliefs, more specifically their willingness to question sources of knowledge or their tendency to accept knowledge passively (Fields, 2006; Schraw et al., 1995; Spiro et al., 1987, 1988). Because the skills required for ill-defined problems are different from those required in well-defined problem solving, students' performance on ill-defined problems will be affected by factors different from those affecting their performance on well-defined problems (Shin et al., 2003), and may even be wholly independent, as shown in Schraw et al. (1995).

For example, a central goal of legal education is to give students a "legal imagination" – that is, teaching them to recognize legally relevant similarities and differences in a set of cases and to exploit ambiguities within them when making arguments. Often the central challenge of an ill-defined problem is *problem recognition* – learning to recognize where conflicts exist and, by extension, how to address them (Jonassen, 1997; Shin et al., 2003). This process of recognition and representation is central to the practice of law and requires unique cognitive and metacognitive skills such as an ability to analogize and distinguish cases, to recognize legally relevant factors, and to anticipate counterarguments.

A well-defined problem such as *Pw* can test students' ability to calculate travel times or access required information, but it does not test their ability to determine what information is relevant or what calculations are necessary in an ambiguous case. Nor would a similarly formulated legal problem test students' ability to craft an appropriate legal ruling in the face of uncertainty. Problems such as *Pi* are closer to those solved by human experts than more well-defined ones. Thus they are both more motivating to students and more diagnostic of their professional skills. The importance of realistic practice has been stressed in the literature on Problem-Based Learning (Belland et al., 2008).

Thus it is important to engage students, particularly advanced students, with ill-defined problems and ill-defined domains, and to support them in the problem-solving process. It is also important for tutors and educational institutions that seek to produce advanced professionals to engage with and support learners in ill-defined domains. In the next section we will turn to the question of how adaptive training technologies can support students, tutors, and educational institutions to this end.

Ill-Definedness and Adaptation

Ill-defined problems are open, challenging, and exhibit conflicting cases and background knowledge not found in well-defined problems. For well-defined problems in educational contexts, the requisite background knowledge can be more easily circumscribed, collected, and added to the syllabus. A solver addressing Pw need only look up suitable answers from a book or compute them using a function. Similarly a tutor or educational institution need only compare students' answers to known acceptable values and solution paths. Such a domain is particularly suited to model-tracing tutoring systems such as the Andes physics tutor (VanLehn et al., 2005).

A solver addressing Pw, however, may draw on, and should heed, a wide range of information, from local customs to recent experiences. They will have to account for a variety of contradictory prior cases and exercise cognitive and metacognitive skills that are not always taught explicitly, if they are taught at all. They are free to form wholly novel solutions, from aerial drops, to bribery, to mule teams (Mauldin, 1945). They are also called on to justify their solution in terms of general principles, and to anticipate hypothetical possibilities. Tutors and institutional actors must be prepared to guide this often chaotic process and to respond to solutions that may draw

on novel experience wholly outside their expertise.

Educational institutions are tasked with preparing professionals, training future doctors or logistical staff officers. To that end they must: identify the requisite background knowledge for the profession; develop a curriculum to disseminate it; and identify suitable assessment mechanisms. In addition to complicating the search for background knowledge, ill-defined problems challenge an institution's ability to assess students' progress. No rigid standard or domain rule will be completely accepted by all instructors. Wholly novel solutions such as a decision to rely on local carriers may be a poor strategic decision – local carriers may taint delivered goods – or a flash of unique insight – they will be less prone to attacks than outsiders, and local hiring can boost the local economy to counter negative press. Judging these solutions without implementing them may be difficult at best, and in the presence of expert disagreement, it may be the case that any expert or group of experts consulted would oppose a solution that others will endorse.

Individual tutors must guide students as they work through a single problem or a series of topics within a domain. Adaptive tutoring technologies commonly provide support via a "two-loop" model where the tutor selects suitable training materials and study problems and then guides students on each step (VanLehn, 2006). In well-defined problems, a partial solution may be compared against an existing solution model to highlight unfinished or incorrect components. Whereas some recent work has shown that tutors can be successful without maintaining an accurate model of students' skills (Chi et al., 2004), other researchers have shown that accurate monitoring is important to tutoring effectiveness (Chi, 2009).

The presence of debatable solutions and wide-ranging background knowledge as well as the need to justify solutions complicates the tutorial process. In the presence of unambiguous solution criteria, it is often possible for a tutor to judge, or at least recognize, a partial solution. This is not guaranteed to be the case in ill-defined domains where students may have imposed several constraints on their solution but not yet be ready to justify or explain it. As a consequence, the tutor may not be able to reliably guide students once they become stuck or recognize when they are really treading down a garden path. Some paths may appear initially contradictory until the students' recharacterization is complete or, as noted by Reitman and Pople, early "failed" decisions may ultimately lead to, or even be, correct solutions (Pople, 1982; Reitman, 1965, 1964). Moreover, in many domains such as policy (Voss et al., 1983) and logistics, it may not be possible to fully judge a solution until it is implemented – a time-consuming and error-prone process in and of itself.

In addition to requiring unique skills many of which, such as argument and metacognition, are rarely taught explicitly, ill-defined domains pose a number of challenges for students. Novices often face difficulty identifying the underlying conflicts in ill-defined problems, notably in legal problems. They also face difficulty in distinguishing relevant from irrelevant background knowledge, anticipating the consequences of a solution, and identifying potential weaknesses. Many of the required skills and solution decisions are interdependent, making it difficult for students to focus on a particular decision or skill, or to recognize what challenges they face.

Two areas in which students require particular support are in justification and structuring. Argument, although important to many fields, is rarely taught explicitly even in domains such as law. And students often face challenges in justifying solutions that they have not yet completed or where the rationale is implicit at best. As noted by Fields, librarians can play a crucial role in helping students structure initially ill-defined problems and identify useful background materials (Fields, 2006).

Despite, or perhaps because of, these manifold challenges, ill-defined problems and domains are commonly used in instruction. Educational institutions have shown success in preparing solvers, sometimes despite the institution's best efforts (Hardy, 1940), and tutors have shown success at supporting students during problem solving. In this section we will discuss tutorial methods that have been successful in ill-defined problems and domains. Some of these methods are specific to adaptive tutoring technologies whereas others have been drawn from human practice.

Well-Defined Models and Skill Transfer

As we discussed earlier, ill-defined problems and domains require unique skills, such as recharacterization, that are not taught by well-defined problems and domains. Ill-defined domains also lack central widely accepted theories that can be used to solve all problems. Well-structured subdomains, and even well-structured problems, however, can be used to teach relevant skills, provided those skills can transfer from the well-defined model to ill-defined domains.

WELL-DEFINED SUBPROBLEMS
AND PROBLEM-SOLVING SKILLS
Well-defined skills such as recall and search are relevant in ill-defined domains such as scientific research. Students working on research problems in organic chemistry, for example, still need to understand basic skills such as computing the molar mass of a compound. Indeed well-defined problems have been used successfully to teach some metacognitive skills. Chi and VanLehn (2008), for example, report on a series of studies in which students were introduced to rigid problem-solving strategies in a restrictive-probability tutor and were then able to transfer those skills to a more open-ended tutor for Physics. Although neither domain is ill-defined, the skills learned, such as a focus on higher-level domain concepts versus lower-level features, are relevant to ill-defined problems. Moreover, Spiro and his colleagues argued that introductory students in ill-defined areas may benefit from more structured representations (Spiro et al., 1987, 1988). Thus, given a clear formulation of the desired skills and their relevance to the target domain, along with

suitable scaffolding for transfer, it is feasible to use well-defined problems with a clear set of problem-solving rules, background information, and solution criteria to scaffold learning in ill-defined domains.

MODEL-BASED DISCOVERY TUTORING

Well-defined problems with clear solution criteria coupled with a limited problem-solving procedure may be used to teach transferrable skills; however, they do not allow students to practice structuring an open domain or to explore novel relationships. Presenting students with a simulated domain, in which the observed behaviors, outcomes, or goals are constrained but the students' actions are not, allows students to practice structuring an open problem while allowing the tutors to scaffold the students' experiences and to control the pedagogical content more effectively.

In medicine, for instance, accurate diagnostic skills combined with a good bedside manner are essential to effective patient care. Medical students typically learn these skills "on the job" by dealing with real patients under the guidance of experienced physicians. Although realistic, this methodology is dependent on the cases at the hospital door. Rather than waiting for patients with Raynaud's disease to present themselves, the University of Pittsburgh's School of Medicine chooses to manufacture them.

Students at the school of medicine participate in simulated doctor-patient sessions. During these sessions they interact with an actor who has been coached to emulate both a set of difficult symptoms and an often trying personality. This process of simulated disease discovery is overseen by the instructor, who prepped the "patient," and by the students' peers. Once the session is over, students are given feedback on their interactions, their examination process, and the correctness of their diagnosis.

A similar approach has been taken in the Sherlock (see Lesgold, Chapter 15) and BiLat (see Lane & Wray, Chapter 10) systems. These tutors teach hardware diagnosis and diplomacy. In the former, students are guided in their work by a model of the hardware system and its user interface. The system also includes an expert model used to guide students in their solution. Ill-defined problems, those that go outside of the machine model, such as crossed circuits, are handled via special-purpose rules. This model permits the students to test a variety of diagnostic and repair tasks and to perceive a range of possible faults without putting existing equipment at risk. Similarly, BiLat places students in a negotiation setting where their task is to enter a village, form relationships with relevant parties, and achieve some diplomatic goal such as selecting a suitable location for a hospital.

This type of *model-based discovery* allows tutors to control the underlying problems so as to ensure that students are adequately challenged and experience a suitable range of test cases. The models can also be constructed, or coached in the medical case, to break their own rules in set ways so as to produce unexpected behavior. At the same time, the use of a simulated environment allows students to engage in free diagnosis and discussion as they would with a real patient. They can even make, and hopefully learn from, irrevocable mistakes such as insulting the local police chief without incurring real-world consequences. One key limitation of this methodology is that the diagnostic and diplomatic lessons learned are limited by the accuracy of the underlying model. As with well-defined problems, such models should be targeted to the key lessons that are expected to transfer.

The benefits of student-driven exploration have been articulated by Seymour Papert who endorsed relatively free exploration in *microworlds* (Papert, 1980), as opposed to the goal-driven exploration of BiLat. Here the model acts like the patient in an earlier medical case and allows for a full range of testing and feedback but with no specific problem in mind. Similar goal-free exploration approaches have been used in well-defined domains such as physics (van Joolingen, 1998) and ill-defined domains such as music (Holland, 2000).

One of the key challenges in model-based instruction is in identifying the pedagogically appropriate level of detail. In Katz et al. (1998), the authors describe a series of studies completed with the Sherlock II system (Lesgold, Chapter 15) for aircraft maintenance. The model used in those studies represented the desired circuitry at a fine level of detail, far finer than was necessary for instruction. The authors concluded that educational models should be tuned to the level at which the students will use them (e.g., at the level of replaceable parts rather than individual pathways), and at the students' level of comprehension suggesting that tutoring systems should begin with relatively coarse, higher-level models and then represent finer grains on an as-needed basis.

WEAK THEORY STRUCTURING

Ill-defined domains lack widely accepted central theories; rather, they are characterized by a number of competing theories each of which partially structures and defines relevant domain concepts and principles. Theories like the aforementioned Pattern Language (Alexander, 1977, 1979) serve to highlight key characteristics of the domain and facilitate the solution of some problems by providing a structural language for the expression of problems and solutions.

In educational contexts, these theories can be used to scaffold the work of novices. First-year architecture students at the University of Oregon, for example, are instructed to read "A Pattern Language" (Alexander, 1977) and then presented with design cases and design problems that they index, solve, and justify according to the language. This scaffolds students' work by making the design language explicit, facilitating both the formation and justification of solutions. As the students advance, they begin to reduce their dependence on the language by designing outside its precepts and critiquing its assumptions.

With model-based discovery, students are free to explore the model through any process or to take any action within the limits of the interface. The underlying model, however, remained constrained. In *weak domain theory* instruction, students are constrained to follow the dictates of a domain

theory but may do so within an unbounded domain. As with the well-structured model, this work is based on selecting a pedagogically relevant domain theory that, like the Pattern Language, teaches transferrable skills.

LARGO (Pinkwart et al., 2007), for example, is an ITS for legal argumentation (see Figure 9.1). It scaffolds students' analysis of oral argumentation using a diagrammatic model of argument with tests and hypothetical cases (Ashley et al., 2008). By restricting students to a predefined language of argument moves and justifications, it permits flexible argument construction, making the problem ill-defined, but retains the ability to scaffold interactions by restricting students to relevant argument moves. It also facilitates automated assessment by providing a shared language for feedback and guidance. LARGO uses the underlying argument model to provide feedback and guidance to the students without requiring a complete model of the domain or the underlying case. As the students mature, and require less immediate feedback, they can graduate to less-structured argument representations with weaker domain models.

Constraint-Based Tutoring

Forming even an incomplete or high-level domain model requires some specification of what a solution, or solution process, *is*. When tutors select relevant cases or provide a weak domain theory, they provide a model that encodes some of the relevant features of the domain and provides a proscriptive structure. In some domains, such as design, this may be an undesirable methodology. Considering *Pi*, a tutor guiding students in the problem-solving process may be willing to permit a range of solutions but not one that violates the existing code of conduct, or fails to deliver even a single meal.

Constraint-based tutors provide a methodology for tutoring based on specific proscriptions and prohibitions. Here the problem is defined in terms of a set of measurable criteria (e.g., supply routes must deliver food) and preferences (e.g., the

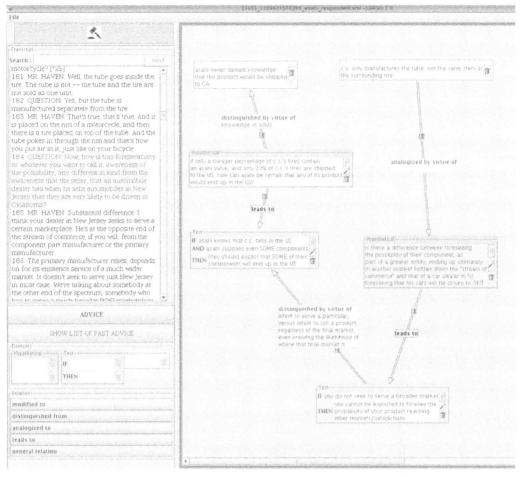

Figure 9.1. A LARGO screenshot showing a partially completed diagram.

fewer vehicles used, the better). These criteria define a class of viable solutions, all of which satisfy the minimal requirements.

According to Mitrovic and Weerasinghe (2009), constraint-based tutors are ideal for ill-defined problems as they permit tutors to restrict students to viable solutions without overly constraining them to an existing model. Their group has applied this methodology to the production of tutors for domains such as database design. In this methodology, students are given fairly free reign to construct their solutions while still permitting a tutor to give feedback when hard constraints are missed or met.

Conditioning

Ill-defined problems and ill-defined domains admit an unbounded space of potentially relevant information. For novice problem solvers this means a potentially indefinite search for relevant materials, whereas for tutors this means that students may present wholly novel and unanticipated solutions drawing on unfamiliar background materials. One approach to this issue is *background conditioning*. In this method, common in law schools, students are presented with a set casebook containing key cases and other background materials. Students are then instructed to generate arguments in a novel case, an ill-defined problem, using those materials. Conditioning the background information in this way scaffolds the students by restricting them to relevant material, according to the standards of the faculty, and supports faculty instruction by guaranteeing that they will be familiar with the materials cited. In many cases the materials may

ILL-DEFINED DOMAINS AND ADAPTIVE TUTORING TECHNOLOGIES

be selected not merely for relevance but to highlight a particular conflict or weakness within the domain. Constraining case materials also supports institutional adaptation by circumscribing the necessary educational materials and testing.

A similar approach is taken in the Rashi system (Dragon & Woolf, 2006). Rashi is an inquiry-based tutor that supports data discovery and hypothesis formation in a range of fields from art history to forestry. The system provides students with a preselected set of authentic materials including interviews and field data. It then allows them to form hypotheses and draw inferences based on them. Like LARGO, Rashi supports only a structured subset of the domain, in this case the relationships and hypotheses identified. Dealing with a limited domain restricts the problem space and permits prestructured feedback. Although this may transform the ill-defined problem into a well-defined one, the use of discovery learning allows students to identify relationships in a flexible manner and, at the same time, develop inquiry skills that can then be transferred to more open domains and materials.

Case-Based Instruction

In many ill-defined domains, case comparison, analogizing and distinguishing prior cases, and justifying decisions based upon them is an important skill that cannot be taught through other means. In some ill-defined domains, even weak theories may be absent, and cases provide the core domain structure. In a series of lectures on the case method, Karl N. Llewellyn asserted: "[N]o case can have a meaning by itself! Standing alone it gives you no guidance" (emphasis in the original). What counts is "that is the background of the other cases in relation to which you must read the one" (Llewellyn, 1960, p. 49). Rand J. Spiro and his colleagues advanced a similar argument when proposing Cognitive Flexibility Theory (Spiro et al., 1987, 1988), asserting that students should study domains through self-directed exploration of related cases in a dynamic case map.

Case-based instruction has been employed in a number of adaptive tutoring contexts. LARGO, as we discussed earlier, scaffolds students' analysis of individual legal cases and case arguments. CATO, by contrast, supports students' case-by-case comparisons (Aleven, 2003, 2006). In these systems, students explored a conditioned set of cases, deriving arguments using cross-case comparisons and legal factors. Cases have also been used in more exploratory contexts. Spiro and his colleagues developed a series of hypertext case exploration systems designed to instruct students in case comparison across history (Spiro & Jehng, 1990), medicine (Spiro et al., 1988), and film criticism (Spiro et al., 1992). In all of these systems, students explore case-by-case relationships in a relatively undirected manner. Cases have also been used, in combination with weak domain models, to provide more detailed feedback than the model could alone (Burke & Kass, 1996).

In case-based instruction, cases are typically selected or produced by an instructor or expert system and then presented to students for analysis. Larson (2005), by contrast, describes the use of student-provided cases for domain exploration. Graffiti is an automated conjecture-making system for extremal graph theory. Researchers using the system define a set of example graphs from which the system induces relevant boundaries. After being presented with a conjecture, the user is asked to accept it or to articulate a counterexample that is then added to the case base. In an educational context, students use the system to explore the domain, allowing the system's conjectures to guide their understanding and to challenge their assumptions.

Apart from a focus on the key cognitive skills of case comparison and the development of cognitive flexibility, case instruction can be more motivating for novice students. Cases drawn from existing practice reflect detailed realistic problems and may be more up to date than older, more static domain theories. Indeed analysis of recent cases is essential for the maintenance of professional skills in many domains. Attorneys track and debate changes in existing caselaw just as medical professionals or research scientists examine and comment on new findings to further their own work.

This structure of case analysis and discussion has been implemented in recent work by the U.S. Army Combined Arms Center (Morris, 2009), which has developed discussion tools to support the presentation and analysis of cases in logistics, tactics, and other domains. This work is an interesting example of adaptation that supports individual learners or continuing professionals in adapting to new experiences by providing a source for recent cases and analysis of those cases. It also supports institutional adaptation by facilitating the collection of current field experiences with analysis. This repository can then be used to derive new institutional wisdom as well as guide future novices.

Process Support

The presence of open-textured or undefined concepts in ill-defined problems and domains makes it difficult to model, or even constrain, solutions to those problems or cases in the domains. In their analysis of policy domains, Voss and his colleagues noted that expert problem solvers followed a structured problem-solving process (Voss, 2006; Voss et al., 1983), separating their work into explicit representation, solving, and justification phases. Other authors, including Shin, Jonassen and McGee (2003) and Fields (2006), have also noted the importance of problem-solving processes in ill-defined domains, whereas Jonassen (1997) articulated a specific seven-step solution process involving specific space representation, solution generation, and monitoring phases.

ICCAT, a tutoring system for intercultural competence, takes a *process support* approach to tutoring (Ogan et al., 2008a, 2009) (see Figure 9.2). Students using the system are presented with a clip taken from a French film and are asked to predicts what will happen next. They then test their predictions by viewing the clip and reflecting on the success or failure of their expectations. This process is called "pause, predict, ponder." ICCAT does not attempt to model the students' analyses or to assess their predictions. Rather, it focuses on structuring their engagement with the task to ensure that they carry out the necessary reflection and analysis. In subsequent work, the system was augmented to support the tutor's interaction with students in an online discussion (Ogan et al., 2008b). Similar work has also been completed by Belland et al. (2008) and Cho and Schunn (2007) to support peer argument in online settings.

Question Prompts

As noted earlier in the chapter, novice problem solvers facing ill-defined problems often fail to engage in crucial cognitive or metacognitive processes such as monitoring and solution assessment. As a consequence they focus on low-level issues and often fail to develop alternative solutions or integrate them effectively. Ge and Land (2003, 2004) proposed a solution framework based in part on question prompts designed to support students' metacognition and reflection. Like ICCAT, this framework is designed to consider the students' solution process by presenting distinct prompts for each of the problem representation, development, justification, and monitoring phases.

Ge and Land delineate three types of question prompts: procedural prompts such as "An example of this..."; elaboration prompts such as "Why is this important?"; and reflection prompts such as "Have our goals changed?" Each prompt type serves distinct cognitive and metacognitive purposes guiding students to either think more deeply about the decisions made, consider alternatives, or monitor their own progress. Question prompts, particularly question prompts that result in self-explanations, have shown success in better-defined domains (Chi et al., 1994). As Ge and Land note, they have been particularly successful with metacognitive skills. They also note, however, that question prompts do not always transfer cleanly across domains, and students' ability to adequately address the

Figure 9.2. An ICCAT screenshot showing student predictions. Copyright © 2008 Amy Ogan. Used with permission.

prompts is limited by their prior knowledge. Moreover, students often give shallow or cursory responses to prompts, thus failing to engage in deeper metacognition.

Study results reported in Ge and Land (2003) show that students who were given question prompts not only performed better on an ill-defined problems but were more successful at each of the solution steps. Subsequent qualitative analysis indicated that students who received the prompts engaged in better metacognitive strategies than the control group. Self-explanation prompts designed to induce metacognition have also been employed in the LARGO system (Pinkwart et al., 2006).

One additional type of prompt, not discussed by Ge and Land, is what we call *expectation prompts*. In this form, suggested by Alan Lesgold (personal communication), the students are prompted to state what they expect to be true if they have identified a successful solution. Alternatively, they may be prompted to make explicit any underlying domain expectations (e.g., students' test performance is based solely on their classroom activities) or to state what consequences they expect from particular solution decisions (e.g., replacing teachers will reduce absenteeism). Doing so would

allow the student to gain interim feedback by testing their expectations (in much the same way as was done in ICCAT (Ogan et al., 2008a, 2009). It would also allow the tutor, or peers, an opportunity to highlight faulty assumptions or solution paths that they have, perhaps subconsciously, discarded.

Peers, Experts, and Critics

In addition to recommending question prompts, Ge and Land (2003, 2004) also discuss the use of peer interactions to guide students' work. Peers, like question prompts, can challenge students, encouraging them to think more deeply about their solutions, engage in metacognition, and consider alternatives. In debate-oriented domains such as law and science, peers provide this support by: presenting counterarguments during class debates or moot court sessions; identifying structural weaknesses in the proposed arguments; or seeking clarification of ambiguous or unstated assumptions. In design domains, peers can present alternate solutions to the same problem and contrast the alternative proposals. Peers can also act in a more collaborative fashion by helping each other structure the problem.

In some cases, such as in a moot court setting, panels of experts will be used in lieu of peers. These experts, typically legal professors, can provide robust feedback in domains where experts may reasonably disagree. As with peer feedback, the presence of multiple experts allows students to receive a range of opinions and to identify multiple perspectives. Indeed, the techniques that are described later in the chapter can easily be applied to a single novice interacting with a set of experts either as peers or judges. In either case the use of peers, or panels of experts, can help tutors adapt to new arenas by presenting them with a raft of solutions to contrast with. It can also help, in some cases, reduce the tutoring load by tasking the other students with providing basic support. At an institutional level, it supports adaptation by allowing assessment to be based on a scholarly community rather than a single, static source.

Ge and Land's discussion was focused on collaborative problem-solving discussions in which peers interacted during the course of problem solving, identifying weaknesses, suggesting alternative solutions, and providing explanations. Similar work on the benefits of peer interaction was presented by Belland et al. (2008) and Kapur and Kinzer (2007). The SWoRD system, by contrast, supports essay writing via anonymous feedback and peer review structured along the lines of a scholarly community (Cho & Schunn, 2007; Cho et al., 2008). In the LARGO system, peer feedback was used in an asynchronous fashion, with students being asked to rate selected portions of other students' annotations and then to review, and possibly revise, their own (Pinkwart et al., 2006).

Peer interactions, however, are not a panacea. As discussed by Kapur & Kinzer (2007), peer groups are prone to a number of problems, such as unequal group participation, that adversely impact their learning. Interestingly, the observed inequity was not driven by the simple tendency of one group member to dominate discussion but by the tendency of the group to focus on the first solution provided rather than challenging it or providing alternatives, especially later in the process. Thus, according to Kapur and Kinzer, it is necessary for developers of collaborative interactions to structure not the group roles but the peer process, encouraging the production of alternate solutions and critiques. Work has been done along these lines using adaptive support models to guide student participation (Kay and Kummerfeld, Chapter 7 in this volume; Walker et al., 2008), or tools to support faculty moderators (Kay et al., 2007; Scheuer and McLaren, 2008).

Conclusions

Ill-defined domains and ill-defined problems such as *Pi* are characterized by unspecified or open-textured concepts, goals, and criteria. Solvers working on them must *recharacterize* the problems or domains to make them solvable. As a consequence, ill-defined domains typically lack well-accepted domain theories, have incomplete definitions of essential domain concepts, and have facially inconsistent cases. Similarly, ill-defined problems have multiple conflicting solutions about which experts can reasonably disagree. As a consequence, it is often necessary for solvers to justify their proposed solutions in terms of past cases and likely outcomes. Moreover, working on ill-defined problems or in ill-defined domains requires unique cognitive and metacognitive skills, such as analogizing cases and monitoring of cognition, that are not tested by well-defined problems. As a result, students, tutors, instructional agencies, and developers of adaptive training technologies face a number of difficulties when dealing with these problems that, as discussed earlier, need to be addressed.

In this chapter we surveyed the unique characteristics of ill-defined problems and domains, discussed their educational relevance, and identified some of the tutorial strategies that have been used to address them. Our goal in this survey was to highlight these unique features and to provide a framework for analysis. Through our survey of prior work we have sought to provide guidance for developers of adaptive training technologies who will work in ill-defined domains or with ill-defined problems. As we have indicated previously, none of these strategies is a panacea, nor will all strategies be appropriate for all contexts. Justifications, while central to law, may be inappropriate for painting or music. Similarly, solution constraints, while important in logistical training, may be unworkable in an open-policy domain.

The authors that we cited earlier have examined one or more of these tutoring techniques. Some of them have made specific recommendations for the development of instruction and instructional systems in ill-defined domains. Where relevant, we have cited those recommendations earlier in the chapter. Rather than rehash them, we will conclude with seven general recommendations of our own for prospective developers and deployers of adaptive training technologies for ill-defined problems and domains:

1. *Support both explicit and implicit framing and recharacterization.* Framing and recharacterization are essential skills for the solution of ill-defined problems and the exploration of ill-defined domains. Tutors and tutoring systems should support students in explicitly framing problems by redefining the essential solution criteria and the recharacterization of domains by helping students identify alternate relationships among the cases or concepts. Prior systems have approached this problem in a number of ways, but the best mechanism remains an open research question.

2. *Support case-based instruction.* Expert problem solvers use cases to structure ill-defined domains extensionally, to guide them when solving ill-defined problems, and to justify the decisions made. Tutors should support students in *analogizing* and *distinguishing* cases within a domain, in using these relationships to retrieve precedents for an ill-defined problem, and in using those examples to guide and justify their solution process.

3. *Focus on skill-specific instruction.* Working in ill-defined domains and on ill-defined problems requires a number of unique skills, some of which, such as argumentation, are rarely taught explicitly. Moreover, many of these skills, particularly metacognitive skills, are interrelated, making them difficult to exercise independently. When designing training in these arenas, it is important to specify what skills are, or should be, taught and to what future problems or domains they are expected to transfer. Rather than developing a tutor for "logistics," it may make more sense, particularly for novice students, to develop individual tutors for relevant skills such as identification of key tactical information, route finding, and intercultural competence. These individual tutors can then segue through scaffolding to a more complex and larger-scale system.

4. *Identify the target level of the adaptation.* Some of the technologies and techniques that we have discussed, such as Web forums and pattern mining, are designed to aid institutions in adapting to a target domain through the collection of current cases. Others, such as peer collaboration, are better targeted to the individual. It is possible for one system to facilitate adaptation at several levels. However, as with the skills desired, it is important to make that clear when developing and deploying the technology so as to avoid incorrect and often costly assumptions.

5. *Model, scaffold, and fade over time.* The needs of novice students differ from those of more advanced problem solvers. Complete novices in ill-defined domains may benefit from a restricted domain of background information and a well-defined problem space. As students advance over time, this rigidity will become constraining and they will be better served by more dynamic mechanisms such as peer review and case-based instruction. Such mechanisms provide less immediate support but allow for a much more realistic

problem-solving experience. This process was discussed extensively in Collins et al. (1989).

6. *Draw from existing human practice.* Despite the manifold challenges of tutoring in ill-defined domains, human tutors have done so for millennia. Although some of the techniques employed, such as textbook memorization, might be detrimental to advanced students, others, such as moot court sessions, have practical utility and can be readily transposed from the classroom to the chatroom. When developing adaptive training in an ill-defined domain, developers should closely examine existing instructional practices to see which practices can be efficiently reused and which should be discarded.

7. *Design for realistic practice.* Ill-defined problems are more realistic than well-defined ones. This is motivating for student problem solvers and facilitates transfer of lessons from the classroom to the field. Adaptive training technologies should be designed, when possible, to mirror professional practice so as to maintain this realism and to facilitate the immediate transfer of skills.

The design of a tutoring system for an ill-defined domain is itself an ill-defined problem. Thus the recommendations that we and other authors have provided should be read, not as hard-and-fast rules, but as guidelines designed to scaffold exploration. To quote Thoreau, "One should not stretch the seams when putting on the coat for it may do good service for him whom it fits."

References

Aleven, V. (2003). Using background knowledge in case-based legal reasoning: A computational model and an intelligent learning environment. *Artificial Intelligence, 150*:183–237.

Aleven, V. (2006). An intelligent learning environment for case-based argumentation. *Technology, Instruction, Cognition, and Learning, 4*(2):191–241.

Aleven, V., Ashley, K. D., Lynch, C., & Pinkwart, N. (Eds.) (2006). *Proceedings of the First International Workshop on Intelligent Tutoring Systems for Ill-Defined Domains.* Held in conjunction with the 8th International conference on Intelligent Tutoring Systems, Jhongli Taiwan.

Alexander, C. (1977). *A Pattern Language.* New York: Oxford University Press.

Alexander, C. (1979). *The Timeless Way of Building.* New York: Oxford University Press.

Ashley, K. D., Lynch, C., Pinkwart, N., & Aleven, V. (2008). A process model of legal argument with hypotheticals. In Francesconi, E., Sartor, G., & Tiscornia, D. (Eds.), *JURIX*, vol. 189 of *Frontiers in Artificial Intelligence and Applications* (pp 1–10). Amsterdam: IOS Press.

Barrows, H. S., & Feltovich, P. J. (1987). The clinical reasoning process. *Medical Education, 21*(2):86–91.

Belland, B. R., Glazewski, K. D., & Richardson, J. C. (2008). A scaffolding framework to support the construction of evidence-based arguments among middle school students. *Education Technology & Research Development, 56*:401–422.

Berman, D. M., & Hafner, C. (1985). Obstacles to the development of logic-based models of legal reasoning. In Walter, C. & Allen, L. E. (Eds.), *Computing Power and Legal Reasoning* (pp. 183–214). Eagan, MN: West Publishing.

Buchanan, B. G. (2001). Creativity at the metalevel: Aaai-2000 presidential address. *AI Magazine, 22*(3):13–28.

Burke, R. D., & Kass, A. K. (1996). Interest-focused tutoring: A tractable approach to modeling in intelligent tutoring systems. Technical Report TR-96–08.

Charlin, B., Boshuizen, H. P., Custers, E. J., & Eltovich, P. J. (2007). Scripts and clinical reasoning. *Medical Education, 41*:1178–1184.

Checkland, P. B. (1985). Formulating problems for systems analysis. In Miser, H. J. & Quade, E. S. (Eds.), *Handbook of Systems Analysis: Overview of Uses, Procedures, Applications, and Practice* (pp. 151–170). New York: North-Holland.

Chi, M. (2009). *Does step-level tutorial decisions matter: Applying reinforcement learning to induce pedagogical tutorial tactics.* PhD thesis, Intelligent Systems Program, University of Pittsburgh.

Chi, M., & VanLehn, K. (2008). Eliminating the gap between the high and low students through meta-cognitive strategy instruction. In Woolf,

B. P., Aïmeur, E., Nkambou, R., & Lajoie, S. P. (Eds.), *Intelligent Tutoring Systems, 9th International Conference, ITS 2008, Montreal, Canada, June 23–27, 2008, Proceedings,* vol. 5091 of *Lecture Notes in Computer Science.* (pp. 603–613). Berlin: Springer.

Chi, M. T. H., deLeeuw, N., Chiu, M.-H., & LaVancher, C. (1994). Eliciting self-explanations improves understanding. *Cognitive Science, 18*(3):439–477.

Chi, M. T. H., Siler, S., & Jeong, H. (2004). Can tutors monitor students' understanding accurately? *Cognition and Instruction, 22*(3):363–387.

Cho, K., Chung, T. R., King, W. R., & Schunn, C. D. (2008). Peer-based computer-supported knowledge refinement: an empirical investigation. *Communications in ACM, 51*(3):83–88.

Cho, K., & Schunn, C. (2007). Scaffolded writing and rewriting in the discipline: A Web-based reciprocal peer review system. *Computers and Education,* 48(3):409–426.

Collins, A., Brown, J. S., & Newman, S. E. (1989). Cognitive apprenticeship: Teaching the craft of reading, writing and mathematics. In Resnick, L. B. (Ed.), *Knowing, Learning and Instruction: Essays in Honor of Robert Glaser* (pp. 453–494). Mahwah, NJ: Lawrence Erlbaum.

Conklin, J. (2006). Chapter 1: Wicked problems & social complexity. In *Dialogue Mapping: Building Shared Understanding of Wicked Problems.* London: Wiley.

Dragon, T., & Woolf, B. P. (2006). Guidance and collaboration strategies in ill-defined domains. In Aleven, V., Ashley, K. D., Lynch, C., & Pinkwart, N. (Eds.), *Proceedings of the First International Workshop on Intelligent Tutoring Systems for Ill-Defined Domains.* Held in conjunction with the 8th International conference on Intelligent Tutoring Systems, Jhongli Taiwan (pp. 65–73).

Fernandes, R., & Simon, H. A. (1999). A study of how individuals solve complex and ill-structured problems. *Policy Sciences,* 32:225–245.

Fields, A. M. (2006). Ill-structured problems and the reference consultation: The librarian's role in developing student expertise. *Reference Services Review,* 34(3):405–420.

Ge, X., & Land, S. M. (2003). Scaffolding students' problem-solving processes in an ill-structured task using question prompts and peer interactions. *Educational Technology Research and Development,* 51(1):21–38.

Ge, X., & Land, S. M. (2004). A conceptual framework for scaffolding ill-structured problem-solving processes using question prompts and peer interactions. *Educational Technology Research and Development,* 52(2):5–22.

Goel, V., & Pirolli, P. (1992). The structure of design problem spaces. *Cognitive Science,* 16:345–429.

Goldin, I., Ashley, K., & Pinkus, R. (2006). Teaching case analysis through framing: Prospects for an its in an ill-defined domain. In Aleven, V., Ashley, K. D., Lynch, C., & Pinkwart, N. (Eds.), *Proceedings of the First International Workshop on Intelligent Tutoring Systems for Ill-Defined Domains.* Held in conjunction with the 8th International conference on Intelligent Tutoring Systems, Jhongli Taiwan (pp. 83–91).

Greeno, J. G. (1976). Indefinite goals in well-structured problems. *Psychological Review,* 83(6):479–491.

Hardy, G. H. (1940). *A Mathematician's Apology.* Cambridge: Cambridge University Press.

Hofstadter, D. R. (1979). *Gödel, Escher, Bach: An Eternal Golden Braid.* New York: Vintage Books.

Holland, S. (2000). Artificial intelligence in music education: A critical review. In Miranda, Eduardo Reck (Ed.), *Readings in Music and Artificial Intelligence* (pp. 239–274). New York: Harwood Academic Publishers.

Jonassen, D. H. (1997). Instructional design models for well-structured and ill-structured learning outcomes. *Educational Technology: Research and Development,* 45(1):65–94.

Kapur, M., & Kinzer, C.K. (2007). Examining the effect of problem type in a synchronous computer-supported collaborative learning (CSCL) environment. *Education Technology & Research Development,* 55:439–459.

Katz, S., Lesgold, A., Hughes, E., Peters, D., Eggan, G., Gordin, M., & Greenberg, L. (1998). Sherlock 2: An intelligent tutoring system built on the lrdc tutor framework. In Bloom, C. P. & Loftin, R. B. (Eds.), *Facilitating the Development and Use of Interactive Learning Environments* (pp. 227–258). Mahwah, NJ: Lawrence Erlbaum Associates.

Kay, J., Reimann, P., & Yacef, K. (2007). Mirroring of group activity to support learning as participation. In Luckin, R., Koedinger, K. R., & Greer, J. E. (Eds.), *AIED,* vol. 158 of *Frontiers in Artificial Intelligence and Applications* (pp. 584–586). Amsterdam: IOS Press.

Lakatos, I. (1976). *Proofs and Refutations.* Cambridge: Cambridge University Press.

Larson, C. E. (2005). A survey of research on automated mathematical conjecturemaking, graphs and discovery. *Proceedings of the American Mathematical Society* (pp. 297–318).

Llewellyn, K. N. (1960). *The Bramble Bush; On Our Law and Its study*. Dobbs Ferry, NY: Oceana Publications.

Luger, G. F. (Ed.) (1995). *Computation & Intelligence: Collected Readings*. Menlo Park, CA and Cambridge, MA: AAAI and MIT Press.

Lynch, C., Ashley, K. D., Aleven, V., & Pinkwart, N. (2006). Defining ill-defined domains; a literature survey. In Aleven, V., Ashley, K. D., Lynch, C., & Pinkwart, N. (Eds.), *Proceedings of the First International Workshop on Intelligent Tutoring Systems for Ill-Defined Domains*. Held in conjunction with the 8th International conference on Intelligent Tutoring Systems, Jhongli Taiwan (pp. 1–10).

Lynch, C., Ashley, K. D., Aleven, V., & Pinkwart, N. (2009). Concepts structures and goals: Redefining ill-definedness. *International Journal of Artificial Intelligence in Education: Special Issue on Ill-Defined Domains*. 19(3):253–266.

Mauldin, B. (1945). *Up Front*. New York: Henry Holt and Company.

McCarthy, J. (1956). The inversion of functions defined by turing machines. In Shannon, J. M. (Ed.), *Automata Studies, Annals of Mathematical Studies*, 34:177–181. Princeton, NJ: Princeton University Press.

McCarthy, J. (1999). Creative solutions to problems. In the AISB Symposium on AI and Scientific Creativity (pp. 44–48).

Minsky, M. (1995). Steps to artificial intelligence. In Luger, G. F. (Ed.), *Computation & Intelligence: Collected Readings*. (pp. 47–90). Menlo Park, CA and Cambridge, MA: AAAI and MIT Press.

Mitrovic, A., & Weerasinghe, A. (2009). Revisiting ill-definedness and the consequences for itss. In Dimitrova, V., Mizoguchi, R., duBoulay, B., & Graesser, A. C. (Eds.), *AIED*, vol. 200 of *Frontiers in Artificial Intelligence and Applications* (pp. 375–382). Amsterdam: IOS Press.

Morris, D. R. (2009). Networked communities in an advanced blended learning framework architecture. Presented at the ARI Workshop on Adaptive Training Technologies.

Newell, A. (1969). Heuristic programming: Ill-structured problems. *Progress in Operations Research*, 3:361–413.

Newell, A., & Simon, H. A. (1995). Gps, a program that simulates human thought. In Luger, G. F. (Ed.), *Computation & Intelligence: Collected Readings*. (pp. 415–428). Menlo Park, CA and Cambridge, MA: AAAI and MIT Press.

Ogan, A., Aleven, V., & Jones, C. (2008a). Pause, predict, and ponder: Use of narrative videos to improve cultural discussion and learning. In Czerwinski, M., Lund, A. M., & Tan, D. S. (Eds.), *CHI* (pp. 155–162). New York: ACM.

Ogan, A., Aleven, V., & Jones, C. (2009). Advancing development of intercultural competence through supporting predictions in narrative video. *International Journal of Artificial Intelligence in Education: Special Issue on Ill-Defined Domains*, 19(3):267–288.

Ogan, A., Walker, E., Aleven, V., & Jones, C. (2008b). Toward supporting collaborative discussion in an ill-defined domain. In Woolf, B. P., Aïmeur, E., Nkambou, R., & Lajoie, S. P. (Eds.), *Intelligent Tutoring Systems, 9th International Conference, ITS 2008, Montreal, Canada, June 23–27, 2008, Proceedings*, vol. 5091 of *Lecture Notes in Computer Science*. (pp. 825–827). Berlin: Springer.

Papert, S. (1980). *Mindstorms: Children, Computers, and Powerful Ideas*. New York: Basic Books.

Pinkwart, N., Aleven, V., Ashley, K. D., & Lynch, C. (2006). Toward legal argument instruction with graph grammars and collaborative filtering techniques. In Ikeda, M., Ashley, K. D., & Chan, T.-W. (Eds.), *Intelligent Tutoring Systems*, vol. 4053 of *Lecture Notes in Computer Science* (pp. 227–236). Berlin: Springer.

Pinkwart, N., Aleven, V., Ashley, K., & Lynch, C. (2007). Evaluating legal argument instruction with graphical representations using largo. In *Proceedings of AIED2007* (pp. 101–108). Marina Del Rey, CA.

Pople, H. E. (1982). Heuristic methods for imposing structure on ill-structured problems: The structuring of medical diagnostics. In Szolovits, P. (Ed.), *AI in Medicine*, Chapter 5. Boulder, CO: Westview Press.

Reitman, W. R. (1964). Heuristic decision procedures, open constraints and the structure of ill-defined problems. In Shelly, II, M. & Bryan, G. L. (Eds.), *Human Judgments and Optimality* (pp. 282–315). New York: John Wiley & Sons.

Reitman, W.R. (1965). *Cognition and Thought: An Information Processing Approach*. New York: John Wiley & Sons.

Rittel, H., & Webber, M. (1973). Dilemmas in a general theory of planning. *Policy Sciences*, 4:155–169.

Scheuer, O., & McLaren, B. M. (2008). Helping teachers handle the flood of data in online student discussions. In Woolf, B. P., Aïmeur, E., Nkambou, R., & Lajoie, S. P. (Eds.), *Intelligent*

Tutoring Systems, 9th International Conference, ITS 2008, Montreal, Canada, June 23–27, 2008, Proceedings, vol. 5091 of *Lecture Notes in Computer Science* (pp. 323–332). Berlin: Springer.

Schraw, G., Dunkle, M. E., & Bendixen, L.D. (1995). Cognitive processes in well-defined and ill-defined problem solving. *Applied Cognitive Psychology*, 9:523–538.

Shin, N., Jonassen, D. H., & McGee, S. (2003). Predictors of well-structured and ill-structured problem solving in an astronomy simulation. *Journal of Research in Science Teaching*, 40(1):6–33.

Simon, H. A. (1973). The structure of ill-structured problems. *Artificial Intelligence*, 4:181–201.

Sipser, M. (1997). *Introduction to the Theory of Computation*. Boston: PWS Publishing Company.

Spiro, R. J., Coulson, R. L., Feltovich, P. J., & Anderson, D. K. (1988). Cognitive flexibility theory: Advanced knowledge acquisition in ill-structured domains. In Patel, V. L. & Croen, G. J. (Eds.), *Program of the Tenth Annual Conference of the Cognitive Science Society* (pp. 375–383). Hillsdale, NJ: Lawrence Earlbaum Associates.

Spiro, R. J., Feltovich, P. J., Jacobson, M. J., & Coulson, R. L. (1992). Cognitive flexibility, constructivism, and hypertext: Random access instruction for advanced knowledge acquisition in ill-structured domains. In Duffy, T. M. & Jonassen, D. H. (Eds.), *Constructivism and the Technology of Instruction* (pp. 57–75). London: Routledge.

Spiro, R. J. & Jehng, J.-C. (1990). Cognitive flexibility and hypertext: Theory and technology for the nonlinear and multidimensional traversal of complex subject matter. In Nix, D. & Spiro, R.(Eds.), *Cognition, Education and Multimedia: Exploring Ideas in High Technology* (pp. 163–205). Hillsdale, NJ: Lawrence Earlbaum Associates.

Spiro, R. J., Vispoel, W. P., Schmitz, J. G., Samarapungavan, A., & Boerger, A. E. (1987). Knowledge acquisition for application: Cognitive flexibility and transfer in complex content domains. In Britton, B. K. & Glynn, S. M. (Eds.), *Executive Control Processes in Reading* (pp. 177–199). Hillsdale, NJ: Lawrence Earlbaum Associates.

Taylor, R. N. (1974). Nature of problem ill-structuredness: Implications for problem formulation and solution. *Decision Sciences*, 5(4):632–643.

van Joolingen, W. R. (1998). Cognitive tools to support discovery learning. In Goettl, B. P., Halff, H. M., Redfield, C. L., & Shute, V. J. (Eds.), *Intelligent Tutoring Systems*, vol. 1452 of *Lecture Notes in Computer Science* (p. 5). Berlin: Springer.

VanLehn, K. (2006). The behavior of tutoring systems. *I. J. Artificial Intelligence in Education*, 16(3):227–265.

VanLehn, K., Lynch, C., Schulze, K. G., Shapiro, J. A., Shelby, R., Taylor, L., Treacy, D., Weinstein, A., & Wintersgill, M. (2005). The andes physics tutoring system: Lessons learned. *I. J. Artificial Intelligence in Education*, 15(3):147–204.

von Clausewitz, G. C. (1873). *Vom Kriege (On War)*. Translated by Colonel J. J. Graham. London: N. Trübner.

Voss, J. F. (2006). Toulmin's model and the solving of ill-structured problems. In Hitchcock, D. & Verheij, B. (Eds.), *Arguing on the Toulmin Model: New Essays in Argument Analysis and Evaluation* (pp. 303–311). Berlin: Springer.

Voss, J. F., Greene, T. R., Post, T. A., & Penner, B. C. (1983). Problem solving skill in the social sciences. *The Psychology of Learning and Motivation*, 17:165–213.

Voss, J. F., & Post, T. A. (1988). On the solving of ill-structured problems: The nature of expertise. In Chi, M. T. H., Glaser, R., & Farr, M. J. (Eds.), *The Nature of Expertise* (pp. 261–285). Hillsdale, NJ: Lawrence Erlbaum Associates.

Walker, E., Ogan, A., Aleven, V., & Jones, C. (2008). Two approaches for providing adaptive support for discussion in an ill-defined domain. In Aleven, V., Ashley, K. D., Lynch, C., & Pinkwart, N. (Eds.), *Proceedings of the Third International Workshop on Intelligent Tutoring Systems for Ill-Defined Domains: Assessment and Feedback in Ill-Defined Domains*. Held in conjunction with the 9th International Conference on Intelligent Tutoring Systems. Montréal Canada (pp. 1–12).

Woolf, B. P., Aïmeur, E., Nkambou, R., & Lajoie, S. P. (Eds.), (2008). *Intelligent Tutoring Systems, 9th International Conference, ITS 2008, Montreal, Canada, June 23–27, 2008, Proceedings*, vol. 5091 of *Lecture Notes in Computer Science*. Berlin: Springer.

CHAPTER 10

Individualized Cultural and Social Skills Learning with Virtual Humans

H. Chad Lane and Robert E. Wray

Introduction

Pedagogical agents usually play the role of tutor (Johnson, Rickel, & Lester, 2000) or peer (Y. Kim & Baylor, 2006) in virtual learning environments. In these roles, the agent works alongside the learner to solve problems, ask questions, hold conversations, and provide guidance. Over the last decade or so, a new breed of pedagogical agents has emerged that do not play the role of expert or peer, however, but rather act as the object of practice. That is, instead of helping on the side, *it is the interaction itself with the virtual character that is intended to have educational value.* Here, the agent is usually a *virtual human* playing a defined social role in an interaction that requires the learner to use specific communicative skills to achieve some goal. For example, to prepare for an international business trip, one might meet with a virtual foreign business partner from the country of interest to negotiate a fictional contract agreement.

The technology challenge is to simulate social encounters in realistic ways and in authentic contexts. The pedagogical challenge is to design scenarios in ways that achieve the learning goals, maintain a high level of accuracy, and stay within an ideal window of challenge (whatever that may be). The basic problems of doing this with virtual humans are eloquently stated by Gratch and Marsella (2005):

> These "virtual humans" must (more or less faithfully) exhibit the behaviors and characteristics of their role, they must (more or less directly) facilitate the desired learning, and current technology (more or less successfully) must support these demands. The design of these systems is essentially a compromise, with little theoretical or empirical guidance on the impact of these compromises on pedagogy. (p. 256)

What are the implications of pedagogical demands on virtual human design? How can virtual humans facilitate learning? This chapter seeks to lay out the space of what is possible in using virtual humans to promote the acquisition of social and intercultural skills and describe a framework for adapting their behaviors to better meet the specific needs of learners.

Table 10.1. Dimensions of Pedagogical Experience Manipulation

	Engagement/Affect	Domain Learning
Configuration	*Provide experiences that motivate and encourage*	*Provide experiences that address specific learner needs*
Dynamic tailoring	*Adjust simulation behaviors to motivate and encourage*	*Adjust simulation behaviors to address specific learner needs*

The tension between fidelity of simulations built for educational purposes and the demands of learning is not new. Authentic practice opportunities are essential both for learner motivation and transfer to real-world contexts (Sawyer, 2006); however, substantial risk is associated with not providing the guidance novices need (Kirschner, Sweller, & Clark, 2006). Beginning learners generally lack the cognitive and metacognitive resources to effectively comprehend, process, or encode their learning experiences. The most common methods of providing the needed guidance are through a human instructor or an intelligent tutoring system (Lane et al., 2008); however, here we focus primarily on complementary methods that involve providing support for learning *through* the virtual human role players. Inspired by anecdotal statements from expert human role players who reported adjusting their behaviors based on observations of learners, we outline the dimensions of what is adjustable in virtual humans and discuss some examples of how virtual human role players might similarly adapt to meet specific learner needs. This line of research falls under the broader notion of *pedagogical experience manipulation*, which involves adjustment of the learning experience based on the evolving needs of the learner (Lane & Johnson, 2008; Wray et al., 2009).

Orchestrated practice can often be viewed as having two loops: an outer loop that involves selecting problems and an inner loop that involves taking a series of steps to solve that problem (VanLehn, 2006). We define pedagogical experience manipulation as encompassing two key methods: *configuration* of the learning experience (the outer loop) and *dynamic tailoring* of the learning experience as it unfolds (the inner loop). Both of these activities can be applied in service to support a learner's affect and/or cognitive learning (Table 10.1), which interact in complex (and not yet fully understood) ways (D'Mello & Graesser, Chapter 6, this volume; Kort, Reilly, & Picard, 2001). Dynamic tailoring comprises not only more familiar methods of directly supporting learning objectives, but also emerging methods that employ narrative adaptation and user-interface manipulations (Magerko, Stensrud, & Holt, 2006; Mott & Lester, 2006; Riedl, Stern, Dini, & Alderman, 2008) to engage and motivate (left column of Table 10.1).

The chapter continues in the next section with a discussion of how humans acquire social and intercultural skills. Developmental models are presented that describe how people tend to progress when learning new intercultural and social skills. This discussion is followed by an overview of virtual human research, including discussion of the technology required to build them, empirical findings regarding their use in learning contexts, and consideration of various methods to adaptively control their behaviors to promote learning. It concludes with pertinent open questions and suggestions for future research on virtual humans.

Acquiring Interpersonal and Intercultural Communication Skills

Whether learning to solve algebra equations, shoot free throws, or play music, there is remarkable consistency in how human beings acquire and develop expertise – in general, people are more alike than they are different (Pashler, McDaniel, Rohrer, & Bjork, 2008). Skill acquisition is believed to occur in three general stages: (1) encoding of declarative knowledge, (2) strengthening of knowledge through practice, and, ultimately, (3) automaticity (Anderson, 2005; Proctor, 2006; VanLehn, 1996). Stage 2, also known as the associative stage, is when learners confront impasses, make errors, and correct their understanding of the domain knowledge. Learning improves according to a power law – in other words, as the amount of practice increases, accuracy in executing the targeted skill improves and time to do it decreases according to a power function (Anderson, 2005, pp. 282–286). Studies have shown that these patterns seem to be universal, across a multitude of domains, cultures, and ages.

In this section, we briefly review related work in the fields of communication and intercultural competence that focuses on learning. Although the skills in question are not as well defined as many of those cited earlier, there is still little reason to believe that the development of interpersonal and intercultural skills is any different.

Acquisition of Social Skills

Social skills (or equivalently, interpersonal skills) form the foundation for both simulation of communicative skills (using a virtual human) and for teaching communicative competence. Although no clear consensus has emerged on a single definition, Segrin & Givertz (2003) state that "one can distill most of these definitions of social skills (and their associated aliases) to the ability to interact with other people in a way that is both appropriate and effective" (p. 136). Given the more specific focus in what follows on intercultural communication, we adopt the more precise definition of social skills as "the ability of an interactant to choose among available communicative behaviors in order that [she or] he may successfully accomplish [her or] his own interpersonal goals during an encounter while maintaining the face and line of his fellow interactants" (Wiemann, 1977, p. 198). It is

worth noting that what constitutes "success" in a social interaction and what interpersonal goals are adopted are not always obvious (Spitzberg & Cupach, 2002).

The concept of social skills can be broken down in many different ways. One of the simplest is to consider two fundamental processes: *message reception* (Wyer & Adaval, 2003) and *message production* (Berger, 2003). The assumption is that humans engage in communication when a desire to receive, deliver, or exchange content (of some kind) exists. Further, this process is usually governed by communicative goals (conscious or not) and an understanding of the kinds of plans that achieve them. These processes can fail in an almost countless number of ways and for equally as many reasons. Message reception and production skills are, nonetheless, the building blocks for participating in communication.

Message reception refers to one's ability to interpret social signals of others and infer meaning from the communicative actions of others. Ultimately, the receiver must both have (1) the motivation to interpret and process the message, and (2) the knowledge necessary to comprehend it (Wyer & Adaval, 2003). Challenges to successful decoding of a message can come from contextual and pragmatic sources in the immediate environment, as well as from internal biases or beliefs. For example, assumptions one makes based on stereotypes can greatly impede message reception. On the message production side, similar challenges arise. How one forms a message (consciously or not) depends again on context, beliefs, biases, and many other influencing variables. Automated communicative skills are deeply rooted and thus difficult to modify in ways that enhance the odds of a producing a message that will be successfully decoded by the hearer.

However, studies on how people acquire novel communicative skills – that is, ones that require modification (or "reprogramming") of automated, even seemingly innate skills – have shown that learning generally follows a power law in a way similar to acquisition of any cognitive skill (Berger, 2003). Thus, although making fundamental changes to our communicative abilities may seem like a learning challenge that poses more hurdles than many others, the same underlying principles for learning any new cognitive skill seem to apply. One such principle is that practice with feedback is an essential component for learning (Anderson, Corbett, Koedinger, & Pelletier, 1995), which is why the development of virtual humans is particularly relevant for intercultural and social skill learning.

Development of Intercultural Competence

Very good examples of biases and beliefs that have high potential to hinder message reception and production come from the domain of intercultural competence. A key aim of many intercultural training programs is to support learners in recognizing how their own beliefs influence their communicative choices, and how those choices are seen and interpreted through the eyes of others. The usual structure of intercultural training programs includes a blend of didactic and experiential components, including methods such as lectures, discussion, film, case study, and role playing (Landis, Bennett, & Bennett, 2004). Many of these methods are based on a classroom instruction model and seek to leverage peer interaction and debate to engage learners. Typically, the goal is to induce changes in knowledge, skills, and/or attitudes. Knowledge includes basic facts about a new culture, such as common values and beliefs, preferences for physical contact, and typical eating and drinking patterns. Skills usually refer to the learner's ability to interact with someone from the new culture, including communicating their desires and interpreting the behaviors of others. Finally, attitudes have to do with basic beliefs a learner has about people of a different culture and whether a positive, neutral, or negative disposition exists toward them. Evaluations of intercultural training programs also tend to focus on these three dimensions (Mendenhall et al., 2006).

The best training programs are grounded in underlying models of individual intercultural development and human learning.

Such models seek to provide a theoretical account for the changes that occur as one experiences a new culture and integrates new knowledge into existing beliefs and understandings. For example, United States Peace Corps (1999) volunteers are told to expect four levels of cultural awareness when they begin a new assignment in a foreign country:

1. **Unconscious incompetence:** minimal awareness of cultural difference or mistakes made; a state of "blissful ignorance."
2. **Conscious incompetence:** basic realization of cultural difference; minimal understanding of underlying reasons or their significance.
3. **Conscious competence:** increased understanding of differences; deliberate behavioral adjustments are made to reduce cultural errors and misunderstandings.
4. **Unconscious competence:** culturally appropriate behavior is more or less automatic; one's "instincts have been reconditioned."

By reifying these stages for consideration by the learner, Peace Corps educators are promoting the idea of self-awareness, which is essential for intercultural growth. For example, to move from unconscious to conscious incompetence, one must begin to realize that what seems "normal" may be considered strange by people from another culture. It must be recognized that any peculiar observed behavior is likely in reaction to the learner. For people with underdeveloped self-awareness, there is a real risk these connections will fail to be made, leading them to conclude the strangeness they perceive is inevitable and beyond their understanding.

A similar but more empirically tested model than the Peace Corps' can be found in Milton Bennett's (1993) *Developmental Model of Intercultural Sensitivity* (DMIS). The DMIS rests on the assertion that as one's ability to *construe* cultural differences evolves, intercultural competence also increases. According to Bennett, "it is the construction of reality as increasingly capable of accommodating cultural difference that constitutes development" (p. 24). The DMIS posits two broad worldview orientations: *ethnocentrism* and *ethnorelativism*, which refers the positioning of one's own culture in relation to others. An ethnocentric orientation implies that one perceives all other cultures relative to his or her own, whereas an ethnorelative perspective implies that one's own culture is understood in the context of others. Three substages are included within each orientation that describe common cognitive and affective states that evolve during development. For Bennett, the goal of intercultural training is to promote gradual movement through the stages and deliver appropriate training given the learner's stage. If, for example, behavioral change is rushed, the learner may develop an impoverished understanding of the new culture. As with learning in most domains, it is important to avoid shallow learning and to develop an underlying conceptual understanding with better chances for retention and transfer.

Theoretical models of intercultural development are not only important for designing training, but also could form a foundation for tracking a learner in an intelligent learning environment (Ogan & Lane, 2010). An environment that adapts virtual human behaviors to meet the needs of the learner will clearly benefit from an estimate of that learner's current stage of development. In the next section, we outline the space of configurability in current virtual human implementations, and the subsequent section, we use the DMIS and Peace Corps models in examples to demonstrate how individualization could be accomplished.

Virtual Humans as Role Players

Live role playing has a long history in education (Kane, 1964) and, because it is interactive and situated, is a common strategy for teaching social interaction skills (Segrin & Givertz, 2003). There are problems, however, with the approach. Role playing in classrooms is not situated in a realistic context, and when done with peers, authenticity concerns are

raised. Expert human role players are generally believed to be the best option, but they are not cost-effective and can be prone to inconsistency (between different role players and due to fatigue). Virtual agents and humanoid robots have been developed to fill a variety of roles and with many different goals in mind. Generally, the purpose is to provide naturalistic communication with human users to establish social presence and support some shared goal. Rich and Sidner (2009) document several prominent examples and describe the expanded space of interaction afforded by humanoid robots and agents in the areas of engagement, emotion, collaboration, and social relationships (pp. 30–31). In this section, however, we review several systems that use virtual role players built specifically for learning.

Examples of Virtual Human Role Players

Because of a widespread and increasing desire for international travel, cultural learning, intercultural communication, and language learning are popular targets for virtual human-based training. For example, BiLAT is a serious game that situates the learner in a narrative context to prepare and meet with a series of virtual humans to solve problems in a fictional Iraqi city. To succeed, it is necessary to understand the underlying narrative context, adhere to cultural expectations, build trust with town officials, and negotiate mutually beneficial agreements (Kim et al., 2009; Lane et al., 2008). A similar structure is used in the Tactical Language family of serious games where the focus is on conversational language, communicative (including gestures), and intercultural competence (Johnson & Valente, 2008). Here, various instructional activities, such as listening and speaking practice, are integrated with immersive learning in three-dimensional simulated environments from various countries. Both of these systems maintain student models and carefully orchestrate scenarios to be appropriate (e.g., in terms of difficulty) for learners as they move through the game.

Another prominent example is the use of virtual humans for clinical training. Again, human role playing is common in doctor training programs to implement "standardized" patients that exhibit consistent symptoms for practice. Controlled studies have shown that virtual patients can be used to train psychiatric students in the classification of post-traumatic stress disorder (PTSD) cases. "Justin" and "Justina" are two such characters that exhibit symptoms of PTSD in their responses to clinician questions (Kenny, Parsons, Gratch, & Rizzo, 2008). In related work, virtual patients have been shown to be as effective as human role players for clinical interviewing skills, including body positioning and eye gaze (Johnsen, Raij, Stevens, Lind, & Lok, 2007).

Many other learning contexts have been used with virtual human role players to teach different kinds of communicative skills in social contexts. Some examples are police officer training in handling the mentally unstable (Hubal, Frank, & Guinn, 2003), healthy play for children with autism (Tartaro & Cassell, 2008), anti-bullying and coping behaviors for school children (Aylett, Vala, Sequeira, & Paiva, 2007; Sapouna et al., 2010), and coping behaviors for mothers of children with serious illness (Marsella, Johnson, & LaBore, 2000). Across the wide spectrum of these applications, most of the individualization that occurs is (1) at the learner's discretion and (2) at the scenario level (e.g., to select appropriate characters to meet with). In other words, learner preferences are incorporated in many instances, but learners are grouped into broad categories for which specialized modes of the system may run. In the sections that follow, we provide some background on how people learn with virtual humans and then explore how the level of individualization might be pushed down into the dynamic behaviors of the characters themselves, toward true individualization.

Foundations of Learning with Virtual Humans

Can virtual humans be effective role players? Building on results from *The Media Equation*, which shows that people treat computers like people (Reeves & Nass,

1996), there is increasing evidence that this result holds even more strongly with virtual humans (Gratch, Wang, Gerten, Fast, & Duffy, 2007; Zanbaka, Ulinski, Goolkasian, & Hodges, 2007). In other words, people treat virtual humans as if they are real. Further, studies on *relational agents* have shown that people can form longer-term bonds with virtual humans that engage in social dialogue, display empathy, discuss future encounters, and more (Bickmore & Picard, 2005). Additionally, characters who provide *personalized* interactions are known to increase feelings of social presence, which in turn enhance learning (Moreno & Mayer, 2004). Learning can also be enhanced when learners choose to adopt social goals (e.g., "come to know your partner") while interacting with virtual humans (Ogan, Kim, Aleven, & Jones, 2009). Together, these results suggest that virtual humans can induce feelings of social presence in learners, that these feelings are enhanced through personalization and simulation of social and relational behaviors, and, ultimately, that we should expect a concomitant improvement in learning.

Early studies of the efficacy of virtual-human-based systems to teach intercultural skills seem to support this conclusion. Significant gains in learning were found for Tactical Iraqi (Surface, Dierdorff, & Watson, 2007) as well as BiLAT (Durlach, Wansbury, & Wilkinson, 2008; Kim et al., 2009; Lane, Hays, Auerbach, & Core, 2010). Unfortunately, these studies do not compare the systems to traditional intercultural training, so there is no way to determine if they are more effective than classroom-based learning.

Adaptability of Virtual Humans

Given the richness and complexity of face-to-face human interaction, it should be no surprise that the space of adjustability in virtual humans is vast. In what follows, we first consider the distinction between nonverbal and verbal behaviors, and then touch on underlying models of cognition, emotion, and language.

Nonverbal behaviors. Observable nonverbal behaviors during interactions with

Figure 10.1. Expressions of skepticism, anger, umbrage, and defensiveness by ICT virtual humans (Kenny et al., 2008; Swartout et al., 2006).

virtual humans are often a primary focus in studies of their communicative competency and fluidity. For example, the role of eye gaze, nodding, and gestures play a significant role in generating feelings of rapport in users (Gratch et al., 2007). When no attempt is made to align nonverbal behaviors with the utterances of users ("noncontingent" responses), feelings of distraction and disfluency in speech follow. The implication for learning with virtual humans is that if their nonverbal behaviors are unnatural to the point of being a distraction, learning may be hindered.

Nonverbal behaviors play a large part in the expression of emotion and it is possible to convey a great deal of implicit feedback through them. There is staggering complexity that emerges from facial expressions alone, but also through gaze, body positioning and movement, and gesturing (examples are shown Figure 10.1). Such signals also come in varying levels of *intensity*, as measured by onset, duration, and length (Ekman, 1993), and so these all represent adjustable parameters that would enable the system to *dampen* or *amplify* nonverbal backchannel feedback from the virtual human.

Content. The information conveyed and the words used to encode a message represent another critical dimension in the space of configurability. A message may have more or less content, more or less meaning, more

or fewer emotive words, more or less explanatory content, and be at a higher or lower rate or tone. The "best" choice of content depends heavily on many factors, including the context of the simulated social situation (e.g., business vs. casual), the culture and personality of the virtual human (e.g., reticent vs. talkative), the familiarity of the character with the user, and more.

Cognitive, communicative, and emotional models. The most sophisticated virtual humans engage in complex, task-based reasoning and engage in coping behaviors that are based on appraisals of situations (i.e., whether something is desirable or should be avoided). Beliefs are formed using underlying representations of the dialogue, their intentions, desires, the task domain, their emotions – communicative behaviors, nonverbal and verbal, flow from these representations (Swartout, et al., 2006). For example, a virtual human in a highly distressed state will display very different nonverbal and verbal behaviors than one who is more hopeful or joyful.

Figure 10.2 shows one possible visualization of an implementation of emotional and personality variables in virtual humans (Marsella & Gratch, 2009; Traum, Swartout, Gratch, & Marsella, 2008). Sliders to the left indicate low-intensity values, whereas those to the right represent high-intensity values. In the figure, the virtual human is set to a maximal state of distress, with low

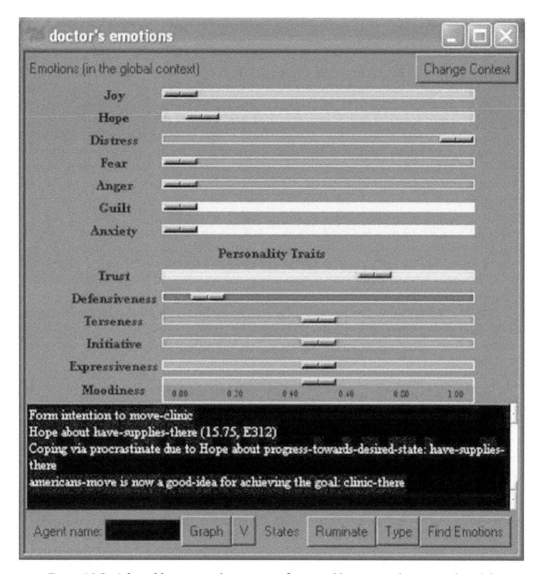

Figure 10.2. Adjustable emotional parameters for virtual humans with emotional models.

values for all other emotions. Emotions can change over the course of an interaction based on the learner's ability to build trust and on what is revealed, promised, and so forth, and the display updates as emotions change. Personality traits are more static and lead directly to different patterns of interaction. The colors of the bars for the emotion dimensions indicate the general categories (red and yellow are more negative while green is positive), whereas the colors on the personality variables change over the course of an interaction depending on the "stance"

of the virtual human. For example, the blue bar for "defensiveness" indicates a positive stance is being taken toward the current course of action (which is tracked in the dialogue manager).

This interface also allows a system user (such an instructor) to modify emotion and personality settings. All of the sliders can be adjusted before a meeting (i.e., configuration) or during (i.e., tailoring). Significantly different values in the character's emotion and personality values can lead to dramatically different reactions, beliefs, and results. In what follows, we discuss a few cases of using this adjustability to address learning goals.

What a human user says also has influence on these various states. For example, a threatening utterance might trigger a withdraw intention, which increases the likelihood of compliance, and culminates in terseness of language, folding of arms, and so on. Of course, the information that a speaker *intends* to communicate may vary greatly from how the message is encoded, as well as how it is decoded by the receiver. Perceived or actual misunderstanding between a learner and a virtual human role player can have a profound effect on the learner's evolving understanding of the skills being practiced. Emotions are believed to play an important role in the adaptivity present in human cognition, and so computational models of emotion may provide a substrate for individualization of virtual human behaviors (Gratch & Marsella, 2005).

Adaptive Training with Virtual Humans

Given the dimensions of adjustability discussed in the previous section, how could virtual human behaviors be adapted to promote learning during an interaction? To override the default behavior requires a belief on the part of the system that the learner will benefit from a particular adaptation as well as a model of what adaptations might pose some threat to the quality or believability of the experience. As discussed in the first section, this highlights the tension between fidelity and learning.

Learner Modeling for Social and Cultural Knowledge

Because of fundamental challenges presented by computationally modeling culture itself, modeling one's acquisition of cultural knowledge poses equal, if not greater, challenges. Systems reviewed earlier maintain learner models that track progress in language and culture learning (Johnson & Valente, 2008) as well as social norms

related to social interaction in international business (Lane et al., 2008). Outside of the learning context, modeling a user's culture has been used to personalize user interfaces. For example, using Hofstede's cultural dimensions (2001), Reinecke and Bernstein (2009) showed that it was possible to predict which user interfaces would be rated most preferable for individual users. The idea of adapting learning environments based on the cultural background of the learner is equally important. For example, various versions of the Tactical Language systems are available for speakers with different cultural backgrounds so that translations are accurate and cultural differences can be appropriately addressed by the system (Johnson, 2009).

To date, however, no intelligent systems model cultural learning or intercultural development at the level of those suggested by the theoretical models of the Peace Corps (1999), Bennett (1993), or any others (Landis et al., 2004). Having an estimate of a learner's stage of intercultural growth can have profound implications on his or her interpretation of observed behaviors, however. For example, a learner at the earliest stage of "unconscious incompetence" will need support in recognizing when cultural differences are apparent and with interpreting signals from others. Also, as discussed earlier, rushing to behavior change too quickly can negatively impact growth. Specifically, a learner may very well be able to learn a new social behavior with minimal instruction; however, teaching that behavior without the underlying conceptual knowledge increases the chance of shallow learning (Bennett, 1993). It should be done at a later stage, when an explanation for why it is appropriate and what cultural values drive the change can be provided and accepted by the learner.

Performing diagnosis to determine which developmental stage a learner may be experiencing poses significant challenges. A variety of psychometric measures have been proposed and evaluated that seek to place individuals at a particular stage of intercultural growth (Paige, 2006). These have proven useful for tracking the perspectives and opinions of learners over extended periods of time during intercultural training, but the results have not yet been integrated meaningfully into educational software for cultural learning. In addition, Bennett (1993) describes various behavioral cues that represent advancement through DMIS stages, as well as behaviors that suggest impasses. Automated detection of these behaviors in a virtual environment would provide stronger evidence for classification of a learner's stage than self-report measures alone and so these advances represent important next steps for the field of intelligent learning environments for culture. In the next two sections, we outline what such an integration would enable and how it is essential for meaningful adaptation of virtual human behaviors.

Techniques for Tailoring Virtual Human Behaviors

Although the focus in this chapter is on the turn-by-turn behaviors of virtual humans, pedagogical experience manipulation applies much more broadly and can be motivated by many factors. Adjustments can be made based on pedagogical strategies (such as fading learning support with time), for purposes of orientation, to manage user engagement, challenge, emotional state, and difficulty, among others (Wray et al., 2009). Thus, adaptation of specific virtual human behaviors should be viewed in service to these broader categories of learning support.

Specific adaptations of virtual human behavior are discussed later in the chapter. These are intended to address the following categories of support for learning social and cultural skills:

- to support *recognition* of errors or when ideal actions are taken;
- to give a *hint* about an action that will have a positive outcome;
- as an *explanation* for observed reactions, emotional state changes, or opinion shifts;
- to elicit a *self-explanation* from the learner to identify relevant domain principles.

Although intended as a framework for delivering feedback implicitly (through a character), these categories are intentionally similar to the goals behind the use of explicit feedback. In fact, implicit and explicit feedback can be viewed as having a shared goal: to provide *formative* feedback with the aim to convey information "to the learner that is intended to modify his or her thinking or behavior for the purpose of improving learning" (Shute, 2008, p. 154). Although this support can certainly be provided by an intelligent tutoring system (Johnson, Vilhjalmsson, & Marsella, 2005; Lane et al., 2008), there may be benefits if pedagogical goals can be achieved organically. For example, it may be less of an interruption to the flow of the experience, or the learner may feel as if she or he did not need excessive support to succeed. There are trade-offs associated with these benefits, which are addressed again in the final section of the chapter.

To provide support for learning through the adaptation of virtual humans, there needs to be (1) a pedagogical purpose (a defined curriculum or learner model can provide this), (2) a tailoring tactic available that achieves the purpose, and (3) heuristics for detecting when and if the adaptations represent a threat to the fidelity of the experience. Tailoring tactics can occur either at the surface level, by adjusting nonverbal behaviors or content, or by adjusting the underlying models in ways that may produce different surface behaviors (see Figure 10.2). In what follows, we organize the suggested tactics according to the pedagogical purposes described earlier and link them to idealized learner model contents.

Recognition. A learner who is in the early stages of exposure to a new culture – especially if it is the first new culture they have experienced – will only have their own culturally biased methods for recognizing and interpreting feedback from people of that culture. For example, if a learner is in the Peace Corps' "unconscious incompetence" stage, she or he has yet to consistently identify when communicative actions fail or succeed. To bring greater attention to such failures or successes, a tactic to *amplify* an existing behavior may be helpful. For example:

- If a learner brings up a taboo topic, angry (or saddened) facial cues and hand gestures could be exaggerated to capture the attention of the user.
- The content of utterances could also be modified to use emotionally charged vocabulary that draws attention to an inappropriate (or just sensitive) topic mentioned by the learner. A prototype system has been implemented using such an agent-based dynamic tailoring architecture (Wray et al., 2009).
- For positive feedback, similar adjustments of facial responses (e.g., smiling) as well as gestures (e.g., hand to heart, or a handshake) could be amplified to reinforce the learner behavior.

Much less obvious manipulations could be made to underlying models that might produce immediate or even delayed feedback. For example, characters in social simulations often model a version of trust of the learner (Johnson et al., 2005; Kim et al., 2009; Swartout et al., 2006). As the interaction progresses, the quality and appropriateness of the learner's actions cause trust to go up and down. Amplifying the positive or negative impact of certain communicative actions could therefore lead to different outcomes, both immediate and in the longer term.

Conversely, in some contexts it may make sense to *dampen* a virtual human reaction to draw attention away from a certain topic. For example, if the user commits a minor cultural error and is concentrating on an advanced communicative skill (e.g., negotiation), it may be preferable to delay discussion of the error until a reflective period. In these instances, recognition is less of a priority. The system may have a belief that the user has the skill and may simply be committing a *slip*. That said, systematic and/or multiple slips may indicate deeper misconceptions and there may be value in helping the learner have practice recovering from such slips. So, this pedagogical approach should be represented in the instructional model and the learner model should be equipped to support such decisions.

Hinting. Sometimes learners reach impasses and cannot progress without some help. Although less intuitive, some limited options are available for allowing virtual humans to make suggestions to the learner. Here, it might be related to a personality trait such as *helpfulness*, or even to an awareness by the virtual human that the learner is "new" to the (virtual) country and would benefit from some friendly advice. However, what constitutes an impasse or success in social contexts varies tremendously (Spitzberg & Cupach, 2002). Also, the goals of the participants and the context can have profound implications on the limits of what is considered realistic. For example, it is unlikely that a person of interest in an investigation is going to give tips on how to properly elicit information from him or herself. However, in a cultural or informal social context, there are some possibilities:

- For learners who are at the "conscious incompetence" stage, hints may be given as friendly advice from the character highlighting an alternative communicative action that would produce a better outcome. For example, a virtual child may indicate that he or she wants candy.
- In a more serious context, a virtual human might ask about what it is the learner should do at a specific time (e.g., "Would you like to ask me about the contract now?"), or simply bring up a topic for conversation that would normally be the learners responsibility.

In some contexts it may even be permissible to allow the learner to *ask* the character what to do. The believability of each of these options depends so much on the context, it is again indicative of the difficultly associated with developing heuristics for detecting threats to fidelity.

Explanation. Pride in one's knowledge and/or culture can be leveraged to provide explanations for observations made by the learner. As usual, these explanations can always come from an external source, like a tutor or Web page; however, something directly from a character may be just as – if not more – impactful given that it is situated in the moment of the interaction. Again, concerns of fidelity greatly depend on the social context (e.g., a child will probably not provide a deep explanation of a cultural value like justice or the importance of family). Some examples of implicit explanations include:

- If mastery of a specific cultural topic tracked by the learner model is estimated as low, the content of the character's utterance could be augmented with some additional information about the relevant concept. This approach has also been implemented using the dynamic tailoring architecture mentioned previously (Wray et al., 2009).
- A learner in a *denial* stage of the DMIS (an early ethnocentric stage) may be unwilling to accept that a cultural difference even exists based on basic interactions with the character. In these instances, a *clarification* of a relevant domain concept (or belief of the character) may support acceptance of that difference. If it is more deeply rooted, it may be necessary to amplify the characters emotions to indicate that a lack of recognition of the difference is upsetting.
- For one in an early stage of development, a character may help establish a causal link between a communicative action and a negative (or positive) result via additional content. For example, the character may state, "I'm not sure why you would ask me if I want a drink when you are aware that people in my country do not approve of alcohol." Similarly, the character could also bring up a communicative action from the past to draw the connection.
- A learner in a later ethnocentric stage may be aware when an error occurs but unwilling to take blame or perhaps prefers to place the onus on the virtual human to be the one who should adapt.

In these circumstances, explanations may be particularly critical.

An advantage that tailored explanations might have over one from a tutor would be that, when used properly, they are situated in practice. Thus, a character who conveys a personal narrative with emotional content can do so as part of the relationship-building process with the learner. Further, more emotionally laden versions of these messages are likely to be more memorable (Gratch & Marsella, 2005).

Self-explanation. Self-explanations enhance a learner's ability to integrate new knowledge with existing knowledge. Further, such explanations can be facilitated when prompted (Chi, Leeuw, Chiu, & LaVancher, 1994). How might a virtual human role player, in the context of a simulated social interaction, elicit self-explanations from a learner? In a way similar to hinting, it may be awkward to imagine a virtual human asking the learner to describe their understanding of the target culture. However, in some contexts it might be plausible:

- A learner in the DMIS stage of *minimization* (where the learner focuses on how his or her culture is similar to the target culture and minimizes the differences) might be engaged in a conversation by the virtual human to discuss their two cultures openly. In this context, the character could ask, "What have you noticed about our cultures that is different?" This might support the learner in understanding that minimization is not equivalent to acceptance, and highlight the need for healthy construal of cultural differences.
- To achieve the integrative benefits of self-explanation, virtual humans could ask the learner to describe their experiences with *other* virtual humans and use that to bridge into eliciting self-explanations about choices made in those interactions.

Natural language dialogue system technology may need to advance in order to achieve the full effect of these tactics, although it is worth noting that pedagogically effective prompting can be achieved with little or no dialogue modeling (Chi et al., 1994). Of course, self-explanations are likely to be occurring in the mind of a learner anyway (as part of their deliberative processes in the communication), and so it may be worthwhile to look for evidence in the content of their contributions or to reserve discussion of them for a reflective period with explicit feedback.

As mentioned earlier, many of the previously described techniques address shared goals with those of a tutor that provides extrinsic feedback (Shute, 2008). There may be times when provision of intrinsic feedback through a character is culturally inappropriate (i.e., the "realism filter" detects an out-of-bounds tailoring action), but there is still a good reason to provide the feedback. For example, if the learner commits a minor gaffe but the virtual role player is interested in helping maintain the learner's face, this would be an ideal situation for feedback because it should probably not go unnoticed. In sum, it seems that intrinsic and extrinsic feedback, while potentially redundant in many cases, may be complementary in many ways – further research is needed to fully explore their relationship.

Given the short span of time that high-fidelity virtual learning environments have been available (Ogan & Lane, 2010), very few systems implement dynamic tailoring or attempt to balance it with explicit feedback from an intelligent tutor. In each of the tailoring examples described in this section, the basic aim is to identify a pedagogical need, identify an appropriate tailoring technique, and then execute it if realism is not threatened. Significant research is needed along each of these dimensions.

Conclusion

It has been suggested that individualized learning experiences and personalized curricula may represent the next evolutionary stage for education (Christensen, Horn, & Johnson, 2008; Collins & Halverson, 2009). The vision of the future is one dominated by self-directed learning with computers playing a significant role in the management and provision of the individualization. For decades, artificial intelligence researchers have pursued this vision through the development of adaptive learning environments that dynamically adjust content and learning support to meet the needs of individual learners (Shute & Zapata-Rivera, 2007). In this chapter, we have explored how these ideas take shape in the context of learning *with* virtual human role players and how they might be adapted to meet specific learner needs.

For virtual human role players to adapt based on pedagogical aims, it is likely that more sophisticated learner models will be necessary. Building learner models for domains such as cultural learning and interpersonal skills is no simple task, but even crude distinctions can be helpful. For example, if an error is made by a true beginner, the character might bring up the underlying cultural difference in their response (a content adjustment). Other learners would get the standard simulation response. We have developed a prototype dynamic tailoring architecture that runs in BiLAT (Kim et al., 2009) to intelligently select and modify character utterances based on their pedagogical content and the evolving skills of the learner (Wray et al., 2009).

An important, recurring question is whether intrinsic adaptations threaten fidelity and the implications to learning when that happens. For example, if a learner comes to rely on intrinsic scaffolding from virtual characters, then the learning in the virtual environment could have a negative effect on far transfer in the field. Similarly, if learners recognize the characters are secretly "helping," does it ruin the fantasy of a realistic conversation? If so, how does this realization impact learner affect and motivation? These concerns are legitimate, and evaluating how to ensure tailoring actions do not break "realism boundaries" remains an important open question. However, three factors reduce the concerns in practice:

1. *The example of adaptive human role players.* As mentioned previously, expert

human role players tend to adapt their behavior to the behavior of their students. We have observed human role players performing some of the adaptive strategies outlined herein. A thorough investigation of the pedagogical adaptations of adaptive human roles players for training would potentially be useful for establishing practical "rules of thumb" for maintaining a realistic experience (or when other factors dominate). However, the primary conclusion is that intrinsic adaptations are already part of the "toolkit" of the best method known for this kind of training.

2. *Wide variation in human behavior.* In informal conversation, human behavior exhibits a vast range of reasonable responses. Two different people may have very different reactions to some statement; the same person may react very differently to the same statement depending on context and mood. The consequence of this variability is that the "realism boundaries" are very broad and more difficult to breach than may first be apparent. Further, because people tend to view virtual humans as real, minor "quirks" in their reactions might be overlooked by the student, making the boundaries fluid and forgiving.

3. *Variation in adaptive delivery.* A conversation consists of a large number of back-and-forth interactions between the student and the virtual character. One potential way to improve the likelihood that "realism bounds" are not violated is to give the pedagogical adaptation system a rich, fine-grained model of the student's capability and a range of adaptation strategies. Any single interaction may have more or less pedagogical content, more or less hinting, more or less nonverbal response. This is the approach taken in the dynamic tailoring architecture mentioned previously. If the virtual character has only a coarse model of the student and a fixed adaptation strategy, then these limitations make it much easier for a student to recognize (and possibly come to depend on) pedagogical adaptations.

4. *The unarticulated relationship between fidelity and learning.* As discussed, the primary risk associated with tailoring lies in the potential to violate loosely defined boundaries of realism. If a character misrepresents a target culture, negative training is possible. However, it is unclear whether and to what extent fidelity concerns truly predominate over pedagogical ones. Just as a batter in baseball will sometimes swing two bats before hitting to make one feel lighter, there may be reason to believe an unrealistically difficult character may provide benefit and insights to the learner. Commercial video games routinely violate the rules of fidelity to maximize interest and motivation. These arguments are anecdotal, but they suggest it may be premature to assume that strict adherence to fidelity is necessary in the development of virtual humans – much empirical research is needed to address these questions.

Finally, current cognitive and social science research is not producing theories and models with such high fidelity that a specific or very narrow range of possible behaviors is mandated in any non-laboratory situation of more than a few seconds. As a consequence, there is no guarantee of realism in intercultural training domains – with or without pedagogical experience manipulation. Until formal validation models of human cultural and interpersonal behaviors become available, the perceived realism of these systems will be largely dependent on the creativity and acumen of their designers and informal feedback from subject-matter experts.

A second open question is whether pedagogical experience manipulation can be as effective as explicit help from a tutoring system. As discussed, use of one form of feedback does not rule out use of the other, so the interplay between explicit feedback (such as that from an intelligent tutor) and implicit feedback from role-playing virtual humans represents another important area for future research. A system providing both methods of support would require some unifying pedagogical model to govern and coordinate the activities of both systems.

Advances also remain necessary in the evaluation of intercultural learning and in the validation, appropriateness, and determination of accuracy of fundamental models like the DMIS. A meta-analysis of many training programs suggests they are effective at teaching cultural knowledge and generating learner satisfaction, but generally fall short in skill acquisition and attitude change (Mendenhall et al., 2006). Although the authors criticize the general lack of rigor in the field and recommend a greater empirical focus, no specific suggestions regarding why skills and attitude effects are more difficult to achieve are given. This may be symptomatic of a general lack of realistic practice opportunities in those training programs and bodes well for the future of virtual human-based environments. Although many of the reviewed studies qualified in terms of rigor, most lacked a strong, experiential component – lectures, assimilators, discussion, and role-play are indicated as the top four types of programs (Mendenhall et al., 2006, p. 134). Given that learning is situated and contextual when interacting with virtual humans, they may also play an important role in the future as an assessment tool to gauge culture-specific learning as well as movement through developmental stages (Ogan & Lane, 2010).

Although many open questions remain regarding the use of virtual humans as role players for the learning of social and intercultural skills, they represent an important class of technology that should continue to remain relevant given the growing importance of such skills. There is a growing global need for intercultural learning and realistic, sustainable practice opportunities. Building a virtual human requires a great deal of effort – artwork, animation, speech, dialogue modeling, cognitive modeling, emotional modeling, task modeling, and more – and it may not be sufficient to only seek to make them realistic. This chapter provided a brief overview of how virtual humans are currently being used as role players in systems for social and intercultural development,

and how they might become specialized for specific learner needs. This represents a possible glimpse of how they may evolve to meet the learning demands of the next several decades.

Acknowledgments

The project or effort described here has been sponsored by the U.S. Army Research, Development, and Engineering Command (RDECOM) and the Air Force Research Laboratory (contract FA8650–08-C-6837). Statements and opinions expressed do not necessarily reflect the position or the policy of the U.S. government, and no official endorsement should be inferred. We thank Daniel Auerbach, Mark Core, Dave Gomboc, Laura Hamel, and Brian Stensrud for the many conversations and e-mails that helped us formulate and refine (and implement some) of these ideas.

References

Anderson, J. R. (2005). *Cognitive psychology and its implications* (6th ed.). New York: Worth Publishers.

Anderson, J. R., Corbett, A. T., Koedinger, K. R., & Pelletier, R. (1995). Cognitive tutors: Lessons learned. *Journal of the Learning Sciences, 4*(2), 167–207.

Aylett, R., Vala, M., Sequeira, P., & Paiva, A. (2007). FearNot! – An emergent narrative approach to virtual dramas for anti-bullying education *International Conference on Virtual Storytelling* (pp. 202–205), Saint Malo, France.

Bennett, M. J. (1993). Towards ethnorelativism: A developmental model of intercultural sensitivity. In R. M. Paige (Ed.), *Education for the intercultural experience* (2nd ed., pp. 21–71). Yarmouth, ME: Intercultural Press.

Berger, C. R. (2003). Message production skill in social interaction. In J. O. Greene & B. R. Burleson (Eds.), *Handbook of communication and social interaction skills* (pp. 257–291). Mahwah, NJ: Lawrence Erlbaum.

Bickmore, T. W., & Picard, R. W. (2005). Establishing and maintaining long-term human-computer relationships. *ACM Transactions on Computer-Human Interaction, 12*(2), 293–327.

Chi, M. T. H., Leeuw, N. D., Chiu, M.-H., & LaVancher, C. (1994). Eliciting self-explanations improves understanding. *Cognitive Science, 18*, 439–477.

Christensen, C. M., Horn, M. B., & Johnson, C. W. (2008). *Disrupting class: How disruptive innovation will change the way the world learns.* New York: McGraw-Hill.

Collins, A., & Halverson, R. (2009). *Rethinking education in the age of technology: The digital revolution and schooling in America.* New York: Teachers College Press.

Durlach, P. J., Wansbury, T. G., & Wilkinson, J. (2008). *Cultural awareness and negotiation skill training: Evaluation of a prototype semi-immersive system.* Paper presented at the Army Science Conference.

Ekman, P. (1993). Facial expression and emotion. *American Psychologist, 48*(4), 384–392.

Gratch, J., & Marsella, S. (2005). Lessons from emotion psychology for the design of lifelike characters. *Applied Artificial Intelligence, 19*, 215–233.

Gratch, J., Wang, N., Gerten, J., Fast, E., & Duffy, R. (2007). *Creating rapport with virtual agents.* Paper presented at the Proceedings of the 7th International Conference on Intelligent Virtual Agents.

Hofstede, G. H. (2001). *Culture's consequences: Comparing values, behaviors, institutions, and organizations across nations.* Thousand Oaks, CA: Sage Publications.

Hubal, R. C., Frank, G. A., & Guinn, C. I. (2003). *Lessons learned in modeling schizophrenic and depressed responsive virtual humans for training.* Paper presented at the Proceedings of the 8th International Conference on Intelligent User Interfaces.

Johnsen, K., Raij, A., Stevens, A., Lind, D. S., & Lok, B. (2007). *The validity of a virtual human experience for interpersonal skills education.* Paper presented at the Proceedings of the SIGCHI Conference on Human Factors in Computing Systems.

Johnson, W. L. (2009). *The politeness effect in an intelligent foreign language tutoring system.* Paper presented at the Proceedings of the 1st Workshop on Culturally-Aware Tutoring Systems at the 9th International Conference on Intelligent Tutoring Systems.

Johnson, W. L., Rickel, J., & Lester, J. C. (2000). Animated pedagogical agents: Face-to-face interaction in interactive learning environments. *International Journal of Artificial Intelligence in Education, 11*, 47–48.

Johnson, W. L., & Valente, A. (2008). *Tactical language and culture training systems: Using artificial intelligence to teach foreign languages and cultures.* Paper presented at the Proceedings of the 20th National Conference on Innovative Applications of Artificial Intelligence – Volume 3.

Johnson, W. L., Vilhjalmsson, H., & Marsella, S. (2005). *Serious games for language learning: How much game, how much AI?* Paper presented at the Proceeding of the 2005 Conference on Artificial Intelligence in Education: Supporting Learning through Intelligent and Socially Informed Technology.

Kane, P. E. (1964). Role playing for educational use. *Speech Teacher, 13*(4), 320–323.

Kenny, P., Parsons, T., Gratch, J., & Rizzo, A. (2008). *Virtual humans for assisted health care.* Paper presented at the Proceedings of the 1st International Conference on PErvasive Technologies Related to Assistive Environments.

Kim, J. M., Hill, R. W., Durlach, P. J., Lane, H. C., Forbell, E., Core, M., et al. (2009). BiLAT: A game-based environment for practicing negotiation in a cultural context. *International Journal of Artificial Intelligence in Education 19*(3), 289–308.

Kim, Y., & Baylor, A. (2006). A social-cognitive framework for pedagogical agents as learning companions. *Educational Technology Research and Development, 54*(6), 569–596.

Kirschner, P. A., Sweller, J., & Clark, R. E. (2006). Why minimal guidance during instruction does not work: An analysis of the failure of constructivist, discovery, problem-based, experiential, and inquiry-based teaching. *Educational Psychologist, 41*(2), 75–86.

Kort, B., Reilly, R., & Picard, R. (2001). *An affective model of interplay between emotions and learning: Reengineering educational pedagogy – building a learning companion.* Paper presented at the Proceedings of the IEEE International Conference on Advanced Learning Technologies.

Landis, D., Bennett, J. M., & Bennett, M. J. (2004). *Handbook of intercultural training.* Thousand Oaks, CA: Sage Publications.

Lane, H. C., Hays, M. J., Auerbach, D., & Core, M. (2010). Investigating the relationship between presence and learning in a serious game. In J. Kay & V. Aleven (Eds.), *Proceedings of the 10th International Conference on Intelligent Tutoring Systems* (pp. 274–284). Berlin: Springer.

Lane, H. C., Hays, M. J., Auerbach, D., Core, M., Gomboc, D., Forbell, E., et al. (2008).

Coaching intercultural communication in a serious game. Paper presented at the 18th International Conference on Computers in Education.

Lane, H. C., & Johnson, W. L. (2008). Intelligent tutoring and pedagogical experience manipulation in virtual learning environments. In J. Cohn, D. Nicholson, & D. Schmorrow (Eds.), *The PSI handbook of virtual environments for training and education* (Vol. 3, Chapter 20, pp. 393–406). Westport, CT: Praeger Security International.

Magerko, B., Stensrud, B., & Holt, L. S. (2006). *Bringing the schoolhouse inside the box – a tool for engaging, individualized training.* Paper presented at the 25th Army Science Conference, Orlando, FL.

Marsella, S. C., & Gratch, J. (2009). EMA: A process model of appraisal dynamics. *Cognitive Systems Research, 10*(1), 70–90.

Marsella, S. C., Johnson, W. L., & LaBore, C. (2000). *Interactive pedagogical drama.* Paper presented at the Proceedings of the Fourth International Conference on Autonomous Agents.

Mendenhall, M. E., Stahl, G. K., Ehnert, I., Oddou, G., Osland, J. S., & Kuhlmann, T. M. (2006). Evaluation studies of cross-cultural training programs: A review of the literature from 1998 to 2000. In D. Landis, J. M. Bennett, & M. J. Bennett (Eds.), *Handbook of intercultural training* (pp. 129–144). Thousand Oaks, CA: Sage.

Moreno, R., & Mayer, R. E. (2004). Personalized messages that promote science learning in virtual environments. *Journal of Educational Psychology, 96*(1), 165–173.

Mott, B. W., & Lester, J. C. (2006). *Narrative-centered tutorial planning for inquiry-based learning environments.* Paper presented at the Proceedings of the 8th International Conference on Intelligent Tutoring Systems.

Ogan, A., Kim, J., Aleven, V., & Jones, C. (2009). *Explicit social goals and learning in a game for cross-cultural negotiation.* Paper presented at the Proceedings of the Workshop on Educational Games, 14th International Conference on Artificial Intelligence in Education.

Ogan, A., & Lane, H. C. (2010). Virtual environments for culture and intercultural competence. In E. Blanchard & D. Allard (Eds.), *Handbook of research on culturally-aware information technology* (pp. 501–519). Hershey, PA: IGI Global.

Paige, R. M. (2006). Instrumentation in intercultural training. In D. Landis, J. M. Bennett, & M. J. Bennett (Eds.), *Handbook of intercultural training* (pp. 85–128). Thousand Oaks, CA: Sage.

Pashler, H., McDaniel, M., Rohrer, D., & Bjork, R. (2008). Learning styles: Concepts and evidence. *Psychological Science in the Public Interest, 9*(3), 105–119.

Proctor, R. W. (2006). Laboratory studies of training, skill acquisition, and retention of performance. In K. A. Ericsson, N. Charness, P. J. Feltovich, & R. R. Hoffman (Eds.), *The Cambridge handbook of expertise and expert performance* (pp. 265–286). Cambridge and New York: Cambridge University Press.

Reeves, B., & Nass, C. (1996). *The media equation: How people treat computers, television, and new media like real people and places.* Cambridge: Cambridge University Press.

Reinecke, K., & Bernstein, A. (2009). *Tell me where you've lived, and i'll tell you what you like: Adapting interfaces to cultural preferences.* Paper presented at the Proceedings of the 17th International Conference on User Modeling, Adaptation, and Personalization.

Rich, C. & Sidner, C. (2009). Robots and Avatars as Hosts, Advisors, Companions and Jesters. *AI Magazine, 30*(1), 29–41.

Riedl, M. O., Stern, A., Dini, D., & Alderman, J. (2008). Dynamic experience management in virtual worlds for entertainment, education, and training. *International Transactions on Systems Science and Applications, Special Issue on Agent Based Systems for Human Learning, 4*(2), 23–42.

Sapouna, M., Wolke, D., Vannini, N., Watson, S., Woods, S., Schneider, W., et al. (2010). Virtual learning intervention to reduce bullying victimization in primary school: A controlled trial. *Journal of Child Psychology and Psychiatry, 51*(1), 104–112.

Sawyer, R. K. (2006). The new science of learning. In R. K. Sawyer (Ed.), *The Cambridge handbook of the learning sciences* (pp. 1–17). Cambridge: Cambridge University Press.

Segrin, C., & Givertz, M. (2003). Methods of social skills training and development. In J. O. Greene & B. R. Burleson (Eds.), *Handbook of communication and social interaction skills* (pp. 135–176). New York: Routledge.

Shute, V. (2008). Focus on formative feedback. *Review of Educational Research, 78*(1), 153–189.

Shute, V., & Zapata-Rivera, D. (2007). Adaptive technologies. In J. M. Spector, M. D. Merrill, J. van Merrienboer, & M. Driscoll (Eds.),

Handbook of research on educational communications and technology (3rd ed., pp. 277–294). New York: Lawrence Erlbaum Associates.

Spitzberg, B. H., & Cupach, W. R. (2002). Interpersonal skills. In M. L. Knapp & J. A. Daly (Eds.), *Handbook of interpersonal communication* (pp. 564–611). Thousand Oaks, CA: Sage.

Surface, E. A., Dierdorff, E. C., & Watson, A. M. (2007). *Special operations language training software measurement of effectiveness study: Tactical Iraqi study final report.* Special Operations Forces Language Office.

Swartout, W., Gratch, J., Hill, R. W., Hovy, E., Marsella, S., Rickel, J., et al. (2006). Toward virtual humans. *AI Magazine, 27*(2), 96–108.

Tartaro, A., & Cassell, J. (2008). *Playing with virtual peers: Bootstrapping contingent discourse in children with autism.* Paper presented at the Proceedings of the 8th International Conference for the Learning Sciences – Volume 2.

Traum, D., Swartout, W., Gratch, J., & Marsella, S. (2008). A virtual human dialogue model for non-team interaction (pp. 45–67). Online at http://www.peacecorps.gov/multimedia/pdf/library/T0087_culturematters.pdf

United States Peace Corps (1999). *Culture matters: The Peace Corps cross-cultural workbook.*

VanLehn, K. (1996). Cognitive skill acquisition. *Annual Review of Psychology, 47*(1), 513–539.

VanLehn, K. (2006). The behavior of tutoring systems. *International Journal of Artificial Intelligence in Education, 16*(3), 227–265.

Wiemann, J. M. (1977). Explication and test of a model of communicative competence. *Human Communication Research, 3,* 195–213.

Wray, R., Lane, H. C., Stensrud, B., Core, M., Hamel, L., & Forbell, E. (2009). *Pedagogical experience manipulation for cultural learning.* Paper presented at the Proceedings of the 2nd Workshop on Culturally Aware Tutoring Systems at the 14th International Conference on Artificial Intelligence in Education.

Wyer, R. S., & Adaval, R. (2003). Message reception skills in social communication. In J. O. Greene & B. R. Burleson (Eds.), *Handbook of communication and social interaction skills* (pp. 291–356). Mahwah, NJ: Lawrence Erlbaum.

Zanbaka, C., Ulinski, A., Goolkasian, P., & Hodges, L. F. (2007). *Social responses to virtual humans: Implications for future interface design.* Paper presented at the Computer Human Interaction 2007 Proceedings.

CHAPTER 11

Emergent Assessment Opportunities

A Foundation for Configuring Adaptive Training Environments

Phillip M. Mangos, Gwendolyn Campbell, Matthew Lineberry, and Ami E. Bolton

Simulation has emerged as a dominant technology in training research and practice, driven in large part by its ability to create a customized, immersive, experiential learning environment (Shute & Zapato-Rivera, 2008; Vincenzi, Wise, Mouloua, & Hancock, 2009). Simulation-based training systems have reached a state of technological maturity capable of supporting real-time, adaptive assessment and training. However, arguably few incorporate an assessment framework necessary to support valid inferences about the latent skills that drive observable performance, and therefore produce meaningful, relevant, and appropriately challenging instructional modifications. Historically, one approach to implementing a formal assessment framework within simulation-based training adopts a top-down perspective, characterized by a time- and resource-intensive comprehensive cognitive task analysis of the domain, and embeds carefully crafted assessment events into the training scenario (Fowlkes, Dwyer, Oser, & Salas, 1998). While there is no doubt that a top-down analysis of a domain will yield a tremendous amount of information highly relevant to conducting an assessment, by itself, this approach lacks the capability to translate performance measures into precise quantitative information about the underlying skills, or latent traits, of the trainees.

More recently, it has been proposed that classical psychometric item analysis, a bottom-up approach, could potentially be integrated with the previously described top-down approach, by treating those embedded scenario events as traditional test items from a paper-and-pencil test (Mangos & Johnston, 2009). Applying classical item analysis in this context would require collecting performance data on an embedded event from a large set of trainees who vary widely in their individual levels of the relevant latent traits. Then these data would be used to develop mathematical functions that probabilistically relate observable performances on this event to levels of latent traits. Once extant, these functions can be applied to assess all future trainees who face the same embedded event. Although this integrated approach does have the benefit of supporting more assessment precision, it should be noted that it is still a fully planned approach to assessment based on events that have been defined (and studied in detail) a priori.

We argue that several key limitations of a purely planned assessment approach emerge when applied to an adaptive, dynamic simulation-based training environment: 1) because of unpredictable changes to the simulation environment in response to trainee actions, no two trainees will ever experience the exact same assessment "item," limiting the application of psychometric models to assess a trainee's competence level; 2) it is often difficult to identify all of the critical features of the environment that affect performance, and thus form the basis for embedded assessments; and 3) even when critical environmental cues have been identified, complex combinations of cues can have unexpected but profound effects on performance, and therefore on the psychometric properties of embedded assessment items.

The purpose of the present study is to address these limitations by proposing a complementary approach to identifying potential assessment content to serve as the basis for opportunistic assessment within adaptive, simulation-based training. Our proposed assessment approach focuses on the application of mathematical modeling strategies to identify complex combinations of cues that can serve as the basis of emergent (versus planned) assessment content with known psychometric properties. We begin by discussing the current state of the practice of adaptive, simulation-based training. We then draw from research and theory on goal pursuit and action control (Gollwitzer, Fujita, & Oettingen, 2004), ecological psychology (Gibson, 1977), and modern psychometrics (Mislevy, Steinberg, & Almond, 2003) to develop a methodology for extracting analogs of assessment items from simulation-based training data and developing psychometric parameters of these items to support latent skill estimation and adaptive training. Finally, we present results from a simulation-based training experiment demonstrating the application of one primary phase of the proposed assessment framework.

Adaptive, Simulation-Based Training

Modern simulations have a number of desirable characteristics making them suitable to support training in complex, high-stakes, or dangerous performance domains. For example, they afford trainers the ability to control the contextual features of the performance environment to isolate challenging problem scenarios or simulate hazardous elements of the environment without actually endangering trainees. Coinciding with the proliferation of digital media and with exponential increases in computing power, simulations have become capable of supporting increasingly sophisticated training functions. Chief among these – and a significant milestone in the evolution of simulations as training tools – is the transfer of control of the training environment from the human trainer to the simulation engine. As a result, adaptive simulation-based training systems have the ability to modify the simulated performance environment itself (as well as other instructional interventions, such as feedback) with little external human intervention. This capability can provide a challenging training experience that addresses the unique configuration of skill strengths and weaknesses a trainee possesses at given point in time during training.

Another critical feature of simulations is the ability to provide experiential learning. An experiential learning system is one that provides an immersive, engaging learning environment for trainees to interact with various problem scenarios seamlessly presented with high fidelity (Freeman, Stacy, Levchuk, Colonna-Romano, & Shebilske, 2009). The defining characteristic of such environments is that they support learning through direct experience of prototypical problem situations. However, an inherent challenge in implementing simulations for experiential learning is the need to plan scenario content in a way that balances instructional objectives and the realism and sense of immersion or presence resulting from the training experience. This conflict becomes even more apparent within adaptive simulations. Adapting the training environment to optimally challenge deficient skills may require modifying contextual features (e.g., changing the source of enemy targets within a military command and control simulation) in a way that interrupts the natural unfolding of events that one might experience in the real world. That is, there are only a limited number of ways to change the source of enemy targets that "make sense" according to the laws of nature and the rules of engagement, and only some or perhaps none of these will address the instructional needs of the trainee given a current assessment of his or her skill strengths and weaknesses.

This conflict – balancing instructional objectives with realism and the natural flow of training environments – has been an inherent challenge to developing adaptive training. The problem is made even more challenging the greater the number of elements that can be varied within the training environment. The sheer complexity of many task domains simulated within simulation-based training systems (e.g., military command and control, urban warfare, emergency/trauma surgery) means that it is often difficult to predict which features will make a task easier or difficult, which ones will activate a different set of cognitive skills, and which ones naturally flow together to make for a realistic experience of the task. Consider an emergency trauma triage simulation – one can alter contextual features related to the patient's long-term medical history, the immediate indicators of trauma (blood pressure, swelling, presence of bleeding, pupil response), the composition of the surgical team, availability of special resources (e.g., specialized radiology equipment), or the physical space and layout of the surgical environment. A trainee may have a strong ability to diagnose patient syndromes that cause sudden and drastic changes in blood pressure, but may have a tendency to overlook risk factors associated with the patient's demographic and medical history. Although it would be easy to alter blood pressure "on the fly" within the simulation, changing presumably stable features such as patient race or sex may compromise the realism of the simulation, and

consequently the trainee's sense of immersion. Moreover, it is difficult to predict the interactive effect of simultaneously changing multiple features that individually would increase the difficulty of the problem – for example, abruptly dropping blood pressure and producing an unreadable X-ray. Is the resulting difficulty level an additive function of the two changes, a multiplicative one, or do the two changes "cancel each other out," resulting in the baseline level of difficulty? Without a formal investigative process for addressing these effects, such questions amount to guesswork, and the more things that can vary within a task domain, the greater the opportunity for bad guesswork.

Reconciling Instruction and Realism: Planned, Embedded Assessments

Simulation-based training systems have benefitted from the use of embedded assessments to make sense of a trainee's skill or knowledge level at critical points during training, affording the possibility of adapting the training environment. As such, an embedded assessment approach to adaptive training can help resolve some of the issues described earlier – to the extent one can strategically, unobtrusively, and accurately measure a trainee's levels of the cognitive skills required for effective performance, one can execute more informed and psychologically meaningful modifications to the task environment. The basic approach for embedded assessments as used historically within simulation-based training contexts can best be characterized as a planned or strategic assessment approach. A prototypical example is the Event-Based Approach to Training (E-BAT), in which strategically timed training events (with key observable response patterns tied to specific skill levels) afford the opportunity for performance measurement and assessment (Fowlkes, Dwyer, Oser, & Salas, 1998).

The effective implementation of such event-based approaches to training has been made possible by the use of comprehensive (but time- and resource-intensive) task-analytic techniques, such as cognitive task analysis. Cognitive task analysis techniques allow one to decompose a task into its composite elements to make informed predictions about how manipulating the task environment (i.e., inserting or removing specific contextual cues) affects the trainee's psychological experience of the task. Although such task-analytic techniques have been used effectively, they are often extremely costly, require significant investments of time and resources, and often suffer from a scalability problem when generalizing to new task domains. A deeper issue, however, relates to the viability of an inherently planned assessment approach within adaptive training contexts. Even if a cognitive task analysis effectively decomposes a task into its cognitively meaningful parts, the very need to plan the assembly of task components to create training events of varying difficulty levels in the real time poses unique challenges to the development of effective, adaptive training systems.

These challenges are apparent when one considers key differences between simulation-based assessment as used in training contexts and more traditional, paper-and-pencil-based educational assessments. First, traditional assessment methods often incorporate many well-defined test items. In contrast, assessment in simulation contexts is, to some extent, inherently opportunistic, capitalizing on temporary combinations of environmental cues or on the use of embedded trigger events that serve as measurement opportunities. Second, test items used in traditional assessment have stable characteristics whereas in simulation-based assessment, the context is constantly evolving in response to both the natural unfolding of scripted events and specific trainee actions. Third, whereas traditional test items are amenable to nonarbitrary psychometric parameters via a well-controlled item-calibration process (Embretson, 2006), training simulations unfold differently over time depending on trainee behaviors; therefore, it is possible that no two trainees will experience embedded assessments the same way, rendering psychometric analysis

difficult. Fourth, it is often difficult to identify all of the critical features of the environment that affect performance, and thus form the basis for embedded assessments. As with the trauma simulation described earlier, even a comprehensive task analysis may not be adequate for identifying all of the features of the performance environment that can be varied to create assessment content. Finally, even when critical environmental cues have been identified relatively thoroughly, complex combinations of cues can have unexpected but profound effects on performance, and therefore on the psychometric properties of embedded assessment items. For example, consider a medical triage scenario that includes multiple indicators of patient trauma (bleeding, disorientation, swelling, delayed pupil response). Even if any one of these indicators increase the difficulty of the scenario when used *alone*, it is impossible to tell how these indicators would affect scenario difficulty when used *together*. It could be that they form an easily recognizable pattern indicative of a common medical syndrome, or that they create an unusual pattern rendering diagnosis difficult. Without a theoretical model linking patterns of cues to scenario psychometric patterns, and an experimental process to refine and validate this model, it is impossible to predict the nonlinear, nonadditive effects of complex cue combinations.

The unique challenges associated with the use of planned assessments and their supporting task-analytic techniques warrant a new look at the development of adaptive training systems with emphasis on innovative ways to create and embed assessment content. Therefore, the purpose of the present study is to propose an approach to identifying potential assessment content to serve as the basis for opportunistic assessment within adaptive, simulation-based training, extending existing approaches that focus primarily on the use of planned assessments. Next, we draw from research and theory on three overlapping domains of psychological research (i.e., goal pursuit and action control theory, ecological psychology, and modern psychometric theory) to articulate the theoretical foundation of the proposed model.

Opportunistic Assessment: Evidence from Three Research Domains

Research on how people set and pursue goals has a considerable history in applied psychology (Locke & Latham, 2002). Research on goal pursuit addresses the mechanisms through which people maintain progress toward goals, recognize and act on opportunities to initiate goal-directed action, and protect goal-directed action from competing action tendencies. A key finding from these streams of research with implications for adaptive training assessments relates to the representation of goals and goal-related action cues in memory. When performing goal-directed actions, people maintain mental representations of active goals in memory. With little task familiarity, these representations may be very abstract, but with increasing task experience, they begin to incorporate key details about the task, such as "if-then" contingencies linking task cues to actions (i.e., implementation intentions; Gollwitzer et al., 2004). Specifically, people have better memory for specific combinations of task cues that afford goal-directed actions, and when such combinations appear during the course of the task, they instigate goal-directed action (often automatically; Gollwitzer et al., 2004). Formal models of goal activation (e.g., Altmann & Trafton, 2002) explore the mechanisms underlying this process. Altmann and Trafton proposed that when individuals are immersed in the task environment and given explicit goals, competing or alternate goals are temporarily inhibited, and the unfolding situation produces retrieval cues that serve as goal-directed action affordances. One finding that has been proposed as evidence for the automatic nature of goal pursuit is the task interruption effect, in which people have better memory for task configurations related to their intentions and goals when interrupted during task performance (Hodgetts & Jones, 2006). Another form of evidence stems from research on automatic goal priming, in which subconsciously primed goals cue action when an individual is placed in a task situation that affords action related to the primed goal (Bargh, Gollwitzer, Lee-Chai, Barndollar, & Trotschel, 2001).

The significance of goal activation and pursuit research for adaptive training assessments is that it offers guidance for intelligently decomposing complex tasks into meaningful sets of cue combinations to be used as a source of assessment content and training scenario adaptations. Such research points to the usefulness of a "bottom-up" approach to task decomposition. The challenge in executing commonly used task analysis techniques to develop adaptive training systems becomes apparent when one considers the intractably large number of cue combinations that could activate goal-directed behavior. To identify meaningful combinations, one could decompose training scenarios into every possible combination of cues and identify which ones affect performance. However, the resulting number of variations could quickly approach infinity, even for moderately complex tasks. Rather than systematically considering every possible cue combination, goal-activation research suggests that only certain cue combinations provide meaningful information about the trainee's cognitive state, and that those same combinations could be translated into diagnostic assessment content. Thus, if one were to simply observe a trainee interacting with a task in a goal-directed manner, one could incisively derive meaningful sets of task cues. Of course, if the trainee being observed is a novice with an immature task schema, he or she may be attending to the wrong cues and/or providing incorrect responses. For example, a novice may not recognize that a sharp drop in blood pressure signals the need to stabilize the patient in a trauma simulation, whereas this cue could instigate almost automatic action from an expert. However, even cue combinations that elicit *incorrect* responses in novices are useful to include within an assessment repertoire. If only those cues that discriminate experts from novices are used for the development of assessment content, training intended for novices would not be able to benefit from this content. Therefore, considering novice errors allows us to sample more comprehensively the universe of cues that could create plausible problem situations ranging in difficulty. (Note: Our consideration of novice decisions distinguishes our theoretical model from others, e.g., Klein's [1997] Recognition-Primed Decision model, that focus primarily on experts' or experienced decision makers' recognition of important cues). By taking "snapshots" of the task environment whenever trainees perform goal-directed actions (i.e., both correct and incorrect ones), one can elicit meaningful cue configurations, make inferences about what cues are associatively linked to performance goals (even those incorrectly linked by novices), and use this information to create a repertoire of problem situations to serve as the basis for diagnostic assessment content.

A second research domain with implications for adaptive training assessments is ecological psychology, the study of human behavior in the context of the environment in which it is situated. A key concept of ecological psychology is that of affordances, that is, action opportunities afforded by the environment (Gibson, 1977). This concept is consistent with notions in theories of goal activation and pursuit, specifically that only specific cue configurations function to elicit goal-directed behavior. We argue that these same cue combinations act as affordances for opportunistic assessment. Our proposed approach to task decomposition suggests that the same cue configurations that initiate goal-directed action also afford assessment of the latent mental states that gave rise to the action. Snapshots of the environment taken when experts (or novices) correctly (or incorrectly) act on their goal-driven intentions serve as effective prototypes for assessment items because they act as affordances to measure the quality of the trainee's mental model that gave rise to the action in the first place. Therefore, when key cue configurations naturally occur during the course of training, this gives us an

opportunity to look at the resulting trainee actions and make valid inferences about the latent knowledge states that caused them.

A third relevant research domain is that of modern psychometric theory. Moving beyond the classical item analysis described earlier in the chapter, Mislevy et al. (2003) proposed a model of evidence-based assessment for use in educational and training settings (e.g., intelligent tutoring systems) that exemplifies this principle. Mislevy and colleagues' Conceptual Assessment Framework (CAF) is an organizing framework for the development and implementation of assessments, which focuses on the use of cumulative, multisource evidence regarding a student's/trainee's emerging knowledge state during training. The source of this evidence is a set of complementary models – for example, representing relationships between task features and emergent task properties (e.g., psychometric properties such as difficulty) – that help form and evaluate hypotheses about the student's knowledge state. Specifically, the student model represents the blueprint for the assessment machinery used to gather, integrate, and evaluate evidence regarding the trainee's knowledge state. The task model functions to develop inferences about features of the task necessary to elicit evidence about the trainee's knowledge state. Underlying these and other components of the framework is the statistical machinery (mathematical models such as item response theory [IRT] models, Bayesian Networks, latent class models) that functions to quantify the various relationships (e.g., task cues and responses) needed to provide assessment-related evidence about the trainee. When applied to dynamic training tasks, these models can effectively translate raw performance data in response to dynamic scenario events into meaningful information on the trainee's latent traits. Therein lies the primary contribution of psychometric theory to adaptive training assessments: It provides a framework for incorporating diagnostic assessments into dynamic training content opportunistically. Planned, embedded training assessments only make use of a small portion of the performance variance that potentially tells a story about underlying latent traits. By leveraging the plethora of available modern psychometric theory models, and by adopting a psychometric worldview that any task cue or response is a potential indicator of underlying latent traits, one can more fully exploit emergent assessment opportunities formed by temporary configurations of task cues.

An Opportunistic Assessment Framework for Adaptive Scenario Modifications

These three lines of research form the basis for our proposed assessment framework: an opportunistic assessment framework designed to complement planned, embedded assessment approaches. Briefly, instead of creating a handful of psychometric models for a small number of planned events, our proposal is to capture the interactive impact of the (constantly changing) environmental cue combinations in mathematical equations that are capable of predicting the psychometric properties of any and all scenario events that emerge as cue values change during the course of a trainee's interaction with the scenario.

More specifically, our solution casts assessment opportunities as emergent properties of the interface between the trainee and the simulated training context in which the trainee is interacting. We posit that immersion in a training simulation creates a goal state in which the trainee is motivated to achieve learning and performance goals. Meaningful combinations of environmental cues serve to activate implementation intentions – mental representations of "if-then" contingencies linking anticipated critical situational cues to instrumental goal-directed responses (Gollwitzer et al., 2004). We argue that the same combinations of environmental cues that afford goal-directed action can also be cast as affordances for opportunistic assessment of the latent mental states that gave rise to the action. Therefore, if one can identify meaningful cue combinations as they periodically emerge and disappear over

the course of a training exercise, this would provide the basis for one to develop robust psychometric parameters for these assessment item analogs, and to use the parameters as the basis for iterative, real-time assessment and adaptive training.

Our proposed framework is shown in Figure 11.1. The framework can be thought of as a general process for assembling task cues, in either a planned or opportunistic manner, into flexibly reconfigurable scenario content's known psychometric parameters (difficulty, discrimination, dimensionality). The two main phases of the process – scenario calibration and scenario-based assessment – correspond roughly to the item calibration and person trait estimation phases of developing and using test items with known psychometric properties (Embretson & Riese, 2000). The scenario-calibration phase involves task analysis via observation and modeling of task cue configurations that elicit goal-directed responses. During this phase, trainees are given the opportunity to perform the task, exploring and interacting with many different scenarios variants. Goal-directed actions are observed and snapshots of the environment when the actions occur are recorded. Modeling techniques including (but not limited to) multiple regression, HLM, fuzzy logic, neural nets, and classification techniques (e.g., cluster analysis) are used to model the relationship between task cues and probabilities of goal-directed actions. The result is a computational task model, corresponding generally to the task model of Mislevy et al.'s (2003) CAF. This computational model can be used to generate a nearly infinite number of task scenarios with predictable psychometric properties. These scenarios are organized into equivalence classes of scenarios with similar properties within the scenario library. During the scenario-based assessment phase, two parallel assessment loops (planned and opportunistic assessment) are used to select, administer, and modify scenarios in real time to obtain iterative information about trainee knowledge states. This information is accumulated by modeling trainee responses to scenario content with known parameters and represented by the iteratively updated

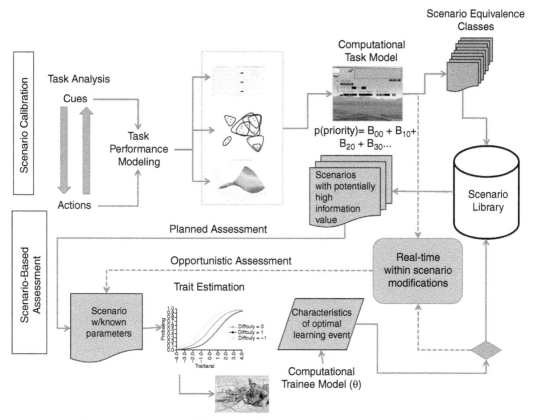

Figure 11.1. Proposed framework for emergent assessment opportunities.

computational trainee model (corresponding to the student model of the CAF). This model is used to infer the characteristics of follow-on scenarios with high potential for addressing deficient skills. A decision point is then reached to either draw new scenarios from the scenario library or modify the existing scenario. The planned assessment path administers scenarios from the scenario library, whereas the opportunistic assessment path modifies scenarios by adding, removing, or changing values of elements within the original scenario environment. This allows for more robust assessment by taking advantage of emergent assessment opportunities and helps ensure an immersive, seamless flow of scenario content. The closed-loop process then allows as many iterations of the embedded subloops as are necessary to meet instructional objectives.

The crux of the scenario-calibration phase is a three-step mathematical modeling process for developing and confirming

the computational task model. The steps are (1) identifying critical combinations of cues likely to activate goal-directed responses, (2) developing synthetic psychometric parameters for assessment items formed by these cue combinations, and (3) estimating actual psychometric parameters of these items to confirm the predicted parameters. Steps 1 and 2 involve the application of mathematical modeling techniques such as multiple regression and hierarchical linear modeling (HLM; Raudenbush & Bryk, 2002) within a policy capturing framework to quantify the effects of various cues on performance (Campbell, Buff, & Bolton, 2002; Dorsey & Coovert, 2003). IRT models (IRT; Embretson & Reise, 2000) are used in Stage 3 to estimate actual psychometric parameters of training events that include meaningful cue combinations identified in Stage 1.

A study was conducted to demonstrate the utility of one portion of the proposed framework, the scenario-calibration phase, by carrying out the three-step modeling process to build the computational task model. We examined the efficacy of this approach using data from a simulation-based training experiment.

Method

Participants. Participants (N = 120) were students at a large, public university participating in the experiment for course credit. Average age of participants, 73 percent of whom were male, was twenty-three years. Most participants had no familiarity with the task or simulation.

Task. Participants performed a Command and Control simulation known as the Forward Observer Personal Computer Simulator, or FOPCSim. The simulation was originally designed as an experimental Command and Control task platform by the Naval Postgraduate School. The simulation is designed to train the task of submitting Calls-for-Fire (CFF) from artillery or other assets with the goal of identifying, prioritizing, and eliminating hostile targets. The trainee takes the perspective of a Forward Observer on the ground, with potentially hostile targets and other objects hidden and emerging from the surrounding area within a photo-realistic 360-degree field of view. Trainees must evaluate those targets based on their physical characteristics, whether or not they are moving and firing, and rate of speed if moving, prioritize the targets, and estimate the distance and azimuth for a target before submitting a CFF to an artillery unit.

The rules of engagement impose a set of prioritization rules that consider three characteristics of potential targets: firing status, mobility status, and proximity. These rules dictate that firing targets are the most important, followed by moving targets, followed by idle targets. If two or more targets exist within the most threatening status tier, the one closest to the forward observer has the highest priority. Trainees' prioritization performance is assessed by considering the priority value of the target currently being engaged at a particular CFF given the other targets currently active in the environment.

Procedure. Trainees began the experiment by completing a brief introduction to the FOPCSim training environment with instructions on the rules of engagement, artillery for specific targets, and the procedure for submitting CFFs (e.g., distance estimation for targeting). They then performed a total of five training scenarios (ten minutes each) that varied in terms of the types and numbers of targets present in the environment. A prototypical snapshot of a training scenario taken at the point of a CFF included three moving targets, two idle targets, a 33 percent chance of any one target engaging in hostile fire, and a proximity of 345 m between the forward observer and the closest target (range 0–1,745 m). The amount, type, and timing of performance feedback was varied systematically across the participants during these training scenarios, resulting in the (highly desirable, from our modeling perspective) exhibition of a wide range of skill levels during the final stage of the experiment – the presentation of three additional test scenarios that ranged in difficulty and had similar target profiles as the training scenarios. Trainees were given opportunities for breaks at various times throughout the experiment.

Results

There are many aspects of performance within this training environment that can be assessed, but in this chapter we focus our analyses on the task of correctly prioritizing among multiple potential targets. We used the previously described three-step modeling strategy to estimate and confirm psychometric parameters of scenarios varying in cue combinations expected to influence the overall level of difficulty of the prioritization task within the scenario.

Model Development. In Step 1, we used HLM to identify critical cue combinations affecting prioritization performance in the five training scenarios. HLM is an extension of multiple regression used for data with an inherently nested structure – for example, in educational settings, in which students are nested within classrooms, classrooms within schools, and schools within districts. HLM allows one to test relationships among variables measured within one level of analysis, as well as between levels. For example, HLM would be suitable for testing the direct effects of individual students' reasoning ability and the moderating influence of class size on average standardized assessment scores for a school. HLM is also appropriate for complex repeated measures designs in which multiple dependent variable measures are considered nested within the individual performer. Our proposed model casts goal-directed behaviors (i.e., CFFs) as opportunities to take snapshots of the environment and to then evaluate the effects of cue configurations on performance. Therefore, HLM is an appropriate strategy for modeling the effects of cue configurations (i.e., presence or absence of specific cues and interactive effects of multiple cues) on various parameters of individual trainees' learning curves for his or her prioritization performance (i.e., intercept, reflecting initial performance; slope, reflecting level of performance change over the course of the training scenarios; and quadratic or other polynomial effects, reflecting rate and patterns of performance change).

We estimated a HLM using 5,488 CFFs nested within 120 participants. Independent variables were measures of various features of cues present in the environment at the time the CFF was submitted, including (among others) (1) number of targets within each of four independent tiers reflecting objective priority level according to the rules of engagement (Tier 1: engaging and moving; Tier 2: engaging and idle; Tier 3: not engaging and moving; Tier 4: not engaging and idle), (2) distance between forward observer and closest target, and (3) difference in distance between the highest-priority target and the next-highest-priority target.

We estimated an initial model containing several possible cue features as independent variables, and then reduced the model by removing nonsignificant effects and variables that resulted in multicollinearity. The final model included significant effects

$(p < .05)$ for a time or practice effect (linear $\beta_{10} = .068$, and quadratic $\beta_{20} = -.001$), the number of firing targets $(\beta_{30} = .787)$, number of moving targets $(\beta_{40} = -.149)$, number of idle targets $(\beta_{50} = -.451)$, proximity of distracter/next highest-priority target $(\beta_{60} = -.117)$, and several interactions involving time and the numbers of targets firing, moving, and idle. Positive parameter estimates mean that higher values of the cue increase the probability of a correct prioritization, and negative estimates mean that higher cue values decrease the probability. For example, for each additional 100 meters difference in the distance from the forward observer to the correct target and its closest distracter, the odds of success are predicted to increase by a factor of 1.1. However, the magnitude and direction of some of these effects varied over time, as indicated by significant interactions with the linear time effect. For example, adding a firing target decreased scenario difficulty early in training but increased scenario difficulty later in training. Figure 11.2 shows patterns for four prototype effects at early (after first CFF) and late points (after twentieth CFF) within training.

These results generally indicated that cues that provided priority information relevant to the rules of engagement consistently influenced prioritization performance.

Model Application. In Step 2, model coefficients from Step 1 were used to estimate expected difficulty levels (i.e., "synthetic" psychometric parameters) of an independent set of scenarios (i.e., the three test scenarios), which used similar sets of cues as the training scenarios but in different combinations and with different values. Of the three scenarios, one was designed to be a lower-difficulty scenario with one target engaging, one moving, and two idle, and the other two scenarios were designed to be more difficult, with one target engaging, three moving, and six idle. Considering the configuration of these scenario cues (along with other cue dimensions captured by the Step 1 HLM model, e.g., target distance), the model predicted that the higher-difficulty test scenarios would

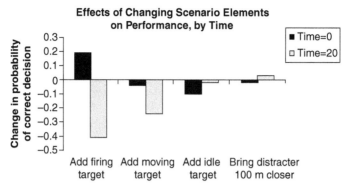

Figure 11.2. Effects of scenario elements on prioritization performance by time.

differ from the lower-difficulty test scenarios by an odds ratio of success of 3.0, with the higher-difficulty scenarios having a lower probability of success. This difference should be evident in differences in the difficulty parameters of the scenarios.

Model Evaluation. In Step 3, we used the two-parameter logistic (2PL) IRT model to estimate actual psychometric parameters (difficulty and discrimination) of the three test scenarios (Embretson & Reise, 2000). Modern psychometric theory provides a wealth of models useful for generating test- and person-invariant estimates of the psychometric properties of scenario content. This supports adaptive training contexts by producing robust, predictable scenario parameters, thereby affording accurate estimation of trainee latent traits in real time and more informed scenario modifications. Although more complex IRT models would be appropriate for the scenarios used in this experiment, the 2PL model offered a reasonable compromise in terms of appropriateness (i.e., allows accurate estimation of the probability of a correct versus incorrect prioritization) and sample size requirements. We then compared the 2PL estimated parameters with the Step 1 model predictions to evaluate and refine the computational task model.

IRT models must be built individually for each test item or, in our case, each scenario event. Given that a trainee's performance early in a scenario impacts the characteristics of the events that he faces later in the scenario, we focused our IRT modeling efforts around the first CFF submitted within each of the three test scenarios. This increases the likelihood that we really are estimating the psychometric difficulty and discrimination parameters for a unitary event.

The 2PL models probabilities of correct item responses (i.e., prioritization performance) as a logistic function of the difference between person trait levels (i.e., prioritization ability) and item difficulty. Difficulty is formally defined as the inflection point on the logistic curve representing the relationship between trait level and probability of a correct response. Specifically, the difficulty level of an item is the trait level at which a person has a 50 percent probability of a correct response to the item.

Figure 11.3 shows item-characteristic curves for the one lower- and two higher-wdifficulty test scenarios, respectively. Difficulty for the lower-difficulty scenario was -3.06, and for the higher-difficulty scenarios .76 and .64, respectively. The difference in difficulties between the higher- and lower-difficulty scenarios meant that an individual with a 50 percent probability of correct prioritization for the more difficult scenarios would have a 92 percent probability of correct prioritization for the easier scenario. This difference translates into an odds ratio of approximately 1.4. Although this value was not identical to the HLM model prediction, the nearly identical difficulties of the harder scenarios and the large difference between these and the lower-difficulty scenario represent a pattern consistent with the HLM model predictions.

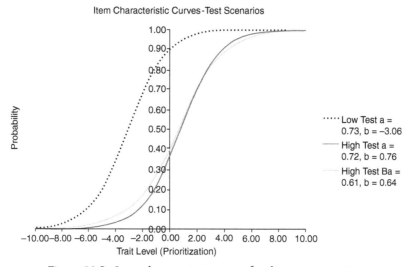

Figure 11.3. Item-characteristic curves for three test scenarios.

Discussion

The first purpose of this study was to propose a framework for incorporating emergent assessment opportunities into adaptive training systems. Our approach involves deriving mathematical models, with variables gleaned from cognitive task analyses of the domain and parameters based on large sets of performance data, that are capable of predicting the psychometric properties of both planned and emergent events. These models can then be used to systematically generate libraries of scenario events with known psychometric properties, as well as to support real-time analysis of the implications of a trainee's performance on an unexpected series of unfolding events.

Additionally, we sought to evaluate one portion of the framework by carrying out the proposed three-step computational task-modeling process. Results of the modeling procedure indicated generally good correspondence between the synthetic and actual psychometric parameters of scenarios. These results are indicative of the utility of the use of multiple, converging modeling strategies to comprehensively sample complex cue configurations and quantify their effects on training performance. Moreover, these results support the applicability of the proposed framework for supporting opportunistic, context-sensitive simulation-based assessment and adaptive training.

The limitations of a purely planned approach to embedded assessments within adaptive training environments were the inspiration for the proposed framework. These limitations are related to the ability to translate complex combinations of simulation environment cues into assessment content with estimable and interpretable psychometric properties. The proposed framework provides an alternative means of extracting assessment items by treating training performance as a connected series of goal-directed actions that allow us to take snapshots of meaningful cue configurations. By identifying and quantifying the psychologically relevant features of situations, our framework provides a means of developing assessments and modifying scenario content opportunistically in real time.

Practical implications. The proposed framework can serve as a schematic for training practitioners to develop adaptive training systems in any domain. It is especially suitable for complex domains in which it is hard to anticipate what characteristics of a scenario affect its difficulty, such as military command and control, medical domains such as emergency room triage, or nuclear power plant control room operations. The proposed task analysis and modeling methodology provides a theoretically grounded, quantitative, and confirmatory approach for addressing this issue. The resulting model allows trainers to produce large amounts of scenario content with predictable psychometric properties – once the environmental cues that affect performance are known, they can be combined in a near-infinite number of ways to create large libraries of scenarios. This can help enhance the efficiency and accuracy of the scenario-generation process in the development of adaptive training systems.

Limitations. The primary limitation of the current study was the use of a relatively limited set of cue combinations within the scenarios examined for the scenario calibration phase. Ideally, a large number of scenarios is needed to ensure that trainees experience many different cue combinations during initial scenario free play. Trainees performed a relatively small number of scenarios during a short time frame and therefore did not have the opportunity to experience the majority of possible cue combinations. This might be impossible in more complex domains; however, the proposed framework suggests that exposure to larger numbers of cue combinations can enhance the quality of the computational task model.

In conclusion, we proposed an approach to identifying content to serve as the basis for opportunistic assessment within adaptive training systems that extends and complements existing approaches to planned, embedded assessments and their associated task-analytic methods. Furthermore, we demonstrated the key role of multiple, convergent mathematical modeling techniques within the proposed approach. The promising results for the initial phase point to the general applicability of the approach to a wide variety of other domains; additional research is needed to evaluate the utility of the full model across such domains.

References

Altmann, E. M., & Trafton, J. G. (2002). Memory for goals: An activation-based model. *Cognitive Science*, 26, 39–83.

Bargh, J. A., Gollwitzer, P. M., Lee-Chai, A., Barndollar, K., & Trotschel, R. (2001). The automated will: Nonconscious activation and pursuit of behavioral goals. *Journal of Personality and Social Psychology*, 81, 1014–1027.

Campbell, G. E., Buff, W. L., & Bolton, A. E. (2002). Traditional mathematical modeling applied to human prioritization judgments: Quicksand for the unwary modeler. Presented at the Eleventh Conference on Computer Generated Forces. May 7–9, 2002, Orlando, FL.

Dorsey, D. W., & Coovert, M. D. (2003). Mathematical modeling of decision making: A soft and fuzzy approach to capturing hard decisions [Special issue]. *Human Factors*, 45, 117–135.

Embretson, S. E. (2006). The continued search for nonarbitrary metrics in psychology. *American Psychologist*, 61, 50–55.

Embretson, S. E., & Reise, S. P. (2000). *Item response theory for psychologists*. Mahwah, NJ: Lawrence Erlbaum Associates.

Fowlkes, J. E., Dwyer, D. J., Oser, R. L., & Salas, E. (1998). Event-based approach to training (EBAT). *International Journal of Aviation Psychology*, 8, 209–221.

Freeman, J., Stacy, W., Levchuk, G., Colonna-Romano, J., & Shebilske, W. (2009). Techniques and technologies for optimizing instructional strategy. In P. M. Mangos & G. Campbell (Chairs), *Innovations in adaptive simulation-based assessment, training, and feedback*. Symposium presented at the 24th Annual Conference of the Society for Industrial and Organizational Psychology, New Orleans, LA.

Gibson, J. J. (1977). The theory of affordances. In R. Shaw & J. Bransford (Eds.), *Perceiving, acting, and knowing*. Hillsdale, NJ: Lawrence Erlbaum Associates.

Gollwitzer, P. M., Fujita, K., & Oettingen, G. (2004). Planning and implementation of goals. In R. F. Baumeister & K. D. Vohs (Eds.), *Handbook of self-regulation: Research, theory, and applications*. New York: Guilford Press.

Hodgetts, H. M., & Jones, D. M. (2006). Interruption of the Tower of London task: Support for a goal-activation approach. *Journal of Experimental Psychology: General*, 135, 103–115.

Klein, G. (1997). The recognition-primed decision (RPD) model: Looking back, looking forward. In C. E. Zsambok & G. Klein (Eds.), *Naturalistic decision making* (pp. 285–292). Mahwah, NJ: Lawrence Erlbaum Associates.

Locke, E. A., & Latham, G. P. (2002). Building a practically useful theory of goal setting and task motivation. *American Psychologist, 57,* 705–717.

Mangos, P. M., & Johnston, J. H. (2009). Performance measurement issues and guidelines for adaptive, simulation-based training. In D. A. Vincenzi, J. A. Wise, M. Mouloua, & P. A. Hancock (Eds.), *Human factors in simulation and training* (pp. 301–320). Boca Raton, FL: Taylor and Francis Group.

Mislevy, R. J., Steinberg, L. S., & Almond, R. G. (2003). On the structure of educational assessments. *Measurement: Interdisciplinary Research and Perspectives, 1,* 3–62.

Raudenbush, S. W., & Bryk, A. S. (2002). *Hierarchical linear models: Applications and data analysis methods.* Thousand Oaks, CA: Sage Publications.

Shute, V. J., & Zapata-Rivera, D. (2008). Adaptive technologies. In J. M. Spector, D. Merrill, J. van Merriënboer, & M. Driscoll (Eds.), *Handbook of research on educational communications and technology* (3rd ed., pp. 277–294). New York: Lawrence Erlbaum Associates, Taylor & Francis Group.

Vincenzi, D. A., Wise, J. A., Mouloua, M., & Hancock, P. A. (Eds.) (2009). *Human factors in simulation and training.* Boca Raton, FL: Taylor and Francis Group.

CHAPTER 12

Semantic Adaptive Training

John Flynn

Introduction

This chapter addresses the potential for the application of emerging Semantic Web technologies to significantly improve the interactions by artificial intelligence characters in game-based training environments. The Semantic Web is an initiative sponsored by the World Wide Web Consortium (W3C), which provides facilities for the markup of data so that the meaning, or semantics, of the data can be directly read and understood by computers. The Semantic Web represents a major advance over the current Web that only presents data in a form for humans to read and understand. Information about the Semantic Web initiative can be found at http://www.w3.org/standards/semanticweb/.

The very best training is obtained when trainees learn and perfect tasks exactly as they will be required to execute them during real-world missions. Of course, real-world environments are not always available, and even when they are, it is often not economically feasible, or even safe, to employ them. Therefore, it is advantageous to make synthetic training environments conform to real-world environments as best as possible. One of the shortfalls in synthetic training environments is the lack of realism afforded to computer-generated characters. This is primarily a reflection of limitations in the current state of the art in the field of artificial intelligence. This chapter explores a Semantic Web–based technology approach to creating virtual characters with human-like characteristics that directly impact how they react in training or teaching environments. While there are many other aspects of training systems that may benefit from using emerging Semantic Web technologies, the following discussion provides some general concepts that introduce the technology and offer food for thought to aid future development in the area of artificial game characters.

A good measure of realism for computer-generated characters is the Turing test proposed by computer scientist Alan Turing in 1950. Its basic premise is that a human carries on a keyboard text-only dialog with two entities located behind a screen – one is another human and the other is a computer.

If the human cannot tell the difference between the two, the computer is said to have passed the Turing test. (More on the Turing test can be found on Wikipedia.) The Loebner Prize has been awarded annually since 1991 to the computer program that best satisfies the objectives of the Turing test. This contest is traditionally won by a class of computer programs called *chat bots* (http://www.loebner.net/Prizef/loebner-prize.html). They are designed to interact with humans in as realistic a manner as possible and represent technology that can improve the computer-generated characters used in synthetic training environments. However, an emerging set of technologies related to the Semantic Web, combined with chat bots, may provide truly revolutionary improvements in the capabilities of artificial intelligence characters.

We will consider two basic types of game character dialog, personal and nonpersonal. Nonpersonal dialog is related to general knowledge. If a person is asked, "What is the highest mountain in Africa?" they would likely respond with the answer, "Mt. Kilimanjaro." The response would not be influenced by any personal factors, such as beliefs, goals, emotions, standards or prejudices, held by the individual. However, if the person is asked, "What do you think of George W. Bush?" the reaction would likely be quite different. Many personal factors would come into play. It is not just that the question is subjective, but that it triggers potentially strong personal feelings. The Artificial Intelligence Markup Language (AIML), described later, offers one reasonable approach for handling nonpersonal dialog. However, capturing and applying personal factors requires an augmented approach. In the following discussion we consider the use of a *formal semantic ontology* for describing individual personal attributes.

Semantic Web Technology – Ontologies

Tim Berners-Lee, creator of the World Wide Web, has expressed a dream of a new Semantic Web in which computers are capable of analyzing all the data on the Web. He states, "I have a dream for the Web [in which computers] become capable of analyzing all the data on the Web – the content, links, and transactions between people and computers. A 'Semantic Web,' which should make this possible, has yet to emerge, but when it does, the day-to-day mechanisms of trade, bureaucracy and our daily lives will be handled by machines talking to machines. The 'intelligent agents' people have touted for ages will finally materialize" (Berners-Lee & Fischetti, 1999). His quote provides an appropriate introduction to the discussion in this section.

The Semantic Web extends the World Wide Web, evolving it from a web of hyperlinked human-readable documents into a web of machine-readable and understandable data interconnected using semantic relationships. The goal of the Semantic Web is to create a vast, distributed, linked data source that has no inherent limitations or boundaries and can be accessed and traversed by humans and machines alike. New technology is rapidly emerging in response to this vision. The Defense Advanced Research Projects Agency (DARPA) was an early investor in research in support of the Semantic Web. The DARPA Agent Markup Language (DAML) project provided the foundation for the World Wide Web Consortium (W3C) standard OWL Web Ontology Language which is based on a formal Descriptive Logic (DL) (http://www.daml.org). The most current version of OWL, OWL 2, was released in October, 2009 (http://www.w3.org/TR/owl2-overview/). However, given that the original version of OWL is still most familiar and widely supported, the examples in this chapter use that version. OWL is designed to create *ontologies*, which are formal descriptions of concepts, terms and relationships within a given knowledge domain. (More on the ontologies can be found on Wikipedia.) Ontologies are expressed in terms of classes, properties, and a variety of formal relationships between these objects. A very simple example is shown in Figure 12.1 using

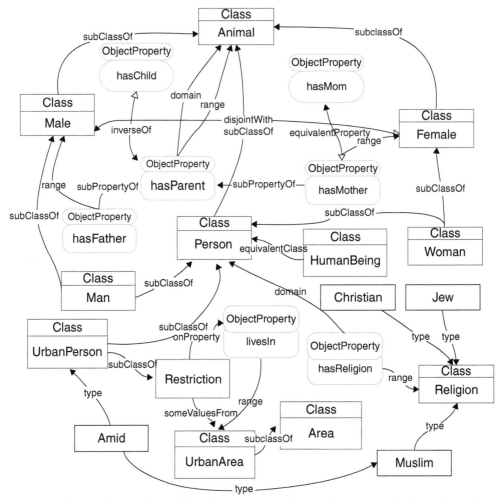

Figure 12.1. An ontology is a formal logical description of a set of concepts and relationships about a specific domain.

the graphical representation VisioOWL (http://www.semwebcentral.org/projects/visioowl).

Think of a *class* as being a formal mathematical set. A *subclass* contains a subset of the members of the original class. Subclasses inherit all of the properties of their parent class. In the example, a Person is a subclass of an Animal and an Urban Person is a subclass of a Person, with the specific property of living in an Urban Area. Amid is a Man and an Urban Person who is further defined as having a Religion, which is Muslim. Because this ontology is written in a formal computer language, OWL, it can be directly processed by a computer program that can

discover, or learn, all of the information represented in the ontology. Ontologies are sometimes referred to as semantic knowledge bases.

The ontology show in Figure 12.1 provides a descriptive logic representation of some very basic aspects of a person. It is easy to see how this simple ontology might be expanded to include significantly more information about Amid and his environment. For example, the concept of Urban Area could be further refined as having some specific minimum population density. Amid's father and mother could be specified, including where they live and their religious affiliation.

In Figure 12.2, the Person ontology has been expanded to include the concepts of *emotions*, *beliefs*, *goals*, *standards*, and *preferences*. It further refines the Emotion class into several emotion pairs that can have values between 10 and –10. For the Disliking-Liking emotion pair, a value of 10 would mean maximum liking and a value of –10 would reflect maximum disliking. A related issue is the *context* of an emotion. In this example, an emotion is placed in the context of an event response, which might be an Audible Event or a Visual Event. This sample ontology could be further expanded to include the representation of more specific Events and also place Emotions in the context of additional properties, such as a DefaultEmotion property that would capture a person's "normal" emotional state. Any specific person might normally express some combination of emotions that reflects his or her basic personality, such as being a "bitter" or "happy" person. That person's normal emotional state could be temporarily modified by external events but would return to the basic personality status after some period of time. In the context of a training game, the external events that may trigger changes in the emotional state of an artificial character are represented by dialog or actions from human participants or other game characters. Additionally, past experiences may predispose a game character to react in some specific fashion. The ontology will allow past experiences to be captured and remembered. Later in the chapter we will discuss how dialog and actions may be interpreted, via rules, to effect emotional changes that, in turn, impact how the artificial character responds to stimuli.

The specific concepts for emotions shown in this example ontology do not represent any consensus among the community of psychologists and others exploring the field of human emotions. However, it may not be necessary to fully understand and duplicate the full complexity of actual human emotions to achieve a level of realism in game characters that is completely adequate for training purposes.

The classes of Goals, Standards, and Preferences could also be expanded to include more detailed descriptions of these human characteristics. To the author's knowledge, no one has attempted to create a full Person ontology that would possess the level of detail necessary to capture enough human characteristics to imbue a game character with the degree of realism to allow that character to function and react in ways basically indistinguishable from a real human. Such an undertaking would not be trivial, and significantly more detail beyond that represented in Figure 12.2 would be needed. A rough estimate of the resources and level of effort required to create a relatively complete, and usable, Person ontology would include a domain expert (a psychologist who has worked in the field of describing human characteristics) and a computer scientist with experience in writing formal descriptive logic ontologies working together over a six-month period of time. A relatively complete Person ontology would provide a template for a host of diverse computer game characters. Only the specific details for each character, such as the person's name, age, religion, emotional values, among others, will change, but the overall Person ontology would support the detailed description of multiple unique individuals. There is also the potential to develop ontologies that reflect generalized characteristics of specific groups. However, the same dangers of overgeneralizing that apply to human profiling can also apply to artificial game characters.

Procedural Language Models – Action Agents

Envision the completion of a much more detailed Person ontology that reflects all of the key characteristics and facts needed to reasonably represent a person in a game-based training environment. A legitimate question is what can be done with the ontology. The ontology is simply a formal logic representation of semantics – the concepts and relationships associated with a person.

240

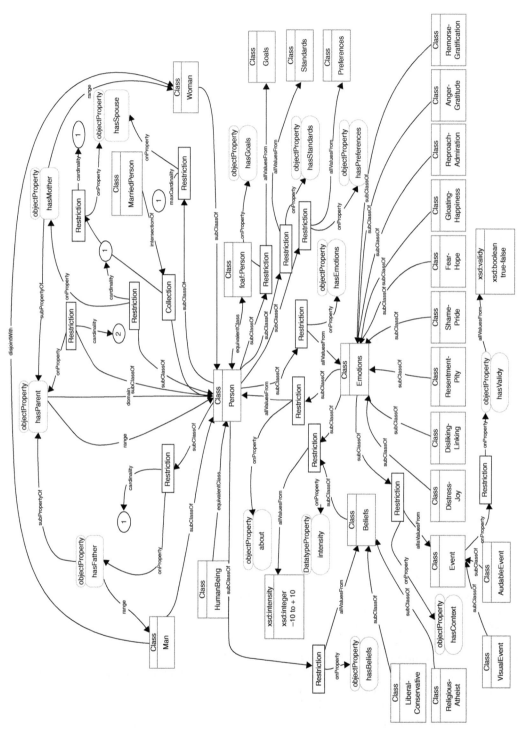

Figure 12.2. This ontology expands the concepts about a Person to include arbitrary sets of emotions and beliefs.

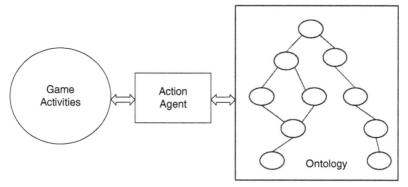

Figure 12.3. Action Agents produce actions for specific ontologies in response to game activities.

It is not actionable because the descriptive logic language OWL does not contain any procedural constructs. We might think of the Person ontology as a being a mind without a body. The mind contains all of the knowledge, emotions, goals, preferences, beliefs, and other attributes of the individual but on its own cannot perform any overt actions in response to outside stimuli. We now have to provide a means for the specific representation of Amid to react to situations or stimuli that may occur during the course of the game. That is, we need to provide the body and its nervous system. This is accomplished through the use of *procedural language modules*, which provide an interface between game actions and the ontology. For ease of reference, these procedural language modules will be called *Action Agents*, as shown in Figure 12.3.

Action Agents can be written using any procedural computer language, such as LISP, C++, Java, or Ruby, including scripted languages such as Perl and PHP. Many of these procedural languages have been extended to support *formal logic reasoning*, which is discussed later.

There may be many different types of Action Agents, each specialized to interpret specific game activities and evaluate the appropriate game character response based on the formal description in the Person ontology. For example, an Action Agent may monitor game activities to detect verbal communications directed to Amid. A human participant, or another game character, may state, "People who live in urban areas are stupid." The Action Agent would examine the Amid Person Ontology, and based on how Amid "feels" about insults to where he lives, the person making the insult, and other pertinent factors, the Action Agent would produce the appropriate reaction. That reaction might range from Amid simply standing there, showing anger, making a verbal response, or taking physical action. We see from this simple example that Action Agents can be complex. An important aspect of Action Agents is they can be truly distributed across the Web environment. One training agency may develop Action Agents that fit their special training needs, whereas another agency could develop their own special Action Agents – both working against a common Person ontology. For example, one training agency may be focused on teaching peaceful resolution of conflict and their version of Action Agents might result in Amid's response to the insult being his refusal to further cooperate with the trainee. Another agency may be interested in training for responses to direct hostile reactions, and as a result might develop Action Agents that would cause Amid to react to the insult with physical force.

The Action Agent architecture illustrated in Figure 12.4 includes processes to *interpret, evaluate,* and *select* appropriate *responses* to a variety of game situations. One of the purposes of these processes is to determine if the input dialog is personal or nonpersonal. Nonpersonal dialog is subject to direct response based on facts stored

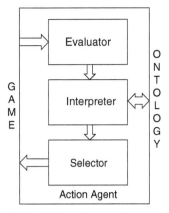

Figure 12.4. Action Agents interpret game actions and provide appropriate responses.

in the knowledge base. Personal dialog is evaluated in the context of specific data extracted from the dialog and the emotional, and other, states stored in the artificial character's ontology. Rules determine how the character's emotions influence specific reactions to the dialog.

There are many potential technical approaches to developing the interpreter, evaluator, and responder modules for an Action Agent. For example, natural language processing might be applied. However, recent research indicates that a brute-force approach may be very practical for most human–game character interactions. The brute-force approach makes no attempt to parse and understand the user's dialog. Instead, it uses pattern-matching techniques and provides facilities to match input queries or statements with predefined specific or random answers.

Although there is a very large set of things people could say that are grammatically correct and semantically meaningful, the number of things people actually do say is surprisingly small. The XML-based Artificial Intelligence Markup Language (AIML) focuses on pattern matching and provides facilities to match input queries or statements with predefined specific or random answers (http://www.alicebot.org/aiml.html). AIML also provides a number of very clever ways to parse the input queries/statements so that different forms of input

that mean the same thing reduce to elicit the same answer. For example, inputs such as, "Hello, what is your name?", "What is your name?", and "Your name please?" all reduce to elicit the same reply, "My name is Amid." AIML was used to develop a computer chat bot called ALICE, which won the Loebner Prize several times as "the most human computer" at the annual Turing Test. ALICE contains more than 40,000 categories of knowledge. Each category combines a question and answer, or stimulus and response, called the *pattern* and *template*, respectively. The AIML software stores the patterns in a tree structure managed by an object called the Graphmaster that implements a pattern storage and matching algorithm. The Graphmaster is compact in memory and permits efficient pattern-matching response times.

The free Pandorabots Web service hosts many different chat bots developed using AIML (http://pandorabots.com). The Pandorabots Web server stores the dialog between humans and the various Chat Bots with approximately 800 million interactions captured to date. Preliminary analysis of these interactions indicates the pattern of dialog follows Zipf's law (http://en.wikipedia.org/wiki/Zipf's_law). Zipf's law is related to the idea of small-world phenomena. For example, the Kevin Bacon game and the idea of six degrees of separation, where given any two random people in a living human population, there is a sequence of typically no more than six steps of acquaintance between any one person and any other randomly named person. Note that this example is constrained by the fact that the scope of the sample is limited to living persons. If it were unconstrained to include all persons who ever lived, the small-world phenomenon would no longer hold. We also see evidence of the small-world phenomenon in Web searches where the most popular key word may get millions of hits whereas the tenth-most popular term may get less than a hundred hits. This type of "the popular boys/girls get all the dates" phenomenon is modeled in terms of Zipfian distributions, where the nth-most popular keyword gets hits that are inversely proportional to n.

Actual dialog between a person and an artificial game character is considerably constrained by the scope and context of the game, especially in a training environment. The Pandorabots dialog analysis indicates that 10,000 questions and 10,000 answers are all that will likely be used in any practical environment. Although this seems considerable, it is very achievable, and once the likely dialog is developed for one specific training environment, relatively few modifications would be needed to extend the robust dialog capabilities to a new environment.

If the nonpersonal, or general-knowledge, dialog between a person and an artificial character can be adequately handled by brute-force pattern matching, as previously discussed, what about the personal dialog that involves analysis of specific emotional and other personal characteristics of the artificial entity? It is feasible that the pattern-matching approach will still suffice to identify those human statements that may elicit a personal reaction from the game character. However, instead of matching the statement or question to a fixed response, the Interpreter would initiate the Analysis process by which an Action Agent would be invoked to examine the specific Person Ontology for characteristics, goals, emotions, beliefs, and other elements that might influence the likely response of the artificial character. The Responder process would then match those personal factors to specific responses and actions appropriate to the context of the situation.

Semantic Technology Supports Reasoning

One of the major advantages of using a formal semantic language and ontology in the development of artificial characters is that such an approach supports *reasoning*. While specific knowledge is an important element in how humans respond and react to their environment, the fact that we can reason greatly expands our ability to formulate appropriate responses when we may not have the complete information directly at hand. A simple example is that we may know that Barack Obama's youngest daughter is named Sacha. We also specifically know that Barack Obama is the President of the United States. However, it is through reasoning that we know that Sacha is also the daughter of the President of the United States, even though we may never have been exposed to that specific fact. Simple reasoning is so natural and intuitive that we hardly give it any thought, but it is responsible for much of our ability to correctly determine new facts based on incomplete information. Consider the preceding simple-reasoning example in the context of information stored in a relational database. The two specifically known facts could be stored in the database; however, there is absolutely no way that the deduced fact that Sacha is the daughter of the president could be determined through relational technology. It is only through the use of a formal logic language like OWL, and the expression of formal logic relationships within the ontology, that automated computer reasoning can be achieved. Simple one-step reasoning is very powerful in its own right; however, computer reasoning can be done across many intermediate steps. One fact can lead to another, which can lead to another, so that a new fact that is not in the actual stored data may be realized that is far removed from the data that allowed the new fact to be obtained via computer reasoning. The computer's capability for keeping track of intermediate reasoning steps may allow artificial game characters to derive new facts far beyond the capacity of humans. This will provide important new capabilities for the computer analysis of information and will improve the realism of artificial intelligence game characters for use in much higher-fidelity training environments.

Conclusions

As in all important undertakings, the devil is always in the details. This cursory introduction and discussion is not intended to provide a specific recipe for how to develop semantic artificial characters in support of adaptive training objectives. However, it is intended to demonstrate that the realization of significantly improved adaptive training environments may be developed within the bounds of new emerging technologies. Semantic Web-related technology is rapidly evolving from a period of worldwide research into the realization of practical adoption in significant new applications. Semantic Web technology does not provide a magical solution to technical development problems, but it does give us important new capabilities that, combined with traditional methods, will allow the development of training environments significantly better than those existing today. It may eventually provide training capabilities far beyond anything we can even imagine.

References

AIML, Dr. Richard Wallace: http://www.alice-bot.org/aiml.html

Berners-Lee, Tim ; Fischetti, Mark (1999). *Weaving the web*. HarperSanFrancisio.

DAML Web site: http://www.daml.org.

John Flynn, VisioOWL: http://www.semwebcentral.org/projects/visioowl.

Loebner Prize: http://www.loebner.net/Prizef/loebner-prize.html

OWL 2 Web Ontology Language, http://www.w3.org/TR/owl2-overview/.

Pandorabots Host Site: http://pandorabots.com

Semantic Web: http://www.w3.org/standards/semanticweb/

Turing Test: http://en.wikipedia.org/wiki/Turing_test

Wikipedia, the free encyclopedia: http://en.wikipedia.org/wiki/Semantic_Web.

Zipf's Law: http://en.wikipedia.org/wiki/Zipf's_law

Part IV

NATURAL LANGUAGE PROCESSING FOR TRAINING

CHAPTER 13

Speech and Language Processing for Adaptive Training

Diane Litman

Introduction

Speech and language processing (also known as natural language processing [NLP], human language technologies [HLT], computational linguistics [CL], etc.) has a fifty-year history as a scientific discipline and a much more recent history as a commercial presence. NLP-based research and applications focused on training environments have followed a similar trajectory. Initial NLP-based work in adaptive training focused on assessing student essay-length and short-answer texts, as well as on developing conversational intelligent tutoring systems. More recently, advances in speech recognition and synthesis have made it possible to include spoken language technologies in both assessments and tutorial dialogue systems. Progress in these traditional areas continues to improve with new innovations in NLP techniques, which include methods ranging from deep linguistic analysis to robust data-driven statistical methods. Commercial products are making their way to the marketplace, and NLP-based systems are being deployed in authentic settings. Continuing software and hardware advances, as well as the amount of language data available on the World Wide Web, have also resulted in the creation of new educational applications of NLP – for example, linguistically detecting then adapting to student metacognitive and emotional states, personalizing texts and spoken artifacts to the needs and interests of particular students, applications automatically generating test questions, and incorporating language into virtual training environments. This chapter first briefly reviews both the research area of NLP and the types of training applications that NLP has contributed to. Next, a case study is presented to illustrate several ways that NLP techniques have been used to develop a spoken-dialogue physics training system that detects and adapts to student uncertainty.

Natural Language Processing

The goal of natural language processing (NLP) is "to get computers to perform useful tasks involving human language, tasks like enabling human – machine

Table 13.1. Knowledge of Language Needed by NLP Applications

Phonetics and Phonology: speech sounds
Morphology: words and their internal structure
Syntax: the structuring of words into larger units
Semantics: meaning
Pragmatics: language in context
Discourse: the study of multiple
  utterances/sentences

Source: Jurafsky & Martin, 2008.

communication, improving human – human communication, or simply doing useful processing of text or speech" (Jurafsky & Martin, 2008). NLP can thus be used to develop adaptive training systems in several ways. For example, knowledge of language can be used to trigger adaptation during training, as well as to personalize adaptation once triggered using the enormous amount of machine-readable text and audio that is now available electronically. In addition, conversational agents are becoming an important human-computer interaction method, including those interactions focused on training.

One distinguishing aspect of NLP applications is that they require knowledge of language, which can be separated into the six categories shown in Table 13.1 (Jurafsky & Martin, 2008). As will be seen in the next section, adaptive training applications have been developed across this spectrum of linguistic knowledge types.

NLP is also distinguished from related fields in that NLP researchers study language from a computational perspective. That is, formal representations are developed to represent linguistic knowledge, which are in turn manipulated via associated algorithms. Popular computational models include state machines, formal rule systems/grammars, and logic (all of which can be made probabilistic if desired), as well as probability theory and Bayesian networks. Associated popular algorithms include search, dynamic programming, and machine learning (Jurafsky & Martin, 2008).

A Brief Survey of NLP for Educational Applications

Assessing Student Language

One of the largest and oldest application areas for NLP in adaptive training involves language assessment, such as for training students to read, write, or speak a first or second language, or for assessing student language responses during other types of adaptive training. Work in this area has primarily used NLP to assess typed or spoken student artifacts with respect to a linguistic dimension from Table 13.1. The computational methods in turn have ranged from statistical methods such as unsupervised learning, Latent Semantic Analysis, and Naive Bayes (e.g., Foltz et al., 1998; Higgins et al., 2006; Jurafsky & Martin, 2008; Kintsch et al., 2000) to highly knowledge-based approaches such as parsing and abductive theorem proving (e.g., Jurafsky & Martin, 2008; Lee & Seneff, 2008; Makatchev et al., 2006).

For example, *syntactic* analysis has been used to detect errors made by nonnative or deaf students, such as incorrect article, preposition, and verb usage (Gamon et al., 2008; Han et al., 2006; Lee & Seneff, 2008; Michaud & McCoy, 2006; Tetreault & Chodorow, 2008). *Semantic* analysis has been used to assess the meaning of both essay-length and short-answer responses, at both fine (e.g., paraphrase or entailment recognition, information extraction) and coarse (e.g., on-topic or off-topic) grained levels of analysis (Higgins et al., 2006; Kintsch et al., 2000; Leacock, 2004; Makatchev et al., 2006; McCarthy et al., 2007; Nielsen et al., 2008, Rosé & VanLehn, 2005; Sukkarieh & Pulman, 2005). Knowledge of *pragmatics* has been used to train nonnative speakers in back-channeling (Ward et al., 2007) and culturally dependent aspects of foreign language learning (Johnson, 2007), whereas knowledge of *discourse* has been used to evaluate the coherence of student essays (Burstein et al., 2003; Foltz et al., 1998; Higgins et al., 2006; Miltsakaki & Kukich, 2004). Finally, knowledge particular to *speech* has been used to assess reading (Beck

& Sison, 2006), speaking (Zechner & Bejar, 2006), and translation (Wang & Seneff, 2007) proficiency.

Teaching Using Language

In addition to being the *domain* of analysis (as was the case in the previous section), language can also be used as the training *method*. Consider the method of tutoring. It has been shown that students working one on one with human tutors often score higher than students working with computer tutors, with both scoring higher than students working on the same topic in classrooms (Anderson et al., 1995; Bloom, 1984). One major difference between human tutors and current computer tutors is that only human tutors participate in unconstrained natural language dialogue with students, which has led to the conjecture that human tutoring might be so effective because of its use of dialogue (Chi et al., 2001; Fox, 1993; Graesser et al., 1995; Merrill et al., 1992). Thus, in recent years, *dialogue*-based training systems following the tutoring paradigm have become increasingly more prevalent (e.g., Evens & Michael, 2006; Graesser et al., 2001; Litman & Silliman, 2004; Rosé & Aleven, 2002; Rosé & Freedman, 2000; VanLehn et al., 2002; Zinn et al., 2002) as one method of attempting to close the performance gap between training by humans and by computers.

In addition to having the training system play the role of the tutor in an interactive natural language dialogue with a student, recent work has explored the use of new conversational roles for training systems, such as student peers (Kersey et al., 2009). For example, one role for peer collaborations in learning is to make deeper meaning better understood. Sometimes, intersubjectivity among students is a better driver of deeper understanding than student-teacher interactions. There has also been increasing interest in using dialogue in training environments in novel ways – for example, to facilitate a student's dialogue with another human as in computer-supported collaborated

learning (Kumar et al., 2007), or to enable a student to observe the training dialogues of other students and/or virtual agents (Chi et al., 2008; Craig et al., 2000; Piwek et al., 2007).

Finally, it has been hypothesized that learning and motivation will be enhanced in more socially realistic training environments. For example, one way that dialogue systems can be made more socially intelligent is to address issues such as politeness and face (Moore et al., 2004; Wang & Johnson, 2008). Another approach is to enable the system to detect and adapt to students' affective and metacognitive states (Aist et al., 2002; Boyer et al., 2008; D'Mello et al., 2008; Pon-Barry et al., 2006a; Ward & Tsukahara, 2003). An example illustrating the detection of positively and negatively valenced students' affective states will be given later in the chapter. Language is also believed to be a crucial modality (Atkinson et al., 2005; Baylor et al., 2003; Moreno et al., 2001) of more socially realistic multimodal training environments, such as those involving pedagogical agents or narrative (Graesser et al., 2001; Johnson, 2007; McQuiggan et al., 2008).

Processing Language

In addition to assessing student linguistic inputs and serving as the trainer's medium of communication, NLP is increasingly being used to (semi)automate and/or personalize the authoring of training systems. This type of work often takes advantage of the large amounts of electronically available examples of spoken and written language that are now found on personal Web sites, in Wikipedia and in online textbooks, and in linguistic repositories such as the Linguistic Data Consortium (http://www.ldc.upenn.edu/) and Talk-Bank (http://talkbank.org/).

For example, various statistical data-driven approaches (e.g., text classification [Rosé et al., 2007] and reinforcement learning [Chi et al., 2009]) have been used to automatically process existing language corpora to gain insights for (or even to actually automate) the authoring of adaptive training systems. An example illustrating the use of corpus-based methods to design adaptive training responses after detecting student uncertainty will be given later in the chapter. With respect to curriculum development, NLP has been used to automatically identify materials to present to students that are tailored to the individual student's reading level and/or topics of interests (Heilman et al., 2007; Miltsakaki & Troutt, 2008; Petersen & Ostendorf, 2009; Pitler & Nenkova, 2008). Furthermore, knowledge of speech has been used to develop tools that allow both students and teachers to appropriately access and process external online lecture materials related to the content of the training system (Glass et al., 2007; Malioutov & Barzilay, 2006). Finally, with respect to assessment, NLP has been used to automatically generate multiple-choice, wordbank, and other types of test questions (Brown et al., 2005; Mitkov et al., 2006).

Adapting Dialogue-Based Training to Student Uncertainty: A Case Study

In this section, a case study is presented to concretely illustrate some of the usages of NLP for adaptive training discussed earlier.[1] The following subsection first introduces ITSPOKE (Litman & Silliman, 2004), which illustrates the use of spoken dialogue technology to build a conversational intelligent tutoring system in the domain of qualitative physics. The next subsection shows how ITSPOKE is being enhanced to process not only *what* the student says, but *how* the student says it, to dynamically detect student states such as uncertainty during the course of tutoring. The final subsection shows how NLP is being used to mine corpora of tutorial dialogues to design the adaptive tutor responses to detected student states in ITSPOKE, as well as to semiautomate

and/or optimize the dialogue behaviors of ITSPOKE and other conversational training systems.

ITSPOKE: A Spoken Tutorial Dialogue System

ITSPOKE (Intelligent Tutoring SPOKEn dialogue system) (Litman & Silliman, 2004) illustrates how spoken dialogue systems technology can be used to implement a computer tutor that can engage in spoken conversations with students. The architecture of ITSPOKE is shown in Figure 13.1. ITSPOKE is built on top of the Why2-Atlas text-based tutor (VanLehn et al., 2002). In Why2-Atlas, a student first provides a natural language answer to a qualitative physics problem (a thought-provoking "why" type question). The Why2-Atlas computer tutor then engages the student in a typed natural language dialogue to provide feedback and correct misconceptions, and to elicit more complete explanations. The dialogues have a Tutor Question–Student Answer–Tutor Response format, implemented with a finite state machine (FSM) dialogue manager. Each dialogue consists of a series of questions about the topics needed to solve the problem. All natural language processing – for example, sentence-level syntactic and semantic analysis (Rosé, 2000), discourse and domain-level processing (Jordan & VanLehn, 2002; Jordan et al., 2003), and finite-state dialogue management (Rosé et al., 2001) – are performed by components in the Why2-Atlas back end.

ITSPOKE is a speech-enhanced version of Why2-Atlas: Student speech is digitized from microphone input using the Sphinx2 speech recognizer (Huang et al., 1993), while tutor utterances are synthesized using the Cepstral text-to-speech system (a commercial outgrowth of the Festival system [Black and Taylor, 1997]) and played to the student using a speaker and/or headphone. ITSPOKE thus tutors the qualitative physics problems via *spoken* dialogue interaction between a student and ITSPOKE. This spoken dialogue interaction between student and computer tutor is mediated via a Web

[1] The research briefly summarized in this section was primarily done in collaboration with Kate Forbes-Riley of the University of Pittsburgh. Full details for the work described in this chapter can be found in the cited publications.

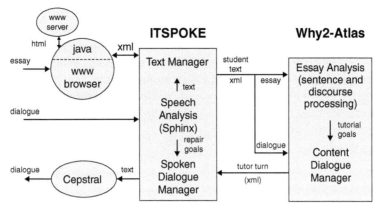

Figure 13.1. The architecture of ITSPOKE.

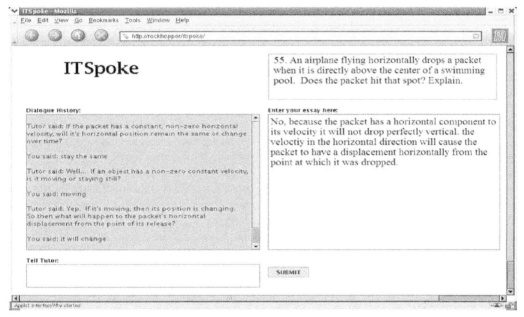

Figure 13.2. Screenshot during human-computer spoken tutoring dialogue (the "Tell Tutor" box is used for typed student login and logout).

interface, supplemented with a high-quality audio link. An example screenshot of this Web interface generated during a dialogue is shown in Figure 13.2. The qualitative physics problem (problem 55) is shown in the upper-right box. The student begins by typing an essay answer to this problem in the middle-right box. When finished with the essay, the student clicks the "SUBMIT" button. The tutor then analyzes the essay and engages the student in the spoken natural language dialogue. The middle-left box in Figure 13.2 records the dialogue history,

where the speech recognition and text-to-speech synthesis components of ITSPOKE provide the "transcriptions." After the dialogue is completed, the student revises the essay, thereby ending the tutoring for that physics problem or causing another round of tutoring/essay revision.

Note that in Why2-Atlas as well as the original nonadaptive version of ITSPOKE, tutor responses (states in the FSM) depended only on the correctness of student answers (transitions between states), and were not adaptive to student affective

Table 13.2. Excerpt of Dialogue with Adaptive ITSPOKE (Punctuation Added for Clarity)

TUTOR1: By the same reasoning that we used for the car, what's the overall net force on the truck equal to?

STUDENT1: The force of the car hitting it?

TUTOR2: That's exactly right, but you seem unsure, so let's sum up. The net force on the truck is equal to the impact force on it. We can prove this just like we did for the car. First, we know that gravity and the normal force on the truck must cancel each other, otherwise the truck would not be at rest vertically. Second, we know that the impact force is the only horizontal force exerted on the truck.

---

and/or metacognitive states. An example dialogue excerpt with a new version of ITSPOKE that adapts its dialogue behaviors after detecting student uncertainty is shown in Table 13.2. The language-processing techniques used to detect states such as student uncertainty (as in STUDENT1), and to adaptively respond to such states once detected (as in TUTOR2), are described in the following two subsections. The natural language processing in the adaptive version of ITSPOKE has also been reimplemented using the TuTalk tutorial dialogue toolkit (Jordan et al., 2007), which supports the authoring and delivery of natural language dialogues in which a computer tutor tries to elicit the main line of reasoning from a student by a series of questions.

Detecting Student Affect on the Basis of Utterances

Whereas *human* tutors can readily detect whether a student is confused, bored, or in some other pedagogically relevant state during a tutorial dialogue, most tutorial dialogue *systems* do not attempt to detect affective/metacognitive student states.[2] Even if they did make such an attempt, most automated

---

[2] Notable exceptions were discussed earlier in the chapter.

tutorial dialogue systems are text-based, and would thus be unable to make use of some of the most important indicators of student states, namely the acoustic and prosodic features of speech.

There has been considerable speech and language research on detecting particular types of user states in naturally occurring spoken dialogue corpora. A standard approach involves hand-labeling naturally occurring utterances for various user states of relevance for the application system (e.g., through the use of judges or self-report), extracting linguistic features (e.g., acoustic and prosodic as well as lexical) from each utterance, then employing machine learning techniques to develop models for predicting a user state for each utterance from the set of utterance features. Such approaches have developed predictive models with performance levels that significantly outperform standard baseline algorithms.

Most work in this area has addressed detecting user states such as anger and frustration, which are particularly relevant to customer care and information-seeking systems. Less work has specifically addressed using linguistic signals to detect learner's affective states in computer-based training, such as boredom, confusion, delight, flow, frustration, and surprise (D'Mello & Graesser, Chapter 6 in this volume). Whether or not these student states can also be detected automatically from linguistic indicators, and whether or not their detection can improve the effectiveness of tutorial dialogue systems, are areas of active research for applying natural language processing to adaptive training.

In our work on ITSPOKE, we have been investigating whether linguistic features that have proved useful for predicting emotion in previous research on (nontutorial) spoken dialogue systems are also useful for predicting educationally relevant user states. We are particularly interested in features that can be computed both *automatically* and in *real time* using speech and language processing, because our goal is to use such features to trigger online adaptation in ITSPOKE based on predicted student emotions.

Table 13.3. Features per Student Turn

- Acoustic-Prosodic Features
  - 4 fundamental frequency (f0): max, min, mean, standard deviation
  - 4 energy (RMS): max, min, mean, standard deviation
  - 4 temporal: amount of silence in turn, turn duration, duration of pause prior to turn, speaking rate
- Lexical Features
  - ITSPOKE-recognized lexical items in the turn
- Identifier Features
  - user
  - gender
  - problem

For example, in a corpus of dialogues between students and ITSPOKE, the features shown in Table 13.3 were used to successfully classify student utterances (i.e., turns) for negative, neutral, and positive emotions (Litman and Forbes-Riley, 2006a).

The acoustic-prosodic features are motivated by previous studies of emotion prediction in spontaneous dialogues (Ang et al., 2002; Batliner et al., 2003; Lee et al., 2001). Fundamental frequency contour (f0) and root mean squared amplitude (RMS) values, representing measures of pitch and loudness, respectively, are computed using Entropic Research Laboratory's pitch tracker.[3] Amount of silence is the percentage of time the student was silent in a turn. Duration within and length of pause between turns can be computed from temporal labels in the system logs associated with system and user turn beginnings and endings. Speaking rate can be approximated by using the number of syllables per second in the string that is output by the automatic speech recognizer. Some studies use the raw values of these acoustic-prosodic features, whereas others normalize each

feature, such as dividing the raw values by the same feature's value for the first student turn in the dialogue, or by the value for the immediately prior student turn.

Whereas acoustic-prosodic features address *how* something is said, lexical features representing *what* is said have also been shown to be useful (Ang et al., 2002; Batliner et al., 2003; Devillers et al., 2003; Lee et al., 2002; Shafran et al., 2003). The lexical feature set represents the system's best speech recognition hypothesis of what is said in each student turn as a word occurrence vector, indicating the lexical items believed to be present in the turn.

Finally, prior studies (Lee et al., 2002; Oudeyer, 2002) have shown that knowing both the user and the user's gender can play an important role in emotion recognition. User and problem are particularly important in a training domain because, in contrast to, for example, call centers, where every caller is distinct, students will use a system repeatedly, and problems are repeated across students.

Using these linguistically motivated features, our predictive models outperformed a majority baseline and shed light on the utility of the different feature types (Litman & Forbes-Riley, 2006a). For example, longer turn durations were good predictors of the negative emotion class. Whereas our highest prediction accuracies were typically obtained using many features, models with few features (particularly the temporal features, e.g. turn duration as noted earlier) often worked nearly as well and have other advantages from an applications perspective (e.g., lexical information is part of the standard output of speech recognizers, while prosodic features are domain-independent).

Although our results show significant improvement in predictive accuracy compared to simple baselines, there is still room for further improvement. One way in which we hope to increase predictive accuracy is to expand our feature sets. For example, we have expanded our initial acoustic-prosodic features to include new turn-based features, as well as features computed at the word level (Nicholas et al., 2006).

---

[3] A pitch tracker takes as input a speech file and outputs an f0 (fundamental frequency) contour (the physical correlate of pitch).

Similar features to ours, as well as others based on more sophisticated lexical analysis (e.g., categorizing lexical items into abstract categories such as hedges and filled pauses), dialogue analysis (e.g., constructing features capturing temporal information, response verbosity and quality, tutor directness), and contextual analysis (e.g., extracting features from not only the current turn but also prior turns) have been used by others to also detect educationally relevant user-affective states in tutorial dialogue (D'Mello et al., 2008; Pon-Barry et al., 2006b; Ward et al., 2007). Although beyond the scope of the ITSPOKE project, the integration of linguistic and nonlinguistic features (e.g., posture and facial features [D'Mello et al., 2008]) to detect affect is also an active area of research.

Adapting Dialogue to Detected Student Affect

It is widely believed that the success of computer-based training systems could be greatly increased if systems were able to adapt to student affect. However, it is still an open question as to how to make a training system actually adaptive to student affect once detected, to improve student learning as well as other types of performance measures.

One approach for developing adaptive dialogue-based training systems is to mine corpora of dialogues between students and effective *human* tutors for insight. In this approach, student turns in a corpus are typically labeled with respect to student affective states, whereas tutor turns are labeled with respect to dialogue behaviors. Such labeling can either be done manually or can be automated by using machine learning and natural language processing to predict the labels from linguistic features as in the preceding subsection. A corpus analysis is then performed to identify how the tutor responds to student affect, which serves as a guide for manually authoring a similarly adaptive computer-based training system.

We have used such a data-driven approach to develop a version of ITSPOKE that can adapt its dialogue behaviors to the student state of uncertainty, over and above correctness (Forbes-Riley & Litman, 2009a). An example dialogue excerpt with this system was shown in Table 13.2. Our approach uses n-gram techniques from statistical natural language processing to identify dependencies between student states and subsequent tutor responses in a manually annotated corpus of human-spoken tutoring dialogues, where the human tutor is performing the same task as the ITSPOKE system. Our student state of interest is uncertainty, the most frequent affective negative state previously labeled using the positive/negative/neutral labeling scheme described in the preceding subsection. Our tutor responses will be formalized using a dialogue act tagset, as each utterance in a dialogue can be viewed as kind of action that speakers use for a particular conversational function – in other words, a dialog act (Jurafsky & Martin, 2008).

Prior to the text-mining study being described here, our corpus had been manually annotated for these student states and tutor responses. To provide a training corpus for building an uncertainty detector (as in the preceding subsection), each *student turn* had been labeled with one of the following four "certainness" tags (Liscombe et al., 2005):

- Uncertain
- Certain
- Mixed
- Neutral

Similarly, as part of a study investigating correlations of tutor dialogue behaviors and learning, each *tutor turn* had previously been labeled with a tutoring-specific dialogue act, using the following hierarchical tagset (Litman & Forbes-Riley, 2006b):

- Feedback Acts
  - Positive
  - Negative
- Question Acts
  - Short Answer
  - Long Answer
  - Deep Answer

- State Acts
  - Restatement
  - Recap
  - Request/Directive
  - Bottom Out
  - Hint
  - Expansion

A wide variety of dialogue acts tagsets have been proposed in the NLP community, but given that tutoring dialogues have a number of tutoring-specific dialogue acts (e.g., hinting), tutorial dialogue research typically uses tutoring-specific tagsets rather than the more domain-independent schemes often used in other NLP applications areas. In our tagset, Question Acts label the type of question in terms of the type of answer required. Feedback Acts label feedback based on the presence of lexical items in the tutor turn, and not only can convey the correctness of the student's prior turn but can also be used for motivational purposes. The State Acts summarize or clarify the state of the student's prior turn or turns.

To develop adaptive tutor responses, we first represented these previously annotated human tutoring dialogues as bigrams of student and tutor turns. This enabled us to use χ^2 analysis to identify dependent bigrams where the student certainty and tutor dialogue act annotations were related in some way other than predicted by chance. Our results showed that statistically significant dependencies existed between many student states and the subsequent dialogue acts of our human tutor (Forbes-Riley & Litman, 2008). For example, after uncertain turns, our human tutor "Bottoms Out" (supplies the complete answer) more than expected, and after neutral turns, less than expected.

Next, we analyzed these dependent bigrams to suggest empirically motivated adaptive strategies, which we implemented in a new version of ITSPOKE that (among other things) adapted to correct but uncertain answers with remediation (Forbes-Riley & Litman, 2009a). (The original ITSPOKE never remediated after correct student answers, even if uttered with uncertainty.) For example, the dependent bigram

analysis indicated that our human tutor responded with a question significantly less than expected after a correct but uncertain answer. We applied this result as follows: If the original ITSPOKE response to incorrect answers was a bottom-out, we now also used this bottom-out after correct but uncertain answers. Otherwise, we authored and used a new bottom-out for use after correct but uncertain answers.

An experimental evaluation showed that an adaptive Wizard of Oz version of ITSPOKE developed using this bigram methodology increased user satisfaction compared to both the original nonadaptive ITSPOKE (for lower expertise students) (Forbes-Riley & Litman, 2009b) and to another adaptive wizarded ITSPOKE developed using a non-NLP approach (for all students) (Forbes-Riley & Litman, 2009a). In our Wizard of Oz system, ITSPOKE's fully automated speech and language components were replaced by a human, to investigate the utility of the text-mining approach for developing adaptive responses under ideal system conditions with respect to speech and language processing.

Note that although our bigram method enables us to derive system adaptations from statistical generalizations about how a human tutor responds to student affect, this approach assumes that the human tutor adapts in a way that positively impacts learning and other performance measures. Others have also made this assumption. For example, Shah et al. (2002) mine a human tutoring corpus for significant dialogue bigrams to aid in the design of adaptive tutor responses to student initiative, whereas Pon-Barry et al. (2006b) develop adaptive tutor responses to student uncertainty using a simpler frequency-based corpus analysis (ignoring statistical significance). To date such corpus-based adaptive systems (even when wizarded) have not yet led to learning improvements, although they have resulted in improvements in user satisfaction and other measures as in our own work discussed earlier. We hypothesize that this is because such approaches typically take into account only *what* the tutor does, but do not confirm whether what the tutor does is actually *effective*.

We are addressing this issue in our current work in two ways. First, we plan to restrict the bigram analysis discussed earlier, to require bigrams to be not only dependent but also predictive of student learning gain (Litman & Forbes-Riley, 2006b) before we use them to derive any system adaptations. Second, we are exploring the use of reinforcement learning as an alternative text-mining method for discovering adaptive strategies based on analysis of an existing annotated human-tutoring dialogue corpus. This approach learns from the potentially nonoptimal actions of our human tutor how responses to particular states in the dialogue could have instead been adapted in ways that optimized a target evaluation metric (e.g., student learning gain) (Tetreault & Litman, 2008). We are also using reinforcement learning to learn more optimal tutor behaviors directly, by making our computer tutoring system exploratory in the types of responses it tries when the optimal decision is not known in advance (Chi et al., 2009). The application of reinforcement learning to both semiautomate and optimize the design of spoken dialogue systems has been an extremely productive data-driven approach for building more adaptive dialogue systems in other application areas.

Summary

This chapter first briefly introduced both the research area of NLP and the many types of training applications that NLP has contributed to. To more concretely illustrate some of these contributions, a case study was presented describing how spoken dialogue technology was used to develop the ITSPOKE conversational physics training system, and how emotional speech and text-mining technology was used to enhance ITSPOKE to detect student uncertainty and adapt dialogue responses accordingly.

Acknowledgments

The author's own research described in this chapter was based on work supported by the National Science Foundation under Grant Nos. 9720359, 0328431, 0325054, and 0631930. Any opinions, findings, and conclusions or recommendations expressed in this material are those of the author and do not necessarily reflect the views of the National Science Foundation. Some of this research was also supported by ONR (N00014-04-1 - 0108).

References

Aist, G., Kort, B., Reilly, R., Mostow, J., & Picard, R. (2002). Experimentally augmenting an intelligent tutoring system with human-supplied capabilities: Adding human-provided emotional scaffolding to an automated reading tutor that listens. In *Proceedings of the ITS 2002 Workshop on Empirical Methods for Tutorial Dialogue Systems* (pp. 16–28). San Sebastian, Spain.

Anderson, J. R., Corbett, A. T., Koedinger, K., & Pelletier, R. (1995). Cognitive tutors: Lessons learned. *The Journal of the Learning Sciences*, 4(2), 167–207.

Ang, J., Dhillon, R., Krupski, A., Shriberg, E., & Stolcke, A. (2002). Prosody-based automatic detection of annoyance and frustration in human-computer dialog. In J. H. L. Hansen & B. Pellom (Eds.), *Proceedings of the International Conference on Spoken Language Processing ICSLP* (pp. 2037–2039). Denver, CO.

Atkinson, R. K., Mayer, R. E., & Merrill, M. M. (2005). Fostering social agency in multimedia learning: Examining the impact of an animated agent's voice. *Contemporary Educational Psychology*, 30(1), 117–139.

Batliner, A., Fischer, K., Huber, R., Spilker, J., & Noth, E. (2003). How to find trouble in communication. *Speech Communication*, 40(1–2), 117–143.

Baylor, A. L., Ryu, J., & Shen, E. (2003). The effect of pedagogical agent voice and animation on learning, motivation, and perceived persona. In *Proceedings of World Conference on Educational Multimedia, Hypermedia and Telecommunications ED-MEDIA* (pp. 452–458). Honolulu, HI.

Beck, J. & Sison, J. (2006). Using knowledge tracing in a noisy environment to measure student reading proficiencies. *International Journal of Artificial Intelligence in Education*, 16, 129–143.

Black, A. & Taylor, P. (1997). Festival speech synthesis system: System documentation (1.1.1). Human Communication Research Centre Technical Report 83, The Centre for Speech Technology Research, University of Edinburgh.

Bloom, B. S. (1984). The 2 Sigma problem: The search for methods of group instruction as effective as one-to-one tutoring. *Educational Researcher, 13*, 4–16.

Boyer, K. E., Phillips, R., Wallis, M., Vouk, M., & Lester, J. (2008). Balancing cognitive and motivational scaffolding in tutorial dialogue. In *Proceedings of International Conference of Intelligent Tutoring Systems ITS* (pp. 239–249). Montreal, Canada.

Brown, J., Frishkoff, G., & Eskenazi, M. (2005). Automatic question generation for vocabulary assessment. In *Proceedings of Human Language Technology Conference and Conference on Empirical Methods in Natural Language Processing HLT/EMNLP* (pp. 819–826). Vancouver, Canada.

Burstein, J., Chodorow, M., & Leacock, C. (2003). CriterionSM online essay evaluation: An application for automated evaluation of student essays. In *Proceedings of Conference on Innovative Applications of Artificial Intelligence AAAI* (pp. 3–10), Acapulco, Mexico.

Chi, M., Jordan, P., VanLehn, K., & Litman, D. (2009). To elicit or to tell: Does it matter? In *Proceedings of International Conference on Artificial Intelligence in Education AIED* (pp. 197–204). Brighton, UK.

Chi, M., Roy, M., & Hausmann, R. (2008). Observing tutorial dialogues collaboratively: Insights about human tutoring effectiveness from vicarious learning. *Cognitive Science: A Multidisciplinary Journal, 32*(2), 301–341.

Chi, M. T. H., Siler, S. A., Jeong, H., Yamauchi, T., & Hausmann, R. G. (2001). Learning from human tutoring. *Cognitive Science, 25*, 471–533.

Craig, S. D., Gholson, B., Ventura, M., Graesser, A. C., & the Tutoring Research Group (2000). Overhearing dialogues and monologues in virtual tutoring sessions: Effects on questioning and vicarious learning. *International Journal of Artificial Intelligence in Education, 11*, 242–253.

Devillers, L., Lamel, L., & Vasilescu, I. (2003). Emotion detection in task-oriented spoken dialogs. In *Proceedings of IEEE International Conference on Multimedia & Expo ICME* (pp. 549–552). Baltimore, MD.

D'Mello, S., Craig, S., Witherspoon, A., McDaniel, B., & Graesser, A. (2008). Automatic detection of learner's affect from conversational cues. *User Modeling and User-Adapted Interaction, 18*(1–2), 45–80.

Evens, M. & Michael, J. (2006). *One-on-one tutoring by humans and computers.* Mahway, NJ: Lawrence Erlbaum Associates.

Foltz, P., Kintsch, W., & Landauer, T. (1998). The measurement of textual coherence with latent semantic analysis. *Discourse Processes, 25*, 285–307.

Forbes-Riley, K. & Litman, D. (2008). Analyzing dependencies between student certainness states and tutor responses in a spoken dialogue corpus. In L. Dybkjaer & W. Minker (Eds.), *Recent Trends in Discourse and Dialogue* (pp. 275–304). Berlin: Springer.

Forbes-Riley, K. & Litman, D. (2009a). Adapting to student uncertainty improves tutoring dialogues. In *Proceedings of International Conference on Artificial Intelligence in Education AIED* (pp. 33–40). Brighton, UK.

Forbes-Riley, K. & Litman, D. (2009b). A user modeling-based performance analysis of a wizarded uncertainty-adaptive dialogue system corpus. In *Proceedings of the International Speech Communication Association Interspeech.* Brighton, UK

Fox, B. A. (1993). *The human tutorial dialogue project.* Hillsdale, NJ: Lawrence Erlbaum Associates.

Gamon, M., Gao, J., Brockett, C., Klementiev, A., Dolan, W., Belenko, D., & Vanderwende, L. (2008). Using contextual speller techniques and language modeling for ESL error correction. In *Proceedings of International Joint Conference on Natural Language Processing IJCNLP* (pp. 449–456). Hyderabad, India.

Glass, J., Hazen, T., Cyphers, S., Malioutov, I., Huynh, D., & Barzilay, R. (2007). Recent progress in the MIT spoken lecture processing project. In *Proceedings of International Speech Communication Association Interspeech* (pp. 2553–2556). Antwerp, Belgium.

Graesser, A., Person, N., Harter, D., & the Tutoring Research Group. (2001). Teaching tactics and dialog in Autotutor. *International Journal of Artificial Intelligence in Education, 12*, 257–279.

Graesser, A., Person, N., & Magliano, J. (1995). Collaborative dialog patterns in naturalistic one-on-one tutoring. *Applied Cognitive Psychology*, 9, 495–522.

Han, N.-R., Chodorow, M., & Leacock, C. (2006). Detecting errors in English article usage by non-native speakers. *Natural Language Engineering*, 12(2), 115–129.

Heilman, M., Collins-Thompson, K., Callan, J., & Eskenazi, M. (2007). Combining lexical and grammatical features to improve readability measures for first and second language texts. In *Companion Proceedings of the Human Language Technology: North American Chapter of the Association for Computational Linguistics HLT/NAACL* (pp. 460–467). Rochester, NY.

Higgins, D., Burstein, J., & Attali, Y. (2006). Identifying off-topic students essays without topic-specific training data. *Natural Language Engineering*, 12(2), 145–159.

Huang, X. D., Alleva, F., Hon, H. W., Hwang, M. Y., Lee, K. F., & Rosenfeld, R. (1993). The SphinxII speech recognition system: An Overview. *Computer, Speech and Language*, 2, 137–148.

Johnson, W. L. (2007). Serious use of a serious game for language learning. In *Proceedings of International Conference on Artificial Intelligence in Education AIED* (pp. 67–74). Marina Del Ray, CA.

Jordan, P., Makatchev, M., & VanLehn, K. (2003). Abductive theorem proving for analyzing student explanations. In U. Hoppe, F. Verdejo, & J. Kay (Eds.), *Proceedings of International Conference on Artificial Intelligence in Education AIED* (pp. 73–80). Sydney, Australia.

Jordan, P. & VanLehn, K. (2002). Discourse processing for explanatory essays in tutorial applications. In *Proceedings of the 3rd SIGdial Workshop on Discourse and Dialogue* (pp. 74–83). Philadelphia, PA.

Jordan, P. W., Hall, B., Ringenberg, M., Cui, Y., & Rosé, C. P. (2007). Tools for authoring a dialogue agent that participates in learning studies. In *Proceedings of International Conference on Artificial Intelligence in Education AIED* (pp. 43–50). Marina Del Rey, CA.

Jurafsky, D. & Martin, J. H. (2008). *Speech and language processing* (2nd ed.). Upper Saddle River, NJ: Prentice-Hall.

Kersey, C., Eugenio, B. D., Jordan, P., & Katz, S. (2009). KSC-PAL: A peer learning agent that encourages students to take the initiative. In *NAACL-HLT 2009 Workshops, The 4th Workshop on Innovative Use of NLP for Building Educational Applications* (pp. 55–63). Boulder, CO.

Kintsch, E., Steinhart, D., Stahl, G., & Group, L. R. (2000). Developing summarization skills through the use of LSA-based feedback. *Interactive Learning Environments*, 8(2), 87–109.

Kumar, R., Rosé, C., Wang, Y., Joshi, M., & Robinson, A. (2007). Tutorial dialogue as adaptive collaborative learning support. In *Proceedings of International Conference on Artificial Intelligence in Education AIED* (pp. 383–290). Amsterdam, The Netherlands.

Leacock, C. (2004). Scoring free-responses automatically: A case study of large-scale assessment. *Examens*, 1(3).

Lee, C., Narayanan, S., & Pieraccini, R. (2001). Recognition of negative emotions from the speech signal. In *Proceedings of IEEE Workshop on Automatic Speech Recognition and Understanding* (pp. 240–243). Trento, Italy.

Lee, C., Narayanan, S., & Pieraccini, R. (2002). Combining acoustic and language information for emotion recognition. In *Proceedings of the International Conference on Spoken Language Processing (ICSLP)* (pp. 873–876). Denver, CO.

Lee, J. & Seneff, S. (2008). Correcting misuse of verb forms. In *Proceedings of Association for Computational Linguistics: Human Language Technologies ACL: HLT* (pp. 174–182). Columbus, OH.

Liscombe, J., Venditti, J., & Hirschberg, J. (2005). Detecting certainness in spoken tutorial dialogues. In *Proceedings of International Speech Communication Association Interspeech* (pp. 1837–1840). Lisbon, Portugal.

Litman, D. & Forbes-Riley, K. (2006a). Recognizing student emotions and attitudes on the basis of utterances in spoken tutoring dialogues with both human and computer tutors. *Speech Communication*, 48(5), 559–590.

Litman, D. & Silliman, S. (2004). ITSPOKE: An intelligent tutoring spoken dialogue system. In *Companion Proceedings of the Human Language Technology: North American Chapter of the Association for Computational Linguistics HLT/NAACL* (pp. 5–8). Boston, MA.

Litman, D. J. & Forbes-Riley, K. (2006b). Correlations between dialogue acts and learning in spoken tutoring dialogues. *Journal of Natural Language Engineering*, 12(2), 161–176.

Makatchev, M., Jordan, P., & VanLehn, K. (2006). Abductive theorem proving for analyzing student explanations and guiding feedback in intelligent tutoring systems. *Journal of Automated Reasoning for Special Issue on Automated Reasoning and Theorem Proving in Education, 32*(3), 187–226.

Malioutov, I. & Barzilay, R. (2006). Minimum cut model for spoken lecture segmentation. In *Proceedings of the Association for Computational Linguistics and International Conference on Computational Linguistics ACL/COLING* (pp. 25–32). Sydney, Australia.

McCarthy, P., Rus, V., Crossley, S., Bigham, S., Graesser, A., & McNamara, D. (2007). Assessing entailer with a corpus of natural language. In *Proceedings of International Florida Artificial Intelligence Research Society Conference FLAIRS* (pp. 247–252). Menlo Park, CA.

McQuiggan, S., Rowe, J., Lee, S., & Lester, J. (2008). Story-based learning: The impact of narrative on learning experiences and outcomes. In *Proceedings of Intelligent Tutoring Systems ITS* (pp. 530–539). Montreal, Canada.

Merrill, D. C., Reiser, B. J., & Landes, S. (1992). Human tutoring: Pedagogical strategies and learning outcomes. Paper presented at the annual meeting of the American Educational Research Association.

Michaud, L. & McCoy, K. (2006). Capturing the evolution of grammatical knowledge in a call system for deaf learners of English. *International Journal of Artificial Intelligence and Education IJAIED, 16*(1), 65–97.

Miltsakaki, E. & Kukich, K. (2004). Evaluation of text coherence for electronic essay scoring systems. *Natural Language Engineering, 10*(1), 25–55.

Miltsakaki, E. & Troutt, A. (2008). Real-time web text classification and analysis of reading difficulty. In *Proceedings of Association for Computational Linguistics ACL Workshop on Innovative Use of NLP for Building Educational Applications* (pp. 89–97). Columbus, OH.

Mitkov, R., Ha, L. A., & Karamanis, N. (2006). A computer-aided environment for generating multiple-choice test items. *Natural Language Engineering, 12*(2), 177–194.

Moore, J. D., Porayska-Pomsta, K., Varges, S., & Zinn, C. (2004). Generating tutorial feedback with affect. In *Proceedings of International Florida Artificial Intelligence Research Society Conference FLAIRS* (pp. 923–928), Miami, FL.

Moreno, R., Mayer, R. E., Spires, H. A., & Lester, J. C. (2001). The case for social agency in computer-based teaching: Do students learn more deeply when they interact with animated pedagogical agents. *Cognition and Instruction, 19*(2), 177–213.

Nicholas, G., Rotaru, M., & Litman, D. J. (2006). Exploiting word-level features for emotion prediction. In *Proceedings of Association for Computational Linguistics IEEE/ACL Workshop on Spoken Language Technology* (pp. 110–113). Palm Beach, Aruba.

Nielsen, R. D., Ward, W., Martin, J. H., & Palmer, M. (2008). Extracting a representation from text for semantic analysis. In *Proceedings of the Association for Computational Linguistics with the Human Language Technology Conference ACL/HLT* (pp. 241–244). Columbus, OH.

Oudeyer, P. (2002). The synthesis of cartoon emotional speech. In *Proceedings of Speech Prosody 2002* (pp. 551–554). Aix-en-Provence, France.

Petersen, S. E. & Ostendorf, M. (2009). A machine learning approach to reading level assessment. *Computer Speech and Language, 23*, 89–106.

Pitler, E. & Nenkova, A. (2008). Revisiting readability: A unified framework for predicting text quality. In *Proceedings of Empirical Methods on Natural Language Processing EMNLP* (pp. 186–195). Honolulu, HI.

Piwek, P., Hernault, H., Prendinger, H., & Ishizuka, M. (2007). T2d: Generating dialogues between virtual agents automatically from text. In *Proceedings of IVA/LNAI* (pp. 161–174). Paris, France.

Pon-Barry, H., Schultz, K., Bratt, E. O., Clark, B., & Peters, S. (2006a). Responding to student uncertainty in spoken tutorial dialogue systems. *International Journal of Artificial Intelligence in Education, 16*, 171–194.

Pon-Barry, H., Schultz, K., Bratt, E. O., Clark, B., & Peters, S. (2006b). Responding to student uncertainty in spoken tutorial dialogue systems. *International Journal of Artificial Intelligence in Education, 16*, 171–194.

Rosé, C. & VanLehn, K. (2005). An evaluation of a hybrid language understanding approach for robust selection of tutoring goals. *International Journal of AI in Education, 15*(4), 325–355.

Rosé, C., Wang, Y., Cuie, Y., Arguello, J., Fischer, F., Weinberger, A., & Stegmann, K. (2007). Analyzing collaborative learning processes automatically: Exploiting the advances of computational linguistics in computer supported collaborative learning. *International*

Journal of Computer-Supported Collaborative Learning, 3(3), 237–271.

Rosé, C. P. (2000). A framework for robust sentence level interpretation. In *Proceedings of the North American Chapter of the Association for Computational Linguistics NAACL* (pp. 1129–1135). Seattle, WA.

Rosé, C. P. & Aleven, V. (2002). *Proceedings of the ITS 2002 workshop on empirical methods for tutorial dialogue systems.* Technical report, San Sebastian, Spain.

Rosé, C. P. & Freedman, R. (2000). Building dialogue systems for tutorial applications. Technical Report FS-00–01 (Working Notes of the Fall Symposium), AAAI.

Rosé, C. P., Jordan, P., Ringenberg, M., Siler, S., VanLehn, K., & Weinstein, A. (2001). Interactive conceptual tutoring in Atlas-Andes. In *Proceedings of Artificial Intelligence in Education AIED* (pp. 256–266). San Antonio, TX.

Shafran, I., Riley, M., & Mohri, M. (2003). Voice signatures. In *Proceedings of the IEEE Automatic Speech Recognition and Understanding Workshop ASRU* (pp. 31–36). St. Thomas, U.S. Virgin Islands.

Shah, F., Evens, M., Michael, J., & Rovick, A. (2002). Classifying student initiatives and tutor responses in human-human keyboard-to-keyboard tutoring sessions. *Discourse Processes, 33*(1), 23–52.

Sukkarieh, J. & Pulman, S. (2005). Information extraction and machine learning:Auto-marking short free text responses to science questions. In *Proceedings of International Conference on Artificial Intelligence in Education AIED* (pp. 629–637). Amsterdam, The Netherlands.

Tetreault, J. & Chodorow, M. (2008). The ups and downs of preposition error detection in ESL writing. In *Proceedings of International Conference on Computational Linguistics COLING* (pp. 865–872). Manchester, UK.

Tetreault, J. R. & Litman, D. J. (2008). A reinforcement learning approach to evaluating state representations in spoken dialogue systems. *Speech Communication* [Special Issue on Evaluating new methods and models for advanced speech – based interactive systems], 50(8–9), 683–696.

VanLehn, K., Jordan, P. W., Rosé, C. P., Bhembe, D., Böttner, M., Gaydos, A., Makatchev, M., Pappuswamy, U., Ringenberg, M., Roque, A., Siler, S., Srivastava, R., & Wilson, R. (2002). The architecture of Why2-Atlas: A coach for qualitative physics essay writing. In *Proceedings of the International Conference on Intelligent Tutoring Systems ITS* (pp. 158–167). Biarritz, France and San Sebastian, Spain.

Wang, C. & Seneff, S. (2007). Automatic assessment of student translations for foreign language tutoring. In *Companion Proceedings of the Human Language Technology: North American Chapter of the Association for Computational Linguistics HLT/NAACL* (pp. 468–475). Rochester, NY.

Wang, N. & Johnson, W. (2008). The politeness effect in an intelligent foreign language tutoring system. In *Proceedings of the International Conference on Intelligent Tutoring Systems ITS* (pp. 270–280). Montreal, Canada.

Ward, N. & Tsukahara, W. (2003). A study in responsiveness in spoken dialog. *International Journal of Human-Computer Studies, 59*(6), 959–981.

Ward, N. G., Escalante, R., Bayyari, Y. A., & Solorio, T. (2007). Learning to show you're listening. *Computer Assisted Language Learning, 20,* 385–407.

Zechner, K. & Bejar, I. I. (2006). Towards automatic scoring of non-native spontaneous speech. In *Companion Proceedings of the Human Language Technology: North American Chapter of the Association for Computational Linguistics HLT/NAACL* (pp. 216–223). New York.

Zinn, C., Moore, J. D., & Core, M. G. (2002). A 3-tier planning architecture for managing tutorial dialogue. In *Proceedings of the International Conference on Intelligent Tutoring Systems ITS* (pp. 574–584). Biarritz, France and San Sebastian, Spain.

CHAPTER 14

The Art and Science of Developing Intercultural Competence

W. Lewis Johnson, LeeEllen Friedland,
Aaron M. Watson and Eric A. Surface

Introduction

As the world becomes more interconnected, it is increasingly common for people to interact and work with others who come from different cultural backgrounds and who speak different native languages. These intercultural interactions require *intercultural competence*: the ability to communicate successfully with people of other cultures (Byram, 1997). Intercultural competence is, therefore, an increasingly important skill for professionals in a range of fields, including management, education, health, and emergency response (Earley, 1987; Kosoko-Lasaki et al., 2008; Schneider et al., 2009; USDHHS, 2008). Intercultural competence is also receiving increasing attention within the military services, as service members take part in overseas deployments and engage in missions that involve frequent contact with people of other cultures (McDonald et al., 2008).

Providing such adult professionals with adequate intercultural competence training can be a difficult challenge. Many believe that cultural proficiency requires extensive education and years of study (NFLC, 2007). Working professionals who are not specialists in linguistics, foreign languages, or cultural analysis typically do not have the time to study foreign languages and cultures extensively. They may have studied a foreign language in school, but by the time they are called on to use their foreign-language skills on the job, those skills have often gone dormant or been forgotten.

This chapter describes a computer-based approach to intercultural competency training that helps learners quickly develop and retain the intercultural skills they need to be effective in their work. This approach is realized in the Alelo family of language and culture training products. It focuses on the particular responsibilities that each learner is preparing for, the situations the learner is likely to encounter in carrying out those responsibilities, and the particular cross-cultural skills that apply to those situations. Learners get the opportunity to practice their skills in computer simulations of realistic work situations and get direct feedback about their levels of effectiveness in those situations. These simulations incorporate artificially intelligent animated characters that represent members of the target culture and that can engage in spoken conversations with learners in the foreign language. We then provide learners with sustainment training tools that help them retain and refresh their communication skills, even after long gaps in training and periods of disuse.

The design of the curricula, and the methods used to implement it, are particularly intended to support and motivate lifelong learners. Unlike students in typical classroom settings, we do not assume that learners are a captive audience. Many are studying in their free time and have many other demands on that time. If they find the training boring, or feel they are making insufficient progress, they may give up and discontinue learning. The training employs a serious game approach (Barrett & Johnson, 2010), utilizing techniques drawn from interactive games to engage learners and maintain their interest and motivation.

This work is informed by, and contributes to, the art and science of cultural competency training, at multiple levels. The training courses advance the state of the art in language and culture training by providing simulations of cross-cultural interactions at an unprecedented level of fidelity. The serious game approach incorporates the work of graphic artists, animators, and other artistic professionals. We conduct scientific analyses of how learners interact with our courses in the field, which helps us determine whether our training methods are effective and prioritize efforts to improve them.

This approach has been realized in computer-based training courses that have been used by tens of thousands of learners around the world to learn to communicate with people of other cultures, mostly in foreign languages. Military service members in particular have benefited greatly from this training, which helps them establish good rapport with local people, increase operational effectiveness, and ultimately avoid conflict and combat casualties.

The chapter is organized as follows. The next section presents some examples from

Alelo courses that illustrate the training methods and technologies employed. After this comes an overview of the instructional design methods that are employed, and a description of some of the particular adaptive technologies that are used to realize them, particularly those for simulated dialog and skill sustainment training. It describes how data collected from field use of Alelo courses are analyzed to measure technology performance and learning effectiveness, and to inform further development effort.

Examples from Alelo Courses

The following examples from Alelo's Operational Dari and Operational Pashto courses and the earlier Tactical Dari course will serve to illustrate the key points in this chapter. These courses are designed to help military service members prepare for deployments to Afghanistan, by acquiring the communication skills that they will need in their encounters with the Afghan people. As shown in Figure 14.1, trainees can practice their skills in encounters with Afghan non-player characters. In this example, the learner plays an American small-unit leader (left) who is meeting with the malek (tribal leader) and other elders in the village to discuss collaborating on a reconstruction project. The learner can select gestures for his character to perform, and speaks in the foreign language on behalf of his character – in this case, in Dari. The system recognizes and interprets what the learner says, and the artificially intelligent non-player characters in the scene respond accordingly. The transcript of the conversation is shown on the top of the screen. In this example, the learner has greeted and introduced himself, and the malek has responded to the greeting and introduced himself. Learners are evaluated in terms of their ability to complete the objectives of the mission and scored on their use of communication skills. The communication score (top right corner of the figure) depends on the number of conversational turns they are able to complete and the amount of scaffolding (i.e., hints and

Figure 14.1. Meeting with the malek in Operational Dari.

assistance; see Seeley Brown et al., 1989) that they must rely on to complete them. In this example, the learner is relying on transcriptions and translations of the malek's phrases to get through the exercise, and so receives a lower score than would be the case if these scaffolds were turned off.

The objective of scenarios such as this is not simply to practice the foreign language, but to develop intercultural competence. To succeed, the learner needs to act and behave in a manner that is culturally appropriate in this situation. This includes such things as making polite and appropriate inquiries about the malek's family, showing reciprocity and mutual respect, and establishing a good relationship and rapport with the malek. The malek character responds positively to each instance of culturally appropriate behavior, and his attitude toward the learner gradually improves. The malek will agree to collaborate on the project with the learner only if the learner has established a sufficient level of rapport. Such scenarios give learners opportunities to practice their skills and help them develop familiarity with these sorts of cross-cultural situations, so that they will be confident and more at ease when they deal with similar situations in real life.

Each course contains a number of such simulated episodes, in what is known as the Mission Game component of the course. Some episodes provide useful practice for anyone working in the foreign country, whereas others, such as the episode shown in Figure 14.1, are aimed more at people with particular mission responsibilities. Before starting the course, each trainee completes a questionnaire in which they indicate their particular mission responsibilities and learning goals. The system then automatically generates a tailored course of instruction, of lesson modules and game episodes. These enable the trainee to quickly and efficiently acquire the particular communication skills that he or she requires.

The course incorporates a combination of lesson materials and learning activities that help learners acquire the knowledge, skills, and attitudes necessary to master these scenarios. These materials can be delivered in a coordinated fashion on a combination of desktop and mobile devices. Figure 14.2 is an example of an exercise delivered on a mobile device – in this case, an iPod Touch.

Figure 14.2. A language-instruction exercise on an iPod Touch.

Here the learner practices one of the basic greetings in Dari, "sa-laam aa-ley-kum." The learner can hear a native Dari speaker say the phrase, speak the phrase into the microphone, and compare their own speech against that of the native speaker. The desktop trainer has a corresponding exercise, which integrates automated speech recognition, to verify that the learner's speech is intelligible and is at an acceptable level of pronunciation accuracy for a beginning language learner.

Once the learner has acquired some basic phrases, he can proceed to simple conversational exercises. Figure 14.3 shows one such exercise, called an Active Dialog, from the desktop training system. Here the learner practices selected communicative skills – in this case, basic greetings and introductions – with his Afghan counterpart. The setting for the dialog is a virtual classroom, suggesting that this is a practice activity rather than a higher-stakes simulated mission. Otherwise, the learner's objectives in the activity are similar to those in the Mission Game episodes. In this case, the learner needs to greet his counterpart and exchange names with him, and in the process he or she receives a communication score based on the number of conversational turns completed and the amount of scaffolding the learner relies on to complete them.

The system tracks the learner's activities and progress on both the desktop trainer and on the mobile trainer. This enables it to dynamically construct refresher training lessons to recover knowledge, skills, and attitudes that may be vulnerable to forgetting and decay (Figure 14.4). Refresher material is selected depending on how recently it has been trained, with spaced practice intervals that progressively increase over time.

To facilitate transfer of communication skills to mission operations in Alelo's military courses, a Virtual Role-Player (VRP) capability has been developed that integrates conversational virtual humans into virtual training and mission rehearsal environments. VRP technology integrates with multiple commonly used mission rehearsal systems, including Virtual Battlespace 2 (VBS2) and RealWorld. VRPs extend the capabilities of these training systems so that trainees can perform the same military actions as before (e.g., maneuver vehicles, fire weapons), but can also engage in conversations with the characters in the scenario, just as in the Mission Game shown in Figure 14.1. Multiple trainees can participate in the virtual environment at any one time, making it possible for teams to carry out simulated missions together (Figure 14.5).

Course Development Methodology and Design Principles

One of the keys to the effectiveness of Alelo courses for lifelong learners is their *focus*:

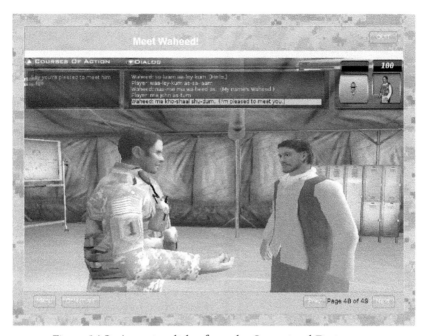

Figure 14.3. An active dialog from the Operational Dari course.

They are designed to concentrate on the skills that learners need to carry out their jobs or missions. In this respect they are similar to courses that teach foreign languages for special purposes (LSP) (Fiorito, 2005) in that they are driven by a needs analysis that determines what skills are most needed by the learners. However, in contrast with LSP courses, they take into consideration the *breadth* of intercultural knowledge, skills, and attitudes (KSAs) required for such purposes (McDonald et al., 2008), not just the language skills. They are designed to promote *transfer* of skills from the learning environment to the real world, for example, through simulated scenarios that allow learners to practice their skills in realistic contexts. Other important considerations for the design of these courses are *accuracy* and *consistency* of the learning material. The courses must reflect current linguistic usage and cultural practices relevant to the intended purposes of the communication skills. Consistency is an issue because the courses incorporate multiple learning activities on multiple learning platforms, which need to treat the intercultural KSAs in a coordinated fashion. It is a particular problem for colloquial and less commonly taught languages, for which there

are often no agreed-on standards of form or orthography.

To ensure that each course meets these objectives, we have developed and implemented a courseware development methodology, called the Situated Culture Methodology, that creates a holistic approach to using the situational context of the learner's job or mission to generate learning objectives, uses those learning objectives to identify key cross-cultural and culture-specific factors and competencies, then applies them in a tailored curriculum focused on the intercultural competence needed to successfully perform the relevant job or mission.

Principles of instructional design guide the creation of innovative curricular components, as illustrated in the examples found in the preceding section. There is also a scientific basis of theory and method from sociocultural and linguistic anthropology (Birdwhistell, 1970; Hall 1966; Hymes 1974, 1987) that shapes the underlying research and data development required to ensure the fidelity of course content in relation to learning objectives.

Ethnographic interviews are conducted with subject matter experts (SMEs) to

Figure 14.4. Dynamic refresher training lessons.

collect data about jobs and missions (Bernard, 1998). This typically includes information about work processes and tasks, as well as the types of contexts in which the work takes place, interactions that commonly occur as part of performing the work tasks, how social and cultural dynamics affect the way one might perform the work in different settings, and criteria for successful performance of tasks. Of prime interest are first-person narratives about how intercultural communication played a role in real-life mission encounters; videos of these narratives are often included in the course to illustrate examples of how principles can apply to specific scenarios.

If language instruction is part of a given course, native speakers of the target language are interviewed in depth, often repeatedly, to collect realistic examples of spoken dialog. This is sometimes supplemented by engaging the native speakers in role playing to prompt them to provide variations and alternative approaches to specific scenario dialogs. These linguistic data are then transcribed and used in creating mission-based lessons and exercises. Usually one or more language SMEs are also used to review course materials and sometimes advise on specific issues pertaining to speech acts or interactions in the curriculum.

Because Alelo takes a situated approach to both language and culture, all curriculum materials are presented in an integrated way that includes information and guidance regarding contextual factors to consider, culturally appropriate practices and behaviors, and the potential consequences of inappropriate behavior. This instruction and the simulated scenarios include a naturalistic combination of factors that are at play during real-world interactions, including verbal and nonverbal behavior, and the use of social space (e.g., distance between people interacting face to face).

Job and mission tasks – based on the ethnographic data collected, and the role that learners will play in the simulated environment (e.g., senior military officer or junior enlisted service member) – are also analyzed in relation to social and cultural factors relevant to the geographic region in which the course is based, as well as sociopolitical, socioeconomic, sociodemographic, and sociocultural characteristics of the place and its people. This analysis is then used to shape the design of lessons, exercises, and interactive scenarios in the course to ensure that appropriate examples, values, and performance criteria are used. Information about the social and cultural factors of the specific region or cultural group is also gathered primarily through ethnographic interviews with natives of the region or cultural group, supplemented by academic research and analysis.

Figure 14.5. Virtual role-player mission rehearsal scenario.

In Figure 14.6, the circle showing cultural factors is labeled with five categories based on a recent framework for operational culture developed by the U.S. Marine Corps (Salmoni & Holmes-Eber, 2008). It should be noted that, although these categories are useful, the Situated Culture Methodology is not dependent on any one categorization or paradigm of social or cultural factors. The methodology can be used with any conceptualization of social and cultural factors based in social theory. Any paradigm or categorization chosen would be represented in the circle shape within the figure and relevant values (e.g., labels, categories, subheadings) would then be used to structure the presentation of information in the course.

Ten Key Design Principles in Alelo Courses

The Situated Culture Methodology provides a proven means of collecting and developing ethnographic linguistic and sociocultural data to use as primary course materials that prepare learners for the roles they will play in real intercultural mission-based situations. The Alelo development methodology for course design includes the following ten key principles:

1. *Task-based learning.* The SCM approach is well aligned with task-based approaches to language learning (Ellis, 2003) in that it focuses on communication necessary to perform real-world tasks, and in that it has learners practice their communication skills in the context of realistic tasks. It assumes that intercultural competence curricula, like other types of curricula, should be based on a task analysis of the skills to be taught and the work situations in which those skills are to be applied (Jonassen et al., 1999). The learning activities in Alelo courses are all task-oriented in this sense. The task-based approach applies to cultural skills training in that the courses focus on situated cultural action.

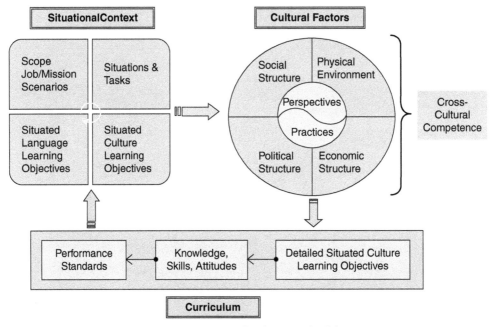

Figure 14.6. Situated culture methodology.

2. *Language in culture*. Alelo products are developed with the understanding that language and culture are inextricably linked and cannot be separated. Communicative skills are taught in the context of face-to-face communication in social situations, in which learners are alerted to the ways in which power relations and social distance influence the use of language in those situations (Brown & Levinson, 1987). The courses cover nonverbal aspects of communication, such as gestures, as well as the verbal aspects. Courses survey the range of cultural factors that are likely to be relevant in the real-world situations that learners are likely to encounter in other countries.

3. *Communicative approach*. Alelo curricula emphasize interaction as the ultimate learning goal, as well as the means to achieve this goal. Curricula are organized around communicative functions in context, and seek to promote communicative competencies in those contexts (Canale & Swain, 1980). They incorporate many activities that involve interaction, particularly with animated characters. Curricula teach individual communicative functions and then progress to tasks and dialogs that involve combinations of these functions.

4. *Tailored curricula*. Alelo courses are tailored to the individual, and this customization takes place at multiple levels. For example, we have developed customized versions of our courses for military and nonmilitary use, and further customize by military organization (e.g., U.S. vs. NATO allies) and branch of military organization (e.g., Army vs. Navy). Each may have differences in terms of situations and missions, and hence differences in curricula. Learning systems further customize the curriculum according to the needs of the individual learner, depending on their military rank, their training objective (proficiency vs. survival), desired training missions, and time available for training.

5. *Localization*. Alelo courses are localized according to the linguistic and other cultural practices of the intended learning community. This helps ensure that learners regard the courses as something

written with them in mind. This includes images, audio recordings, cultural content, and translation into the native language of the learners, but extends beyond that to the norms of usage in particular communities. This comes up particularly in courses for military services, each of which tends to develop slightly different practices in the use of titles, forms of address, and specialized jargon. It also relates to choice of artwork in the animated scenarios, for example, uniforms and physical appearance of the animated characters.

6. *Immersive learning.* Immersive environments play an important role in providing the context for communication and facilitate skill transfer to real-world situations, in accordance with theories of situated cognition (Lave, 1988) and constructivist learning (Vygotsky, 1986). Immersive environments also provide the context for game-based learning where learners develop the contextualized skills and confidence they need to succeed.

7. *Scaffolding.* Alelo employs an elaborate scaffolding methodology within our courses (page-level, lesson-level, and course-level) to progressively develop the skills of the learner and reduce their reliance on hints, assistance, and other forms of support. Courses employ a scaffolding-and-fading approach, in which scaffolding is gradually removed until learners are able to complete the task unassisted (Seeley Brown et al., 1989). Scaffolding takes the form of translations and transcriptions, hints, and other signals that the learner's action was consistent or inconsistent with cultural practice. It is also integrated into the feedback from pedagogical agents (virtual coaches and virtual conversational partners). Virtual coaches help learners prepare for practice scenarios and give learners feedback on their performance. The reactions of the conversational partners are highlighted to help learners recognize when they have acted in a culturally inappropriate way. Learners first develop their skills in practice scenarios where scaffolding is added and then test their skills in assessment scenarios where the scaffolding is removed.

8. *Feedback.* The frequency, timing, and type of feedback given to a learner is critical during language instruction. In our courses, feedback takes the form of evaluation and scoring of the learner's performance, reactions of the animated characters to culturally correct or incorrect behavior, or feedback from virtual coaches. Because many activities are highly interactive and game-based, particular attention is paid to ensure that feedback is provided in a way that does not disrupt the flow of the learning activity. This helps get learners into a flow state of engaged activity (Csikszentmihalyi, 1990) and helps promote conversational fluency. We therefore employ a two-loop model in providing feedback. Feedback in the outer loop, between learning activities, encourages reflection on the preceding learning activity and drawing lessons learned. Feedback in the inner loop, in the midst of the learning activity, is action-oriented, rapid, and designed to maintain the flow of the activity. Other researchers such as VanLehn (2006) employ a two-loop model in providing feedback, but do not place as much emphasis on maintaining flow in the inner loop.

9. *Learner motivation.* Alelo courses are designed throughout to promote and maintain learner motivation. Motivation is a common problem in second-language courses, which many learners find tedious and boring. It is a particular issue in courses for lifelong learners, who are frequently attempting to learn a language in their spare time. Such learners are likely to lose interest and discontinue learning if the learning activities are not sufficiently engaging and motivating. Research has shown some foreign-language learners who lack confidence in their language skills are more likely to disengage from the

training environment compared to those with greater confidence (Bienkowski, Watson, & Surface, 2010). Following the work of researchers on motivation in learning (e.g., Lepper, 1988), learning activities are designed to optimize learner confidence and sense of control, and optimize the level of challenge. This is achieved in part through the use of feedback that offers encouragement and adheres to norms of politeness (Wang et al., 2008). The principles and design techniques of game-based learning (Gee, 2003; Prensky, 2001) are employed throughout to promote sustained engagement.

10. *Skill sustainment.* Courses are designed not just to develop communication skills, but to sustain them as well. This is a particular concern for courses that attempt to impart skills in a compressed period of time. The contextualization of learning helps promote sustainment because it supports the formation of associations in memory that both promote retention and facilitate recall (Neisser, 1984). In accordance with research on spaced practice and memory (Baddely & Longmand, 1978; Bahrick, 1979; Melton, 1970), we have developed methods for dynamically selecting refresher learning materials based on the learner's past training history, to help learners retain their communication skills better and quickly recover them when they start to lose them. We provide sustainment training on mobile devices, so that learners can refresh their skills anywhere, anytime.

Technology Architecture Overview

The following is an overview of the technology architecture used to author and deliver these courses. The remainder of the chapter focuses on selected adaptive technologies within this architecture. More detail about the other technologies described here may be found in Johnson (2010) and Johnson and Valente (2009).

Authors develop courses using a set of collaborative authoring tools named Kona and accessed using a Web-based portal named Hilo.[1] Kona maintains a repository of course content, including specifications of learning activities and a collection of art assets (images, sound recordings, animations, etc.) used in these learning activities. A multidisciplinary team of authors utilize these tools, including linguists, anthropologists, media specialists, animators, software engineers, and experts in the language and culture subject matter of the particular course.

Course content specifications are represented in XML and specify the learning content in a platform-independent manner. This makes it possible to deliver learning materials on both desktop computers and mobile devices, and to create integrated suites of learning materials across multiple platforms. Each content element is tagged with metadata to indicate whether it applies to all delivery platforms or is intended for a specific platform such as a mobile device. In a typical course, most content applies to all platforms, but it is sometimes necessary to tag selected elements for a particular device to reflect the specifics of how the course is delivered on that device. For example, our iPhone application does not yet include a Mission Game, so references to the Mission Game in the course materials must be marked as desktop-only.

The content specifications can support multiple source languages, which helps us achieve the Localization goal mentioned in the previous section. For example, Alelo has developed a multilingual Web site for Voice of America to teach American English language and culture, named goEnglish.me. This course has so far been developed for Chinese and Farsi speakers, and localizations for speakers of other languages are planned for the near future.

The content specifications also include metadata to specify the intended audience

---

[1] A number of the component names in this architecture, as well as the company name Alelo, have Hawaiian origins. Hawaii provides an example of the type of harmonious interchange between cultures that Alelo as a company seeks to promote.

of a particular learning activity. For example, the Operational Dari lesson on introducing your team has different versions of content for U.S. Marines, other U.S. service members, and other NATO allies operating in Afghanistan, each using different names for military ranks. U.S. Marine learners learn how to say Marine-specific military ranks such as gunnery sergeant or lance corporal in Dari, whereas the other services do not. This enables us to employ a mass customization approach to content development and plays an essential role in achieving the Tailored Curricula goal mentioned in the previous section.

To create the individual learning products, a build system named Kapili converts content into shared content packages that can be loaded onto particular delivery platforms. Each delivery platform has a runtime player that can play the content on that particular device. For example, the scenarios in Figure 14.1 and the dialog in Figure 14.3 were delivered using the Lapu desktop runtime platform, built on top of the Unreal Engine from Epic Games. The language-instruction activity in Figure 14.2 and the refresher training activity in Figure 14.4 were delivered using the Uku mobile runtime platform on the Apple iOS operating system for iPhones, iPod Touches, and iPads.

Each learning product typically uses some combination of the available runtime platforms, depending on the needs of the particular learning organization and the computing resources available to them. A front-end portal for the learning package, named Puka, enables learners to select the particular learning modules they require, based on their particular learning goals and needs. Puka can then download the content packages for those particular learning modules, providing each learner with a customized course of instruction.

Finally, an important element of the technology architecture is the support for data collection and analysis. We have developed a common framework for logging learner activities, influenced by Mostow and Beck's (2009) model of educational data logging. Each runtime player includes a logging

mechanism consistent with this framework. These data can be uploaded to a learning management system so that instructors can track learners' progress. We also can import the logging data into a data warehouse named Hoahu for detailed analysis (Johnson et al., 2010). This enables us to investigate how the learners are using the systems, study trajectories of learning over time, and derive measures of learning gains and system performance. This makes possible an iterative cycle of course development, evaluation, and improvement, where lessons learned from deployed versions of learning systems help inform the development of successive versions. Data collected from training sites is incorporated into the training corpora for some of the underlying technologies such as automated speech recognition, resulting in progressive improvement of recognition performance over time.

Adaptive Curriculum Tailoring

As indicated earlier, most Alelo curricula are designed to support a range of different learning requirements, with the understanding that not all learners have the same learning needs. Some of this variation in learning requirements is captured by classifying learners into different groups – for example, different military services – and tagging learning content according to the group it is intended to support. This results in a family of learning products for a given topic, each tailored for a particular group of learners. Adaptive curriculum-tailoring methods are then employed to further tailor the curriculum according to the learning goals of smaller groups of learners as well as individual learners.

The particular set of learning modules in the curriculum for a given course is determined by the course of instruction (COI). Courses of instruction can be selected and changed at runtime, according to choices made by the instructor and/or the learner. Using the learning management system (Kahu in Figure 14.7), an instructor can select a course of instruction for his or her

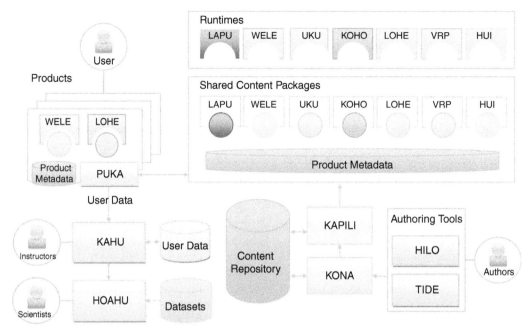

Figure 14.7. Alelo technology architecture.

class or small unit and download it to the learning portal (Puka) on each learner's training device. Then when the learner uses the training device, he or she will then see a tailored course curriculum, separated into required or recommended learning modules (included in the COI) and optional learning modules (not included in the COI). The COI is shared across the available training devices. So for example, if the course includes both a desktop runtime player and a mobile runtime player, learners will see the same COI on both runtime players.

COIs can be further tailored according to the needs and preferences of each individual learner, and in the case of self-paced learning, this is the primary tailoring mechanism. At the beginning of the course, learners can complete a questionnaire in which they indicate their particular role in their organization, the range of jobs or missions that they are training for, the particular region they are interested in, and, in some courses, the level of communicative proficiency they are aiming for. Puka then selects a recommended course of instruction for the learner based on those choices. If during the course learners decide to change their learning

objectives, they can go back and change their questionnaire answers and obtain a revised COI. The latter feature was introduced based upon feedback from Marine trainees who had trained with the Tactical Iraqi language and culture trainer. Some of these trainees were originally assigned to complete a compressed predeployment training course, but as their language skills increased, their training ambitions also increased, and they started getting interested in preparing for a language proficiency test so that they could obtain college credit and bonus pay. The latest versions of the Iraqi Arabic and sub-Saharan French courses now allow the trainee to expand their learning objectives at any time and switch from a predeployment training COI to a language proficiency training COI.

The following examples, taken from the Virtual Cultural Awareness Trainer for the Horn of Africa (VCAT-HOA), further illustrate how courses of instruction are tailored based on learner questionnaire choices. VCAT is intended for use by military service members and other government personnel on assignment to the Horn of Africa region.

- Learners can choose from among thirteen countries of interest within the Horn of Africa region. The COI will then include a combination of modules pertaining to the Horn of Africa region as a whole and modules specific to the country of choice.
- Learners can select a level of responsibility: Junior, Mid-Level, and Senior. Junior enlisted personnel fall into the junior category, noncommissioned officers fall into the mid-level category, and officers fall into the senior category. The COI will then include learning modules relating to the particular types of situations that learners at that level are likely to encounter; for example, senior personnel complete modules covering the cultural issues relating to meetings with host country's leaders.
- Learners can select a type of mission to train for: civil affairs, security operations, humanitarian assistance operations, and noncombatant evacuation operations. Based on this choice, training modules relating to those particular types of missions are included in the COI.

Based on these choices, each learner can receive one of 156 possible tailored courses of instruction.

Conversational Virtual Humans as Adaptive Learning Technologies

Adaptive technologies are also integrated into the individual learning activities within a course of instruction. These include the speech and multimodal communication technologies that enable us to create conversational virtual humans that engage in face-to-face dialog with learners, as illustrated in Figures 14.1 and 14.3. These play a critical role in providing learners with opportunities to practice their culturally appropriate communication skills. For their behavior to be culturally appropriate, it is important that they adapt to the learner. The virtual humans are designed to model the way people adapt their interaction with

other people based on the changing power and social-distance relationships between them. If learners demonstrate knowledge of culturally appropriate behavior and develop rapport with the animated characters, the characters will reciprocate and become more friendly and cooperative. This makes it possible to model intercultural interaction scenarios such as the meeting with the malek in Operational Dari, where appropriate cultural action is essential for a successful mission outcome. In addition, virtual humans play an essential role in providing feedback to the learner. The manner in which virtual humans react to what learners say and do provides learners with cues as to whether or not they are behaving in a socially appropriate way, as in real life. These reactions can be highly salient learning experiences, particularly if the virtual human reacts emotionally to what the learner has said.

The virtual humans can engage in simulated multimodal conversation with language learners. The virtual humans need to be able to react to nonverbal actions such as gestures that the learners might perform, actions that they might perform on objects in the virtual world, as well as their spoken utterances. In most Alelo products, the user selects gestures and actions from on-screen menus, which then causes the learner's avatar in the scenario to perform the action. Spoken utterances are input via microphone, except in products that lack a spoken input channel, in which case learners choose utterances from menus of options. The conversational virtual human then interprets the inputs in a manner consistent with the culture and generates a response.

Unlike many spoken language processing systems designed for use by native speakers, Alelo spoken dialog systems are specifically designed to process and understand *learner language*, that is, language forms produced by language learners (Ellis & Barkhuizer, 2005). All components of the spoken dialog system architecture, from automated speech recognition through virtual human response, are designed with the characteristics of learner language in mind, particularly for novice-to-intermediate language learners, as defined on the ACTFL spoken proficiency scale (ACTFL, 1983). This is necessary to ensure that the dialog system is robust enough to interpret the learner's speech in spite of mispronunciations and other errors. Another objective is to detect and categorize errors when they occur, so that the system can assess learner performance and provide feedback.

Interpreting learner language can be challenging for people (ACTFL, 1983), and even more so for computers. However, by taking into account the particular characteristics of the speech of the target learners, it is possible to maximize understanding rates. The acoustic models used in the automated speech recognizer are trained on samples of learner speech as well as native speech, to ensure that the recognizer is tolerant of learner accents. Analysis of interaction logs and speech recordings collected from the courses make it possible to understand in detail the properties of the learners' language as they progress through the course. The following are some key properties that the framework takes advantage of:

- limited vocabulary, primarily drawn from the courses themselves and therefore somewhat predictable;
- frequent use of memorized phrases, drawn from the curriculum, which makes the language even more predictable; and
- limited use of complex, multi-phrase utterances, so that the meaning of most utterances can be characterized as simple speech acts.

Figure 14.8 gives an overview of the conversational virtual human architecture. The architecture is built on top of game engine platforms that manage the virtual worlds in which the simulations take place, including the physical environment, objects, and animated characters. It is independent of any particular game engine, but relies on the game engine interface to provide the conversational interface that receives the learners' inputs (speech, gestures and other action choices, and locomotion), outputs the virtual humans' spoken responses, and animates the movements of the animated characters and objects in the scene.

The automated speech recognizer takes the learner's speech and attempts to recognize it as an utterance in the foreign language. It utilizes the Julius open-source speech recognition decoder (Lee & Kawahara, 2009), applied to recognition models developed specifically for learner language. It utilizes a grammar-based recognition approach in which the recognition grammars are generated automatically from the database of foreign-language utterances within Kona that is constructed by the course authors as they develop each course. Depending on the type of learning material, the grammar may recognize ill-formed utterances in addition to well-formed utterances, enabling the system to recognize and respond to learner mistakes. In addition to the recognition model, there is a "garbage model" that will match with low probability against any input utterance. This helps ensure that the speech recognizer will report an utterance as recognized if it is recognized with sufficiently high probability. This helps reject unintelligible learner speech, in which cases the virtual human generates responses such as "Excuse me?" or "I didn't understand you" in the foreign language. It also helps avoid situations where the system misinterprets the learner as saying something that he or she did not say, which learners find frustrating and lowers their confidence in the reliability of the recognition system.

Next, the virtual human takes the learner's behavior – that is, the learner's utterance, gestures, and other actions – and attempts to interpret the communicative intent of that behavior. Communicative intents are presented as communicative acts, like speech acts, but not limited to speech. Following the work of Traum and Hinkelman (1992), each includes a *core function* (to greet, ask, inform, request, etc.) and *grounding* function – in other words, the act's role in coordinating the conversation (e.g., to initiate a conversation, continue, acknowledge the other speaker, etc.). Interpretation depends on the particular culture being modeled, as well as the dialog context. If the learner says

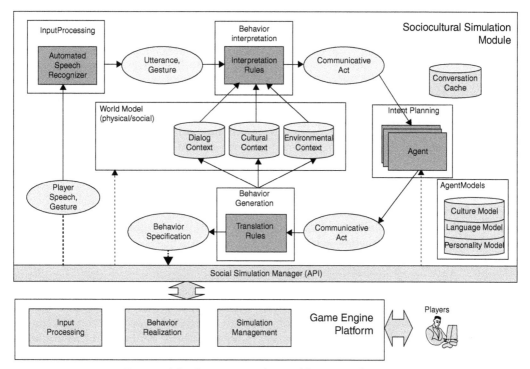

Figure 14.8. Conversational virtual human architecture.

something that does not make sense in the current dialog context, the virtual human may respond as if he or she does not understand the learner, just as people do in similar circumstances.

Once the system interprets the learner's behavior, the virtual humans in the conversation or within earshot in the vicinity choose a communicative act to perform in response, in the intent-planning phase. The communicative act is then realized as a coordinated set of behaviors on the part of the virtual human, which may comprise a spoken utterance, one or more gesture animations, lip animation, and other animated actions. These depend on the particular culture, the dialog state, states of objects in the virtual world, as well as the virtual human's current attitudes toward the learner. This results in a high level of adaptivity and flexibility in the virtual human behavior.

Depending on the type of learning activity, portions of the overall architecture may be used. In the simplest case, called *language-instruction pages*, just the automated speech recognition component is used. Learners

are prompted to say the phrase and receive feedback as to whether the learner's utterance matches the phrase. This type of exercise is illustrated in Figure 14.2. (Note that automated speech recognition is currently available only in the desktop runtime platforms, not the iPhone, so on the iPhone, the platform plays back the learner's speech and the native speaker's speech, and lets the learner compare the two.)

In another common type of activity, called *mini-dialogs*, learners practice individual conversational turns and get feedback on the accuracy and appropriateness of their response, frequently provided by a Virtual Coach. Learners build up their skills by practicing conversational turns in mini-dialogs and then combine them in more extended dialogs. For the mini-dialogs, only the automated speech recognition and behavior interpretation phases of the pipeline are required. Because the context of the exercise is more constrained than in an open-ended dialog, it is possible to expand the range of ill-formed or inappropriate utterances that the system is prepared to recognize and give learners feedback regarding those errors when they occur (Kumar et al., 2009). Thus the bulk of the coached practice on language forms and language use occurs in the context of these mini-dialogs.

Evaluating Virtual Human Performance

Getting the behavior right for the virtual humans requires collaboration among social scientists, instructional designers, animators, engineers – in fact, pretty much the entire multidisciplinary team. The front-end analysis of the culture results in libraries of culturally appropriate behaviors, which in turn are created and sequenced by trained animators. The resulting virtual human behavior must be appropriate from a social science standpoint (e.g., are the malek character's gestures appropriate for an Afghan of that social standing in that situation?), from an artistic standpoint (e.g., are they fluid and natural?), as well as from a pedagogical standpoint (e.g., will a novice-level trainee be able to recognize and interpret the cultural cues in the malek's behavior?). Scaffolding is sometimes added to the virtual human's behavior, in the form of visual and auditory signals and callout commentaries, to help novice learners with limited intercultural competence interpret the situation and the behaviors of the virtual humans correctly.

To make accurate assessments of the performance of the spoken dialog system, it is necessary to collect and analyze data from actual dialogs between learners and virtual humans, in the context of field use of the systems. Field data is essential for an accurate assessment because speech recognition rates depend on the accuracy of the learners' speech, and learners continually adapt their speech as a result of their interactions with the system.

As an illustration, the following are some evaluation results from field data collected in late 2009 (Johnson et al., 2010; Sagae et al., in press). Forty-five active-duty Navy subjects were recruited as volunteers to undergo self-study training with Tactical Iraqi and Tactical French. Subjects were asked to train for extended periods of time over the course of several months. The purpose of this was to obtain longitudinal data on learner and system performance, to see how the performance of the dialog system changes as learners develop and improve their language skills. As it turned out, many of the subjects were unable to take significant amounts of time out of their busy training schedule for this volunteer study. A total of thirteen subjects trained for four or more hours: eight out of twenty-five Arabic trainees and five out of twenty French trainees. Analysis focused on these subjects.

One useful overall measure of dialog system performance is the *meaningful response rate*, that is, the frequency of virtual human responses that indicated that the virtual human understood what the learner said, and did not produce responses like "Sorry, I didn't understand you." The virtual human may fail to have a meaningful response for a number of reasons: the microphone may have failed to pick up the learner's voice, the automated speech recognizer may have been unable to recognize the learner's utterance, or the virtual human may have been unable to interpret the meaning of the utterance in the context of the dialog.

If the virtual human did not understand what the learner said, the learner would need to repeat or rephrase what he or she said – in other words, perform additional *utterance attempts* – until the virtual human understood and was able to respond and complete the dialog turn. So another useful measure of dialog system performance is the number of utterance attempts per dialog turn, or the number of utterance attempts per meaningful response. If the learner must repeat themselves multiple times to be understood, a *dialog breakdown* is said to have occurred. Dialog breakdowns inevitably occur in real life when language learners attempt to communicate with native speakers. However, severe breakdowns with multiple speech attempts can cause learner frustration and should be avoided if possible, for example, by hints that help learners rephrase what they are trying to say to be understood.

In this particular study, the meaningful response rate for the French learners was 59 percent and the meaningful response rate for the Arabic learners was 58 percent. The number of utterance attempts per dialog turn was 1.64 for French, and 1.73 for Arabic. Of the total number of dialog terms, 7.1 percent of the French dialog turns were severe breakdowns involving four or more dialog attempts, whereas 6.5 percent of the Arabic dialog turns were severe breakdowns.

These statistics indicate that learners had to repeat themselves from time to time, but usually were able to make themselves understood with relatively few attempts. These frequencies are likely not greatly different from what beginning learners would experience in real life when engaging in conversations with native speakers. However, a small fraction of the dialog turns were severe and brought down the overall meaningful response rate. Further study of these breakdown occurrences revealed that even when the learners received hints, in the form of possible foreign-language utterance texts for the learner to say, they continued to experience difficulty being understood, especially if the utterances were in French. The learners apparently were confused by the written French hints, which is not surprising given that French spelling is somewhat idiosyncratic and includes letters that are pronounced differently from how they are pronounced in English. As an outcome of this analysis, the hint system in the new Operational courses has been improved to provide more spoken hints, to help learners improve their pronunciation and overcome serious breakdowns.

Although these measures provide useful overall indicators of dialog performance, they do not distinguish failures due to system performance problems from failures resulting from poor learner speech. Therefore, two annotators were recruited to review learner recordings out of the sample set and judge the accuracy of the system's interpretations of the French learners' speech. Two sets of dialogs were selected for comparison in this study: one set of beginner-level dialogs and one set of intermediate-level dialogs. Annotators were asked first to indicate whether they agreed with the system as to whether or not the learner's speech was intelligible (i.e., recognizable utterance vs. garbage) and whether they agreed with the system's interpretation of the utterance as a communicative act. A total of 345 dialog turns were annotated. Overall inter-annotator agreement for this task, as measured by Cohen's Kappa, was 0.8, which is good.

Overall, there were very few instances where the annotators judged that the system had misunderstood the learners by inappropriately assigning a communicative act to the learner's speech. Less than 1 percent of the dialog turns were considered unintelligible by the annotators but interpreted by the system. For 3.5 percent of the dialog turns (eight for annotator 1, eighteen for annotator 2), the system assigned a communicative act interpretation and the annotators assigned a different interpretation. In the remaining cases where the system assigned an interpretation to the dialog turn (167 or 48.4 percent for annotator 1, 160 or 46.4 percent for annotator 2), the annotators agreed with the system's interpretations.

The annotators were able to assign interpretations to a number of utterances that the system rejected as garbage (94 or 27.2 percent for annotator 1, 134 or 38.8 percent for annotator 2). To understand the causes for these disagreements, the annotators were asked to revisit these cases and judge whether the utterance had a pronunciation error, a grammatical error, or was free of errors. Most of these cases (58 out of 94, or 62 percent, for annotator 1, 85 out of 134, or 63 percent, for annotator 2) were judged as having pronunciation errors, and very few (0 for annotator 1, 2 for annotator 2) were judged as having grammatical errors. Remaining cases (36 or 10.4 percent of the total for annotator 1, 47 or 13.6 percent for annotator 2) were judged as well-formed, and therefore the system should have interpreted them, assuming they were appropriate to the context of the dialog.

These results indicate that the Alelo dialog systems investigated in this study are quite successful at avoiding misunderstandings, where the system thinks the learner said something that he or she did not mean to say. This is a significant advance over the speech recognizer used in the first version of Tactical Iraqi, which lacked a garbage model and therefore tended to misunderstand learner speech frequently, causing considerable learner frustration.

The results also suggest that dialog performance could be further improved by increasing the system's tolerance for mispronunciations – or by providing improved training so that learners improve their pronunciation. For the reasons noted earlier, the current focus of development at Alelo is on improving pronunciation hints. Improving tolerance for mispronunciations in automated speech recognition may be useful as well; however, it likely is not necessary to achieve the same level of tolerance for error as the annotators in this study. For one thing, it may be useful for pedagogical purposes to require learners to strive for greater pronunciation accuracy, to avoid the plateau and fossilization effects that many language learners experience (Han & Odlin, 2006). The results also indicate that the current system rejects some well-formed utterances, and so further effort may be needed to reduce this rejection rate – as long as it does not increase misunderstanding rates as a side effect.

Adaptive Technologies for Sustainment Training

The next set of technologies that we discuss relate to the problem of adapting curricula to meet the needs of skill sustainment and refresher training. As we attempt to meet the needs of lifelong learners to develop communication skills quickly, there is risk that they might also lose them quickly if they have not trained them sufficiently. We are employing adaptive training in two ways to help address the skill sustainment problem.

- The sequence of training activities presented to the learner is adapted dynamically until the learner has mastered the skills being trained, so that the learned

skills are resistant to forgetting and skill decay.
- After long gaps in training, learners receive compressed and tailored curricula that help them quickly regain the skills that they may have lost.

Adaptive technologies have the potential for revolutionizing refresher training for language and other communicative skills. Language learners typically experience skill decay after periods of disuse of their language skills, but most language curricula are aimed at initial acquisition of language skills, not refresher training. It is difficult to design a good refresher language training course that meets the needs of all learners, because the effectiveness of the course depends on the knowledge, skills, and attitudes that each individual learner brings to the course – what they have previously learned as well as what skills have since decayed. However, through adaptive technologies it is possible to customize curricula based on each learner's skill profile and training history, so that learners can recover their skills as quickly and efficiently as possible.

This is a good example of where scientific analysis of field use of Alelo's learning environments has led to their further improvements. By analyzing the pattern of skill acquisition and decay in learners who use our courses for extended periods, with gaps in their training, it was possible to design improved adaptive training methods that resist and counteract skill decay, which are now being integrated into the new versions of Alelo's training systems.

Background: Research in Skill Acquisition and Decay

The research literature describes skill decay over time. Research has also identified learning conditions and principles that can reduce decay (i.e., increase retention) across a variety of skills. For instance, spaced practice can help lessen the effects of skill decay (e.g., Baddely & Longmand, 1978; Bahrick, 1979; Melton, 1970). Although massed practice may enhance performance in the training context, research suggests such a strategy often does not translate to enhanced retention after periods of time without using the skill (e.g., Bahrick, 1979; Estes, 1955). Spaced practice, however, tends to result in slower, incremental improvements in performance during training (relative to massed), but higher levels of retention after some time interval (e.g., Baddely & Longmand, 1978; Bahrick, 1979; Melton, 1970). This is the basis for many flashcard-based language-learning algorithms that promote rote memorization of vocabulary items.

However, learning communicative language skill is more complex and involved than rote memorization of declarative knowledge. From a general skill acquisition perspective (e.g., Anderson, 1982), learners must acquire knowledge, proceduralize that knowledge creating initial skill (Neves & Anderson, 1981), compile the skill, automatize the skill, and apply the skill. Furthermore, communicative competence involves a combination of a number of component skills, including pronunciation skills, skill in producing well-formed utterances, listening comprehension skills, ability to recognize cultural cues, and so on. Skill decay can therefore potentially manifest itself in multiple ways. Learners may retain the ability to recognize vocabulary items, but lose fluency. They may retain the ability to pronounce foreign-language phrases, but lose the ability to use those skills effectively in conversation.

Research points to various strategies that can be employed to alleviate decay in complex cognitive skills, and which may apply to communicative skills. Variable practice (i.e., practicing a set of skills across a range of potential situations) has been found to be beneficial across many skill domains (see Ghodsian et al., 1997), such as extending knowledge and skills acquired to novel situations (see Van Rossum, 1990 for review) and a variety of motor learning tasks (Catalano & Kleiner, 1984; Kerr & Booth, 1978). Furthermore, retention can be enhanced by constructing practice environment(s) to match real-world contexts in which learners will use their skills. Such training approaches

will call for trainees to process information and produce skills under the same conditions they will encounter after leaving training (Morris, Bransford, & Franks, 1977). Encoding specificity theory (Cormier, 1987), which states information is better recalled under conditions similar to those in which it was originally processed and encoded, suggests that learning and practicing skills in an environment similar to the transfer context will enhance retention.

Overlearning, or the act of continuing to train and practice a skill after it has been learned, has been proposed to lead to skill automaticity (i.e., requiring fewer attentional demands to retrieve and perform) (Schneider, 1985; Shiffrin & Schneider, 1977). Research evidence suggests overlearning has a moderate effect on retention of both cognitive and physical tasks (see Driskell, Willis, & Cooper, 1992). However, the evidence also suggests this effect weakens as the retention interval lengthens (Driskell, Willis, & Cooper, 1992).

Approaches such as variable practice and overlearning can be thought of as adaptive in nature, in that they require training content to adjust (or adapt) according to learner behaviors. For example, one cannot begin to *overlearn* a skill until he or she has first sufficiently demonstrated the skill has been learned. The major challenge in implementing such adaptive approaches is customizing them to fit the unique (yet volatile) skill profiles of individual learners. These skill profiles can change both during periods of training and during periods of disuse of the learned skills.

Empirical Study of Skill Decay in Tactical Iraqi

To the extent possible, Alelo curricula are designed with these findings in mind, to maximize retention. Learners overlearn key phrases, such as greetings, to maximize retention, and practice vocabulary in a range of phrases and contexts to provide variable practice. However, the goal of providing effective training in a compressed amount of time makes it necessary to find the right mix of learning activities and to make trade-offs between these various activities. The research literature does not provide clear indications of how to make these trade-offs. For example, how much training time should be devoted to overlearning of key phrases, and how much should be devoted to variable practice in a range of phrases?

To address these questions, Alelo collaborated with SWA Consulting Inc. to analyze archival data from trainees who worked for extended periods with Alelo's Tactical Iraqi language and culture trainer. The subject trainees were U.S. Marines who had trained at the Marine Corps Air Ground Combat Center (MCAGCC) at Twentynine Palms, California.

We retrieved a total of 294 separate trainee profiles from Twentynine Palms. Out of these, thirty-four had trained for at least a month and had skipped at least a week at some point during their training. Many of these trainees had conducted extensive training with Tactical Iraqi, at least twenty-five Skill Builder lessons. These learners were native English speakers who trained with Tactical Iraqi between October 2007 and September 2008. The final data set consisted of 9,615 unique speech attempts made during the course of training.

This study focused on patterns of successful speech attempts (or utterances) produced by learners. We identified skill decay as instances in which learners failed to reproduce an utterance they previously had produced correctly. Several potential predictors of utterance success in the practice setting of the Tactical Language Training System (TLTS) Skill Builder were identified and operationalized for this empirical study. The follow variables were calculated from log data for this study:

- The number of previous speech attempts, both in general and for specific target utterances, was calculated.
- The number of previous successful utterances was also calculated for each target utterance. This variable could reflect the degree of overlearning undertaken by the learner, with a larger number of successful attempts indicating greater overlearning.
- The time elapsed (in real time) since a learner's last successful utterance for each target utterance was computed. This variable reflects a retention interval–the amount of time that passed since the learner last produced the target utterance successfully.
- Training pages that both provide example speech clips and require learners to repeat those same utterances were differentiated from pages that require learners to produce speech from memory.
- The number of other target utterances attempted between two attempts of a specific target utterance was calculated. To the extent that the other utterances were semantically similar to the target utterance, this variable may reflect interference.

To examine the role of training context characteristics and learner behaviors on language acquisition and attrition, hierarchical linear modeling (HLM) for a binary outcome was employed. The models estimated are similar to common logistic regression models, with the exception that model intercepts were allowed to vary across groups, or clusters, of related observations. Analyses were carried out using the GLIMMIX procedure in SAS for generalized linear mixed models. The three-level multilevel analysis considered speech attempts nested within target utterances nested within speakers, with the probability of success (vs. failure) of each speech attempt constituting the predicted outcome of the model. Only speech attempts for which learners had at least one successful previous attempt for that specific target utterance (i.e., had demonstrated the ability to produce the utterance correctly) were included in the analysis. As is customary in multilevel modeling, a series of models was estimated to determine (1) the observed unconditional variability (i.e., not controlling for any explanatory variables) in the probability of successful speech attempts across target utterances (after controlling for between-speaker differences), and

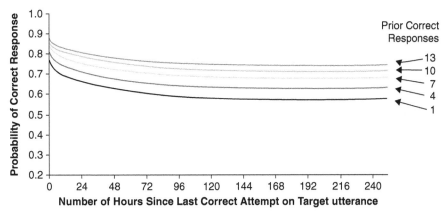

Figure 14.9. Time elapsed since last correct attempt and probability of a correct response.[2]

(2) the predictive roles of various explanatory variables entered into the model.

Across the 9,615 speech attempts, there was significant variability in the probability of speech success between target utterances and within speakers. The following are some of the factors that were related to successful or unsuccessful attempts at speech production. The amount of time since one's last correct attempt (on a given target) was negatively related to the probability of success on any given attempt. The impact of time lessened as the time interval increased, with the largest decrease occurring during the first 50 hours, followed by a more gradual decrease up until 150 hours (at which point time since the last correct attempt was unrelated to future success). This relationship is presented in Figure 14.9, which also depicts the role of prior successes with respect to the target utterance. This plot shows that skill decay due to elapsed time was more pronounced in learners who had fewer prior correct utterances than those who had more correct utterances. That is, advanced learners' skills were somewhat less susceptible to decay compared to those of novice learners.

The complexity (or difficulty) of the target phrase was also related to skill decay. The probability of a correct response varied by the degree of difficulty of the phrase, both in terms of utterance length and the frequency of difficult phonemes. As utterance length increased, the probability of a correct response reached a maximum at a length of twenty-one characters (approximately the length of common phrases such as "as-salaamu 'aleykum" and "wa 'aleykum as-salaam"), and then decreased significantly thereafter (see Figure 14.9). This may reflect the tendency of novice learners to memorize and repeat short phrases. Also, the proportion of non-English phonemes in a target utterance was negatively related to the probability of success.

These findings show promise for incorporating an automated process for tracking which language skills are most susceptible to decay for individual learners at a given time during training.

Adaptive Presentation of Learning Activities for Sustainment

Based on the lessons learned from this and similar analyses, we are developing new methods for dynamically customizing each learner's course of instruction and sequence of learning activities, based on the learner's trajectory of learning and predicted forgetting. The first version, illustrated in Figure 14.4, integrated into the Alelo's mobile training platform, prompts learners to review language-instruction pages that the learner has previously studied, to ensure that the learner has properly mastered these

---

[2]   Reported probabilities calculated holding all other model variables constant at their grand mean.

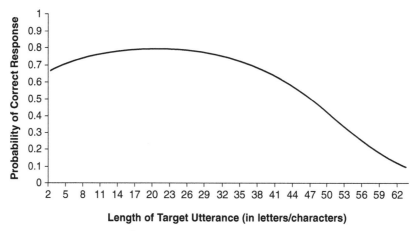

Figure 14.10. Length of target utterance and probability of a correct response.

phrases. It keeps track of each language-instruction page that the trainee has visited, and the amount of time that has elapsed since it was visited. If a page has not been visited for sufficient amount of time, it is included in a set of pages for the trainee to review. Each time the learner reviews a page, the time interval until the next review increases, resulting in spaced practice.

The next version will track each learner's progress of language acquisition and decay, and dynamically generate a tailored curriculum that helps them quickly achieve or regain mastery of the language skills that they need for a particular purpose, such as completing a particular mission. Material will be organized by topic, as in the current curricula, but the material included under each topic will change dynamically based on what the learner has previously mastered or is in danger of forgetting. If the system judges that the learner has fully mastered a particular topic, it will encourage the learner to skip it. Later, if the learner has stopped training on a particular topic for a period of time, the system will provide the trainee with a focused set of exercises that will help them quickly recover their skills (Figure 14.10).

The key to the approach is a detailed learner model that tracks the learner's degree of mastery of each phrase and topic, based on the theoretical language acquisition model and empirical studies of skill

decay such as the one described in the previous section. For each phrase and vocabulary item, the learner model will track the type of skill the learner has demonstrated (recognition and recall, pronunciation, use in conversation) and the level of mastery demonstrated (declarative level vs. automatized, overlearned level). This requires tracking both the number of correct and incorrect attempts, as in the study in the previous section, as well as the amount of time the learner requires to complete a particular exercise. Each exercise and activity will be tagged with metadata indicating what language skills it teaches and/or tests. If an exercise involves language skills that the learner has already mastered, the system will let the learner skip the exercise and focus on the exercises that cover skills where the learner is weaker.

If the learner has stopped training for an extended period of time, the mastery estimates in the learner model may no longer be valid due to skill decay. In such cases the learner will be encouraged to complete a summary quiz or practice scenario covering a particular topic, and use the data to recalibrate the learner model. This will enable the system to recommend refresher and remedial training to trainees who have failed to master certain skills or are in the process of losing those skills. We also plan to incorporate a mechanism for predicting skill decay, precalibrated from analyses of archival learner data, so that the system is better able to make recommendations of refresher training activities without having to first retest the learner's skills.

We plan to continue to collect data from field use of this sustainment training model and use it to iteratively improve the personalized refresher training mechanism. This will involve progressively improving the ability of the learner model to account for and predict skill acquisition and decay, both statistically for the population of learners as a whole and for each individual learner. In the longer term, we anticipate that individual differences in learner skill acquisition and decay patterns will emerge, which may be indicative of differences in learning strategies, metacognitive skill, and/or aptitude.

Summary

This chapter summarized the approach to developing intercultural competence underlying Alelo courses and described some of the adaptive technologies used to implement this approach. The approach is particularly suited to the needs of lifelong learners who may have specific needs for intercultural competence in their job or work and relatively little free time to study and train. Course designs adhere to ten key principles, grounded in research in learning science, psychology, anthropology, and applied linguistics: task-based learning, language in culture, communicative approach, customization, localization, immersive learning, scaffolding, feedback, learner motivation, and skill sustainment. Courses are developed in accordance with the Situated Culture Methodology, which is based on theories and methods from sociocultural and linguistic anthropology. An integrated technology architecture, incorporating adaptive technologies, supports authoring and delivery of the courses using computer game engines, Web browsers, and mobile devices. Data from field use of the courses is used to measure system performance and effectiveness, and to identify areas for further improvement.

Experience indicates that when used properly, these courses can be very effective in promoting intercultural competence. For example, the 3rd Battalion, 7th Marines used Tactical Iraqi to prepare for its deployment to Iraq in 2006 and 2007. Each squad of thirteen Marines included at least two trainees who had trained for forty hours with the course prior to deployment. This battalion did not suffer a single combat casualty during this deployment, the first Marine battalion to do so in the Iraq war. The Marine Corps Center for Lessons Learned interviewed the officers and surveyed the enlisted personnel afterward (MCCLL, 2008). The study uncovered evidence that the level of intercultural competence of these Marines upon arrival in Iraq was much higher than that of previous units, and that this helped establish a positive relationship between the Marines and the local people and contributed significantly to mission effectiveness.

Future plans call for further expanding the utilization of the products described here, particularly the new mobile solutions. We plan to further develop the personalized refresher training capabilities. Meanwhile we aim to expand the approach to new products aimed at additional learner communities, languages, and cultures.

Acknowledgments

The author wishes to express his thanks to the various members of the Alelo team who contributed to this work. Mike Emonts edited and commented on the manuscript. This work was sponsored by USMC PMTRASYS, Voice of America, Office of Naval Research, and DARPA. Opinions expressed here are those of the authors and not of the sponsors or the U.S. government.

References

American Council for the Teaching of Foreign Languages (ACTFL) (1983). *ACTFL proficiency guidelines*. Hastings-on-Hudson, NY: ACTFL Materials Center.

L

Anderson, J. (1982). Acquisition of cognitive skill. *Psychological Review, 89*(4), 369–406.

Austin, J. L. (1975). *How to do things with words.* Cambridge, MA: Harvard University Press.

Baddely, A. D. & Longman, D. J. A. (1978). The influence of length and frequency of training session on the rate of learning to type. *Ergonomics, 21,* 627–635.

Bahrick, H. P. (1979). Maintenance of knowledge: Questions about memory we forgot to ask. *Journal of Experimental Psychology: General, 108,* 296–308.

Barrett, K. A. & Johnson, W. L. (2011). Developing serious games for learning language-in-culture. In Information Resources Management Association (Ed.), *Gaming and simulations: Concepts, methodologies, tools and applications* (pp. 1313–1343). Hershey, PA: IGI Global.

Bernard, H. Russell (Ed.) (1998). *Handbook of methods in cultural anthropology.* Lanham, MD: AltaMira Press.

Bienkowski, S. C., Watson, A. M., & Surface, E. A. (2010). Performance-avoid goal orientation and task engagement: Moderating effect of self-efficacy. Paper presented at the American Psychological Association Convention, August, San Diego, CA.

Birdwhistell, R. L. (1970). *Kinesics and context: Essays on body motion communication.* Philadelphia: University of Pennsylvania Press.

Brown, P. & Levinson, S. C. (1987). *Politeness: Some universals in language usage.* New York: Cambridge University Press.

Byram, M. (1997). *Teaching and assessing intercultural communicative competence.* Clevedon: Multilingual Matters.

Canale, M. & Swain, M. (1980). Theoretical bases of communicative approaches to second language teaching and testing. *Applied Linguistics, 1,* 1–47.

Catalano, J. F. & Kleiner, B. M. (1984). Distant transfer in coincident timing as a function of variability of practice. *Perceptual & Motor Skills, 58,* 851–856.

Cormier, S. M. (1987). The structural processes underlying transfer of training. In S. M. Cormier & J. D. Hagman (Eds.), *Transfer of learning: Contemporary research and applications* (pp. 152–182). San Diego, CA: Academic Press.

Csikszentmihalyi, M. (1990). *Flow: The psychology of optimum experience.* New York: Harper Perennial.

Driskell, J. E., Willis, R. P., & Copper, C. (1992). Effect of overlearning on retention. *Journal of Applied Psychology, 77,* 615–692.

Earley, P. C. (1987). Intercultural training for managers: A comparison of documentary and interpersonal methods. *The Academy of Management Journal, 30*(4), 685–698.

Ellis, R. (2003). *Task-based language learning and teaching.* New York: Oxford University Press.

Ellis, R. & Barkhuizen, G. (2005). *Analyzing learner language.* Oxford: Oxford University Press.

Estes, W. K. (1955). Statistical theory of distributional phenomena in learning. *Psychological Review, 62,* 369–377.

Fiorito, L. (2005). Teaching English for Special Purposes (ESP). Available at http://www.usingenglish.com/articles/teaching-english-for-specific-purposes-esp.html

Gee, J. P. (2003). What video games have to teach us about learning and literacy. *Computers in Entertainment (CIE), 1*(1), 17–27

Ghodsian, D., Bjork, R. A., & Benjamin, A. S. (1997). Evaluating training during training: Obstacles and opportunities. In M. A. Quinones & A. Ehrenstein (Eds.), *Training for a rapidly changing workplace* (pp. 63–88). Washington, DC: American Psychological Association.

Hall, E. T. (1966). *The hidden dimension.* Garden City, NY: Doubleday.

Han, Z. & Odlin, T. (2006). *Studies of fossilization in second language acquisition.* Clevedon: Multilingual Matters.

Hymes, D. (1974). *Foundations in sociolinguistics: An ethnographic approach.* Philadelphia: University of Pennsylvania Press.

Hymes, Dell (1987). Communicative competence. In Ulrich Ammon, Norbert Dittmar, & Klaus J. Mattheier (Eds.), *Sociolinguistics: An international handbook of the science of language and society* (pp. 219–229). Berlin: Walter de Gruyter.

Johnson, W. L. (2010). Using immersive simulations to develop intercultural competence. In Toru Ishida (Ed.), *Culture and computing,* LNCS 6295 (pp. 1–15). Berlin: Springer-Verlag.

Johnson, W. L. & Valente, A. (2009). Tactical language and culture training systems: Using AI to teach foreign languages and cultures. *AI Magazine, 30*(2), 72–84.

Johnson, W. L, Ashish, N., Bodnar, S., & Sagae, A. (2010). Expecting the unexpected: Warehousing and analyzing data from ITS field use. In V. Aleven, J. Kay, & J. Mostow (Eds.), *ITS 2010, Part II,* LNCS 6095 (pp. 352–354). Berlin: Springer-Verlag.

Jonassen, D. H., Tessmer, M., & Hannum, W. H. (1999). *Task analysis methods for instructional design.* Mahwah, NJ: Lawrence Erlbaum.

Kerr, R. & Booth, B. (1978). Specific and varied practice of motor skill. *Perceptual & Motor Skills, 46,* 395–401.

Kosoko-Lasaki, S., Cook, C. T., & O'Brien, R. L. (2008). *Cultural proficiency in addressing health disparities.* Boston: Jones & Bartlett.

Kumar, R., Sagae, A., & Johnson, W. L. (2009). Evaluating an authoring tool for mini-dialogs. In *Proceedings of AIED* 2009. Berlin: Springer-Verlag.

Lantolf, J. P. & Thorne, S. L. (2006). *Sociocultural theory and the genesis of second language development.* Oxford: Oxford University Press.

Lave, J. (1988). *Cognition in practice.* New York: Cambridge University Press.

Lee, A. & Kawahara, T. (2009). Recent development of open-source speech recognition engine Julius. In *Proceedings of Asia-Pacific Signal and Information Processing Association Annual Summit and Conference.* Sapporo, Japan, October 4–7, 2009.

Lepper, M. R. (1988). Motivational considerations in the study of instruction. *Cognition and Instruction,* 289–309.

Marine Corps Center for Lessons Learned (MCCLL) (2008). Tactical Iraqi language and culture training system. *Marine Corps Center for Lessons Learned Newsletter, 4*(8), 4.

McDonald, D. P., McGuire, G., Johnson, J., Selmeski, B., & Abbe, A. (2008). Developing and managing cross-cultural competence within the Department of Defense: Recommendations for learning and assessment. Technical report, RACCA WG.

Melton, A. W. (1970). The situation with respect to the spacing of repetitions and memory. *Journal of Verbal Learning and Verbal Behavior, 9,* 596–606.

Morris, C. D., Bransford, J. D., & Franks, J. J. (1977). Levels of processing versus transfer appropriate processing. *Journal of Verbal Learning and Verbal Behavior, 16,* 519–533.

Mostow, J. & Beck, J. (2009). What, how, and why should tutors log? In *Proceedings of EDM 2009,* pp. 269–278.

National Foreign Language Center (NFLC) (2007). Cultural Proficiency Guidelines (3.2). Available at http://www.nflc.org/culture-prof-guide_3–2.pdf

Neisser, U. (1984). Interpreting Harry Bahrick's discovery: What confers immunity against forgetting? *Journal of Experimental Psychology: General, 113,* 32–35.

Neves, D. M., & Anderson, J. R. (1981). Knowledge compilation: Mechanisms for the automatization of cognitive skills. In J. R. Anderson (Ed.), *Cognitive skills and their acquisition* (pp. 57–84). Hillsdale, NJ: Erlbaum.

Prensky, M. (2001). *Digital game-based learning.* Columbus, OH: McGraw-Hill.

Sagae, A., Johnson, W. L., & Bodnar, S. (2010). Validation of a dialog system for language learners. In *Proceedings of the SIGDIAL 2010 Conference* (pp. 241–244). Tokyo: Association for Computational Linguistics..

Salmoni, B. & Holmes-Eber, P. (2008). *Operational culture for the Warfighter.* Quantico, VA: Marine Corps University Press.

Schneider, P. & Sadowski, D. (2009). The effects of intercultural collaboration strategies on successful PhD education. Paper presented at the 2009 International Workshop on Intercultural Collaboration, Palo Alto, CA.

Schneider, W. (1985). Training high-performance skills: Fallacies and guidelines. *Human Factors, 27,* 285–300.

Seeley Brown, J., Collins, A., & Deguid, P. (1989). Situated cognition and the culture of learning. *Educational Research, 18*(1), 32–42.

Shiffrin, R. M. & Schneider, W. (1977). Controlled and automatic human information processing: Perceptual learning, automatic attending, and a general theory. *Psychological Review, 84,* 127–190.

Traum, D., & Hinkelman, E. (1992). Conversation acts in task-oriented spoken dialogue. *Computational Intelligence, 8,* 575–599.

U.S. Department of Health and Human Services (USDHHS) (2008). Cultural competency curriculum for disaster preparedness and crisis response. Available at https://cccdpcr.thinkculturalhealth.org/

VanLehn, K. (2006). The behavior of tutoring systems. *International Journal of Artificial Intelligence in Education, 16*(3), 227–265.

Van Rossum, J. H. (1990). Schmidt's schema theory: The empirical base of the variability of practice hypothesis: A critical analysis. *Human Movement Science, 9,* 387–435.

Vygotsky, L. S. (1986). *Thought and language.* Cambridge, MA: MIT Press.

Wang, N., Johnson, W. L., Mayer, R. E., Rizzo, P., Shaw, E., & Collins, H. (2008). The politeness effect: Pedagogical agents and learning outcomes. *International Journal of Human Computer Studies, 66*(2), 98–112.

Part V

CULMINATIONS

CHAPTER 15

Practical Issues in the Deployment of New Training Technology

Alan M. Lesgold

My purpose in this chapter is to pass on the lessons learned during the development of five generations of intelligent coached apprenticeship systems, along with subsequent work designing and implementing training for a number of different complex jobs. My colleagues and I had a rare privilege: being able to refine and test a number of generations of intelligent training systems over multiple job applications. Whereas some of what we learned could be learned in any intensive training development effort, some outcomes only become apparent when one is enmeshed in an extended process of iterative refinement and improvement of training.

Between 1984 and about 1998, my colleagues and I developed five generations of intelligent computer systems to prepare technicians for complex electronics jobs (Gott & Lesgold, 2000; Lesgold & Nahemow, 2001). The first two generations were systems to train people to repair avionics test stations in the U.S. Air Force. These test stations are devices that automatically perform a range of tests on avionics (electronics for aircraft) modules that have failed in use. The automated testing makes it relatively easy for technicians with a year or two of post-high-school training to determine common failures of the modules and either repair or replace them. Unfortunately, when the test station itself fails, a complex diagnostic process must be applied by the technician – it is not implicit in the way the device operates. Our training systems focused on this harder diagnostic task. Our goal was to prepare technicians to confront and diagnose failures in aspects of systems that they did not directly manipulate from day to day. The third through fifth generations of our systems prepared technicians at Intel Corporation to repair failures in the equipment used to place layers (Generation 4) or write circuits (Generation 5) on computer chips.

Another way of thinking about the jobs our systems addressed is that they involved artifacts experienced every day but aspects of those artifacts and system knowledge that seldom were experienced. On rare occasions of breakdown in the infrastructure of work systems, however, the cost of that knowledge being missing is huge. On those occasions, the cost of system downtime is substantial – thousands of dollars per hour or battles lost – and the time needed for diagnosis and repair on the order of hours or days. On-the-job learning of these particular skills takes a long time, because opportunities to learn occur only when relatively rare work system infrastructure failures occur, and there is always pressure to let the best expert fix the problem rather than let the novice gain experience. For example, one of our systems produced the same amount of improvement in skill after twenty-five hours of training as occurred on average in four years on the job, but our best estimates were that four years on the job provided only about ten-to-twelve hours of the kinds of experiences encapsulated in our simulated training environment. The task we addressed, then, was training technicians to do well in the 0.2 percent of work time that involved restoring the technically complex infrastructure of the work environment. This is similar to preparing pilots for events they may experience only once or twice in their careers but that absolutely require the right response.

Overall, we developed an approach to training of expertise in confronting rare but critical tasks that was extremely valuable. For example, the improvement in mean time to repair one of the chip-making devices after training on our fifth-generation system was more than ten hours; the savings from one trainee using the trained knowledge once equaled the entire cost of developing that system. However, being effective and efficient is not enough. Our systems did not continue to be employed, at least in the years immediately after their development, although the approach is coming back into favor today to some extent. Overall, then, we learned lessons both about how to train and about how difficult it is to get effective approaches implemented.

In this chapter, I briefly outline the approach to training that we used, the basic level of success, and the lessons we learned along the way.

Learning by Doing with Reflection

The basic approach we took is not unique to our work. Indeed, it would be quite familiar to those who have read the work of Donald Schön (1983). It consists of learning by doing, followed by reflection. The experience of using one of our systems, then, included the following components:

- a realistic simulated work environment in which hard problems can be confronted;
- supportive coaching providing a scaffold for the trainee that assured that every trainee could solve every problem task;
- tools to support reflection after solving a problem and to compare one's solution to that of an expert.

This approach, however, stands in contrast to much of traditional training that involves decomposing complex knowledge into small pieces and then providing an opportunity to learn each piece separately.

The overall scenario of work by the trainee using our system is described in detail by Lesgold and Nahemow (2001). Here is a brief summary. First, the trainee confronts a problem in a simulated work environment, in this case a partly robotic system that puts layers onto wafers that eventually are cut up into computer processor chips. The displays that present the problem reproduce what would be seen on consoles in the work environment. Then, the technician can examine schematic circuit or system diagrams of the device to be diagnosed and repaired. Those diagrams show the connections among electrical and mechanical components as well as paths followed by gases and by heat in the chip-making equipment. The schematics are dynamic, and simulated actions are accomplished by clicking on the representations of components that the technician wants to manipulate.

Figure 15.1 shows one of many views in one of our simulations. In that view, the troubleshooting trainee has clicked on an element in the diagram, accessing a menu that affords opportunities for actions as well as the possibility of component-specific

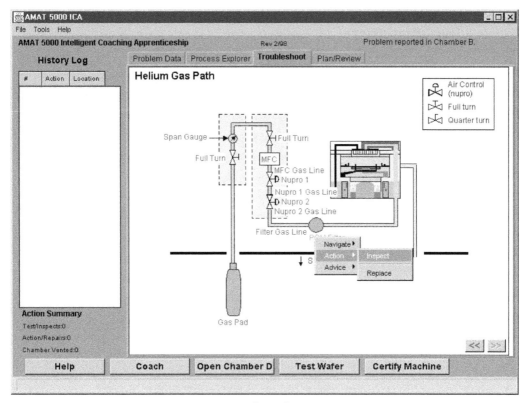

Figure 15.1. View of simulation environment.

advice on the problem. Other tabs along the top of the screen can be clicked to show the displays that would have alerted the trainee to a problem in the machine, the process explorer (discussed later), and an outline of the steps taken so far in addressing the problem, which also is the means for getting overall advice on how to proceed (see Lesgold & Nahemow, 2001 for a more detailed account).

Even complex actions, like sequences of programmed robotic movements, can be requested by the trainee, by clicking on consecutive locations to which a wafer should be transported, as shown in Figure 15.2. Indeed, any action likely to be relevant to diagnosing and repairing the device could be carried out easily by clicking on the representation of a device component in the schematic displays and then choosing alternatives from pop-up menus.

A core idea behind learning by doing with reflection is that the trainee is never left unable to make progress in solving a

problem. So, we needed to have ways in which a trainee who got stumped could get help. We developed two basic approaches to this. One was an opportunity to review brief descriptions of fault-causing phenomena that might be relevant to the situation at hand. This we called the *process explorer* (see Lesgold & Nahemow, 2001 for details). The process explorer presented a matrix whose rows corresponded to variables that might be relevant to the fault being diagnosed (e.g., silane flow) and whose columns corresponded to symptoms that might be relevant to the case at hand (e.g., grit deposited on a wafer). Within the cells of the matrix, symbols indicated what perturbation of a given variable might produce a given symptom. Clicking on one of these symbols produced a brief explanation of the relationship summarized by the symbol and its underlying cause. In essence, the process explorer provided just-in-time delivery of basic knowledge relevant to the problem at hand. Although the overall matrix of causes and

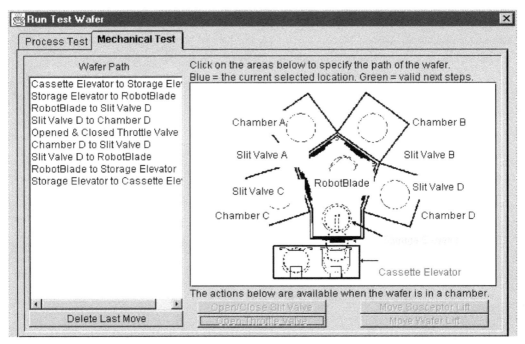

Figure 15.2. Programming a simulated robotic sequence via the schematic interface.

symptoms might be huge – at least 10,000 cells for the restricted range of problems we used – it was straightforward to select a small, relevant subset that included every cause related to the symptoms at hand and every symptom related to those causes.

Note that this is an interesting form of adaptive training. In principle, huge amounts of physical chemistry, electronics, mechanics, quantum physics, and silicon chemistry might be relevant to the work that technicians do with the devices in question. It is not feasible to teach all of these subjects completely to technicians with perhaps two years of post-high-school training. So, we engineered ways to deliver the particular tidbits of these subjects that might be relevant to a problem at hand, using language grounded in the work environment rather than in basic science. The "time" for this "just-in-time" delivery of knowledge was set by the trainee – we taught minimal science that was relevant to the problem-solving work of the trainee at the moment the trainee thought it might be relevant.

The other form of tutorial help also was tailored to the trainee's needs and metered by the trainee's request. If stumped, the trainee was shown a structured summary of actions already taken, with the structuring based on application of an expert model to the data already gathered by the trainee plus the data in the original problem statement. He could click on any action and see a list of questions the intelligent tutor was prepared to answer, as shown in Figure 15.3. As was the case in all five generations of our training systems, technicians were always able to complete every problem successfully, after a sufficient amount of tutorial help. In contrast to the less motivating areas of school learning addressed by other intelligent tutoring systems, trainees in the work environments we operated in were able to limit their help seeking appropriately and did not push the system to solve problems for them – their motivation was to master fault diagnosis, not simply to be labeled as being masters.

After completing a problem, trainees were able to review their performance, further access the process explorer for just-in-time

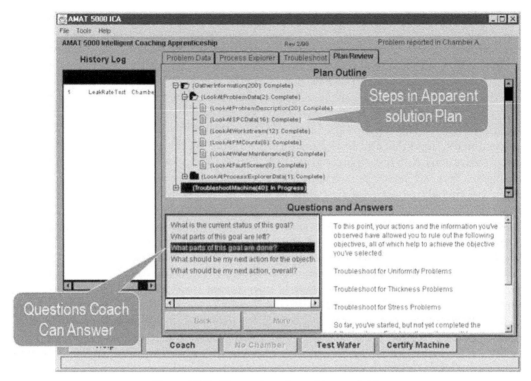

Figure 15.3. Illustration of coaching available.

basic science knowledge, and compare their performance to that of an expert system that we had developed (although such a system might, in principle, not be able to diagnose every possible system failure, it was more than adequate for the range of failures that we used in the problem sets we developed for the training we delivered). This was the reflection component of our method. Katz et al. (2003) have shown that post-problem reflection enhances learning from tutored problem solving.

We have reported evidence previously (Gott & Lesgold, 2000; Lesgold & Nahemow, 2001) that showed the value of the approach we developed. This can be measured several different ways. First, in our assessments of the first two generations of (Sherlock) tutors, we found that the tutored problem solving scheme that lasted twenty to twenty-five hours produced about the same improvement in performance on the difficult diagnostic tasks as about four more years of on-the-job experience. Also, in tests

of our last generations, we found that a half-day of training produced improvements in mean time to diagnose a problem and restore system function of about ten hours. As noted earlier, the whole cost of the final generation of our systems was recovered the first time one trainee used the acquired knowledge once.

So, the approach of learning by doing with reflection, supported by intelligent coached simulated work environments, seems quite cost-effective. Of course, while each generation paid for itself in improved performance, there was a steep learning curve for cost of development. The first generation cost about $2 million to produce, partly because the techniques were not yet developed and mostly because programming tools and hardware and software platforms were not yet advanced enough to support the approach. By the fifth generation, cost of development was about $70,000. So, in economic terms, learning by doing with reflection is extremely effective.

Lessons Learned

We learned many lessons along the way in this work, both about how to train and about how organizations adapt to new possibilities. Many of the lessons involved the inevitable negotiations that occur when an organization is paying for development of instructional systems that are novel. Because the organizations had no experience with intelligent coached learning-by-doing systems, and initially we did not have much either, it was difficult for them to do the normal monitoring of progress and evaluation of product that any prudent, well-run organization requires. Thus, they would ask for information and sometimes prescribe details of the training that did not match with our best ideas. Over the course of resolving these various impasses, we learned many important lessons.

Remain Driven by Core Learning Principles

Our sponsors had staff who were experienced in traditional training approaches. They also knew a lot about the culture in which our systems would be embedded. So, they often had ideas about how our systems should be designed. For example, when we began the first version of our system, Sherlock I, we considered a reflection option in which we showed the sequence of actions carried out by the trainee, with markings alongside the actions to show how well they matched with an expert's actions. In particular, actions clearly inconsistent with expert performance were marked with a red X, and the trainee could click on the X to see an explanation of why the action was ill advised. This was vetoed by our clients because red X's were used in their world to indicate very extreme violations of mandated procedure, and they felt that simply making an inefficient problem-solving move did not rise to the level of miscreance that the red X connoted.

We honored the client request to eliminate the red X scheme. We did this because even though the principle of post-problem reflection was a key part of our instructional design that we felt was supported by research, the specific approach of using red X's was not. More generally, we made many compromises on the look and feel of the system and related matters, so long as we did not feel we were compromising on effectiveness.

Some of these were judgment calls, of course. For example, we sometimes provided more visual fidelity of the simulation to the real work environment than we felt was instructionally necessary because it helped the client organization become comfortable with the training system. We also responded to the client's request to measure success using realistic problem-solving tests that struck us as too close to the training tasks we had developed. Our goal was far transfer, but the organizational need to assure success required us to focus mostly on near transfer. However, we found ways to meet our assessment goals without omitting goals important to our clients.

Sometimes, we discovered that something seen as extremely important by clients did not really matter. For example, trainees generally needed rather minimal hints to get through tough problems. Often, they could eventually figure out what to do but just could not manage the overall process of getting to a solution because their capabilities were automated inadequately and thus could not support the high mental load of problem solving. In such cases, it was possible to keep them on track in solving problems, and therefore getting needed practice, with minimal problem-solving help. Indeed, in our first system, more than half of the time, all that was needed was to remind the trainee of the steps he had taken so far, after which he could complete the problem solution. The actual range of coaching potentially available in our earlier generations of systems substantially exceeded the amount either needed or used. This was necessary to build client confidence. As we demonstrated the efficacy of our systems, we gained greater license to restrict the available expert advice to that which was used and useful.

Overall, we learned quickly to accommodate client desires when possible. If the client wanted something that we knew was counterproductive, we made that case. If the client wanted something that we knew did not matter, we pointed this out if we had good data to back up our claims. In the many cases where we did not think the client's desires were relevant, we politely gave our views, gave honest estimates of the minimal cost of accommodating the request, and then did so if the client wanted it still.

The Best System Does Not Always Win

By the time we were on the second of the five generations of systems we built, we had clear evidence that the approach worked and that it was worth the investment. By the time we built Generation Five, we knew that the return on investment was absolutely huge. A number of systems are extant that are based on the approach we took. For example, although developed completely independent of us and equipped with many affordances we could not have such as speech understanding, *Tactical Iraqi* (Johnson & Beal, 2005) uses the same basic approach and much more extensive artificial intelligence. Still, we have not seen businesses running to build intelligent coached apprenticeship systems. Indeed, the systems did not survive in either environment where they were introduced. There are lessons to be learned from this.

First, it is important to note that decisions to develop training systems are made by individuals in the end. A training director, in most cases, must decide to build such a system. On the one hand, the approach works well and provides a huge return on investment. On the other hand, the approach still is somewhat exotic in the training world, which consists mostly of didactic methods and primary reliance on print or Web media to deliver relatively static and unintelligent content. Further, even after five generations of development and even with a huge return on investment, our experience has been that building an intelligent coached learning environment requires a financial investment that is more than twice as great as for many standard training approaches.

So, when a training director is considering the possibility of an intelligent coached learning environment, he faces a decision to spend more than twice the usual amount on technology that is unfamiliar. Such an investment will be exceptionally visible. At the same time, it involves technology that the director may not understand, and there is plenty of evidence that software projects can, without extremely talented management, cascade out of control (e.g., Brooks, 1975). The risks taken by the decision maker may exceed his personal gains for a successful project. Indeed, I do not believe that we will see routine development of intelligent learning by doing systems until (1) the approach is extremely well documented and systematized, both in the operation and in the development of training systems; (2) a significant number of people are trained in developing such systems; and perhaps (3) tools support rapid prototyping and final development of the systems. In the interim, there appears to be room for third-party organizations to assume the risks of training development, although few start-up organizations have the funding base to take such risks.

Be Platform-Free

Another lesson we learned was that it is essential to build systems that are platform-independent and can run on any operating system. Here are some reasons why. In our last three generations, we tested and fielded our systems in multiple sites of the company. No two sites had the same versions of operating system and network SQL servers (our systems were distributed over multiple servers and a client component). We would arrive at a site not knowing what versions of operating systems were running, and we generally had only a few hours to set up. Because we were platform-independent, this was not a problem, but even the slightest deviation from reliance on standards would have assured failure in some of our sites.

Later, after we went on to somewhat different instructional systems development, we agreed to field learning systems at multiple overseas sites. The contract called for the systems to work on PCs running current versions of Windows. A week before I sent staff overseas to install these systems, we were informed that several generations of Apple computers were what we should expect. Fortunately, all of our systems were then written using Java. While it was the beginning of the Java era and we had to debug a few Java functions that were not yet reliable on Apple computers, we got that done and the systems were installed on time and worked.

I am very proud of the software development teams I have had – they were wizards. In the end, however, no amount of wizardry could have made up for being platform-free, adhering to all standards, and always testing and retesting everything we developed in every environment we encountered. We stretched the wizardry to the limit in the first generation. Our clients wanted us to use a particular videodisk system for which driver software was not being kept current by the manufacturer. In the end, we had to reverse-engineer the drivers from compiled object code and write updated ones. The moral for future work, however, is to insist on relatively standard platforms for training system delivery.

Another Way of Considering Our Approach

There is no real magic in our training approach. We simulate the few teachable moments from the hardest aspects of real work and allow students to make the most of those moments. Most of real life is routine and engaged at a level of minimal attention and effort. The occasions where hard thought is required are rare. Moreover, because the stakes are high on those occasions, novices often are kept away from the work environment so that trained experts can work quickly. But engaging novel problems, persisting until solving them, and

learning to consider the relative cost and benefit of different choices requires practice, reflection, and feedback delivered just in time. Our approach is, for complex diagnostic jobs, what simulator exercises are for pilots – a safe way to get supervised, critiqued practice that can be reflected on and learned from.

When we first introduced our approach, traditional trainers found it hard to accommodate. After all, training time for most jobs, especially the military jobs we were dealing with in our first generations of work, is tightly allocated. Every new training component must compete with the content already being delivered. At the time, for the electronics jobs we were addressing, almost all the training time was given over to basic electronics theory. So, we kept getting asked which elements of theory we would address with our systems. Although we did embed small elements of theory in our later systems (such as the process explorer [Lesgold & Nahemow, 2001]), we mostly saw our task as addressing the development of ability to solve emergent problems that could never be predicted. Von Clausewitz saw the difference, but it took a while for the training world to see it:

> Theory cannot equip the mind with formulas for solving problems, nor can it mark the narrow path on which the sole solution is supposed to lie by planting a hedge of principles on either side. But it can give the mind insight into the great mass of phenomena and of their relationships, then leave it free to rise into the higher realms of action. There the mind can use its innate talents to capacity, combining them all so as to seize on what is right and true. (von Clausewitz, 1976, pp. 577–578)

Competence in "the higher realms of action," I argue, must be practiced, and that is what the intelligent coached apprenticeship model is really all about. In an ideal world, with infinite time for training and an unlimited supply of talent, one might be able to teach all relevant theory first and then begin to prepare trainees to solve novel, emergent problems. Such ideals never exist, so it is essential that we learn how to produce high-end "fixers" who can approach problems never before seen and solve them efficiently. Some of that capability comes from practice, but the practice must include exposure to unpredictable problems.

Whereas this happens in many training environments, the training world also is influenced by the school culture. Just as in school, training often involves periods of didactic interspersed with somewhat more modest opportunities for learning by doing. It also involves tests. Whereas it is quite possible to model student knowledge from the pattern of solution on simulated problems, little training is completely devoid of tests. Students have certain expectations of tests, as do teachers. Two important expectations are that tests will be fair and that students will not cheat. However, in the school world, what is fair and what constitutes cheating have become overly constrained. Tests that students cannot cram for seem unfair. Work done in collaboration seems like cheating. But the kinds of training my colleagues and I worked on is preparation for the unfairness of life, so the tasks used for training must, by the simplistic view of both teachers and students, be "unfair." Furthermore, it is reasonable to expect that as maintenance of increasingly complex systems comes to require combinations of knowledge that span individual workers, collaboration will be a necessity, requiring training that encompasses it. Fortunately, some of these concerns are being addressed by the best of recent thinking about "twenty-first-century skills."

Football Coaching Is the Right Metaphor

I have been struck by how closely our approach to intelligent coached apprenticeship matches with how the best coaches improve their football teams. Coaching during a game is very terse, with the focus being on *how* to perform. Coaches call plays and briefly note actions that require reflection. But the reflection does not happen during the game. Small amounts may occur during halftime, but a coach never calls a timeout to walk players through a major learning exercise. Players learn to play football largely by actually playing the game, with all its difficulties. There is a little part training, such as kickers practicing punts on the sidelines, but even that is tied to actual game participation. The real task motivates any part-skill practice, and the real task comes first.

At the same time, football at its highest professional level also includes substantial reflection. Monday morning film review sessions are extensive. Powerful scene-indexing systems are used to gather multiple examples of a performance detail that needs to be refined. If there is a hole in the defensive line, teams and coaches will review play after play to identify how the hole arises and how it might be filled. Substantial investments are made in software to assemble the right mix of reminders of experience for review, reflection, and coaching. Alternative approaches to the situations being reviewed are discussed, and decisions are made about how to practice certain plays to improve performance for the next game.

This idea that during performances coaching should be terse and focused on what to do in the immediate context while post-performance reflection can be more extensive and can include consideration of why one action or plan might be better than another seems to fit with the way trainees prefer to learn, too. Katz, Allbritton, and Connelly (2003) have examined trainee preferences in tasks like those used in our intelligent coached apprenticeship systems and have found that trainees prefer "how to" information while working on a problem and "why" information after they have finished and are in a reflective mode.

The scheme of terse "how to" coaching during performance with extended "why" explanations during reflection also is consistent with emerging ideas about the role of cognitive load during learning and performance (cf. van Merriënboer & Sweller, 2005). During performances at the limits of one's ability (or beyond), there is no cognitive capacity left to handle any thinking beyond that needed to move forward with the performance. Hence, explanations either will not be processed or will cause the performance to deteriorate further. Neither outcome is productive or satisfying. So, any explanation and effort toward conceptual understanding needs to wait till the performance is completed.

The problem, of course, is that the situation that might prompt explanation or reflection has passed once the problem is completed, so there is need to restore the context that can support the explanation. This is why forms of replay are so important during post-problem reflection. At various times in the five generations of tutors we built, we used slightly different devices to restore a context for reflection. The simplest approach was simply to list the actions taken by the trainee and then make expert advice available when any step in the list was clicked on.

A more complex scheme that proved helpful was to list the trainee's steps alongside an expert's steps (generated by our expert model) and make commentary available about both. In the latest generations of our systems, we also added access to the process explorer. This allowed the trainee to get comments on what he/she had done during problem solution, compare to an expert's actions, get comments and justifications of any expert step, and then turn to the process explorer for an explanation of the underlying science that was relevant. Because the situation representations for any of these efforts were maintained in the post-problem displays, and because the trainee could access any of the information sources in any order as desired, cognitive load was managed effectively, and, we believe, opportunities for learning were relatively optimal.

Experts and System Designers Also "Learn by Teaching"

Especially in our later work on training the repair of chip-making machines, we were training in an area where expertise was not completely developed. These machines are of recent vintage, and as each new generation of chip fabrication plant is built, new versions of the machines are developed for it. Several times in the evolution of computer chips, the technology of fabrication has had to change substantially to achieve smaller components. As a result, it has not been possible to have the long period of practice and learning that traditionally characterizes expertise.

This exposed an important fact about the value of different training approaches. Put simply, expert knowledge of how to repair the chip-making machines was imperfect. We started our expert model-building efforts by doing the standard interviews with experts (see the PARI method described in Gott & Lesgold, 2000). However, as we built the expert model (cf. Lesgold & Nahemow, 2001), my colleague Martin Nahemow, a manufacturing plasma physicist with patents related to the processes used by the chip-making machines, noticed that some of the expert rules were nonoptimal. We ended up modifying the expert model to provide better explanations and to propose more optimal solutions to the problems posed in our simulations.

This situation, in which expertise is fragmentary and incomplete, is not uncommon in our rapidly changing world. The experts in the plant, after all, tended to have two to four years of tertiary education plus a lot of experience with chip-making equipment. They also had attended classes conducted by the manufacturers of the equipment. It could well be that no one person had all the relevant knowledge for optimal performance. The manufacturer knew how the system was designed and how it worked, and had some amount of experience with equipment failures, especially early in the equipment life cycle. The technician experts dealt with the equipment every day and had built up, through "combat experience," a lot of practical knowledge that was extremely useful.

What happened when we built the expert model was that we started with the rules extracted from performances and think-alouds of the top technicians and then massaged the rule set based on Nahemow's expertise in applying the various relevant sciences to the building of devices. We could have operated on a broader scale, negotiating the knowledge of technicians and of the designers and manufacturers of the equipment, but instead we did our own quick merger of Nahemow's knowledge with that of the most experienced technicians. The result was that the expert model, and hence the coaching in the system, was a bit better than that of the current working experts. Put another way, it is possible for experts to learn by building tutors that capture their expertise, especially if the expertise is newly developed and anchored in practice rather than design.

One could argue that had we worked with the equipment designers rather than the technicians, we would have achieved an optimal expert model right away, without having to tap Nahemow's wisdom. I believe this to be unlikely. Modern equipment is so complex that it often is impossible to predict entirely how it will fail after extended use. Designers can develop tests for individual components and optimal procedures for component replacement, but emergent problems will, over time, be less likely to be the ones predicted by the designers, even when they use sophisticated schemes to predict how systems eventually will fail (as happens, for example, in the aircraft industry). It may well be that developing an expert model for training technicians to handle difficult, unpredictable, emergent failures is a good way to crystalize knowledge that might be distributed across multiple sources: designers, manufacturers, operators, and maintenance technicians.

What to Teach

Which bodies of knowledge/expertise are best conveyed with an intelligent coached apprenticeship system? Such systems, even though economically feasible, still are somewhat costly. Even with the approach just described, one might argue that the real learning conveyed by our systems was not simply acquisition of the rules in the expert model. In reality, we were preparing technicians for situations that go beyond any feasible set of rules. Expert models are, mostly, anchored in models of the systems on which the expertise rests. System failures in sophisticated and well-designed systems come from situations outside those models. For example, heat in one component might melt insulation on a cable that is part of a different subsystem, prompting a short circuit that creates a connection between two subsystems that have no logical connection. Unless this specific problem reflects an inherent design fault, there will be no rule for it. If the cable was removed and then improperly replaced while doing a previous repair, there likely is no rule to detect this problem unless improper installation of that particular cable is a recurrent occurrence.

We built our systems believing that complex systems that fail do so relatively uniquely, just as Tolstoy (in *Anna Karenina*) observed that "happy families are all alike; every unhappy family is unhappy in its own way." I suggest that if you can model a body of expertise completely and track it perfectly, a machine can do it, so there is no need to invest in an intelligent training system. Rather, intelligent coached apprenticeship must drive students beyond that which we can track perfectly. Far transfer has to be the goal. For this reason, our evaluations of our tutors (Gott & Lesgold, 2000; Lesgold & Nahemow, 2001) focused on far transfer. It also is likely that our approach of coached practice followed by reflection had the effect of producing practice focused specifically on going beyond one's knowledge while remaining systematic in ways constrained by that knowledge.

The Cost of Starting Too Soon

In retrospect, we probably started our efforts too soon. Certainly in the mid-1980s, the barriers to good system development were many. Programming was too hard, hardware too impoverished, and the results too idiosyncratic. Initially, we did not have the ability to use databases that could be edited by nonprogrammers. Often, we had to use faster heuristics that were somewhat superficial, especially in the early years of the work. At the same time, the level of difficulty in building the first systems had some positive effects, too. We were forced to spend a lot of time doing careful reflective work, because designs were harder to change on the fly. Furthermore, our limited student-modeling capability led us to build systems that relied more on the intelligence of the trainee to get the right information at the right time. Our strategy of providing a wealth of coaching resources and leaving to the trainee much of the choice of which one to use and when to use it was quite successful for the highly motivated technicians with whom we worked. With students who are more reluctant to try out different learning tools, to explore beyond a problem's solution, or to remain motivated through extended practice, refined student modeling may be more important.

Interface

We invested a lot of effort in interface development, partly because there were few tools for building good interfaces and partly because we set as our goal that no instruction manual should be needed to use our tutors (we came pretty close to meeting that goal, although brief familiarization sessions proved at least socially helpful).[1]

One interface feature that we developed leveraged the fact that system diagrams, which were a primary means of communication with the trainee, are relatively hierarchical. Main systems could be captured as computational objects that had subsystems nested inside of them. Subsystems in turn had smaller assemblies nested in their objects. The basic idea, quite standard in

developing complex displays, is that each level of object had a procedure for responding to a command to display itself. We added one small twist to this standard approach. Each object's capability for drawing itself was parameterized to depend on how important that object was at the instant in the course of problem solution at which it was to be displayed. Each object also had a subprocedure for optimizing how much detail it displayed depending on how much screen space it was allocated. So, when an object represented something an expert would be thinking about in the current context, it took more of the total display space and then asked its components to draw themselves within the space allocated. If an object represented an area of the system that would not be on the expert's mind at that instant, it took less space and often did not even display its individual components.

This produced displays that were highly tailored to the situation at hand and that focused attention on areas of the system that merited it. There are two ideas embedded in this approach that are worth noting. First, it is possible to scaffold performance through subtle variations in displays. Such scaffolding is implicit, because the trainee is never told that the display might be highlighting an area worth examining, and in reality, the sense of the trainee generally was that the displays did not have that purpose. Second, this approach represents an example of an adaptive technique one might call adaptive hyperdisplay. Each object displayed on the screen could be clicked on and "opened" if it had components that were not displayed initially. So, the whole system diagram was always accessible to the trainee, but it just happened that there was more detail shown in areas that an expert might be focused on. As students come to do more online searching for information, we are seeing this kind of approach used more frequently, and with more sophisticated algorithms to decide what to display first.

Modeling, Mining, and Data Collection

As our systems were refined, we built in progressively more logging of trainee activity. What we could not do back then was to

---

[1] This is no small issue. When we first began, we assigned the task of developing an introduction to the tutor for trainees to an assistant who was well trained in standard instructional design. We ended up not using that introduction because we felt that the training to use the system should be at least an order of magnitude shorter than the time that would be spent learning on the system afterward.

extensively model that activity in real time. Even today, there are more potential analyses that might become evident after a tutor is deployed than are apparent at the time it is developed. One important use of increased data logging and automatic data reduction and interpretation is to capture, within a training system, the seeds for its successor. If I were starting a tutor project today, I would certainly include as much data logging as possible and find ways to get the data into a permanent repository. Increasingly, it will turn out that intelligent coached apprenticeship systems can be developed in part by trying out approaches on already-captured data from previous systems. In this regard, the work of the Pittsburgh Science of Learning Center (http://www.learnlab.org) is especially noteworthy. They are already supporting studies that use as data the performance information logged by tutors and other instructional systems already in use.

Implications for the Future

I end with a few suggestions for future work. Although there are counterarguments to this approach, I do think we did some good by taking on the intelligent tutoring task a bit early. However, that is only because we were continually willing to scrap portions of our effort and redesign them. The danger in taking on a problem before it is ripe for solution is that one becomes wed to the approximations and heuristics used to overcome computational inadequacy. The antidote to this danger is to see research as partly the creative destruction of suboptimal past approaches. That is sometimes difficult for an individual. It is extremely difficult for organizations.

Each of the five generations of systems we built was seen by the sponsoring organization as a substantial investment in a technology they hoped to keep reusing for other training problems. Even though we tried to be honest in portraying the work as an exploration, as projects went through multiple layers of bureaucracy, they became represented increasingly as being efforts to produce a body of reusable technology. Especially in the early generations, this impeded the organizational ability to use the results of the work. After all, they had just, in their view, bought a technology, and now they were being told that it was not quite right and that parts of the approach would need to be reinvented for future use. A small number of leaders within the sponsoring organization understood that, but it was harder for purchasing offices and managers further removed from the projects to understand.

Success itself also is hard for an organization to absorb. At the beginning of our work, sponsors welcomed large effects because they justified the investment. As we got better at tutor development, however, the effects were visibly large enough that they were harder to believe. One small example illustrates this. Our last-generation system produced effects that were economically huge. People trained on the system often took ten hours less to repair a machine than those not so trained. That meant that factories using the system to train their technicians would recover the entire cost of training if even one trainee used the trained knowledge to restore a manufacturing line.

However, the effect was so large as to be hard to believe. Studies were even conducted of the net profit of a plant before and after the training was administered. There were improvements detected, but even these were hard to believe. Numerous accounts were offered for why the profitability improvement could have come from other changes in the factory environment over the same time period.

None of this is unreasonable. It is essential to understand how real any training effect is – in both knowledge terms and utility terms such as profitability. The company was doing exactly what it should do – challenge every claim. I suspect, however, that our culturally shared sense of the pace and effectiveness of training will continue for a while to have trouble accommodating the belief that coached learning by doing with reflection really can work.

Even when our society accepts the power of coached learning in adaptive simulated environments, other barriers to use will remain. To be accepted, a training regimen must fit into an existing culture. In the case of training, this means fitting two cultures. The approach must become comfortable to training departments and schools, or these organizations will resist it. Also, the approach must be assimilated into the broader organizational culture and even society at large. Otherwise, effectiveness will not trump the belief that reading manuals is enough or that simulations can never substitute for reality.

We see this today in school systems, especially in cities. Computer support for learning is affordable if one builds a school system from scratch, but a mesh of habits, beliefs, union contracts, and organizational design makes use of the accumulated results of twenty-five years of system developments almost impossible. That will not continue permanently, but it remains unclear whether existing organizations will soon make use of adaptive learning environments that include rich simulations or whether new organizations will need to arise to take advantage of the tools that have been and are being built.

References

Brooks, Jr., F. P. (1975). *The mythical man-month: Essays on software engineering*. Boston: Addison-Wesley.

von Clausewitz, C. (1976). *On War*. Michael Howard and Peter Paret (Eds. & Trans.). Princeton, NJ: Princeton University Press.

Gott, S. P., & Lesgold, A. M. (2000). Competence in the workplace: How cognitive performance models and situated instruction can accelerate skill acquisition. In R. Glaser (Ed.), *Advances in instructional psychology* (pp. 239–327). Hillsdale, NJ: Erlbaum.

Johnson, W. L., & Beal, C. (2005). Iterative evaluation of a large-scale intelligent game for language learning. In C. Looi, G. McCalla, B. Bredeweg, & J. Breuker (Eds.), *Artificial intelligence in education: Supporting learning through intelligent and socially informed technology* (pp. 290–297). Amsterdam: IOS Press.

Katz, S., Allbritton, D., & Connelly, J. (2003). Going beyond the problem given: How human tutors use post-solution discussions to support transfer. *International Journal of Artificial Intelligence in Education, 13*(1), 79–116.

Lesgold, A., & Nahemow, M. (2001). Tools to assist learning by doing: Achieving and assessing efficient technology for learning. In D. Klahr & S. Carver (Eds.), *Cognition and instruction: Twenty-five years of progress* (pp. 307–346). Mahwah, NJ: Erlbaum.

van Merriënboer, J. J. G., & Sweller, J. (2005). Cognitive load theory and complex learning: Recent developments and future directions. *Educational Psychology Review, 17*(2), 147–177.

Schön, D. (1983). *The reflective practitioner*. New York: Basic Books.

CHAPTER 16

A Model-Driven Instructional Strategy

The Benchmarked Experiential System for Training (BEST)

Georgiy Levchuk, Wayne Shebilske, and Jared Freeman

Introduction

The military, the aviation industry, and other commercial enterprises increasingly use simulations to train and maintain skills. Such "experiential training" (c.f., Ness, Tepe, & Ritzer, 2004; Silberman, 2007) deeply engages learners with realistic environments, technologies, and often with the teammates with which they must execute real-world missions.

However, these simulations are not training systems in a formal sense. The environments generally are not imbued with the capability to measure human performance or the instructional intelligence to improve it (Freeman, MacMillan, Haimson, Weil, Stacy, & Diedrich, 2006) through the selection of feedback (cf. Shebilske, Gildea, Freeman, & Levchuk, 2009) or training scenarios (addressed in this chapter). It is the trainees and trainers who exercise instructional strategy in these simulations. Trainees are notoriously poor instructional strategists, however. They often invest less time on task than is optimal, exercise poor learning strategies, and engage in other undesirable learning practices (Steinberg, 1989; Williams, 1993).

Significant advances have been made in developing Intelligent Tutoring Systems (ITS), which automate the application of instructional strategy. ITS designed around systematic application of instructional strategies (e.g., Chi & VanLehn's [2007] focus on principles and dynamic scaffolding) or computational models of human cognition and learning have improved learning by individuals in well-defined domains. For example, the LISP programming tutor (Anderson, Conrad, & Corbett, 1989) reduced training time by 30 percent and increased scores by 43 percent relative to a control group, with a particularly strong effect for the poorest students. There is little literature, however, that tests methods of scaling ITS student models up from individual instruction to team training, and little concerning their application in ill-defined domains – those domains in which there is disagreement over solution methods and solutions for a given problem.

Scaling up an ITS to teams is a problem because the literature is scant and not altogether helpful with respect to modeling instructional strategy for team training. Most formal models used for team training are, ironically, models of individual performers that serve as simulated teammates and/or instructor to a single trainee (c.f., Eliot & Wolf, 1995; Freeman, 2002; Freeman, Haimson, Diedrich, & Paley, 2005; Miller, Yin, Volz, Ioerger, & Yen, 2000; Rickel & Johnson, 1999). Because these models generally represent domain experts, not instructional experts, their ability to enforce sound instructional strategy is limited.

Ill-defined domains, likewise, are a little-explored frontier for ITS. The literature includes reports of marked success in automated tutoring of algebra (Anderson, Douglass, & Qin, 2004), LISP (Anderson et al., 1989), and probability and physics (Chi & VanLehn, 2008). Some systems are designed to train people to diagnose unique failures in seemingly well-defined domains such as electronics (Lesgold, Lajoie, Bunzo, & Eggan, 1992). Recent work explores performance and learning in complex domains, such as those that can be characterized as dynamical systems (Dutt & Gonzalez, 2008). However, there is scant literature concerning the application of ITS with strong didactic models to ill-defined domains, including military mission planning and execution.

We are attempting to automate the management of instructional strategy in simulation-based team training within ill-defined domains such as military command and control. To accomplish this, we are developing and empirically testing the effects of (1) models that assess team performance in these domains, and (2) models that adapt instructional strategy to the team on the basis of these assessments. We call this the Benchmarked Experiential System for Training (BEST).

To assess performance, we have applied optimization techniques that generate benchmarks against which to evaluate team performance, as well as animated feedback based on these benchmarks. This model-based approach to benchmarking and feedback reliably increases learning, holding learning trials constant (Shebilske, Gildea, Freeman, & Levchuk, 2009), and it is arguably more efficient than engaging domain experts in developing solutions to large numbers of scenarios. To adapt instructional strategy, we have extended Atkinson's (1972) application of optimal control theory to sequence instructional experiences. This chapter focuses on the sequencing model and its effects in two experiments.

A POMDP Model of Instructional Strategy

BEST selects, from a large and structured library of scenarios, the scenario that is most likely to increase team expertise given the team's performance in the previous scenario. In practice, this optimal scenario-sequencing policy is expressed in a simple lookup table that specifies the next scenario to administer given any plausible combination of a prior scenario and a performance score. We generate this table by applying the modeling technique described earlier to historical data or expert estimates of selected parameters. Generating the table is computationally intensive, and so it is created before training is delivered. During training, instructors can navigate the table rapidly to select a scenario (Figure 16.1a); software can do so instantaneously. The intended effect of this customized, optimized scenario sequencing is to increase the level of expertise students achieve in a fixed period of training, or to accelerate progress to a given level of expertise. We describe the optimization strategy here, then turn to an empirical test of its effects.

The problem of sequencing instructional experiences has all the elements of planning under uncertainty: The system has observables, hidden dynamics, and control measures that need to be planned. The true state of trainee knowledge and skill cannot be directly observed, but only estimated from measures of process and outcome. The effect of a training experience on expertise cannot be reliably predicted; it, too, is probabilistic. Finally, the challenge at hand is to select training events that produce the fastest or

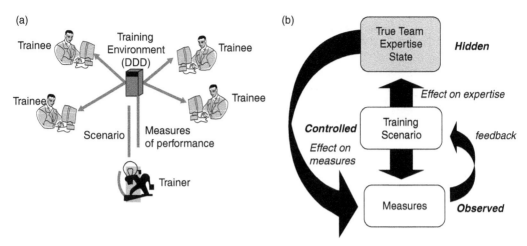

Figure 16.1. The problem of training and conceptual POMDP solution.

largest change in expertise. To represent and solve this complex problem systematically and reliably, we invoke a computational modeling strategy.

To model the evolution of team expertise, we assume that the space of team expertise can be represented using a finite-state machine; that is, we discretize expertise state into a finite set of team expertise states. This is a simplifying assumption, but it enables us to study complex temporal expertise dynamics and develop efficient system control strategies.

To develop optimal instructional strategy for navigating this space, we utilize the Partially Observable Markov Decision Processes (POMDP; Kaelbling, Littman, & Cassandra, 1998; see a tutorial at http://www.cs.brown.edu/research/ai/pomdp/tutorial/index.html; see Figure 16.1). The POMDP is well suited to decision-theoretic planning under uncertainty. It has several advantages.

First, the POMDP formulation captures the dynamic nature of team and individual skills via a Markov decision process graph. Within the graph, a single finite discrete variable indexes the current team expertise state, and external actions control expertise changes. For example, the state of team's expertise may represent the proficiency of each team member at their tasks (such as accurately prioritizing enemy targets) and their ability to collaborate (e.g., efficiently communicate with other team members). The state changes approximate the dynamics of the team expertise when the model applies a specific control action to a team. In our context, a control action corresponds to selecting a training scenario. Expertise changes are described by a table of transition probabilities that statistically represent the uncertain effect on expertise of selecting a specific training scenario for a team.

Second, POMDP formulation allows us to make training decisions under partial observability of the true state of team expertise. Although observations about team and individual performance influence our belief about achieved team skills, the actual ("true") state of skills is not observable. Thus, we can only estimate the expertise state, interpreting it as "partially observable."

Third, the POMDP formulation allows our model to treat scenario selection as both the control mechanism to change the skills and the testing mechanisms to obtain more knowledge of the true state of team expertise.

More formally, the POMDP model is described using the following variables:

- a finite set of states, S;
- a finite set of control actions, A;
- a finite set of observations, Z;
- a state transition function, $\tau: S \times A \to \Pi(S)$, where $\Pi(\cdot)$ is the probability distribution over some finite set;

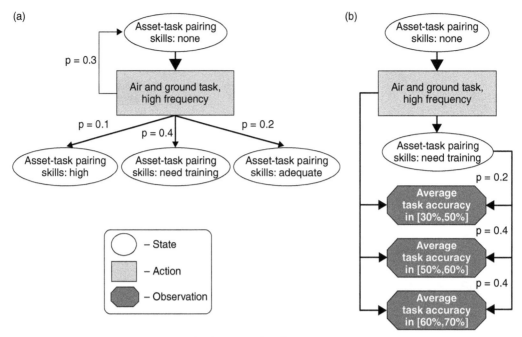

Figure 16.2. An example of POMDP structure.

- an observation function, $o: S \times A \to \Pi(Z)$; and
- an immediate reward function, $r: S \times A \to R$.

In the present application, the set S represents all possible states of team expertise. The team can be in only one state at a given time. The set A represents all of the available training/testing scenarios. The set Z consists of all possible observations about trainees, that is, all possible values of normalized performance and process measures. The state transition function τ models the uncertainty in the evolution of expertise states (learning), while the observation function o relates the observed measures to the true underlying expertise state and scenario selection actions. The immediate utility of performing a control action in each of the true states of the environment is given by the immediate reward function r, which can incorporate a cost of training and a benefit of attaining expertise.

Thus, the dynamics of team expertise are represented in a state-action model (see Figure 16.2a) equivalent to Markov Decision Process (MDP) graph, where the

instructional actions change the team expertise with some uncertainty. The state-action model is uniquely described with a set of team expertise states S, a set of selectable training scenarios A, and state transition function τ. That is, if $S = \{s_1, s_2, ..., s_N\}$ and $A = \{a_1, a_2, ..., a_M\}$, then transition function $\tau: S \times A \to \Pi(S)$ defines the probability $\tau(s_i, a_k, s_j) = \Pr\{s_j | s_i, a_k\}$ that team expertise will change to state s_j if scenario instruction a_k is applied when team expertise is in state s_i.

1. *The state-action model* illustrates how the controlled instructions of the trainer can affect the dynamics of the team expertise. For example, if the team does not have any skills in pairing assets (such as weapons) to tasks (such as enemy targets), then playing a mission scenario containing air and ground task classes with high appearance frequency would have 30 percent probability of not achieving any effects, 10 percent probability of achieving high level of skills, 40 percent probability of acquiring some skills for which further training is required, and 20 percent probability that adequate skills are achieved.

2. *The observation model* illustrates an example of how observations from the *average task accuracy* measure are related to the selection of scenarios (represented as task classes and task frequencies) and the true state of expertise resulting from executing a new scenario. For example, there is a 40 percent probability that average task accuracy will range from 60 percent to 70 percent, given that the new scenario contained air and ground task classes with high appearance frequency and that the team achieves some asset-task pairing skills that require training.

The true states that team expertise takes over time (i.e., states of MDP) are not known to the trainer or the instructional model. They obtain only partial observations about current state of expertise in the form of performance and/or process measures. The observation-state relationships are captured using an observation model (see Figure 16.2b) described by the state set, action set, and observation function o. That is, if the set of measure outcomes is $Z = \{z_1, z_2, ..., z_L\}$, then an observation function defines the probability $\Pr\{z_j | s_i, a_k\}$ that a normalized performance/process measure outcome z_j is obtained when instruction action a_k (a scenario) is applied and team expertise transitions to state s_i. (In another formulation, this probability reflects the dependence of measures on only the true expertise state, that is, the probability $\Pr\{z_j | s_i\}$.)

The training policy should produce substantial learning while minimizing the cost of training sessions. The cost and reward can be quantified using the scoring of team's skills, as we have done in the present research, and other factors such as the duration of training or complexity of scenario development and training session preparation. However, because the true states of expertise of the team are not known, we cannot compute precise cost-reward measure of the training policy. Instead, we use an objective of expected cost-reward measure, called *expected utility*, which incorporates the beliefs about state of expertise.

The POMDP solution objective is to derive a control policy, an instructional strategy that achieves the greatest amount of expected utility (expected reward of training) over some number of decision steps (training events). This control policy can be expressed as a policy graph, where nodes are beliefs about true state of team's expertise, each such node contains a training scenario to be executed, and links correspond to probabilities of moving to a new belief state.

If the states of expertise were observable, this policy could be specified as a training action to be performed at the currently attained state of expertise s. The problem of finding the team training policy then simplifies to a Markov Decision Process (MDP). The MDP solution is significantly easier to obtain than a POMDP solution, with algorithms running in time square of state space size time per iteration or cube of state space size for a closed-form solution (Bellman, 1957).

In case of partial observability, the intelligent tutoring system (ITS) at time $t + 1$ does not know the current state $s[t+1]$ of the team's expertise/knowledge. Instead, the ITS has an initial belief about the expertise state (potentially from prior assessments), the history of observations $z^{t+1} = \{z[1], z[2], ..., z[t+1]\}$, and ITS's own actions $a^t = \{a[1], a[2], ..., a[t]\}$. The ITS can act optimally on this information by conditioning the training policy on its current belief about the state of the team expertise/ knowledge at every time step. The belief state at time t is represented as a vector of probabilities $b[t] = (b_1[t], b_2[t], ..., b_N[t])$, where $b_i[t]$ is equal to the probability that state of the team's knowledge is s_i at time $t \left(\sum_{i=1}^{N} b_i[t] = 1 \right)$.

These beliefs are probability distributions over the states $i \in S$ and are sufficient statistics to act optimally. The POMDP-based scenario training policy is then defined on the belief state, so that we specify the training scenario $\pi(b) \in A$ to be performed at belief state b.

Optimal algorithms for POMDP are significantly more computationally complex than the solutions for MDP formulation, and the problem of finding optimal policies is PSPACE-complete (Papadimitriou & Tsitsiklis, 1987). There exist two main classes of approximate algorithms for POMDP: value-function methods that seek to approximate the value of belief states – probability distributions over the environment states (Hauskrecht, 2000); and policy-based methods that search for a good policy within some restricted class of policies.

Due to the large size of the belief state space, the optimal policy to maximize the objective function cannot be derived using conventional means. Currently, problems of a few hundred states are at the limits of tractability for optimal POMDP algorithms (Smith & Simmons, 2004). This is because most exact algorithms for general POMDPs use a form of dynamic programming, which has a computational explosion in the belief state space (Cassandra, Littman, & Zhang, 1997). Still, these algorithms provide a useful finding that a value function can be given by a piecewise linear and convex representation and transformed into a new such function iteratively over time. And while the set of belief states is infinite, the structure of the POMDP problem allows efficient clustering of all beliefs into a limited set of states.

Several algorithms that use dynamic-programming (DP) updates of the value function have been developed, such as one pass (Sondik, 1971), exhaustive enumeration (Monahan, 1982), linear support (Cheng, 1988), and witness. Out of these algorithms, the witness algorithm has been shown to have superior performance. Combining the benefits of Monahan's enumeration and witness algorithms, a more superior optimal algorithm called incremental pruning has been developed in Zhang and Liu (1996) and enhanced in Cassandra, Littman, and Zhang (1997).

To overcome the solution complexity of optimal algorithms, efficient approximate solutions to POMDP have been proposed. These algorithms use replicated Q-learning or linear Q-learning to update the belief

state-action vectors during the search in belief state.

Another approximate technique is a Heuristic Search Value Iteration (HSVI) algorithm proposed by Smith and Simmons (2004). This is an anytime algorithm that returns an approximate policy and a provable bound on its error with respect to optimal policy. HSVI combines two well-known techniques: attention-focusing search heuristics and piecewise linear convex representations of the value function. On some of the benchmarking problems, HSVI displayed higher than 100-time improvement in solution time compared to state of the art POMDP value iteration algorithms (Smith & Simmons, 2004). In addition, HSVI was able to solve problems ten times larger than those reported previously.

Recently, researchers have examined new methods that restrict the set of states the POMDP policy solution can have (Aberdeen & Baxter, 2002; Poupart, Ortiz, & Boutilier, 2001; Sutton et al., 2000). One such solution using an internal-state policy-gradient algorithm (Aberdeen, 2003) was shown to solve the problem with tens of thousands of possible environment states in reasonable time (e.g., thirty minutes). (Recall that the BEST POMDP solution is computed offline once for all students in advance of training; thus the time to compute a solution does not influence training.) This algorithm uses the concept of finite-state stochastic controller (FSSC), which provides efficient near-optimal policy identification and model training by trading off the optimality with complexity and adapting the solution to new evidence over time. FSSC solution is attractive because the number of its internal states can be significantly smaller than the number of possible states of team expertise or state beliefs, and new states can be added and old deleted as new evidence is received. As the internal states start describing the beliefs about the team expertise and the transition probabilities become deterministic, the FSSC approaches the optimal solution to POMDP problem.

The preceding algorithms describe the main features of POMDP solution approaches. Optimal algorithms can only be applied to solve small-scale POMDP problems, and approximate iterative solutions must be used for larger-scale situations. In our research, we experimented with small spaces of eleven expertise states, and therefore used the optimal value iteration solutions. However, we envision a need to move to approximate solutions for real-world applications. The recent advances in heuristic value iteration, stochastic controller models, and error-bounding state space reduction methods promise to achieve needed trade-offs between optimality and complexity of POMDP modeling.

Experimental Validation

Testing the Application of a POMDP to Team Training

We conducted two, similar experiments to compare a control condition to the POMDP adaptive training system. In the control condition, the experimenters applied a single, predetermined sequence of scenarios. In the POMDP condition, the experimenters assessed team performance and then used that assessment and the scenario identity to select the next scenario from a simple table generated by the POMDP solver. In each experiment, a single team used the POMDP instructional strategy to learn one new experience and the control instructional strategy to learn another new experience. The two experiments counterbalanced the order of the two instructional strategies.

The experiments trained teams to execute the tasks of an Air Force Dynamic Targeting Cell (DTC). The role of the DTC is to rapidly adjust air operations to strike time-sensitive targets (TSTs), which are unexpected hazards (threats) and opportunities (targets) that may demand immediate action. These actions should minimally disrupt the current mission plan for prosecuting other targets and defending against other threats (cf. Shebilske et al., 2009).

Pilot studies suggested to us that in this domain, whole-task training would be less effective than hierarchical part-task training,

which is one of a few part-task training sequences that have afforded an advantage over whole-task training (Fredericksen & White, 1989). Accordingly, the training scenarios systematically and independently vary the number of threats and targets to develop student skill at each part of their task: defense and offense. The control condition and adaptive POMDP condition drew on the same library of scenarios.

To increase the relevance of this work to field training and operations, the experiment simulated (1) experienced DTC teams (2) training for new experiences in which a) the current enemy escalated or changed tactics, b) new enemies arose, and c) enemies were confronted in different contexts (Shebilske et al., 2009). To replicate experienced DTC teams, we used a paradigm in which two teams participated for many hours to learn many more complex scenarios. These teams attained the proficiency of a moderately or highly skilled operational DTC, in the judgment of scientists who had performed the task analysis of DTC teams in operational settings and of our simulated team. We focused on training for new experiences because this is the emphasis of most operational training. Such training is analogous to professional football players training each week for their next opponent (Corrington & Shebilske, 1995).

We started developing our POMDP model after we had about fifty hours of data on participants in Experiment 1, who were trained to perform like DTC teams, and after developing a system to enable experts to rate trainee performance, as described by Shebilske et al. (2009). This empirical foundation was not enough to estimate parameters for the POMDP model from historical data alone, but it was enough to build expert judgments about parameters, thus: When reviewing the historical assessments from each training scenario (a1), the experts thought of their ratings as observations (o1) at the end of the scenario, which reflected the state of expertise (s2) the team obtained while performing the current scenario. The experts then estimated the Observation Probability (Pr {o1 | s2, a1}) and Transition

Probabilities (P {s2 | s1, a1}), which reflect how the team expertise changes from one state to another when the team performs a current scenario.

The experts did not have data for all possible combinations of transitions from one difficulty level to another, but they noticed a tendency that enabled them to estimate by extrapolation. The tendency concerned the probability of transitioning from a lower state to a higher state as a function of the combination of TSTs with enemy defenses (such as Surface-to-Air Missiles), which constitute threats to our strike force. Having a low number of TSTs or Threats raised the probability of better performance on a component task in the short run, but in the long run, having a medium to high number increased overall performance as reflected by ratings on the most comprehensive of our training objectives: to coordinate attack assets. The experts also noticed another tendency that guided their estimations of the transition probability (P) for a team that was given a scenario (a1) that had a difficulty of medium to high TST/ threat combinations. They found high variability in the probability that a team that was given such a scenario would advance from one state of expertise (s1) to a more advanced state of expertise (s2) in a single performance of the scenario. The estimated advancement included assessment of the team's state of expertise with respect to (1) recognizing TSTs, (2) taking into account other threats, and (3) submitting a plan to prosecute TST while disrupting other mission priorities minimally. The expert's final estimates for this transition probability (P {s2 | s1, a1}) included estimates of states of expertise before and after the scenario. The POMDP model was thus able to hold a team at the same scenario difficulty level when their state had not changed as a result of performance on the current scenario, or to advance the team to a higher scenario difficulty level when their measured expertise state had improved.

The POMDP model assigned scenarios that were challenging but achievable. That is, the POMDP model kept training in the team's zone of proximal development (Vygotsky, 1978). The hierarchical part-task training strategy used in the control condition also was designed to keep the trainees in their proximal zone. However, it used a more conservative predetermined sequence as shown in Figure 16.3. The triangles in the figure show that, for both experiments, the hierarchical part-task control strategy gradually increased the number of TSTs and then increased the other Threats that were present in the mission. The logic was that a DTC team must learn to detect TSTs before it can design strike packages that take into account the TST in the context of the other Threats. Accordingly, detecting TSTs is a less advanced skill in the hierarchy. This is consistent with the logic of the hierarchical part-task strategy, which conservatively keeps challenges low for more advanced skills in the hierarchy until a skill less advanced in the hierarchy is learned well. Then it holds the challenges for the less advanced skill at a consistently high level and gradually increases the challenge for the more advanced skill. In contrast, circles in the figure show that the POMDP training strategy increased TSTs and Threats less conservatively and more efficiently by changing both before the less advanced TST skill had reached its highest level. Specifically, the control strategy and the POMDP strategy started with the same TST/Threat combination and ended with same TST/Threat combination, but the POMDP strategy took the more direct diagonal path. Because the POMDP was not predetermined, it was able to use inferred state of expertise before and after each scenario to advance the challenge of both TSTs and Threats or to hold the participants at the same challenge level of TSTs and Threats. The circles that overlap represent the same combination of TSTs and Threats. Specifically, in Experiment 1, the team was held for two scenarios of ten TSTs and thirty-five Threats, for two scenarios of eleven TSTs and forty Threats, and for two scenarios of twelve TSTs and forty-five Threats. In Experiment 2, the POMDP diagonal path looks similar. A critical difference, however, is where the POMDP model told the experimenters to hold the team or to advance them. Specifically, the team

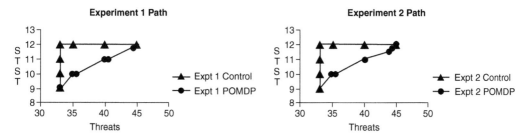

Figure 16.3. Training sequences for control and POMDP conditions.

was held for two scenarios at ten TSTs and thirty-five Threats and for three scenarios at twelve TSTs and forty-five threats. We hypothesized that the POMDP training path would be more effective than the control hierarchical part-task training path.

We tested this hypothesis in two single-team experiments. The team in Experiment 1 was 7 undergraduate college students (2 women and 5 men, mean age = 22.6 years), who were paid $7.25 per hour for 117 hours each. The team in Experiment 2 was 7 undergraduate college students (2 women and 5 men, mean age = 20 years), who were paid $7.25 per hour for 45 hours each. The participation in both experiments was part of responsibilities as research assistants, but teams did not know the purpose of the experiment until they had completed the research. Shebilske et al. (2009) describe the work stations and Aptima's Dynamic Distributed Decision-making (DDD, see http://www.aptima.com) synthetic task environment used to simulate Air Force Intelligence, Surveillance, and Reconnaissance (ISR) and the DTC task. The dependant variable was the quality of the proposed strike package for each TST, which was determined by expert ratings of the strike package. The ratings evaluated the plan of the whole team, as opposed to evaluating each individual, making each experiment a single-team design (cf., Shebilske et al., 2009).

Although the main purpose for two experiments was to counterbalance the order of presenting the two instructional strategies, the second experiment also decreased the amount of training before the teams learned new experiences. Each experiment had three phases. Phase I was background

training; Phase II was performing missions with the same enemy using the same attack strategy; Phase III was performing missions that exposed the teams to new, and putatively more difficult experiences defending against new, and qualitatively different, attack strategies. Sessions in all three Phases of both experiments consisted of planning (10 min), mission execution (40 min), and debriefing (10 min). Phase I was 50 hours in Experiment 1 and 16 hours in Experiment 2. Phase II was 49 hours in Experiment 1 and 11 hours in Experiment 2. Difficulty increased gradually in Phase II as described by Shebilske et al. (2009). Phase III was 18 hours in Experiments 1 and 2.

Extended training produced experienced teams, but at time scales that are unusually long for typical laboratory training studies. For example, the scale of training interventions in the present experiment was the scenario. In Phase III, for instance, 18 scenario interventions occurred in 18 hours of training, or 1 intervention per hour for 18 hrs. The ratio, 1/18, is not as unusual as the time scale. If we apply the same ratio to 18 interventions in a typical laboratory task in which all training occurs in 1 hour, we get a more familiar timescale: 1 training intervention per 3.3 minutes in 60 minutes. Research is needed to determine the best ratio of interventions per time unit for longer training intervals.

Results during Initial Training in Phases I and II

Time was reduced in Phases I and II of Experiment 2 because Experiment 1 had shown that the team was so close to asymptotic performance on the pre-test in Phase

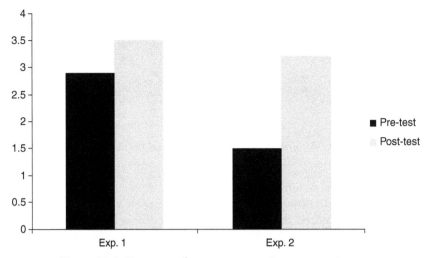

Figure 16.4. Pre-test and post-test scores in two experiments.

II that the pre-test and post-test difference was not statistically significant. Figure 16.4 shows this result and shows that the reduction of Phase I and II times in Experiment 2 was effective. It resulted in much lower pre-test performance in Phase II, the same asymptotic performance on the post-test, and a significant difference between the pre-test and post-test $(t(35) = 3.13, p < .01)$. Note that the pre-tests and post-tests were similar to one another and were counterbalanced across experiments. The scores on all pre-tests and post-tests were ratings of the most comprehensive training objective, which was to coordinate an attack asset.

Phase III: Testing the POMDP Approach for an Experienced Team to Learn a New Experience

Phase III was critical because it compared the Control training protocol and the POMDP training protocol for the same team learning two, new experiences that varied with respect to enemy strategy. For example, during New Experience 1 at the beginning in Phase III, the enemy destroyed the refueling tankers, and did so consistently. This forced the DTC to choose different attack package patterns and gave them repeated practice doing so. During New Experience 2 in Phase III, a different strategic variation was presented and practiced. The order of

training the two new experiences was the same in both experiments. The only difference in Phase III was in the order of testing the Control training protocol and the POMDP training protocol. In Experiment 1, the team had the Control training protocol for New Experience 1 and the POMDP training protocol for New Experience 2. In Experiment 2, the team had the POMDP training protocol for New Experience 1 and the Control protocol for New Experience 2. As a result, over the two experiments, the POMDP and Control Condition had both orders of new experiences and pre-test–post-test combinations.

Results during Phase III

The results from both experiments supported the hypothesis. Figure 16.5 shows that the post-test minus pre-test difference for the POMDP training strategy was greater than that difference for the Control Training Strategy in both experiments. That is, the POMDP training strategy produced more learning whether it was used for learning the first or second new experience, or whether it was used with the first or second pre-test–post-test combination. The standard errors for the post-tests were consistently smaller than those for the pre-tests. We used SPSS to conducted conservative t-tests, which are robust to unequal variance. In Experiment

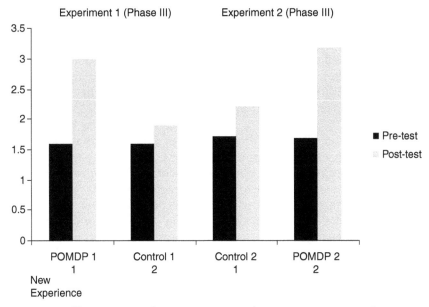

Figure 16.5. Difference scores for new experiences between treatments and experiments.

1, on the POMDP post-test, accuracy of the plan to coordinate attack assets rose significantly, from 1.6 on the pre-test to 3.0 on the post-test ($t(31)$ = 3.11, $p < .01$). Between the POMDP post-test and New Experience 2 for the Control Pre-test, performance fell from 3.0 to 1.6 ($t(27)$ = 2.83, $p < .01$). On the Control protocol Post-test, the slight rise from 1.6 to 1.9 was not significant ($t(34)$ = 0.48, $p > .05$). In Experiment 2, on the Control post-test, attack plan accuracy rose insignificantly, from 1.7 on the pre-test to 2.2 on the post-test ($t(41)$ = .86, $p > .05$). Between the Control post-test and New Experience 2 for the POMDP Pre-test, performance fell insignificantly from 2.2 to 1.7 ($t(40)$ = .94, $p > .05$). On the POMDP protocol Post-test, the increase in attack plan accuracy from 1.7 to 3.2 was significant ($t(40)$ = 2.70, $p < .01$).

Discussion

One potential disadvantage of single-team designs is the possibility of serial correlation, which would violate the independence assumption required for many standard statistics, including those used in the present experiment. Anderson (2001) reviews misunderstandings about this potential risk,

which result in failures to realize the potential advantages of single-person (or in this case, single-team) designs. He also discusses evidence and conditions in which the independence assumption seems reasonable. For example, we isolated the observations in our rating procedure by rating each plan relative to the circumstances that existed when the plan was made regardless of earlier or later circumstances. Accordingly, we cautiously made the independence assumption until future experiments yield enough data to test it with time-series analyses (see West, 2006).

Another disadvantage of the single team A-B design is that neither the order nor the materials can be counterbalanced. We addressed this problem by counterbalancing order and materials between Experiments 1 and 2 and by minimizing the similarity of strategic countermeasures in Phases II and III. Learning with the Control protocol second in Experiment 1 was potentially facilitated by general knowledge of the tendency for the enemy to change strategies. However, this was a potential bias in favor of the Control protocol and made the observed POMDP advantage more defensible. We cautiously conclude that the POMDP protocol facilitated experienced teams learning new experiences in both Experiments and that the Control protocol did not. Accordingly, we argue that the advantage for POMDP in Experiments 1 and 2 was due to the instructional strategy (scenario selection) driven by a POMDP model, and not to differences in order of new experiences or in pre-tests and post-tests.

The advantage of the POMDP-drive strategy is that it exposes a team to as much complexity as the team can learn from given its state of expertise.[1] This is not true of static instructional strategies such as the control condition tested here. Further, the use of POMDPs is arguably more effective than instruction guided by the trainee or by a trainer who (typically) has domain knowledge but not instructional expertise. It also may be more cost-effective than an ITS, which can require development of an instrumented instructional environment, a rule-based (and, thus, domain-specific) model of expert performance, a rule-based model that diagnoses student performance, and a model of instructional strategy (Polson & Richardson, 1988). By contrast, the present POMDP training protocol requires only an instructional environment with a library of systematically defined training scenarios; instrumentation – automated or observer-based – to assess trainee performance; a generalized POMDP solver; and a model of the rate of human learning given the scenario library, based on historical performance scores and/or expert assessments of trainee state before and after a training scenario. In sum, the present experiments demonstrate both the potential instructional effectiveness of a POMDP adaptive training system and its technical feasibility.

The research reported here is a foundation for future experiments. These could test information-processing accounts of

the observed advantage of POMDP-driven instructional sequences. The findings would also increase our understanding of team performance in ill-defined domains. One hypothesis for such research is this: The responsiveness of the POMDP sequences to team state enables students to learn from scenarios with higher counts of TSTs and threats, and these combinations are advantageous over training with a lower number of either TSTs or threats. The literature on part-task/whole-task training provides a useful perspective on these combinations. Having a lower number of either TSTs or threats is similar to part-task training, whereas having higher TST/threat combinations is similar to whole-task training. Whole-task training is generally better than part-task training, especially when training with the whole task facilitates the learning of critical input/output ensembles (e.g. Fredericksen & White, 1989; Gopher, Weil, & Siegel, 1989). Ieoger, Shebilske, Yen, and Volz (2005) set the stage for applying this principle to teamwork on complex tasks such as the present task, which is a dynamical system in the sense that the components are interdependent and interactive. They argue that teams understand system dynamics by processing collective variables, which are all uncontrolled variables that depend on the reciprocal interactions among an organism (in this case, the team), its components (in this case, team members), and its environment (in this case, the DDD/DTC simulation environment). For example, an input/output ensemble in the present task might include as input understanding a communication such as: "Would it be better to prosecute the present TST with the jet that we had planned to use to attack the nearby enemy tank, or with the jet that we had planned to use to attack the nearby enemy aircraft?" A response, output, might be, "Use the jet for the tank because we can replace it more easily." The collective variables for this case include the two team members, the TST, and the other threats, the enemy tank and enemy jet. They are uncontrolled in the sense that they are free to vary over a wide range of possibilities. These collective

[1] Although the state of expertise is evaluated before and after each scenario, no assumption is made that the change in expertise state during a scenario depended only on events in that scenario. The change in expertise may have been influenced by all prior experience, but it occurred in the context of the evaluation period, which was a scenario for this experiment.

variables become more complex when the number of TSTs and threats increase together. That is, when the DTC environment includes high-TST/high-threat combinations, team members must recognize more complex patterns in enemy and friendly weapons. They must also engage in more complex patterns of communication to form a unified team plan. The plan might include, for instance, combinations of two relevant TSTs, four relevant threats, and many more objects that must be seen as irrelevant to a specific input/output ensemble. These more complex input/response patterns of collective variables must be integrated into functional input/response ensembles. Medium to high TST/threat combinations enable the formation of these ensembles and facilitate learning. The present research did not measure these collective variables. However, future research will investigate whether these collective variables are best learned with the POMDP adaptive training system using medium to high TST/threat combinations. Future experiments will also compare the collective variables for high TST/threat combinations with and without the POMDP adaptive training system. We hypothesize that the adaptive feature will be necessary to enable effective use of the high TST/treat combinations. Finally, we believe that information processing models of collective variables will explain this advantage of the POMDP adaptive training system.

The present experiment also provides a foundation for future development of a POMDP adaptive training system. The technologies employed here to leverage POMDP for training were a mix of manual and automated methods. Defining the POMDP for DTC was a laborious process. Technologies are needed that simplify and accelerate subject-matter-expert work to parameterize a POMDP for a new domain. Applying the POMDP during training was slowed by manual assessment of performance. Automated measurement and assessment of team performance could remove the expert from the loop where that produces reliable and valid measures, and in so doing it would

accelerate training. Further, automated measurements (observations), related scenarios (actions), and other data could be stored and used to manually or automatically refine the POMDP model to improve its training recommendations.

Finally, the speed and effectiveness of training administered here may have been limited by the large size of the training event: a scenario. This limitation was imposed by the present experimental procedures and not by the POMDP approach itself. The POMDP approach could be revised to select smaller training events such as vignettes that would be automatically composed into scenarios. Alternatively, the POMDP could specify training objectives that a scenario generation technology could translate into vignettes and dynamically construct into scenarios (c.f., MacMillan, Stacy, & Freeman, in press). Such a wedding of POMDP with dynamic scenario generation technology would ensure that training consists of only those events that are relevant to a team's training needs. This would necessarily be more efficient than selection from a library of predefined scenarios, none of which is guaranteed to address all and only a team's current training needs.

Conclusion

The research reported here employed a POMDP model to inject rigorous, real-time instructional strategy into simulation-based team training in an ill-defined domain. POMDP-driven adaptive selection of training experiences enhanced learning, relative to ordering scenarios in a predetermined sequence using a hierarchical part-task training strategy. This work demonstrated the feasibility of a POMDP-driven adaptive training system. Finally, it set the stage for experiments that test information-processing accounts of the POMDP effectiveness, and for development of technology that marries POMDP scenario-specification techniques with automated scenario-generation technology that adapts instruction within as well as between scenarios.

This research program is also distinguished by its logical progression in integrating field research, laboratory research, and field applications. One starting point for the present research was field study of DTC teams in operational settings. Based on these task analyses, we simulated DTC operations using the DDD synthetic task environment and applied a POMDP model to adaptively select training experiences in the laboratory. The products of this research include a large number of challenging training scenarios and a model-driven instructional strategy that, we believe, should be of direct benefit, not only to future research, but also to Air Force DTC staff training in operational settings.

Acknowledgments

This research was supported in part by an STTR from the Air Force Office of Scientific Research.

References

Aberdeen, D. (2003). Policy-gradient algorithms for partially observable markov decision processes. PhD Thesis, The Australian National University, April.

Aberdeen, D., & J. Baxter. (2002). Scalable internal-state policy-gradient methods for POMDPs. *Proceedings of the International Conference on Machine Learning*, pp. 3–10.

Anderson, J. R., Conrad, F. G., & Corbett, A. T. (1989). Skill acquisition and the LISP Tutor. *Cognitive Science, 13*, 467–506.

Anderson, J. R., Douglass, S., & Qin, Y. (2004). How should a theory of learning and cognition inform instruction? In A. Healy (Ed.), *Experimental cognitive psychology and it's applications*. Washington, DC: American Psychological Association.

Anderson, N. H. (2001). *Empirical direction in design and analysis*. Mahwah, NJ: Lawrence Erlbaum Associates.

Atkinson, Richard C. (1972). Ingredients for a theory of instruction. *American Psychologist, 27*(10), 921–931.

Bellman, R. (1957). *Dynamic programming*. Princeton, NJ: Princeton University Press.

Cassandra, A. R., Littman, M. L., & Zhang, N. L. (1997). Incremental pruning: A simple, fast,

exact method for partially observable Markov decision processes. *Uncertainty in Artificial Intelligence* (UAI).

Cheng, H. T. (1988). Algorithms for partially observable Markov decision processes. PhD thesis, University of British Columbia.

Chi, M., & VanLehn, K. (2007). Accelerated future learning via explicit instruction of a problem solving strategy. In K. R. Koedinger, R. Luckin & J. Greer (Eds.), *Artificial intelligence in education* (pp. 409–416). Amsterdam: IOS Press.

Chi, Min, & VanLehn, Kurt (2008). Eliminating the gap between the high and low students through meta-cognitive strategy instruction. *Proceedings of ITS 2008*, Montreal, Canada.

Corrington, K., & Shebilske, W. L. (1995). Complex skill acquisition: Generalizing laboratory-based principles to football. *Applied Research in Coaching and Athletics Annual*, 54–69.

Dutt, Varun, & Gonzalez, Cleotilde (2008). Human perceptions of climate change. *Proceedings of the 2008 System Dynamics Conference*, Athens, Greece.

Eliot, C., & Woolf, B.P. (1995). An adaptive student centered curriculum for an intelligent training system. *User Modeling and User-Adapted Instruction, 5*, 67–86.

Fredericksen, J., & White, B. (1989). An approach to training based upon principled task decomposition. *Acta Psychologica, 71*, 89–146.

Freeman, J., Haimson, C., Diedrich, F., & Paley, M., (2005). Training teamwork with synthetic teams. In Clint Bowers, Eduardo Salas, & Florian Jentsch (Eds.), *Creating high-tech teams: Practical guidance on work performance and technology*. Washington, DC: APA Press.

Freeman, J., MacMillan, J., Haimson, C., Weil, S., Stacy, W., & Diedrich, F. (2006). From gaming to training. *Society for Advanced Learning Technology*, February 8–10, Orlando, FL.

Freeman, Jared (2002). I've got synthers. Who could ask for anything more? *Proceedings of the 46th Annual Meeting of the Human Factors and Ergonomics Society*, Baltimore, MD.

Gopher, D., Weil, M., & Siegel, D. (1989). Practice under changing priorities: An approach to the training of complex skills. *Acta Psychologica, 71*, 147–177.

Hauskrecht, M. (2000). Value-function approximations for partially observable Markov decision processes. *Journal of Artificial Intelligence Research, 13*, 33–94.

Ieoger, T., Shebilske, W., Yen, J., & Volz, R. (2005). Agent-based training of distributed command and control teams. *Proceedings of the 49th*

Annual Meeting of Human Factors Society, Orlando, FL.

Kaelbling, L. P., Littman, M. L., & Cassandra, A. R. (1998). Planning and acting in partially observable stochastic domains. *Artificial Intelligence, 101,* 99–134.

Lesgold, A. M., Lajoie, S. P., Bunzo, M., & Eggan, G. (1992). SHERLOCK: A coached practice environment for an electronics troubleshooting job. In J. Larkin & R. Chabay (Eds.), *Computer assisted instruction and intelligent tutoring systems: Shared issues and complementary approaches* (pp. 201–238). Hillsdale, NJ: Erlbaum.

MacMillan, J., Stacy, W., & Freeman, J. (in press). The design of synthetic experiences for effective training: Challenges for DMO. *Proceedings of Distributed Mission Operations Training,* Mesa, AZ.

Miller, M., Yin, J., Volz, R. A., Ioerger, T. R., & Yen, J. (2000). Training teams with collaborative agents. *Proceedings of the Fifth International Conference on Intelligent Tutoring Systems,* (ITS-2000), 63–72.

Monahan, G. E. (1982). A survey of partially observable Markov decision processes: Theory, models and algorithms. *Management Science, 28*(1), .

Ness, J. W., Tepe, V., & Ritzer, D. R., (2004). *The science and simulation of human performance.* Amsterdam: Elsevier.

Papadimitriou, C. H., & Tsitsiklis, J. N. (1987). The complexity of Markov decision processes. *Mathematics of Operations Research, 12*(3), 441–450.

Polson, Martha, & Richardson, J. Jeffrey (1988). *Foundations of intelligent tutoring systems.* Hillsdale, NJ: Lawrence Erlbaum Associates.

Poupart. P., Ortiz, L. E., & Boutilier, C. (2001). Value-directed sampling methods for monitoring POMDPs. *Uncertainty in Artificial Intelligence,* Retrieved June 10, 2008, from www.citeseer.nj.nec.com/445996.html

Rickel, J., & Johnson, W. L. (1999). Virtual humans for team training in virtual reality. *Proceedings of the Ninth World Conference on AI in Education.* Amsterdam: IOS Press.

Shebilske, W., Gildea, K., Freeman, J., & Levchuk, G. (2009). Optimizing instructional strategies: A benchmarked experiential system for training (BEST). *Theoretical Issues in Ergonomic Science. Special Issue on Optimizing Virtual Training Systems, 10*(3), 267–278.

Silberman, Melvin (Ed.) (2007). *The handbook of experiential learning.* New York: Wiley & Sons.

Smith, T., & Simmons, R. G. (2004). Heuristic search value iteration for POMDPs. *Proceedings of the 20th Conference on Uncertainty in Artificial Intelligence (UAI).* ACM International Conference Proceeding Series, Vol. 70.

Sondik, E. J. (1971). The optimal control of partially observable Markov processes. PhD thesis, Stanford University.

Steinberg, E. R. (1989). Cognition and learner control: A literature review, 1977–1988. *Journal of Computer-Based Instruction, 16,* 117–121.

Sutton, R. S., McAllester, D., Singh, S., & Mansour, Y. (2000). Policy gradient methods for reinforcement learning with function approximation. *Advances in Neural Information Processing Systems, 12,* 1057–1063.

Vygotsky, L. (1978). *Mind in society.* Cambridge, MA: Harvard University Press.

West, B. J. (2006). *Where medicine went wrong: Rediscovering the path to complexity.* Mahwah, NJ: World Scientific.

Williams, M. D. (1993). A comprehensive review of learner control: The Role of Learner Characteristics. *Proceedings of Selected Research and Development Presentations at the Convention of the Association for Educational Communications and Technology Sponsored by the Research and Theory Division* (15th), January 13–17, New Orleans, LA.

Zhang, N. L., & Liu, W. (1996). Planning in stochastic domains: Problem characteristics and approximations. Technical Report HKUST-CS96-31, Department of Computer Science, The Hong Kong University of Science and Technology.

CHAPTER 17

Exploring Design-Based Research for Military Training Environments

Marie Bienkowski

Online training is developing faster in response to needs than approaches to training are being proven effective. The modern military training environment is evolving to meet the needs of soldiers in both current operations and those operations that are expected to arise. The length of time in which a soldier must be training is shifting: from the relatively slow pace of the classroom where learners are assumed to learn at the same pace, to the pace of the individual as developers work toward the goal of just-in-time and adaptive training. Difficult-to-define skills such as leadership, critical thinking, adaptability, and creative problem solving are in demand as training topics. Soldiers have less predictable needs and this leads to a call for training faster, and shrinking budgets necessitate training with less cost. These drivers impel researchers and developers to apply technological solutions to the training problem (continuing a decades-long approach to military training [Fletcher, 2009]) but not necessarily to adopt them with careful attention to their evidence of effectiveness. As an example of this impulse, although meta-analyses have only recently shown online learning to be effective (Means, Toyama, Murphy, Bakia, & Jones, 2009), prior to obtaining proof of effectiveness, hundreds of thousands of soldiers began taking distance-learning courses.

Developing a training solution that meets the previously described needs is a complex endeavor. Not only are the needs rapidly evolving, but also the constraints are significant. The state-of-the-art in Intelligent Computer-Aided Instruction (ICAI) (Fletcher, 2009) is advanced, but the low adoption rate of technologies based on this approach, developed over years of funding, suggests that that "return on investment" should be clearly spelled-out and that any barriers to adoption be well understood and addressed during development, not after development is completed. Furthermore, as training goals evolve, methods that work for domains with well-structured content such as physics and mathematics, that have been the subject of computer-aided instruction for many years, must yield to new techniques as soldiers grapple with learning twenty-first-century skills such as effective teamwork and communication, conducting counterinsurgencies, and lessening kinetic operations by deftly applying cultural knowledge to a tense situation.

The range of skills needing to be trained is expanding against a compressed time for training, and today's soldiers are trained for the *most likely* mission, not a *known* mission (NRC, 2008). Trainees need to leave training sessions with knowledge to apply to near and far-transfer situations, skills to apply and hone over time, and demonstrated abilities. If the U.S. Army Training and Doctrine Command defines *precision learning* as focusing on the student, tailoring methods and contents to the needs of the soldier, and being responsive to changing needs (Durlach & Tierney, 2009), then *precision training* must focus on soldiers' developing knowledge, skills, and abilities (KSAs) and *precision feedback* must help them monitor their own development and align future learning with their needs. Precise feedback must be supported by custom assessments that cannot be rendered as standard multiple-choice tests for topics such as cultural competence, leadership, critical thinking, and interpersonal skills.

Underpinning this broad vision for training is a process of tool development, application, testing, and verification. Typically this design process follows a top-down, requirements-first approach, similar to that used in the early days of engineering and computer science design. As outlined in Cohn et al. (2008), first training needs are analyzed against job performance, a training system is designed, and then metrics are collected that measure the performance of a trainee against some standard of operation. This top-down approach works well in situations where KSAs are well defined, where timing allows a more leisurely consideration of background information (e.g., task analysis, target users, and training environment), and where schedules permit cycles of development of training materials and multiple iterations on implementation and testing. In new contexts, where traditional technology-based training falls short, this approach may fail to support discovery and innovation.

Defining Design-Based Research

The field of learning sciences has recently begun to codify an approach to the study of learning that draws on current engineering, software, and industrial design practices such as agile design (Highsmith, 2002), rapid prototyping, participatory design, and user-centered design (Norman & Draper, 1986). This approach, initially termed "design experimentation" (Brown, 1992) but now called "design-based research," allows for the simultaneous development and refinement of theory, artifact, and practice in natural learning contexts.

Barab and Squire (2004) characterize design-based research as not one but "a series of approaches, with the intent of producing new theories, artifacts, and practices that account for and potentially impact learning and teaching in naturalistic settings" (p. 2). Of importance in their definition is the idea of a family of methods and the research-and-development goals of the studies conducted with these methods.

Kelly, Lesh, and Baek (2008) view design processes as "systematic, creative, dynamic, generative, and directed at solutions to real problems" (p. xiii). Their contrast with controlled experimental methods that are "systematized, rule-governed, tied to standards of evidence and warrant, and directed at establishing principles, theories, and laws" highlights a topic that has been the subject of much discussion in the literature: identifying the kinds of claims for which design-based research can provide warrants (Cobb, Confrey, diSessa, Lehrer, & Schauble, 2003; Dede, 2004, 2005).

Van den Akker, Gravemeijer, McKenney, and Nieveen (2006) provide us with characteristics of design-based research that identify traits of studies that bear a family resemblance, as follows:

- Interventionist: The study creates or engineers an intervention (tool, artifact, practice) that is tested and that operates in a real context.
- Iterative: The study uses a cyclic approach of design, evaluation, and revision.

- Process-oriented: The study does not just measure inputs and outputs (as in a "black box" model) but instead emphasizes understanding conditions for success and failure.
- Utility-oriented: The merit of the design being studied is measured, in part, by how practical users judge it to be when it is used in their natural context.
- Theory-oriented: The study begins with an investigation of theoretical propositions that are brought to bear on the design, and the field testing of the design, in turn, feeds back in to theory building (p. 4).

These definitions together create a characterization of design-based research that aligns well with innovation practices (West & Farr, 1990) in that this methodology supports an intentional introduction of something new that is designed to benefit the target audience.

Why consider design-based research? As with other "interventionist" fields of study, design-based research recognizes the need to acknowledge the intuitions of those deeply involved in the end-user environment about what might work, and to support innovators trying to introduce new approaches, such as gaming and simulation-based training. As the pace of training accelerates to match the need for teaching – for example, regional knowledge that lends itself to agile in-country responses – the pace of training development must accelerate also. Design-based research can match this pace. It can also, when executed well, satisfy the divergent goals of both vendor-driven and science-driven investigations into efficiency and effectiveness (NRC, 2008). It offers promise to find a balance between applying technological advances that seem promising (technology-centric) and the needs of a learner (learner-centric).

Although design-based research was developed in the K-12 education context, where the content that is to be learned (e.g., science, mathematics, and social studies) does not change radically over time, it has been used to study other topics in K-12

learning that suggest it may be applicable more widely. For example, as reported in Barab and Squire (2004), studies have focused on student learning of interdisciplinary content and the nature of scientific work, teacher professional development, and student citizenship in communities. diSessa and Cobb (2004) report on their design-based research on learning supports: students competency with scientific representation and the role of classroom discussions in learning mathematics. In this chapter, I present design-based research as a promising method for doing research on designed innovations in military training.

Characterizing Design-Based Research

Design-based research encompasses differentiated stages of work that overlap and inform one another, including theory development, design and testing of an artifact or practice, assessment design to create instructionally sensitive measures of learning, and evaluation of the effects of the artifact or practice in the local and broader contexts in which it will be used. One variant of design-based research is co-design (Penuel, Roschelle, & Shechtman, 2007), characterized by a research-and-development process in which a team of researchers, developers, and teachers work together in well-defined roles to design and build a prototype and work to ensure that the innovation is a good fit with the teachers/district/school's concrete goals for students learning. Using this co-design approach, Penuel, Roschelle, and Shechtman found that teachers are more likely to adopt the innovation.

In K-12 education research, design-based research supports directly the goal of translating research into practice. As an iterative design process, it allows a research team to build successive approximations of a solution to a problem and, given sufficient time, to feel confident that the result will be useful to learners. It allows developer teams to build a tool that is very sensitive to context but also to consider how to generalize the tool in order to move the design to scale.

Context encompasses broad considerations such as the setting (e.g., classroom, informal space, self-directed), the teachers, learners, and their background (e.g., grade level, cultural and family background, motivation, and identity), and classroom activity structures and norms (e.g., group work, whole-class discussion, formative assessment). In design-based research, multiple context variables are allowed to vary during implementation rather than being held constant as in randomized controlled trials.

When considering tools or innovations that can be the subject of design-based research in military contexts, intelligent tutoring systems (ITSs) are a possibility. ITSs are formalized as encoding specific content knowledge (the expert model), a model of student thinking, and pedagogical moves into a computer-based system that can interact with a student to tutor or guide them in learning or accomplishing a task. Design-based research with such systems could study early prototypes, or built-out, vertical slices of the systems' functionality in the target environment.

To support agile and cost-effective training, distance or online learning applications have been proposed. These approaches make the context of a classroom less important and instead highlight the need for a design team to consider the characteristics of learners who will use the system and their background in terms of prior knowledge and learning abilities. Online learning may not provide a group context for practice and reflection and may not account for likely distractions or time lapses between training sessions. At the same time, if we define design broadly to encompass more than just a tool or artifact, such as an online course, we can study how interventions play out in classroom instruction, individual/self-paced learning, and field- and team-based practice. This orientation of design-based research toward rapid design and study in context is consistent with applications of design engineering and with recommendations for military training approaches, for example, in Boldovici, Bessemer, and Bolton (2002).

In defining design-based research, the literature on design experiments and design research makes contrasts with laboratory research, psychological studies (Brown, 1992) and randomized controlled experiments (Kelly, Lesh, & Baek, 2008). In contrast to these approaches, design-based research is conducted in natural settings (not a laboratory), includes social interaction (not only the psychology of the individual), and trades off generalizability through random assignment for discovery through *in situ* experimentation. Design-based research also differs from formative evaluation, for whereas both methodologies foreground iterative development and testing cycles with end-users, design-based research includes a strong focus on theory development. Design-based research has been likened to the design sciences such as aeronautics and acoustics, in contrast to natural sciences such as biology and physics (Collins, Joseph, & Bielaczyc, 2004). These comparisons are useful for defining the term and can also highlight methods or practices from these other sciences (e.g., the development of airplanes that could break the sound barrier, as reported in Phillips & Dolle [2006]) that could serve as compelling examples in learning sciences.

Here, for the sake of argument, I outline the top-down training system design methods described in Cohn et al. (2008) as a contrast with design-based research. As presented in their chapter, training is designed using a method analogous to designing a large software system. They list several major stages in the method, framed as questions:

1. Does the design meet the training needs? This is answered through interviews with subject-matter experts, student questionnaires, background information reviews (from doctrine and field manuals), focus groups, and task analysis. These activities lead to user profiles that characterize trainee's background, claims about what performance is lacking (the gap or training needs), and ideas for what can be done to close the gap (the intervention or the training).

Outputs of this stage are "work models, performance metrics, fidelity requirements, and use scenarios" (p. 90).

2. How are the training needs addressed? This stage encompasses design of the training considering many factors: the delivery platform, the needed fidelity, development cost, and the progression of the trainee from novice to expert.

3. How is training effectiveness measured? This final stage produces and validates metrics that link the training to changes in soldier capabilities. Measures of effectiveness and measures of performance, the standards for military operational requirements, can be used, according to Cohn et al. (2008), to derive measures that are operationally meaningful.

The method sketched here does not exhaustively cover the design methods used in military training but rather typifies them. Design-based research has not yet been applied in this context – at least not *formally* applied. Yet it holds promise for discovery in areas where existing practices fail. Also, top-down methods do not work well when a researcher has an innovation that already exists that he or she wants to apply to a specific context. Consider, for example, the growth in the application of virtual reality or simulation-based training systems. People have a sense that they will be effective (sometimes, only "scant evidence" as described in Mayo [2009]) and are willing to take a calculated risk that they will work in a training environment. Design-based research can give some early evidence for effectiveness and shape the artifact to the environment, thus mitigating risk. For example, Roschelle, Tatar, and Kaput (2008) in their review of the scaling up of the SimCalc approach to teaching the mathematics of change (conducted since 1994) describe how SimCalc started with the observation that a dynamic representation implemented on affordable technology could support learning complex math. This led to early experiments with video games, but as they learned, this was "a design element that has largely dropped out of the SimCalc project, as none of these

games proved compelling in small-scale trials with students.... Neither large-scale research nor a sophisticated methodology was needed to rule out innovations with little potential" (p. 375).

A further benefit of adopting a design-based research methodology is its explicit consideration of learning science theory (as called for by the National Research Council [2008]). Design-based researchers attend to prior research in the design decisions that they make in determining the design procedure, in analyzing the problem to be solved, or in making decisions about the design itself (Edelson, 2006). As Edelson points out, design-based research can be used to test prior research but the caution of Kelly (2006) in the same volume bears consideration as well: It works in the area of discovery and not verification. Hypothesis testing (canonically, examining the effects of independent variables on dependent variables) remains the purview of experimental methods, but design-based research can be used to present richly textured cases if sufficient and systematic documentation is captured during the research. The intended outcome, in addition to a potentially workable and effective artifact or process, is a warranted theory of learning with that artifact or process from which principles for future designs can occur (Collins, Joseph, & Bielaczyc, 2004; Edelson, 2006; NRC, 2008).

Stages of Design-Based Research

Design-based research, as I described in the opening, draws inspiration and techniques from many disciplines. Bannan-Ritland (2003) created a useful framework by overlaying general phases on top of the individual detailed phases in these methodologies: instructional design, product design, usage-centered design, diffusion of innovations, and established educational research. The major phases of design-based research she describes are informed exploration, design enactment, local impact (implementation research), and broader impact (scaling and summative evaluation). In the following, I employ the general outline of her framework to present an approach to design-based research (although some tasks I present in earlier phases than does Bannan-Ritland).

Informed Exploration

Informed exploration lays the groundwork for design-based studies, encompassing not just a review of the literature, but also needs analysis and theory development. In some ways, this phase is similar to preparatory work in summative evaluation that lays out the program theory or impact theory (sometimes called the "logic model" as it expresses the "logic" behind the program) at the outset. Program theories typically describe sequences of preconditions, causes, and effects that represent the intended implementation of the program. The evaluator's job is to elicit this theory, or model, from the program designers and from the program-as-implemented. In design-based research, this program theory is a proposed implementation in a specific context that will have a specific impact. Considering an output of this stage to be analogous to a program theory can both capture the goals for the innovation and serve as a touchstone for keeping on course as the implementation evolves. The program theory can describe any assumptions about the target audience (e.g., grade level, literacy status) and implementation factors. For example, in their studies on the use of handheld computers to support formative assessment tasks, Penuel and Yarnall (2005) consciously addressed implementation factors related to information overload for teachers reviewing assessment data and resistance to changes in classroom practices.

Informed exploration includes a survey of the context, addressing questions such as:

- What is the current practice?
- What needs are we addressing with the innovation?
- What are the specific learning goals?

This phase also includes a characterization of the content to be learned and the end-users:

- What background do they have?
- What context of use does the intervention support?
- What content are they learning, related to what background knowledge, and in what progression?

In military training environments, trainees are expected to be self-directed learners and, when they are not *doing*, they are *training*. However, although motivation to learn can be assumed (because the consequences of not being trained can be costly), factors such as fatigue and compressed time for learning can be mediating factors to success or failure.

Finally, theory development is begun in the informed exploration phase by considering questions such as:

- What is the theory of learning on which we base the work?
- What evidence exists for effectiveness of this kind of training?

Design-based researchers vary in the amount of attention they pay to theory development. Those who pay more attention take a firm stance on the role of design-based research vis-à-vis theory, typified by statements such as "Design experiments are conducted to develop theories, not merely to empirically tune 'what works'" (Cobb et al., 2003). Cobb and colleagues describe design-based research as creating good conditions for developing theories that are *prospective* in predicting what will happen in the implementation phase while at the same supporting a *reflective* review of those predictions about learning. Similarly, in 2008, a National Research Council (NRC) committee called for behavioral research to "create a science of learning that is relevant to issues in military training, guides instructional design of technology-based training in the military, and identifies and assesses instructional methods that have large effects on learning" (NRC, 2008, p. 16).

If the design-based research is using or adapting existing technology (such as a virtual environment or serious game), a model of the use, couched in a narrative scenario (or context), can be built at this exploration phase. These use cases can serve as preliminaries to design documents for developers and as ways to create shared expectations with stakeholders. Stakeholders in design-based research include professionals from many areas: domain experts, developers, instructors, researchers, and learners/end-users. In military training, the set of stakeholders may seem small (e.g., the soldier and his or her trainer and superior officer), but in fact stakeholder may be defined broadly to include agents such as experts who possess the knowledge to which the soldier aspires, the unit to which the soldier is assigned, present and future team members, the branch of the service of which the soldier is a member, and the nation as a whole. Design-based research thus addresses the need for interdisciplinary teams called for in Graesser and King (2008) (but which can be difficult to accomplish when the end-users are soldiers who deploy soon after training).

Often, it is useful to begin thinking about measurement at the informed exploration phase. Once the program theory is in place, researchers can explore what factors are most influential and thus most necessary to measure. Although it may not be possible to articulate every factor in the theory, using results from the research literature, information from stakeholder, and observations and pilot testing, the theory can be a reasonable first pass on how the learning occurs and what context factors need to be sampled to explain how the intervention works or not. Choice of measurement is guided by program goals and constrained by budget.

Once the design is supported by a program theory, the stage is set to either embed an innovation into a context (if working with existing technology) or to develop and deploy an innovation. Design-based research, as a methodology, differs from formative user testing because it is more extensive – the object of consideration is not just the artifact and someone interfacing with it, but also the context features that affect implementation, user experience, and social/cognitive factors. For example, in studying handheld augmented reality games for learning, O'Shea, Mitchell, Johnston, and Dede (2009) began from theories about learning in authentic settings and through social interaction, cooperation, and motivation. Their formative studies uncovered not only logistical difficulties, but also design features that led to students competing (vs. cooperating) and seeking only the "correct" answer (vs. holding tentative ideas based on available data).

Design Enactment

Design enactment is the part of design-based research that is most analogous to instructional design methods. It is here that the "vendor-driven" approach could be given prominence with an additional distinctive feature: a program theory or conceptual model of how the program confers a benefit for stakeholders. As the National Research Council report points out, "decisions about how to design technology-based training are often based on intuitions and opinions of persons with technological development skills rather than on research evidence and a research-based theory of how people learn" (NRC, 2008, p. 41). The methodology of design-based research corrects this oversight by relying on theory work, as previously described, prior to enactment.

There are no hard and fast rules about which tasks are done in which phase, and design-based research is iterative and cyclic. For example, preliminary domain or content modeling, knowledge elicitation from subject-matter experts, or task analysis is often needed during informed exploration to build shared assumptions with stakeholders and to set boundaries for the extent of the intervention. In cases where a knowledge canon is available (e.g., chapters from an Advanced Placement textbook, as in Chaudhri et al. [2007]), establishing the scope of the training content may be simpler than in cases where knowledge, skills, and abilities are not so codified, as in domains of cultural norms (e.g., McFarland, 2005), leadership, teamwork, and flexible decision making. In either case, design enactment includes detailed work on the domain.

Techniques generally employed at this stage include user experience testing, user interface reviews, and review of goals/outcomes and indicators of progress toward them. With the advent of Internet collaboratories, it is also possible to expose the prototype intervention to a wider audience. Unlike product design, which is proprietary, this wider view can refine the intervention through review by a larger set of possible users and/or stakeholders. Formative evaluation also takes place during design enactment. Formative evaluation is sometimes depicted as seamless with evaluation of local impact (Bannan-Ritland, 2008), but our view is that formative evaluation is done as the design is enacted and is more or less simultaneous with the implementation. In this way, designs can be revisited during the enactment phase owing to changes from the evaluation.

Assessment Design

The design-based research literature does not specifically call out the design of assessments as a core part of its methodology, although the choice between standardized versus researcher-designed assessments is important for studying innovations in learning (Penuel, 2005). Especially when research is innovating in supporting learning for new or ill-defined areas, standard assessments may not be sensitive to the instruction given or may not even test what is being taught. In educational research, although preference is given to assessments that are standardized and regarded as valid in measuring learning of basic skills, researcher-designed assessments can be much better aligned with program design and opportunities to learn.

It is useful to pause a moment to distinguish evaluation and assessment, as used here. Evaluation, as I describe in the next section, is undertaken to study the effectiveness and impact of a specific intervention in a specific environment, either naturally occurring or structured to control variables and test hypotheses. Assessment is the specific technique used to determine whether learning objectives have been met through some form of testing or observation. Assessment may be embedded or administered after the fact, and may be used for formative or summative purposes. Assessment cannot be developed without a very clear understanding of the learning objectives for a particular session of learning (of whatever length), so assessment design can begin as early as the informed exploration phase of design-based research.

When decomposing a military training environment to understand how training can be effective, we have to first consider the training intervention, or the *what* of the training. First, what are the training goals and learning objectives? What knowledge, skills, and abilities do we expect the learner to acquire? Second, what resources and materials will be used in the training, and what instructional activities (e.g., lecture, game, simulation) are available and appropriate? Finally, we need to understand the social context in which the training takes place: What are the consequences of success and failure for the learner with respect to how well or completely the material is learned? How is the training situated in the organizational culture? Understanding all of these answers helps set the stage for assessment design.

When the content being learned is new or novel and seems complex to define, a period of initial study guided by the goal of designing valid assessments can be useful to help clarify what the measurable expectations are for learners. This contrasts with an approach guided by the goal of designing training according to some theoretical approach followed by the development of assessment "after the fact." Building an assessment can be a systematic process that designs activities that elicit solid evidence of knowledge, skills, and abilities (KSAs). Such an approach is embodied in, for example, the Principled Assessment Design for Inquiry (PADI) system based on evidence-centered design (Mislevy & Haertel, 2006). PADI is an online design support system for building assessment blueprints as a foundation for full assessment implementation. Threaded throughout the PADI design process is the driving question: How can we judge what a learner knows and can do? Evidence-centered design, the theoretical underpinning of PADI, views assessment as an argument – from evidence – about learning. PADI design begins with a clear and agreed-on statement of what KSAs are the target of the learning, and from that defines what observables would constitute evidence of the learning having taken place. These first two tasks provide input for the third – designing ways of gathering evidence (such as placing the learner in a situation where she must use the KSAs to complete a task) – and the evidence so gathered serves as warrants for claims about learning.

Evaluation and Local Impact

Evaluation is the process of working with a client to understand their goals for a programmatic intervention and also those of the various stakeholders in the process. Although the design-based research literature does not explicitly highlight the role of evaluation, projects that develop and test interventions can use impartial evaluation at an early (formative) and terminal (summative) stage of the research, and evaluation teams on projects typically participate throughout the research. Evaluation can be an ongoing process, not just what researchers do at the end of the design enactment phase. In informed exploration, for example, beginning to consider evaluation can inform program design and set the stage for analyzing implementation of the design.

As I described previously, evaluation begins with developing an impact or program theory. The components of the program theory yield factors that guide the evaluator to understand the conditions that are required for high-quality implementation and may indicate whether the intervention will be so sensitive to implementation that implementation fidelity needs to be measured. Implementation measures include logs, observations, and self-reporting (e.g., on surveys).

Evaluation is largely concerned with assessing the impact of an intervention on specified outcomes in such a way (ultimately) that causality can be strongly inferred. Sometimes, outcome measures can be existing instruments that are important to the training stakeholders. In other cases, existing measures will not be sensitive to the KSAs for which the design is intended. In such cases, evaluators develop outcome measures that are sensitive to likely effects. This requires the same rigor of assessment design as described above.

Evaluation of local impact in design-based research is done early enough that it can give evidence of efficacy of a less mature or less reliable design, which can provide evidence of a potential return on investment and help focus resources on promising designs that should be subject to larger experimental research. This more formative evaluation, also called "diagnostic evaluation" (e.g., in Boldovici, Bessemer, & Bolton, 2002), can indeed "diagnose" early problems, and early studies can also help identify and recruit populations that can participate in later random-assignment experiments to rigorously assess impact and outcomes.

Scaling Up and Broader Impacts

In considering the application of design-based research to military training environments, most of the stages, as we have described earlier, appear to transfer well. Evaluating the broader impact of the design as it scales up to more contexts may not have the same requirements in military training as it does in the K-12 setting. For example, researchers who work on scale in education often foresee policy problems as they consider scaling up "the scattered, successful 'islands of innovation' empowered by instructional technology into universal improvements in schooling" (Dede, 1998, p. 199). Such policy problems are not an issue if the training is mandated. If no mandate exists (e.g., if a unit commander does not see the value of training on a particular skill such as negotiation), training will not take place no matter how effective the innovation. Failing to consider the organizational structure within which the innovation is to be adopted can lead to little to no uptake (Durlach, Wansbury, & Wilkinson, 2008). Promising methods for increasing adoption, in addition to understanding the context, include co-design (Penuel, Roschelle, & Shechtman, 2007) and expanding the scope of the design to encompass ease of adoption, scalability, and sustainability as design factors to consider up front (Fishman, Marx, Blumenfeld, Krajcik, & Soloway, 2004).

Design-based research that identifies promising innovations that succeed in local contents should culminate in more rigorous tests in a randomized controlled experiment. Populations identified throughout the earlier stages can be recruited for participation, and validated assessments developed during the design can be used as measures that are instructionally sensitive. However, some have argued that waiting to think about scaling until the final stage of research is too late and that, instead, a third view of education research is required. Instead of simply considering "what works" (via experimentation) or "what could work" via design-based research, Roschelle, Tatar, and Kaput (2008) argue that, from the outset, considering "what could scale up" builds in the need for answering different kinds of questions. Asking whether the design is sufficiently well specified such that it can be implemented as expected in many contexts is a key question, for in scaling a design, handpicked instructors and trainees will not be the only ones teaching and learning.

Design-Based Research Obstacles and Affordances

What is unique about military environments for evaluation and assessment? Scaling up an innovation may be more likely to succeed given the standardization already present in the military training context. It is also likely that the constraints placed on the problem by the needs of the end-users make a noticeable difference; the need to learn quickly, learn anywhere, and learn at a low cost places restrictions on the way training is delivered and requires innovation in thinking about KSA acquisition and testing. For example, consider the example of preparing for in-country activities by studying cultural KSAs. A novice soldier cannot become an expert through crammed classroom training prior to deployment. One approach would be to add more training opportunities: to increase the dosage of the treatment. However, research tells us that learning design techniques such as preparation for future learning, peer learning, and reflection can help retention. Beginning from these research findings, an innovation may be developed to focus not on learning and recitation of all of the necessary KSAs, but instead to lay the groundwork for in-country learning that is organized in such a way that social-networking techniques are used to support reflection and peer learning.

Design-based research may appear to carry a lot of risk: Military training designers justifiably feel that they have just one chance to get training built, and they want to be sure training works before putting people at risk on being unprepared. In cases where an approach works well, conducting design-based research offers little reward for the risk. On the other hand, if existing approaches are known to be inadequate, the risk seems minor compared to having no solution at all. For example, ITSs are offered as a possibility for military training, but in new situations, there may be no expert model to encode for the student to learn. In such cases, such as leading a team with different areas of expertise to a novel solution, design-based research could create new solutions based on co-design with teams.

Organizations cannot have innovation without risk, and if the design-based research draws from research results, risk may be mitigated (Edelson, 2006). Yet a challenge in applying the design-based research methodology to military training is that, although training is "deeply embedded in military culture as a core mission" (NRC, 2008, p. 39), it can be difficult to obtain soldiers to participate in experimental testing (e.g., Durlach, Wansbury, & Wilkinson, 2008).

The main affordance of design-based research is that it supports innovation and lets researchers know early if a method shows promise, saving potential investment costs. It is a good method for getting traction on tackling ill-defined problems, and a good bridge between laboratory studies and the real world with its multiple varying factors. It gives a methodological context for using good formative evaluation that can provide course corrections for designs. The potential downside is that a research team falls into the trap of continuing to make the "next change" to improve a design and never acknowledges that the design just did not work (Dede, 2005).

One useful view of design-based research, presented by Edelson (2006), is from an engineer's perspective, in which designers work with knowledge of context, constraints, and affordances, and they consider "the implications of alternative design decisions." He lists the following as areas that designers have to consider:

- Design process – who is involved and what are the steps?
- Design context – what are the goals and constraints that the design must take into account, from all stakeholders and all relevant situations?
- Design decisions – approaches, alternatives, trade-offs, cost, efficiency, and the like.

Considering design from this perspective allows a fresh look at instructional design and can be a starting point for adapting design-based research for military training.

Recommendations

I argued that even though design-based research is not yet formally applied to military training, opportunities exist in technology-rich designs such as virtual games, simulation-based training, and online learning. Design-based research does not obviate the need for hard work in research and development of adaptive training approaches

and tools, including domain analysis, user-centered design, and careful assessment design. As Walker (2006) describes, the research must "balance boldness and caution" in ways that support innovation more than can be obtained from strict experimental designs. Balance is required, because being overly cautious in avoiding errors can dampen innovation and lead to more cost and development time, whereas overly bold strategies can lead to complex designs that have many possible effects.

Two promising areas should be pursued now. First, more theory development would help frame problems, identify variables for later experimental study, and lay the groundwork for summative evaluations. The National Research Council report (2008) recommends basing the design of technology-based training on "a research-based theory of how people learn." Reviewing the cognitive and psychological literature on how people learn and how skill and expertise develop is a good first step in grounding the innovation in theory. Design-based research then provides us with techniques for capturing and explaining the theory to be applied and suggests that these "research-based theories" should be held as tentative and be revisited during formative work so that development and usability do not overtake the theoretical grounding. Also, these theories cannot supplant or ignore current practices of training or organizational context in order for the innovation to scale.

The second area of promise is evaluation of local impacts prior to expanding to a summative evaluation. Formative evaluations should shed light in both directions of the methodological path: back toward the theory to verify its continued explanatory power, and ahead to proposed changes to the designed tool or practice to increase its usability and range of support for learning. Formative evaluations can also investigate whether the design is implemented as intended (implementation fidelity). Well-designed summative evaluations should uncover the factors that lead to success or failure, and the way organization's culture affects implementation. Taking heed of these practices will lead to stronger designs for later scaling.

References

Bannan-Ritland, B. (2003). The role of design in research: The integrative learning design framework. *Educational Researcher, 32*(1), 21–24.

Bannan-Ritland, B. (2008). Investigating the act of design in design research: The road taken. In A. E. Kelly, R. A. Lesh, & J. Y. Baek (Eds.), *Handbook of design research methods in education: Innovations in science, technology, engineering, and mathematics learning and teaching* (pp. 299–319). New York and London: Routledge.

Barab, S., & Squire, K. (2004). Design-based research: Putting a stake in the ground. *The Journal of the Learning Sciences, 13*(1), 1–14.

Boldovici, J. A., Bessemer, D. W., & Bolton, A. E. (2002). *The elements of training evaluation.* Alexandria, VA: US Army Research Institute for the Behavioral and Social Sciences.

Brown, A. L. (1992). Design experiments. Theoretical and methodological challenges in evaluating complex interventions in classroom settings. *The Journal of the Learning Sciences, 2*(2), 141–178.

Chaudhri, V. K., John, B. E., Mishra, S., Pacheco, J., Porter, B., & Spaulding, A. (2007). *Enabling experts to build knowledge bases from science textbooks.* Paper presented at the Proceedings of the 4th international conference on knowledge capture. Whistler, BC, Canada.

Cobb, P., Confrey, J., diSessa, A., Lehrer, R., & Schauble, L. (2003). Design experiments in educational research. *Educational Researcher, 32*(1), 9–13.

Cohn, J., Stanney, K. M., Milham, L. M., Jones, D. L., Hale, K. S., Darken, R. P., & Sullivan, J. (2008). Training evaluation of virtual environments. In E. Baker, J. Dickieson, W. Wulfeck, & H. F. O'Neil (Eds.), *Assessment of problem solving using simulations* (pp. 81–105). New York: Lawrence Erlbaum Associates.

Collins, A., Joseph, D., & Bielaczyc, K. (2004). Design research: Theoretical and methodological issues. *The Journal of the Learning Sciences, 13*(1), 15–42.

Dede, C. (1998). The scaling-up process for technology-based educational innovations. In C. Dede (Ed.), *Learning with technology: ACSD Yearbook 1998* (pp. 199–215). Alexandria, VA: Association for Supervision and Curriculum Development.

Dede, C. (2004). If design-based research is the answer, what is the question? *The Journal of the Learning Sciences, 13*(1), 105–114.

Dede, C. (2005). Why design-based research is both important and difficult. *Educational Technology, 45*(1), 5–8.

diSessa, A., & Cobb, P. (2004). Ontological innovation and the role of theory in design experiments. *The Journal of the Learning Sciences, 13*(1), 77–103.

Durlach, P. J., & Tierney, D. (2009). *Developing adaptive technologies for army training and education.* Presented at the U.S. Army Research Institute Workshop on Adaptive Training Technologies, March, Charleston, S.C.

Durlach, P. J., Wansbury, T. G., & Wilkinson, J. G. (2008). Cultural awareness and negotiation skills training: Evaluation of a prototype semi-immersive system. *Proceedings of the 26th Army Science Conference*, Orlando, FL.

Edelson, D. C. (2006). Balancing innovation and risk: Assessing design research proposals. In v. d. J. Akker, K. Gravemeijer, & S. McKenney (Eds.), *Educational design research* (pp. 100–106). New York: Routledge.

Fishman, B., Marx, R. W., Blumenfeld, P., Krajcik, J., & Soloway, E. (2004) Creating a framework for research on systemic technology innovations, *The Journal of the Learning Sciences, 13*(1), 43–76.

Fletcher, J. (2009). Education and training technology in the military. *Science, 323*(5910), 72–75.

Graesser, A. C., & King, B. (2008). Technology-based training. In J. J. Blascovich & C. R. Hartel (Eds.), *Human behavior in military contexts*. Committee on Opportunities in Basic Research in the Behavioral and Social Sciences for the U.S. Military. Board on Behavioral, Cognitive, and Sensory Sciences and Education, Division of Behavioral and Social Sciences and Education. Washington, DC: The National Academies Press.

Highsmith, J. (2002). What is agile software development? *CrossTalk: The Journal of Defense Software Engineering* (October), 4–9.

Kelly, A. E. (2006). Quality criteria for design research. In v. d. J. Akker, K. Gravemeijer, & S. McKenney (Eds.), *Educational design research* (pp. 107–118). New York: Routledge.

Kelly, A. E., Lesh, R. A., & Baek, J. Y. (2008). *Handbook of design research methods in education: Innovations in science, technology, engineering, and mathematics learning and teaching.* New York and London: Routledge.

McFarland, M. (2005). Military cultural education. *Military Review*, 62–69.

Mayo, M. J. (2009). Video games: A route to large-scale STEM education? *Science, 323*, 79–82.

Means, B., Toyama, Y., Murphy, R., Bakia, M., & Jones, K. (2009). *Evaluation of evidence-based practices in online learning: A Meta-analysis and review of online-learning studies.* Washington, DC: U.S. Department of Education.

Mislevy, R. J., & Haertel, G. D. (2006). *Implications of evidence-centered design for educational testing.* Menlo Park, CA: SRI International.

National Research Council (NRC) (2008). *Human behavior in military contexts.* Committee on Opportunities in Basic Research in the Behavioral and Social Sciences for the U.S. Military. James J. Blascovich and Christine R. Hartel, Editors. Board on Behavioral, Cognitive, and Sensory Sciences and Education, Division of Behavioral and Social Sciences and Education. Washington, DC: The National Academies Press.

Norman, D. A., & Draper, S. W. (Eds.) (1986). *User centered system design: New perspectives on human-computer Interaction.* Hillsdale, NJ: Erlbaum.

O'Shea, P., Mitchell, R., Johnston, C., & Dede, C. (2009). Lessons learned about designing augmented realities. *International Journal of Gaming and Computer-Mediated Simulations, 1*(1), 1–15.

Penuel, W. R. (2005). *Recommendations for evaluation research within educational innovations.* Paper presented at the Joint Conference of the Canadian Evaluation Society and the American Evaluation Association, Toronto, Ontario, Canada.

Penuel, W. R., & Yarnall, L. (2005). Designing handheld software to support classroom assessment: An analysis of conditions for teacher adoption. *Journal of Technology, Learning, and Assessment, 3*(5). Available at http://www.jtla.org

Penuel, W. R., Roschelle, J. R., & Shechtman, N. (2007). Designing formative assessment software with teachers: An analysis of the co-design process. *Research and Practice in Technology Enhanced Learning, 2*(1), 51–74.

Phillips, D., & Dolle, J. (2007). From Plato to Brown and beyond: Theory, practice, and the promise of design experiments. In E. de Corte & L. Verschaffel (Eds.), *Instructional psychology: Past, present, and future trends: sixteen essays in honor of Erik de Corte.* (pp. 277–293). Amsterdam: Elsevier.

Puntambekar, S., & Sandoval, W. (2009). Design research: Moving forward. *The Journal of the Learning Sciences, 18*(3), 323–326.

Roschelle, J., Tatar, D., & Kaput, J. (2008). Getting to scale with innovations that deeply restructure how students come to know mathematics. In A. E. Kelly, R. A. Lesh & J. Y. Baek (Eds.), *Handbook of design research methods in education: Innovations in science, technology, engineering, and mathematics learning and teaching* (pp. 369–395). New York and London: Routledge.

van den Akker, J., Gravemeijer, K., McKenney, S., & Nieveen, N. (2006). Introducing educational design research. In J. van den Akker, K. Gravemeijer, S. McKenney, & N. Nieveen (Eds.), *Educational design research* (pp. 3–7). New York: Routledge.

Walker, D. (2006). Toward productive design studies. In J. van den Akker, K. Gravemeijer, & S. McKenney (Eds.), *Educational design research* (pp. 8–13). New York: Routledge.

West, M., & Farr, J. (1990). Innovation at work. In M. West & J. Farr (Eds.), *Innovation and creativity at work: Psychological and organizational strategies.* (pp. 3–13). New York: Wiley.

CHAPTER 18

A Road Ahead for Adaptive Training Technology

Paula J. Durlach

One-on-one tutoring is considered the gold standard in education and training; but just as one-on-one human tutoring is resource intensive, so is the path to engineering computer-based tutors. To achieve the same kind of effectiveness as expert human tutors, technology-based training must customize content and feedback based on each student's unique combination of aptitude, knowledge, motivations, and other relevant characteristics, and employ pedagogical strategies known to support student mastery. For an adult training audience who will need to apply their learning in their professional life, "mastery" must be more than performance on a test during a training episode; it must be retained and transferred to real-world situations.

As system developers and education and training providers, we need to deliver training effectively and efficiently within cost and time constraints. So how should an organization responsible for providing training for more than 500,000 people per year (such as the U.S. Army) allocate its research dollars in this area? Contributors to this book, as well as participants from industry and the U.S.

Department of Defense research-and-development community, were asked to consider four specific issues to help answer this question. Although targeted to the needs of the U.S. Army, the discussion is relevant to the training needs of any large organization. To address the questions, discussion groups were convened on the topics presented later in the chapter, and the results of each discussion group were presented to the entire gathering for further input and comment. This chapter provides a summary of each discussion group's conclusions, supplemented with comments from the feedback session to the entire assembly of participants. The assigned topics were as follows:

Student models: What specific skills, knowledge, abilities, and characteristics of the learner need to be represented in student models to produce effective adaptive training technology? How do we measure these?

Pedagogical models: Assuming we had all the information we need in the student model, how do we translate this into adaptive experiential training?

Training efficiency: What types of adaptations in training technology could provide the biggest payoff in training efficiency?

Training applications: What type of Department of Defense training requirements could best be filled by adaptive training technology?

Each group was also asked to discuss knowledge gaps and the types of research required to fill the gaps. Lastly, they were asked to discuss any novel technologies or approaches not currently being used in educational contexts, which might be brought to bear on the problem.

Student Models

What specific skills, knowledge, abilities, and characteristics of the learner need to be represented in student models to produce effective adaptive training technology?

The general consensus was that anything that could affect learning and drive adaptation should be measured. This includes student data that we currently do not know how to act on because they might prove useful in the future (especially if subjected to data-mining techniques). The desire to measure everything was tempered by an appreciation that this might be impractical and may have potential adverse impact on the student and his or her learning experience. With regard to the latter, it was stressed that in an authentic training situation, sacrificing time on task or student engagement for purposes of data collection was not desirable. As a rule of thumb, intrusiveness should be avoided – it is not appropriate to impose measurement demands on the student that interfere with concentration on the training task itself. Moreover, the privacy and confidentiality of student data must be maintained. In a simulated or experimental training situation (i.e., conducted to address research questions with recruited participants rather than the target training audience), more flexibility could be allowed for data collection, and of course the normal methods of ensuring participant confidentiality must be adhered to.

There was agreement on what data are essential: the student's domain knowledge (knowledge, skills, and abilities, or KSAs). The goal of training is to develop mastery, and the trajectory of that mastery should influence how a training system adapts. The best-proven adaptive technique is mastery learning (making sure the student masters the current learning objectives before continuing on). Consequently, continuous assessment of student competence in the training domain is required. Data need to include not only what the student has mastered with regard to the learning objectives, but also specific weaknesses or misconceptions, because these can be targeted and repaired with adaptive training. To obtain these data, assessment of the student's domain knowledge should occur at the start of training and subsequently be tracked during the course of training. Patterns of student performance should be analyzed for evidence of knowledge gaps and misconceptions, and the training content adapted to address these. Analysis of within-problem behavior can provide insight into level of mastery, as novices tend to approach a problem differently from more experienced problem solvers.

Although necessary, performance and mastery tracking were not seen as sufficient. The student model ought to have a form of episodic memory representing aspects of the student's interaction with the system. This includes things like requests for help if the system supports this, use of available reference materials, such as a glossary, use of help information on system navigation, and so forth. These data can provide insight into what kind of help the student seeks, whether the student is trying to "game" the system, or whether there are significant human factors issues with the user interface. Ideally, the student should be able to concentrate on the training task and not have to expend significant effort on how the training system itself works (e.g., how to operate an avatar in a virtual environment).

In addition to domain-relevant KSAs and system-interaction data, focus group members indicated that student models should include information on student traits and states. These are data considered potentially important for adapting training, although the precise ways to do the adaptation based on the information may not be well understood yet. Under student states (i.e., characteristics that tend to vary during individual learning experiences), frustration, boredom, and other forms of affect that might impact learning were mentioned. Relatively persistent but still malleable student aspects mentioned included metacognitive skills and various attitudes (such as attitudes toward computer-based training). Under traits (i.e., relatively stable attributes of the student), any physical limitations (e.g., color blindness), learning style (e.g., visual vs. verbal), aptitudes (e.g., spatial ability), and demographic information (e.g., gender) were mentioned.

Among these, metacognitive skills were highlighted as particularly important. Metacognitive skills are actions and strategies students use to evaluate their own comprehension and learning. Learning is facilitated when the learner automatically applies skills or deliberately selects strategies intended to monitor and improve the process of learning. Examples of metacognitive activities include: regulating and directing attention (was my mind wandering?); self-reflection (am I understanding?); self-explanation (why is that the right way to do it?); and schema creation (how is this related to what I already know?). Metacognitive activities also involve adapting behavior when the learning process breaks down (e.g., asking for help, avoiding distractions). Good metacognition about one's own learning tends to enhance learning, retention, and transfer. Consequently, knowing something about a student's metacognitive abilities could feed into adaptive interventions to both compensate for weaknesses in those skills in the short run and to directly enhance those skills for the long run.

Collecting, archiving and analyzing student data, even data not used by the training system that collects it, was seen as a necessary step to truly understanding the variables affecting learning. Group members suggested that educational data-mining techniques could be applied to discover associations among these variables and their relations with learning outcomes. These associations could then be used to create better student models and adaptive interventions. For this strategy to succeed, it would be important to include contextual information with the student data collected (e.g., the training domain, the pedagogical strategy in force when the data were collected, and other relevant information). Group members also indicated that student data could also be submitted to psychometric analysis, which could provide normative information not already available. For example, for simulation training where the relative difficulty of specific training scenarios has not been established, performance data could be used in spiral development so that a later version could select scenarios for students based on empirically established challenge levels. A vision of a second-order adaptive system was even discussed: This type of training system would learn from its own data and adjust the way it adapts to students based on what works (i.e., what maximizes mastery).

How Do We Measure Student KSAs and Other Student Data?

The most common method of collecting data for the student model is through monitoring and logging the student's interaction with the training system. Thus, any overt action the student performs can be a source of data; however, knowing how to interpret those overt actions depends on inference. Even when the student responds directly to a question about their knowledge (e.g., is the following statement true or false?), the response requires interpretation. If the student gets the answer right, does it reflect underlying knowledge or was it just a lucky guess? Indeed, the function of a student model is to help make better inferences about underlying knowledge than could be accomplished by examining each student-system interaction in isolation.

A student model can take into account multiple student-system interactions in context, to build up a model of the student's current cognitive model of the target training domain. Intelligent tutoring systems (ITS) work well when they can infer thought processes from analyzing the steps students take in solving problems (e.g., in algebra or physics). Forcing students to "show their work" is one way to obtain the data for the model; however, various domains lend themselves more or less naturally to requiring the student to behaviorally reveal the way they go about solving problems. This might be natural for problems with discrete steps (like solving algebraic equations), but it is rather less natural for problems where the solution does not necessarily follow a linear progression of discrete operations.

A method to gain additional insight about the current state of the students' understanding is by directly asking them. This can take the form of tests, questions concerning their own opinion about their knowledge (e.g., how confident do you feel about your understanding of the law of large numbers?), or it might take the form of requests for explanations about why they took certain actions (e.g., why did you decide to take the northern route to the objective?). Moreover, such questioning can be interactive or of mixed initiative so as to stimulate metacognitive processes. The student may be asked for elaboration, clarification, or hypothetical thinking. The technical ability to understand open-ended student responses will be bounded by the system's ability to interpret natural language, however. As an alternative, the student could be offered response options; however, this changes the nature of the task from generation to recognition and could become unwieldy if the options become too numerous.

"Stealth measurement" is a potential alternative (or compliment) to overt questioning. Here, the stream of overt student-system interactions is used to infer what the student knows (or how they feel), but the measurement process is covert, in that no overt questioning is involved (hence the term "stealth"). The challenge is interpreting how the stream of interactions relates to student state. One approach is to use Bayesian modeling to create probabilistic linkages between observed behaviors and inferred student state (e.g., because the student did x, y, and z, the probability is .75 that he understands how to analyze a route for possible ambush sites). This method holds promise, but it has yet to be proven successful in other than fairly simple training simulations.

Neuropsychological measures were another source of data nominated for collection and potential inclusion in student models. Various neurophysiological sensors (requiring various levels of obtrusiveness) could be used to gain insight not only into student affect (e.g., stress, boredom, frustration), but also various cognitive states such as attention and recognition. Measures being investigated include eye movements, posture, facial expression, galvanic skin response, and brain waves. Like overt behavior, neuropsychological measures must be interpreted (e.g., what is the significance of a particular posture?), which may require both pattern analysis over time and integration of data from multiple streams.

Finally, another method of obtaining information about the student is to exploit data captured outside the training system itself. In real time, this can only occur if the system can access other repositories of data about students, and if the privacy and confidentiality issues raised by this possibility are resolved. For research purposes, however, such interoperability of systems is not required, and student records held in various forms may be of use in mining for relationships between student attributes and their learning outcomes. Nevertheless, the issue of learner control over data access remains an issue. Into the future, as the potential for persistent student models increases, the issue of whether a student should be able to inspect, censor, or correct data in their student model will require resolution.

What are the gaps and what research needs to be conducted to fill the gaps? What novel technologies or approaches require development?

The group highlighted the need for carefully controlled, systematic studies to determine the relation between student states and traits and learning outcomes. Data must be collected and reported in such a way that meta-analysis is possible. In addition we need improved educational data-mining techniques, as well as better Bayesian reasoning software for stealth modeling. Without data that can be used for modeling, and strong modeling techniques, we will continue to rely on idiosyncratic handcrafted models. We need the data and methods to analyze it so that student models can be created automatically using machine learning techniques.

We need improved capabilities in natural language processing. This will open the door to better interactive dialogs and allow the student to provide better insight into what they are thinking or considering doing. It would allow for guided hypothetical thinking exercises and Socratic-like approaches to automated training and education.

Finally, we need to start thinking about the development and use of persistent student models that stay with the learner over a lifetime. Issues to be established include the nature of the information in the model, interoperability with multiple training and educational applications, data privacy, and learner control over their own data. One immediate practical use highlighted was the aid a persistent student model could contribute to computer-based natural language processing, were it to include a personalized language corpus for each student. Statistical linguistic analysis on such a corpus could then be used to improve interpretation of student language inputs.

Pedagogical Models

Assuming we had all the information we need in the student model, how do we translate this into adaptive experiential training?

The group used an example to ground the discussion: Assuming we had different profiles for subgroups of the training audience, the question is how do we adapt the training differently for each subgroup to maximize the benefit in knowledge acquisition for each? For example, suppose we identified one subgroup as "Competitors," who want to win or outperform everyone else, and another subgroup as "Explorers," who want to understand how the simulation works and maybe break it. How would we adapt to each subgroup? We should be able to do things like alter content and feedback style, select media, tailor the particular combination of didactic versus experiential content, adjust strategy according to student affect, and so forth, all in the service of maximizing retention and transfer.

How to adapt to such subgroups is not currently known, although the goal for adaptation was generally agreed to be keeping the student in the "sweet spot," where there is some motivating challenge, at just the right level: not too easy and not too difficult (analogous to the zone of proximal development). The goal of adaptation should be to create the proverbial carrot, leading the learner on through the incentive of discovery and mastery, not the stick, simply forcing the student reluctantly forward. But supposing we knew what motivated each student, and how far we could challenge him or her without leaving the sweet spot; we have not yet mastered how to use this knowledge to adapt content, feedback, scaffolding, and other instructional interventions. On the other hand, there are things we know we need to understand before we could ever hope to do it. We have been told we know everything we need to know about the student, so presumably we have an accurate assessment of their state of knowledge, which means we already have a good assessment model in place. To this we need to add a really good understanding of the training domain and its psychometric properties (what is prerequisite to what, what is related to what, what is easy, what is difficult, perhaps dependent on subgroup). Without this domain model we cannot decide what next challenge might be inside or outside the student's sweet spot. In addition, we need to be able to translate our knowledge of what is motivating to each student with how the instructional interventions and experiences are presented (e.g., if a student is a "Competitor," then be sure to give comparative performance feedback). Perhaps this is the component we currently know least about, because in reality we certainly do not know everything there is to know about our students.

Accepted best practices for providing effective training tend to be heuristic, leaving details of implementation up to the instructor or software designer. In addition, it is not obvious how heuristics derived from laboratory (trial-based) research can be applied in scenario-based experiential training. Finally, such guidelines tend to be one-size-fits-all (not adaptive). "Spaced trials are better than massed" and "Provide corrective feedback" are examples of such rules. Precisely how such rules are implemented in software tends to be more of an art than a science. In the context of experiential learning, for example, there are many ways that feedback can be given. Empirical data supporting one strategy versus another is lacking (see discussion later in the chapter).

If the goal is to promote retention and transfer of domain mastery, the content should be aimed at teaching principles, not just procedures. Employing interventions to promote metacognitive and general learning skills (like self-explanation) can be useful in this regard. Such skills can aid students in applying their knowledge in novel situations. It must be remembered that merely doing well *during* the training session does not guarantee transfer.

Based on cognitive load theory, instruction needs to adapt to the learner based on their level of workload in real time (e.g., adapt pedagogical interventions to current level of mental challenge). This means that the way feedback is given or scaffolding is implemented will need to adapt to the learner's current level of mastery (keeping the student in that zone). Therefore, effective adaptation of instructional strategy is highly dependent on a student model that can accurately characterize student knowledge, workload, and affective state.

What are the gaps and what research needs to be conducted to fill the gaps? What novel technologies or approaches require development?

We have heuristics, rules of thumb about how to intervene instructionally; when it comes to implementing them, however, we do not have the details to guide all the decisions required. For example, with feedback, it is not clear when during experiential training is the best time to give it. Should you allow the student to observe the consequences of their bad decisions, or stop them immediately and give corrective feedback? Just how far into difficulties do you let them get? When is there a danger of impairing their motivational state, disrupting the flow of a scenario and engagement in the exercise? How do you prevent "sucking the fun" out of a serious game? Research is needed to explore the effects of implicit versus explicit feedback in scenario-based training. Perhaps the benefits of allowing students to observe the results of their decisions (implicit feedback) depends on how obviously the decision and outcome are linked (are the effects subtle or clear, are they immediate or delayed?). Carefully controlled, systematic studies of which feedback tactics work best for effective experiential learning are required.

Conducting such research is difficult: There tends to be a limited amount of time with students to apply experimental training manipulations, and an even more limited access when it comes to collecting retention and transfer data. Moreover, the research requires sensitive assessment measures. To evaluate the relative impact of different instructional interventions requires far more sensitive measures than ones designed merely to establish pre-training to post-training improvement. Consequently, more attention will need to be given to designing assessment measures that can discriminate levels of improvement; a more psychometric approach needs to be taken to assessment construction.

From a technology point of view, work needs to be conducted on how to adapt scenarios automatically without losing narrative coherence. If a goal is to customize the learning objectives addressed in a scenario for each student, this will require either a huge library of pre-scripted scenarios, or techniques to adapt scenarios on the fly.

Also from a technology standpoint, there needs to be links to the Web 3.0 or learning object repositories to supplement existing content when it is needed, on an individual basis; or there needs to be at least a link to human advisors or networked communities of practice. When an ITS does not have the content the student needs, there should be a way to direct the student where to find it.

As capabilities in natural language processing grow, instructional methods to take best advantage of these improvements should be pursued. This could open the door to far better automated understanding of student explanations and better ability to conduct interactive learning dialogs. Better natural language processing could also be applied to creating an automated facilitator – an agent that could facilitate discussions among distributed students.

Whereas the discussion mainly focused on adapting to the student, the issue of adapting the content of training to stay current with changing circumstances in the real world was also considered. It was suggested that data mining and communities of practice might be used to get the content required. It was acknowledged that domain experts and communities of practice need to be involved more in the training design process.

An important unsolved issue is how to cope with less-than-well-defined domains. Can we use artificial intelligence (AI) to find patterns in the art of the ill-defined domains and put some structure on it? Work using AI, ontologies, and the semantic web to create a semantic web subject-matter expert should be initiated to test the extent of the power of these techniques. Such an expert could then be called on to answer student questions in the relevant domain.

Training Efficiency

What types of adaptations in training technology could provide the biggest payoff in training efficiency?

The reason to invest in adaptive technology is to make training more effective and/or efficient. In terms of efficiency, it is normally assumed that there is a trade-off between mastery and retention on the one hand and time and cost on the other. However, the discussion questioned this assumption, suggesting that both improvements in mastery and retention *and* time and cost could be achieved at the same time. This is only early days as far as technology-based training; each generation has seen incredible advances in what can be done. Each generation of development gets less costly and time-consuming.

It would be desirable to have a model providing guidance on which training approaches are best for teaching which competencies. There are several approaches available: classroom, simple simulations, virtual reality, and ITS. Each serves a specific need. There is a danger of jumping on a bandwagon and overgeneralizing a new approach. Instead, each needs to be applied where it is best suited. No specific type of training approach should be excluded. Each has its own advantages and disadvantages. Some types of content need small-group interaction with live instructors. For others, you just need to read a manual. So, in terms of training technology, the goal should be to apply it to cases where it provides the biggest advantages relative to other methods.

Because of limited resources, investments in innovative training technology need to be prioritized. The best place to start is where there are existing inefficiencies or bottlenecks. Adaptive training technology should be developed for declarative training (to keep people out of classrooms, live instructors are unnecessary). Adaptive hypermedia may be ideal for this. It can get the student to the right piece of content at the right time, including video and simulation. Refresher training is also a good target for adaptive training technology. Some initial level of knowledge can be assumed, but each student will have a unique pattern of memory decay. So, adapting to each student could be really useful. It could take the student from vaguely remembering back to the fluency they originally had.

Another area where adaptive training technology should be targeted is in preparing people for live training exercises, so that when they do get there, they really can get the full benefits from that experience. Technology-based simulation training should be used to prepare people for live practice. For team-based simulation training, whether live or virtual, there is a real need for technological support. Good ways to replay the experience from different perspectives are needed. Adaptive technology could aid in deciding what is recorded and how it is reviewed depending on who is doing the learning. If the same group exercise can be replayed differently for each participant, it could ensure a focus on *their* high-priority training objectives. This is particularly needed for large-scale simulations, in which participants come from multiple units and echelons, to ensure that all participants receive a training benefit as opposed to merely acting as role players in support of the learning of others.

What are the gaps and what research needs to be conducted to fill the gaps? What novel technologies or approaches require development?

The group asked for a model to understand which approaches are best in terms of both mastery and efficiency for teaching different types of content and competencies. The model should specify how sophisticated the training technology needs to be for different training domains. It should provide answers to questions like: When training is technology-based, should it be blended with classroom training, or can it stand on its own? When do you really need a student model? When can you train using well-chosen worked-out examples and stories rather than an interactive simulation? What is the best way to train in an ill-defined domain? When is it crucial to be able to interact with peers? This model should initially be based

on what is currently considered best practice, but it then needs to be followed up with evaluations, because it is unlikely that currently available guidelines address all the technological possibilities.

Given that interactive simulations will be used for some training, the group asked for improved methods of creating scenarios to support the development of competencies (as opposed to merely training on procedures). These scenarios need to be well-characterized so that trainers understand the learning objectives they target. A goal should be to address multiple competencies with the minimum number of simulation exercises. It was suggested that this would require authoring tools for scenarios, improved methods of knowledge elicitation, and collaboration between subject-matter experts and instructional designers. There is a conflict between getting new training out the door faster and vetting and validating content. It might help if there were standardization across training systems, interfaces, and architectures, because modules could be shared, but getting the validators involved in the authoring process might be the best solution.

Having great training technology is not the only issue. Organizational acceptance is crucial. An organization's training community needs to be involved in the development of new training approaches, so it will not be viewed as a threat; and the training audience needs to be involved to ensure that the design fits into their other activities. Great training does not do any good if no one has the time to participate in it.

Training applications

What type of Department of Defense training requirements could best be filled by adaptive training technology? What are the gaps and what research needs to be conducted to fill the gaps? What novel technologies or approaches require development?

The essential challenge is how to train a diverse training audience with fewer resources and less time. Training needs to address both occupational specialties and cross-situational competencies. For training to be adaptive, it is not enough for the training to adjust to trainee KSAs; it must also adjust to a rapidly changing world where operational environments, missions, enemies, tactics, techniques, procedures, and equipment are constantly evolving. It must also foster the cognitive agility to cope under these continuously changing conditions. However, the problem is bigger than how to design adaptive training technology or what domains to apply it to. Training is ubiquitous and we need to somehow integrate what are currently isolated stovepipes: professional military education, occupational specialty training, and operational training.[1] We also need to view job aides, training, and education as a continuum, not separate unrelated things. Sometimes all we need is performance support, not training. A person doing their tax return wants help filling in the form; they do not want to learn the tax code. We need to figure out when intervention needs to support task completion as opposed to training. Finally, we need training content that is not only adaptable, but also reusable, shareable, and deployable across multiple contexts.

The problem is not only how to design the technology; certain organizational changes need to occur. A significant challenge is getting the organization to embrace a student-centered approach to training and education, and to refashion an assignment and personnel system to deal with students obtaining a diverse set of qualifications and credentials at different times. A big challenge is that the requirements-generation process does not fit with the training development

process; but that is where the money is. To compete for funding in the current environment requires evidence of benefits – in other words, making a strong return-on-investment (ROI) case. But the training community does not have that kind of data. Along with many other large organizations, the U.S. Army has been poor at measuring performance and maintaining training records. There has been little systematic tracking of the correlation between entry-level KSAs, training performance, initial job success, and organizational retention. These data need to be collected and fed into databases and then models, to be able to make an ROI case with real data. Along the way, this would create a strong data source for persistent student models. Later this could be integrated with a federation of training technology applications. A shared ontology among student models and training applications would support automated updating of student data as new training is completed, as well as recommendations to the student about what training is available and which might be appropriate to master next.

The Road Ahead: Data and Models

These final paragraphs attempt to provide a bottom line on the foregoing: There is no single silver-bullet technique that is going to solve every training issue. Training technology does not have to be adaptive in every aspect, and we need to be selective in targeting when and how to adapt to reap the most gains. We need to lay out the space of potential adaptive strategies and to indicate the conditions under which their use produces significant gains in learning outcomes, compared with nonadaptive approaches. If we do not know this, then we need carefully controlled, systematic research to fill in our knowledge gaps. We should also broaden our ideas about where adaptive techniques might provide benefits to areas beyond traditional training, such as in real-time performance support and mission rehearsal tools. Moreover, we should broaden our conception of adaptability to include not just

---

[1] Professional military education focuses on leadership, management, military history, operational doctrine, national defense policy, planning and decision making, legal responsibilities, and professional ethics. Traditionally it consists of classroom training, attended by career military officers and noncommissioned officers (NCOs) of the Armed Forces of the United States every three to five years during their career. Occupational specialty training provides education and training for a specific job (e.g., helicopter maintenance). Operational training prepares units to carry out the specific missions they must be prepared to conduct.

adapting to students, but also adapting to changing training needs.

When it comes to adapting to students, making instructional decisions needs to be less of an art and more of a science. We need to get better at collecting, organizing, and analyzing training data: data about students, their performance, and how it compares to expert performance. We cannot develop good student models or assessments without this. Assessment is at the very heart of adaptive training and education. If we do not establish how to measure what is novice, intermediate, and expert performance in a domain, if we do not establish what is normatively easy or challenging, if we cannot relate prior experience to expected domain performance, our ability to adapt effectively to the student will always fall short of the mark. We will not be able to accurately assess where the student currently stands in their mastery or what the next best training experience should be for them. Moreover, without sensitive and valid measures, it will be difficult to interpret the results of research on the relative effectiveness of different training strategies. This is because a real difference in the effectiveness of two training interventions might not be detectable if measured by a poorly designed, insensitive assessment instrument. Thus, improved methods to create valid and sensitive assessments are absolutely essential to progress in creating adaptive training technology. These methods use mathematical techniques like item response theory and Bayesian modeling to select assessment elements. These methods are highly dependent on data for model creation, and so, returning to where this summary started, we need to improve the ability of training designers, especially psychometricians and modelers, to get their hands on sufficient student data to create the models that will underlie the adaptive training of the future.

Another initiative should be to invest in improving model creation capabilities (as well as other tools to assist in creating the components of adaptive technology-based training). The preceding paragraph highlighted the need for data; modeling is what it is needed for. Adaptive training currently has a heavy dependence on handcrafted models used in one-off, domain-specific training technology applications (an example is BiLat, discussed in Chapter 10 by Lane and Wray). This technology is expensive to create and difficult to update, and each new prototype advances our overall capabilities to create good training rather little. In addition, it is highly dependent on the creativity and insights of the training developers. An alternative may be using data (from both students and domain experts) to drive model creation. Applying educational data mining, machine learning, and other modeling techniques to data can reveal information to support pedagogical decisions required for training system design. Educational data mining is a relatively new discipline, however, and educational data-mining methods are not particularly user-friendly to those who are not already experts in data mining. Thus, progress may be gained by supporting the development of tools that are more accessible for those with instructional design intentions, who may be lacking expertise in artificial intelligence and machine learning.

Index

For EU product safety concerns, contact us at Calle de José Abascal, 56–1°, 28003 Madrid, Spain or eugpsr@cambridge.org.